The Postal Service Guide to U.S. Stamps

27th Edition
Updated Stamp Values

HarperResource
An Imprint of HarperCollins*Publishers*

HarperCollins books may be purchased for educational, business, or sales
promotional use. For information please write: Special Markets Department,
HarperCollins Publishers Inc., 10 East 53rd Street, New York, NY 10022.

Printed in the United States of America.

Library of Congress Control Number: 00-134570

ISBN 0-06-095854-5

00 01 02 03 04 RRD 10 9 8 7 6 5 4 3 2 1

Table of Contents

An Amazing Universe

Stamp collecting offers a galaxy of enjoyment

There's a vast universe out there just waiting to be explored. It's called stamp collecting and it can take you to places and show you things you've only dreamed about.

There's something thrilling about watching a space launch. Every time the space shuttle blasts into orbit, millions of people are captivated by the adventure and the excitement. In their own small way, stamps help capture some of that excitement and certainly record the history of those moments. They can show us the vastness of space, the thrill of walking on the moon, or the excitement of bold new scientific achievements. Many facets of life and culture are reflected in postage stamps.

Stamp collecting can be a lifelong hobby. It's fun and educational for all ages. And it's easy to start your own collection without a big investment. Read on to find out how to start or build your very own collection.

SPACE ACHIEVEMENT AND EXPLORATION

WORLD STAMP EXPO 2000

33 USA

33 USA

EGG NEBULA

GALAXY NGC 1316

USA 33

Zachary Canter, age 9

What is philately?

The word philately (fi-látt-eh-lee) means the study of stamps and other postal materials. Stamp collectors are sometimes called philatelists.

How do I start collecting stamps?

It's easy. You can start by simply saving stamps from letters, packages, and postcards. Ask your friends and family to save stamps from their mail.

Neighborhood businesses that get a lot of mail—banks, stores, travel agencies, and others—might save their envelopes for you, too.

Or, start your collection by choosing one or two favorite subjects. Then, collect stamps that fit your theme—art, history, sports, transportation, science, animals, and others—whatever you choose! This is called topical or thematic stamp collecting. See the stamps pictured in these feature articles for ideas to get you started on a space theme!

Will it cost me a lot to start a collection?

No! Start with used stamps and a few inexpensive accessories (such as a small album and a package of stamp hinges), and you can have a great time on a limited budget. Remember to put stamps, albums, and hinges on your birthday and holiday wish lists, too!

What kinds of stamps are there?

There are a number of different types of stamps. Their purposes can be described as commemorative, definitive, or special; their formats can be in sheets, booklets, or coils. And all of these now exist with conventional adhesive (the "lick-and-stick" gum) or self-adhesive (the "no-lick, peel-and-stick" type).

Definitive stamps (also called "regular issues") are the most common type of postage stamp. They feature everything from statesmen to animals and from the American flag to historic vehicles. They tend to be fairly small (generally less than an inch square), with denominations (the face value printed on the stamp) from one cent to many dollars. They are printed in large quantities, often more than once, and tend to be available for several years.

Commemorative stamps are usually larger and more colorful than definitives. They are printed in smaller quantities and typically are printed only once. They remain on sale for a limited period of time, generally about a year; many post offices

Francis Hopkinson Flag USA 33
1777
2000

2000

carry them for only a few months. They are issued for specific rates, most often the prime letter rate. They honor, or commemorate, important people, events, or subjects, all of which reflect some aspect of American culture.

Special stamps supplement the regular issues and tend to be more commemorative in appearance (larger and more colorful), while meeting specific needs. They may be reprinted, but tend to remain on sale for only the life of the specific rate for which they are issued. These include Christmas and Love stamps, Holiday Celebration stamps, international rate stamps (previously known as airmail stamps), Priority Mail, and Express Mail stamps.

Sheet stamps are printed as large press sheets, then trimmed into smaller units called panes, most of which measure less than eight by ten inches. Panes generally contain twenty stamps,

but may contain up to a hundred or as few as one stamp; smaller commemorative panes, with fewer than ten stamps, are often called souvenir sheets, depending on their purpose. Individual stamps tend to have perfs (perforations) or die-cut edges (generally with a wavy pattern) on all sides.

Booklet stamps are designed to be folded into a convenient unit. Booklets generally contain twenty stamps and may contain separate panes of stamps in a small folder or may be issued in a flat unit designed to be folded into a booklet by the customer. Most individual booklet stamps have at least one straight edge (no perfs or die-cuts) and some-times two adjacent straight edges.

Coil stamps are issued in rolls. Customers often buy them

Definitive

Commemorative

Special

Booklet

Coil

in rolls of a hundred stamps; business mailers can buy them in rolls of up to ten thousand stamps. Individual coil stamps usually have two straight edges on opposite sides.

How do I remove stamps from envelopes?

If you wish, you can save whole envelopes with stamps on them and store them anywhere—from shoe boxes to special albums. These are called "covers." Collecting entire envelopes reflects a specialty called "postal history." It's a good idea to save the whole envelope if there's something special about the address or return address (famous places or people for example), or the postmark (a date or location of some historic significance). See also the information below on collectible "first day covers" later in this article.

If you want to remove stamps from envelopes, it pays to be careful. The best way to remove stamps from envelopes is to soak them. Here's how:

1. Tear or cut off the upper right-hand corner of the envelope, leaving enough margin around the stamps to ensure they aren't damaged.

2. Place it, stamp side down, in a small pan of warm (not hot) water. If the stamp is affixed to a piece of colored envelope, use colder water; it may take longer, but any dyes from the paper are less likely to run and discolor the stamp. After a few minutes, the stamp should

sink to the bottom. Remove the envelope piece from the water as soon as the stamp is off.

3. Wait a few more minutes for any remaining gum to dislodge from the stamp. The newer self-adhesive gums tend to take a bit longer.

4. Lift the stamp out. If you use your fingers, be sure your hands are clean, since oil from your skin can hasten discoloration of the stamps over time. Tongs—a good stamp-collecting tool like tweezers—can be used to minimize contact.

How do I collect First Day Covers?

The fastest way to get a First Day Cover is to buy the stamp yourself (it will usually go on sale the day after the first day of issue), attach it to your own envelope (or cover), and send it to the first day post office for cancellation. You can submit up to fifty envelopes, up to thirty days after the stamp's issue date. Here's how:

1. Write your address in the lower right-hand corner of each first day envelope, at least 5/8 inch from the bottom. Leave plenty of room for the stamp(s) and cancellation. Use a peel-off label if you prefer.
2. Insert a piece of cardboard (about as thick as a postcard) into each envelope. You can tuck the flap in or seal the envelope.
3. Affix your stamp(s) to your first day envelope(s).
4. Put your first day envelope(s) inside another, larger envelope and mail it to "Customer-Affixed Envelopes" in care of the postmaster of the first day city. Your envelopes will be canceled and returned.

Or, you can purchase a plain envelope with the stamp(s) already affixed and canceled. These are now sold directly by mail order through the U.S. Postal Service.

The White House
2000   USA 33

Wet stamps are delicate and should be handled carefully.

5. Place the stamp between two paper towels and put a heavy object, such as a book, on top. This will keep the stamp from curling as it dries. Leave the stamp there overnight.

6. If the stamp shows signs of remaining adhesive, even after lengthy soaking, dry it face down on a single paper towel with nothing touching the back. If necessary, it can be flattened after it's dried; otherwise, it may stick to surfaces when drying.

How should I organize my stamps?

However you want to, of course—it's your collection. But be sure to protect them so they don't get damaged or lost. You can attach your stamps to loose-leaf paper and put them in a three-ring binder. Or, arrange them in a more formal album, which you can buy in stores or by mail order.

What kinds of stamp albums can I buy?

Some stamp albums feature specific categories with pictures of the stamps that should appear on each page. You may want to select one with loose-leaf pages so you can add pages as your collection grows. Personal computers can help you design your own pages, featuring your collection in a totally personalized manner. Software programs can help you

with stamp-album pages, and common page-design programs can help you customize any design.

A *stock book* is an album with plastic or paper pockets on each page. There are no pictures of stamps, so you can organize the stock book in any way. These books are especially useful for holding duplicate stamps, stamps for trading, and stamps that you've saved but haven't yet had time to put in the album containing your permanent collection.

How do I put a stamp in the album?

It's best to use a stamp hinge— a small strip of thin material (often glassine) with gum on one side. Unlike tape or glue (which should *never* be used), hinges let you peel the stamp off the page without damaging it. Hinges come either folded or unfolded. Here's how to use a folded hinge:

1. Lightly moisten about three fourths of the short end of the hinge, leaving the area nearest the fold unmoistened. Press the hinge to the back of the stamp, placing the fold about 1/8 inch from the top of the stamp; that way, it can't be seen once the stamp is mounted in the album.

2. Lightly moisten most of the

11

OHIO CLASS
USA 55

long end of the hinge (again, leaving the area closest to the fold unmoistened), position the stamp where you want it in the album, and press down to secure it.

3. Using tongs, gently lift the stamp from the bottom to make sure it's not stuck to the page.

If you have an unfolded hinge, simply fold it about one third the length (gummed side out), giving you short and long ends, and proceed as above.

Instead of a hinge, you can insert the entire stamp into a mount—a small, clear plastic sleeve. Mounts are more expensive than hinges, but they protect stamps from air, dirt, and moisture. Hinges are fine for used stamps (stamps without adhesive that you've removed from mail), but mounts offer better protection for mint stamps (new stamps with adhesive, such as those you buy from the post office).

Is there anything else I need?

Here's a list of other materials and accessories you may find helpful:

Glassine envelopes are made of a special thin, see-through paper that protects stamps from grease and air. You can use them to keep stamps until you put them in your album.

A *stamp catalog* is a reference book with illustrations to help you identify stamps (like this book). It also lists the values of used and unused (mint) stamps.

A *magnifying glass* (or *loupe*) helps you examine stamps by making them appear larger. Sometimes it's important to examine certain details of stamps more closely.

A *perforation gauge* measures perforations along the edges of stamps. Sometimes the size and number of perfs are needed to identify stamps. The same principle can be used to measure the distance between peaks or ridges on newer die-cut self-adhesive stamps, with wavy die cuts that simulate perforations.

A *watermark tray* (and *watermark fluid*) help make watermarks on stamps more visible. A watermark is a design or pattern that is pressed into some stamp paper during manufacturing. This equipment is necessary only with stamps—mostly older stamps—with watermarks that help to identify them.

How can I tell what a stamp is worth?

Ask yourself two questions: "How rare is it?" and "What condition is it in?" The price listed in a stamp catalog gives you some idea of how rare it is. However,

GATO CLASS

Light Cancel–Very Fine

Superb

Medium Cancel–Fine

Very Fine

Heavy Cancel

Fine

Good

How should I judge the condition of a stamp?

Stamp dealers put stamps into categories according to their condition. Look at the pictured examples to see the differences among categories. A stamp in mint condition is the same as when purchased from the post office. An unused stamp has no cancellation but may not have any gum on the back. Mint stamps are usually worth more than unused stamps. Hinge marks on mint stamps can reduce value, which is why the use of stamp mounts is recommended for mint stamps.

You can begin to judge the condition of a stamp by examining the front of it. Are the colors bright or faded? Is the stamp clean, dirty, or stained? Is the stamp torn or creased? Torn stamps are not considered "collectible," but you may want to keep an example as a space filler until you get a better copy.

Are all the perforations intact? Has the stamp been canceled? A stamp with a light cancellation is in better condition than one with heavy marks across it.

Is the stamp design centered on the paper, crooked, or off to one side? In the examples pictured, this centering can range from "superb" (perfectly centered on the stamp) to "good" (the design on at least one side is marred somewhat by the perfs). Anything less would be graded "fair" or "poor" and,

the stamp may sell at more or less than the catalog price, depending on its condition. Catalog prices and condition are discussed further below.

Always try to find stamps in the best possible condition.

like torn copies, should be saved only as space fillers. Centering varies widely on older stamps; modern production techniques make it unlikely that copies with less than "fine" centering could be found.

Now look at the back of the stamp. Is there a thin spot in the paper? If so, it may have been caused by careless removal from a hinge or envelope.

The values listed in this book are for used and unused stamps in "very fine" condition that may have been hinged.

Where else can I find stamps?

Check the classified ads in philatelic newspapers and magazines at your local library. Some are listed under "publications" in this book (see page 524), and most will send you a free sample copy on request. There also are a number of stamp-related sites on the Internet, which can be accessed through most search programs and services.

What other stamp materials can I collect?

Postal stationery products are popular among some collectors. These have the stamp design printed and/or embossed (with an impressed or raised image) directly on them.

Stamped envelopes were first issued in the United States in 1853. More than five hundred million of them are printed each year.

Stamped cards (also called *postal cards*) were first issued in 1873. The first U.S. multicolored commemorative stamped cards were released in 1956. Several different stamped card designs are issued each year.

Aerogrammes (also called *air letters*) are designed to be letters and envelopes all in one. They are specially stamped, marked for folding, and gummed for sealing.

Other philatelic collectibles include:

Plate numbers (including *plate blocks*) appear on or adjacent to stamps. These are most common on sheet stamps. Plate blocks are the group of stamps (usually four) which have the printing plate numbers in the adjoining selvage—or margin (usually in the corner of the pane). On coils, these numbers appear in the margins of the stamps themselves, and collectors may save a *plate number strip* of three or five stamps with the number on the center stamp. On booklets, the plate numbers

usually appear on the booklet "tab" by which the panes are affixed to the booklet cover.

Booklet Panes are panes of stamps affixed in, or as part of, a thin folder to form a booklet. With self-adhesive stamps, a newer convertible booklet format has been created, so that the stamps, liner, and booklet are all one unit. Usually, collectors of booklet panes save the entire pane or the entire booklet.

Marginal blocks (including *copyright blocks*) feature marginal inscriptions other than the plate numbers. The most common is the copyright block, which features the copyright symbol ©, copyright date, and U.S. Postal Service information. All U.S. stamp designs since 1978 are copyrighted.

First Day Covers (FDCs) are envelopes bearing new stamps that are postmarked on the first day of sale. For each new postal issue, the U.S. Postal Service generally selects one location, usually related to the stamp subject, as the place for the first day dedication ceremony and the first day postmark. See page 10 for information on how to collect these covers.

First Day Ceremony Programs are given to persons who attend first day ceremonies. They contain a list of participants,

information on the stamp subject, and the actual stamp attached and postmarked.

Are there any stamp groups I can join?

Yes! Stamp clubs can be a great source for new stamps and stamp collecting advice. These clubs often meet at schools, libraries, and community centers. Ask your local postmaster or librarian for the locations of stamp clubs in your area and other contact information (including Internet sites, in some cases).

Exploring Space

Stamps with a space theme are almost boundless

Outer space and the dreams of humanity—both are boundless. It's no wonder that space is probably the most popular thematic topic for stamp collectors. It captures the imagination and it records an amazing—and ongoing—part of our history.

More than thirty years ago, in 1969, the first human beings set foot on the Moon. Nearly twenty years ago, in 1981, the first space shuttle launch began an era of regular manned space flights, leading to recent accomplishments like the orbiting Hubble Space Telescope and the start of the International Space Station. Throughout this space age, with its roots back in the 1950s, U.S. space efforts have continued to "push the envelope"—and stamps along with them.

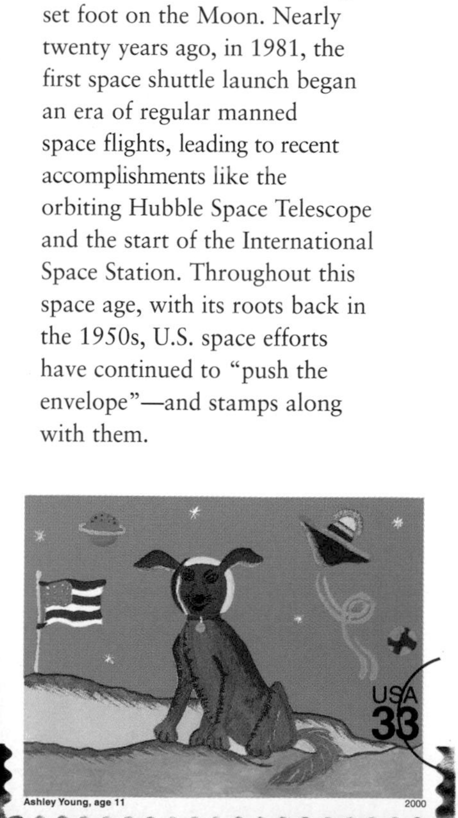

Ashley Young, age 11

2000

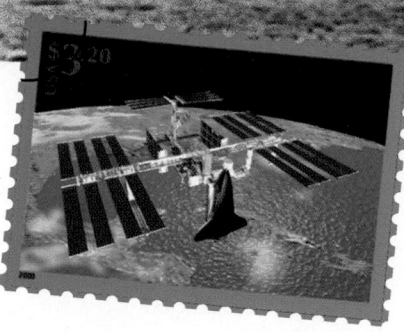

As we moved into the new millennium, the U.S. Postal Service issued some truly groundbreaking stamps. The most breathtaking is a group of five souvenir sheets honoring Space Achievement and Exploration. They feature the first holographic stamps in U.S. postal history, and their printed images on these pages cannot do them justice. But a description of the precedent-setting features of these new stamps may help to explain their beauty and innovation.

The uncut press sheet, offered to collectors, includes all five of the souvenir sheets and the fifteen stamps they contain. Focusing on the theme of Space Achievement and Exploration, the sheet contains the first U.S. postage stamps ever to be produced as holograms (four of the fifteen stamps are holographic). The sheet also features the first circular and pentagonal stamps ever produced by the United States.

Central to the sheet is the circular holographic stamp featuring a three-dimensional view of the Earth from space. It repeats the theme "Space Achievement and Exploration."

When it is viewed side to side, the viewer can actually see the Earth rotate up to twenty-five degrees east and west!

In the upper left corner of the press sheet is the souvenir sheet "Landing on the Moon." This holographic image features the lunar landing craft and celebrates the remarkable achievements that allowed astronauts to explore the Moon.

The souvenir sheet in the lower right corner is titled "Escaping the Gravity of Earth" and celebrates the accomplishments of a new breed of workers—those who work in space on shuttle missions, including those who contribute to the construction of the visionary International Space Station. These two stamps are also holographic images.

In the lower left souvenir sheet, "Exploring the Solar System," are five pentagonal stamps featuring different views of our sun. These pentagonal shapes were created using special perforating dies, resulting in the first five-sided stamps in U.S. history.

Morgan Hill, age 9

Lastly, in the upper right souvenir sheet, there are six images of "Probing the Vastness of Space." These stamps honor the role of observatories, telescopes, and satellite technology in the American space program.

The achievements of one such effort, the Hubble Space Telescope, were celebrated on another set of five stamps issued earlier in 2000. This telescope is the largest and most complex astronomical observatory ever placed into Earth orbit. The pane of stamps pays tribute to the remarkable astronomer Edwin Powell Hubble for whom the telescope is named. The five stamps feature spectacular images of space phenomena captured by the telescope.

Finally, there are our future visionaries. The U.S. Postal Service held a design contest for children ages eight through twelve, and the four winning designs offer an interesting vision of the future as only our next generation can imagine it. The results are featured on four special commemorative stamps titled "Stampin' The Future."™

This is only the beginning. Space will offer us everything our imaginations can dream and possibly even more. The future is boundless.

18

Celebrating Space Achievements

U.S. postage stamps have paid tribute to the pioneering spirit of American space exploration for many years. They provide a colorful record of U.S. space accomplishments and offer a window into the future as well. You might wonder about the first stamp on the list, but the 1948 commemorative for Fort Bliss features an early rocket missile launch.

Skylab

Pushing the Envelope:

The Art of the Postage Stamp

The 2000 *Postal Service Guide to U.S. Stamps* offers readers an insider's preview of a new museum exhibition. "Pushing the Envelope: The Art of the Postage Stamp" celebrates the contributions of more than seventy outstanding artists and designers whose images reflect a rapidly changing world, breathing new life into time-honored icons. This exciting exhibition spans forty years of illustration history and will be on view at the Norman Rockwell Museum in Stockbridge, Massachusetts, from November 11, 2000, through May 28, 2001.

Founded in 1969, the Norman Rockwell Museum is dedicated to the enjoyment and study of Rockwell's work and regularly showcases the importance of illustration in American culture. Exhibitions often include magazine covers, book illustrations, advertisements—and now

postage stamps.

Selected from the U.S. Postal Service's extensive collection, "Pushing the Envelope" will include a broad range of images that explore science and technology, arts and entertainment, transportation, athletic achievement, American heroes, and North American flora and fauna. Additional information about the stamps included in the show is found throughout the 2001 *Guide*. Each stamp subject is described within its historical context with the original issuance and the artist identified for ease of reference.

Inside you will find more information about each of the Celebrate The Century® stamp panes. Learn more about David Wallechinsky, who wrote the text for all ten stamp panes, and the individual artists who created the illustrations for specific decades.

The second issuance of the

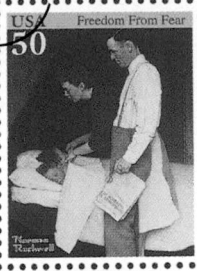

Nature of America series is also featured in the *Guide* and in the upcoming exhibition. Turn to the *Guide* for more information about the stamp pane design and some of its important visual elements.

Another U.S. Postal Service first is showcased in this year's *Guide:* the U.S. Navy Submarines prestige booklet. Working with the U.S. Navy, as well as with naval and submarine historians, the Postal Service developed a

1997 Classic American Aircraft, and Ted Rose's 1999 All Aboard!: Twentieth-Century Trains stamps.

We hope that you will enjoy this year's unique *Postal Service Guide to U.S. Stamps*—and we hope to see you in Stockbridge.

brief history of the submarine service. The *Gato*-class submarine stamp art will be included in the "Pushing the Envelope" exhibit, and more information on that stamp design is also provided.

Philatelists will be especially pleased to see several examples of art used for engraved stamps in the exhibition, including two original drawings by Norman Rockwell. Other stamps of particular interest are John Dallison's 1995 Antique Automobiles, Bill Phillips's

This exhibition has been made possible by BerkshireBank.

2000 Issues
U.S. Postage Stamps & Postal Stationery

Year 2000

Lunar New Year
(Year of the Dragon)

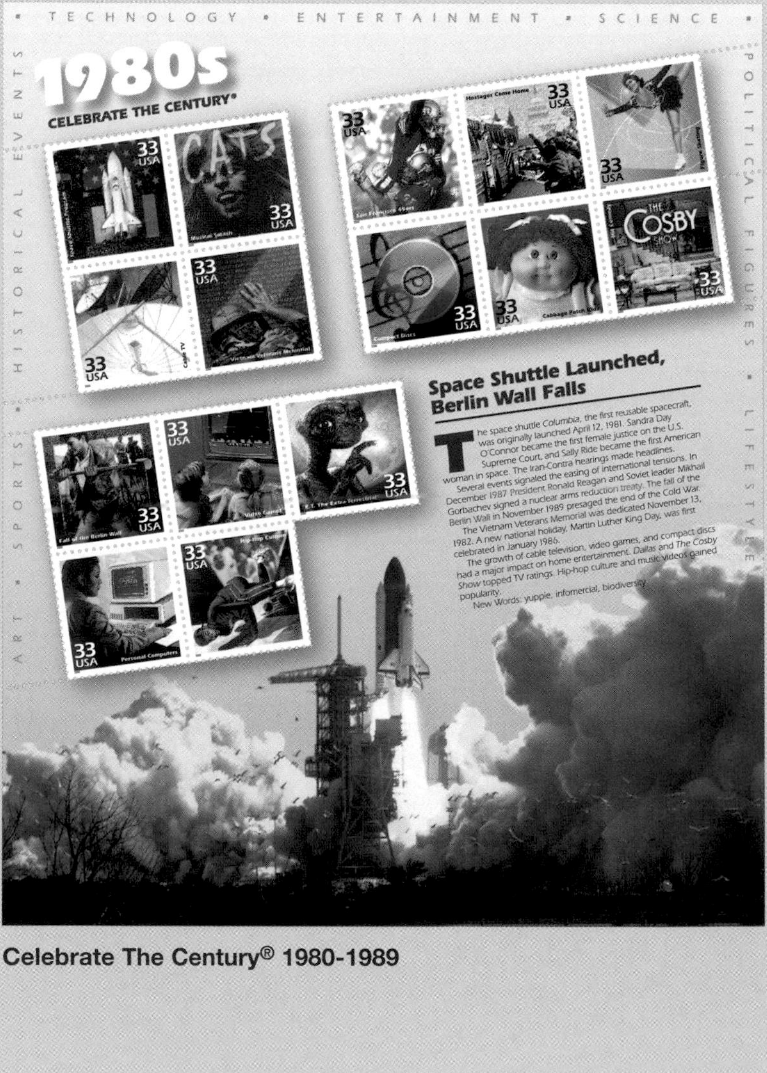

TECHNOLOGY ◦ *ENTERTAINMENT* ◦ *SCIENCE*

1980s
CELEBRATE THE CENTURY®

Space Shuttle Launched, Berlin Wall Falls

The space shuttle Columbia, the first reusable spacecraft, was originally launched April 12, 1981. Sandra Day O'Connor became the first female justice on the U.S. Supreme Court, and Sally Ride became the first American woman in space. The Iran-Contra hearings made headlines. Several events signaled the easing of international tensions. In December 1987 President Ronald Reagan and Soviet leader Mikhail Gorbachev signed a nuclear arms reduction treaty. The fall of the Berlin Wall in November 1989 presaged the end of the Cold War.

The Vietnam Veterans Memorial was dedicated November 13, 1982. A new national holiday, Martin Luther King Day, was first celebrated in January 1986.

The growth of cable television, video games, and compact discs had a major impact on home entertainment. *Dallas* and *The Cosby Show* topped TV ratings. Hip-hop culture and music videos gained popularity.

New Words: yuppie, infomercial, biodiversity

Celebrate The Century® 1980-1989

22

Year 2000   #3369

The Postal Service commemorated the beginning of the year 2000 with a stamp featuring a celebratory image of a baby ringing in the New Year. This illustration by J.C. Leyendecker (1874-1951) originally appeared on the cover of the January 2, 1937, issue of *The Saturday Evening Post*. For nearly 40 years, Leyendecker—a role model for the young Norman Rockwell—illustrated covers featuring the New Year's baby for *The Saturday Evening Post*.

Date of Issue: December 27, 1999   Illustrator: J.C. Leyendecker
Place of Issue: Washington, DC   Printing: Offset/Microprint
Designer: Carl Herrman   ("USA")

Lunar New Year (Year of the Dragon)   #3370

The dragon is the fifth of the twelve animals associated with the Chinese lunar calendar. People born in the Year of the Dragon are described as having a strong and energetic character. They are self-confident and curious, and they work toward perfection.

Clarence Lee, an American of Chinese descent, combines calligraphy with a paper-cut design in these intricate arrangements. The first stamp in the series was Year of the Rooster, followed by Year of the Dog, Boar, Rat, Ox, Tiger, and Hare.

The Lunar New Year is celebrated by people of Chinese, Korean, Vietnamese, Tibetan, and Mongolian heritage.

Date of Issue: January 6, 2000   Illustrator: Clarence Lee
Place of Issue: San Francisco, CA   Printing: Offset/Microprint
Designer: Clarence Lee   (dragon)

Celebrate The Century® 1980-1989   #3190, 3190a-o

The space shuttle Columbia, the first reusable spacecraft, was originally launched April 12, 1981. Sandra Day O'Connor became the first female justice on the U.S. Supreme Court, and Sally Ride became the first American woman in space. The Iran-Contra hearings made headlines.

Several events signaled the easing of international tensions. In December 1987 President Ronald Reagan and Soviet leader Mikhail Gorbachev signed a nuclear arms reduction treaty. The fall of the Berlin Wall in November 1989 presaged the end of the Cold War.

The Vietnam Veterans Memorial was dedicated November 13, 1982. A new national holiday, Martin Luther King Day, was first celebrated in January 1986.

The growth of cable television, video games, and compact discs had a major impact on home entertainment. *Dallas* and *The Cosby Show* topped TV ratings. Hip-hop culture and music videos gained popularity. New Words: yuppie, infomercial, biodiversity.

Date of Issue: January 12, 2000   Illustrator: Robert Rodriguez
Place of Issue: Titusville, FL   Printing: Offset
Designer: Carl Herrman

Grand Canyon   #C135

Carved by the rushing waters of the Colorado River over the course of a few million years, the Grand Canyon is one of the most spectacular natural landmarks in the United States. Through the exposure of multiple layers of earth, the canyon provides one of the world's best records of geologic history. In 1919 Congress officially created Grand Canyon National Park, located in northwestern Arizona, where more than five million people visit each year. The Grand Canyon is 277 miles long and more than a mile deep in places.

Date of Issue: January 20, 2000
Place of Issue: Grand Canyon, AZ
Designer: Ethel Kessler

Photographer: Tom Till
Printing: Offset/Microprint
("USA")

Patricia Harris   #3371

With this 23rd stamp in the Black Heritage series, the Postal Service honors Patricia Roberts Harris, the first African-American woman to serve as a member of a presidential cabinet.

In 1977 President Jimmy Carter named Patricia Roberts Harris Secretary of Housing and Urban Development. Two years later he appointed her Secretary of Health, Education and Welfare.

Among her other significant accomplishments, Harris was the first African-American woman to serve as a U.S. ambassador—President Johnson named her ambassador to Luxembourg in 1965—and the first woman to serve as dean of Howard University Law School.

Date of Issue: January 27, 2000
Place of Issue: Washington, D.C.

Designer: Richard Sheaff
Printing: Offset

University of Utah   #UX312

This stamped card commemorates the 150th anniversary of the founding of the University of Utah on February 28, 1850. Originally named the University of Deseret, it was the first university established west of the Missouri River.

The stamped card depicts the neoclassical John R. Park Building, one of several historic buildings located around Presidents Circle. The Park Building was placed on the National Register of Historic Places on April 20, 1978.

Date of Issue: February 28, 2000
Place of Issue: Salt Lake City, UT
Designer: Ethel Kessler

Illustrator: Allen Garns
Printing: Offset

Fruit Berries   #3294a, 3295a, 3296a, 3297c, 3297d

These definitive stamps, featuring blueberries, strawberries, raspberries and blackberries, were issued in a two-sided pressure sensitive adhesive (PSA). These designs were previously issued in single-sided convertible booklets and in coils of 100, both PSAs.

Date of Issue: March 15, 2000
Place of Issue: Ponchatoula, LA
Designer: Howard Paine

Illustrator: Ned Seidler
Printing: Gravure

Grand Canyon

Patricia Roberts Harris

University of Utah

Fruit Berries

Ryman Auditorium

U.S. Navy Submarines

U.S. Navy Submarines
Los Angeles **Class**

Ryman Auditorium   #UX313

Ryman Auditorium, originally called the Union Gospel Tabernacle, is best known as a former home of the Grand Ole Opry. Construction of the tabernacle began in 1889 by Captain Thomas Ryman; upon his death in 1904, it was renamed Ryman Auditorium. It was placed on the National Register of Historic Places in May 1971. After renovation in 1994, Ryman Auditorium reopened as a theater.

The stamp art features an original oil painting by Mike Summers. The painting, completed in 1994, now hangs in the Ryman Auditorium. It depicts how the building looked around the turn of the century.

Date of Issue: March 18, 2000   Illustrator: Mike Summers
Place of Issue: Nashville, TN   Printing: Offset
Designer: Richard Sheaff

9a. U.S. Navy Submarines   #BK279, 3377a, 3373-3377
Prestige Booklet

The five stamp designs in this prestige booklet depict different periods in submarine technology. In 1900, with the purchase of *Holland*, the U.S. Navy acquired its first submarine. The S-class submarine shows the change in technology and size that occurred after USS *Holland*. The *Gato* class sub represents the contributions that submarines made to American naval superiority in the Pacific during WWII. *Los Angeles* class attack subs are nuclear powered. The *Ohio* class submarine—560 feet long with 24 Trident ballistic missiles—represents an ever present deterrent to possible military aggression.

9b. U.S. Navy Submarines   #3372
Los Angeles Class

The *Los Angeles Class* commemorative stamp depicted in this booklet can be purchased separately.

Date of Issue: March 27, 2000   Illustrator: James Griffiths
Place of Issue: Groton, CT   Printing: Offset
Designer: Carl Herrman

Pacific Coast Rain Forest   #3378, 3378a-j

The Pacific Coast Rain Forest stamp pane is the second in an educational series designed to promote appreciation of North America's major plant and animal communities (the first in this series was the Sonoran Desert).

The rain forest of the Pacific Northwest is one of the largest remaining temperate rain forests in the world and is considered by some to be the most spectacular. This is an old-growth forest, with giant trees hundreds of years old. The understory of the rain forest (as illustrated in the artwork) is especially lush.

The artwork highlights the diversity of life in the coastal temperate rain forest and includes 26 common animal and plant species. The scene includes an aquatic component because streams, rivers, and the life they support, are critical parts of this ecosystem.

Date of Issue: March 29, 2000   Illustrator: John D. Dawson
Place of Issue: Seattle, WA   Printing: Offset
Designer: Ethel Kessler

Louise Nevelson   #3379-3383, 3383a

Louise Nevelson (1899-1988), one of the most gifted sculptors of the 20th century, introduced a new form of sculpture that consisted of carved, recycled, and painted wood objects arranged in boxes to create entire sculptural walls. During her 50-year career, she produced an impressive and influential body of work.

Each stamp is a photographic reproduction that shows a detail of a larger Nevelson sculpture. The sculptures featured on the stamps are (from left to right): *Silent Music I*, *Royal Tide I*, *Black Chord*, *Nightsphere-Light*, and *Dawn's Wedding Chapel I*. The selvage photo of Nevelson was taken by Arnold Newman.

Date of Issue: April 6, 2000   Designer: Ethel Kessler
Place of Issue: New York, NY   Printing: Offset

Coral Pink Rose   #3052E

Roses are one of the most favored and beloved flowers throughout the world. The rose depicted here is coral pink with a rounded form and abundant petals and is similar to the "America" variety of rose that was named in honor of the United States bicentennial. This stamp was previously issed in a different format.

Date of Issue: April 7, 2000   Illustrator: Ned Seidler
Place of Issue: New York, NY   Printing: Gravure
Designer: Derry Noyes

Pacific Coast Rain Forest

Louise Nevelson

Coral Pink Rose

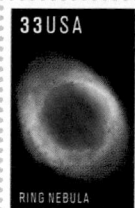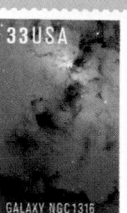

Edwin Powell Hubble/Telescope

American Samoa

Library of Congress

Edwin Powell Hubble/Telescope   #3384-3388, 3388a

Edwin Powell Hubble was an eminent American astronomer whose work furthered our understanding of the universe. Born November 20, 1889, in Marshfield, Missouri, Hubble determined that galaxies (very large groups of stars and associated matter) exist outside of and are receding from our own galaxy, the Milky Way.

The Hubble Space Telescope (HST), launched in April 1990, orbits the Earth and sends images of astronomical objects back to scientists. The HST can see farther into the universe than Earth-based observation tools and provides astronomers with stunningly clear images.

The five stamp images-Eagle Nebula, Ring Nebula, Lagoon Nebula, Egg Nebula, and Galaxy NGC 1316-were captured by the Hubble Space Telescope. The images are visual representations of data taken by the HST that have been processed, and in some cases colorized, for scientific purposes.

Date of Issue: April 10, 2000   Designer: Phil Jordan
Place of Issue: Greenbelt, MD   Printing: Gravure

American Samoa   #3389

This stamp commemorates 100 years of political affiliation between the United States and the territory of American Samoa in the South Pacific. In April 1900, local Samoan chiefs ceded the islands of Tutuila and Aunuu to the United States. The stamp art depicts an "alia," the traditional double canoe, sailing with the prevailing easterly wind. Sunuitao Peak, on the island of Ofu, can be seen in the background.

Date of Issue: April 17, 2000   Illustrator: Herb Kane
Place of Issue: Pago Pago, AS   Printing: Offset/Microprint
Designer: Howard Paine   ("Samoa")

Library of Congress   #3390

Established by an act of Congress on April 24, 1800, the Library of Congress marks its bicentennial with a national celebration of all libraries. The bicentennial goal of the world's largest library is "to inspire creativity in the century ahead by stimulating greater use of the Library of Congress and libraries everywhere."

The Postal Service is joining in the celebration with the issuance of this commemorative stamp that features a 1980 photograph of the interior dome and several of the arched windows in the Main Reading Room in the Thomas Jefferson Building. A historic photograph of the exterior of the Thomas Jefferson Building was used on the selvage.

Date of Issue: April 24, 2000   Photographer: Michael Freeman
Place of Issue: Washington, D.C.   Printing: Offset
Designer: Ethel Kessler

Wile E. Coyote and Road Runner   #3391, 3392

The fourth stamp in the Postal Service's Looney Tunes series features Wile E. Coyote and Road Runner.

Wile E. Coyote has appeared in more than 40 cartoons with Road Runner, the speedy object of his appetite. Wile E. Coyote is a lovable antihero. His confidence and ambition never cease in his pursuit of the elusive Road Runner who, relying on an instinctive gift for survival, effortlessly thwarts all his schemes.

Date of Issue: April 26, 2000
Place of Issue: Phoenix, AZ
Designer: Ed Wleczyk,
        Warner Bros.

Character Art: Frank Espinosa,
        Warner Bros.
Printing: Offset/Microprint

Celebrate The Century® 1990-1999   #3191, 3191a-o

The Soviet Union collapsed, effectively ending the Cold War. Troops were deployed by the United States in the Persian Gulf, in Somalia, and in the Balkans. In 1992-often called the Year of the Woman-a record number of women were elected to political office.

American astronauts joined Russian cosmonauts on the Mir space station, and Mars Pathfinder and Mars Global Surveyor sent back extraordinary images of the red planet. A grouping of planets resembling our solar system was found by astronomers.

The World Wide Web and e-mail revolutionized communications. Millions of American bought cellular phones as service expanded.

In Washington, D.C., the Holocaust Museum drew huge crowds, while in Los Angeles, the Getty Center's architecture got rave reviews. Moviegoers flocked to see *Titanic* and *Jurassic Park*.

Extreme sports, such as snowboarding and BMX biking, attracted young people, and the U.S. women's softball, soccer, and basketball teams proved themselves the best in the world.

New words: e-commerce, Web site, Y2K

Date of Issue: May 2, 2000
Place of Issue: Escondido, CA
Designer: Howard Paine

Illustrator: Drew Struzan
Printing: Offset

Wile E. Coyote and Road Runner

Celebrate The Century® 1990-1999

Distinguished Soldiers

Summer Sports

Adoption

Middlebury College

Distinguished Soldiers   #3393-3396, 3396a

Commemorated for their heroism and leadership in World War I and World War II, the Postal Service honors distinguished soldiers Alvin C. York, John L. Hines, Audie L. Murphy, and Omar N. Bradley.

The stamp art features black-and-white photographs of these four men. Color photographs of shoulder sleeve insignia are used as design motifs to indicate units the soldiers served in during their illustrious careers.

Date of Issue: May 3, 2000   Designer: Phil Jordan
Place of Issue: Washington, D.C.   Printing: Offset

Summer Sports   #3397

Taken by noted sports photographer David Madison, the photo used for the stamp design graphically portrays the swift pace of a summer track event. The camera captured only a blur of legs as the runners raced past.

Date of Issue: May 5, 2000   Photographer: David Madison
Place of Issue: Spokane, WA   Printing: Offset/Microprint
Designer: Richard Sheaff

Adoption   #3398

With the issuance of the Adoption stamp, the Postal Service continues its tradition of raising awareness of social issues.

The stamp design combines the colorful art of Greg Berger with text. Berger, who was adopted himself, provides his personal interpretation of this issue. Recalling memories of his own childhood, he used fundamental shapes, simple forms, and bright colors to create a happy, hopeful image. This graphic design attempts to convey a visual balance between reality and the fantasy of what might be; it also shows that childhood is a delicate and influential part of life.

Date of Issue: May 10, 2000   Illustrator: Greg Berger
Place of Issue: Los Angeles, CA   Printing: Offset/Microprint
Designer: Greg Berger

Middlebury College   #UX316

This stamped card commemorates the 200th anniversary of Middlebury College. The charter for the college was officially granted on November 1, 1800, and classes began five days later. Middlebury College is the oldest operating institution of higher education in Vermont and the second oldest in terms of charter.

The Middlebury College stamped card features a painting of the east side of Old Stone Row, which was placed on the National Register of Historic Places on September 18, 1997. The buildings of Old Stone Row are primarily significant because they embody the architectural characteristics of the early 19th-century stone mill building type, as adapted to educational purposes.

Date of Issue: May 19, 2000   Illustrator: Arnold Holeywell
Place of Issue: Middlebury, VT   Printing: Offset
Designer: Howard Paine

Youth Team Sports   #3399-3402, 3402a

The Youth Team Sports stamp pane depicts a variety of team sports popular with American children between the ages of 6 and 17.

The photographs used in each stamp design were chosen to convey the action and excitement of team play: William Sallaz's photograph depicts the athleticism of basketball, Mike Powell's image portrays a football player running with the ball, Zoran Milich's photograph features two soccer players competing for possession of the ball, and Bob Wickley's image captures a baseball pitch in mid-flight.

Date of Issue: May 27, 2000   Designer: Derry Noyes
Place of Issue: Lake Buena Vista, FL   Printing: Offset

The Stars & Stripes   #3403

With this stamp pane, the U.S. Postal Service pays tribute to the American flag and its unique history. Composed of 20 different flags, the pane loosely charts the evolution of the Stars and Stripes from colonial times to the present. Among the flags displayed are the Continental Colors and the Star-Spangled Banner, in addition to many regional and military flags. These flags were selected for their significance in American history as well as for their aesthetic value.

Date of Issue: June 14, 2000   Designer: Richard Sheaff
Place of Issue: Baltimore, MD   Printing: Offset

Youth Team Sports

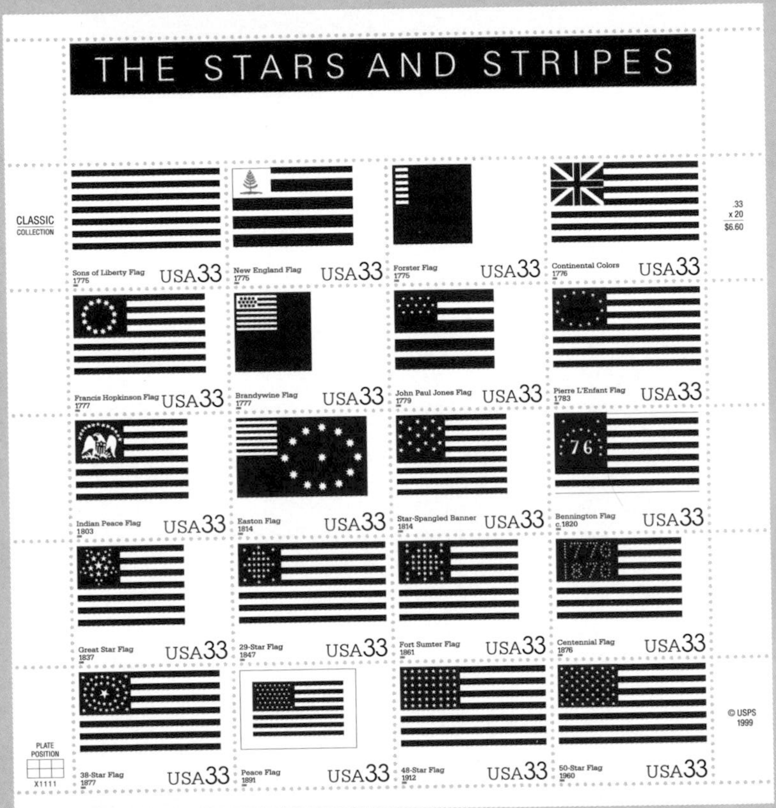

THE STARS AND STRIPES

CLASSIC COLLECTION

.33 x 20 $6.60

Sons of Liberty Flag 1775 — USA 33
New England Flag 1775 — USA 33
Forster Flag 1775 — USA 33
Continental Colors 1776 — USA 33

Francis Hopkinson Flag 1777 — USA 33
Brandywine Flag 1777 — USA 33
John Paul Jones Flag 1779 — USA 33
Pierre L'Enfant Flag 1783 — USA 33

Indian Peace Flag 1803 — USA 33
Easton Flag 1814 — USA 33
Star-Spangled Banner 1814 — USA 33
Bennington Flag c.1820 — USA 33

Great Star Flag 1837 — USA 33
29-Star Flag 1847 — USA 33
Fort Sumter Flag 1861 — USA 33
Centennial Flag 1876 — USA 33

PLATE POSITION
X1111

38-Star Flag 1877 — USA 33
Peace Flag 1891 — USA 33
48-Star Flag 1912 — USA 33
50-Star Flag 1960 — USA 33

© USPS 1999

The Stars & Stripes

Fruit Berries

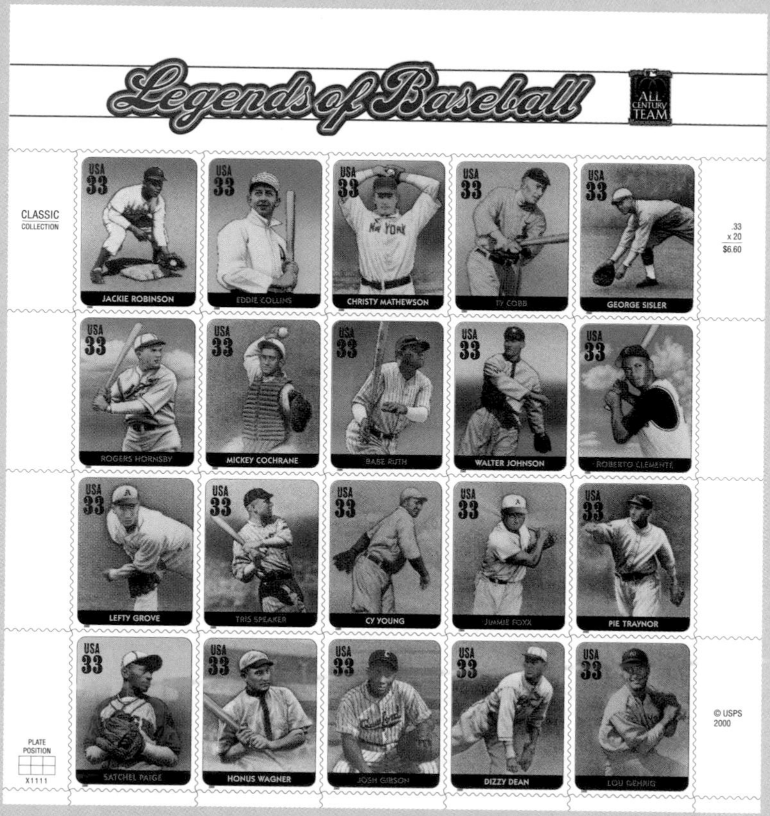

Legends of Baseball

ALL CENTURY TEAM

CLASSIC
COLLECTION

.33
x 20
$6.60

USA 33	USA 33	USA 33	USA 33	USA 33
JACKIE ROBINSON	EDDIE COLLINS	CHRISTY MATHEWSON	TY COBB	GEORGE SISLER
ROGERS HORNSBY	MICKEY COCHRANE	BABE RUTH	WALTER JOHNSON	ROBERTO CLEMENTE
LEFTY GROVE	TRIS SPEAKER	CY YOUNG	JIMMIE FOXX	PIE TRAYNOR
SATCHEL PAIGE	HONUS WAGNER	JOSH GIBSON	DIZZY DEAN	LOU GEHRIG

PLATE
POSITION

X1111

© USPS
2000

Legends of Baseball

Fruit Berries

These definitive stamps were also issued in a linerless coil of 100.

Date of Issue: June 16, 2000
Place of Issue: Buffalo, NY
Designer: Howard Paine

Illustrator: Ned Seidler
Printing: Gravure

Legends of Baseball

In this Classic Collection, the U.S. Postal Service honors 20 nominees for the Major League Baseball® All-Century Team™. These players embody the glory and tradition of our national pastime. Tales of their extraordinary abilities and larger-than-life personalities have made them much more than just ballplayers: They are legends.

Date of Issue: July 6, 2000
Place of Issue: Atlanta, GA
Designer: Phil Jordan

Illustrator: Joe Saffold
Printing: Offset

Space Achievement and Exploration

These stamp designs educate the world about the accomplishments, wonder, and excitement of the American space program. They display the achievements of our space program, as well as the infinite possibilities of future space endeavor.

The **upper left quadrant** commemorates the Apollo program that culminated in landing American astronauts on the moon. The background image is from the Apollo 16 mission.

The **upper right quadrant** addresses the exploration of deep space.

The stamp in the **central panel** is the first circular hologram stamp ever issued by the Postal Service. It features a view of Earth from the Apollo 17 spacecraft and shows the continents of Africa and Antarctica.

Moving farther from Earth, the **lower left quadrant** represents the exploration of our solar system. These stamps are the first pentagonal stamps ever issued by the Postal Service.

The **lower right quadrant** represents American technology solving the problems of escaping the gravitational pull of Earth and learning how to send missions into Earth's orbit.

Dates of Issue: July 7-16
Place of Issue: Anaheim, CA
  World Stamp Expo 2000

Designer: Richard Sheaff
Printing: Gravure

Space Achievement and Exploration
Full Press Sheet Poster of 15 Stamps

Landing on The Moon

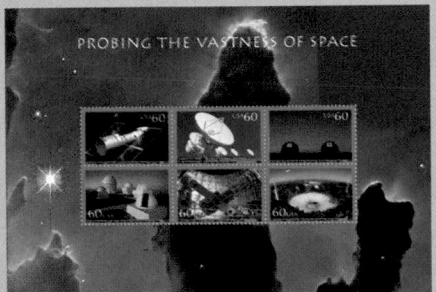

Probing the Vastness of Space

 **Achievement and Exploration**

Exploring the Solar System

Escaping the Gravity of Earth

Stampin' the Future™

Joseph W. Stilwell

Claude Pepper

Stampin' the Future™

In celebration of the approaching 21st century,the Postal Service held Stampin' the Future, a youth stamp design contest for children 8 to 12 years of age. Kids from the United States and its various territories and possessions were invited to submit designs based on their visions of the 21st century.

Date of Issue: July 13, 2000
Place of Issue: Anaheim, CA

Designer: Richard Sheaff
Printing: Offset

Joseph W. Stilwell

General Joseph W. "Vinegar Joe" Stilwell (1883-1946) was the senior American military commander in the China-Burma-India theater during World War II. He also served as chief of staff to Generalissimo Chiang Kai-shek and as deputy supreme commander of the newly established South East Asia Command.

Date of Issue: August 27, 2000
Place of Issue: Providence, RI
Designer: Richard Sheaff

Illustrator: Mark Summers
Printing: Offset Intaglio

Claude Pepper

On the 100th anniversary of the year of his birth, the Postal Service honors Claude Pepper, a champion of rights for the elderly.

In a political career that spanned 60 years, Claude Pepper, served in both the U.S. Senate (1936-1951) and the U.S. House of Representatives (1963-1989). From 1977 to 1983, he was chairman of the House Select Committee on Aging, continuing his strong support of the Social Security and Medicare programs.

Date of Issue: September 7, 2000
Place of Issue: Tallahassee, FL
Designer: Richard Sheaff

Illustrator: Mark Summers
Printing: Intaglio

California Statehood

With the issuance of this stamp in 2000, the Postal Service commemorates California's sesquicentennial.

The stamp features a photograph of cliff tops at the southern end of the Big Sur coastline with iceplant blooming in the foreground. The photograph captures the beauty and grandeur of California's coastal environment.

Date of Issue: September 8, 2000   Photographer: Art Wolfe
Place of Issue: Sacramento, CA   Printing: Gravure
Designer: Carl Herrman

Edward G. Robinson

This is the sixth stamp issued in the Legends of Hollywood series. Edward G. Robinson (1893-1973), stage and screen actor, renowned art collector, philanthropist, and humanitarian, is best remembered for his classic portrayals of gangsters in *Little Caesar* (1931) and several other films. The versatile actor appeared in some 90 movies, including *Double Indemnity* (1944) and *Key Largo* (1948). He received an Academy Award for his lifetime achievement in films in 1973.

Date of Issue: September 14, 2000   Illustrator: Drew Struzan
Place of Issue: Burbank, CA   Printing: Gravure
Designer: Howard Paine

Deep Sea Creatures

The deep sea is the most expansive animal habitat on Earth, and the dominant physical factors are darkness, cold, and high pressure. In response to these conditions, the creatures there possess significant modifications that differ greatly from creatures that inhabit more benign regions. These adaptations include bizarre body forms and unusual lifestyles.

The five life-forms represented on these stamps—fanfin anglerfish, sea cucumber, fangtooth, amphipod, and medusa—provide a glimpse into a vast and alien world seen by few people. Adults as well as children are fascinated by the strange appearance and adaptations of these creatures of the deep sea.

Date of Issue: October 2, 2000   Photographers:
Place of Issue: Monterey, CA   Bruce Robison
(National Stamp Collecting Month)   Laurence P. Madin
Designer: Greg Berger   Printing: Gravure

California Statehood

Edward G. Robinson

Deep Sea Creatures

Thomas Wolfe

The White House

The New York Public Library

Thomas Wolfe

The issuance of this commemorative stamp celebrates the 100th anniversary of the birth of Thomas Wolfe, who is considered one of the greatest American autobiographical novelists of the 20th century.

Born October 3, 1900, Wolfe is best known for his novel *Look Homeward, Angel* (1929), which is based on his early life in North Carolina. He also wrote *Of Time and the River* (1935), *The Web and the Rock* (1939), and *You Can't Go Home Again* (1940). His last two books were published posthumously. Wolfe died September 15, 1938, at the age of 37.

Artist Michael J. Deas brings to light a pensive Thomas Wolfe, complementing the author's image with that of an angel and the titles of some of his literary works.

Date of Issue: October 3, 2000
Place of Issue: Asheville, NC
Designer: Phil Jordan

Illustrator: Michael Deas
Printing: Offset

The White House

John Adams, second President of the United States, moved into the unfinished "President's House" in November 1800, eight years after the first stone was laid. The U.S. Postal Service joins the White House in commemorating the 200th anniversary of the first residency of the White House, an enduring symbol of the American presidency. The pristine blanket of snow in the serene photograph of the north facade belies the Executive Mansion's multiple functions: bustling office, site of official state ceremonies, and home to our Chief Executive and his family.

Date of Issue: TBD
Place of Issue: Washington, D.C.
Designer: Derry Noyes

Photographer: Patricia Fisher
Printing: Offset

The New York Public Library

This definitive stamp depicts one of the two lions guarding the entrance to the New York Public Library. Sculpted by Edward Clark Potter, these trademarked beasts, nicknamed Patience and Fortitude—have been adopted by the library as its official mascots.

Date of Issue: November 9, 2000
Place of Issue: New York, New York
Designer Carl Herrman

Illustrator: Nancy Stahl
Printing: Gravure

Explanation of Catalog Prices

The United States Postal Service sells only the commemoratives and special issues released during the past few years. Current postal stationery and regular issues remain on sale for longer periods of time. Prices in this book are called "catalog prices" by stamp collectors. Collectors use catalog prices as guidelines when buying or trading stamps. **It is important to remember the prices are simply guidelines to the stamp values. Stamp condition is very important in determining the actual value of a stamp.**

Prices are Estimated

Listed prices are estimates of how much you can expect to pay for a stamp from a dealer. **A 15-cent minimum valuation has been established that represents a fair-market price to have a dealer locate and provide a single stamp to a customer. Dealers may charge less per stamp to provide a group of such stamps, and may charge less for such a single stamp. Similarly, a $1.00 minimum has been established for First Day Covers (FDCs).** If you sell a stamp to a dealer, he or she may offer

you much less than the catalog price. Dealers pay based on their interest in owning a particular stamp. If they already have a full supply, they may only buy additional stamps at a low price.

Condition Affects Value

The catalog prices are given for unused (mint) stamps and used (canceled) stamps that have been hinged and are in "very fine" condition. Stamps in "superb" condition that have never been hinged may cost more than the listed price. Stamps in less than "fine" condition may cost less.

The prices for used stamps are based on a light cancellation; a heavy cancellation lessens a stamp's value. Canceled stamps may be worth more than uncanceled stamps. This happens if the cancellation is of a special type or for a significant date. Therefore, it is important to study an envelope before removing a stamp and discarding its "cover." Additional information about and examples of stamp conditions can be found in the Introduction to this book.

Sample Listing

				Un	U	PB/LP/PNC	#	FDC	Q(M)
3069	32¢	Georgia O'Keefe	05/23/96	.60	.15	2.40	(4)	1.25	156

Scott Catalog Number (bold type indicates stamp is pictured)

Description

Denomination

Date of Issue

Unused Catalog Price

Used Catalog Price

Plate Block Price, Line Pair Price or **Plate Number** Coil Price

Number of stamps in Plate Block, Line Pair or Plate Number Coil

First Day Cover Price

Quantity Issued in **Millions** (where known)

3069

Understanding the Listings

■ Prices in **regular type** for single unused and used stamps are taken from the *Scott 2000 Specialized Catalogue of U.S. Stamps & Covers*, whose editors have based these prices on **actual retail values** as they found them in the marketplace. The Scott numbering system for stamps is used in this book. Prices quoted for unused and used stamps are for "very fine" condition, except where "very fine" is not available.

■ Stamp values in *italic* generally refer to items difficult to value accurately.

■ A dash (—) in a value column means the item is known to exist but information is insufficient for establishing a value.

■ The stamp listings contain a number of additions designated "*a*," "*b*," "*c*," etc. These represent recognized variations of stamps as well as errors. These listings are as complete as space permits.

Occasionally, a new stamp or major variation may be inserted by the catalog editors into a series or sequence where it was not originally anticipated. These additions are identified by capital letters "*A*," "*B*" and so forth. For example, a new stamp which logically belonged between 1044 and 1045 is designated 1044A, even though it is entirely different from 1044. The insertion was preferable to a complete renumbering of the series.

■ Prices for Plate Blocks, First Day Covers, American Commemorative Panels and Souvenir Pages are taken from *Scott 2000 Specialized Catalogue of U.S. Stamps & Covers*.

Sample Variation Listing

			Un	U	PB/LP/PNC	#	FDC	Q(M)
2281	25¢ Honeybee	09/02/88	.45	.15	3.25	(3)	1.25	
a	Imperf. pair		45.00					
b	Black omitted		65.00					
d	Pair, imperf. between		1,000.00					

Scott Catalog Number (bold type indicates stamp is pictured)

Description Denomination

Date of Issue

Unused Catalog Price

Used Catalog Price

Plate Block Price, Line Pair Price or **Plate Number Coil Price**

Number of stamps in plate Block, Line Pair or Plate Number Coil

First Day Cover Price

Quantity Issued in **Millions** (where known)

2281

Commemorative and Definitive Stamps

1847-1861

1

2

3

4

5

11

12

14

17

Issues of 1847

		Un	U
	Thin, Bluish Wove Paper, July 1, Imperf., Unwmkd.		
1	5¢ Benjamin Franklin	5,250.00	600.00
b	5¢ orange brown	6,500.00	850.00
c	5¢ red orange	12,500.00	5,000.00
	Pen cancel		300.00
	Double transfer of top or top and bottom frame lines		725.00
	Double transfer of top, bottom and left frame lines and numerals		3,000.00
2	10¢ George Washington	26,000.00	1,400.00
	Pen cancel		750.00
	Vertical line through second "F" of "OFFICE"	—	1,600.00
	With "stick pin" in tie, or with "harelip"	—	1,900.00
	Double transfer in lower right "X," or of left and bottom frame lines	—	2,000.00
	Double transfer in "POST OFFICE"	—	2,300.00

Issues of 1875, Reproductions of 1 and 2, Bluish Paper, Without Gum

		Un	U
3	5¢ Franklin	850.00	—
4	10¢ Washington	1,100.00	—

5¢. On the originals, the left side of the white shirt frill touches the oval on a level with the top of the "F" of "Five." On the reproductions, it touches the oval about on a level with the top of the figure "5."

10¢. On the originals, line of coat points to "T" of TEN and right line of coat points between "T" and "S" of CENTS.

On the reproductions left, line of coat points to right tip of "X" and right line of coat points to center of "S" of CENTS.

On the reproductions, the eyes have a sleepy look, the line of the mouth is straighter, and in the curl of hair near the left cheek is a strong black dot, while the originals have only a faint one.

Issues of 1851-57, Imperf.

		Un	U
5	1¢ Franklin, type I	175,000.00	35,000.00
5A	1¢ blue, type Ib	12,000.00	5,000.00
	#6-9: Franklin (5), 1851		
6	1¢ dark blue, type Ia	30,000.00	9,000.00
7	1¢ blue, type II	1,000.00	160.00
	Cracked plate	1,250.00	360.00
8	1¢ blue, type III	10,000.00	2,500.00
8A	1¢ blue, type IIIa	4,000.00	950.00
9	1¢ blue, type IV	650.00	125.00
	Triple transfer, one inverted	800.00	175.00

Issues of 1851-57

#10-11, 25-26a all had plates on which at least four outer frame lines (and usually much more) were recut, adding to their value.

		Un	U
10	3¢ orange brown Washington, type I (11)	2,750.00	100.00
	3¢ copper brown	3,250.00	170.00
	On part-India paper	—	500.00
11	3¢ Washington, type I	240.00	10.00
	3¢ deep claret	325.00	18.00
	Double transfer, "GENTS" for "CENTS"	375.00	35.00
12	5¢ Jefferson, type I	16,000.00	1,250.00
13	10¢ green Washington, type I (14)	13,000.00	750.00
14	10¢ green, type II	3,250.00	225.00
15	10¢ Washington, type III	3,250.00	225.00
16	10¢ green, type IV (14)	22,500.00	1,500.00
17	12¢ Washington	4,000.00	325.00

Issues of 1857-61, Perf. 15.5 (Issued in 1857 except #18, 27, 28A, 29, 30, 30A, 35, 36b, 37, 38, 39)

		Un	U
	#18-24: Franklin (5)		
18	1¢ blue, type I	1,500.00	500.00
19	1¢ blue, type Ia	16,000.00	4,500.00
20	1¢ blue, type II	850.00	240.00
21	1¢ blue, type III	11,000.00	1,800.00
22	1¢ blue, type IIIa	1,600.00	425.00
23	1¢ blue, type IV	6,250.00	575.00
24	1¢ blue, type V	175.00	40.00
	"Curl" on shoulder	240.00	67.50
	"Earring" below ear	350.00	95.00
	Long double "curl" in hair	300.00	80.00
b	Laid paper	—	
	#25-26a: Washington (11)		
25	3¢ rose, type I	2,000.00	75.00
	Major cracked plate	3,400.00	500.00
26	3¢ dull red, type II	75.00	5.00
	3¢ brownish carmine	140.00	16.00
	3¢ claret	170.00	21.00
	Left or right frame line double	110.00	15.00
	Cracked plate	750.00	225.00
26a	3¢ dull red, type IIa	200.00	45.00
	Double transfer	300.00	100.00
	Left frame line double	—	140.00

5
Bust of Benjamin
Franklin.

Detail of **#7, 20** Type II

Lower scrollwork
incomplete (lacks little
balls and lower plume
ornaments). Side orna-
ments are complete.

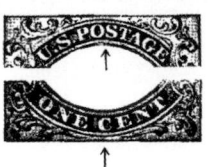

Detail of **#9, 23** Type IV

Similar to Type II, but
outer lines recut top,
bottom or both.

Detail of **#5, 18, 40**
Type I

Has curved, unbroken
lines outside labels.
Scrollwork is substan-
tially complete at top,
forms little balls at
bottom.

Detail of **#8, 21** Type III

Outer lines broken in
the middle. Side orna-
ments are substantially
complete.

Detail of **#8A, 22**
Type IIIa

Outer lines broken top
or bottom but not
both.

Detail of **#24** Type V

Similar to Type III of
1851-57 but with side
ornaments partly cut
away.

Detail of **#6, 19** Type Ia

Same as Type I at bot-
tom but top ornaments
and outer line partly
cut away. Lower scroll-
work is complete.

Detail of **#5a** Type Ib

Lower scrollwork is
incomplete, the little
balls are not so clear.

3¢ Washington Types I-IIa, series 1851-57, 1857-61, 1875

10

Bust of George Washington

Detail of **#10, 11, 25, 41**
Type I

There is an outer frame line
at top and bottom.

Detail of **#26** Type II

The outer frame line
has been removed at top
and bottom. The side frame
lines were recut so as to be
continuous from the top to
the bottom of the plate.

Detail of **#26a** Type IIa

The side frame lines ex-
tended only to the bottom
of the stamp design.

5¢ Jefferson Types I-II, Series 1851-57, 1857-61

12

Portrait of Thomas Jefferson

Detail of **#12, 27-29** Type I

There are projections on all
four sides.

Detail of **#30-30A** Type II

The projections at top and
bottom are partly cut away.

10¢ Washington Types I-IV, series 1851-57, 1857-61, 1875

15

Portrait of George
Washington

Detail of **#13, 31, 43** Type I

The "shells" at the lower
corners are practically
complete. The outer line
below the label is very
nearly complete. The outer
lines are broken above the
middle of the top label and
the "X" in each upper corner.

Detail of **#14, 32** Type II

The design is complete at
the top. The outer line at the
bottom is broken in the
middle. The shells are partly
cut away.

Detail of **#15, 33** Type III

The outer lines are broken
above the top label and the
"X" numerals. The outer line
at the bottom and the shells
are partly cut away, as in
Type II.

Detail of **#16, 34** Type IV

The outer lines have been recut at top or bottom or both.
Types I, II, III and IV have
complete ornaments at the
sides of the stamps and
three pearls at each outer
edge of the bottom panel.

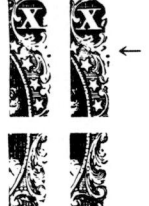

Detail of **#35** Type V

(Two typical examples).
Side ornaments slightly cut
away. Outer lines complete
at top except over right "X."
Outer lines complete at bottom and shells nearly so.

Issues of 1857-61	Un	U
Perf. 15.5		
#27-29: Jefferson (12)		
27	5¢ brick red, type I	*19,000.00*	1,200.00
28	5¢ red brown, type I	3,500.00	450.00
b	5¢ brt. red brn., type I	3,750.00	625.00
28A	5¢ Indian red, type I	*25,000.00*	2,750.00
29	5¢ brown, type I	2,000.00	325.00
	Defective transfer	—	—
30	5¢ orange brown, type II	1,100.00	1,000.00
30A	5¢ brown, type II (30)	1,500.00	260.00
b	Printed on both sides	*4,000.00*	*4,250.00*
	#31-35: Washington (15)		
31	10¢ green, type I	14,000.00	750.00
32	10¢ green, type II	4,250.00	275.00
33	10¢ green, type III	4,250.00	275.00
	"Curl" on forehead		
	or in left "X"		350.00
34	10¢ green, type IV	*27,500.00*	2,100.00
35	10¢ green, type V	275.00	65.00
	Small "curl" on forehead	325.00	77.50
	"Curl" in "e" or		
	"t" of "Cents"	350.00	90.00
	Plate I Outer frame lines complete		
36	12¢ blk. Washington		
	(17), plate I	1,200.00	190.00
	Triple transfer	1,500.00	
36b	12¢ black, plate III	725.00	170.00
	Vertical line		
	through rosette	900.00	250.00
37	24¢ gray lilac	1,250.00	325.00
a	24¢ gray	1,250.00	325.00
38	30¢ orange Franklin	1,600.00	425.00
	Recut at bottom	1,850.00	550.00
39	90¢ blue Washington	2,500.00	*5,500.00*
	Double transfer		
	at top or bottom	2,600.00	—
	90¢ Same, with pen cancel		1,250.00

Note: Beware of forged cancellations of #39. Genuine cancellations are rare

Issues of 1875	Un	U
Government Reprints, White Paper		
Without Gum, Perf. 12		
40	1¢ bright blue Franklin (5)	*550.00*	
41	3¢ scarlet Wash. (11)	*2,400.00*	
42	5¢ orange brown		
	Jefferson (30)	*1,000.00*	
43	10¢ blue green		
	Washington (14)	*2,000.00*	
44	12¢ greenish black		
	Washington (17)	*2,500.00*	
45	24¢ blackish violet		
	Washington (37)	*2,500.00*	
46	30¢ yellow orange		
	Franklin (38)	*2,500.00*	
47	90¢ deep blue		
	Washington (39)	*3,750.00*	
48-54	Not assigned		
Issue of 1861, Thin,		
Semi-Transparent Paper		
#55-62 are no longer considered postage stamps. Many experts consider them to be essays and/or trial color proofs.		
62B	10¢ dark green		
	Washington (58)	*6,000.00*	750.00

30

37

38

39

40

62B

Have you noticed? The Perf listings have changed from fractions to decimals. For example, Perf 10-1/2 is now 10.5. This is the first step taken toward giving you a more precise perf gauge which currently may only be precise to the nearest 0.5.

63   **64**   **65**   **67**

68   **69**   **70**   **71**

72   **73**   **77**

Details

Issues of 1861-62, 1861-66, 1867 and 1875

Detail of **#63, 86, 92**

There is a dash in 63, 86 and 92 added under the tip of the ornament at the right of the numeral in upper left corner.

Detail of **#67, 75, 80, 95**

There is a leaf in 67, 75, 80 and 95 added to the foliated ornaments at each corner.

Detail of **#69, 85E, 90, 97**

In 69, 85E, 90 and 97, ovals and scrolls have been added at the corners.

Detail of **#64-66, 74, 79, 82-83, 85, 85C, 88, 94**

In 64-66, 74, 79, 82-83, 85, 85C, 88 and 94, ornaments at corners have been enlarged and end in a small ball.

Detail of **#68, 85D, 89, 96**

There is an outer line in 68, 85D, 89 and 96 cut below the stars and an outer line added to the ornaments above them.

Detail of **#72, 101**

In 72 and 101, parallel lines form an angle above the ribbon containing "U.S. Postage"; between these lines a row of dashes has been added, along with a point of color to the apex of the lower line.

1861-1867

Issues of 1861-62		Un	U
	Perf. 12		
63	1¢ blue Franklin	300.00	27.50
a	1¢ ultramarine	675.00	240.00
b	1¢ dark blue	500.00	70.00
c	Laid paper	—	—
d	Vert. pair, imperf. horiz.	—	—
e	Printed on both sides		2,500.00
	Double transfer	—	40.00
	Dot in "U"	325.00	32.50
64	3¢ pink Washington	6,000.00	675.00
a	3¢ pigeon blood pink	15,000.00	3,250.00
b	3¢ rose pink	450.00	125.00
65	3¢ rose Washington	125.00	2.50
b	Laid paper	—	—
d	Vertical pair, imperf. horizontally	3,500.00	750.00
e	Printed on both sides	2,000.00	1,600.00
f	Double impression		6,000.00
	Cracked plate	—	—
	Double transfer	140.00	5.50
66	3¢ lake Washington is considered a Trial Color Proof		
67	5¢ buff Jefferson	15,000.00	750.00
68	10¢ yellow green Washington	500.00	47.50
	10¢ deep yellow green on thin paper	625.00	55.00
a	10¢ dark green	550.00	50.00
b	Vert. pair, imperf. horiz.		3,500.00
	Double transfer	550.00	52.50
69	12¢ blk. Washington	900.00	85.00
	12¢ intense black	925.00	90.00
	Double transfer of top or bottom frame line	950.00	100.00
	Double transfer of top and bottom frame lines	975.00	105.00
70	24¢ red lilac Washington	1,400.00	135.00
a	24¢ brown lilac	1,250.00	115.00
b	24¢ steel blue	6,500.00	475.00
c	24¢ violet	9,000.00	900.00
d	24¢ grayish lilac	2,500.00	600.00
	Scratch under "A" of "POSTAGE"		—
71	30¢ orange Franklin	1,100.00	130.00
a	Printed on both sides		—
72	90¢ bl. Washington	2,200.00	375.00
a	90¢ pale blue	2,200.00	375.00
b	90¢ dark blue	2,400.00	425.00
	Issues of 1861-66		
73	2¢ blk. Andrew Jackson	325.00	50.00
	Double transfer	375.00	55.00
	Major double transfer of top left corner and "POSTAGE"		12,500.00
	Cracked plate	—	—

Issues of 1861-66		Un	U
	Perf. 12		
	#74 3¢ scarlet Washington was not regularly issued and is considered a Trial Color Proof.		
75	5¢ red brown Jefferson (67)	3,750.00	425.00
76	5¢ brown Jefferson (67)	800.00	100.00
a	5¢ dark brown	900.00	115.00
	Double transfer of top or bottom frame line	875.00	115.00
77	15¢ blk. Lincoln	1,200.00	130.00
	Double transfer	1,250.00	140.00
78	24¢ lilac Washington (70)	800.00	90.00
c	24¢ blackish violet	30,000.00	1,750.00
	Scratch under "A" of "POSTAGE"	—	—
	Grills on U.S. Stamps		
	Between 1867 and 1870, postage stamps were embossed with pyramid-shaped grills that absorbed cancellation ink to prevent reuse of canceled stamps.		
	Issues of 1867, With Grills		
	Grills A, B and with C: Points Up		
	A. Grill Covers Entire Stamp		
79	3¢ rose Washington (56)	3,750.00	850.00
b	Printed on both sides		—
80	5¢ brown Jefferson (57)	—	80,000.00
a	5¢ dark brown		80,000.00
81	30¢ orange Franklin (61)		50,000.00
	B. Grill about 18 x 15mm		
82	3¢ rose Washington (56)		160,000.00
	C. Grill about 13 x 16mm		
83	3¢ rose Washington (56)	4,250.00	850.00
	Double grill	5,500.00	2,100.00
	Grills, D, Z, E, F with Points Down		
	D. Grill about 12 x 14mm		
84	2¢ black Jackson (73)	13,000.00	2,250.00
85	3¢ rose Washington (56)	4,750.00	800.00
	Split grill		875.00
	Z. Grill about 11 x 14mm		
85A	1¢ blue Franklin (55)		935,000.00
85B	2¢ black Jackson (73)	5,250.00	800.00
	Double transfer	5,750.00	850.00
85C	3¢ rose Washington (56)	8,500.00	2,250.00
	Double grill	10,000.0	
85D	10¢ grn. Washington (58)		90,000.00
85E	12¢ blk. Washington (59)	7,000.00	1,000.00
	Double transfer of top frame line		1,100.00
85F	15¢ black Lincoln (77)		220,000.00
	E. Grill about 11 x 13mm		
86	1¢ blue Franklin (55)	2,500.00	425.00
a	Double grill	—	550.00
	Split grill	2,650.00	475.00

	Issues of 1867	Un	U
	With Grills, Perf. 12		
87	2¢ black Jackson (73)	950.00	110.00
	2¢ intense black	1,050.00	130.00
	Double grill	—	—
	Double transfer	1,000.00	120.00
88	3¢ rose Washington (65)	600.00	15.00
a	3¢ lake red	650.00	19.00
	Double grill	—	—
	Very thin paper	625.00	16.00
89	10¢ grn. Washington (68)	3,500.00	275.00
	Double grill	4,500.00	475.00
90	12¢ blk. Washington (69)	3,750.00	325.00
	Double transfer of top		
	or bottom frame line	3,900.00	350.00
91	15¢ black Lincoln (77)	7,500.00	625.00
	Double grill	—	950.00
	F. Grill about 9 x 13mm		
92	1¢ blue Franklin (63)	900.00	160.00
	Double transfer	950.00	190.00
	Double grill	—	300.00
93	2¢ black Jackson (73)	375.00	37.50
	Double grill	—	145.00
	Very thin paper	425.00	45.00
94	3¢ red Washington (65)	300.00	5.00
c	Vertical pair,		
	imperf. horizontally	*1,050.00*	
d	Printed on both sides	*1,150.00*	
	Double grill		—
	End roller grill		325.00
	Quadruple split grill	550.00	125.00
95	5¢ brown Jefferson (67)	2,400.00	650.00
a	5¢ dark brown	2,600.00	775.00
	Double transfer		
	of top frame line	—	—
	Double grill	—	—
96	10¢ yellow green		
	Washington (68)	1,900.00	200.00
	Double transfer	—	—
	Quadruple split grill		625.00
97	12¢ blk. Washington (69)	2,250.00	200.00
	Double transfer of top		
	or bottom frame line	2,400.00	210.00
	Triple grill		—
98	15¢ black Lincoln (77)	2,500.00	275.00
	Double transfer of		
	upper right corner	—	—
	Double grill	—	425.00
	Quadruple split grill	3,250.00	575.00
99	24¢ gray lilac		
	Washington (70)	4,500.00	650.00
100	30¢ orange Franklin (71)	4,500.00	650.00
	Double grill	6,000.00	1,350.00
101	90¢ bl. Washington (72)	7,000.00	1,150.00
	Double grill	*10,000.00*	

	Issues of 1875	Un	U
	Reissue of 1861-66 Issues,		
	Without Grill, Perf. 12		
102	1¢ blue Franklin (63)	*650.00*	*950.00*
103	2¢ black Jackson (73)	*2,750.00*	*4,500.00*
104	3¢ brown red		
	Washington (65)	*3,000.00*	*5,000.00*
105	5¢ brown Jefferson (67)	*2,250.00*	*2,750.00*
106	10¢ grn. Washington (68)	*2,400.00*	*4,500.00*
107	12¢ blk. Washington (69)	*3,250.00*	*5,250.00*
108	15¢ black Lincoln (77)	*3,250.00*	*5,500.00*
109	24¢ deep violet		
	Washington (70)	*4,000.00*	*7,000.00*
110	30¢ brownish orange		
	Franklin (71)	*4,250.00*	*8,000.00*
111	90¢ bl. Washington (72)	*5,250.00*	*40,000.00*
	Issues of 1869, With Grill,		
	Hardware Paper		
	G. Grill about 9.5 x 9mm		
112	1¢ buff Franklin	650.00	140.00
b	Without grill	*4,000.00*	
	Double grill	1,000.00	310.00
113	2¢ br. Post Horse and		
	Rider	600.00	50.00
	Split grill	750.00	70.00
	Double transfer		65.00
114	3¢ Locomotive	300.00	20.00
a	Without grill	950.00	
d	Double impression		3,500.00
	Triple grill	—	—
	Sextuple grill	—	3,250.00
	Gray paper	—	95.00
115	6¢ Washington	2,000.00	180.00
	Quadruple split grill	—	700.00
116	10¢ Shield and Eagle	1,600.00	140.00
	End roller grill	—	—
117	12¢ S.S. Adriatic	1,750.00	150.00
	Split grill	2,100.00	165.00
118	15¢ Columbus Landing,		
	type I	6,000.00	600.00
119	15¢ type II (118)	2,500.00	250.00
b	Center inverted	*275,000.00*	*18,500.00*
c	Center double, one inverted		*35,000.00*
120	24¢ Declaration of		
	Independence	5,500.00	700.00
b	Center inverted	*275,000.00*	*20,000.00*
121	30¢ Shield, Eagle		
	and Flags	5,500.00	550.00
b	Flags inverted	*210,000.00*	*65,000.00*
	Double grill	—	1,100.00
122	90¢ Lincoln	7,500.00	2,100.00
	Split grill	—	—
	Issues of 1875, Reissue of 1869 Issue,		
	Without Grill, Hard White Paper, Perf. 12		
123	1¢ buff (112)	475.00	325.00
124	2¢ brown (113)	600.00	450.00
125	3¢ blue (114)	*4,500.00*	*14,000.00*
126	6¢ blue (115)	1,200.00	1,400.00

112

113

114

115

116

117

118

120

121

122

Details

15¢ Landing of Columbus, Types I-III, Series 1869-75

Detail of **#118** Type I

Picture unframed.

Detail of **#119** Type II

Picture framed.

#129 Type III

Same as Type I but without fringe of brown shading lines around central vignette.

134   **135**   **136**   **137**

138   **139**   **140**   **141**

142   **143**   **144**

156   **157**   **158**

Details

Detail of #**134, 145**

Detail of #**135, 146**

Detail of #**136, 147**

Detail of #**156, 167, 182, 192**

1¢. In the pearl at the left of the numeral "1" there is a small crescent.

Detail of #**157, 168, 178, 180, 183, 193**

2¢. Under the scroll at the left of "U.S." there is small diagonal line. This mark seldom shows clearly.

Detail of #**158, 169, 184, 194**

3¢. The under part of the upper tail of the left ribbon is heavily shaded.

Issues of 1875		Un	U
127	10¢ yellow (116)	1,850.00	1,600.00
128	12¢ green (117)	2,000.00	*2,500.00*
129	15¢ brown and blue,		
	type III (118)	1,750.00	1,000.00
a	Imperf. horizontally	2,500.00	—
130	24¢ grn. & violet (120)	1,750.00	1,200.00
131	30¢ bl. & carmine (121)	2,500.00	2,250.00
132	90¢ car. & black (122)	4,500.00	5,250.00
	Issue of 1880, Reissue of 1869		
	Issue, Soft Porous Paper		
133	1¢ buff (112)	300.00	200.00
a	1¢ brown orange,		
	issued without gum	225.00	175.00
	Issues of 1870-71		
	With Grill, White Wove Paper,		
	No Secret Marks		
	H. Grill about 10 x 12mm		
134	1¢ Franklin	1,600.00	100.00
	End roller grill		475.00
135	2¢ Jackson	950.00	60.00
136	3¢ Washington	675.00	17.50
	Cracked plate	—	82.50
137	6¢ Lincoln	3,600.00	500.00
	Double grill	—	850.00
138	7¢ Edwin M. Stanton	2,500.00	400.00
139	10¢ Jefferson	4,000.00	650.00
140	12¢ Henry Clay	*19,000.00*	2,750.00
141	15¢ Daniel Webster	4,750.00	1,100.00
142	24¢ Gen. Winfield Scott	—	6,500.00
143	30¢ Alexander Hamilton	10,000.00	2,000.00
144	90¢ Commodore Perry	11,500.00	1,350.00
	Split grill	—	1,400.00

Issues of 1870-71		Un	U
	Without Grill, White Wove		
	Paper, No Secret Marks		
145	1¢ ultra. Franklin (134)	390.00	12.00
146	2¢ red brn. Jackson (135)	275.00	7.50
147	3¢ grn. Washington (136)	275.00	1.10
148	6¢ carmine Lincoln (137)	575.00	22.50
	6¢ violet carmine	600.00	27.50
149	7¢ verm. Stanton (138)	675.00	85.00
150	10¢ brown Jefferson (139)	575.00	20.00
151	12¢ dull violet Clay (140)	1,425.00	130.00
152	15¢ brt. or. Webster (141)	1,550.00	130.00
153	24¢ purple Scott (142)	1,425.00	130.00
154	30¢ black Hamilton (143)	3,750.00	150.00
155	90¢ carmine Perry (144)	3,400.00	275.00
	Issues of 1873, Without Grill,		
	White Wove Paper, Thin to Thick,		
	Secret Marks		
156	1¢ ultra. Franklin	200.00	3.00
	Paper with silk fibers	—	21.00
f	Imperf. pair	—	*550.00*
157	2¢ br. Jackson	360.00	15.00
	Double paper	475.00	30.00
c	With grill	*1,800.00*	*700.00*
158	3¢ gr. Washington	125.00	.40
	olive green	*375.00*	15.00
	Cracked plate	—	32.50

To celebrate the opening of the **National Postal Museum**, the newest member of the Smithsonian Institution family, the U.S. Postal Service in 1993 issued four stamps highlighting periods in American history when the mails played a significant role. The first stamp features **Benjamin Franklin**, the first Postmaster General appointed by the Continental Congress, and three images emblematic of

his career and mail delivery in the early days of the United States: a printing press, colonial post rider, and Independence Hall. Included on the other three stamps in this issue are such varied images as a Pony Express rider, Charles Lindbergh, 1931 Model A Ford mail truck, and a modern bar code.

The National Postal Museum stamps were illustrated by Richard Schlecht, who has worked on many projects for the Postal Service, including stamps commemorating Ponce de León (1983), Junipero Serra (1985), and The First Voyage of Christopher Columbus (1992).

Issues of 1873	Un	U
Without Grill, White Wove Paper, Thin to Thick, Secret Marks		
159 6¢ dull pk. Lincoln	425.00	17.50
b With grill	1,800.00	
160 7¢ or. verm. Stanton	875.00	75.00
Ribbed paper	—	90.00
161 10¢ br. Jefferson	575.00	17.50
162 12¢ bl. vio. Clay	1,500.00	90.00
163 15¢ yel. or. Webster	1,650.00	95.00
a With grill	4,500.00	
164 24¢ pur. Scott	—	
165 30¢ gray blk. Hamilton	1,750.00	95.00
166 90¢ rose carm. Perry	2,750.00	250.00
Issues of 1875, Special Printing, Hard, White Wove Paper, Without Gum, Secret Marks		
Although perforated, these stamps were usually cut apart with scissors. As a result, the perforations are often much mutilated and the design is frequently damaged.		
167 1¢ ultra. Franklin (156)	9,500.00	
168 2¢ dk. br. Jackson (157)	4,250.00	
169 3¢ blue green Washington (158)	11,000.00	—
170 6¢ dull rose Lincoln (159)	10,000.00	
171 7¢ reddish vermilion Stanton (160)	2,500.00	
172 10¢ pale brown Jefferson (161)	10,000.00	
173 12¢ dark vio. Clay (162)	3,750.00	

Issues of 1875	Un	U
174 15¢ bright orange Webster (163)	10,000.00	
175 24¢ dull pur. Scott (142)	2,400.00	5,000.00
176 30¢ greenish black Hamilton (143)	7,500.00	
177 90¢ vio. car. Perry (144)	9,000.00	
Regular Issue, Yellowish Wove Paper		
178 2¢ verm. Jackson (157)	325.00	8.50
c With grill	500.00	
179 5¢ Zachary Taylor, June	475.00	17.50
Cracked plate	—	150.00
Double paper	550.00	
c With grill	1,500.00	
Paper with silk fibers	—	27.50
Special Printing, Hard, White Wove Paper, Without Gum		
180 2¢ carmine vermilion Jackson (157)	26,000.00	
181 5¢ br. bl. Taylor (179)	42,500.00	
Issues of 1879, Soft, Porous Paper, Thin to Thick, Perf. 12		
182 1¢ dark ultramarine Franklin (156)	250.00	2.25
183 2¢ verm. Jackson (157)	120.00	2.25
a Double impression	—	500.00

The second First Lady and mother of the sixth President, **Abigail Adams** was self-reliant, self-educated, and outspoken. In 1985, the Postal Service commemorated this important figure in American history with a stamp illustrated by Bart Forbes.

She was a devoted partner to John Adams, whom she married in 1764 when he was a young lawyer. Abigail raised their children amid long separations resulting from his career as a circuit judge, delegate to the Continental Congress, and envoy to Europe.

From 1784 until 1788, she and Adams lived in Paris and London where he served as a diplomat for the new nation. Abigail honed her entertaining skills overseas, which came in handy during John Adams' years as Vice President and President. During the final year of his Presidency, the Adamses moved into the still-uncompleted President's House in the new capital.

John Adams consulted Abigail on important decisions. She was an early advocate of women's rights, earning her the title of "Mrs. President" from those who believed women should not be involved in government. Following his unsuccessful bid for a second term, the couple retired to their beloved home in Quincy, Massachusetts. There, until her death in 1818, they enjoyed their remaining years together.

159

160

161

162

163

179

Details

Detail of **#137, 148**

Detail of **#138, 149**

Detail of **#139, 150, 187**

Detail of **#159, 170, 186, 195**

6¢.The first four vertical lines of the shading in the lower part of the left ribbon have been strengthened.

Detail of **#160, 171, 196**

7¢. Two small semicircles are drawn around the ends of the lines that outline the ball in the lower righthand corner.

Detail of **#161, 172, 188, 197**

10¢. There is a small semi-circle in the scroll at the right end of the upper label.

Detail of **#140, 151**

Detail of **#141, 152**

Detail of **#143, 154, 165, 176**

Detail of **#162, 173, 198**

12¢. The balls of the figure "2" are crescent-shaped.

Detail of **#163, 174, 189, 199**

15¢. In the lower part of the triangle in the upper left corner two lines have been made heavier, forming a "V". This mark can be found on some of the Continental and American (1879) printings, but not all stamps show it.

Detail of **#190**

30¢. In the "S" of "CENTS," the vertical spike across the middle section of the letter has been broadened.

| 205 | 206 | 207 | 208 |

| 209 | 210 | 211 | 212 |

| 219 | 220 | 221 | 222 | 223 | 224 |

| 225 | 226 | 227 | 228 | 229 |

Details

Issues of 1881-82, Re-engravings of 1873 Designs

Detail of #206

1¢. Upper vertical lines have been deepened, creating a solid effect in parts of background. Upper arabesques shaded.

Detail of #207

3¢. Shading at sides of central oval is half its previous width. A short horizontal dash has been cut below th "TS" of "CENTS."

Detail of #208

6¢. Has three vertical lines instead of four between the edge of the panel and the outside of the stamp.

Detail of #209

10¢. Has four vertical lines instead of five between left side of oval and edge of the shield. Horizontal lines in lower part of background strengthened.

	Issues of 1879	Un	U
184	3¢ grn. Washington (158)	95.00	.30
	Double transfer	—	—
	Short transfer	—	5.75
185	5¢ blue Taylor (179)	475.00	12.00
186	6¢ pink Lincoln (159)	825.00	19.00
187	10¢ brown Jefferson		
	(139) (no secret mark)	1,650.00	25.00
188	10¢ brown Jefferson		
	(161) (with secret mark)	1,200.00	25.00
	black brown	1,300.00	37.50
	Double transfer		45.00
189	15¢ red or. Webster (163)	325.00	22.50
190	30¢ full blk. Hamilton (143)	1,000.00	55.00
191	90¢ carmine Perry (144)	2,000.00	250.00

**Issues of 1880, Special Printing,
Soft Porous Paper, Without Gum, Perf. 12**

		Un	U
192	1¢ dark ultramarine		
	Franklin (156)	14,000.00	
193	2¢ blk. br. Jackson (157)	7,000.00	
194	3¢ blue green		
	Washington (158)	22,500.00	
195	6¢ dull rose		
	Lincoln (159)	14,000.00	
196	7¢ scarlet vermilion		
	Stanton (160)	2,750.00	
197	10¢ deep brown		
	Jefferson (161)	14,000.00	
198	12¢ blk. pur. Clay (162)	4,250.00	
199	15¢ or. Webster (163)	14,000.00	
200	24¢ dk. vio. Scott (142)	4,250.00	
201	30¢ greenish black		
	Hamilton (143)	10,000.00	
202	90¢ dull carmine		
	Perry (144)	11,000.00	
203	2¢ scarlet vermilion		
	Jackson (157)	22,500.00	
204	5¢ dp. bl. Taylor (179)	40,000.00	

Issues of 1882, Perf. 12

		Un	U
205	5¢ Garfield, Apr. 10	210.00	7.00

**Special Printing, Soft Porous
Paper, Without Gum, Perf. 12**

		Un	U
205C	5¢ gray brown		
	Garfield (205)	25,000.00	

**Issues of 1881-82, Designs
of 1873 Re-engraved**

		Un	U
206	1¢ Franklin, Aug. 1881	60.00	.75
	Double transfer	80.00	5.00
207	3¢ Washington,		
	July 16, 1881	65.00	.40
	Double transfer	—	9.00
	Cracked plate	—	
208	6¢ Lincoln, June 1882	450.00	70.00
a	6¢ brown red	400.00	100.00
209	10¢ Jefferson, Apr. 1882	130.00	4.25
	10¢ pur. or olive brown	140.00	4.50
b	10¢ black brown	500.00	40.00

	Issues of 1883	Un	U
210	2¢ Washington, Oct. 1	45.00	.30
	Double transfer	50.00	1.50
211	4¢ Jackson, Oct. 1	220.00	12.50
	Cracked plate	—	

Special Printing, Soft Porous Paper, Perf. 12

		Un	U
211B	2¢ pale red brown		
	Washington (210)	550.00	—
c	Horizontal pair,		
	imperf. between	2,000.00	
211D	4¢ deep blue green		
	Jackson (211) no gum	22,500.00	

Issues of 1887, Perf. 12

		Un	U
212	1¢ Franklin, June	95.00	1.10
	Double transfer		—
213	2¢ green Washington		
	(210), Sept. 10	35.00	.35
b	Printed on both sides		—
	Double transfer	—	3.25
214	3¢ vermilion Washington		
	(207), Oct. 3	75.00	55.00

Issues of 1888, Perf. 12

		Un	U
215	4¢ carmine		
	Jackson (211), Nov.	200.00	17.50
216	5¢ indigo		
	Garfield (205), Feb.	200.00	10.00
217	30¢ orange brown		
	Hamilton (165), Jan.	425.00	95.00
218	90¢ pur. Perry (166),		
	Feb.	1,100.00	225.00

Issues of 1890-93, Perf. 12

		Un	U
219	1¢ Franklin, Feb. 22, 1890	25.00	.30
	Double transfer	—	
219D	2¢ lake Washington		
	(220), Feb. 22, 1890	190.00	.80
	Double transfer	—	—
220	2¢ Washington, 1890	20.00	.30
a	Cap on left "2"	65.00	2.25
c	Cap on both "2s"	250.00	17.50
	Double transfer	—	3.25
221	3¢ Jackson, Feb. 22, 1890	65.00	7.00
222	4¢ Lincoln, June 2, 1890	67.50	2.50
	Double transfer	82.50	
223	5¢ Grant, June 2, 1890	65.00	2.50
	Double transfer	80.00	3.00
224	6¢ Garfield, Feb. 22, 1890	67.50	19.00
225	8¢ Sherman, Mar. 21, 1893	52.50	12.00
226	10¢ Webster,		
	Feb. 22, 1890	140.00	3.00
	Double transfer	—	—
227	15¢ Clay, Feb. 22, 1890	180.00	19.00
	Double transfer	—	—
	Triple transfer	—	—
228	30¢ Jefferson,		
	Feb. 22, 1890	300.00	27.50
	Double transfer	—	—
229	90¢ Perry, Feb. 22, 1890	450.00	120.00
	Short transfer at bottom	—	—

	ssues of 1893		Un	U	PB	#	FDC	Q(M)
Columbian Exposition Issue, Printed by The American Bank Note Co., Perf. 12								
230	1¢ Columbus in Sight of Land	01/02/93	25.00	40	350.00	(6)	4,000.00	449
	Double transfer		30.00	.75				
	Cracked plate		95.00					
231	2¢ Landing of Columbus	01/02/93	22.50	.20	275.00	(6)	3,500.00	1,464
	Double transfer		27.50	.30				
	Triple transfer		67.50	—				
	Quadruple transfer		100.00					
	Broken hat on third							
	figure left of Columbus		65.00	.30				
	Broken frame line		24.00	.25				
	Recut frame lines		24.00	—				
	Cracked plate		95.00	—				
232	3¢ *Santa Maria*, Flagship	01/02/93	62.50	15.00	750.00	(6)	6,000.00	12
	Double transfer		82.50	—				
233	4¢ ultramarine, Fleet	01/02/93	87.50	7.50	1,050.00	(6)	9,500.00	19
a	4¢ blue (error)		19,000.00	5,500.00	87,500.00	(4)		
	Double transfer		125.00	—				
234	5¢ Columbus Soliciting							
	Aid from Isabella	01/02/93	95.00	8.00	1,400.00	(6)	16,000	35
	Double transfer		145.00	—				
235	6¢ Columbus Welcomed							
	at Barcelona	01/02/93	90.00	22.50			20,000.00	5
a	6¢ red violet		90.00	22.50	1,250.00	(6)		
	Double transfer		115.00	30.00				
236	8¢ Restored to Favor	03/93	80.00	11.00	875.00	(6)		11
	Double transfer		92.50	—				
237	10¢ Presenting Natives	01/02/93	135.00	8.00	3,250.00	(6)	7,500.00	17
	Double transfer		175.00	12.50				
	Triple transfer		—					
238	15¢ Columbus							
	Announcing His Discovery	01/02/93	240.00	65.00	3,750.00	(6)		2
	Double transfer		—	—				
239	30¢ Columbus at La Rábida	01/02/93	300.00	85.00	8,500.00	(6)		0.6
240	50¢ Recall of Columbus	01/02/93	600.00	160.00	13,000.00	(6)		0.2
	Double transfer		—	—				
	Triple transfer		—	—				
241	$1 Isabella							
	Pledging Her Jewels	01/02/93	1,500.00	650.00	45,000.00	(6)		0.05
	Double transfer		—	—				
242	$2 Columbus in Chains	01/02/93	1,550.00	600.00	65,000.00	(6)	52,500.00	0.05
243	$3 Columbus Describing							
	His Third Voyage	01/02/93	2,400.00	1,000.00				0.03
a	$3 olive green		2,400.00	1,000.00	85,000.00	(6)		
244	$4 Isabella and Columbus	01/02/93	3,250.00	1,350.00				0.03
a	$4 rose carmine		3,250.00	1,350.00	240,000.00	(6)		
245	$5 Portrait of Columbus	01/02/93	3,750.00	1,600.00	190,000.00	(6)		0.03

230

231

232

233

234

235

236

237

238

239

240

241

242

243

244

245

246 **248** **253**

254 **255** **256**

257 **258** **259**

Details

2¢ Washington Types I-III, Series 1894-98

Triangle of **#248-50, 265**
Type I

Triangle of **#251, 266**
Type II

Triangle of **#252, 267, 279B-279Be** Type III

Horizontal lines of uniform thickness run across the triangle.

Horizontal lines cross the triangle, but are thinner within than without.

The horizontal lines do not cross the double frame lines of the triangle.

Issues of 1894		Un	U	PB	#

Unwmkd., Perf. 12

Bureau Issues Starting in 1894 and continuing until 1979, the Bureau of Engraving and Printing in Washington produced all U.S. postage stamps except #909-21, 1335, 1355, 1410-18 and 1789. Beginning in 1979, security printers in addition to the Bureau of Engraving and Printing started producing postage stamps under contract with the U.S. Postal Service.

#	Description		Un	U	PB	#
246	1¢ Franklin	10/94	29.00	4.00	325.00	(6)
	Double transfer		32.50	5.00		
247	1¢ blue Franklin (246)	11/94	60.00	2.00	575.00	(6)
	Double transfer		—	3.50		
248	2¢ pink Washington, type I	10/94	25.00	3.00	225.00	(6)
	Double transfer		—	—		
249	2¢ carmine lake, type I (248)	10/94	130.00	2.25	1,250.00	(6)
	Double transfer		—	2.75		
250	2¢ carmine, type I (248)		27.50	.50	275.00	(6)
c	Vertical pair, imperf. horizontally		1,500.00			
d	Horizontal pair, imperf. between		1,500.00			
	Double transfer		—	1.50		
251	2¢ carmine, type II (248)		230.00	3.50	2,250.00	(6)
252	2¢ carmine, type III (248)		110.00	3.75	1,250.00	(6)
b	Horizontal pair, imperf. vertically		1,350.00		—	
d	Horizontal pair, imperf. between		1,500.00			
253	3¢ Jackson	09/94	95.00	8.00	1,000.00	(6)
254	4¢ Lincoln	09/94	120.00	3.75	1,350.00	(6)
255	5¢ Grant	09/94	90.00	4.75	825.00	(6)
c	Vertical pair, imperf. horiz.		1,750.00			
	Worn plate, diagonal lines missing in oval background		110.00	5.50		
	Double transfer		115.00	5.50		
256	6¢ Garfield	07/94	140.00	21.00	2,100.00	(6)
a	Vertical pair, imperf. horizontally		850.00		12,500.00	(6)
257	8¢ Sherman	03/94	130.00	14.00	1,200.00	(6)
258	10¢ Webster	09/94	225.00	10.00	2,500.00	(6)
	Double transfer		260.00	11.50		
259	15¢ Clay	10/94	275.00	45.00	4,000.00	(6)

Standing six feet tall and blessed with a captivating voice, **Sojourner Truth** used her extraordinary oratorical talents to condemn slavery and extol the importance of women's rights and religious salvation. She bore the mental and physical scars of a traumatic childhood spent under the yoke of slavery.

After gaining her freedom, she began looking for ways to express her sense of moral outrage and religious conviction. Sojourner Truth traveled throughout the country exhorting audiences to support abolition, suffrage, and other social reforms. During the Civil War, she worked directly with freed slaves and recruited for Michigan's black regiment.

In 1986, the Postal Service honored Sojourner Truth with a stamp in the **Black Heritage** series. The stamp's illustrator, Jerry Pinkney, created several Black Heritage stamps, including Harriet Tubman, Jackie Robinson, and Carter G. Woodson.

	Issues of 1894		Un	U	PE	
260	50¢ Jefferson	11/94	400.00	95.00	8,000.00	(6)
261	$1 Perry, type I	11/94	850.00	275.00	15,000.00	(6)
261A	$1 black Perry, type II (261)	11/94	2,000.00	600.00	22,500.00	(6)
262	$2 James Madison	12/94	2,850.00	875.00	32,500.00	(6)
263	$5 John Marshall	12/94	4,250.00	1,900.00	19,500.00	(3)
	Issues of 1895, Wmkd. (191), Perf. 12					
264	1¢ blue Franklin (246)	04/95	6.00	.25	190.00	(6)
265	2¢ carmine Washington,					
	type I (248)	05/95	27.50	.80	340.00	(6)
	Double transfer		40.00	3.25		
266	2¢ carmine, type II (248)		27.50	3.00	375.00	(6)
267	2¢ carmine, type III (248)		5.00	.25	160.00	(6)
268	3¢ purple Jackson (253)	10/95	35.00	1.10	600.00	(6)
	Double transfer		42.50	2.75		
269	4¢ dark brown Lincoln (254)	06/95	37.50	1.60	650.00	(6)
	Double transfer		42.50	3.00		
270	5¢ chocolate Grant (255)	06/11/95	35.00	1.90	550.00	(6)
	Double transfer		42.50	3.25		
	Worn plate, diagonal lines					
	missing in oval background		37.50	2.50		
271	6¢ dull brown Garfield (256)	08/95	85.00	4.25	2,100.00	(6)
	Very thin paper		95.00	4.50		
a	Wmkd. USIR		2,250.00	400.00		
272	8¢ violet brown Sherman (257)	07/95	60.00	1.25	700.00	(6)
a	Wmkd. USIR		1,750.00	110.00	7,000.00	(3)
	Double transfer		75.00	2.75		
273	10¢ dark green Webster (258)	06/95	85.00	1.50	1,400.00	(6)
	Double transfer		105.00	3.50		
274	15¢ dark blue Clay (259)	09/95	200.00	9.00	3,100.00	(6)
275	50¢ orange Jefferson (260)	11/95	275.00	20.00	5,250.00	(6)
a	50¢ red orange		300.00	24.00	5,400.00	(6)
276	$1 black Perry, type I (261)	08/95	600.00	65.00	11,500.00	(6)
276A	$1 black Perry, type II (261)	08/95	1,200.00	140.00	22,500.00	(6)
277	$2 bright blue Madison (262)	08/95	1,000.00	300.00	18,000.00	(6)
a	$2 dark blue		1,000.00	300.00		
278	$5 dark green Marshall (263)	08/95	2,250.00	425.00	67,500.00	(6)

260   261

262   263

277

Watermark 191
Double-line "USPS"
in capital letters;
detail at right.

Details

$1 Perry, Types I-II, Series 1894

Detail of **#261, 276** Type I   Detail of **#261A, 276A**
                                              Type I

The circles enclosing $1   The circles enclosing $1
are broken.   are complete.

1898-1900

	Issues of 1898-1900		Un	U	PB	#	FDC	Q(M)
	Wmkd. (191), Perf. 12							
279	1¢ deep grn. Franklin (246)	01/98	9.00	.25	175.00	(6)		
	Double transfer		12.00	.85				
279B	2¢ red Washington, type III (248)	01/98	9.00	.25	200.00	(6)		
c	2¢ rose carmine, type III		240.00	65.00	2,650.00	(6)		
d	2¢ orange red, type III		10.00	.30	210.00	(6)		
e	Booklet pane of 6	04/16/00	425.00	425.00				
f	2¢ carmine type IV		10.00	.25	210.00	(6)		
280	4¢ rose brn. Lincoln (254)	10/98	30.00	.90				
a	4¢ lilac brown		30.00	.90				
b	4¢ orange brown		30.00	.90	600.00	(6)		
	Extra frame line at top		50.00	4.00				
281	5¢ dark blue Grant (255)	03/98	35.00	.75	600.00	(6)		
	Double transfer		45.00	2.00				
	Worn plate, diagonal lines missing in oval background		40.00	.90				
282	6¢ lake Garfield (256)	12/98	45.00	2.50	800.00	(6)		
a	6¢ purple lake		60.00	3.50	1,000.00	(6)		
	Double transfer		57.50	3.50				
282C	10¢ brown Webster (258), type I	11/98	180.00	2.50	2,250.00	(6)		
	Double transfer		200.00	4.25				
283	10¢ orange brown Webster (258), type II		110.00	2.00	1,600.00	(6)		
284	15¢ olive grn. Clay (259)	11/98	150.00	7.50	2,000.00	(6)		
	Issues of 1898, Trans-Mississippi Exposition Issue							
285	1¢ Marquette on the Mississippi	06/17/98	30.00	6.00	300.00	(6)	11,000.00	71
	Double transfer		40.00	7.25				
286	2¢ Farming in the West	06/17/98	25.00	1.50	275.00	(6)	11,000.00	160
	Double transfer		37.50	2.25				
	Worn plate		27.50	1.75				
287	4¢ Indian Hunting Buffalo	06/17/98	140.00	21.00	1,400.00	(6)	27,500.00	5
288	5¢ Frémont on the Rocky Mountains	06/17/98	130.00	20.00	1,300.00	(6)	16,000.00	8
289	8¢ Troops Guarding Wagon Train	06/17/98	175.00	37.50	2,750.00	(6)	—	3
a	Vertical pair, imperf. horizontally		19,000.00		75,000.00	(4)		
290	10¢ Hardships of Emigration	06/17/98	170.00	22.50	3,000.00	(6)	27,500.00	5
291	50¢ Western Mining Prospector	06/17/98	625.00	180.00		(6)	22,500.00	0.5
292	$1 Western Cattle in Storm	06/17/98	1,250.00	525.00	45,000.00	(6)	—	0.06
293	$2 Mississippi River Bridge	06/17/98	2,100.00	900.00	130,000.00	(6)		0.06

282C

285

286

287

288

289

290

291

292

293

Details

10¢ Webster Types I-II, Series 1898

Detail of **#282C** Type I

The tips of the foliate ornaments do not impinge on the white curved line below "TEN CENTS."

Detail of **#283** Type II

The tips of the ornaments break the curved line below the "E" of "TEN" and the "T" of "CENTS."

The Subscription Series Program

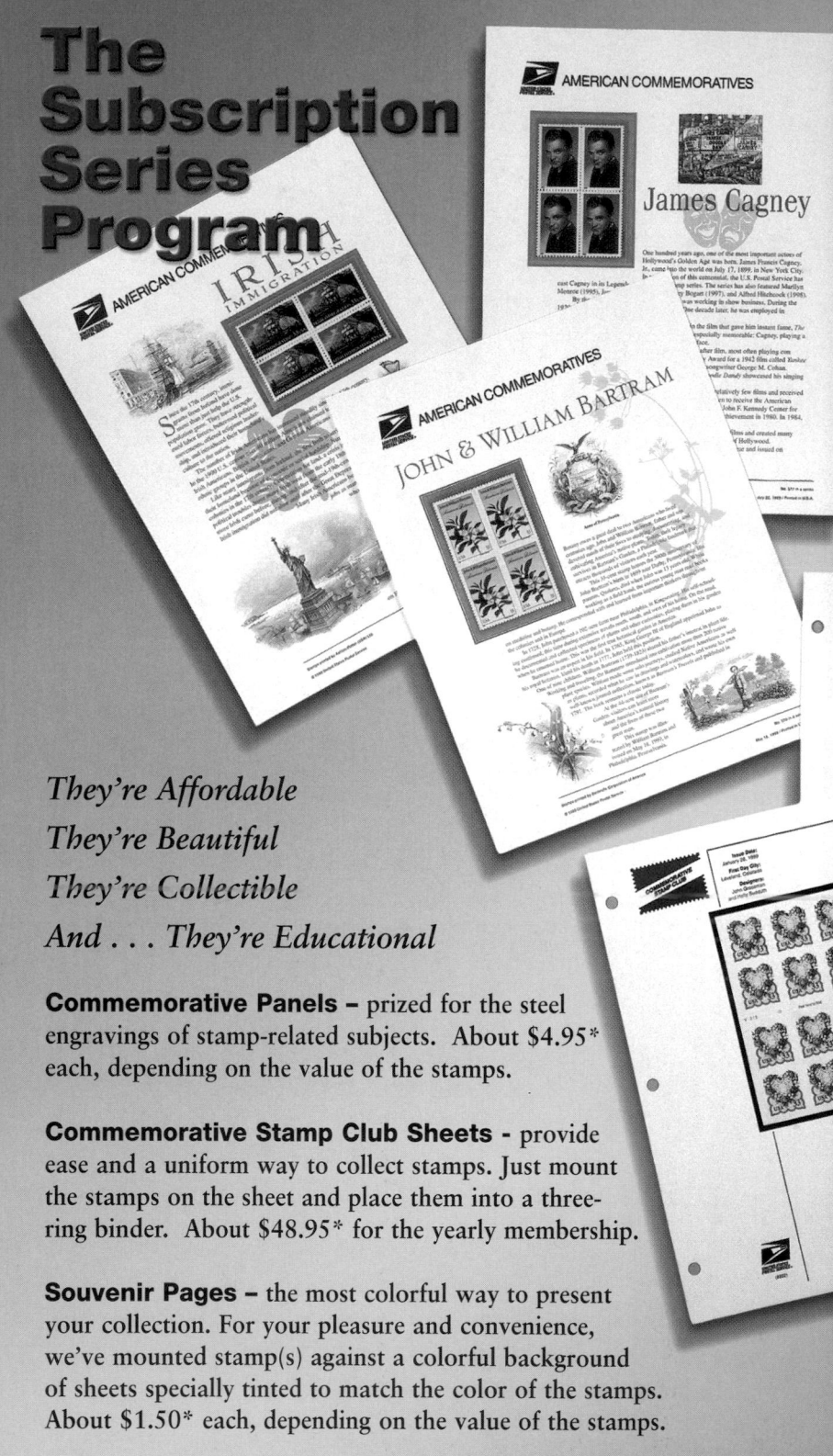

They're Affordable
They're Beautiful
They're Collectible
And . . . They're Educational

Commemorative Panels – prized for the steel
engravings of stamp-related subjects. About $4.95*
each, depending on the value of the stamps.

Commemorative Stamp Club Sheets - provide
ease and a uniform way to collect stamps. Just mount
the stamps on the sheet and place them into a three-
ring binder. About $48.95* for the yearly membership.

Souvenir Pages – the most colorful way to present
your collection. For your pleasure and convenience,
we've mounted stamp(s) against a colorful background
of sheets specially tinted to match the color of the stamps.
About $1.50* each, depending on the value of the stamps.

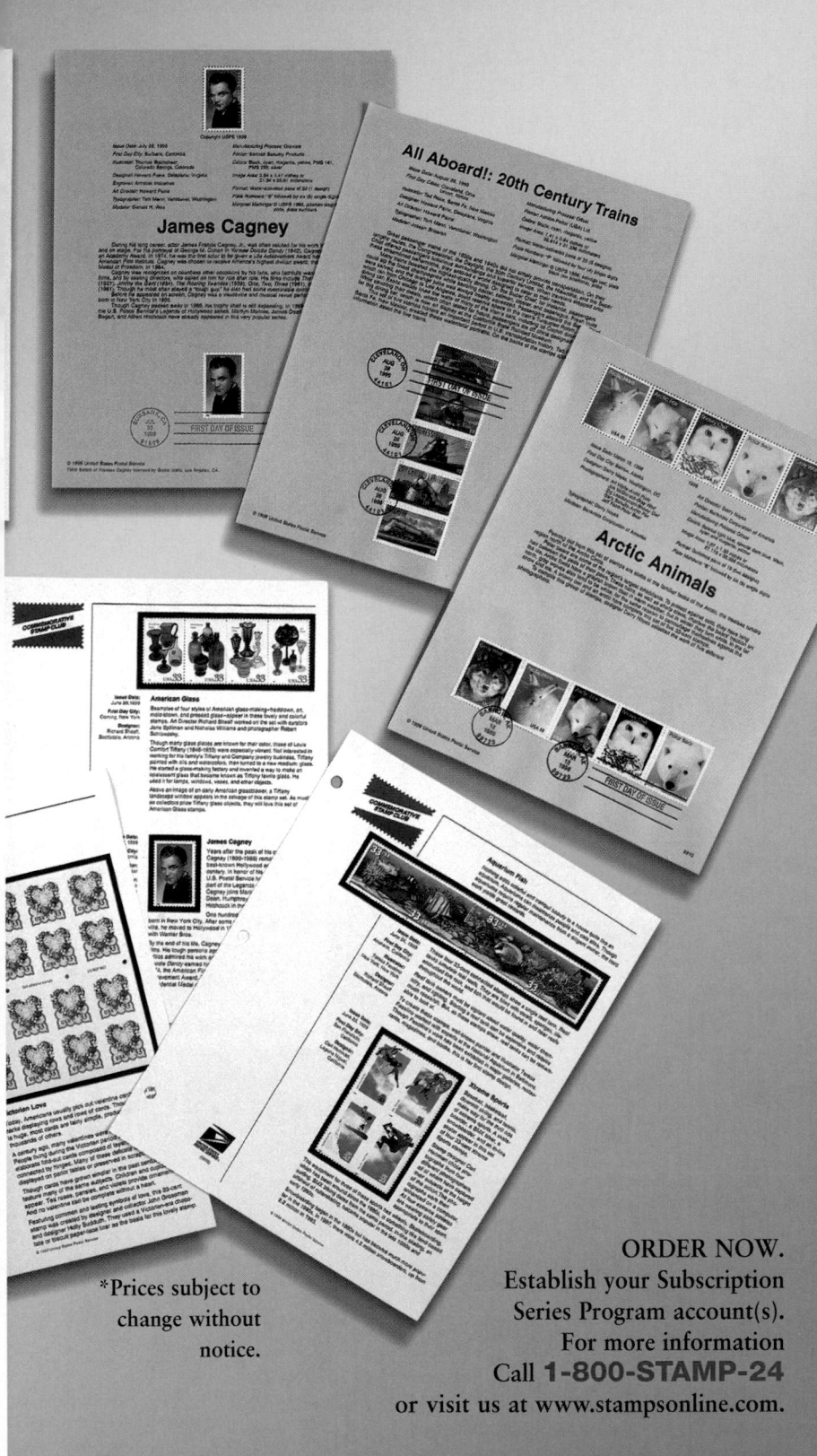

*Prices subject to change without notice.

294   295   296

297   298   299

300 301 302 303

304 305 306 307

308 309 310

311 312 313

	Issues of 1901-03		Un	U	PB	#	FDC	Q(M)
	Issues of 1901, Pan-American Exposition Issue, Perf. 12							
294	1¢ Great Lakes Steamer	05/01/01	18.00	3.00	240.00	(6)	*4,500.00*	91
a	Center inverted		*10,000.00*	*7,000.00*	*75,000.00*	(4)		
295	2¢ An Early Locomotive	05/01/01	17.50	1.00	250.00	(6)	*2,750.00*	210
a	Center inverted		*37,500.00*	*15,000.00*	*250,000.00*	(4)		
296	4¢ Automobile	05/01/01	80.00	15.00	2,250.00	(6)		6
a	Center inverted		*21,000.00*		*110,000.00*	(4)		
297	5¢ Bridge at Niagara Falls	05/01/01	95.00	14.00	2,500.00	(6)	*15,000.00*	7
298	8¢ Canal Locks at							
	Sault Ste. Marie	05/01/01	120.00	50.00	*4,250.00*	(6)		5
299	10¢ American Line Steamship	05/01/01	170.00	25.00	7,000.00	(6)		5
	Wmkd. (191), Perf. 12 (All issued in 1903 except #300b, 306, 308)							
300	1¢ Franklin	02/03	10.00	.20	175.00	(6)		
b	Booklet pane of 6	03/06/07	525.00	—				
	Double transfer		15.00	1.00				
	Worn plate		11.00	.30				
	Cracked plate		12.00	.30				
301	2¢ Washington	01/17/03	14.00	.20	210.00	(6)	*2,750.00*	
c	Booklet pane of 6	01/24/03	450.00	—				
	Double transfer		24.00	1.00				
	Cracked plate		—	1.00				
302	3¢ Jackson	02/03	50.00	2.75	650.00	(6)		
	Double transfer		70.00	3.75				
	Cracked plate		—	—				
303	4¢ Grant	02/03	55.00	1.25	675.00	(6)		
	Double transfer		70.00	2.75				
304	5¢ Lincoln	01/03	55.00	1.50	675.00	(6)		
305	6¢ Garfield	02/03	65.00	2.50	775.00	(6)		
	6¢ brownish lake		65.00	2.50				
	Double transfer		70.00	3.50				
306	8¢ M. Washington	12/02	40.00	2.00	600.00	(6)		
	8¢ lavender		50.00	2.75				
307	10¢ Webster	02/03	60.00	1.40	900.00	(6)		
308	13¢ B. Harrison	11/18/02	45.00	7.50	550.00	(6)		
309	15¢ Clay	05/27/03	150.00	4.75	2,750.00	(6)		
	Double transfer		190.00	9.00				
310	50¢ Jefferson	03/23/03	425.00	22.50	*6,250.00*	(6)		
311	$1 David G. Farragut	06/05/03	700.00	55.00	*16,000.00*	(6)		
312	$2 Madison	06/05/03	1,100.00	170.00	*27,500.00*	(6)		
313	$5 Marshall	06/05/03	2,900.00	675.00	*80,000.00*	(6)		

For listings of #312 and 313 with perf. 10, see #479 and 480.

	Issues of 1906-08		Un	U	PB/LP		FDC	Q(M)
	Imperf. (All issued in 1908 except #314)							
314	1¢ bl. grn. Franklin (300)	10/02/06	20.00	15.00	180.00	(6)		
314A	4¢ brown Grant (303)	04/08	27,500.00	22,500.00				
	#314A was issued imperforated, but all copies were privately perforated at the sides.							
315	5¢ blue Lincoln (304)	05/12/08	290.00	475.00	2,750.00	(6)		
	Coil Stamps, Perf. 12 Horizontally							
316	1¢ bl. grn. pair Franklin (300)	02/18/08	100,000	—	165,000.00	(2)		
317	5¢ blue pair Lincoln (304)	02/24/08	12,500.00	—	28,000.00	(2)		
	Coil Stamp, Perf. 12 Vertically							
318	1¢ bl. grn. pair Franklin (300)	07/31/08	10,000.00	—	17,000.00	(2)		
	Issues of 1903, Perf. 12							
319	2¢ Washington	11/12/03	5.25	.15	95.00	(6)		
a	2¢ lake, type I		—	—				
b	2¢ carmine rose, type I		7.00	.35	135.00	(6)		
c	2¢ scarlet, type I		5.25	.25	85.00	(6)		
d	Vertical pair, imperf.							
	Horizontal		3,500.00					
e	Vertical pair, imperf.							
	between		1,250.00					
f	2¢ lake, type II		6.75	.25	210.00	(6)		
g	Booklet pane of 6,							
	carm., type I,	12/03/03	110.00	150.00				
h	Booklet pane of 6,							
	carm., type II		240.00					
i	2¢ carmine, type II		25.00	50.00				
q	Booklet pane of 6, lake,							
	type II		190.00	300.00				
	Issues of 1906, Washington (319), Imperf.							
320	2¢ carmine	10/02/06	19.00	12.00	225.00	(6)		
a	2¢ lake, die II		50.00	40.00	750.00	(6)		
b	2¢ scarlet		19.00	12.50	225.00	(6)		
	Double transfer		26.00	16.00				
	Issues of 1908, Coil Stamp (319), Perf. 12 Horizontally							
321	2¢ carmine pair	02/18/08	125,000.00					
	Coil Stamp, Perf. 12 Vertically							
322	2¢ carmine pair	07/31/08	8,000.00	5,500.00	9,000.00	(2)		
	Issues of 1904, Louisiana Purchase Exposition Issue, Perf. 12							
323	1¢ Robert R. Livingston	04/30/04	30.00	4.00	275.00	(6)	6,000.00	80
	Diagonal line through left "1"		50.00	11.00				
324	2¢ Thomas Jefferson	04/30/04	27.50	1.50	275.00	(6)	4,500.00	193
325	3¢ James Monroe	04/30/04	90.00	30.00	950.00	(6)	5,000.00	5
326	5¢ William McKinley	04/30/04	95.00	25.00	1,000.00	(6)	22,500.00	7
327	10¢ Map of Louisiana							
	Purchase	04/30/04	180.00	27.50	2,250.00	(6)	24,000.00	4
	Issues of 1907, Jamestown Exposition Issue, Wmkd. (191), Perf. 12							
328	1¢ Captain John Smith	04/26/07	30.00	4.00	275.00	(6)	6,000.00	78
	Double transfer		35.00	5.00				
329	2¢ Founding of							
	Jamestown, 1607	04/26/07	35.00	3.50	375.00	(6)	9,000.00	149
330	5¢ Pocahontas	04/26/07	135.00	27.50	2,600.00	(6)		

319

323

324

325

326

327

328

329

330

Details

2¢ Washington Die I-II, Series 1903

Detail of **#319a, 319b, 319g** Die I

Detail of **#319c, 319f, 319h, 319i** Die II

331   332   333   334

335   336   337   338

339   340   341   342

Details

3¢ Washington Types I-IV, Series 1908-19

Detail of #**333, 345, 359, 376, 389, 394, 426, 445, 456, 464, 483, 493, 501-01b** Type I

Top line of toga rope is weak and rope shading lines are thin. Fifth line from left is missing. Line between lips is thin.

Detail of #**484, 494, 502, 541** Type II

Top line of toga rope is strong and rope shading lines are heavy and complete. Line between lips is heavy.

Detail of #**529** Type III

Top row of toga rope is strong but fifth shading line is missing as in Type I. Toga button center shading line consists of two dashes, central dot. "P," "O" of "POSTAGE" are separated by line of color.

Detail of #**530, 535** Type IV

Toga rope shading lines are complete. Second, fourth toga button shading lines are broken in middle, third line is continuous with dot in center. "P," "O" of "POSTAGE" are joined.

ssues of 1908-09			Un	U	PB/LP	#
Wmkd. (191) Perf. 12 (All issued in 1908 except #336, 338-42, 345-47)						
331	1¢ Franklin	12/08	7.00	.15	75.00	(6)
a	Booklet pane of 6	12/02/08	160.00	*140.00*		
	Double transfer		9.00	.60		
332	2¢ Washington	11/08	6.50	.15	67.50	(6)
a	Booklet pane of 6	11/16/08	135.00	*125.00*		
	Double transfer		12.00	—		
	Cracked plate		—	—		
333	3¢ Washington, type I	12/08	32.50	2.50	325.00	(6)
334	4¢ Washington	12/08	40.00	1.00	400.00	(6)
	Double transfer		52.50	—		
335	5¢ Washington	12/08	50.00	2.00	500.00	(6)
336	6¢ Washington	01/09	62.50	5.00	725.00	(6)
337	8¢ Washington	12/08	47.50	2.50	475.00	(6)
	Double transfer		55.00	—		
338	10¢ Washington	01/09	67.50	1.40	800.00	(6)
a	"China Clay" paper		*1,000.00*			
	Very thin paper		—			
339	13¢ Washington	01/09	40.00	19.00	475.00	(6)
	Line through "TAG"					
	of "POSTAGE"		65.00	—		
340	15¢ Washington	01/09	65.00	5.50	600.00	(6)
a	"China Clay" paper		*1,000.00*			
341	50¢ Washington	01/13/09	325.00	20.00	*6,500.00*	(6)
342	$1 Washington	01/29/09	500.00	75.00	*13,000.00*	(6)
	Imperf.					
343	1¢ green Franklin (331)	12/08	5.75	4.50	55.00	(6)
	Double transfer		12.00	7.00		
344	2¢ carmine Washington (332)	12/10/08	7.00	3.00	85.00	(6)
	Double transfer		13.50	4.00		
	Foreign entry,					
	design of 1¢		*1,250.00*	—		
	#345-47: Washington (333-35)					
345	3¢ deep violet, type I	1809	13.00	20.00	170.00	(6)
	Double transfer		25.00	—		
346	4¢ orange brown	02/25/09	22.50	22.50	200.00	(6)
	Double transfer		45.00	—		
347	5¢ blue	02/25/09	40.00	32.50	325.00	(6)
	Cracked plate		—			
Issues of 1908-10, Coil Stamps, Perf. 12 Horizontally						
#350-51, 354-56: Washington (Designs of 334-35, 338)						
348	1¢ green Franklin (331)	12/29/08	30.00	17.00	230.00	(2)
349	2¢ carmine Washington (332)	01/09	60.00	10.00	425.00	(2)
	Foreign entry, design of 1¢		—	*1,750.00*		
350	4¢ orange brown	08/15/10	135.00	90.00	975.00	(2)
351	5¢ blue	01/09	150.00	125.00	1,000.00	(2)
Issues of 1909, Coil Stamps, Perf. 12 Vertically						
352	1¢ green Franklin (331)	01/09	67.50	35.00	500.00	(2)
	Double transfer		—	—		

	Issues of 1909		Un	U	PB/LP	#	FDC	Q(M)
	Coil Stamps, Perf. 12 Vertically							
353	2¢ carmine Washington (332)	01/12/09	75.00	10.00	500.00	(2)		
354	4¢ orange brown	02/23/09	165.00	75.00	1,200.00	(2)		
355	5¢ blue	02/23/09	175.00	90.00	1,200.00	(2)		
356	10¢ yellow	01/07/09	2,250.00	1,050.00	9,000.00	(2)		
	Bluish Paper, Perf. 12, #359-66: Washington (Designs of 333-40)							
357	1¢ green Franklin (331)	02/16/09	95.00	100.00	1,000.00	(6)		
358	2¢ carmine Washington (332)	02/16/09	90.00	100.00	975.00	(6)		
	Double transfer		—					
359	3¢ deep violet, type I	1909	1,800.00	2,250.00	20,000.00	(6)		
360	4¢ orange brown	1909	20,000.00		92,500.00	(3)		
361	5¢ blue	1909	4,500.00	6,500.00	40,000.00	(6)		
362	6¢ red orange	1909	1,350.00	1,900.00	15,000.00	(6)		
363	8¢ olive green	1909	21,500.00		95,000.00	(3)		
364	10¢ yellow	1909	1,600.00	2,100.00	27,500.00	(6)		
365	13¢ blue green	1909	2,800.00	2,250.00	27,500.00	(6)		
366	15¢ pale ultramarine	1909	1,350.00	1,600.00	10,000.00	(6)		
	Lincoln Memorial Issue, Wmkd. (191)							
367	2¢ Bust of Abraham Lincoln	02/12/09	5.50	1.75	150.00	(6)	500.00	148
	Double transfer		7.50	2.50				
	Imperf.							
368	2¢ carmine (367)	02/12/09	22.50	20.00	200.00	(6)	11,000.00	1
	Double transfer		45.00	27.50				
	Bluish Paper							
369	2¢ carmine (367)	02/09	225.00	240.00	2,900.00	(6)		0.6
	Alaska-Yukon Pacific Exposition Issue							
370	2¢ Willam H. Seward	06/01/09	9.00	2.00	225.00	(6)	1,800.00	153
	Double transfer		11.00	4.50				
	Imperf.							
371	2¢ carmine (370)	06/09	28.00	22.50	250.00	(6)		0.5
	Double transfer		42.50	27.50				
	Hudson-Fulton Celebration Issue, Wmkd. (191)							
372	2¢ *Half Moon & Clermont*	09/25/09	13.00	4.50	300.00	(6)	750.00	73
	Double transfer		16.00	4.75				
	Imperf.							
373	2¢ carmine (372)	09/25/09	32.50	25.00	280.00	(6)	—	0.2
	Double transfer		47.50	30.00				
	Issues of 1910-11, Wmkd. (190) #376-82: Washington (Designs of 333-38, 340)							
374	1¢ green Franklin (331)	11/23/10	6.50	.20	75.00	(6)		
a	Booklet pane of 6	10/07/10	140.00	100.00				
	Double transfer		13.00	—				
	Cracked plate		—	—				
375	2¢ carmine Washington (332)	11/23/10	6.50	.20	82.50	(6)		
	2¢ lake		250.00					
a	Booklet pane of 6	11/30/10	95.00	85.00				
	Cracked plate		—	—				
	Double transfer		11.00	—				
	Foreign entry, design of 1¢		—	1,000.00				
376	3¢ deep violet, type I	01/16/11	19.00	1.40	190.00	(6)		

367

370

370

USPS

Watermark 190
Single-line
"USPS"
in capital letters;
detail at right.

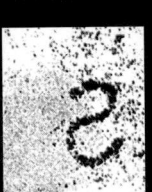

397

398

399

400

Issues of 1911		Un	U	PB/LP	#	FDC	Q(M)
Wmkd. (190), Perf. 12							
377	4¢ brown	01/20/11	30.00	.50	265.00	(6)		
	Double transfer		—	—				
378	5¢ blue	01/25/11	30.00	.50	320.00	(6)		
	Double transfer							
379	6¢ red orange	01/25/11	35.00	.70	460.00	(6)		
380	8¢ olive green	02/08/11	110.00	12.50	1,050.00	(6)		
381	10¢ yellow	01/24/11	100.00	3.75	1,100.00	(6)		
382	15¢ pale ultramarine	03/01/11	260.00	15.00	2,250.00	(6)		
Issues of 1910, Imperf.							
383	1¢ green Franklin (331)	12/10	2.60	2.00	47.50	(6)		
	Double transfer		6.75	—				
384	2¢ carmine Washington (332)	12/10	4.25	2.50	140.00	(6)		
	Foreign entry, design of 1¢		1,500.00					
	Double transfer		8.00	—				
	Rosette plate, crack on head		100.00	—				
Issues of 1910, Coil Stamps, Perf. 12 Horizontally							
385	1¢ green Franklin (331)	11/01/10	30.00	15.00	375.00	(2)		
386	2¢ carmine Washington (332)	11/01/10	55.00	20.00	675.00	(2)		
Issues of 1910-11, Coil Stamps, Wmkd. (190), Perf. 12 Vertically							
387	1¢ green Franklin (331)	11/01/10	125.00	50.00	525.00	(2)		
388	2¢ carmine Washington (332)	11/01/10	750.00	350.00	5,000.00	(2)		
389	3¢ deep violet Washington, type I (333)	01/24/11	52,500.00	10,000.00	115,000.00	(2)		
Issues of 1910-13, Coil Stamps, Perf. 8.5 Horizontally							
390	1¢ green Franklin (331)	12/12/10	4.50	6.00	32.50	(2)		
	Double transfer		—	—				
391	2¢ carmine Washington (332)	12/23/10	35.00	12.50	220.00	(2)		
Coil Stamps, Perf. 8.5 Vertically #394-96: Washington (Designs of 333-35)							
392	1¢ green Franklin (331)	12/12/10	20.00	19.00	150.00	(2)		
	Double transfer		—	—				
393	2¢ carmine Washington (332)	12/16/10	40.00	7.75	260.00	(2)		
394	3¢ deep violet, type I	09/18/11	50.00	47.50	360.00	(2)		
395	4¢ brown	04/15/12	50.00	42.50	360.00	(2)		
396	5¢ blue	03/13	50.00	42.50	360.00	(2)		
Issues of 1913, Panama Pacific Exposition Issue, Wmkd. (190), Perf. 12							
397	1¢ Vasco Nunez de Balboa	01/01/13	17.50	1.50	175.00	(6)	5,000.00	167*
	Double transfer		22.50	2.50				
398	2¢ Pedro Miguel Locks, Panama Canal	01/13	21.00	.50	275.00	(6)		251*
	2¢ carmine lake		575.00					
	Double transfer		40.00	2.00				
399	5¢ Golden Gate	01/01/13	75.00	9.50	1,900.00	(6)	21,000.00	14*
400	10¢ yellow Discovery of San Francisco Bay	01/01/13	125.00	20.00	2,400.00	(6)	—	8*
400A	10¢ orange (400)	08/13	210.00	16.00	12,000.00	(6)		
*Includes perf. 10 printing quantities.							

Issues of 1914-15			Un	U	PB/LP	#
Perf. 10						
401	1¢ green (397)	12/14	25.00	5.50	340.00	(6)
402	2¢ carmine (398)	01/15	75.00	1.50	2,000.00	(6)
403	5¢ blue (399)	02/15	175.00	15.00	4,000.00	(6)
404	10¢ irabge (400)	07/15	925.00	62.50	12,500.00	(6)
Issues of 1912-14, Wmkd. (190), Perf. 12						
405	1¢ green	02/12	5.50	.15	80.00	(6)
a	Vertical pair,					
	imperf. horizontally		650.00	—		
b	Booklet pane of 6	02/08/12	60.00	45.00		
	Cracked plate		13.00	—		
	Double transfer		6.50	—		
406	2¢ carmine, type I	02/12	5.50	.15	100.00	(6)
	2¢ lake		350.00	—		
a	Booklet pane of 6	02/08/12	60.00	60.00		
b	Double impression		—			
	Double transfer		7.50	—		
407	7¢ black	04/14	80.00	11.00	1,200.00	(6)
Imperf. #408-13: Washington (Designs of 405-6)						
408	1¢ green	03/12	1.15	.55	20.00	(6)
	Double transfer		2.50	1.00		
	Cracked plate		—	—		
409	2¢ carmine, type I	02/12	1.40	.60	40.00	(6)
	Cracked plate		15.00	—		
Coil Stamps, Perf. 8.5 Horizontally						
410	1¢ green	03/12	6.00	4.00	30.00	(2)
	Double transfer		—	—		
411	2¢ carmine, type I	03/12	10.00	3.75	55.00	(2)
	Double transfer		12.50	—		
Coil Stamps, Perf. 8.5 Vertically						
412	1¢ green	03/18/12	25.00	5.50	120.00	(2)
413	2¢ carmine, type I	03/12	42.50	1.10	240.00	(2)
	Double transfer		45.00	—		
Perf. 12						
414	8¢ Franklin	02/12	45.00	1.25	450.00	(6)
415	9¢ Franklin	04/14	55.00	12.50	625.00	(6)
416	10¢ Franklin	01/12	45.00	.40	475.00	(6)

405   **406**   **407**   **414**   **415**   **416**

2¢ Washington, Types I-VII, Series 1912-21

Detail of #406-06a, 411, 413, 425-25e, 442, 444, 449, 453, 461, 463-63a, 482, 499-99f Type I

One shading line in first curve of ribbon above left "2" and one in second curve of ribbon above right "2". Toga button has only a faint outline. Top line of toga rope, from button to front of the throat, is very faint. Shading lines of face end in the front of the ear, with little or no joining, to form lock of hair.

Detail of #482a, 500 Type Ia

Similar to Type I but all lines are stronger.

Detail of #454, 487, 491, 539 Type II

Shading lines in ribbons as in Type I. Toga button, rope and rope shading lines are heavy. Shading lines of face at lock of hair end in strong vertical curved line.

Detail of #450, 455, 488, 492, 540, 546 Type III

Two lines of shading in curves of ribbons.

Detail of #526, 532 Type IV

Top line of toga rope is broken. Toga button shading lines form "DID". Line of color in left "2" is very thin and usually broken.

Detail of #527, 533 Type V

Top line of toga is complete. Toga button has five vertical shading lines. Line of color in left "2" is very thin and usually broken. Nose shading dots are as shown.

Detail of #528, 534 Type Va

Same as Type V except third row from bottom of nose shading dots has four dots instead of six. Overall height of design is 1/3mm shorter than Type V.

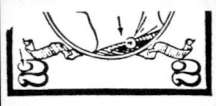

Detail of #528A, 534A Type VI

Generally same as Type V except line of color in left "2" is very heavy.

Detail of #528B, 534B Type VII

Line of color in left "2" is continuous, clearly defined and heavier than in Type V or Va but not as heavy as Type VI. An additional vertical row of dots has been added to upper lip. Numerous additional dots appear in hair at top of head.

417

418

419

420

421

423

434

After 1915 (from 1916 to date),
all postage stamps, except #519 and 832b,
are on unwatermarked paper.

Issues of 1912-14			Un	U	PB	#
417	12¢ Franklin	04/14	50.00	4.25	600.00	(6)
	Double transfer		55.00	—		
	Triple transfer		72.50	—		
418	15¢ Franklin	02/12	85.00	3.50	800.00	(6)
	Double transfer		—	—		
419	20¢ Franklin	04/14	200.00	15.00	1,900.00	(6)
420	30¢ Franklin	04/14	125.00	15.00	1,450.00	(6)
421	50¢ Franklin	08/14	425.00	17.50	9,500.00	(6)
	Wmkd. (191)					
422	50¢ Franklin (421)	02/12/12	250.00	15.00	4,500.00	(6)
423	$1 Franklin	02/12/12	525.00	60.00	11,000.00	(6)
	Double transfer		550.00			
Issues of 1914-15, Wmkd. (190), Perf. 10 #424-30: Wash. (Designs of 405-06, 333-36, 407)						
424	1¢ green	09/05/14	2.30	.20	40.00	(6)
	Cracked plate		—	—		
	Double transfer		4.50	—		
	Experimental precancel, New Orleans			—		
a	Perf. 12 x 10		2750.00	2,500.00		
b	Perf. 10 x 12			950.00		
c	Vertical pair, imperf. horizontally		425.00	250.00		
d	Booklet pane of 6		4.75	3.00		
e	As "d", imperf.		1,600.00			
425	2¢ rose red, type I	09/05/14	2.20	.20	27.50	(6)
	Cracked plate		9.50	—		
	Double transfer		—	—		
c	Perf. 10 x 12			—		
d	Perf. 12 x 10		6,500.00	3,500.00		
e	Booklet pane of 6	01/06/14	16.00	12.50		
426	3¢ deep violet, type I	09/18/14	14.00	1.25	180.00	(6)
427	4¢ brown	09/07/14	35.00	.50	500.00	(6)
	Double transfer		45.00	—		
428	5¢ blue	09/14/14	32.50	.50	400.00	(6)
a	Perf. 12 x 10			5,500.00		
429	6¢ red orange	09/28/14	47.50	1.40	525.00	(6)
430	7¢ black	09/10/14	85.00	4.00	950.00	(6)
	#431-33, 435, 437-40: Franklin (414-21, 423)					
431	8¢ pale olive green	09/26/14	35.00	1.50	475.00	(6)
	Double impression		—			
432	9¢ salmon red	10/06/14	50.00	7.50	700.00	(6)
433	10¢ orange yellow	09/09/14	47.50	.40	825.00	(6)
434	11¢ Franklin	08/11/15	22.50	7.50	250.00	(6)
435	12¢ claret brown	09/10/14	26.00	4.00	300.00	(6)
a	12¢ copper red		29.00	4.00	325.00	(6)
	Double transfer		32.50	—		
	Triple transfer		37.50	—		
436	Not assigned					
437	15¢ gray	09/16/14	125.00	7.25	1,100.00	(6)
438	20¢ ultramarine	09/19/14	210.00	4.00	3,250.00	(6)
439	30¢ orange red	09/19/14	250.00	16.00	4,000.00	(6)
440	50¢ violet	12/10/15	550.00	16.00	13,500.00	(6)

	Issues of 1914		Un	U	PB/LB	#
	Coil Stamps, Perf. 10 Horizontally #441-59: Wash.					
	(Designs of 405-06, 333-35; Flat Press, 18.5-19 x 22mm)					
441	1¢ green	11/14/14	1.00	1.00	7.75	(2)
442	2¢ carmine, type I	07/22/14	8.00	6.00	47.50	(2)
	Coil Stamps, Perf. 10 Vertically					
443	1¢ green	05/29/14	22.50	5.00	135.00	(2)
444	2¢ carmine, type I	04/25/14	35.00	1.50	240.00	(2)
445	3¢ violet, type I	12/18/14	220.00	125.00	1,200.00	(2)
446	4¢ brown	10/02/14	120.00	42.50	675.00	(2)
447	5¢ blue	07/30/14	42.50	27.50	240.00	(2)
	Issues of 1915-16, Coil Stamps, Perf. 10 Horizontally					
	(Rotary Press, Designs 18.5-19 x 22.5mm)					
448	1¢ green	12/12/15	6.00	3.25	40.00	(2)
449	2¢ red, type I	12/05/15	2,600.00	450.00	*15,000*	(2)
450	2¢ carmine, type III	02/16	9.50	3.00	75.00	(2)
451	Not assigned					
	Issues of 1914-16, Coil Stamps, Perf. 10 Vertically (Rotary Press, Designs 19.5 20 x 22mm)					
452	1¢ green	11/11/14	9.50	2.00	70.00	(2)
453	2¢ carmine rose, type I	07/03/14	125.00	4.25	625.00	(2)
	Cracked plate		—	—		
454	2¢ red, type II	06/15	82.50	10.00	425.00	(2)
455	2¢ carmine, type III	12/15	8.50	1.00	50.00	(2)
456	3¢ violet, type I	02/02/16	240.00	90.00	1,150.00	(2)
457	4¢ brown	02/18/16	25.00	17.50	150.00	(2)
	Cracked plate		35.00	—		
458	5¢ blue	03/09/16	30.00	17.50	180.00	(2)
	Issue of 1914, Horizontal Coil Stamp, Imperf.					
459	2¢ carmine, type I	06/30/14	250.00	*900.00*	1,100.00	(2)
	Issues of 1915, Wmkd. (191), Perf. 10					
460	$1 violet black Franklin (423)	02/08/15	800.00	85.00	*11,500.00*	(6)
	Double transfer		850.00	—		
	Perf. 11					
461	2¢ pale carmine red Washington					
	(406), type I	06/17/15	125.00	*250.00*	*1,300.00*	(6)
	Privately perforated copies of #409 have been made to resemble 461.					
	Issues of 1916-17, Unwmkd., Perf. 10 #462-69: Wash. (Designs of 405-06, 333-36, 407)					
462	1¢ green	09/27/16	6.50	.35	150.00	(6)
	Experimental precancel, Springfield, MA,					
	or New Orleans, LA			10.00		
a	Booklet pane of 6	10/15/16	9.00	*2.50*		
463	2¢ carmine, type I	09/25/16	4.25	.25	130.00	(6)
	Experimental precancel, Springfield, MA			22.50		
a	Booklet pane of 6	10/08/16	90.00	*45.00*		
	Double transfer		6.00	—		
464	3¢ violet, type I	11/11/16	75.00	12.50	1,400.00	(6)
	Double transfer in "CENTS"		*90.00*	—		
465	4¢ orange brown	10/07/16	45.00	1.70	675.00	(6)
466	5¢ blue	10/17/16	75.00	1.70	950.00	(6)
	Experimental precancel, Springfield, MA			175.00		
467	5¢ carmine (error in plate of 2¢)		550.00	675.00		
468	6¢ red orange	10/10/16	95.00	7.00	1,400.00	(6)
	Experimental precancel, Springfield, MA			175.00		
469	7¢ black	10/10/16	120.00	11.00	1,400.00	(6)
	Experimental precancel, Springfield, MA			175.00		

	Issues of 1916-17		Un	U	PB/LP	#	FDC
	#470-78: Franklin (Designs of 414-16, 434, 417-21, 423)						
470	8¢ olive green	11/13/16	57.50	5.50	575.00	(6)	
	Experimental precancel, Springfield, MA			165.00			
471	9¢ salmon red	11/16/16	57.50	14.00	775.00	(6)	
472	10¢ orange yellow	10/17/16	105.00	1.25	1,400.00	(6)	
473	11¢ dark green	11/16/16	37.50	16.00	375.00	(6)	
	Experimental precancel, Springfield, MA			575.00			
474	12¢ claret brown	10/10/16	50.00	5.00	650.00	(6)	
	Double transfer		60.00	6.00			
	Triple transfer		72.50	9.00			
475	15¢ gray	11/16/16	190.00	10.50	3,250.00	(6)	
476	20¢ light ultramarine	12/05/16	240.00	12.00	3,750.00	(6)	
476A	30¢ orange red		4,000.00	—	—	(6)	
477	50¢ light violet	03/02/17	950.00	60.00	55,000.00	(6)	
478	$1 violet black	12/22/16	725.00	16.00	13,000.00	(6)	
	Double transfer		775.00	20.00			
479	$2 dark blue Madison (312)	03/22/17	300.00	40.00	4,250.00	(6)	
480	$5 light green Marshall (313)	03/22/17	240.00	42.50	3,100.00	(6)	
	Issues of 1916-17, Imperf.						
	#481-96: Washington (Designs of 405-06, 333-35)						
481	1¢ green	11/16	1.00	.55	14.00	(6)	
	Double transfer		2.50	1.25			
482	2¢ carmine, type I	12/08/16	1.50	1.25	25.00	(6)	
482A	2¢ deep rose, type Ia			12,000.00			
483	3¢ violet, type I	10/13/17	14.00	7.50	125.00	(6)	
	Double transfer		18.50	—			
484	3¢ violet, type II		11.00	5.00	100.00	(6)	
	Double transfer		13.50	—			
485	5¢ carmine (error in plate of 2¢) 03/17		—		140.00	(6)	
	Issues of 1916-22, Coil Stamps, Perf. 10 Horizontally						
486	1¢ green	01/18	.90	.25	4.75	(2)	
	Double transfer		2.25	—			
487	2¢ carmine, type II	11/15/16	14.00	3.00	110.00	(2)	
488	2¢ carmine, type III	1919	2.50	1.75	15.00	(2)	
	Cracked plate		12.00	7.50			
489	3¢ violet, type I	10/10/17	5.00	1.50	32.50	(2)	
	Coil Stamps, Perf. 10 Vertically						
490	1¢ green	11/17/16	.55	.25	3.50	(2)	
	Cracked plate (horizontal)		7.50	—			
	Cracked plate (vertical) retouched		9.00	—			
	Rosette crack		50.00	—			
491	2¢ carmine, type II	11/17/16	2,100.00	550.00	10,500.00	(2)	
492	2¢ carmine, type III		9.00	.25	52.50	(2)	
493	3¢ violet, type I	07/23/17	16.00	3.00	110.00	(2)	
494	3¢ violet, type II	02/04/18	10.00	1.00	75.00	(2)	
495	4¢ orange brown	04/15/17	10.00	4.00	75.00	(2)	
	Cracked plate		25.00	—			
496	5¢ blue	01/15/19	3.50	1.00	30.00	(2)	
497	10¢ orange yellow						
	Franklin (416)	01/31/22	20.00	10.50	140.00	(2)	4,500.00

Issues of 1917-19			Un	U	PB	#
Perf. 11, #498-507: Washington (Designs of 405-06, 333-36, 407)						
498	1¢ green	03/17	.35	.25	17.50	(6)
a	Vertical pair, imperf. horizontally		175.00			
b	Horizontal pair, imperf. between		100.00			
d	Double impression		175.00			
e	Booklet pane of 6	04/06/17	2.50	.50		
f	Booklet pane of 30	09/17	*1,000.00*			
g	Perf. 10 top or bottom		—			
	Cracked plate		7.50	—		
499	2¢ rose, type I	03/17	.35	.25	17.50	(6)
a	Vertical pair, imperf. horizontally		150.00			
b	Horizontal pair, imperf. vertically		275.00	*150.00*		
e	Booklet pane of 6	03/31/17	4.00	*1.00*		
f	Booklet pane of 30	09/17	*27,500.00*			
g	Double impression		160.00	—		
	Double transfer		6.00	—		
500	2¢ deep rose, type Ia		250.00	180.00	2,000.00	(6)
	Pair, types I and Ia		*1,275.00*			
501	3¢ light violet, type I	03/17	11.00	.25	125.00	(6)
b	Booklet pane of 6	10/17/17	70.00	*30.00*		
d	Double impression		275.00			
502	3¢ dark violet, type II		14.00	.40	150.00	(6)
b	Booklet pane of 6	02/28/18	60.00	*30.00*		
c	Vertical pair, imperf. horizontally		250.00	125.00		
e	Perf. 10, top or bottom		—	3,500		
503	4¢ brown	03/17	10.00	.25	140.00	(6)
504	5¢ blue	03/17	9.00	.25	130.00	(6)
	Double transfer		11.00	—		
505	5¢ rose (error in plate of 2¢)		375.00	500.00		
506	6¢ red orange	03/17	12.50	.25	175.00	(6
507	7¢ black	03/17	27.50	1.10	260.00	(6)
#508-12, 514-18: Franklin (Designs of 414-16, 434, 417-21, 423)						
508	8¢ olive bister	03/17	12.00	.50	175.00	(6)
c	Perf. 10 top or bottom			*875.00*		
509	9¢ salmon red	03/17	14.00	1.75	150.00	(6)
510	10¢ orange yellow	03/17	17.00	.15	190.00	(6)
511	11¢ light green	05/17	9.00	2.50	130.00	(6)
	Double transfer		12.50	3.25		
512	12¢ claret brown	05/17	9.00	.35	130.00	(6)
a	12¢ brown carmine		9.50	.40		
b	Perf. 10, top or bottom		—	*2,250.00*		
513	13¢ apple green	01/10/19	11.00	6.00	130.00	(6)
	13¢ deep apple green		12.50	6.50		
514	15¢ gray	05/17	37.50	1.00	575.00	(6)
515	20¢ light ultramarine	05/17	47.50	.25	625.00	(6)
	20¢ deep ultramarine		50.00	.25		
b	Vertical pair, imperf. between		*325.00*			
516	30¢ orange red	05/17	37.50	1.00	600.00	(6)
a	Perf. 10 top or bottom		*5,000.00*	—		
517	50¢ red violet	05/17	67.50	.50	1,650.00	(6)
c	Perf. 10, top or bottom			*4,500.00*		
518	$1 violet brown	05/17	52.50	1.50	1,350.00	(6)
b	$1 deep brown		*1,600.00*	*1,000.00*		

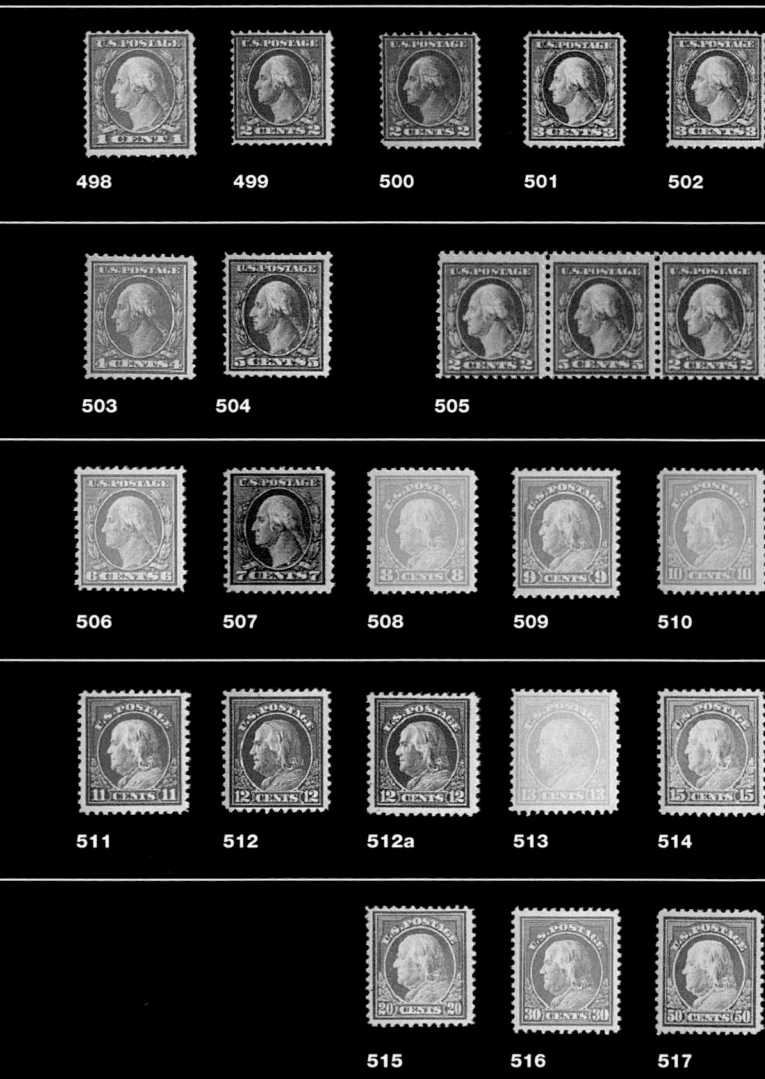

498   499   500   501   502

503   504   505

506   507   508   509   510

511   512   512a   513   514

515   516   517

*We redesigned and expanded the new issues
just for you! Read about the newest issues in the
"2000 Issues—New U.S. Postage Stamps" section.*

523

524

537

	ssue of 1917		Un	U	PB		FDC	Q(M)
	Wmkd. (191), Perf. 11							
519	2¢ carm. Washington (332)	10/10/17	400.00	*700.00*	2,700.00	(6)		
	Privately perforated copies of #344 have been made to resemble #519.							
520-22	Not assigned							
	Issues of 1918, Unwmkd.							
523	$2 Franklin	08/19/18	625.00	230.00	*12,000.00*	(8)		
524	$5 Franklin	08/19/18	220.00	35.00	4,250.00	(8)		
	Issues of 1918-20 #525-35: Washington (Designs of 405-06, 333)							
525	1¢ gray green	12/18	2.50	.50	25.00	(6)		
	1¢ Emerald		3.50	1.00				
a	1¢ dark green		2.75	.95				
d	Double impression		27.50	25.00				
526	2¢ carmine, type IV	03/06/20	27.50	3.50	250.00	(6)	*750.00*	
	Gash on forehead		40.00	—				
	Malformed "2" at left		37.50	6.00				
527	2¢ carmine, type V	03/20/20	20.00	1.00	175.00	(6)		
a	Double impression		60.00	10.00				
	Line through "2" and "EN"		30.00	—				
528	2¢ carmine, type Va	05/04/20	9.00	.25	85.00	(6)		
c	Double impression		27.50	—				
528A	2¢ carmine, type VI	06/24/20	52.50	1.50	550.00	(6)		
d	Double impression		160.00					
528B	2¢ carmine, type VII	11/03/20	22.50	.35	165.00	(6)		
e	Double impression		70.00					
	Retouched on cheek		400.00	—				
529	3¢ violet, type III	03/18	3.25	.25	60.00	(6)		
a	Double impression		32.50	—				
b	Printed on both sides		*450.00*					
530	3¢ purple, type IV		1.60	.20	18.50	(6)		
a	Double impression		20.00	6.00	—			
b	Printed on both sides		*250.00*					
	"Blister" under "U.S."		4.50	—				
	Recut under "U.S."		4.50	—				
	Imperf.							
531	1¢ green	01/19	9.00	8.00	90.00	(6)		
532	2¢ carmine rose, type IV	03/20	40.00	27.50	350.00	(6)		
533	2¢ carmine, type V	05/04/20	140.00	80.00	1,250.00	(6)		
534	2¢ carmine, type Va	05/25/20	11.00	6.50	110.00	(6)		
534A	2¢ carmine, type VI	07/26/20	40.00	22.50	350.00	(6)		
534B	2¢ carmine, type VII	12/02/20	1,900.00	850.00	*15,000.00*	(6)		
535	3¢ violet, type IV	1918	9.00	5.00	77.50	(6)		
a	Double impression		100.00	—				
	Issues of 1919, Perf. 12.5							
536	1¢ gray green							
	Washington (405)	08/15/19	19.00	20.00	175.00	(6)		
a	Horizontal pair, imperf. vertically		*700.00*					
	Perf. 11							
537	3¢ Allied Victory	03/03/19	9.50	3.25	100.00	(6)	*750.00*	100
a	deep red violet		*600.00*	*150.00*	4,250.00	(6)		
c	red violet		40.00	12.00				
	Double transfer		—	—				

	Issues of 1919		Un	U	PE		FDC	Q(M)
	Issues of 1919, George Washington, Unwmkd., Perf. 11 x 10							
538	1¢ green	06/19	12.00	8.50	115.00	(4)		
a	Vertical pair, imperf. horizontally		50.00	100.00	900.00	(4)		
	Double transfer		17.50	—				
539	2¢ carmine rose, type II		2,800.00	3,750.00	15,000.00	(4)		
540	2¢ carmine rose, type III	06/14/19	14.00	8.50	110.00	(4)		
	Double transfer		22.50	—				
a	Vertical pair, imperf. horizontally		50.00	100.00	750.00	(4)		
b	Horizontal pair, imperf. vertically		750.00					
541	3¢ violet, type II	06/19	42.50	30.00	375.00	(4)		
	Issue of 1920, Perf. 10 x 11							
542	1¢ green	05/26/20	13.50	1.10	170.00	(6)	1,250.00	
	Issues of 1921, Perf. 10							
543	1¢ green	05/21	.50	.25	15.00	(4)		
a	Horizontal pair, imperf. between		1,100.00					
	Double transfer			—				
	Triple transfer		—	—				
	Issue of 1922, Perf. 11							
544	1¢ green		13,500.00	3,250.00				
	Issues of 1921, Perf. 11							
545	1¢ green	05/21	175.00	160.00	1,050.00	(4)		
546	2¢ carmine rose, type III	05/21	110.00	150.00	725.00	(4)		
a	Perf. 10 at left		—					
	Recut in hair		125.00	175.00				
	Issues of 1920, Perf. 11							
547	$2 Franklin	11/01/20	190.00	40.0	4,300.00	(8)		
	Pilgrim Tercentenary Issue							
548	1¢ The Mayflower	12/21/20	4.50	2.25	45.00	(6)	800.00	138
	Double transfer		—	—				
549	2¢ Landing of the Pilgrims	12/21/20	6.50	1.60	65.00	(6)	650.00	196
550	5¢ Signing of the Compact	12/21/20	42.50	12.50	475.00	(6)	—	11
	Issues of 1922-25, Perf. 11 (See also #581-91, 594-606, 622-23, 631-42, 658-79, 684-87, 692-701, 723)							
551	½¢ Nathan Hale	04/04/25	.15	.15	6.00	(6)	20.00	(4)
	"Cap" on fraction bar		.75	.15				
552	1¢ Franklin	01/17/23	1.40	.15	25.00	(6)	30.00	(2)
a	Booklet pane of 6	08/11/23	6.00	1.50				
	Double transfer		3.50	—				
553	1½¢ Harding	03/19/25	2.60	.15	30.00	(6)	30.00	(2)
554	2¢ Washington	01/15/23	1.40	.15	22.50	(6)	42.50	
a	Horizontal pair, imperf. vertically		200.00					
b	Vertical pair, imperf. horizontally		500.00					
c	Booklet pane of 6	02/10/23	6.50	2.00				
	Double transfer		2.50	.80				
555	3¢ Lincoln	02/12/23	18.00	1.00	160.00	(6)	35.00	
556	4¢ M. Washington	01/15/23	19.00	.25	170.00	(6)	60.00	
b	Perf. 10, top or bottom		2,250.00	—				
557	5¢ T. Roosevelt	10/27/22	19.00	.20	190.00	(6)	150.00	
a	Imperf. pair		1,500.00					
c	Perf. 10, top or bottom		—	3,250.00				
558	6¢ Garfield	11/20/22	35.00	.85	400.00	(6)	250.00	
	Double transfer		55.00	2.00				
	Same, recut		55.00	2.00				

547

548   549   550

551   552

553   554

555   556

 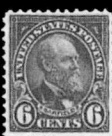

557   558

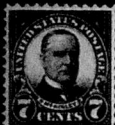

559

560

561

562

563

564

565

566

567

568

569

570

571

572

573

ssues of 1922-23			Un	U	PE		FDC
559	7¢ McKinley	05/01/23	9.00	.55	70.00	(6)	175.00
	Double transfer		—	—			
560	8¢ Grant	05/01/23	47.50	.60	600.00	(6)	210.00
	Double transfer		—	—			
561	9¢ Jefferson	01/15/23	13.50	1.10	160.00	(6)	210.00
	Double transfer		—	—			
562	10¢ Monroe	01/15/23	18.00	.15	200.00	(6)	190.00
a	Vertical pair, imperf. horizontally		*1,250.00*				
b	Imperf. pair		*1,250.00*				
c	Perf. 10 at top or bottom			*2,250.00*			
563	11¢ Hayes	10/04/22	1.30	.40	30.00	(6)	600.00
564	12¢ Cleveland	03/20/23	6.00	.15	72.50	(6)	210.00
a	Horizontal pair, imperf. vertically		*1,000.00*				
565	14¢ American Indian	05/01/23	4.00	.75	50.00	(6)	450.00
	Double transfer		—	—			
566	15¢ Statue of Liberty	11/11/22	22.50	.15	250.00	(6)	600.00
567	20¢ Golden Gate	05/01/23	21.00	.15	240.00	(6)	*500.00*
a	Horizontal pair, imperf. vertically		*1,500.00*				
568	25¢ Niagara Falls	11/11/22	18.00	.45	250.00	(6)	*700.00*
b	Vertical pair, imperf. horizontally		*850.00*				
c	Perf. 10 at one side		*3,000.00*				
569	30¢ Buffalo	03/20/23	32.50	.35	240.00	(6)	*900.00*
	Double transfer		55.00	—			
570	50¢ Arlington Amphitheater	11/11/22	55.00	.15	650.00	(6)	*1,250.00*
571	$1 Lincoln Memorial	02/12/23	45.00	.45	325.00	(6)	*7,000.00*
	Double transfer		90.00	1.50			
572	$2 U.S. Capitol	03/20/23	90.00	9.00	750.00	(6)	*15,000.00*
573	$5 Head of Freedom,						
	Capitol Dome	03/20/23	150.00	15.00	1,900.00	(8)	*25,000.00*
574	Not assigned						
	Issues of 1923-25, Imperf.						
575	1¢ green Franklin (552)	03/20/23	7.50	5.00	77.50	(6)	
576	1½¢ yel. brn. Harding (553)	04/04/25	1.60	1.50	20.00	(6)	45.00
577	2¢ carmine Washington (554)		1.75	1.25	27.50	(6)	
	Issues of 1923, Perf. 11 x 10						
578	1¢ green Franklin (552)	1923	95.00	*140.00*	750.00	(4)	
579	2¢ carmine Washington (554)	1923	85.00	*125.00*	575.00	(4)	
	Recut in eye		*105.00*	*150.00*			
	Issues of 1923-26, Perf. 10 (See also #551-73, 622-23, 631-42, 658-79, 684-87, 692-701, 723)						
580	Not assigned						
581	1¢ green Franklin (552)	04/21/23	9.50	.65	105.00	(4)	*5,750.00*
582	1½¢ brn. Harding (553)	03/19/25	4.50	.60	37.50	(4)	40.00
	Pair with full horiz. gutter between		*135.00*				
583	2¢ carm. Wash. (554)	04/14/24	2.50	.25	27.50	(4)	
a	Booklet pane of 6	08/27/26	85.00	27.50			*1,500.00*
584	3¢ violet Lincoln (555)	08/01/25	26.50	2.25	220.00	(4)	55.00
585	4¢ yellow brown Martha						
	Washington (556)	03/25	16.00	.45	200.00	(4)	55.00
586	5¢ blue T. Roosevelt (557)	12/24	16.00	.25	190.00	(4)	57.50
587	6¢ red orange Garfield (558)	03/25	7.50	.35	77.50	(4)	60.00
588	7¢ black McKinley (559)	05/29/26	10.50	5.50	90.00	(4)	70.00

	Issues of 1925-26		Un	U	PB/LP		FDC	Q(M)
	Perf. 11 x 10							
589	8¢ olive grn. Grant (560)	05/29/26	25.00	3.50	200.00	(4)	72.50	
590	9¢ rose Jefferson (561)	05/29/26	5.00	2.25	42.50	(4)	72.50	
591	10¢ orange Monroe (562)	06/08/25	60.00	.25	500.00	(4)	95.00	
592-93	Not assigned							
	Issues of 1923, Perf. 11							
594	1¢ green Franklin (552), design 19.75 x 22.25mm	1923	*18,000.00*	5,500.00				
595	2¢ carmine Washington (554), design 19.75 x 22.25mm	1923	275.00	300.00	1,950.00	(4)		
596	1¢ green Franklin (552), design 19.25 x 22.5mm	1923		*60,000.00*				
	Issues of 1923-29, Coil Stamps, Perf. 10 Vertically							
597	1¢ green Franklin (552)	07/18/23	.30	.15	2.25	(2)	*600.00*	
	Gripper cracks or double transfer		2.60	1.00				
598	1½¢ brown Harding (553)	03/19/25	1.00	.15	*4.75*	(2)	60.00	
599	2¢ carmine Washington (554), type I	01/23	.40	.15	2.30	(2)	*1,500.00*	
	Double transfer		1.90	1.00				
	Gripper cracks		2.30	2.00				
599A	2¢ carmine Washington (554), type II	03/29	125.00	11.00	675.00	(2)		
600	3¢ violet Lincoln (555)	05/10/24	7.25	.15	24.00	(2)	60.00	
601	4¢ yellow brown M. Washington (556)	08/05/23	4.50	.35	30.00	(2)		
602	5¢ dark blue T. Roosevelt (557)	03/05/24	1.75	.15	10.00	(2)	82.50	
603	10¢ orange Monroe (562)	12/01/24	4.00	.15	26.00	(2)	100.00	
	Coil Stamps, Perf. 10 Horizontally							
604	1¢ yel. grn. Franklin (552)	07/19/24	.35	.15	3.75	(2)	90.00	
605	1½¢ yel. brn. Harding (553)	05/09/25	.35	.15	3.50	(2)	70.00	
606	2¢ carmine Washington (554)	12/31/23	.35	.20	2.60	(2)	100.00	
607-09	Not assigned							
	Issues of 1923, Harding Memorial Issue, Perf. 11							
610	2¢ blk. Harding	09/01/23	.65	.15	20.00	(6)	30.00	1,459
a	Horizontal pair, imperf. vertically		*1,750.00*					
	Double transfer		1.75	.50				
	Imperf.							
611	2¢ blk. Harding (610)	11/15/23	6.50	4.00	80.00	(6)	90.00	0.8
	Perf. 10							
612	2¢ blk. Harding (610)	09/12/23	17.50	1.75	290.00	(4)	100.00	100
	Perf. 11							
613	2¢ black Harding (610)	1923		*25,000.00*				
	Issues of 1924, Huguenot-Walloon Tercentary Issue, May 1							
614	1¢ Ship Nieu Nederland	01/05/24	3.00	3.25	35.00	(6)	45.00	51
615	2¢ Walloons' Landing at Fort Orange (Albany)	01/05/24	6.00	2.10	65.00	(6)	55.00	78
	Double transfer		12.50	3.50				
616	5¢ Huguenot Monument to Jan Ribault at Mayport, Florida	01/05/24	25.00	12.50	250.00	(6)	82.50	6

599   610

614   615   616

Details

2¢ Washington Types I-II, Series 1923-29

Detail of **#599, 634** Type I

No heavy hair lines at top center of head.

Detail of **#599A, 634A** Type II

Three heavy hair lines at top center of head.

617

618

619

620

621

622

623

627

628

629

630

ssues of 1925			Un	U	PB	#	FDC	Q(M)
Lexington-Concord Issue, Perf. 11								
617	1¢ Washington at Cambridge	04/04/25	2.80	2.40	40.00	(6)	40.00	16
618	2¢ "The Birth of Liberty,"							
	by Henry Sandham	04/04/25	5.50	3.90	67.50	(6)	42.50	27
619	5¢ "The Minute Man,"							
	by Daniel Chester French	04/04/25	22.50	12.50	225.00	(6)	100.00	5
	Line over head		45.00	18.50				
	Norse-American Issue							
620	2¢ Sloop *Restaurationen*	05/18/25	4.00	3.00	190.00	(8)	30.00	9
621	5¢ Viking Ship	05/18/25	15.00	10.50	550.00	(8)	45.00	2
	Issues of 1925-26 (See also #551-79, 581-91, 594-606, 631-42, 658-79, 684-87, 692-701, 723)							
622	13¢ B. Harrison	01/11/26	13.50	.45	150.00	(6)	25.00	
623	17¢ Wilson	12/28/25	15.00	.25	170.00	(6)	30.00	
624-26 Not assigned								
	Issues of 1926							
627	2¢ Independence							
	Sesquicentennial Exposition	05/10/26	3.25	.50	37.50	(6)	10.00	308
628	5¢ John Ericsson Memorial	05/29/26	6.50	3.25	80.00	(6)	30.00	20
629	2¢ Battle of White Plains	10/18/26	2.25	1.70	35.00	(6)	6.25	41
a	Vertical pair, imperf. between		—					
	International Philatelic Exhibition Souvenir Sheet							
630	2¢ Battle of White Plains,							
	sheet of 25 with selvage							
	inscription (629)	10/18/26	400.00	450.00			1,500.00	0.1
	Dot over first "S" of "States"		425.00	475.00				
	Imperf. (See also #551-79, 581-91, 594-606, 622-23, 658-79, 684-87, 692-701, 723)							
631	1½¢ yellow brown							
	Harding (553)	08/27/26	2.00	1.70	62.50	(4)	30.00	
	Issues of 1926-34, Perf. 11 x 10.5 (See also #551-73, 575-79, 581-91, 594-606, 622-23, 631-42, 684-87, 692-701, 723)							
632	1¢ green Franklin (552)	06/10/27	.15	.15	2.00	(4)	45.00	
a	Booklet pane of 6	11/02/27	5.50	*1.50*			*3,000.00*	
b	Vertical pair, imperf. between		1,600.00	125.00				
	Pair with full vertical gutter between		150.00	—				
	Cracked plate		—	—				
633	1½¢ yellow brown							
	Harding (553)	05/17/27	2.00	.15	65.00	(4)	45.00	
634	2¢ carmine Washington							
	(554), type I	12/10/26	.15	.15	1.75	(4)	47.50	
	Pair with full vertical gutter between		200.00					
b	2¢ carmine lake, type I		—	—	—	(4)		
c	Horizontal pair, imperf. between		*2,000.00*					
d	Booklet pane of 6	02/25/27	1.75	.90				
634A	2¢ carmine Washington							
	(554), type II	12/28/27	350.00	13.50	2,000.00	(4)		
	Pair with full vertical or							
	horizontal gutter between		1,000.00	—				
635	3¢ violet Lincoln (555)	02/03/27	.45	.15	10.00	(4)	47.50	
a	3¢ bright violet Lincoln	02/07/34	.25	.15	5.50	(4)	25.00	
	Gripper cracks		3.25	2.00				
636	4¢ yellow brown Martha							
	Washington (556)	05/17/27	2.25	.15	75.00	(4)	50.00	
	Pair with full vertical gutter between		*200.00*					
637	5¢ dark blue Theodore							
	Roosevelt (557)	03/24/27	2.25	.15	15.00	(4)	50.00	
	Pair with full vertical gutter between		*275.00*					

ssues of 1927-31			Un	U	PB/LE			DC	Q(M)
	Perf. 11 x 10.5								
638	6¢ red orange Garfield (558)	07/27/27	2.25	.15	15.00	(4)		57.50	
	Pair with full vert. gutter between		200.00						
639	7¢ black McKinley (559)	03/24/27	2.25	.15	15.00	(4)		57.50	
a	Vertical pair, imperf.								
	between		275.00	85.00					
640	8¢ olive green Grant (560)	06/10/27	2.25	.15	15.00	(4)		62.50	
641	9¢ orange red Jefferson (561)	1931	2.25	.15	15.00	(4)		72.50	
642	10¢ orange Monroe (562)	02/03/27	3.75	.15	22.50	(4)		90.00	
	Double transfer		—	—					
	Perf. 11								
643	2¢ Vermont Sesquicentennial	08/03/27	1.40	.80	37.50	(6)		6.00	40
644	2¢ Burgoyne Campaign	08/03/27	3.50	2.10	32.50	(6)		12.50	26
	Issues of 1928								
645	2¢ Valley Forge	05/26/28	1.05	.40	25.00	(6)		4.00	101
	Perf. 11 x 10.5								
646	2¢ Battle of Monmouth/								
	Molly Pitcher	10/20/28	1.10	1.10	32.50	(4)		15.00	10
	Wide spacing, vertical pair		50.00	—					
	Hawaii Sesquicentennial Issue								
647	2¢ Washington (554)	08/13/28	5.00	4.50	125.00	(4)		15.00	6
	Wide spacing, vertical pair		100.00						
648	5¢ Theodore Roosevelt (557)	08/13/28	14.50	13.50	260.00	(4)		22.50	1
	Aeronautics Conference Issue, Perf. 11								
649	2¢ Wright Airplane	12/12/28	1.25	.80	10.00	(6)		7.00	51
650	5¢ Globe and Airplane	12/12/28	5.25	3.25	50.00	(6)		10.00	10
	Plate flaw "prairie dog"		27.50	12.50					
	Issues of 1929								
651	2¢ George Rogers Clark	02/25/29	.65	.50	10.00	(6)		6.00	17
	Double transfer		4.25	2.25					
652	Not assigned								
	Perf. 11 x 10.5								
653	½¢ olive brown Nathan								
	Hale (551)	5/25/29	.15	.15	1.50	(4)		25.00	
	Electric Light's Golden Jubilee Issue, Perf. 11								
654	2¢ Thomas Edison's First Lamp	06/05/29	.70	.70	27.50	(6)		10.00	32
	Perf. 11 x 10.5								
655	2¢ carmine rose (654)	06/11/29	.65	.15	35.00	(4)		80.00	210
	Coil Stamp, Perf. 10 Vertically								
656	2¢ carmine rose (654)	06/11/29	14.00	1.75	75.00	(2)		90.00	133
	Perf. 11								
657	2¢ Sullivan Expedition	06/17/29	.70	.60	25.00	(6)		4.00	51
	2¢ lake		500.00	—					

643   644   645

646   647   648

649   650

651

654   657

658   **669**

680   **681**

682   **683**

684   **685**

	Issues of 1929		Un	U	PB/LP		FDC	Q(M)
	#658-68 overprinted "Kans.," Perf. 11 x 10.5							
	(See also #551-73, 575-79, 581-91, 594-606, 622-23, 631-42, 684-87, 692-701, 723)							
658	1¢ Franklin	05/01/29	2.50	2.00	35.00	(4)	50.00	13
a	Vertical pair, one without overprint		325.00					
659	1½¢ brown Harding (553)	05/01/29	4.00	2.90	150.00	(4)	52.50	8
	Wide spacing, pair		70.00					
660	2¢ carmine Washington (554)	05/01/29	4.50	1.10	47.50	(4)	52.50	87
661	3¢ violet Lincoln (555)	05/01/29	22.50	15.00	210.00	(4)	60.00	3
662	4¢ yellow brown Martha Washington (556)	05/01/29	22.50	9.00	210.00	(4)	62.50	2
663	5¢ deep blue T. Roosevelt (557)	05/01/29	14.00	9.75	150.00	(4)	70.00	3
664	6¢ red orange Garfield (558)	05/01/29	32.50	18.00	450.00	(4)	80.00	1
665	7¢ black McKinley (559)	05/01/29	30.00	27.50	500.00	(4)	80.00	1
666	8¢ olive green Grant (560)	05/01/29	110.00	75.00	825.00	(4)	125.00	2
667	9¢ light rose Jefferson (561)	05/01/29	16.00	11.25	190.00	(4)	140.00	1
668	10¢ orange yel. Monroe (562)	05/01/29	25.00	12.00	350.00	(4)	165.00	3
	#669-79 overprinted "Nebr."							
669	1¢ Franklin	05/01/29	4.00	2.25	50.00	(4)	50.00	8
a	Vertical pair, one without overprint		—					
670	1½¢ brown Harding (553)	05/01/29	3.75	2.50	52.50	(4)	50.00	9
671	2¢ carmine Washington (554)	05/01/29	3.75	1.30	42.50	(4)	55.00	73
672	3¢ violet Lincoln (555)	05/01/29	15.00	12.00	165.00	(4)	65.00	2
673	4¢ yellow brown Martha Washington (556)	05/01/29	22.50	15.00	250.00	(4)	70.00	2
	Wide spacing, pair		120.00					
674	5¢ deep blue T. Roosevelt (557)	05/01/29	20.00	15.00	275.00	(4)	75.00	2
675	6¢ red orange Garfield (558)	05/01/29	47.50	24.00	525.00	(4)	100.00	1
676	7¢ black McKinley (559)	05/01/29	27.50	18.00	300.00	(4)	100.00	0.8
677	8¢ olive green Grant (560)	05/01/29	37.50	25.00	400.00	(4)	125.00	1
678	9¢ light rose Jefferson (561)	05/01/29	42.50	27.50	550.00	(4)	140.00	0.5
679	10¢ orange yel. Monroe (562)	05/01/29	135.00	22.50	1,050.00	(4)	175.00	2
	Warning: Excellent forgeries of the Kansas and Nebraska overprints exist.							
	Perf. 11							
680	2¢ Battle of Fallen Timbers	09/14/29	.80	.80	22.50	(6)	3.50	29
681	2¢ Ohio River Canalization	10/19/29	.70	.65	15.00	(6)	3.50	33
	Issues of 1930							
682	2¢ Mass. Bay Colony	04/08/30	.60	.50	22.50	(6)	3.50	74
683	2¢ Carolina-Charleston	04/10/30	1.20	1.20	42.50	(6)	3.50	25
	Perf. 11 x 10.5							
684	1½¢ Warren G. Harding	12/01/30	.35	.15	1.75	(4)	4.50	
	Pair with full horizontal gutter between		175.00					
	Pair with full vertical gutter between		—					
685	4¢ William H. Taft	06/04/30	.90	.15	11.00	(4)	6.00	
	Gouge on right "4"		2.10	.60				
	Recut right "4"		2.10	.65				
	Pair with full horizontal gutter between		—					
	Coil Stamps, Perf. 10 Vertically							
686	1½¢ brn. Harding (684)	12/01/30	1.80	.15	6.50	(2)	5.00	
687	4¢ brown Taft (685)	09/18/30	3.25	.45	13.00	(2)	20.00	

			Un	U	PB		FDC	Q(M)
	Issues of 1930							
	Perf. 11							
688	2¢ Battle of Braddock's Field	07/09/30	1.00	.85	30.00	(6)	4.00	26
689	2¢ Gen. von Steuben	09/17/30	.55	.55	20.00	(6)	4.00	66
a	Imperf. pair		2,500.00		12,000.00	(6)		
	Issues of 1931							
690	2¢ General Pulaski	01/16/31	.30	.15	10.00	(6)	4.00	97
691	Not assigned							
	Perf. 11 x 10.5 (See also #551-73, 575-79, 581-91, 594-606, 622-23, 631-42, 658-79, 684-87, 723)							
692	11¢ light bl. Hayes (563)	09/04/31	2.60	.15	13.50	(4)	100.00	
	Retouched forehead		6.75	1.00				
693	12¢ brown violet Cleveland (564)	08/25/31	5.50	.15	27.50	(4)	100.00	
694	13¢ yellow green Harrison (622)	09/04/31	2.00	.15	12.50	(4)	100.00	
695	14¢ dark blue American Indian (565)	09/08/31	3.75	.25	22.50	(4)	100.00	
696	15¢ gray Statue of Liberty (566)	08/27/31	8.00	.15	40.00	(4)	125.00	
	Perf. 10.5 x 11							
697	17¢ black Wilson (623)	07/25/31	4.50	.15	27.50	(4)	2,750.00	
698	20¢ carmine rose Golden Gate (567)	09/08/31	8.75	.15	40.00	(4)	325.00	
	Double transfer		20.00	—				
699	25¢ blue green Niagara Falls (568)	07/25/31	9.00	.15	47.50	(4)	2,750.00	
700	30¢ brown Buffalo (569)	09/08/31	17.50	.15	72.50	(4)	325.00	
	Cracked plate		27.50	.85				
701	50¢ lilac Arlington Amphitheater (570)	09/04/31	40.00	.15	200.00	(4)	450.00	
	Perf. 11							
702	2¢ Red Cross	05/21/31	.25	.15	1.90	(4)	3.00	99
a	Red cross omitted		40,000.00					
703	2¢ Yorktown	10/19/31	.40	.25	2.25	(4)	3.50	25
a	2¢ lake and black		4.50	.65				
b	2¢ dark lake and black		375.00		2,000.00	(4)		
c	Pair, imperf. vertically		5,000.00					
	Issues of 1932, Washington Bicentennial Issue, Perf. 11 x 10.5							
704	½¢ Portrait by Charles W. Peale	01/01/32	.15	.15	5.00	(4)	5.00 (4)	88
	Broken circle		.75	.20				
705	1¢ Bust by Jean Antoine Houdon	01/01/32	.15	.15	4.25	(4)	4.00 (2)	1,266
706	1½¢ Portrait by Charles W. Peale	01/01/32	.40	.15	14.50	(4)	4.00 (2)	305
707	2¢ Portrait by Gilbert Stuart	01/01/32	.15	.15	1.50	(4)	4.00	4,222
	Gripper cracks		1.75	.65				
708	3¢ Portrait by Charles W. Peale	01/01/32	.55	.15	15.00	(4)	4.00	456
709	4¢ Portrait by Charles P. Polk	01/01/32	.25	.15	5.50	(4)	4.00	151
	Broken bottom frame line		1.50	.50				
710	5¢ Portrait by Charles W. Peale	01/01/32	1.60	.15	15.00	(4)	4.00	171
	Cracked plate		5.25	1.10				
711	6¢ Portrait by John Trumbull	01/01/32	3.25	.15	50.00	(4)	4.00	112
712	7¢ Portrait by John Trumbull	01/01/32	.25	.15	7.00	(4)	4.00	83
713	8¢ Portrait by Charles B.J.F. Saint Memin	01/01/32	2.75	.50	50.00	(4)	4.50	97
	Pair, full vert. gutter between		—					
714	9¢ Portrait by W. Williams	01/01/32	2.40	.15	30.00	(4)	4.50	76
715	10¢ Portrait by Gilbert Stuart	01/01/32	10.00	.15	95.00	(4)	4.50	147

688

689

690

702

703

704

705

706

707

708

709

710

711

712

713

714

715

716

717

718

719

720

724

725

726

727

728

729

730

731

732

733

734

ssues of 1932		Un	U	PB/LP	#	FDC	Q(M)
Olympic Winter Games Issue, Perf. 11							
716	2¢ Ski Jumper 01/25/32	.40	.20	10.00	(6)	6.00	51
	Recut	3.50	1.50				
	Colored "snowball"	25.00	5.00				
Perf. 11 x 10.5							
717	2¢ Arbor Day 04/22/32	.15	.15	6.50	(4)	4.00	100
Olympic Summer Games Issue, Perf. 11 x 10.5							
718	3¢ Runner at Starting Mark 06/15/32	1.40	.15	11.50	(4)	6.00	168
	Gripper cracks	4.25	.75				
719	5¢ Myron's Discobolus 06/15/32	2.20	.20	20.00	(4)	8.00	53
	Gripper cracks	4.25	1.00				
720	3¢ Washington 06/16/32	.15	.15	1.30	(4)	7.50	
	Pair with full vertical or horizontal gutter between	200.00					
b	Booklet pane of 6 07/25/32	37.50	7.50			100.00	
c	Vertical pair, imperf. between	325.00	250.00				
	Recut lines on nose	2.00	.75				
Coil Stamp, Perf. 10 Vertically							
721	3¢ deep violet (720) 06/24/32	2.75	.15	10.00	(2)	15.00	
	Recut lines around eyes	—	—				
Coil Stamp, Perf. 10 Horizontally							
722	3¢ deep violet (720) 10/12/32	1.50	.35	6.25	(2)	15.00	
Coil Stamp, Perf. 10 Vertically (See also #551-73, 575-79, 581-91, 594-606, 622-23, 631-42, 684-87, 692-701)							
723	6¢ deep orange Garfield (558) 08/18/32	11.00	.30	60.00	(2)	15.00	
Perf. 11							
724	3¢ William Penn 10/24/32	.25	.15	8.00	(6)	3.25	49
a	Vertical pair, imperf. horizontally	—					
725	3¢ Daniel Webster 10/24/32	.30	.25	16.50	(6)	3.25	49
Issues of 1933							
726	3¢ Georgia Settlement 02/12/33	.25	.20	10.00	(6)	3.25	61
Perf. 10.5 x 11							
727	3¢ Peace of 1783 04/19/33	.15	.15	4.00	(4)	3.50	73
Century of Progress Issue							
728	1¢ Restoration of Fort Dearborn 05/25/33	.15	.15	1.90	(4)	3.00 (3)	348
	Gripper cracks	2.00	—				
729	3¢ Federal Building at Chicago 05/25/33	.15	.15	2.25	(4)	3.00	480
American Philatelic Society Issue Souvenir Sheets, Without Gum, Imperf.							
730	1¢ sheet of 25 (728) 08/25/33	27.50	27.50			100.00	0.4
a	Single stamp from sheet	.75	.45			3.25 (3)	11
731	3¢ sheet of 25 (729) 08/25/33	25.00	25.00			100.00	0.4
a	Single stamp from sheet	.65	.45			3.25	11
Perf. 10.5 x 11							
732	3¢ NRA 08/15/33	.15	.15	1.50	(4)	3.25	1,978
	Gripper cracks	1.50	—				
	Recut at right	2.00					
Perf. 11							
733	3¢ Byrd Antarctic Expedition II 10/09/33	.50	.50	14.00	(6)	10.00	5
	Double transfer	2.75	1.00				
734	5¢ Kosciuszko 10/13/33	.55	.25	27.50	(6)	4.50	45
a	Horizontal pair, imperf. vertically	2,250.00	25,000.00	(8)			

	Issues of 1934		Un	U	PB		FDC	Q(M)
	National Stamp Exhibition Issue Souvenir Sheet, Without Gum, Imperf.							
735	3¢ sheet of 6 (733)	02/10/34	12.50	10.00			40.00	0.8
a	Single stamp from sheet		2.00	1.65			5.00	4
	Perf. 11							
736	3¢ Maryland Tercentenary	03/23/34	.15	.15	6.00	(6)	1.60	46
	Double transfer		—	—				
	Mothers of America Issue, Perf. 11 x 10.5							
737	3¢ Portrait of his Mother,							
	by James A. McNeill Whistler	05/02/34	.15	.15	1.00	(4)	1.60	193
	Perf. 11							
738	3¢ deep violet (737)	05/02/34	.15	.15	4.25	(6)	1.60	15
739	3¢ Wisconsin Tercentenary	07/07/34	.15	.15	3.00	(6)	1.10	64
a	Vert. pair, imperf. horiz.		350.00					
b	Horiz. pair, imperf. vert.		450.00					
	National Parks Issue, Unwmkd.							
740	1¢ El Capitan, Yosemite							
	(California)	07/16/34	.15	.15	1.00	(6)	2.25	84
	Recut		1.50	.50				
a	Vertical pair, imperf.							
	horizontally, with gum		450.00					
741	2¢ Grand Canyon (Ariz.)	07/24/34	.15	.15	1.25	(6)	2.25	74
a	Vertical pair, imperf.							
	horizontally, with gum		450.00					
b	Horizontal pair, imperf.							
	vertically, with gum		425.00					
	Double transfer		1.25	—				
742	3¢ Mirror Lake, Mt. Rainier							
	(Washington)	08/03/34	.15	.15	1.75	(6)	2.50	95
a	Vertical pair, imperf.							
	horizontally, with gum		425.00					
743	4¢ Cliff Palace, Mesa Verde							
	(Colorado)	09/25/34	.35	.40	7.00	(6)	2.25	19
a	Vertical pair, imperf.							
	horizontally, with gum		700.00					
744	5¢ Old Faithful, Yellowstone							
	(Wyoming)	07/30/34	.70	.65	8.75	(6)	2.25	30
a	Horizontal pair, imperf.							
	vertically, with gum		500.00					
745	6¢ Crater Lake (Oregon)	09/05/34	1.10	.85	15.00	(6)	3.00	16
746	7¢ Great Head, Acadia							
	Park (Maine)	10/02/34	.60	.75	10.00	(6)	3.00	15
a	Horizontal pair, imperf.							
	vertically, with gum		700.00					
747	8¢ Great White Throne,							
	Zion Park (Utah)	09/18/34	1.60	1.50	15.00	(6)	3.25	15
748	9¢ Glacier National Park							
	(Montana)	08/27/34	1.50	.65	15.00	(6)	3.50	17
749	10¢ Great Smoky Mountains							
	(North Carolina)	10/08/34	3.00	1.25	22.50	(6)	6.00	18
	American Philatelic Society Issue Souvenir Sheet, Imperf.							
750	3¢ sheet of 6 (742)	08/28/34	30.00	27.50			40.00	0.5
a	Single stamp from sheet		3.50	3.25			3.25	3
	Trans-Mississippi Philatelic Exposition Issue Souvenir Sheet							
751	1¢ sheet of 6 (740)	10/10/34	12.50	12.50			35.00	0.7
a	Single stamp from sheet		1.40	1.60			3.25 (3)	4

735

736

737

739

740

741

742

744

743

745

746

747

748

749

750

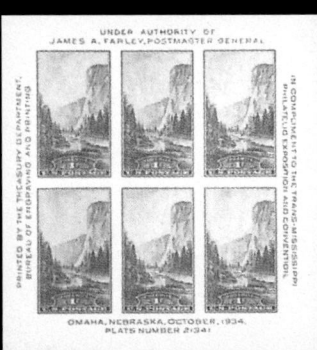

751

113

Examples of Special Printing Position Blocks

Gutter Block 752

Centerline Block 754

Line Block 756

Arrow Block 763

Cross-Gutter Block 768

114

ssues of 1935			Un	U	PB	#	FDC	Q(M)
Special Printing (#752-71), Without Gum, Perf. 10.5 x 11								
752	3¢ violet Peace of 1783 (727)	03/15/35	.15	.15	15.00	(4)	5.00	3
	Perf. 11							
753	3¢ blue Byrd Expedition II (733)	03/15/35	.50	.45	17.50	(6)	6.00	2
	Imperf.							
754	3¢ dp. vio. Whistler's Mother (737)	03/15/35	.55	.55	16.00	(6)	6.00	2
755	3¢ deep violet Wisconsin (739)	03/15/35	.55	.55	16.00	(6)	6.00	2
756	1¢ green Yosemite (740)	03/15/35	.20	.20	5.25	(6)	6.00	3
757	2¢ red Grand Canyon (741)	03/15/35	.25	.25	6.00	(6)	6.00	3
	Double transfer		—					
758	3¢ deep violet Mt. Rainier (742)	03/15/35	.50	.45	15.00	(6)	6.00	2
759	4¢ brown Mesa Verde (743)	03/15/35	.95	.95	20.00	(6)	6.50	2
760	5¢ blue Yellowstone (744)	03/15/35	1.50	1.30	25.00	(6)	6.50	2
	Double transfer		—					
761	6¢ dark blue Crater Lake (745)	03/15/35	2.40	2.10	35.00	(6)	6.50	2
762	7¢ black Acadia (746)	03/15/35	1.50	1.40	30.00	(6)	6.50	2
	Double transfer		—					
763	8¢ sage green Zion (747)	03/15/35	1.60	1.50	37.50	(6)	7.50	2
764	9¢ red orange Glacier (748)	03/15/35	1.90	1.65	42.50	(6)	7.50	2
765	10¢ gray black Smoky Mts. (749)	03/15/35	3.75	3.25	50.00	(6)	7.50	2
766	1¢ yellow grn. (728), pane of 25	03/15/35	25.00	25.00			250.00	0.1
a	Single stamp from pane		.70	.40			5.50 (3)	2
767	3¢ violet (729), pane of 25	03/15/35	23.50	23.50			250.00	0.09
a	Single stamp from pane		.60	.40			5.50	2
768	3¢ dark blue (733), pane of 6	03/15/35	20.00	15.00			250.00	0.3
a	Single stamp from pane		2.80	2.40			6.50	2
769	1¢ green (740), pane of 6	03/15/35	12.50	11.00			250.00	0.3
a	Single stamp from pane		1.85	1.80			4.00	2
770	3¢ deep violet (742), pane of 6	03/15/35	30.00	24.00			250.00	0.2
a	Single stamp from pane		3.25	3.10			5.00	1
771	16¢ dark blue Great Seal of U.S.	03/15/35	2.25	2.25	52.50	(6)	12.50	1

For perforate variety, see #CE2.

A number of position pieces can be collected from the panes or sheets of the 1935 Special Printing issues, including horizontal and vertical gutter (#752, 766-70) or line (#753-65, 771) blocks of four (HG/L and VG/L), arrow-and-guideline blocks of four (AGL) and crossed-gutter or centerline blocks of four (CG/L). Pairs sell for half the price of blocks of four. Arrow-and-guideline blocks for #753 are top or bottom only.

	HG/L	VG/L	AGL	CG/L		HG/L	VG/L	AGL	CG/L
752	11.00	18.00		47.50	762	8.50	7.50	8.25	14.00
753	4.50	50.00	52.50	57.50	763	7.50	9.50	11.00	17.50
754	3.50	2.80	3.00	7.25	764	10.00	9.00	10.50	22.50
755	3.50	2.80	3.00	7.25	765	18.00	21.00	24.00	30.00
756	.90	1.10	1.25	3.00	766	11.00	14.00		15.00
757	1.40	1.10	1.25	3.50	767	10.50	13.50		15.00
758	2.80	2.50	2.75	5.25	768	15.00	18.00		20.00
759	5.50	4.50	4.75	8.50	769	12.00	14.00		15.00
760	7.00	8.50	9.00	15.00	770	25.00	22.00		30.00
761	13.00	11.00	12.50	20.00	771	13.00	11.00	12.50	50.00

ssues of 1935		Un	U	PE		D	Q(M)
Perf. 11 x 10.5							
Beginning with #772, unused values are for never-hinged stamps.							
772	3¢ Connecticut	04/26/35	.15	.15	1.40	(4)	9.00	71
	Defect in cent design		1.00	.25				
773	3¢ California Pacific							
	International Expo	05/29/35	.15	.15	1.25	(4)	8.00	101
	Pair with full vertical gutter between		—					
Perf. 11							
774	3¢ Boulder Dam	09/30/35	.15	.15	1.65	(6)	10.00	74
Perf. 11 x 10.5							
775	3¢ Michigan Statehood	11/01/35	.15	.15	1.25	(4)	8.00	76
Issues of 1936							
776	3¢ Republic of Texas	03/02/36	.15	.15	1.10	(4)	17.50	124
Perf. 10.5 x 11							
777	3¢ Rhode Island	05/04/36	.15	.15	1.10	(4)	8.00	67
	Pair with full gutter between		200.00					
Third International Philatelic Exhibition Issue Souvenir Sheet, Imperf.							
778	Sheet of 4 different stamps							
	(#772, 773, 775 and 776)	05/09/36	1.75	1.75			13.00	3
a-d	Single stamp from sheet		.40	.30				3
779-81	Not assigned							
Perf. 11 x 10.5							
782	3¢ Arkansas Statehood	06/15/36	.15	.15	1.10	(4)	8.00	73
783	3¢ Oregon Territory	07/14/36	.15	.15	1.10	(4)	8.50	74
	Double transfer		1.00	.50				
784	3¢ Susan B. Anthony	8/26/36	.15	.15	.75	(4)	5.00	270
	Period missing after "B"		.75	.25				

In 1982 the U.S. Postal Service issued four stamps illustrated by Charles Harper portraying sources of energy. The stamps commemorated the 1982 Knoxville World's Fair, whose theme was energy. Two of the stamps depicted **synthetic and fossil fuels**.

During the energy crisis of the 1970s, the United States looked for alternatives to imported oil, including synthetic fuels produced from coal and shale. Solar and nuclear power were other new sources of energy proposed for development.

Fossil fuels come in three major forms: coal, oil, and natural gas. They were formed millions of years ago from prehistoric plants and animals. When these organisms died, they decomposed and became buried deep in the earth under layers of mud, rock, and sand. Over millions of years this plant and animal debris formed fossil fuels. Fossil fuels are not renewable: once they are used, they cannot be remade.

772

773

774

775

776

777

778

782

783

784

785

786

787

788

789

790

791

792

793

794

795

796

798

799

800

801

802

Issues of 1936-37		Un	U	PB		FDC	Q(M)
Perf. 11 x 10.5, Army Issue							
785	1¢ George Washington, Nathaniel Green and Mount Vernon	12/15/36	.15	.15	.85	(4)	5.00	105
	Pair with full vertical gutter between		—					
786	2¢ Andrew Jackson, Winfield Scott and The Hermitage	01/15/37	.15	.15	.85	(4)	5.00	94
787	3¢ Generals Sherman, Grant and Sheridan	02/18/37	.20	.15	1.10	(4)	5.00	88
788	4¢ Generals Robert E. Lee and "Stonewall" Jackson and Stratford Hall	03/23/37	.30	.15	8.00	(4)	5.50	36
789	5¢ U.S. Military Academy at West Point	05/26/37	.60	.15	8.50	(4)	5.50	37
Perf. 11 x 10.5, Navy Issue							
790	1¢ John Paul Jones, John Barry, *Bon Homme Richard* and *Lexington*	12/15/36	.15	.15	.85	(4)	5.00	105
791	2¢ Stephen Decatur, Thomas Macdonough and Saratoga	01/15/37	.15	.15	.75	(4)	5.00	92
792	3¢ David G. Farragut and David D. Porter, *Hartford* and *Powhatan*	02/18/37	.15	.15	1.00	(4)	5.00	93
793	4¢ Admirals William T. Sampson, George Dewey and Winfield S. Schley	03/23/37	.30	.15	8.50	(4)	5.50	35
794	5¢ Seal of U.S. Naval Academy and Naval Cadets	05/26/37	.60	.15	8.50	(4)	5.50	37
Issues of 1937							
795	3¢ Northwest Territory Ordinance	07/13/37	.15	.15	1.10	(4)	6.00	85
Perf. 11							
796	5¢ Virginia Dare	08/18/37	.20	.20	6.50	(6)	7.00	25
Society of Philatelic Americans Issue Souvenir Sheet, Imperf.							
797	10¢ blue green (749)	08/26/37	.60	.40			6.00	5
Perf. 11 x 10.5							
798	3¢ Constitution Sesquicentennial	09/17/37	.15	.15	1.00	(4)	6.50	100
Territorial Issues, Perf. 10.5 x 11							
799	3¢ Hawaii	10/18/37	.15	.15	1.25	(4)	7.00	78
Perf. 11 x 10.5							
800	3¢ Alaska	11/12/37	.15	.15	1.25	(4)	7.00	77
	Pair with full gutter between		—					
801	3¢ Puerto Rico	11/25/37	.15	.15	1.25	(4)	7.00	81
802	3¢ Virgin Islands	12/15/37	.15	.15	1.25	(4)	7.00	76
	Pair with full vertical gutter between	275.00						

ssues of 1938-39			Un	U	PE		FDC

Presidential Issue Perf. 11 x 10.5 (#804b, 806b, 807a issued in 1939, 832b in 1951, 832c in 1954, rest in 1938; see also 839-51)

			Un	U	PE		FDC
803	½¢ Benjamin Franklin	05/19/38	.15	.15	.35	(4)	2.25
804	1¢ George Washington	04/25/38	.15	.15	.25	(4)	2.50
b	Booklet pane of 6	01/27/39	2.00	.35			15.00
	Pair with full vertical gutter between		160.00	—			
805	1½¢ Martha Washington	05/05/38	.15	.15	.20	(4)	2.50
b	Horizontal pair, imperf. between		175.00	30.00			
	Pair with full horizontal gutter between		175.00				
806	2¢ John Adams	06/03/38	.15	.15	.30	(4)	2.50
b	Booklet pane of 6	01/27/39	4.75	.85			15.00
	Recut at top of head		3.00	1.50			
807	3¢ Thomas Jefferson	06/16/38	.15	.15	.25	(4)	2.50
a	Booklet pane of 6	01/27/39	8.50	1.25			18.00
b	Horizontal pair, imperf. between		900.00	—			
c	Imperf. pair		2,500.00				
808	4¢ James Madison	07/01/38	.75	.15	3.75	(4)	2.50
809	4½¢ The White House	07/11/38	.15	.15	1.50	(4)	2.50
810	5¢ James Monroe	07/21/38	.20	.15	1.00	(4)	2.50
811	6¢ John Quincy Adams	07/28/38	.20	.15	1.00	(4)	2.50
812	7¢ Andrew Jackson	08/04/38	.25	.15	1.25	(4)	2.50
813	8¢ Martin Van Buren	08/11/38	.30	.15	1.40	(4)	2.50
814	9¢ William H. Harrison	08/18/38	.30	.15	1.40	(4)	3.00
	Pair with full vertical gutter between		—				
815	10¢ John Tyler	09/02/38	.25	.15	1.25	(4)	3.00
816	11¢ James K. Polk	09/08/38	.65	.15	3.00	(4)	3.00
817	12¢ Zachary Taylor	09/14/38	.90	.15	4.25	(4)	3.00
818	13¢ Millard Fillmore	09/22/38	1.25	.15	6.50	(4)	3.00
819	14¢ Franklin Pierce	10/06/38	.90	.15	4.50	(4)	3.00
820	15¢ James Buchanan	10/13/38	.40	.15	1.90	(4)	3.00
821	16¢ Abraham Lincoln	10/20/38	.90	.25	4.50	(4)	5.00
822	17¢ Andrew Johnson	10/27/38	.85	.15	4.50	(4)	5.00
823	18¢ Ulysses S. Grant	11/03/38	1.75	.15	8.75	(4)	5.00
824	19¢ Rutherford B. Hayes	11/10/38	1.25	.35	6.25	(4)	5.00
825	20¢ James A. Garfield	11/10/38	.70	.15	3.50	(4)	5.00
826	21¢ Chester A. Arthur	11/22/38	1.25	.15	7.00	(4)	5.00
827	22¢ Grover Cleveland	11/22/38	1.00	.40	9.50	(4)	5.00
828	24¢ Benjamin Harrison	12/02/38	3.50	.20	17.00	(4)	5.00
829	25¢ William McKinley	12/02/38	.60	.15	3.00	(4)	6.00
830	30¢ Theodore Roosevelt	12/08/38	3.75	.15	18.00	(4)	7.50
831	50¢ William Howard Taft	12/08/38	5.75	.15	26.00	(4)	10.00

803    804    805    806    807

808    809    810    811    812

813    814    815    816    817

818    819    820    821    822

823   824   825   826   827

828   829   830   831

832   833   834

835   837   838

836

852   853   854

855   856

858

857

	ssues of 1938-54		Un	U	PB/LF		FDC	Q(M)
	Perf. 11							
832	$1 Woodrow Wilson	08/29/38	7.00	.15	35.00	(4)	50.00	
a	Vertical pair, imperf. horizontally		1,600.00					
b	Watermarked "USIR" (1951)		250.00	65.00	1,550.00	(4)		
c	$1 red violet and black	08/31/54	6.00	.15	30.00	(4)	25.00	
d	As "c," vert. pair, imperf. horiz.		1,250.00					
e	Vertical pair, imperf. between		2,750.00					
f	As "c," vert. pair, imperf. between		7,000.00					
833	$2 Warren G. Harding	09/29/38	20.00	3.75	95.00	(4)	100.00	
834	$5 Calvin Coolidge	11/17/38	95.00	3.00	440.00	(4)	150.00	
a	$5 red, brown and black		3,250.00	1,500.00				
	Issues of 1938, Perf. 11 x 10.5							
835	3¢ Constitution Ratification	06/21/38	.25	.15	3.50	(4)	6.50	73
	Perf. 11							
836	3¢ Swedish-Finnish Tercentenary	06/27/38	.15	.15	2.50	(6)	6.00	59
	Perf. 11 x 10.5							
837	3¢ Northwest Territory	07/15/38	.15	.15	7.50	(4)	6.00	66
838	3¢ Iowa Territorial Centennial	08/24/38	.15	.15	5.00	(4)	6.00	47
	Pair with full vertical gutter between		—					
	Issues of 1939, Coil Stamps, Perf. 10 Vertically							
839	1¢ green Washington (804)	01/20/39	.30	.15	1.40	(2)	5.00	
840	1½¢ bister brn.							
	Martha Washington (805)	01/20/39	.30	.15	1.50	(2)	5.00	
841	2¢ rose carmine							
	John Adams (806)	01/20/39	.40	.15	1.75	(2)	5.00	
842	3¢ deep violet Jefferson (807)	01/20/39	.50	.15	2.00	(2)	5.00	
	Gripper cracks		—					
	Thin, translucent paper		2.50	—				
843	4¢ red violet Madison (808)	01/20/39	8.00	.40	27.50	(2)	5.00	
844	4½¢ dark gray							
	White House (809)	01/20/38	.70	.40	5.00	(2)	5.00	
845	5¢ bright blue Monroe (810)	01/20/39	5.00	.35	27.50	(2)	5.00	
846	6¢ red orange							
	John Quincy Adams (811)	01/20/39	1.10	.20	7.50	(2)	7.00	
847	10¢ brown red Tyler (815)	01/20/39	11.00	.50	42.50	(2)	9.00	
	Coil Stamps, Perf. 10 Horizontally							
848	1¢ green Washington (804)	01/27/39	.85	.15	2.75	(2)	5.00	
849	1½¢ bister brn.							
	Martha Washington (805)	01/27/39	1.25	.30	4.50	(2)	5.00	
850	2¢ rose carmine							
	John Adams (806)	01/27/39	2.50	.40	6.50	(2)	5.00	
851	3¢ deep violet Jefferson (807)	01/27/39	2.25	.35	6.25	(2)	6.00	
	Perf. 10.5 x 11							
852	3¢ Golden Gate Exposition	02/18/39	.15	.15	1.25	(4)	6.00	114
853	3¢ New York World's Fair	04/01/39	.15	.15	1.75	(4)	12.50	102
	Perf. 11							
854	3¢ Washington's Inauguration	04/30/39	.40	.15	3.50	(6)	6.00	73
	Perf. 11 x 10.5							
855	3¢ Baseball	06/12/39	1.75	.15	7.50	(4)	35.00	81
	Perf. 11							
856	3¢ Panama Canal	08/15/39	.25	.15	3.00	(6)	6.50	68
	Perf. 10.5 x 11							
857	3¢ Printing	09/25/39	.15	.15	1.00	(4)	5.00	71
	Perf. 11 x 10.5							
858	3¢ 50th Anniversary of Statehood							
	(Montana, North Dakota, South							
	Dakota, Washington)	11/02/39	.15	.15	1.10	(4)	5.00	67

	ssues of 1940		Un	U	PB		FDC	Q(M)
	Famous Americans Issue, Perf. 10.5 x 11							
	Authors							
859	1¢ Washington Irving	01/29/40	.15	.15	.95	(4)	2.00	56
860	2¢ James Fenimore Cooper	01/29/40	.15	.15	.95	(4)	2.00	53
861	3¢ Ralph Waldo Emerson	02/05/40	.15	.15	1.25	(4)	2.00	53
862	5¢ Louisa May Alcott	02/05/40	.30	.20	8.25	(4)	3.00	22
863	10¢ Samuel L. Clemens (Mark Twain)	02/13/40	1.65	1.20	35.00	(4)	4.50	13
	Poets							
864	1¢ Henry W. Longfellow	02/16/40	.15	.15	1.75	(4)	2.00	52
865	2¢ John Greenleaf Whittier	02/16/40	.15	.15	1.75	(4)	2.00	52
866	3¢ James Russell Lowell	02/20/40	.15	.15	2.25	(4)	2.00	52
867	5¢ Walt Whitman	02/20/40	.35	.15	9.00	(4)	4.00	22
868	10¢ James Whitcomb Riley	02/24/40	1.75	1.25	30.00	(4)	6.00	12
	Educators							
869	1¢ Horace Mann	03/14/40	.15	.15	1.90	(4)	2.00	52
870	2¢ Mark Hopkins	03/14/40	.15	.15	1.25	(4)	2.00	52
871	3¢ Charles W. Eliot	03/28/40	.15	.15	2.25	(4)	2.00	52
872	5¢ Frances E. Willard	03/28/40	.40	.20	9.00	(4)	4.00	21
873	10¢ Booker T. Washington	04/07/40	1.25	1.10	25.00	(4)	6.50	14
	Scientists							
874	1¢ John James Audubon	04/08/40	.15	.15	.95	(4)	2.00	59
875	2¢ Dr. Crawford W. Long	04/08/40	.15	.15	.95	(4)	2.00	58
876	3¢ Luther Burbank	04/17/40	.15	.15	1.10	(4)	2.00	58
877	5¢ Dr. Walter Reed	04/17/40	.25	.15	6.00	(4)	3.00	24
878	10¢ Jane Addams	04/26/40	1.10	.85	20.00	(4)	5.00	15
	Composers							
879	1¢ Stephen Collins Foster	05/03/40	.15	.15	1.00	(4)	2.00	57
880	2¢ John Philip Sousa	05/03/40	.15	.15	1.00	(4)	2.00	58
881	3¢ Victor Herbert	05/13/40	.15	.15	1.10	(4)	2.00	56
882	5¢ Edward A. MacDowell	05/13/40	.40	.20	9.25	(4)	3.00	21
883	10¢ Ethelbert Nevin	06/10/40	3.75	1.35	32.50	(4)	5.00	13
	Artists							
884	1¢ Gilbert Charles Stuart	09/05/40	.15	.15	1.00	(4)	2.00	54
885	2¢ James A. McNeill Whistler	09/05/40	.15	.15	.95	(4)	2.00	54
886	3¢ Augustus Saint-Gaudens	09/16/40	.15	.15	1.00	(4)	2.00	55
887	5¢ Daniel Chester French	09/16/40	.50	.20	8.00	(4)	3.00	22
888	10¢ Frederic Remington	09/30/40	1.75	1.25	25.00	(4)	5.00	14
	Inventors							
889	1¢ Eli Whitney	10/07/40	.15	.15	1.90	(4)	2.00	48
890	2¢ Samuel F.B. Morse	10/07/40	.15	.15	1.10	(4)	2.00	53
891	3¢ Cyrus Hall McCormick	10/14/40	.25	.15	1.75	(4)	2.00	54
892	5¢ Elias Howe	10/14/40	1.10	.30	12.50	(4)	3.00	20
893	10¢ Alexander Graham Bell	10/28/40	11.00	2.00	65.00	(4)	7.50	14

859 860 861 862 863

864 865 866 867 868

869 870 871 872 873

874 875 876 877 878

879 880 881 882 883

884 885 886 887 888

889 890 891 892 893

894

895

896

897

898

899

900

901

902

903

904

905

906

907

908

	Issues of 1940		Un	U	PB	#	FDC	Q(M)
894	3¢ Pony Express	04/03/40	.25	.15	2.75	(4)	5.00	46
	Perf. 10.5 x 11							
895	3¢ Pan American Union	04/14/40	.20	.15	2.75	(4)	4.50	48
	Perf. 11 x 10.5							
896	3¢ Idaho Statehood	07/03/40	.15	.15	1.75	(4)	4.50	51
	Perf. 10.5 x 11							
897	3¢ Wyoming Statehood	07/10/40	.15	.15	1.50	(4)	4.50	50
	Perf. 11 x 10.5							
898	3¢ Coronado Expedition	09/07/40	.15	.15	1.50	(4)	4.50	61
	National Defense Issue							
899	1¢ Statue of Liberty	10/16/40	.15	.15	.45	(4)	4.25	
a	Vertical pair, imperf. Between		650.00	—				
b	Horizontal pair, imperf. between		40.00	—				
	Pair with full vertical gutter between		200.00					
	Cracked plate		3.00					
	Gripper cracks		3.00					
900	2¢ 90mm Antiaircraft Gun	10/16/40	.15	.15	.45	(4)	4.25	
a	Horizontal pair, imperf. between		40.00	—				
	Pair with full vertical gutter between		275.00					
901	3¢ Torch of Enlightenment	10/16/40	.15	.15	.60	(4)	4.25	
a	Horizontal pair, imperf. between		30.00	—				
	Pair with full vertical gutter between		—					
	Perf. 10.5 x 11							
902	3¢ Thirteenth Amendment	10/20/40	.20	.15	3.00	(4)	7.50	44
	Issue of 1941, Perf. 11 x 10.5							
903	3¢ Vermont Statehood	03/04/41	.15	.15	1.75	(4)	7.00	55
	Issues of 1942							
904	3¢ Kentucky Statehood	06/01/42	.15	.15	1.10	(4)	4.00	64
905	3¢ Win the War	07/04/42	.15	.15	.40	(4)	3.75	
b	3¢ purple		—	—				
	Pair with full vertical or horizontal gutter between		175.00					
906	5¢ Chinese Resistance	07/07/42	.30	.20	8.75	(4)	6.00	21
	Issues of 1943							
907	2¢ Allied Nations	01/14/43	.15	.15	.30	(4)	3.50	1,700
	Pair with full vertical or horizontal gutter between		225.00					
908	1¢ Four Freedoms	02/12/43	.15	.15	.60	(4)	3.50	1,200

In 1991 the U.S. Postal Service issued ten stamps commemorating the American contribution to World War II. The first stamp depicted the Burma Road, China's lifeline to the outside world in 1941.

The **Burma Road** was constructed by China after Japan had captured China's seaports. Initially connecting Lashio, Burma, with Kunming, China, the Burma Road carried arms and food across deep gorges and around hairpin turns to the besieged Chinese people. Eventually the Burma Road extended 2,100 miles from Rangoon on the Bay of Bengal to Chungking, the capital of free China.

Illustrated by William H. Bond, these stamps, issued annually from 1991-1995, commemorate the 50th anniversary of American involvement in World War II. His other projects for the Postal Service include Alaska Statehood (1984) and several stamps in the Transportation series (1985-1987).

Issues of 1943-44		Un	U	PE		FDC	Q(M)
Overrun Countries Issue, Perf. 12							
909	5¢ Poland	06/22/43	.20	.15	4.50*	(4)	7.50	20
910	5¢ Czechoslovakia	07/12/43	.20	.15	2.75*	(4)	4.00	20
911	5¢ Norway	07/27/43	.15	.15	1.40*	(4)	4.00	20
912	5¢ Luxembourg	08/10/43	.15	.15	1.30*	(4)	4.00	20
913	5¢ Netherlands	08/24/43	.15	.15	1.30*	(4)	4.00	20
914	5¢ Belgium	09/14/43	.15	.15	1.15*	(4)	4.00	20
915	5¢ France	09/28/43	.15	.15	1.25*	(4)	4.00	20
916	5¢ Greece	10/12/43	.35	.25	11.00*	(4)	4.00	15
917	5¢ Yugoslavia	10/26/43	.25	.15	4.50*	(4)	4.00	15
918	5¢ Albania	11/09/43	.20	.15	4.25*	(4)	4.00	15
919	5¢ Austria	11/23/43	.20	.15	3.75*	(4)	4.00	15
920	5¢ Denmark	12/07/43	.20	.15	5.75*	(4)	4.00	15
921	5¢ Korea	11/02/44	.15	.15	4.75*	(4)	5.00	15
	"KORPA" plate flaw		17.50	12.50				
*Instead of plate numbers, the selvage is inscribed with the name of the country.							
Issues of 1944, Perf. 11 x 10.5							
922	3¢ Transcontinental Railroad	05/10/44	.20	.15	1.40	(4)	6.00	61
923	3¢ Steamship	05/22/44	.15	.15	1.25	(4)	4.00	61
924	3¢ Telegraph	05/24/44	.15	.15	.90	(4)	3.50	61
925	3¢ Philippines	09/27/44	.15	.15	1.10	(4)	3.50	50
926	3¢ Motion Pictures	10/31/44	.15	.15	.90	(4)	4.00	53

Allies in Normandy, D-Day, June 6, 1944

Illustrated by William H. Bond, the **Allies in Normandy, D-Day** stamp was one of ten issued in 1994 commemorating the 50th anniversary of World War II. Allied operations in Normandy began with the June 6, 1944 invasion, known as D-Day.

The Allied invasion of Normandy was an enormous undertaking, requiring an unprecedented amount of troops, supplies, and planning. Before the attack German defenses were pounded by bombers and naval barrages and elaborate ruses were constructed to fool German spies. Despite threatening weather and fierce resistance, Allied troops were able to establish beachheads and make enough gains to insure the success of the invasion. The amphibious landing on the beaches was complemented by behind-the-lines actions by airborne troops. These brave soldiers landed at night by parachute and glider. They captured key bridges and occupied important road junctions.

909

910

911

912

913

914

915

916

917

918

919

920

921

922

923

924

925

926

927

928

929

930

931

932

933

934

935

936

937

938

939

940

941

942

943

944

945

946

947

	Issues of 1945, Perf. 11 x 10.5		Un	U	PB	#	FDC	Q(M)
927	3¢ Florida Statehood	03/03/45	.15	.15	.50	(4)	4.50	62
928	5¢ United Nations Conference	04/25/45	.15	.15	.45	(4)	5.00	76
	Perf. 10.5 x 11							
929	3¢ Iwo Jima (Marines)	07/11/45	.15	.15	.40	(4)	10.00	137
	Issues of 1945-46, Franklin D. Roosevelt Issue, Perf. 11 x 10.5							
930	1¢ Roosevelt and Hyde Park Residence	07/26/45	.15	.15	.15	(4)	3.50	128
931	2¢ Roosevelt and "The Little White House" at Warm Springs, Ga.	08/24/45	.15	.15	.25	(4)	3.50	67
932	3¢ Roosevelt and White House	06/27/45	.15	.15	.30	(4)	3.50	134
933	5¢ Roosevelt, Map of Western Hemisphere and Four Freedoms	01/30/46	.15	.15	.45	(4)	3.50	76
934	3¢ Army, Sept. 28	09/28/45	.15	.15	.30	(4)	6.00	128
935	3¢ Navy	10/27/45	.15	.15	.30	(4)	6.00	136
936	3¢ Coast Guard	11/10/45	.15	.15	.30	(4)	6.00	112
937	3¢ Alfred E. Smith	11/26/45	.15	.15	.35	(4)	2.50	309
	Pair with full vertical gutter between	—						
938	3¢ Texas Statehood	12/29/45	.15	.15	.30	(4)	4.00	171
	Issues of 1946							
939	3¢ Merchant Marine	02/26/46	.15	.15	.30	(4)	5.00	136
940	3¢ Veterans of World War II	05/09/46	.15	.15	.35	(4)	4.00	260
941	3¢ Tennessee Statehood	06/01/46	.15	.15	.30	(4)	1.50	132
942	3¢ Iowa Statehood	08/03/46	.15	.15	.30	(4)	1.50	132
943	3¢ Smithsonian Institution	08/10/46	.15	.15	.30	(4)	1.50	139
944	3¢ Kearny Expedition	10/16/46	.15	.15	.30	(4)	1.50	115
	Issues of 1947, Perf. 10.5 x 11							
945	3¢ Thomas A. Edison	02/11/47	.15	.15	.30	(4)	3.00	157
	Perf. 11 x 10.5							
946	3¢ Joseph Pulitzer	04/10/47	.15	.15	.30	(4)	1.50	120
947	3¢ Postage Stamps Centenary	05/17/47	.15	.15	.30	(4)	1.50	127

In the winter of 1945, as the war in the Pacific neared its climax, a tiny ash heap of an island took on great importance. Iwo Jima's location made it prime real estate for U.S. military planners.

On February 19, 1945, the Marines landed on **Iwo Jima**. Iwo was won with sweat and blood. The stamp shows a Marine patrol raising the American flag on the crest of Mt. Suribachi. The scene was captured by AP photographer Joe Rosenthal, and became perhaps the most celebrated picture of the war. Most of the nearly 7,000 Americans who died in the battle were Marines, making it the costliest battle in their history.

Illustrated by William H. Bond, this stamp was one of ten on a 1995 sheet, one of five annual stamp sheets issued to commemorate the 50th anniversary of American involvement in World War II.

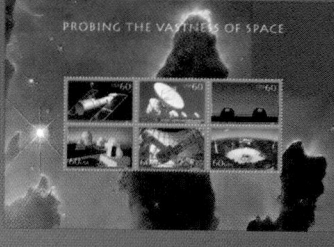

**Buy and collect
all five panes and
the uncut press sheet.**

To order or for more information visit us at
www.stampsonline.com
or Call 1-800-STAMP-24

LANDING ON THE MOON

PROBING THE VASTNESS OF SPACE

ESCAPING THE GRAVITY OF EARTH

EXPLORING THE SOLAR SYSTEM

SPACE ACHIEVEMENT AND EXPLORATION
WORLD STAMP EXPO 2000

Space Achievement and Exploration

United States Postal Service Firsts!!!

The *first circular stamp*

The *first hologram stamps*

The *first pentagonal stamps*

And, three out-of-this-world sets of horizontal stamps

In All—Fifteen Space Achievement and Exploration stamps commemorating the United States space program.

BUY

■ the $11.75 Space Achievement and Exploration circular commemorative stamp featuring a holographic image of the earth. Item No. 111700

■ the $3.20 Escaping the Gravity of Earth commemorative stamps—a pane of two Priority Mail hologram stamps. One features a design of a computer-generated NASA image and the other a design based on a NASA artist's conception of the International Space Station. Item No. 111600

■ the $11.75 Landing on the Moon stamp with a hologram of a lunar lander. The stamp features a selvage photograph of Charles M. Duke, Jr., on the surface of the moon taken by astronaut John W. Young during the Apollo 16 mission in April 1972. Item No. 111800

■ the pane of five pentagonal $1.00 Exploring the Solar System commemorative stamps—portraying the exploration of our solar system. Item No. 108100

■ the pane of six individual 60-cent Probing the Vastness of Space stamps. Issued in international rate denominations, these stamps commemorate the use of observatories and telescopes in the exploration of deep space. Item No. 500800.

BUY

■ the special $38.50 Uncut Press Sheet of Space Achievement and Exploration commemorative stamps *including all five space issues:* "Probing the Vastness of Space," "Escaping the Gravity of Earth," "Exploring the Solar System," "Landing on the Moon," and a fifth central circular pane, "Space Achievement and Exploration." Item No. 500300

	ssues of 1947		Un	U	PE		FDC	Q(M)
	Centenary International Philatelic Exhibition Issue Souvenir Sheet, Imperf.							
948	Souvenir sheet of 2							
	stamps (#1-2)	05/19/47	.55	.45			2.00	10
a	5¢ single stamp from sheet		.20	.20				
b	10¢ single stamp from sheet		.25	.25				
	Perf. 11 x 10.5							
949	3¢ Doctors	06/09/47	.15	.15	.30	(4)	2.50	133
950	3¢ Utah Settlement	07/24/47	.15	.15	.30	(4)	1.00	132
951	3¢ U.S. Frigate *Constitution*	10/21/47	.15	.15	.30	(4)	5.00	131
	Perf. 10.5 x 11							
952	3¢ Everglades National Park	12/05/47	.15	.15	.30	(4)	1.00	122
	Issues of 1948							
953	3¢ Dr. G.W. Carver	01/05/48	.15	.15	.35	(4)	1.00	122
	Perf. 11 x 10.5							
954	3¢ California Gold	01/24/48	.15	.15	.30	(4)	1.00	131
955	3¢ Mississippi Territory	04/07/48	.15	.15	.30	(4)	1.00	123
956	3¢ Four Chaplains	05/28/48	.15	.15	.30	(4)	3.00	122
957	3¢ Wisconsin Statehood	05/29/48	.15	.15	.30	(4)	1.00	115
958	5¢ Swedish Pioneer	06/04/48	.15	.15	.45	(4)	1.00	64
959	3¢ Progress of Women	07/19/48	.15	.15	.30	(4)	1.00	118
	Perf. 10.5 x 11							
960	3¢ William Allen White	07/31/48	.15	.15	.40	(4)	1.00	78
	Perf. 11 x 10.5							
961	3¢ U.S.-Canada Friendship	08/02/48	.15	.15	.30	(4)	1.00	113
962	3¢ Francis Scott Key	08/09/48	.15	.15	.30	(4)	1.00	121
963	3¢ Salute to Youth	08/11/48	.15	.15	.30	(4)	1.00	78
964	3¢ Oregon Territory	08/14/48	.15	.15	.35	(4)	1.00	52
	Perf. 10.5 x 11							
965	3¢ Harlan F. Stone	08/25/48	.15	.15	.60	(4)	1.00	54
966	3¢ Palomar Observatory	08/30/48	.15	.15	.95	(4)	2.00	61
a	Vertical pair, imperf. between		550.00					
	Perf. 11 x 10.5							
967	3¢ Clara Barton	09/07/48	.15	.15	.30	(4)	3.00	58

On January 24, 1848, carpenter James Marshall discovered gold at Sutter's Mill on the American River near Sacramento. He didn't know it at the time, but the largest gold rush in the history of the United States was about to begin.

Within a few years, gold seekers were everywhere, and California's population had swollen to an estimated 250,000. Promising their families new prosperity, young men left their jobs to look for gold along the rocky banks of Sierra streams and in gulches and canyons. The work was tedious and backbreaking, but gold fever often surmounted discomfort and discouragement.

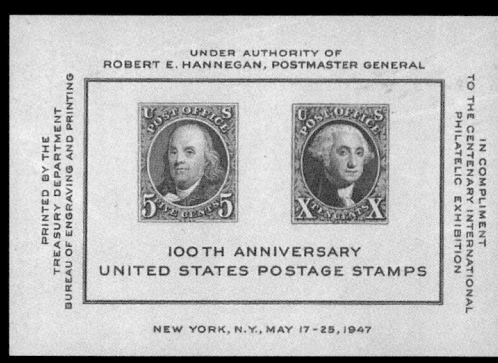

948

949

950

951

952

953

954

955

956

957

958

959

960

961

962

963

964

965

966

967

968

969

970

971

972

973

974

975

976

977

978

979

980

981

982

983

984

985

986

987

988

	ssues of 1948		Un	U	PB	#	FDC	Q(M)
968	3¢ Poultry Industry	09/09/48	.15	.15	.35	(4)	1.25	53
	Perf. 10.5 x 11							
969	3¢ Gold Star Mothers	09/21/48	.15	.15	.35	(4)	1.00	77
	Perf. 11 x 10.5							
970	3¢ Fort Kearny	09/22/48	.15	.15	.35	(4)	1.00	58
971	3¢ Volunteer Firemen	10/04/48	.15	.15	.35	(4)	7.00	56
972	3¢ Indian Centennial	10/15/48	.15	.15	.35	(4)	1.00	58
973	3¢ Rough Riders	10/27/48	.15	.15	.40	(4)	1.00	54
974	3¢ Juliette Gordon Low	10/29/48	.15	.15	.30	(4)	2.25	64
	Perf. 10.5 x 11							
975	3¢ Will Rogers	11/04/48	.15	.15	.40	(4)	1.50	67
976	3¢ Fort Bliss	11/05/48	.15	.15	1.10	(4)	2.00	65
	Perf. 11 x 10.5							
977	3¢ Moina Michael	11/09/48	.15	.15	.35	(4)	1.00	64
978	3¢ Gettysburg Address	11/19/48	.15	.15	.35	(4)	1.00	63
	Perf. 10.5 x 11							
979	3¢ American Turners	11/20/48	.15	.15	.30	(4)	1.00	62
980	3¢ Joel Chandler Harris	12/09/48	.15	.15	.55	(4)	1.25	57
	Issues of 1949, Perf. 11 x 10.5							
981	3¢ Minnesota Territory	03/03/49	.15	.15	.30	(4)	1.00	99
982	3¢ Washington and Lee University	04/12/49	.15	.15	.30	(4)	1.00	105
983	3¢ Puerto Rico Election	04/27/49	.15	.15	.30	(4)	1.00	109
984	3¢ Annapolis Tercentenary	05/23/49	.15	.15	.30	(4)	1.00	107
985	3¢ Grand Army of the Republic	08/29/49	.15	.15	.30	(4)	1.00	117
	Perf. 10.5 x 11							
986	3¢ Edgar Allan Poe	10/07/49	.15	.15	.45	(4)	1.25	123
	Thin outer frame line at top, inner frame line missing		6.00					
	Issues of 1950, Perf. 11 x 10.5							
987	3¢ American Bankers	01/03/50	.15	.15	.30	(4)	2.00	131
	Perf. 10.5 x 11							
988	3¢ Samuel Gompers	01/27/50	.15	.15	.30	(4)	1.00	128

Gunfights, gold rushes, trailblazing expeditions—the Old West lives on in history and in legend. In 1994, the U.S. Postal Service commemorated this era with the Legends of the West stamps. The 20 illustrations by Mark Hess, feature prominent figures and unforgettable scenes from the Wild West.

William Frederick Cody (1846–1917), better known as "Buffalo Bill," was a Pony Express rider, buffalo hunter, and Indian fighter. Known as "Wild Bill," **James Butler Hickok** (1837–1876) was a Union scout and spy before becoming a sheriff in Kansas. He later went to the Dakota Territory, where gold had been discovered. **Sacagawea** (c. 1787–1812) was taken captive as a child and sold to a French-Canadian fur trapper who married her. After the United States acquired vast expanses of land through the Louisiana Purchase, Sacagawea guided Lewis and Clark's expedition—while transporting her infant son on her back. Born in Ireland, **Nellie Cashman** (c. 1849–1925) emigrated to America and took part in many mining expeditions. During a gold strike in British Columbia, Cashman organized a relief expedition for scurvy-stricken miners. She later joined gold rushes in the Klondike and Alaska.

Issues of 1950		Un	U	PE		FDC	Q(M)
National Capital Sesquicentennial Issue, Perf. 10.5 x 11, 11 x 10.5							
989	3¢ Statue of Freedom on Capitol Dome	04/20/50	.15	.15	.30	(4)	1.00	132
990	3¢ Executive Mansion	06/12/50	.15	.15	.40	(4)	1.00	130
991	3¢ Supreme Court	08/02/50	.15	.15	.30	(4)	1.00	131
992	3¢ U.S. Capitol	11/22/50	.15	.15	.40	(4)	1.00	130
	Gripper cracks		1.00	.50				
	Perf. 11 x 10.5							
993	3¢ Railroad Engineers	04/29/50	.15	.15	.30	(4)	1.00	122
994	3¢ Kansas City, MO	06/03/50	.15	.15	.30	(4)	1.00	122
995	3¢ Boy Scouts	06/30/50	.15	.15	.30	(4)	5.00	132
996	3¢ Indiana Territory	07/04/50	.15	.15	.30	(4)	1.00	122
997	3¢ California Statehood	09/09/50	.15	.15	.30	(4)	1.00	121
	Issues of 1951							
998	3¢ United Confederate Veterans	05/30/51	.15	.15	.30	(4)	1.00	119
999	3¢ Nevada Settlement	07/14/51	.15	.15	.30	(4)	1.00	112
1000	3¢ Landing of Cadillac	07/24/51	.15	.15	.30	(4)	1.00	114
1001	3¢ Colorado Statehood	08/01/51	.15	.15	.30	(4)	1.00	114
1002	3¢ American Chemical Society	09/04/51	.15	.15	.30	(4)	2.00	117
1003	3¢ Battle of Brooklyn	12/10/51	.15	.15	.30	(4)	1.00	116
	Issues of 1952							
1004	3¢ Betsy Ross	01/02/52	.15	.15	.35	(4)	1.00	116
1005	3¢ 4-H Club	01/15/52	.15	.15	.30	(4)	1.00	116
1006	3¢ B&O Railroad	02/28/52	.15	.15	.40	(4)	1.75	113
1007	3¢ American Automobile Association	03/04/52	.15	.15	.30	(4)	1.00	117

In 1991 the Postal Service issued a stamp honoring the **American eagle**, commonly known as the bald eagle. As our national bird, its likeness appears on many stamps and on the Great Seal of the United States.

The bald eagle is a large bird of prey with a dark body, white head and tail, and large yellow bill. Bald eagles are usually found beside rivers and lakes where they fish and hunt for waterfowl, small mammals, and carrion. Bald eagles establish pair bonds through spectacular aerial displays and are monogamous once they have chosen a mate. They build large nests, to which they often return year after year.

Severe declines in bald eagle populations led to this species being officially classified as endangered. Recovery programs have significantly increased the number of nesting pairs. Bald eagles, once threatened with extinction, now have a promising future.

990

989

991

992

993

994

995

996

997

998

999

1000

1001

1002

1003

1004

1005

1006

1007

1008

1009

1010

1011

1012

1013

1014

1015

1016

1017

1018

1019

1020

1021

1022

1023

1024

1025

1026

1027

1028

1029

	Issues of 1952		Un	U	PB	#	FDC	Q(M)
1008	3¢ NATO	04/04/52	.15	.15	.30	(4)	1.00	2,900
1009	3¢ Grand Coulee Dam	05/15/52	.15	.15	.30	(4)	1.00	115
1010	3¢ Arrival of Lafayette	06/13/52	.15	.15	.30	(4)	1.00	113
	Perf. 10.5 x 11							
1011	3¢ Mt. Rushmore Memorial	08/11/52	.15	.15	.35	(4)	1.00	116
	Perf. 11 x 10.5							
1012	3¢ Engineering	09/06/52	.15	.15	.30	(4)	1.00	114
1013	3¢ Service Women	09/11/52	.15	.15	.30	(4)	1.00	124
1014	3¢ Gutenberg Bible	09/30/52	.15	.15	.30	(4)	1.00	116
1015	3¢ Newspaper Boys	10/04/52	.15	.15	.30	(4)	1.00	115
1016	3¢ International Red Cross	11/21/52	.15	.15	.30	(4)	1.50	136
	Issues of 1953							
1017	3¢ National Guard	02/23/53	.15	.15	.30	(4)	1.00	115
1018	3¢ Ohio Statehood	03/02/53	.15	.15	.35	(4)	1.00	119
1019	3¢ Washington Territory	03/02/53	.15	.15	.30	(4)	1.00	114
1020	3¢ Louisiana Purchase	04/30/53	.15	.15	.30	(4)	1.00	114
1021	5¢ Opening of Japan	07/14/53	.15	.15	.65	(4)	1.00	89
1022	3¢ American Bar Association	08/24/53	.15	.15	.30	(4)	5.00	115
1023	3¢ Sagamore Hill	09/14/53	.15	.15	.30	(4)	1.00	116
1024	3¢ Future Farmers	10/13/53	.15	.15	.30	(4)	1.00	115
1025	3¢ Trucking Industry	10/27/53	.15	.15	.30	(4)	1.00	124
1026	3¢ General George S. Patton	11/11/53	.15	.15	.40	(4)	4.00	115
1027	3¢ New York City	11/20/53	.15	.15	.35	(4)	1.00	116
1028	3¢ Gadsden Purchase	12/30/53	.15	.15	.30	(4)	1.00	116
	Issue of 1954							
1029	3¢ Columbia University	01/04/54	.15	.15	.30	(4)	1.00	119

The **Rural America** stamps, issued in 1973 and 1974, were illustrated by John Falter and F.C. Murphy and show three important scenes in the development of American agriculture.

The first stamp, illustrated by F.C. Murphy, honors the centennial of Angus beef's introduction to the United States. Noted for their fine quality of beef, Angus cattle, or Aberdeen Angus as they are sometimes known, originated in northern Scotland. This polled, or naturally hornless, breed was introduced to American ranchers at a Kansas City, Missouri, livestock show in 1873. It has become an important and popular source of beef around the world.

The centennial of hard winter wheat's introduction to American soil by Mennonites was celebrated by the Postal Service in 1974 with a stamp illustrated by John Falter. Fleeing persecution in Russia, Mennonite settlers brought with them seeds from hardy strains of wheat they had cultivated on the Russian steppes. Many Mennonites settled in the Midwest, often buying land from American railroad companies. The varieties of wheat they planted on their new farms flourished in the fertile soils and helped shape the landscape of the plains today.

1954-1967

	Issues of 1954-67		Un	U	PB		FDC
	Liberty Issue, Perf. 11 x 10.5, 10.5 x 11						
1030	½¢ Franklin	10/20/55	.15	.15	.25	(4)	1.00
1031	1¢ Washington	03/56	.15	.15	.20	(4)	
	Pair with full vertical or						
	horizontal gutter between		150.00				
b	Wet printing		.15	.15	.20	(4)	1.00
	Perf. 10.5 x 11						
1031A	1¼¢ Palace of the Governors	06/17/60	.15	.15	.45	(4)	1.00
1032	1½¢ Mt. Vernon	02/22/56	.15	.15	1.75	(4)	1.00
	Perf. 11 x 10.5						
1033	2¢ Jefferson	09/15/54	.15	.15	.22	(4)	1.00
	Pair with full vertical or						
	horizontal gutter between		—				
1034	2½¢ Bunker Hill	06/17/59	.15	.15	.50	(4)	1.00
1035	3¢ Statue of Liberty	06/24/54	.15	.15	.25	(4)	
a	Booklet pane of 6	06/30/54	4.00	.90			5.00
b	Tagged	07/06/66	.25	.25	5.00	(4)	15.00
c	Imperf. pair		2,000.00				
d	Horizontal pair, imperf. between		—				
e	Wet printing	06/24/54	.15	.15	.30	(4)	1.00
f	As "a," untagged		5.00	1.10			
1036	4¢ Lincoln	11/19/54	.15	15	.35	(4)	
a	Booklet pane of 6	07/31/58	2.75	.80			4.00
b	Tagged	11/02/63	.50	.40	6.50	(4)	50.00
	Perf. 10.5 x 11						
1037	4½¢ The Hermitage	03/16/59	.15	.15	.65	(4)	1.00
	Perf. 11 x 10.5						
1038	5¢ James Monroe	12/02/54	.15	.15	.45	(4)	1.00
	Pair with full vertical gutter between		200.00				
1039	6¢ T. Roosevelt	11/18/55	.25	.15	1.10	(4)	
a	Wet printing	11/18/55	.40	.15	1.65	(4)	1.00
1040	7¢ Wilson	01/10/56	.20	.15	1.00	(4)	1.00
	Perf. 11						
1041	8¢ Statue of Liberty	04/09/54	.25	.15	2.25	(4)	1.00
a	Carmine double impression		650.00				
1042	8¢ Statue of Liberty, redrawn	03/22/58	.20	.15	.90	(4)	1.00
	Perf. 11 x 10.5						
1042A	8¢ Gen. John J. Pershing	11/17/61	.20	.15	.90	(4)	1.00
	Perf. 10.5 x 11						
1043	9¢ The Alamo	06/14/56	.30	.15	1.30	(4)	1.50
1044	10¢ Independence Hall	07/04/56	.25	.15	1.10	(4)	1.00
d	Tagged	07/06/66	2.00	1.00	35.00	(4)	15.00
	Perf. 11						
1044A	11¢ Statue of Liberty	06/15/61	.30	.15	1.25	(4)	1.00
c	Tagged	01/11/67	2.00	1.60	35.00	(4)	22.50

1031A

1030

1031

1032

1033

1034

1037

1035

1036

1038

1039

1040

1041

1042

1042A

1043

1044

1044A

1045   1046   1047

1048   1049

1050   1051

1052   1053

ssues of 1954-67		Un	U	PB/LF		FDC
Perf. 11 x 10.5						
1045 12¢ Benjamin Harrison	06/06/59	.35	.15	1.50	(4)	1.00
a Tagged	1968	.35	.15	4.00	(4)	25.00
1046 15¢ John Jay	12/12/58	.60	.15	3.00	(4)	1.00
a Tagged	07/06/66	1.10	.35	12.50	(4)	20.00
Perf. 10.5 x 11						
1047 20¢ Monticello	04/13/56	.40	.15	1.75	(4)	1.20
Perf. 11 x 10.5						
1048 25¢ Paul Revere	04/18/58	1.10	.15	4.75	(4)	1.30
1049 30¢ Robert E. Lee	09/21/55	.70	.15	3.50	(4)	
a Wet printing	09/21/55	1.10	.15	5.00	(4)	2.00
1050 40¢ John Marshall	04/58	1.50	.15	7.50	(4)	
a Wet printing	09/24/55	2.25	.25	12.50	(4)	2.00
1051 50¢ Susan B. Anthony	04/58	1.50	.15	6.75	(4)	
a Wet printing	08/25/55	1.75	.15	10.00	(4)	6.00
1052 $1 Patrick Henry	10/58	5.00	.15	21.00	(4)	
a Wet printing	10/07/55	5.00	.15	21.00	(4)	10.00
Perf. 11						
1053 $5 Alexander Hamilton	03/19/56	75.00	6.75	325.00	(4)	65.00
Issues of 1954-73, Coil Stamps, Perf. 10 Vertically						
1054 1¢ dark green						
Washington (1031)	08/57	.20	.15	1.00	(2)	
b Imperf. pair		2,500.00	—			
c Wet printing	10/08/54	.35	.20	1.75	(2)	1.00
Coil Stamp, Perf. 10 Horizontally						
1054A 1¼¢ turquoise Palace						
of the Governors (1031A)	06/17/60	.15	.15	2.25	(2)	1.00
Coil Stamps, Perf. 10 Vertically						
1055 2¢ rose carmine						
Jefferson (1033)	05/57	.15	.15	.75	(2)	
a Tagged	05/06/68	.15	.15	.75	(2)	11.00
b Imperf. pair (Bureau precanceled)			550.00			
c As "a," imperf. pair		575.00				
d Wet printing	10/22/54	.40	.15	3.50	(2)	1.00
1056 2½¢ gray blue						
Bunker Hill (1034)	09/09/59	.25	.25	3.50	(2)	2.00
1057 3¢ deep violet Statue of						
Liberty (1035)	10/56	.15	.15	.55	(2)	
a Imperf. pair		1,750.00	—	2,750.00	(2)	
b Tagged	06/26/67	1.00	.50	25.00	(2)	
c Wet printing	07/20/54	.30	.15	2.00	(2)	1.00
1058 4¢ red violet Lincoln (1036)	07/31/58	.15	.15	2.00	(2)	1.00
a Imperf. pair		120.00	70.00	200.00	(2)	
b Wet printing (Bureau precanceled)		27.50	.50	375.00	(2)	
Coil Stamp, Perf. 10 Horizontally						
1059 4½¢ blue green						
The Hermitage (1037)	05/01/59	1.50	1.20	14.00	(2)	1.75
Coil Stamp, Perf. 10 Vertically						
1059A 25¢ green Revere (1048)	02/25/65	.50	.30	2.00	(2)	1.25
b Tagged	04/03/73	.65	.20	3.00	(2)	14.00
Dull finish gum	1980	.65		3.00	(2)	
c Imperf. pair		50.00		100.00	(2)	

Issues of 1954		Un	U	PB		FDC	Q(M)
Perf. 11 x 10.5							
1060 3¢ Nebraska Territory	05/07/54	.15	.15	.30	(4)	1.00	116
1061 3¢ Kansas Territory	05/31/54	.15	.15	.30	(4)	1.00	114
Perf. 10.5 x 11							
1062 3¢ George Eastman	07/12/54	.15	.15	.30	(4)	1.00	128
Perf. 11 x 10.5							
1063 3¢ Lewis and Clark Expedition	07/28/54	.15	.15	.30	(4)	1.00	116
Issues of 1955, Perf. 10.5 x 11							
1064 3¢ Pennsylvania Academy of the Fine Arts	01/15/55	.15	.15	.30	(4)	1.00	116
Perf. 11 x 10.5							
1065 3¢ Land-Grant Colleges	02/12/55	.15	.15	.30	4)	1.00	120
1066 8¢ Rotary International	02/23/55	.20	.15	.95	(4)	3.00	54
1067 3¢ Armed Forces Reserve	05/21/55	.15	.15	.30	(4)	1.00	176
Perf. 10.5 x 11							
1068 3¢ New Hampshire	06/21/55	.15	.15	.35	(4)	1.00	126
Perf. 11 x 10.5							
1069 3¢ Soo Locks	06/28/55	.15	.15	.30	(4)	1.00	122
1070 3¢ Atoms for Peace	07/28/55	.15	.15	.35	(4)	1.00	134
1071 3¢ Fort Ticonderoga	09/18/55	.15	.15	.30	(4)	1.00	119
Perf. 10.5 x 11							
1072 3¢ Andrew W. Mellon	12/20/55	.15	.15	.30	(4)	1.00	112

When the Communist government of North Korea attacked South Korea in 1950, President Harry Truman decided to commit American troops to lead a United Nations force against the North Koreans in a "police action" rather than ask Congress to declare war. By the war's indecisive end in 1953, 1.5 million American men and women had served; around 54,000 lost their lives in what is sometimes called the "Forgotten War."

In October 1986 Congress authorized the creation of a memorial in Washington, D.C., for **veterans of the Korean War**. On June 14, 1992, President George Bush formally broke ground at a site on the National Mall. The completed memorial was dedicated on July 27, 1995, the 42nd anniversary of the armistice that ended the war.

This 1985 stamp by Robert A. Anderson commemorates the veterans of the Korean War—those who served and still remember, and those who never came home.

1060

1061

1062

1063

1064

1065

1066

1067

1068

1069

1070

1071

1072

1073

1074

1075

1076

1077

1078

1079

1080

1081

1082

1083

1084

1085

	ssues of 1956		Un	U	PB		FDC	Q(M)
1073	3¢ Benjamin Franklin	01/17/56	.15	.15	.30	(4)	1.00	129
	Perf. 11 x 10.5							
1074	3¢ Booker T. Washington	04/05/56	.15	.15	.30	(4)	1.25	121
	Fifth International Philatelic Exhibition Issues Souvenir Sheet, Imperf.							
1075	Sheet of 2 stamps							
	(1035, 1041)	04/28/56	2.00	2.00			5.00	3
a	3¢ (1035), single stamp from sheet		.80	.80				
b	8¢ (1041), single stamp from sheet		1.00	1.00				
	Perf. 11 x 10.5							
1076	3¢ New York Coliseum and							
	Columbus Monument	04/30/56	.15	.15	.30	(4)	1.00	120
	Wildlife Conservation Issue							
1077	3¢ Wild Turkey	05/05/56	.15	.15	.35	(4)	1.50	123
1078	3¢ Pronghorn Antelope	06/22/56	.15	.15	.35	(4)	1.50	123
1079	3¢ King Salmon	11/09/56	.15	.15	.35	(4)	1.50	109
	Perf. 10.5 x 11							
1080	3¢ Pure Food and Drug Laws	06/27/56	.15	.15	.30	(4)	1.00	113
	Perf. 11 x 10.5							
1081	3¢ Wheatland	08/05/56	.15	.15	.30	(4)	1.00	125
	Perf. 10.5 x 11							
1082	3¢ Labor Day	09/03/56	.15	.15	.30	(4)	1.00	118
	Perf. 11 x 10.5							
1083	3¢ Nassau Hall	09/22/56	.15	.15	.30	(4)	1.00	122
	Perf. 10.5 x 11							
1084	3¢ Devils Tower	09/24/56	.15	.15	.30	(4)	1.00	118
	Pair with full horizontal gutter between		—					
	Perf. 11 x 10.5							
1085	3¢ Children's Stamp	12/15/56	.15	.15	.30	(4)	1.00	101

Coral Reefs are vibrant, undersea communities that support a dizzying array of life. The defining organism of the reef is the coral itself, an invertebrate that leaves underwater skeletal deposits as it grows and dies. Given time and the right conditions, coral can build up enough to shape the sea bed or form land masses. Four types of coral were featured on the 1980 Coral Reefs issuance, illustrated by Chuck Ripper.

Named for its tendency to grow in ridged, hemispherical domes, brain coral inhabits a wide range of marine environments. Found in several shapes and colors, this coral thrives on the lagoon side of reefs. Finger coral is just one of many kinds of branching and pillar coral that can be found in a variety of forms and colors as well. These two beautiful examples of coral act as a reminder of the fragility of a complex and fascinating ecosystem.

ssues of 1957			Un	U	PB		FDC	Q(M)
1086	3¢ Alexander Hamilton	01/11/57	.15	.15	.30	(4)	1.00	115
	Perf. 10.5 x 11							
1087	3¢ Polio	01/15/57	.15	.15	.30	(4)	1.00	187
	Perf. 11 x 10.5							
1088	3¢ Coast and Geodetic Survey	02/11/57	.15	.15	.30	(4)	1.00	115
1089	3¢ American Institute							
	of Architects	02/23/57	.15	.15	.30	(4)	1.00	107
	Perf. 10.5 x 11							
1090	3¢ Steel Industry	05/22/57	.15	.15	.30	(4)	1.00	112
	Perf. 11 x 10.5							
1091	3¢ International Naval Review-							
	Jamestown Festival	06/10/57	.15	.15	.30	(4)	1.00	118
1092	3¢ Oklahoma Statehood	06/14/57	.15	.15	.35	(4)	1.00	102
1093	3¢ School Teachers	07/01/57	.15	.15	.30	(4)	2.00	102
	Perf. 11							
1094	4¢ Flag	07/04/57	.15	.15	.35	(4)	1.00	84
	Perf. 10.5 x 11							
1095	3¢ Shipbuilding	08/15/57	.15	.15	.30	(4)	1.00	126
	Champion of Liberty Issue, Ramon Magsaysay, Perf. 11							
1096	8¢ Bust of Magsaysay on Medal	08/31/57	.20	.15	.85	(4)	1.00	39
	Plate block of 4, ultramarine # omitted		—					
	Perf. 10.5 x 11							
1097	3¢ Lafayette	09/06/57	.15	.15	.30	(4)	1.00	123
	Perf. 11							
1098	3¢ Wildlife Conservation	11/22/57	.15	.15	.35	(4)	1.00	174
	Perf. 10.5 x 11							
1099	3¢ Religious Freedom	12/27/57	.15	.15	.30	(4)	1.00	114
	Issues of 1958							
1100	3¢ Gardening-Horticulture	03/15/58	.15	.15	.30	(4)	1.00	123
1101-03	Not assigned							
	Perf. 11 x 10.5							
1104	3¢ Brussels Universal and							
	International Exhibition	04/17/58	.15	.15	.30	(4)	1.00	114
1105	3¢ James Monroe	04/28/58	.15	.15	.30	(4)	1.00	120
1106	3¢ Minnesota Statehood	05/11/58	.15	.15	.30	(4)	1.00	121
	Perf. 11							
1107	3¢ International Geophysical							
	Year	05/31/58	.15	.15	.35	(4)	1.00	126
	Perf. 11 x 10.5							
1108	3¢ Gunston Hall	06/12/58	.15	.15	.30	(4)	1.00	108

When Norman Rockwell (1894–1978) illustrated the stamp commemorating the 50th anniversary of the **Boy Scouts of America** in 1960, he was continuing his lifelong association with the organization. Rockwell was working with the Boy Scouts as early as 1913, when he became art editor for Boy's Life magazine. He illustrated nearly every official Boy Scouts calendar for decades.

Rockwell's work has appeared on several other stamps celebrating quintessential American topics, including the 1963 City Mail Delivery stamp and the 1972 Tom Sawyer stamp. A commemorative stamp featured his self-portrait in 1994, the same year his famous Four Freedoms were issued as a souvenir sheet. In 1999, one of his paintings also appeared on a stamp honoring the Peace Corps as a part of the Celebrate The Century: The 1960s stamp pane.

1086

1087

1088

1089

1090

1091

1092

1093

1094

1095

1096

1097

1098

1099

1100

1104

1105

1106

1107

1108

1958-1959

1109

1110

1111

1112

1113

1114

1115

1116

1117

1118

1119

1120

1121

1122

1123

1124

1125

1126

1127

1128

1129

1130

1131

Issues of 1958		Un	U	PB	#	FDC	Q(M)
Perf. 10.5 x 11							
1109 3¢ Mackinac Bridge	06/25/58	.15	.15	.30	(4)	1.00	107
Champion of Liberty Issue, Simon Bolivar							
1110 4¢ Bust of Bolivar on Medal	07/24/58	.15	.15	.35	(4)	1.00	115
Perf. 11							
1111 8¢ Bust of Bolivar on Medal	07/24/58	.20	.15	1.25	(4)	1.00	39
Plate block of four, ocher # only		—					
Perf. 11 x 10.5							
1112 4¢ Atlantic Cable	08/15/58	.15	.15	.35	(4)	1.00	114
Issues of 1958-59, Lincoln Sesquicentennial Issue, Perf. 10.5 x 11							
1113 1¢ Portrait by George Healy	02/12/59	.15	.15	.20	(4)	1.00	120
1114 3¢ Sculptured Head by Gutzon Borglum	02/27/59	.15	.15	.30	(4)	1.00	91
Perf. 11 x 10.5							
1115 4¢ Lincoln and Stephen Douglas Debating, by Joseph Boggs Beale	08/27/58	.15	.15	.35	(4)	1.00	114
1116 4¢ Statue in Lincoln Memorial by Daniel Chester French	05/30/59	.15	.15	.40	(4)	1.00	126
Champion of Liberty Issue, Lajos Kossuth, Perf. 10.5 x 11							
1117 4¢ Bust of Kossuth on Medal	09/19/58	.15	.15	.30	(4)	1.00	120
Perf. 11							
1118 8¢ Bust of Kossuth on Medal	09/19/58	.20	.15	1.10	(4)	1.00	44
Perf. 10.5 x 11							
1119 4¢ Freedom of the Press	09/22/58	.15	.15	.30	(4)	1.00	118
Perf. 11 x 10.5							
1120 4¢ Overland Mail	10/10/58	.15	.15	.30	(4)	1.00	125
Perf. 10.5 x 11							
1121 4¢ Noah Webster	10/16/58	.15	.15	.30	(4)	1.00	114
Perf. 11							
1122 4¢ Forest Conservation	10/27/58	.15	.15	.30	(4)	1.00	156
Perf. 11 x 10.5							
1123 4¢ Fort Duquesne	11/25/58	.15	.15	.30	(4)	1.00	124
Issues of 1959							
1124 4¢ Oregon Statehood	02/14/59	.15	.15	.30	(4)	1.00	120
Champion of Liberty Issue, José de San Martin, Perf. 10.5 x 11							
1125 4¢ Bust of San Martin on Medal	02/25/59	.15	.15	.30	(4)	1.00	133
a Horizontal pair, imperf. between		1,500.00					
Perf. 11							
1126 8¢ Bust of San Martin on Medal	02/25/59	.20	.15	.85	(4)	1.00	45
Perf. 10.5 x 11							
1127 4¢ NATO	04/01/59	.15	.15	.30	(4)	1.00	122
Perf. 11 x 10.5							
1128 4¢ Arctic Explorations	04/06/59	.15	.15	.40	(4)	1.00	131
1129 8¢ World Peace Through World Trade	04/20/59	.20	.15	.85	(4)	1.00	47
1130 4¢ Silver Centennial	06/08/59	.15	.15	.30	(4)	1.00	123
Perf. 11							
1131 4¢ St. Lawrence Seaway	06/26/59	.15	.15	.35	(4)	1.00	126
Pair with full horizontal gutter between		—					

	Issues of 1959		Un	U	PE		FDC	Q(M)
1132	4¢ 49-Star Flag	07/04/59	.15	.15	.40	(4)	1.00	209
1133	4¢ Soil Conservation	08/26/59	.15	.15	.35	(4)	1.00	121
	Perf. 10.5 x 11							
1134	4¢ Petroleum Industry	08/27/59	.15	.15	.30	(4)	1.00	116
	Perf. 11 x 10.5							
1135	4¢ Dental Health	09/14/59	.15	.15	.40	(4)	2.75	118
	Champion of Liberty Issue, Ernst Reuter, Perf. 10.5 x 11							
1136	4¢ Bust of Reuter on Medal	09/29/59	.15	.15	.30	(4)	1.00	112
	Perf. 11							
1137	8¢ Bust of Reuter on Medal	09/29/59	.20	.15	.85	(4)	1.00	43
	Perf. 10.5 x 11							
1138	4¢ Dr. Ephraim McDowell	12/03/59	.15	.15	.40	(4)	1.50	115
a	Vertical pair, imperf. between		450.00					
b	Vertical pair, imperf. horizontally		350.00					
	Issues of 1960-61, American Credo Issue, Perf. 11							
1139	4¢ Quotation from Washington's Farewell Address	01/20/60	.15	.15	.40	(4)	1.25	126
1140	4¢ Benjamin Franklin Quotation	03/31/60	.15	.15	.40	(4)	1.25	125
1141	4¢ Thomas Jefferson Quotation	05/18/60	.15	.15	.45	(4)	1.25	115
1142	4¢ Francis Scott Key Quotation	09/14/60	.15	.15	.45	(4)	1.25	122
1143	4¢ Abraham Lincoln Quotation	11/19/60	.15	.15	.50	(4)	1.25	121
	Pair with full horizontal gutter between		—					
1144	4¢ Patrick Henry Quotation	01/11/61	.15	.15	.50	(4)	1.25	113
	Issues of 1960							
1145	4¢ Boy Scouts	02/08/60	.15	.15	.40	(4)	4.00	139
	Olympic Winter Games Issue, Perf. 10.5 x 11							
1146	4¢ Olympic Rings and Snowflake	02/18/60	.15	.15	.40	(4)	1.00	124
	Champion of Liberty Issue, Thomas G. Masaryk							
1147	4¢ Bust of Masaryk on Medal	03/07/60	.15	.15	.30	(4)	1.00	114
a	Vertical pair, imperf. between		3,250.00					
	Perf. 11							
1148	8¢ Bust of Masaryk on Medal	03/07/60	.20	.15	.95	(4)	1.00	44
a	Horizontal pair, imperf. between		—					
	Perf. 11 x 10.5							
1149	4¢ World Refugee Year	04/07/60	.15	.15	.30	(4)	1.00	113
	Perf. 11							
1150	4¢ Water Conservation	04/18/60	.15	.15	.35	(4)	1.00	122
	Perf. 10.5 x 11							
1151	4¢ SEATO	05/31/60	.15	.15	.35	(4)	1.00	115
a	Vertical pair, imperf. between		175.00					

1132

1133

1134

1135

1136

1137

1138

1139

1140

1141

1142

1143

1144

1145

1146

1147

1148

1149

1150

1151

1960

1152

1153

1154

1155

1156

1157

1158

1159

1160

1161

1162

1163

1164

1165

1166

1167

1168

1169

1170

1171

1172

1173

ssues of 1960		Un	U	PB	#	FDC	Q(M)
Perf. 11 x 10.5							
1152 4¢ American Woman	06/02/60	.15	.15	.30	(4)	1.00	111
Perf. 11							
1153 4¢ 50-Star Flag	07/04/60	.15	.15	.30	(4)	1.00	153
Perf. 11 x 10.5							
1154 4¢ Pony Express	07/19/60	.15	.15	.40	(4)	1.00	120
Perf. 10.5 x 11							
1155 4¢ Employ the Handicapped	08/28/60	.15	.15	.30	(4)	1.00	118
1156 4¢ 5th World Forestry Congress	08/29/60	.15	.15	.30	(4)	1.00	118
Perf. 11							
1157 4¢ Mexican Independence	09/16/60	.15	.15	.30	(4)	1.00	112
1158 4¢ U.S.-Japan Treaty	09/28/60	.15	.15	.30	(4)	1.00	125
Champion of Liberty Issue, Ignacy Jan Paderewski, Perf. 10.5 x 11							
1159 4¢ Bust of Paderewski on Medal	10/08/60	.15	.15	.30	(4)	1.00	120
Perf. 11							
1160 8¢ Bust of Paderewski on Medal	10/08/60	.20	.15	.90	(4)	1.00	43
Perf. 10.5 x 11							
1161 4¢ Sen. Robert A. Taft Memorial	10/10/60	.15	.15	.35	(4)	1.00	107
Perf. 11 x 10.5							
1162 4¢ Wheels of Freedom	10/15/60	.15	.15	.30	(4)	1.00	110
Perf. 11							
1163 4¢ Boys' Clubs of America	10/18/60	.15	.15	.30	(4)	1.00	124
1164 4¢ First Automated Post Office	10/20/60	.15	.15	.30	(4)	1.00	124
Champion of Liberty Issue, Gustaf Mannerheim, Perf. 10.5 x 11							
1165 4¢ Bust of Mannerheim on Medal	10/26/60	.15	.15	.30	(4)	1.00	125
Perf. 11							
1166 8¢ Bust of Mannerheim on Medal	10/26/60	.20	.15	.80	(4)	1.00	42
1167 4¢ Camp Fire Girls	11/01/60	.15	.15	.30	(4)	1.00	116
Champion of Liberty Issue, Giusseppe Garibaldi, Perf. 10.5 x 11							
1168 4¢ Bust of Garibaldi on Medal	11/02/60	.15	.15	.30	(4)	1.00	126
Perf. 11							
1169 8¢ Bust of Garibaldi on Medal	11/02/60	.20	.15	.85	(4)	1.00	43
Perf. 10.5 x 11							
1170 4¢ Sen. Walter F. George Memorial	11/05/60	.15	.15	.35	(4)	1.00	124
1171 4¢ Andrew Carnegie	11/25/60	.15	.15	.35	(4)	1.00	120
1172 4¢ John Foster Dulles Memorial	12/06/60	.15	.15	.35	(4)	1.00	117
Perf. 11 x 10.5							
1173 4¢ Echo I-Communications for Peace	12/15/60	.15	.15	.65	(4)	2.00	124

	Issues of 1961		Un	U	PE		FDC	Q(M)
	Champion of Liberty Issue, Perf. 10.5 x 11							
1174	4¢ Bust of Gandhi on Medal	01/26/61	.15	.15	.30	(4)	1.00	113
	Perf. 11							
1175	8¢ Bust of Gandhi on Medal	01/26/61	.20	.15	1.00	(4)	1.00	42
1176	4¢ Range Conservation	02/02/61	.15	.15	.40	(4)	1.00	111
	Perf. 10.5 x 11							
1177	4¢ Horace Greeley	02/03/61	.15	.15	.30	(4)	1.00	99
	Issues of 1961-65, Civil War Centennial Issue, Perf. 11 x 10.5							
1178	4¢ Fort Sumter	04/12/61	.15	.15	.65	(4)	2.00	101
1179	4¢ Shiloh	04/07/62	.15	.15	.50	(4)	2.00	125
	Perf. 11							
1180	5¢ Gettysburg	07/01/63	.15	.15	.60	(4)	2.00	80
1181	5¢ The Wilderness	05/05/64	.15	.15	.60	(4)	2.00	125
1182	5¢ Appomattox	04/09/65	.25	.15	1.15	(4)	2.00	113
a	Horizontal pair, imperf. vertically	4,500.00						
1183	4¢ Kansas Statehood	05/10/61	.15	.15	.35	(4)	1.00	106
	Perf. 11 x 10.5							
1184	4¢ Sen. George W. Norris	07/11/61	.15	.15	.35	(4)	1.00	111
1185	4¢ Naval Aviation	08/20/61	.15	.15	.35	(4)	1.00	117
	Pair with full vertical gutter between	150.00						
	Perf. 10.5 x 11							
1186	4¢ Workmen's Compensation	09/04/61	.15	.15	.35	(4)	1.00	121
	With plate # inverted				.60	(4)		
	Perf. 11							
1187	4¢ Frederic Remington	10/04/61	.15	.15	.40	(4)	1.00	112
	Perf. 10.5 x 11							
1188	4¢ Republic of China	10/10/61	.15	.15	.45	(4)	1.50	111
1189	4¢ Naismith-Basketball	11/06/61	.15	.15	.45	(4)	6.00	109
	Perf. 11							
1190	4¢ Nursing	12/28/61	.15	.15	.45	(4)	5.00	145
	Issues of 1962							
1191	4¢ New Mexico Statehood	01/06/62	.15	.15	.30	(4)	1.00	113
1192	4¢ Arizona Statehood	02/14/62	.15	.15	.30	(4)	1.00	122
1193	4¢ Project Mercury	02/20/62	.15	.15	.35	(4)	3.00	289
1194	4¢ Malaria Eradication	03/30/62	.15	.15	.30	(4)	1.00	120
	Perf. 10.5 x 11							
1195	4¢ Charles Evans Hughes	04/11/62	.15	.15	.30	(4)	1.00	125

On May 22, 1986, at the AMERIPEX '86 international stamp show in Chicago, the Postal Service issued 36 stamps by Jerry Dadds honoring American Presidents. One stamp commemorated the 35th President, **John F. Kennedy**.

John F. Kennedy 1961-1963

He was the youngest man and first Roman Catholic to be elected President and, tragically, the youngest to die in office.

Kennedy narrowly defeated Richard M. Nixon in the 1960 presidential election. In his Inaugural Address, he exhorted Americans to "ask not what your country can do for you—ask what you can do for your country." His presidency was identified with the New Frontier program, an ambitious legislative agenda promoting education, social welfare, and economic growth. He also faced challenges such as the struggle over civil rights in the South and the construction of Soviet missile bases in Cuba. His assassination on November 22, 1963, was a devastating loss to the nation.

1174

1175

1176

1177

1178

1179

1180

1181

1182

1183

1184

1185

1186

1187

1188

1189

1190

1191

1192

1193

1194

1195

1962-1963

1196

1197

1198

1199

1200

1201

1202

1203

1204

1205

1206

1207

1208

1209

1213

1230

1231

1232

1233

1234

Issues of 1962		Un	U	PB/LP	#	FDC	Q(M)
Perf. 11							
1196 4¢ Seattle World's Fair	04/25/62	.15	.15	.30	(4)	1.00	147
1197 4¢ Louisiana Statehood	04/30/62	.15	.15	.30	(4)	1.00	119
Perf. 11 x 10.5							
1198 4¢ Homestead Act	05/20/62	.15	.15	.30	(4)	1.00	123
1199 4¢ Girl Scout Jubilee	07/24/62	.15	.15	.30	(4)	4.00	127
Pair with full vertical gutter between		250.00					
1200 4¢ Sen. Brien McMahon	07/28/62	.15	.15	.30	(4)	1.00	131
1201 4¢ Apprenticeship	08/31/62	.15	.15	.30	(4)	1.00	120
Perf. 11							
1202 4¢ Sam Rayburn	09/16/62	.15	.15	.30	(4)	1.00	121
1203 4¢ Dag Hammarskjold	10/23/62	.15	.15	.30	(4)	1.00	121
1204 4¢ black, brown and yellow (yellow inverted), Dag Hammarskjold, special printing	11/16/62	.15	.15	1.10	(4)	6.00	40
Christmas Issue							
1205 4¢ Wreath and Candles	11/01/62	.15	.15	.30	(4)	1.00	862
1206 4¢ Higher Education	11/14/62	.15	.15	.35	(4)	1.50	120
1207 4¢ Winslow Homer	12/15/62	.15	.15	.45	(4)	1.00	118
a Horizontal pair, imperf. between		6,750.00					
Issue of 1963-66							
1208 5¢ Flag over White House	01/09/63	.15	.15	.40	(4)	1.00	
a Tagged	08/25/66	.20	.15	2.00	(4)	11.50	
b Horizontal pair, imperf. between		1,500.00					
Pair with full horizontal gutter between		—					
Issues of 1962-66, Perf. 11 x 10.5							
1209 1¢ Andrew Jackson	03/22/63	.15	.15	.20	(4)	1.00	
a Tagged	07/06/66	.15	.15	.40	(4)	5.75	
Pair with full vertical gutter between		—					
1210-12 Not assigned							
1213 5¢ George Washington	11/23/62	.15	.15	.40	(4)	1.00	
a Booklet pane of 5 + label		3.00	1.75			4.00	
b Tagged	10/28/63	.50	.20	4.50	(4)	5.75	
c As "a," tagged	10/28/63	2.00	1.50			125.00	
1214-24 Not assigned							
Coil Stamps, Perf. 10 Vertically							
1225 1¢ green Jackson (1209)	05/31/63	.15	.15	2.25	(2)	1.00	
a Tagged	07/06/66	.15	.15	.75	(2)	5.00	
1226-28 Not assigned							
1229 5¢ dark blue gray Washington (1213)	11/23/62	1.25	.15	4.00	(2)	1.00	
a Tagged	10/28/63	1.25	.15	4.00	(2)	20.00	
b Imperf. pair		450.00		1,250.00	(2)		
Issues of 1963, Perf. 11							
1230 5¢ Carolina Charter	04/06/63	.15	.15	.40	(4)	1.00	130
1231 5¢ Food for Peace-Freedom from Hunger	06/04/63	.15	.15	.40	(4)	1.00	136
1232 5¢ West Virginia Statehood	06/20/63	.15	.15	.40	(4)	1.00	138
1233 5¢ Emancipation Proclamation	08/16/63	.15	.15	.40	(4)	1.00	132
1234 5¢ Alliance for Progress	08/17/63	.15	.15	.40	(4)	1.00	136

1963-1964

ssues of 1963		Un	U	PB		FDC	Q(M)
1235 5¢ Cordell Hull	10/05/63	.15	.15	.40	(4)	1.00	131
Perf. 11 x 10.5							
1236 5¢ Eleanor Roosevelt	10/11/63	.15	.15	.40	(4)	1.00	133
Perf. 11							
1237 5¢ The Sciences	10/14/63	.15	.15	.40	(4)	1.00	130
1238 5¢ City Mail Delivery	10/26/63	.15	.15	.50	(4)	1.00	128
1239 5¢ International Red Cros	10/29/63	.15	.15	.40	(4)	1.00	119
Christmas Issue							
1240 5¢ National Christmas							
Tree and White House	11/01/63	.15	.15	.40	(4)	1.00	1,300
a Tagged	11/02/63	.65	.40	4.00	(4)	60.00	
Pair with full horizontal gutter between		—					
1241 5¢ John James Audubon,							
(See also #C71)	12/07/63	.15	.15	.40	(4)	1.00	175
Issues of 1964, Perf. 10.5 x 11							
1242 5¢ Sam Houston	01/10/64	.15	.15	.45	(4)	1.00	126
Perf. 11							
1243 5¢ Charles M. Russell	03/19/64	.15	.15	.40	(4)	1.00	128
Perf. 11 x 10.5							
1244 5¢ New York World's Fair	04/22/64	.15	.15	.40	(4)	2.00	146
Perf. 11							
1245 5¢ John Muir	04/29/64	.15	.15	.40	(4)	1.00	120
Perf. 11 x 10.5							
1246 5¢ President John Fitzgerald							
Kennedy Memorial	05/29/64	.15	.15	.55	(4)	3.50	512
Perf. 10.5 x 11							
1247 5¢ New Jersey Settlement	06/15/64	.15	.15	.40	(4)	1.00	124
Perf. 11							
1248 5¢ Nevada Statehood	07/22/64	.15	.15	.40	(4)	1.00	123
1249 5¢ Register and Vote	08/01/64	.15	.15	.45	(4)	1.00	453
Perf. 10.5 x 11							
1250 5¢ Shakespeare	08/14/64	.15	.15	.40	(4)	1.50	123
1251 5¢ Doctors William and							
Charles Mayo	09/11/64	.15	.15	.50	(4)	1.50	123
Perf. 11							
1252 5¢ American Music	10/15/64	.15	.15	.40	(4)	1.00	127
a Blue omitted		1,000.00					
1253 5¢ Homemakers	10/26/64	.15	.15	.40	(4)	1.00	121

In 1963 the U.S. Post Office Department issued a stamp by Antonio Frasconi honoring **The Sciences** and the centennial of the National Academy of Sciences. President Abraham Lincoln signed the congressional charter that established the academy on March 3, 1863. The academy's mandate was to investigate,

examine, experiment, and report on any subject of science or art, whenever called upon by any department of the government.

The National Academy of Sciences is now part of a complex of associated organizations collectively known as the National Academies, which consists of the National Research Council (established in 1916), the National Academy of Engineering (established in 1964), and the Institute of Medicine (established in 1970). The National Academies are private, nonprofit organizations that provide a public service by offering independent advice to the federal government on scientific and technological issues.

1235

1236

1237

1238

1239

1240

1241

1242

1243

1244

1245

1246

1247

1248

1249

1250

1251

1252

1253

1254   **1255**

1258

1259

1260

1256   **1257**   **1257b**

1261

1262

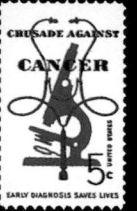

1263

1264

1265

1266

1267

1268

1269

1270

1271

1272

1273

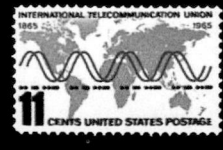

1274

1275

1276

	Issues of 1964		Un	U	PB	#	FDC	Q(M)
	Christmas Issue, Perf. 11							
1254	5¢ Holly	11/09/64	.25	.15			1.00	352
1255	5¢ Mistletoe	11/09/64	.25	.15			1.00	352
1256	5¢ Poinsettia	11/09/64	.25	.15			1.00	352
1257	5¢ Sprig of Conifer	11/09/64	.25	.15			1.00	352
b	Block of four, #1254-57		1.10	1.10	1.25	(4)	3.00	
c	As "b," tagged		2.50	2.00			57.50	
	Perf. 10.5 x 11							
1258	5¢ Verrazano-Narrows Bridge	11/21/64	.15	.15	.40	(4)	1.00	120
	Perf. 11							
1259	5¢ Fine Arts	12/02/64	.15	.15	.40	(4)	1.00	126
	Perf. 10.5 x 11							
1260	5¢ Amateur Radio	12/15/64	.15	.15	.40	(4)	1.00	122
	Issues of 1965, Perf. 11							
1261	5¢ Battle of New Orleans	01/08/65	.15	.15	.40	(4)	1.00	116
1262	5¢ Physical Fitness-Sokol	02/15/65	.15	.15	.50	(4)	1.00	115
1263	5¢ Crusade Against Cancer	04/01/65	.15	.15	.40	(4)	1.00	120
	Perf. 10.5 x 11							
1264	5¢ Winston Churchill Memorial	05/13/65	.15	.15	.40	(4)	1.50	125
	Perf. 11							
1265	5¢ Magna Carta	06/15/65	.15	.15	.40	(4)	1.00	120
	Corner block of four, black PB# omitted		—					
1266	5¢ International Cooperation Year-United Nations	06/26/65	.15	.15	.40	(4)	1.00	115
1267	5¢ Salvation Army	07/02/65	.15	.15	.40	(4)	2.50	116
	Perf. 10.5 x 11							
1268	5¢ Dante Alighieri	07/17/65	.15	.15	.40	(4)	1.00	115
1269	5¢ President Herbert Hoover Memorial	08/10/65	.15	.15	.45	(4)	1.00	115
	Perf. 11							
1270	5¢ Robert Fulton	08/19/65	.15	.15	.40	(4)	1.00	116
1271	5¢ Florida Settlement	08/28/65	.15	.15	.45	(4)	1.00	117
a	Yellow omitted		425.00					
1272	5¢ Traffic Safety	09/03/65	.15	.15	.45	(4)	1.00	114
1273	5¢ John Singleton Copley	09/17/65	.15	.15	.50	(4)	1.00	115
1274	11¢ International Telecommunication Union	10/06/65	.35	.20	3.25	(4)	1.00	27
1275	5¢ Adlai E. Stevenson Memorial	10/23/65	.15	.15	.40	(4)	1.00	128
	Christmas Issue							
1276	5¢ Angel with Trumpet (1840 Weather Vane)	11/02/65	.15	.15	.40	(4)	1.00	1,140
a	Tagged	11/15/65	.75	.25	5.00	(4)	42.50	
1277	Not assigned							

Issues of 1965-78			Un	U	PB		FDC
Prominent Americans Issue, Perf. 11 x 10.5, 10.5 x 11 (See also #1299, 1303-05C)							
1278	1¢ Jefferson	01/12/68	.15	.15	.20	(4)	1.00
a	Booklet pane of 8	01/12/68	1.00	.50			2.50
b	Bklt. pane of 4 + 2 labels	05/10/71	.80	.30			12.50
c	Untagged (Bureau precanceled)			.15			
1279	1¼¢ Albert Gallatin	01/30/67	.15	.15	7.50	(4)	1.00
1280	2¢ Frank Lloyd Wright	06/08/66	.15	.15	.25	(4)	1.00
a	Booklet pane of 5 + label	01/08/68	1.25	.60			4.00
b	Untagged (Bureau precanceled)			.15			
c	Booklet pane of 6	05/07/71	1.00	.50			15.00
	Pair with full vertical gutter between		—				
1281	3¢ Francis Parkman	09/16/67	.15	.15	.25	(4)	1.00
a	Untagged (Bureau precanceled)			.15			
1282	4¢ Lincoln	11/19/65	.15	.15	.40	(4)	1.25
a	Tagged	12/01/65	.15	.15	.55	(4)	20.00
	Pair with full horizontal gutter between		—				
1283	5¢ Washington	02/22/66	.15	.15	.50	(4)	1.00
a	Tagged	02/23/66	.15	.15	.60	(4)	22.50
1283B	5¢ redrawn	11/17/67	.15	.15	.50	(4)	1.00
	Dull finish gum		.20		1.40	(4)	
d	Untagged (Bureau precanceled)			.15			
1284	6¢ Roosevelt	01/29/66	.15	.15	.60	(4)	1.00
a	Tagged	12/29/66	.15	.15	.80	(4)	20.00
b	Booklet pane of 8	12/28/67	1.50	.75			3.00
c	Booklet pane of 5 + label	01/09/68	1.50	.75			100.00
1285	8¢ Albert Einstein	03/14/66	.20	.15	.85	(4)	3.00
a	Tagged	07/06/66	.20	.15	.85	(4)	14.00
1286	10¢ Jackson	03/15/67	.20	.15	1.00	(4)	1.00
b	Untagged (Bureau precanceled)			.20			
1286A	12¢ Henry Ford	07/30/68	.25	.15	1.00	(4)	1.25
c	Untagged (Bureau precanceled)			.25			
1287	13¢ John F. Kennedy	05/29/67	.30	.15	1.50	(4)	2.50
a	Untagged (Bureau precanceled)			.35			
1288	15¢ Oliver Wendell Holmes	03/08/68	.30	.15	1.25	(4)	1.00
a	Untagged (Bureau precanceled)			.30			
	Booklet Stamp, Perf. 10						
1288B	15¢ magenta, tagged						
	(1288), Single from booklet		.30	.15			1.00
c	Booklet pane of 8	06/14/78	2.50	1.75			3.00
e	As "c," vert. imperf. between		—				
	Perf. 11 x 10.5, 10.5 x 11						
1289	20¢ George C. Marshall	10/24/67	.40	.15	1.75	(4)	1.00
a	Tagged	04/03/73	.40	.15	1.75	(4)	12.50
1290	25¢ Frederick Douglass	02/14/67	.55	.15	2.25	(4)	1.25
a	Tagged	04/03/73	.45	.15	2.00	(4)	14.00
1291	30¢ John Dewey	10/21/68	.60	.15	2.75	(4)	1.25
a	Tagged	04/03/73	.50	.15	2.25	(4)	14.00
1292	40¢ Thomas Paine	01/29/68	.80	.15	3.25	(4)	2.00
a	Tagged	04/03/73	.65	.15	2.75	(4)	15.00
1293	50¢ Lucy Stone	08/13/68	1.00	.15	4.25	(4)	3.25
a	Tagged	04/03/73	.80	.15	3.50	(4)	20.00
1294	$1 Eugene O'Neill	10/16/67	2.25	.15	10.00	(4)	7.50
a	Tagged	04/03/73	1.65	.15	6.75	(4)	22.50

1278 1279

1281

1280

1282 1283 1283B

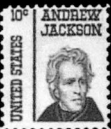

1284

1285 1286

1286A

1287 1288

1291

1289 1290

1292 1293 1294

1295   1305

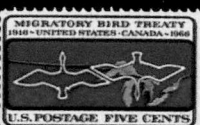

1306   1307

1310

1308   1309

1311

1314

1312   1313

	Issues of 1965-78		Un	U	PB/LP	#	FDC	Q(M)
	Perf. 11 x 10.5, 10.5 x 11							
1295	$5 John Bassett Moore	12/03/66	9.50	2.25	40.00	(4)	40.00	
a	Tagged	04/03/73	8.00	2.00	32.50	(4)	65.00	
1296	Not assigned							
	Issues of 1967-75, Coil Stamps, Perf. 10 Horizontally							
1297	3¢ violet Parkman (1281)	11/04/75	.15	.15	.45	(2)	1.00	
a	Imperf. pair		30.00		55.00	(2)		
b	Untagged (Bureau precanceled)			.15				
c	As "b," imperf. pair			6.00	25.00	(2)		
1298	6¢ Roosevelt (1284)	12/28/67	.15	.15	1.25	(2)	1.00	
a	Imperf. pair		2,250.00					
	Issues of 1966-81, Coil Stamps, Perf. 10 Vertically (See also #1279-96)							
1299	1¢ green Jefferson (1278)	01/12/68	.15	.15	.25	(2)	1.00	
a	Untagged (Bureau precanceled)			.15				
b	Imperf. pair		30.00	—	60.00	(2)		
1300-02	Not assigned							
1303	4¢ blk. Lincoln (1282)	05/28/66	.15	.15	.75	(2)	1.00	
a	Untagged (Bureau precanceled)			.15				
b	Imperf. pair		900.00		2,000.00	(2)		
1304	5¢ bl. Washington (1283)	09/08/66	.15	.15	.40	(2)	1.00	
a	Untagged (Bureau precanceled)			.15				
b	Imperf. pair		175.00		400.00	(2)		
e	As "a," imperf. pair			450.00	900.00	(2)		
1304C	5¢ redrawn (1283B)	1981	.15	.15	1.25	(2)		
d	Imperf. pair		1,000.00					
1305	6¢ gray brown Roosevelt	02/28/68	.15	.15	.55	(2)	1.00	
a	Imperf. pair		75.00		130.00	(2)		
b	Untagged (Bureau precanceled)			.20				
1305E	15¢ magenta, Type I (1288)	06/14/78	.25	.15	1.25	(2)	1.00	
	Dull finish gum		.60		2.00	(2)		
f	Untagged (Bureau precanceled)			.30				
g	Imperf. pair		30.00		75.00	(2)		
h	Pair, imperf. between		225.00		600.00	(2)		
1305C	$1 dull purple Eugene O'Neill (1294)	01/12/73	1.75	.20	5.00	(2)	5.00	
d	Imperf. pair		2,250.00		4,000.00	(2)		
	Issues of 1966, Perf. 11							
1306	5¢ Migratory Bird Treaty	03/16/66	.15	.15	.40	(4)	1.00	117
1307	5¢ Humane Treatment of Animals	04/09/66	.15	.15	.40	(4)	1.00	117
1308	5¢ Indiana Statehood	04/16/66	.15	.15	.40	(4)	1.00	124
1309	5¢ American Circus	05/02/66	.15	.15	.50	(4)	4.00	131
	Sixth International Philatelic Exhibition Issue							
1310	5¢ Stamped Cover	05/21/66	.15	.15	.40	(4)	1.00	122
	Souvenir Sheet, Imperf.							
1311	5¢ Stamped Cover (1310) and Washington, D.C., Scene	05/23/66	.15	.15			1.00	15
	Perf. 11							
1312	5¢ The Bill of Rights	07/01/66	.15	.15	.45	(4)	1.00	114
	Perf. 10.5 x 11							
1313	5¢ Poland's Millennium	07/30/66	.15	.15	.45	(4)	1.00	128
	Perf. 11							
1314	5¢ National Park Service	08/25/66	.15	.15	.45	(4)	1.00	120
a	Tagged	08/26/66	.30	.25	2.00	(4)	20.00	

	Issues of 1966		Un	U	PB		FDC	Q(M)
1315	5¢ Marine Corps Reserve	08/29/66	.15	.15	.45	(4)	2.00	125
a	Tagged		.30	.20	2.00	(4)	25.00	
b	Black and bister omitted		16,000.00					
1316	5¢ Women's Clubs	09/12/66	.15	.15	.45	(4)	1.00	115
a	Tagged	09/13/66	.30	.20	2.00	(4)	22.50	
	American Folklore Issue, Johnny Appleseed							
1317	5¢ Johnny Appleseed and Apple	09/24/66	.15	.15	.45	(4)	1.50	124
a	Tagged	09/26/66	.30	.20	2.00	(4)	22.50	
1318	5¢ Beautification of America	10/05/66	.15	.15	.45	(4)	1.00	128
a	Tagged		.30	.20	2.00	(4)	20.00	
1319	5¢ Great River Road	10/21/66	.15	.15	.45	(4)	1.00	128
a	Tagged	10/22/66	.30	.20	2.00	(4)	22.50	
1320	5¢ Savings Bond-Servicemen	10/26/66	.15	.15	.45	(4)	1.00	116
a	Tagged	10/27/66	.30	.20	2.00	(4)	22.50	
b	Red, dark bl. and blk. omitted		5,000.00					
c	Dark blue omitted		9,000.00					
	Christmas Issue							
1321	5¢ Madonna and Child, by Hans Memling	11/01/66	.15	.15	.40	(4)	1.00	1,174
a	Tagged	11/02/66	.30	.20	1.75	(4)	9.50	
1322	5¢ Mary Cassatt	11/17/66	.15	.15	.60	(4)	1.00	114
a	Tagged		.30	.25	2.00	(4)	20.00	
	Issues of 1967							
1323	5¢ National Grange	04/17/67	.15	.15	.40	(4)	1.00	121
a	Tagging omitted		5.00	—				
1324	5¢ Canada	05/25/67	.15	.15	.40	(4)	1.00	132
1325	5¢ Erie Canal	07/04/67	.15	.15	.40	(4)	1.00	119
1326	5¢ Search for Peace	07/05/67	.15	.15	.40	(4)	1.00	122
1327	5¢ Henry David Thoreau	07/12/67	.15	.15	.40	(4)	1.00	112
1328	5¢ Nebraska Statehood	07/29/67	.15	.15	.40	(4)	1.00	117
a	Tagging omitted		6.00	—				
1329	5¢ Voice of America	08/01/67	.15	.15	.40	(4)	1.00	112
	American Folklore Issue, Davy Crockett							
1330	5¢ Davy Crockett	08/17/67	.15	.15	.40	(4)	1.25	114
a	Vertical pair, imperf. between		6,000.00					
b	Green omitted		—					
c	Black and green omitted		—					
d	Yellow and green omitted		—					
e	Tagging omitted		5.00					
	Accomplishments in Space Issue							
1331	5¢ Space-Walking Astronaut	09/29/67	.55	.15			3.00	60
a	Attached pair, #1331-32		1.25	1.25			8.00	
1332	5¢ Gemini 4 Capsule and Earth	09/29/67	.55	.15	2.75	(4)	3.00	60
1333	5¢ Urban Planning	10/02/67	.15	.15	.50	(4)	1.00	111
1334	5¢ Finland Independence	10/06/67	.15	.15	.50	(4)	1.00	111

1315

1316

1317

1318

1319

1320

1321

1322

1323

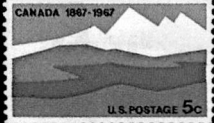

1324

1325

1326

1327

1328

1329

1330

1331   1332   1331a

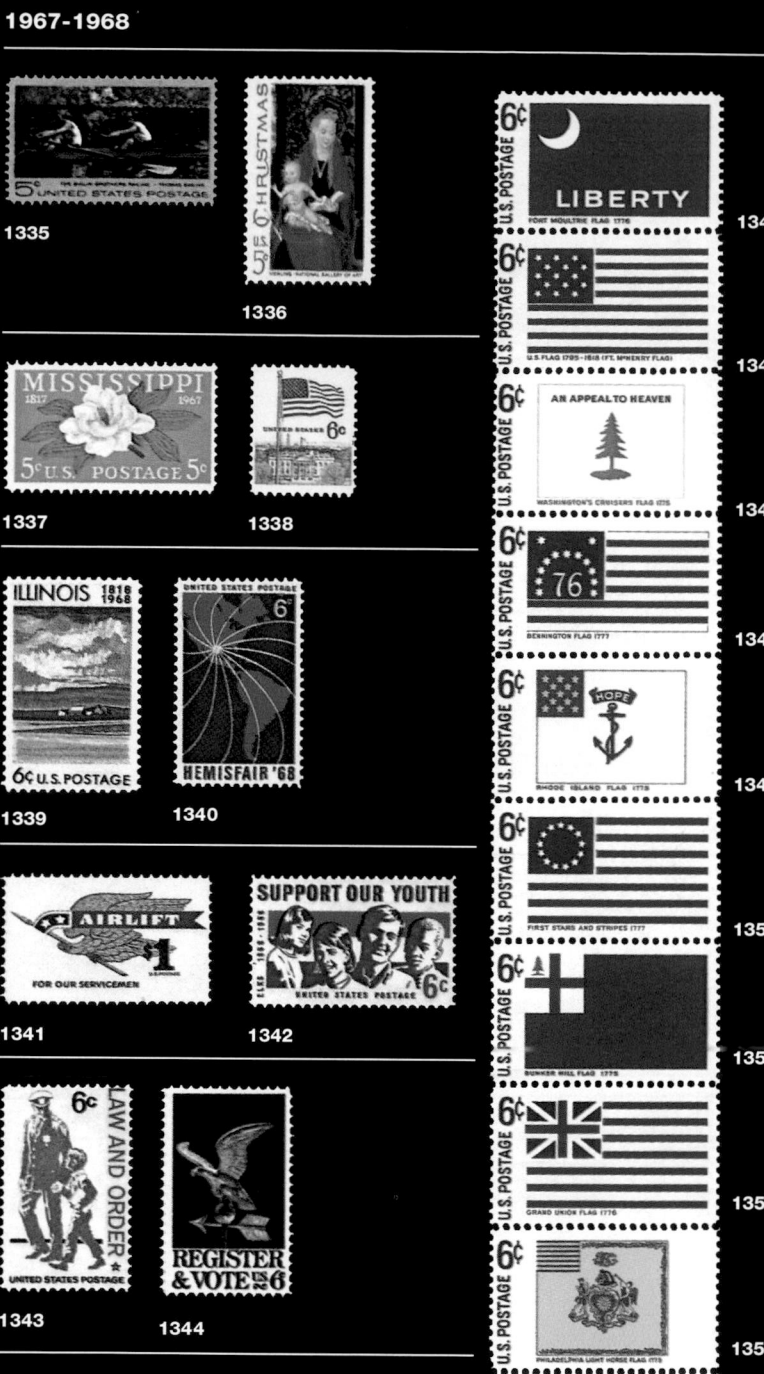

1335

1336

1337

1338

1339

1340

1341

1342

1343

1344

1355

1345

1346

1347

1348

1349

1350

1351

1352

1353

1354

1354a

ssues of 1967		Un	U	PB	#	FDC	Q(M)
Perf. 12							
1335 5¢ Thomas Eakins	11/02/67	.15	.15	.50	(4)	1.00	114
Christmas Issue, Perf. 11							
1336 5¢ Madonna and Child,							
by Hans Memling	11/06/67	.15	.15	.40	(4)	1.00	1,209
1337 5¢ Mississippi Statehood	12/11/67	.15	.15	.50	(4)	1.00	113
Issues of 1968-1971							
1338 6¢ Flag over White House							
(design 19 x 22mm)	01/24/68	.15	.15	.45	(4)	1.00	
k Vertical pair, imperf. between		550.00					
Coil Stamp, Perf. 10 Vertically							
1338A 6¢ dk bl, rd and grn (1338)	05/30/69	.15	.15	.30	(2)	1.00	
b Imperf. pair		500.00					
Perf. 11 x 10.5							
1338D 6¢ dark blue, red and green							
(1338, design 18.25 x 21mm)	08/07/70	.15	.15	2.60	(20)	1.00	
e Horizontal pair, imperf. between		175.00					
1338F 8¢ dk bl, rd and slt grn (1338)	05/10/71	.15	.15	3.00	(20)	1.00	
i Imperf., vertical pair		50.00					
j Horizontal pair, imperf. between		60.00					
Coil Stamp, Perf. 10 Vertically							
1338G 8¢ dk bl, rd and slt grn (1338)	05/10/71	.20	.15	.40	(2)	1.00	
h Imperf. pair		55.00					
Issues of 1968, Perf. 11							
1339 6¢ Illinois Statehood	02/12/68	.15	.15	.50	(4)	1.00	141
1340 6¢ HemisFair '68	03/30/68	.15	.15	.50	(4)	1.00	144
a White omitted		1,400.00					
1341 $1 Airlift	04/04/68	2.25	1.25	10.00	(4)	6.50	
Pair with full horizontal gutter between							
1342 6¢ Support Our Youth-Elks	05/01/68	.15	.15	.50	(4)	1.00	147
1343 6¢ Law and Order	05/17/68	.15	.15	.50	(4)	1.50	130
1344 6¢ Register and Vote	06/27/68	.15	.15	.50	(4)	1.00	159
Historic Flag Issue							
1345 6¢ Ft. Moultrie Flag, 1776	07/04/68	.40	.25			3.00	23
1346 6¢ Ft. McHenry (U.S.)							
Flag, 1795-1818	07/04/68	.30	.25			3.00	23
1347 6¢ Washington's							
Cruisers Flag, 1775	07/04/68	.25	.25			3.00	23
1348 6¢ Bennington Flag, 1777	07/04/68	.25	.25			3.00	23
1349 6¢ Rhode Island Flag, 1775	07/04/68	.25	.25			3.00	23
1350 6¢ First Stars and							
Stripes, 1777	07/04/68	.25	.25			3.00	23
1351 6¢ Bunker Hill Flag, 1775	07/04/68	.25	.25			3.00	23
1352 6¢ Grand Union Flag, 1776	07/04/68	.25	.25			3.00	23
1353 6¢ Philadelphia Light Horse							
Flag, 1775	07/04/68	.25	.25			3.00	23
1354 6¢ First Navy Jack, 1775	07/04/68	.25	.25			3.00	23
a Strip of 10, #1345-54		2.75	2.75	6.50	(20)	15.00	
Perf. 12							
1355 6¢ Walt Disney	09/11/68	.15	.15	.70	(4)	12.50	153
a Ocher omitted		700.00	—				
b Vertical pair, imperf. horizontally		750.00					
c Imperf. pair		675.00					
d Black omitted		2,000.00					
e Horizontal pair, imperf. between		4,750.00					
f Blue omitted		2,250.00					
g Tagging omitted		10.00					

Issues of 1968		Un	U	PB		FDC	Q(M)
Perf. 11							
1356 6¢ Father Marquette	09/20/68	.15	.15	.50	(4)	1.00	133
American Folklore Issue, Daniel Boone							
1357 6¢ Pennsylvania Rifle, Powder Horn,							
Tomahawk, Pipe and Knife	09/26/68	.15	.15	.50	(4)	1.25	130
a Tagging omitted		—					
1358 6¢ Arkansas River Navigation	10/01/68	.15	.15	.50	(4)	1.00	132
1359 6¢ Leif Erikson	10/09/68	.15	.15	.50	(4)	1.00	129
Perf. 11 x 10.5							
1360 6¢ Cherokee Strip	10/15/68	.15	.15	.60	(4)	1.00	125
a Tagging omitted		5.00	—				
Perf. 11							
1361 6¢ John Trumbull	10/18/68	.15	.15	.60	(4)	1.00	128
1362 6¢ Waterfowl Conservation	10/24/68	.15	.15	.65	(4)	2.00	142
a Vertical pair, imperf. between		550.00					
b Red and dark blue omitted		1,100.00					
Christmas Issue							
1363 6¢ Angel Gabriel, from							
"The Annunciation," by							
Jan Van Eyck	11/01/68	.15	.15	2.00	(10)	1.00	1,411
a Untagged	11/02/68	.15	.15	2.00	(10)	6.50	
b Imperf. pair tagged		250.00					
c Light yellow omitted		85.00					
d Imperf. pair (untagged)		325.00					
1364 6¢ American Indian	11/04/68	.15	.15	.70	(4)	1.25	125
Issues of 1969, Beautification of America Issue							
1365 6¢ Capitol, Azaleas and Tulips	01/16/69	.35	.15			1.00	48
1366 6¢ Washington Monument,							
Potomac River and Daffodils	01/16/69	.35	.15			1.00	48
1367 6¢ Poppies and Lupines							
along Highway	01/16/69	.35	.15			1.00	48
1368 6¢ Blooming Crabapple Trees							
Lining Avenue	01/16/69	.35	.15			1.00	48
a Block of 4, #1365-68		1.65	1.75	1.75	(4)	4.00	
b As "a," tagging omitted		—					
1369 6¢ American Legion	03/15/69	.15	.15	.45	(4)	1.00	149
American Folklore Issue, Grandma Moses							
1370 6¢ "July Fourth" by							
Grandma Moses	05/01/69	.15	.15	.50	(4)	1.00	139
a Horizontal pair, imperf. between		225.00					
b Black and Prussian blue omitted		900.00					
1371 6¢ Apollo 8	05/05/69	.15	.15	.65	(4)	3.00	187
1372 6¢ W.C. Handy	05/17/69	.15	.15	.45	(4)	1.00	126
a Tagging omitted		6.00	—				
1373 6¢ California Settlement	07/16/69	.15	.15	.45	(4)	1.00	144
1374 6¢ John Wesley Powell	08/01/69	.15	.15	.45	(4)	1.00	136
1375 6¢ Alabama Statehood	08/02/69	.15	.15	.45	(4)	1.00	151

1356

1357

1358

1359

1360

1361

1362

1365

1366

1363

1364

1367

1368

1368a

1369

1370

1371

1372

1373

1374

1375

	Issues of 1970-74		Un	U	PB/LF			FDC	Q(M)
1393	6¢ Eisenhower	08/06/70	.15	.15	.50	(4)		1.00	
a	Booklet pane of 8		1.50	.65				3.00	
b	Booklet pane of 5 + label		1.50	.65				1.50	
c	Untagged (Bureau precanceled)			.15					
	Perf. 10.5 x 11								
1393D	7¢ Franklin	10/20/72	.15	.15	.60	(4)		1.00	
e	Untagged (Bureau precanceled)			.15					
	Perf. 11								
1394	8¢ Eisenhower	05/10/71	.15	.15	.60	(4)		1.00	
	Pair with full vertical gutter between		—						
	Perf. 11 x 10.5								
1395	8¢ deep claret Eisenhower								
	1394), Single from booklet		.20	.15				1.00	
a	Booklet pane of 8	05/10/71	1.80	1.25				3.00	
b	Booklet pane of 6	05/10/71	1.25	.90				3.00	
c	Booklet pane of 4 + 2 labels	01/28/72	1.65	.80				2.25	
d	Booklet pane of 7 + label	01/28/72	1.90	1.00				2.00	
1396	8¢ U.S. Postal Service	07/01/71	.15	.15	2.00	(12)		1.00	
1397	14¢ Fiorello H. LaGuardia	04/24/72	.25	.15	1.15	(4)		1.00	
a	Untagged (Bureau precanceled)			.25					
1398	16¢ Ernie Pyle	05/07/71	.30	.15	1.25	(4)		1.25	
a	Untagged (Bureau precanceled)			.35					
1399	18¢ Dr. Elizabeth Blackwell	01/23/74	.35	.15	1.50	(4)		1.25	
1400	21¢ Amadeo P. Giannini	06/27/73	.40	.15	1.65	(4)		1.00	
	Coil Stamps, Perf. 10 Vertically								
1401	6¢ dark blue gray Eisenhower (1393)	08/06/70	.15	.15	.50	(2)		1.00	
a	Untagged (Bureau precanceled)			.15					
b	Imperf. pair		2,000.00		—	(2)			
1402	8¢ deep claret Eisenhower (1394)	05/10/71	.15	.15	.55	(2)		1.00	
a	Imperf. pair		45.00		70.00	(2)			
b	Untagged (Bureau precanceled)			.15					
c	Pair, imperf. between		6,250.00						
1403-04	Not assigned								
	Issues of 1970, Perf. 11								
1405	6¢ Edgar Lee Masters	08/22/70	.15	.15	.50	(4)		1.00	138
a	Tagging omitted		30.00	—					
1406	6¢ Woman Suffrage	08/26/70	.15	.15	.50	(4)		1.00	135
1407	6¢ South Carolina Settlement	09/12/70	.15	.15	.50	(4)		1.00	136
1408	6¢ Stone Mountain Memorial	09/19/70	.15	.15	.50	(4)		1.00	133
1409	6¢ Ft. Snelling	10/17/70	.15	.15	.50	(4)		1.00	135
	Anti-Pollution Issue, Perf. 11 x 10.5								
1410	6¢ Save Our Soil								
	Globe and Wheat Field	10/28/70	.20	.15				1.25	40
1411	6¢ Save Our Cities								
	Globe and City Playground	10/28/70	.20	.15				1.25	40
1412	6¢ Save Our Water								
	Globe and Bluegill Fish	10/28/70	.20	.15				1.25	40
1413	6¢ Save Our Air								
	Globe and Seagull	10/28/70	.20	.15				1.25	40
a	Block of 4, #1410-13		1.00	1.25	2.25	(10)		3.00	

1393

1393D

1394

1396

1397

1398

1399

1400

1405

1406

1407

1408

1409

1410

1411

1412

1413

1413a

1414

1414a

1415　1416

1417　1418　1418b

1419

1420

1421　1422　1421a

1423

1424

1425

1426

1427　1428

1429　1430　1430a

	Issues of 1970		Un	U	PB	#	FDC	Q(M)
	Christmas Issue, Perf. 10.5 x 11							
1414	6¢ Nativity, by Lorenzo Lotto	11/05/70	.15	.15	1.10	(8)	1.40	639*
a	Precanceled		.15	.15	1.90	(8)	10.00	358
b	Black omitted		650.00					
c	As "a," blue omitted		1,500.00					

#1414a-18a were furnished to 68 cities. Unused prices are for copies with gum and used prices are for copies with or without gum but with an additional cancellation.
*Includes #1414a.

	Perf. 11 x 10.5							
1415	6¢ Tin and Cast-iron Locomotive	11/05/70	.30	.15			1.40	122
a	Precanceled		.75	.15				110
b	Black omitted		2,500.00					
1416	6¢ Toy Horse on Wheels	11/05/70	.30	.15			1.40	122
a	Precanceled		.75	.15				110
b	Black omitted		2,500.00					
c	Imperf. pair			4,000.00				
1417	6¢ Mechanical Tricycle	11/05/70	.30	.15			1.40	122
a	Precanceled		.75	.15				110
b	Black omitted		2,500.00					
1418	6¢ Doll Carriage	11/05/70	.30	.15			1.40	122
a	Precanceled		.75	.15				110
b	Block of 4, #1415-18		1.25	1.50	3.25	(8)	3.50	
c	Block of 4, #1415a-18a		3.25	3.25	6.50	(8)	6.00	
d	Black omitted		2,500.00					
	Perf. 11							
1419	6¢ United Nations	11/20/70	.15	.15	.50	(4)	1.50	128
	Pair with full horizontal gutter between		—					
1420	6¢ Landing of the Pilgrims	11/21/70	.15	.15	.50	(4)	1.00	130
a	Orange and yellow omitted		900.00					
	Disabled American Veterans and Servicemen Issue							
1421	6¢ Disabled American Veterans Emblem	11/24/70	.15	.15			1.50	67
a	Attached pair, #1421-22		.25	.30	1.00	(4)	2.50	
1422	6¢ U.S. Servicemen	11/24/70	.15	.15			1.50	67
	Issues of 1971							
1423	6¢ American Wool Industry	01/19/71	.15	.15	.50	(4)	1.00	136
a	Tagging omitted		7.00					
1424	6¢ Gen. Douglas MacArthur	01/26/71	.15	.15	.50	(4)	1.25	135
1425	6¢ Blood Donor	03/12/71	.15	.15	.50	(4)	1.25	131
a	Tagging omitted		9.00					
	Perf. 11 x 10.5							
1426	8¢ Missouri Statehood	05/08/71	.15	.15	2.00	(12)	1.00	161
	Wildlife Conservation Issue, Perf. 11							
1427	8¢ Trout	06/12/71	.20	.15			1.25	44
1428	8¢ Alligator	06/12/71	.20	.15			1.25	44
1429	8¢ Polar Bear	06/12/71	.20	.15			1.25	44
1430	8¢ California Condor	06/12/71	.20	.15			1.25	44
a	Block of 4, #1427-30		.80	.90	.90	(4)	3.00	
b	As "a," light green and dark green omitted from #1427-28		4,500.00					
c	As "a," red omitted from #1427, 1429-30		9,000.00					

	Issues of 1971		Un	U	PB		FDC	Q(M)
1431	8¢ Antarctic Treaty	06/23/71	.15	.15	.65	(4)	1.00	139
a	Tagging omitted		7.00					
	American Revolution Bicentennial Issue							
1432	8¢ Bicentennial Commission Emblem	07/04/71	.20	.15	.85	(4)	1.00	138
a	Gray and black omitted		700.00					
b	Gray omitted		1,250.00					
1433	8¢ John Sloan	08/02/71	.15	.15	.70	(4)	1.00	152
a	Tagging omitted		—					
	Space Achievement Decade Issue							
1434	8¢ Earth, Sun and Landing Craft on Moon	08/02/71	.15	.15				88
c	Tagging omitted		25.00					
1435	8¢ Lunar Rover and Astronauts	08/02/71	.15	.15	.65	(4)		88
a	Tagging omitted		25.00					
1436	8¢ Emily Dickinson	08/28/71	.15	.15	.65	(4)	1.00	143
a	Black and olive omitted		800.00					
b	Pale rose omitted		7,500.00					
1437	8¢ San Juan, Puerto Rico	09/12/71	.15	.15	.65	(4)	1.00	149
a	Tagging omitted		7.50					
	Perf. 10.5 x 11							
1438	8¢ Prevent Drug Abuse	10/04/71	.15	.15	1.00	(6)	1.00	139
1439	8¢ CARE	10/27/71	.15	.15	1.25	(8)	1.00	131
a	Black omitted		4,750.00					
b	Tagging omitted		5.00					
	Historic Preservation Issue, Perf. 11							
1440	8¢ Decatur House, Washington, D.C.	10/29/71	.15	.15			1.25	43
1441	8¢ Whaling Ship *Charles W. Morgan*, Mystic, Connecticut	10/29/71	.15	.15			1.25	43
1442	8¢ Cable Car, San Francisco	10/29/71	.15	.15			1.25	43
1443	8¢ San Xavier del Bac Mission, Tucson, Arizona	10/29/71	.15	.15			1.25	43
a	Block of 4, #1440-43		.75	.85	.85	(4)	3.00	
b	As "a," black brown omitted		2,750.00					
c	As "a," ocher omitted		—					
d	As "a," tagging omitted		60.00					
	Christmas Issue, Perf. 10.5 x 11							
1444	8¢ Adoration of the Shepherds, by Giorgione	11/10/71	.15	.15	1.75	(12)	1.00	1,074
a	Gold omitted		600.00					
1445	8¢ Partridge in a Pear Tree	11/10/71	.15	.15	1.75	(12)	1.00	980

1431

1433

1432

1434   1435   1434a

1436   1437   1438   1439

1440   1441

1442   1443   1443a

1444   1445

1446   1447

1448   1449

1452

1450   1451 1451a

1454

1453

1456   1457

1455

1458   1459   1459a

1460   1461   1462

1463

ssues of 1972		Un	U	PB	#	FDC	Q(M)
1446 8¢ Sidney Lanier	02/03/72	.15	.15	.65	(4)	1.00	137
Perf. 10.5 x 11							
1447 8¢ Peace Corps	02/11/72	.15	.15	1.00	(6)	1.00	150
National Parks Centennial Issue, Cape Hatteras, (See also #C84)							
1448 2¢ Ship at Sea	04/05/72	.15	.15				43
1449 2¢ Cape Hatteras Lighthouse	04/05/72	.15	.15				43
1450 2¢ Laughing Gulls on							
Driftwood	04/05/72	.15	.15				43
1451 2¢ Laughing Gulls and Dune	04/05/72	.15	.15				43
a Block of 4, #1448-51		.25	.25	.50	(4)	2.00	
b As "a," black omitted		2,750.00					
Wolf Trap Farm							
1452 6¢ Performance at							
Shouse Pavilion	06/26/72	.15	.15	.55	(4)	1.00	104
1453 8¢ Old Faithful, Yellowstone	03/01/72	.15	.15	.70	(4)	1.00	164
a Tagging omitted		15.00					
Mount McKinley							
1454 15¢ View of Mount McKinley							
in Alaska	07/28/72	.30	.20	1.30	(4)	1.00	54

Note: Beginning with this National Parks Centennial issue, the USPS began to offer stamp collectors first day cancellations affixed to 8" x 101/2" souvenir pages. The pages are similar to the stamp announcements that have appeared on Post Office bulletin boards beginning with Scott #1132. See "Souvenir Pages" listed in the back of this book (see Table of Contents)

1455 8¢ Family Planning	03/18/72	.15	.15	.65	(4)	1.00	153
a Yellow omitted		1,650.00					
b Dark brown and olive omitted		—					
American Bicentennial Issue, Colonial American Craftsmen, Perf. 11 x 10.5							
1456 8¢ Glassblower	07/04/72	.15	.15			1.00	50
1457 8¢ Silversmith	07/04/72	.15	.15			1.00	50
1458 8¢ Wigmaker	07/04/72	.15	.15			1.00	50
1459 8¢ Hatter	07/04/72	.15	.15			1.00	50
a Block of 4, #1456-59		.65	.75	.75	(4)	2.50	
Olympic Games Issue, (See also #C85)							
1460 6¢ Bicycling and Olympic							
Rings	08/17/72	.15	.15	1.25	(10)	1.00	67
Cylinder flaw (broken red ring)		10.00					
1461 8¢ Bobsledding and							
Olympic Rings	08/17/72	.15	.15	1.60	(10)	1.00	180
1462 15¢ Running and Olympic							
Rings	08/17/72	.30	.20	3.00	(10)	1.00	46
1463 8¢ Parent Teachers							
Association	09/15/72	.15	.15	.65	(4)	1.00	180

The tallest mountain in North America, **Mount McKinley** is an important landmark in Denali National Park and Preserve. Originally established in 1917 as Mount McKinley National Park, the park was given its current name in 1980. Covering more than six million acres, Denali is one of the most popular tourist attractions in the state of Alaska.

Besides the 20,320-foot tall Mount McKinley, the park is also home to grizzly bears, wolves, moose, and herds of caribou. Denali's unspoiled wilderness was designated an International Biosphere Reserve in 1974 by the United Nations.

This Mount McKinley stamp was issued in 1972 as part of the National Parks Centennial issuance. James Barkley illustrated the stamp.

	ssues of 1972		Un	U	PE		FDC	Q(M)
	Wildlife Conservation Issue, Perf. 11							
1464	8¢ Fur Seals	09/20/72	.15	.15			1.50	50
1465	8¢ Cardinal	09/20/72	.15	.15			1.50	50
1466	8¢ Brown Pelican	09/20/72	.15	.15			1.50	50
1467	8¢ Bighorn Sheep	09/20/72	.15	.15			1.50	50
a	Block of 4, #1464-67		.65	.75	.75	(4)	3.00	
b	As "a," brown omitted		4,000.00					
c	As "a," green and blue omitted		4,750.00					
	Note: With this Wildlife Conservation issue the USPS introduced the "American Commemorative Series" Stamp Panels. Each panel contains a block of four or more mint stamps with text and background illustrations. See pages 493-497 for a complete listing.							
1468	8¢ Mail Order Business	09/27/72	.15	.15	1.75	(12)	1.00	185
	Perf. 10.5 x 11							
1469	8¢ Osteopathic Medicine	10/09/72	.15	.15	1.00	(6)	1.00	162
	American Folklore Issue, Tom Sawyer, Perf. 11							
1470	8¢ Tom Sawyer Whitewashing a Fence, by Norman Rockwell	10/13/72	.15	.15	.65	(4)	1.00	163
a	Horizontal pair, imperf. between		4,500.00					
b	Red and black omitted		2,250.00					
c	Yellow and tan omitted		2,400.00					
	Christmas Issue, Perf. 10.5 x 11							
1471	8¢ Angels from "Mary, Queen of Heaven" by the Master of the St. Lucy Legend	11/09/72	.15	.15	1.75	(12)	1.00	1,003
a	Pink omitted		200.00					
b	Black omitted		4,000.00					
1472	8¢ Santa Claus	11/09/72	.15	.15	1.75	(12)	1.00	1,017
	Perf. 11							
1473	8¢ Pharmacy	11/10/72	.15	.15	.65	(4)	5.50	166
a	Blue and orange omitted		1,000.00					
b	Blue omitted		2,250.00					
c	Orange omitted		2,250.00					
1474	8¢ Stamp Collecting	11/17/72	.15	.15	.65	(4)	1.00	167
a	Black omitted		1,000.00					
	Issues of 1973, Perf. 11 x 10.5							
1475	8¢ Love	01/26/73	.15	.15	1.00	(6)	2.50	320
	American Bicentennial Issue, Communications in Colonial Times, Perf. 11							
1476	8¢ Printer and Patriots Examining Pamphlet	02/16/73	.15	.15	.65	(4)	1.00	166
1477	8¢ Posting a Broadside	04/13/73	.15	.15	.65	(4)	1.00	163
	Pair with full horizontal gutter between		—					
1478	8¢ Postrider	06/22/73	.15	.15	.65	(4)	1.00	159
1479	8¢ Drummer	09/28/73	.15	.15	.65	(4)	1.00	147
	Boston Tea Party							
1480	8¢ British Merchantman	07/04/73	.15	.15			1.00	49
1481	8¢ British Three-Master	07/04/73	.15	.15			1.00	49
1482	8¢ Boats and Ship's Hull	07/04/73	.15	.15			1.00	49
1483	8¢ Boat and Dock	07/04/73	.15	.15			1.00	49
a	Block of 4, #1480-83		.65	.75	.75	(4)	3.00	
b	As "a," blk. (engraved) omitted		1,500.00					
c	As "a," blk. (lithographed) omitted		1,500.00					

1464   **1465**

1468

1466   **1467**   **1467a**

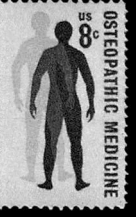

1469   **1470**

1471   **1472**   **1473**   **1474**

1475   **1476**   **1477**

1478   **1479**

1480   **1481**

1482   **1483**   **1483a**

1484

1485

1486

1487

1488

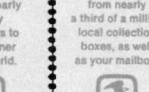

1489

1490

1491

1492

1493

Nearly 27 billion
U.S. stamps
are sold yearly
to carry
your letters to
every corner
of the world.

People Serving You

Mail is
picked up
from nearly
a third of a million
local collection
boxes, as well
as your mailbox.

People Serving You

More than
87 billion letters
and packages
are handled
yearly—almost
300 million every
delivery day.

People Serving You

The People
in your
Postal Service
handle and
deliver more
than 500 million
packages yearly.

People Serving You

Thousands of
machines, buildings,
and vehicles
must be operated
and maintained
to keep your
mail moving.

People Serving You

1494

1495

1496

1497

1498

The skill
of sorting mail
manually
is still vital
to delivery of
your mail.

People Serving You

Employees
use modern, high-
speed equipment
to sort and process
huge volumes of
mail in central
locations.

People Serving You

Thirteen billion
pounds of mail are
handled yearly by
postal employees
as they speed
your letters and
packages.

People Serving You

Our customers
include
54 million urban
and 12 million
rural families,
plus 9 million
businesses.

People Serving You

Employees
cover
4 million miles
each delivery day
to bring mail to
your home or
business.

People Serving You

ssues of 1973		Un	U	PB	#	FDC	Q(M)
American Arts Issue, Perf 11							
1484 8¢ George Gershwin and Scene							
from "Porgy and Bess"	02/28/73	.15	.15	1.75	(12)	1.00	139
a Vertical pair, imperf. horizontally		250.00					
1485 8¢ Robinson Jeffers, Man and Children							
of Carmel with Burro	08/13/73	.15	.15	1.75	(12)	1.00	128
a Vertical pair, imperf. horizontally		250.00					
1486 8¢ Henry Ossawa Tanner,							
Palette and Rainbow	09/10/73	.15	.15	1.75	(12)	1.00	146
1487 8¢ Willa Cather, Pioneer Family							
and Covered Wagon	09/20/73	.15	.15	1.75	(12)	1.00	140
a Vertical pair, imperf. horizontally		275.00					
1488 8¢ Nicolaus Copernicus	04/23/73	.15	.15	.65	(4)	1.75	159
a Orange omitted		1,000.00					
b Black omitted		1,300.00					
Postal Service Employees Issue, Perf. 10.5 x 11							
1489 8¢ Stamp Counter	04/30/73	.15	.15			1.00	49
1490 8¢ Mail Collection	04/30/73	.15	.15			1.00	49
1491 8¢ Letter Facing on Conveyor	04/30/73	.15	.15			1.00	49
1492 8¢ Parcel Post Sorting	04/30/73	.15	.15			1.00	49
1493 8¢ Mail Canceling	04/30/73	.15	.15			1.00	49
1494 8¢ Manual Letter Routing	04/30/73	.15	.15			1.00	49
1495 8¢ Electronic Letter Routing	04/30/73	.15	.15			1.00	49
1496 8¢ Loading Mail on Truck	04/30/73	.15	.15			1.00	49
1497 8¢ Carrier Delivering Mail	04/30/73	.15	.15			1.00	49
1498 8¢ Rural Mail Delivery	04/30/73	.15	.15			1.00	49
a Strip of 10, #1489-98		1.50	1.75	3.00	(20)	5.00	

#1489-98 were the first United States postage stamps to have printing on the back.
(See also 1559-62.)

Love stamps have become an eagerly anticipated part of the commemorative stamp program—but it all began with one design. In 1973, the U.S. Postal Service featured the work of pop artist Robert Indiana on the very first Love stamp. The simple, colorful design was enormously successful, and more than 300

million of the stamps were printed. Indiana's artwork, created in the 1960s, became widely recognized by the public, earning a place in philatelic history as well.

Today, the iconic design that was featured on the 1973 Love stamp appears in a wide variety of forms—including a popular sculpture at Kennedy Plaza in Philadelphia, "the city of brotherly love." Robert Indiana's works can be found in many museums and public places, including the Whitney Museum of American Art and the Museum of Modern Art in New York, and the Smithsonian Institution in Washington, D.C.

Issues of 1973		Un	U	PB		FDC	Q(M)
Perf. 11							
1499 8¢ Harry S. Truman	05/08/73	.15	.15	.65	(4)	1.00	157
Progress in Electronics Issue, (See also #C86)							
1500 6¢ Marconi's Spark							
Coil and Gap	07/10/73	.15	.15	.55	(4)	1.00	53
1501 8¢ Transistors and Printed							
Circuit Board	07/10/73	.15	.15	.70	(4)	1.00	160
a Black omitted		700.00					
b Tan and lilac omitted		1,250.00					
1502 15¢ Microphone, Speaker, Vacuum							
Tube, TV Camera Tube	07/10/73	.30	.15	1.30	(4)	1.00	39
a Black omitted		1,500.00					
1503 8¢ Lyndon B. Johnson	08/27/73	.15	.15	1.90	(12)	1.00	153
a Horizontal pair, imperf. vertically		350.00					
Issues of 1973-74, Rural America Issue							
1504 8¢ Angus and Longhorn Cattle,							
by F.C. Murphy	10/05/73	.15	.15	.65	(4)	1.00	146
a Green and red brown omitted		1,000.00					
b Vertical pair, imperf. between		—					
1505 10¢ Chautauqua Tent and							
Buggies	08/06/74	.20	.15	.85	(4)	1.00	151
1506 10¢ Wheat Fields and Train	08/16/74	.20	.15	.85	(4)	1.00	141
a Black and blue omitted		900.00					
Issues of 1973, Christmas Issue, Perf. 10.5 x 11							
1507 8¢ Small Cowper Madonna,							
by Raphael	11/07/73	.15	.15	1.75	(12)	1.00	885
Pair with full vertical gutter between		—					
1508 8¢ Christmas Tree in							
Needlepoint	11/07/73	.15	.15	1.75	(12)	1.00	940
a Vertical pair, imperf. between		300.00					
Pair with full horizontal gutter between		—					
Issues of 1973-74, Perf. 11 x 10.5							
1509 10¢ 50-Star and							
13-Star Flags	12/08/73	.20	.15	4.25	(20)	1.00	
a Horizontal pair, imperf. between		60.00	—				
b Blue omitted		175.00					
c Imperf. pair		1,150.00					
1510 10¢ Jefferson Memorial	12/14/73	.20	.15	.85	(4)	1.00	
a Untagged (Bureau precanceled)			.20				
b Booklet pane of 5 + label		1.65	.55			2.25	
c Booklet pane of 8		1.65	.70			2.50	
d Booklet pane of 6	08/05/74	5.25	1.00			3.00	
e Vertical pair, imperf. horizontally		525.00					
f Vertical pair, imperf. between		—					

1499

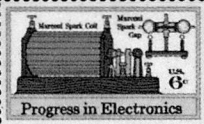

1500

1501

1502

1503

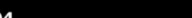

1504

1505

1506

1507

1508

1509

1510

1974

1511   1518

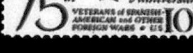

1525

1526

1527

1528   1529

1530   1531   1532   1533

1534   1535   1536   1537   1537a

Issues of 1973-74		Un	U	PB/LP		FDC	Q(M)
1511 10¢ ZIP Code	01/04/74	.20	.15	1.75	(8)	1.00	
a Yellow omitted		65.00					
Pair with full horizontal gutter between		—					
1512-17 Not assigned							
Coil Stamps, Perf. 10 Vertically							
1518 6.3¢ Liberty Bell	10/01/74	.15	.15	.80	(2)	1.00	
a Untagged (Bureau precanceled)			.15	.80	(2)		
b Imperf. pair		225.00		600.00	(2)		
c As "a," imperf. pair			110.00	250.00	(2)		
1519 10¢ red and blue Flags (1509)	12/08/73	.20	.15			1.00	
a Imperf. pair		37.50					
1520 10¢ blue Jefferson Memorial (1510)	12/14/73	.25	.15	.75	(2)	1.00	
a Untagged (Bureau precanceled)			.25				
b Imperf. pair		42.50		70.00	(2)		
1521-24 Not assigned							
Issues of 1974, Perf. 11							
1525 10¢ Veterans of Foreign Wars	03/11/74	.20	.15	.85	(4)	2.00	149
Perf. 10.5 x 11							
1526 10¢ Robert Frost	03/26/74	.20	.15	.85	(4)	1.00	145
Perf. 11							
1527 10¢ Expo '74 World's Fair	04/18/74	.20	.15	2.50	(12)	1.00	135
Perf. 11 x 10.5							
1528 10¢ Horse Racing	05/04/74	.20	.15	2.50	(12)	2.00	156
a Blue omitted		1,000.00					
b Red omitted		—					
Perf. 11							
1529 10¢ Skylab	05/14/74	.20	.15	.85	(4)	1.50	164
a Vertical pair, imperf. between		—					
Universal Postal Union Issue							
1530 10¢ Michelangelo, from "School of Athens," by Raphael	06/06/74	.20	.15			1.00	24
1531 10¢ "Five Feminine Virtues," by Hokusai	06/06/74	.20	.15			1.00	24
1532 10¢ "Old Scraps," by John Fredrick Peto	06/06/74	.20	.15			1.00	24
1533 10¢ "The Lovely Reader," by Jean Etienne Liotard	06/06/74	.20	.15			1.00	24
1534 10¢ "Lady Writing Letter," by Gerard Terborch	06/06/74	.20	.15			1.00	24
1535 10¢ Inkwell and Quill, from "Boy with a Top," by Jean-Baptiste Simeon Chardin	06/06/74	.20	.15			1.00	24
1536 10¢ Mrs. John Douglas, by Thomas Gainsborough	06/06/74	.20	.15			1.00	24
1537 10¢ Don Antonio Noriega, by Francisco de Goya	06/06/74	.20	.15			1.00	24
a Block of 8, #1530-37		1.60	1.60	3.50	(16)	4.00	
b As "a," imperf. vertically		7,500.00					

	ssues of 1974		Un	U	PE		FDC	Q(M)
	Mineral Heritage Issue, Perf. 11							
1538	10¢ Petrified Wood	06/13/74	.20	.15			1.00	42
a	Light blue and yellow omitted		—					
1539	10¢ Tourmaline	06/13/74	.20	.15			1.00	42
a	Light blue omitted		—					
b	Black and purple omitted		—					
1540	10¢ Amethyst	06/13/74	.20	.15			1.00	42
a	Light blue and yellow omitted		—					
1541	10¢ Rhodochrosite	06/13/74	.20	.15			1.00	42
a	Block of 4, #1538-41		.80	.90	.90	(4)	2.50	
b	As "a," light blue and yellow omitted		2,000.00					
c	Light blue omitted		—					
d	Black and red omitted		—					
1542	10¢ First Kentucky Settlement-Ft. Harrod	06/15/74	.20	.15	.85	(4)	1.00	156
a	Dull black omitted		900.00					
b	Green, black and blue omitted		3,750.00					
c	Green omitted		—					
d	Green and black omitted		—					
	American Bicentennial Issue, First Continental Congress							
1543	10¢ Carpenters' Hall	07/04/74	.20	.15			1.00	49
1544	10¢ "We Ask but for Peace, Liberty and Safety"	07/04/74	.20	.15			1.00	49
1545	10¢ "Deriving Their Just Powers from the Consent of the Governed"	07/04/74	.20	.15			1.00	49
1546	10¢ Independence Hall	07/04/74	.20	.15			1.00	49
a	Block of 4, #1543-46		.80	.90	.90	(4)	2.75	
1547	10¢ Energy Conservation	09/23/74	.20	.15	.85	(4)	1.00	149
a	Blue and orange omitted		900.00					
b	Orange and green omitted		750.00					
c	Green omitted		750.00					
	American Folklore Issue, The Legend of Sleepy Hollow							
1548	10¢ Headless Horseman and Ichabod Crane	10/10/74	.20	.15	.85	(4)	2.00	157
1549	10¢ Retarded Children	10/12/74	.20	.15	.85	(4)	1.00	150
	Christmas Issue, Perf. 10.5 x 11							
1550	10¢ Angel from Perussis Altarpiece	10/23/74	.20	.15	2.10	(10)	1.00	835
	Perf. 11 x 10.5							
1551	10¢ "The Road-Winter," by Currier and Ives	10/23/74	.20	.15	2.50	(12)	1.00	883
	Precanceled Self-Adhesive, Imperf.							
1552	10¢ Dove Weather Vane atop Mount Vernon	11/15/74	.20	.15	4.25	(20)	1.00	213
	Issues of 1975, American Arts Issue, Perf. 10.5 x 11							
1553	10¢ Benjamin West, Self-Portrait	02/10/75	.20	.15	2.10	(10)	1.00	157
	Perf. 11							
1554	10¢ Paul Laurence Dunbar and Lamp	05/01/75	.20	.15	2.10	(10)	1.00	146
a	Imperf. pair		1,300.00					
1555	10¢ D.W. Griffith and Motion-Picture Camera	05/27/75	.20	.15	.85	(4)	1.00	149
a	Brown omitted		750.00					

1538

1539

1540

1541   1541a

1542

1543   1544

1545   1546   1546a

1547

1548

1549

1550

1551

1552

1553

1554

1555

1556

1557

1558

1559

1560

1561

YOUTHFUL HEROINE
On the dark night of April 26, 1777, 16-year-old Sybil Ludington rode her horse "Star" alone through the Connecticut countryside rallying her father's militia to repel a raid by the British on Danbury.

GALLANT SOLDIER
The conspicuously courageous actions of black foot soldier Salem Poor at the Battle of Bunker Hill on June 17, 1775, earned him citations for his bravery and leadership ability.

FINANCIAL HERO
Businessman and broker Haym Salomon was responsible for raising most of the money needed to finance the American Revolution and later to save the new nation from collapse.

1562

1563

1564

FIGHTER EXTRAORDINARY
Peter Francisco's strength and bravery made him a legend around campfires. He fought with distinction at Brandywine, Yorktown and Guilford Court House.

1565 **1566** **1569**

1570 **1569a**

1567 **1568** **1568a**

ssues of 1975		Un	U	PB	#	FDC	Q(M)
Space Issues, Perf. 11							
1556	10¢ Pioneer 10 Passing						
	Jupiter 02/28/75	.20	.15	.85	(4)	2.00	174
a	Red and yellow omitted	1,500.00					
b	Blue omitted	950.00					
1557	10¢ Mariner 10, Venus						
	and Mercury 04/04/75	.20	.15	.85	(4)	2.00	159
a	Red omitted	600.00					
b	Ultramarine and bister omitted	2,000.00					
1558	10¢ Collective Bargaining 03/13/75	.20	.15	1.75	(8)	1.00	153
	Imperfs. of #1558 exist from printer's waste						
American Bicentennial Issue, Contributors to the Cause, Perf. 11 x 10.5							
1559	8¢ Sybil Ludington						
	Riding Horse 03/25/75	.15	.15	1.50	(10)	1.00	63
a	Back inscription omitted	275.00					
1560	10¢ Salem Poor Carrying						
	Musket 03/25/75	.20	.15	2.10	(10)	1.00	158
a	Back inscription omitted	225.00					
1561	10¢ Haym Salomon						
	Figuring Accounts 03/25/75	.20	.15	2.10	(10)	1.00	167
a	Back inscription omitted	250.00					
b	Red omitted	250.00					
1562	18¢ Peter Francisco						
	Shouldering Cannon 03/25/75	.35	.20	3.60	(10)	1.00	45
Battle of Lexington & Concord, Perf. 11							
1563	10¢ "Birth of Liberty,"						
	by Henry Sandham 04/19/75	.20	.15	2.50	(12)	1.00	144
a	Vertical pair, imperf. horizontally	425.00					
Battle of Bunker Hill							
1564	10¢ "Battle of Bunker						
	Hill," by John Trumbull 06/17/75	.20	.15	2.50	(12)	1.00	140
Military Uniforms							
1565	10¢ Soldier with Flintlock						
	Musket, Uniform Button 07/04/75	.20	.15			1.00	45
1566	10¢ Sailor with Grappling						
	Hook, First Navy Jack, 1775 07/04/75	.20	.15			1.00	45
1567	10¢ Marine with Musket,						
	Full-Rigged Ship 07/04/75	.20	.15			1.00	45
1568	10¢ Militiaman with						
	Musket, Powder Horn 07/04/75	.20	.15			1.00	45
a	Block of 4, #1565-68	.85	.90	2.50	(12)	2.50	
Apollo Soyuz Space Issue							
1569	10¢ Apollo and Soyuz						
	after Docking and Earth 07/15/75	.20	.15			3.00	81
a	Attached pair, #1569-70	.45	.40	2.50	(12)	5.00	
b	As "a", tagging omitted	30.00					
c	As "a," vertical pair,						
	imperf. horizontally	2,000.00					
	Pair with full horizontal gutter between	—					
1570	10¢ Spacecraft before Docking,						
	Earth and Project Emblem 07/15/75	.20	.15			3.00	81

	ssues of 1975		Un	U	PB		FDC	Q(M)
	Perf. 11 x 10.5							
1571	10¢ International							
	Women's Year	08/26/75	.20	.15	1.30	(6)	1.00	146
	Postal Service Bicentennial Issue							
1572	10¢ Stagecoach and							
	Trailer Truck	09/03/75	.20	.15			1.00	42
1573	10¢ Old and New							
	Locomotives	09/03/75	.20	.15			1.00	42
1574	10¢ Early Mail Plane and Jet	09/03/75	.20	.15			1.00	42
1575	10¢ Satellite for Mailgrams	09/03/75	.20	.15			1.00	42
a	Block of 4, #1572-75		.85	.90	2.50	(12)	1.25	
b	As "a," red "10¢" omitted		9,500.00					
	Perf. 11							
1576	10¢ World Peace Through Law	09/29/75	.20	.15	.85	(4)	1.25	147
	Banking and Commerce Issue							
1577	10¢ Engine Turning, Indian Head							
	Penny and Morgan Silver Dollar	10/06/75	.20	.15			1.00	73
a	Attached pair, #1577-78		.40	.40	.85	(4)	1.25	
b	Brown and blue omitted		2,250.00					
c	As "a," brn., blue and yel. omitted		2,750.00					
1578	10¢ Seated Liberty Quarter, $20							
	Gold Piece and Engine Turning	10/06/75	.20	.15			1.00	73
	Christmas Issue							
1579	(10¢) Madonna and Child,							
	by Domenico Ghirlandaio	10/14/75	.20	.15	2.50	(12)	1.00	739
a	Imperf. pair		110.00					
	Plate flaw ("d" damaged)		5.00	—				
1580	(10¢) Christmas Card,							
	by Louis Prang, 1878	10/14/75	.20	.15	2.50	(12)	1.00	879
a	Imperf. pair		120.00					
b	Perf. 10.5 x 11		.60	.15	15.00	(12)		
	Issues of 1975-81, Americana Issue, Perf. 11 x 10.5 (Designs 18.5 x 22.5mm; #1590-90a, 17.5 x 20mm; see also 1606, 1608, 1610-19, 1622-23, 1625, 1811, 1813, 1816)							
1581	1¢ Inkwell & Quill	12/08/77	.15	.15	.25	(4)	1.00	
a	Untagged (Bureau precanceled)			.15				
1582	2¢ Speaker's Stand	12/08/77	.15	.15	.25	(4)	1.00	
a	Untagged (Bureau precanceled)			.15				
1583	Not assigned							
1584	3¢ Early Ballot Box	12/08/77	.15	.15	.30	(4)	1.00	
a	Untagged (Bureau precanceled)			.15				
1585	4¢ Books, Eyeglasses	12/08/77	.15	.15	.40	(4)	1.00	
a	Untagged (Bureau precanceled)			1.25				
1586-89	Not assigned							
	Booklet Stamp							
1590	9¢ Capitol Dome (1591), single from							
	booklet (1623a)	03/11/77	.45	.20			1.00	
	Booklet Stamp, Perf. 10							
a	Single (1591) from booklet (1623c)		20.00	12.50				
	#1590 is on white paper; #1591 is on gray paper.							
	Perf. 11 x 10.5							
1591	9¢ Capitol Dome	11/24/75	.20	.15	.85	(4)	1.00	
a	Untagged (Bureau precanceled)			.20				
1592	10¢ Contemplation of Justice	11/17/77	.20	.15	.90	(4)	1.00	
a	Untagged (Bureau precanceled)			.25				
1593	11¢ Printing Press	11/13/75	.20	.15	.90	(4)	1.00	
1594	12¢ Torch	04/08/81	.25	.15	1.25	(4)	1.00	

1571

1572 **1573**

1574 **1575** **1575a**

1576

1577 **1578** **1577a**

1579

1580

1581 **1582**

1584 **1585**

1591 **1592**

1593 **1594**

1596   **1595**

1597   **1599**

1603   **1604**

1605   **1606**

1608   **1610**

1611   **1612**

1613   **1614**   **1615**   **1615C**

	Issues of 1975-79		Un	U	PB/LP	#	FDC

Americana Issue (continued), Perf. 11 x 10.5 (See also #1581-82, 1584-85, 1590-99, 1603-08, 1610-19, 1622-23, 1625, 1811, 1813, 1816)

			Un	U	PB/LP	#	FDC
1595	13¢ Liberty Bell, single from booklet		.25	.15			1.00
a	Booklet pane of 6	10/31/75	1.90	.75			2.00
b	Booklet pane of 7 + label		1.75	.75			2.75
c	Booklet pane of 8		2.00	*1.00*			2.50
d	Booklet pane of 5 + label	04/02/76	1.50	.75			2.25
	Perf. 11						
1596	13¢ Eagle and Shield	12/01/75	.25	.15	3.25	(12)	1.00
a	Imperf. pair		*50.00*	—			
b	Yellow omitted		*200.00*				
1597	15¢ Ft. McHenry Flag	06/30/78	.30	.15	1.90	(6)	1.00
a	Imperf. pair		*20.00*				
b	Gray omitted		*700.00*				
	Booklet Stamp, Perf. 11 x 10.5						
1598	15¢ Ft. McHenry Flag (1597), single from booklet		.35	.15			1.00
a	Booklet pane of 8	06/30/78	3.50	*.80*			2.50
1599	16¢ Head of Liberty	03/31/78	.35	.15	1.90	(4)	1.00
1600-02	Not assigned						
1603	24¢ Old North Church	11/14/75	.45	.15	1.90	(4)	1.00
1604	28¢ Ft. Nisqually	08/11/78	.55	.15	2.40	(4)	1.25
	Dull finish gum		1.10		10.00	(4)	
1605	29¢ Sandy Hook Lighthouse	04/14/78	.55	.15	2.75	(4)	1.50
	Dull finish gum		2.00		15.00	(4)	
1606	30¢ One-Rm. Schoolhouse	08/27/79	.55	.15	2.40	(4)	1.25
1607	Not assigned						
	Perf. 11						
1608	50¢ Whale Oil Lamp	09/11/79	.85	.15	3.75	(4)	1.50
a	Black omitted		*300.00*				
b	Vertical pair, imperf. horizontally		*1,750.00*				
c	Tagging omitted		*10.00*				
1609	Not assigned						
1610	$1 Candle and Rushlight Holder	07/02/79	1.75	.20	7.50	(4)	3.00
a	Brown omitted		*275.00*				
b	Tan, orange and yellow omitted		*350.00*				
c	Brown inverted		*15,000.00*				
1611	$2 Kerosene Table Lamp	11/16/78	3.25	.75	14.00	(4)	5.00
1612	$5 Railroad Lantern	08/23/79	7.50	1.75	31.00	(4)	12.50
	Coil Stamps, Perf. 10 Vertically						
1613	3.1¢ Guitar	10/25/79	.15	.15	1.50	(2)	1.00
a	Untagged (Bureau precanceled)			.50			
b	Imperf. pair		*1,400.00*		*3,600.00*	(2)	
1614	7.7¢ Saxhorns	11/20/76	.20	.15	1.00	(2)	1.00
a	Untagged (Bureau precanceled)			.35			
b	As "a," imperf. pair			*1,600.00*	*4,400.00*	(2)	
1615	7.9¢ Drum	04/23/76	.20	.15	.75	(2)	1.00
a	Untagged (Bureau precanceled)			.20			
b	Imperf. pair		*600.00*				
1615C	8.4¢ Piano	07/13/78	.20	.15	3.25	(2)	1.00
d	Untagged (Bureau precanceled)			.30			
e	As "d," pair, imperf. between			75.00	140.00	(2)	
f	As "d," imperf. pair			17.50	35.00	(2)	

ssues of 1975-81		Un	U	PB/LP	#	FDC
Americana Issue (continued), Perf. 10 Vertically (See also #1581-82, 1584-85, 1590-99, 1603-05, 1811, 1813, 1816)						
1616	9¢ slate green Capitol Dome (1591) 03/05/76	.20	.15	1.00	(2)	1.00
a	Imperf. pair	175.00		400.00	(2)	
b	Untagged (Bureau precanceled)		.35			
c	As "b," imperf. pair	700.00		—	(2)	
1617	10¢ purple Contemplation of Justice (1592) 11/04/77	.20	.15	1.10	(2)	1.00
a	Untagged (Bureau precanceled)		.25			
b	Imperf. pair	70.00		140.00	(2)	
	Dull finish gum	.30		2.75	(2)	
1618	13¢ brown Liberty Bell (1595) 11/25/75	.25	.15	.70	(2)	1.00
a	Untagged (Bureau precanceled)		.45			
b	Imperf. pair	25.00		65.00	(2)	
g	Pair, imperf. between	—				
1618C	15¢ Ft. McHenry Flag (1597) 06/30/78	.40	.15			1.00
d	Imperf. pair	25.00				
e	Pair, imperf. between	150.00				
f	Gray omitted	40.00				
1619	16¢ blue Head of Liberty (1599) 03/31/78	.35	.15	1.50	(2)	1.00
a	Huck Press printing (white background with a bluish tinge, fraction of a millimeter smaller) .50		.15	2.00	(2)	
1620-21	Not assigned					
	Perf. 11 x 10.5					
1622	13¢ Flag over Independence Hall 11/15/75	.25	.15	5.75	(20)	1.00
a	Horizontal pair, imperf. between	55.00				
b	Imperf. pair	1,100.00				
c	Perf. 11 1981	.65	.15	60.00	(20)	
d	As "c," vertical pair, imperf.	150.00				
e	Horizontal pair, imperf. vertically	—				
	Booklet Stamps					
1623	13¢ Flag over Capitol, single from booklet (1623a)	.25	.15			1.00
a	Booklet pane of 8, (1 #1590 and 7 #1623) 03/11/77	2.25	1.10			25.00
	Booklet Stamps, Perf. 10					
b	13¢ Single from booklet	1.00	1.00			
c	Booklet pane of 8, (1 #1590a and 7 #1623b)	26.00	—			12.50
	#1623, 1623b issued only in booklets. All stamps are imperf. at one side or imperf. at one side and bottom.					
	Booklet Stamps, Perf. 11 x 10.5					
d	Attached pair, #1590 and 1623	.70	.70			
	Booklet Stamps, Perf. 10					
e	Attached pair, #1590a and 1623b	22.50	20.00			
1624	Not assigned					
	Coil Stamp, Perf. 10 Vertically					
1625	13¢ Flag over Independence Hall (1622) 11/15/75	.25	.15			1.00
a	Imperf. pair	25.00				

1622

1623a

1976

1632

1629   **1630**   **1631**   **1631a**

BICENTENNIAL ERA 1776-1976   BICENTENNIAL ERA 1776-1976   BICENTENNIAL ERA 1776-1976

1633   **1634**   **1635**

BICENTENNIAL ERA 1776-1976   BICENTENNIAL ERA 1776-1976

1636   **1637**

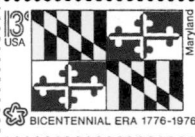

BICENTENNIAL ERA 1776-1976   BICENTENNIAL ERA 1776-1976   BICENTENNIAL ERA 1776-1976

1638   **1639**   **1640**

BICENTENNIAL ERA 1776-1976   BICENTENNIAL ERA 1776-1976

1641   **1642**

BICENTENNIAL ERA 1776-1976   BICENTENNIAL ERA 1776-1976   BICENTENNIAL ERA 1776-1976

1643   **1644**   **1645**

BICENTENNIAL ERA 1776-1976   BICENTENNIAL ERA 1776-1976

1646   **1647**

	ssues of 1976		Un	U	PE		FDC	Q(M)
	American Bicentennial Issue, The Spirit of '76, Perf. 11							
1629	13¢ Drummer Boy	01/01/76	.20	.15			1.25	73
1630	13¢ Old Drummer	01/01/76	.20	.15			1.25	73
1631	13¢ Fife Player	01/01/76	.20	.15			1.25	73
a	Strip of 3, #1629-31		.60	.65	2.50	(12)	2.00	
b	As "a," imperf.		1,300.00					
c	Imperf. pair, #1631		800.00					
1632	13¢ Interphil 76	01/17/76	.20	.15	1.00	(4)	1.00	158
	State Flags							
1633	13¢ Delaware	02/23/76	.25	.20			1.50	9
1634	13¢ Pennsylvania	02/23/76	.25	.20			1.50	9
1635	13¢ New Jersey	02/23/76	.25	.20			1.50	9
1636	13¢ Georgia	02/23/76	.25	.20			1.50	9
1637	13¢ Connecticut	02/23/76	.25	.20			1.50	9
1638	13¢ Massachusetts	02/23/76	.25	.20			1.50	9
1639	13¢ Maryland	02/23/76	.25	.20			1.50	9
1640	13¢ South Carolina	02/23/76	.25	.20			1.50	9
1641	13¢ New Hampshire	02/23/76	.25	.20			1.50	9
1642	13¢ Virginia	02/23/76	.25	.20			1.50	9
1643	13¢ New York	02/23/76	.25	.20			1.50	9
1644	13¢ North Carolina	02/23/76	.25	.20			1.50	9
1645	13¢ Rhode Island	02/23/76	.25	.20			1.50	9
1646	13¢ Vermont	02/23/76	.25	.20			1.50	9
1647	13¢ Kentucky	02/23/76	.25	.20			1.50	9

During World War II, the United States, called by President Franklin D. Roosevelt the "arsenal of democracy," faced the daunting task of supplying and financing the lion's share of the Allied war effort. To help finance the war, the Treasury Department sold war bonds. These were essentially loans by a citizen to the government.

Purchasing bonds allowed Americans on the home front to participate actively in the war effort. Aggressive campaigns used many methods to sell war bonds, such as rallies, celebrity caravans, posters, and booths in public places.

In 1966 the U.S. Post Office Department issued a stamp commemorating the 25th anniversary of **U.S. Savings Bonds**. The stamp also honored Americans who served in the armed forces. It was illustrated by the late Stevan Dohanos, whose many projects for the U.S. Post Office Department and U.S. Postal Service included John F. Kennedy (1967) and Vietnam Veterans (1979).

	ssues of 1976		Un	U	DC	Q(M)
	American Bicentennial Issue (continued), State Flags					
1648	13¢ Tennessee	02/23/76	.25	.20	1.50	9
1649	13¢ Ohio	02/23/76	.25	.20	1.50	9
1650	13¢ Louisiana	02/23/76	.25	.20	1.50	9
1651	13¢ Indiana	02/23/76	.25	.20	1.50	9
1652	13¢ Mississippi	02/23/76	.25	.20	1.50	9
1653	13¢ Illinois	02/23/76	.25	.20	1.50	9
1654	13¢ Alabama	02/23/76	.25	.20	1.50	9
1655	13¢ Maine	02/23/76	.25	.20	1.50	9
1656	13¢ Missouri	02/23/76	.25	.20	1.50	9
1657	13¢ Arkansas	02/23/76	.25	.20	1.50	9
1658	13¢ Michigan	02/23/76	.25	.20	1.50	9
1659	13¢ Florida	02/23/76	.25	.20	1.50	9
1660	13¢ Texas	02/23/76	.25	.20	1.50	9
1661	13¢ Iowa	02/23/76	.25	.20	1.50	9
1662	13¢ Wisconsin	02/23/76	.25	.20	1.50	9
1663	13¢ California	02/23/76	.25	.20	1.50	9
1664	13¢ Minnesota	02/23/76	.25	.20	1.50	9
1665	13¢ Oregon	02/23/76	.25	.20	1.50	9
1666	13¢ Kansas	02/23/76	.25	.20	1.50	9
1967	13¢ West Virginia	02/23/76	.25	.20	1.50	9

In 1970, the 350th anniversary of the **Pilgrims' Landing in America**, the Postal Service issued a stamp celebrating this event. The story of the *Mayflower* and its passengers has become a familiar part of American history: colonists braving a dangerous transatlantic journey in order to practice their religion in peace, the generous Native American, Squanto, sharing his knowledge of fishing and planting crops, and the Mayflower Compact, an early expression of American democracy.

Seeking religious freedom, the Pilgrims, an English religious group, decided to relocate to the New World. Accompanied by another group of settlers recruited by English merchants, the Pilgrims departed for Virginia in 1620. After a harrowing voyage across the North Atlantic, the Pilgrims arrived in what became Massachusetts, far from their original destination.

Because they ended up outside the bounds of Virginia, some of the settlers thought that they were no longer obligated to accept the authority of the Pilgrim leaders. Recognizing the need for a framework of government, the Pilgrims drew up the Mayflower Compact, which established a "civil body politic" to enact "just and equal laws." All the male passengers signed it. From this auspicious beginning the Pilgrims became an important part of America's democratic history and tradition.

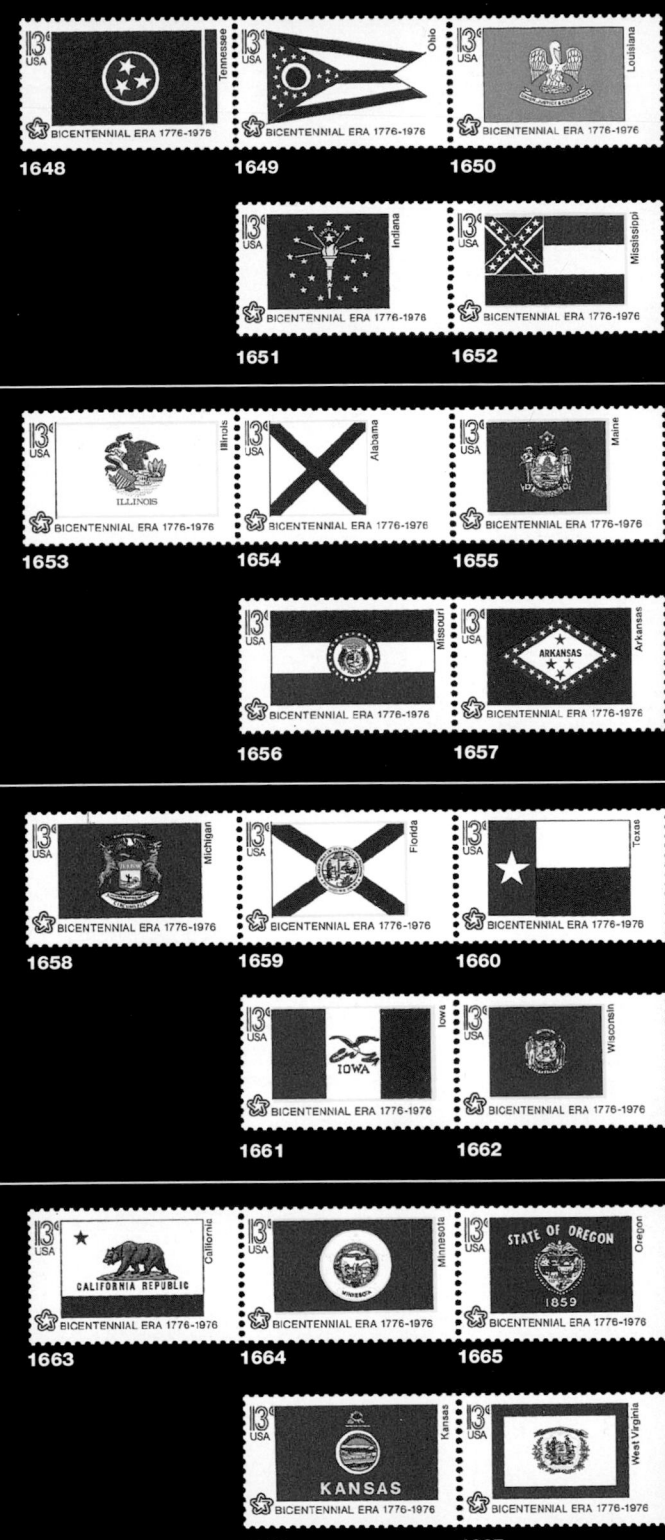

1648

1649

1650

1651

1652

1653

1654

1655

1656

1657

1658

1659

1660

1661

1662

1663

1664

1665

1666

1667

13¢ USA Nevada — BICENTENNIAL ERA 1776-1976
1668

13¢ USA Nebraska — BICENTENNIAL ERA 1776-1976
1669

13¢ USA Colorado — BICENTENNIAL ERA 1776-1976
1670

13¢ USA North Dakota — BICENTENNIAL ERA 1776-1976
1671

13¢ USA South Dakota — BICENTENNIAL ERA 1776-1976
1672

13¢ USA Montana — BICENTENNIAL ERA 1776-1976
1673

13¢ USA Washington — BICENTENNIAL ERA 1776-1976
1674

13¢ USA Idaho — BICENTENNIAL ERA 1776-1976
1675

13¢ USA Wyoming — BICENTENNIAL ERA 1776-1976
1676

13¢ USA Utah — BICENTENNIAL ERA 1776-1976
1677

13¢ USA Oklahoma — OKLAHOMA — BICENTENNIAL ERA 1776-1976
1678

13¢ USA New Mexico — BICENTENNIAL ERA 1776-1976
1679

13¢ USA Arizona — BICENTENNIAL ERA 1776-1976
1680

13¢ USA Alaska — BICENTENNIAL ERA 1776-1976
1681

13¢ USA Hawaii — BICENTENNIAL ERA 1776-1976
1682

Issues of 1976		Un	U	FDC	Q(M)
American Bicentennial Issue (continued), State Flags					
1668	13¢ Nevada	02/23/76	.25	.20	1.50	9
1669	13¢ Nebraska	02/23/76	.25	.20	1.50	9
1670	13¢ Colorado	02/23/76	.25	.20	1.50	9
1671	13¢ North Dakota	02/23/76	.25	.20	1.50	9
1672	13¢ South Dakota	02/23/76	.25	.20	1.50	9
1673	13¢ Montana	02/23/76	.25	.20	1.50	9
1674	13¢ Washington	02/23/76	.25	.20	1.50	9
1675	13¢ Idaho	02/23/76	.25	.20	1.50	9
1676	13¢ Wyoming	02/23/76	.25	.20	1.50	9
1677	13¢ Utah	02/23/76	.25	.20	1.50	9
1678	13¢ Oklahoma	02/23/76	.25	.20	1.50	9
1679	13¢ New Mexico	02/23/76	.25	.20	1.50	9
1680	13¢ Arizona	02/23/76	.25	.20	1.50	9
1681	13¢ Alaska	02/23/76	.25	.20	1.50	9
1682	13¢ Hawaii	02/23/76	.25	.20	1.50	9
a	Pane of 50, #1633-82		13.00	—	27.50	

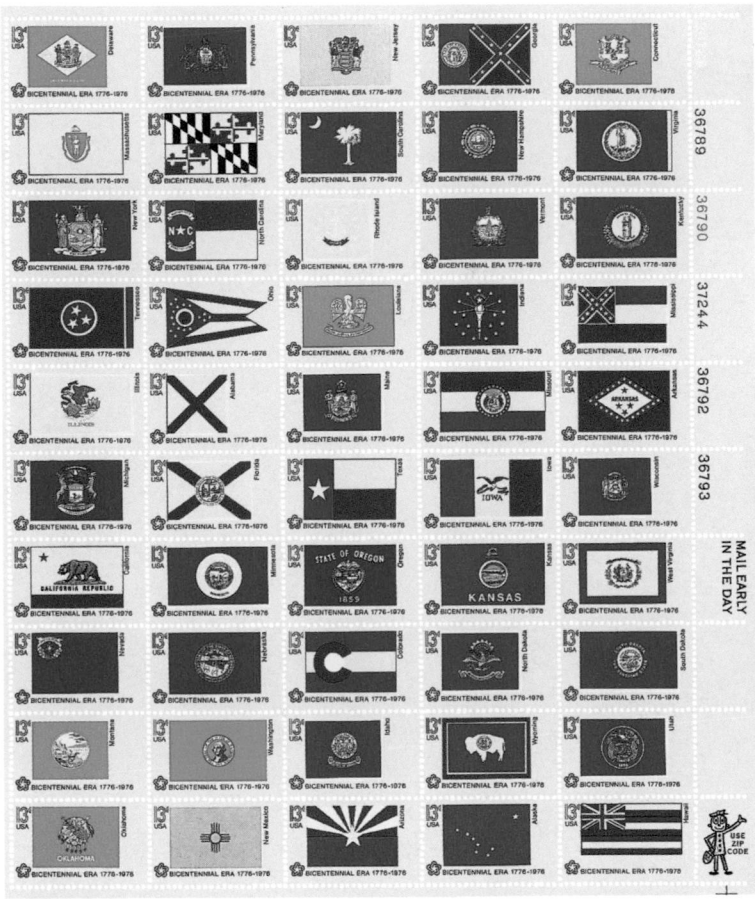

Example of 1682a

1976

	ssues of 1976		Un	U	PB		FDC	Q(M)
1683	13¢ Telephone Centennial	03/10/76	.25	.15	1.10	(4)	1.00	158
1684	13¢ Commercial Aviation	03/19/76	.25	.15	2.75	(10)	1.00	156
1685	13¢ Chemistry	04/06/76	.25	.15	3.25	(12)	2.00	158
	Pair with full vertical gutter between		—					

American Bicentennial Issue Souvenir Sheets, 5 stamps each, Perf. 11

1686	13¢ The Surrender of Lord Cornwallis at Yorktown, by John Trumbull	05/29/76	3.25	—			6.00	2
a	13¢ Two American Officers		.45	.40				2
b	13¢ Gen. Benjamin Lincoln		.45	.40				2
c	13¢ George Washington		.45	.40				2
d	13¢ John Trumbull, Col. David Cobb, General Friedrich von Steuben, Marquis de Lafayette and Thomas Nelson		.45	.40				2
e	13¢ Alexander Hamilton, John Laurens and Walter Stewart		.45	.40				2
f	"USA/13¢" omitted on "b," "c" and "d," imperf.		—	2,250.00				
g	"USA/13¢" omitted on "a" and "e"		450.00	—				
h	Imperf. (untagged)			2,250.00				
i	"USA/13¢" omitted on "b," "c" and "d"		450.00					
j	"USA/13¢" double on "b"		—					
k	"USA/13¢" omitted on "c" and "d"		800.00					
l	"USA/13¢" omitted on "e"		500.00					
m	"USA/13¢" omitted, imperf. (untagged)			—				
n	As "g", imperf., untagged			—				
1687	18¢ The Declaration of Independence, 4 July 1776 at Philadelphia, by John Trumbull	05/29/76	4.25	—			7.50	2
a	18¢ John Adams, Roger Sherman and Robert R. Livingston		.55	.55				2
b	18¢ Thomas Jefferson and Benjamin Franklin		.55	.55				2
c	18¢ Thomas Nelson, Jr., Francis Lewis, John Witherspoon and Samuel Huntington		.55	.55				2
d	18¢ John Hancock and Charles Thomson		.55	.55				2
e	18¢ George Read, John Dickinson and Edward Rutledge		.55	.55				2
f	Design and marginal inscriptions omitted		3,000.00					
g	"USA/18¢" omitted on "a" and "c"		800.00					
h	"USA/18¢" omitted on "b," "d" and "e"		500.00					
i	"USA/18¢" omitted on "d"		550.00	500.00				
j	Black omitted in design		2,000.00					
k	"USA/18¢" omitted, imperf. (untagged)		3,000.00					
m	"USA/18¢" omitted on "b" and "e"		500.00					

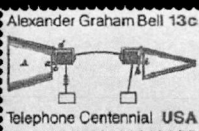

1683   **1684**   **1685**

The Surrender of Lord Cornwallis at Yorktown
From a Painting by John Trumbull

1686

The Declaration of Independence, 4 July 1776 at Philadelphia
From a Painting by John Trumbull

1687

Washington Crossing the Delaware
From a Painting by Emanuel Leutze / Eastman Johnson

1688

Washington Reviewing His Ragged Army at Valley Forge
From a Painting by William T. Trego

1689

ssues of 1976		Un	U	FDC	Q(M)
American Bicentennial Issue (continued) Souvenir Sheets, 5 stamps each					
1688	24¢ Washington Crossing the Delaware, by Emanuel Leutze/ Eastman Johnson 05/29/76	5.25	—	8.50	2
a	24¢ Boatmen	.70	.70		2
b	24¢ George Washington	.70	.70		2
c	24¢ Flagbearer	.70	.70		2
d	24¢ Men in Boat	.70	.70		2
e	24¢ Steersman and Men on Shore	.70	.70		2
f	"USA/24¢" omitted, imperf.	3,500.00			
g	"USA/24¢" omitted on "d" and "e"	500.00	450.00		
h	Design and marginal inscriptions omitted	3,250.00			
i	"USA/24¢" omitted on "a," "b" and "c"	500.00	—		
j	Imperf. (untagged)	3,000.00			
k	"USA/24¢" inverted on "d" and "e"	—			
1689	31¢ Washington Reviewing His Ragged Army at Valley Forge, by William T. Trego 05/29/76	6.25	—	9.50	2
a	31¢ Two Officers	.85	.85		2
b	31¢ George Washington	.85	.85		2
c	31¢ Officer and Brown Horse	.85	.85		2
d	31¢ White Horse and Officer	.85	.85		2
e	31¢ Three Soldiers	.85	.85		2
f	"USA/31¢" omitted, imperf.	2,750.00			
g	"USA/31¢" omitted on "a" and "c"	450.00			
h	"USA/31¢" omitted on "b," "d" and "e"	450.00	—		
i	"USA/31¢" omitted on "e"	500.00			
j	Black omitted in design	2,000.00			
k	Imperf. (untagged)		2,250.00		
l	"USA/31¢" omitted on "b" and "d"	—			
m	"USA/31¢" omitted on "a," "c" and "e"	—			
n	As "m," imperf. (untagged)	—			
p	As "h," imperf. (untagged)		2,500.00		
q	As "g," imperf. (untagged)	2,750.00			
r	"USA/31¢" omitted on "d" & "e"	—			
s	As "f", untagged	2,250.00			

	Issues of 1976		Un	U	PB		FDC	Q(M)
	American Bicentennial Issue, Benjamin Franklin, Perf. 11							
1690	13¢ Bust of Franklin, Map							
	of North America, 1776	06/01/76	.25	.15	1.10	(4)	1.00	165
a	Light blue omitted		300.00					
	Declaration of Independence, by John Trumbull							
1691	13¢ Delegates	07/04/76	.25	.15			1.00	41
1692	13¢ Delegates and John Adams	07/04/76	.25	.15			1.00	41
1693	13¢ Roger Sherman, Robert R.							
	Livingston, Thomas Jefferson							
	and Benjamin Franklin	07/04/76	.25	.15			1.00	41
1694	13¢ John Hancock, Charles							
	Thomson, George Read,							
	John Dickinson and							
	Edward Rutledge	07/04/76	.25	.15			1.00	41
a	Strip of 4, #1691-94		1.00	1.10	5.50	(20)	2.00	
	Olympic Games Issue							
1695	13¢ Diver and Olympic Rings	07/16/76	.25	.15			1.00	46
1696	13¢ Skier and Olympic Rings	07/16/76	.25	.15			1.00	46
1697	13¢ Runner and Olympic							
	Rings	07/16/76	.25	.15			1.00	46
1698	13¢ Skater and Olympic							
	Rings	07/16/76	.25	.15			1.00	46
a	Block of 4, #1695-98		1.10	1.10	3.25	(12)	2.00	
b	As "a," imperf.		700.00					
1699	13¢ Clara Maass	08/18/76	.25	.15	3.25	(12)	2.00	131
a	Horizontal pair, imperf. vertically		475.00					
1700	13¢ Adolph S. Ochs	09/18/76	.25	.15	1.10	(4)	1.00	158
	Christmas Issue							
1701	13¢ Nativity, by							
	John Singleton Copley	10/27/76	.25	.15	3.25	(12)	1.00	810
a	Imperf. pair		100.00					
1702	13¢ "Winter Pastime,"							
	by Nathaniel Currier	10/27/76	.25	.15	2.75	(10)	1.00	482*
a	Imperf. pair		100.00					
	*Includes #1703 printing							
1703	13¢ as #1702	10/27/76	.25	.15	6.00	(20)	1.00	
a	Imperf. pair		110.00					
b	Vertical pair, imperf. between		—					
c	Tagging omitted		12.50					

#1702 has overall tagging. Lettering at base is black and usually ½mm below design. As a rule, no "snowflaking" in sky or pond. Pane of 50 has margins on 4 sides with slogans. #1703 has block tagging the size of the printed area. Lettering at base is gray-black and usually ¾mm below design. "Snowflaking" generally in sky and pond. Pane of 50 has margin only at right or left and no slogans.

	Issues of 1977, American Bicentennial Issue, Washington at Princeton							
1704	13¢ Washington, Nassau Hall,							
	Cannon and 13-star Flag, by							
	Charles Willson Peale	01/03/77	.25	.15	2.75	(10)	1.00	150
a	Horizontal pair, imperf. vertically		550.00					
1705	13¢ Sound Recording	03/23/77	.25	.15	1.10	(4)	1.00	177

1690

JULY 4,1776 JULY 4,1776 JULY 4,1776 JULY 4,1776

1691　　　　1692　　　　1693　　　　1694　1694a

1695　　　　1696

1699

1700

1697　　　　1698　　1698a

1701　　　　　　1702　　　　　　1703

1704

1705

1706 **1707**

1708 **1709** **1709a**

1710

1711

1712 **1713**

1714 **1715** **1715a**

1716

1717 **1718**

1719 **1720** **1720a**

1721

ssues of 1977			Un	U	PB		FDC	Q(M)
American Folk Art Issue, Pueblo Pottery, Perf. 11								
1706	13¢ Zia Pot	04/13/77	.25	.15			1.00	49
1707	13¢ San Ildefonso Pot	04/13/77	.25	.15			1.00	49
1708	13¢ Hopi Pot	04/13/77	.25	.15			1.00	49
1709	13¢ Acoma Pot	04/13/77	.25	.15			1.00	49
a	Block of 4, #1706-09		1.00	1.00	2.75	(10)	2.00	
b	As "a," imperf. vertically		2,500.00					
1710	13¢ Solo Transatlantic Flight	05/20/77	.25	.15	3.25	(12)	3.00	209
a	Imperf. pair		1,250.00					
1711	13¢ Colorado Statehood	05/21/77	.25	.15	3.25	(12)	1.00	192
a	Horizontal pair, imperf. between		600.00					
b	Horizontal pair, imperf. vertically		900.00					
c	Perf. 11.2		.35	.25				
	Butterfly Issue							
1712	13¢ Swallowtail	06/06/77	.25	.15			1.00	55
1713	13¢ Checkerspot	06/06/77	.25	.15			1.00	55
1714	13¢ Dogface	06/06/77	.25	.15			1.00	55
1715	13¢ Orange-Tip	06/06/77	.25	.15			1.00	55
a	Block of 4, #1712-15		1.00	1.00	3.25	(12)	2.00	
b	As "a," imperf. horizontally		15,000.00					
	American Bicentennial Issue, Lafayette's Landing in South Carolina							
1716	13¢ Marquis de Lafayette	06/13/77	.25	.15	1.10	(4)	1.00	160
	Skilled Hands for Independence							
1717	13¢ Seamstress	07/04/77	.25	.15			1.00	47
1718	13¢ Blacksmith	07/04/77	.25	.15			1.00	47
1719	13¢ Wheelwright	07/04/77	.25	.15			1.00	47
1720	13¢ Leatherworker	07/04/77	.25	.15			1.00	47
a	Block of 4, #1717-20		1.00	1.00	3.25	(12)	1.75	
	Perf. 11 x 10.5							
1721	13¢ Peace Bridge	08/04/77	.25	.15	1.10	(4)	1.00	164

Commemorated on a pair of 1975 postage stamps, the rendezvous between the American Apollo and Soviet Soyuz spacecraft was a diplomatic and techno-logical breakthrough. The stamps' illustrator, Robert McCall, has worked on several space projects for the Postal Service, including stamps depicting Skylab (1974), Pioneer 10 (1975), and the Viking Mission to Mars (1978).

Successfully completing the **Apollo-Soyuz** rendezvous required extensive cooperation between the two nations. Before the docking could take place, these Cold War rivals had to agree on complex cultural and scientific differ-ences: incompatible docking systems, differing cabin pressures, language dif-ferences, and even the name of the mission itself.

The Apollo spacecraft was manned by three American astronauts, Thomas Stafford, Vance Brand, and Donald Slayton, while cosmonauts Aleksey Leonov and Valeriy Kubasov manned the Soyuz. Despite the challenges facing the project, it went off largely without a hitch and the ships remained linked for two days. In perhaps the most significant moment of the mission, the two crews shook hands while millions watched on live television.

2000 Stamp Yearbook

**Look for this year's
2000 STAMP YEARBOOK**
containing a phenomenal 64 pages
and 99 stamps augmented by
beautiful designs and illustrations.

*Get these and dozens of other
commemorative stamps in the*
2000 STAMP YEARBOOK

- *spectacular* Edwin Powell Hubble
- *incomparable* Legends of Baseball
- *awesome* Deep Sea Creatures
- *creative* Stampin' The Future™
- *patriotic* The Stars and Stripes
- *heroic* Distinguished Soldiers
- *glamorous* Edward G. Robinson
- *reflective* Thomas Wolfe and . . .
- *leading this year's issues—*
  The Year 2000 and
  Lunar New Year.

ssues of 1977		Un	U		PB		FDC	Q(M)
American Bicentennial Issue, Battle of Oriskany, Perf. 11								
1722	13¢ Herkimer at Oriskany,							
	by Frederick Yohn	08/06/77	.25	.15	2.75	(10)	1.00	156
	Energy Issue							
1723	13¢ Energy Conservation	10/20/77	.25	.15			1.25	79
a	Attached pair, #1723-24		.50	.50	3.25	(12)	1.25	
1724	13¢ Energy Development	10/20/77	.25	.15			1.25	79
1725	13¢ First Civil Settlement							
	Alta, California	09/09/77	.25	.15	1.10	(4)	1.00	154
	American Bicentennial Issue, Articles of Confederation							
1726	13¢ Members of Continental							
	Congress in Conference	09/30/77	.25	.15	1.10	(4)	1.00	168
1727	13¢ Talking Pictures	10/06/77	.25	.15	1.10	(4)	1.50	157
	American Bicentennial Issue, Surrender at Saratoga							
1728	13¢ Surrender of Burgoyne,							
	by John Trumbull	10/07/77	.25	.15	2.75	(10)	1.00	154
	Christmas Issue							
1729	13¢ Washington at Valley							
	Forge, by J.C. Leyendecker	10/21/77	.25	.15	5.75	(20)	1.00	882
a	Imperf. pair		75.00					
1730	13¢ Rural Mailbox	10/21/77	.25	.15	2.75	(10)	1.00	922
a	Imperf. pair		300.00					
	Issues of 1978							
1731	13¢ Carl Sandburg	01/06/78	.25	.15	1.10	(4)	1.00	157
	Captain Cook Issue							
1732	13¢ Capt. James Cook							
	Alaska, by Nathaniel Dance	01/20/78	.25	.15			2.00	101
1733	13¢ *Resolution* and *Discovery*							
	Hawaii, by John Webber	01/20/78	.25	.15			2.00	101
a	Vertical pair, imperf. horizontally		—					
b	Attached pair, #1732-33		.50	.50	1.10	(4)	3.00	
c	As " b," imperf. between		4,500.00					
1734	13¢ Indian Head Penny	01/11/78	.25	.15	1.25	(4)	1.00	
	Pair with full horizontal gutter between		—					
a	Horizontal pair, imperf. vertically		300.00					
1735	(15¢) "A" Stamp	05/22/78	.25	.15	1.25	(4)	1.00	
a	Imperf. pair		110.00					
b	Vertical pair, imperf. horizontally		750.00					
	Booklet Stamp, Perf. 11 x 10.5							
1736	(15¢) "A" orange Eagle (1735),							
	single from booklet	05/22/78	.25	.15			1.00	
a	Booklet pane of 8	05/22/78	2.25	.90			2.50	
	Roses Booklet Issue, Perf. 10							
1737	15¢ Roses, single from							
	booklet	07/11/78	.25	.15			1.00	
a	Booklet pane of 8	07/11/78	2.25	.90			2.50	
b	As "a," imperf.							
c	As "a," tagging omitted		40.00					

#1736-37 issued only in booklets. All stamps are imperf. on one side or on one side and bottom.

1723

1722

1725

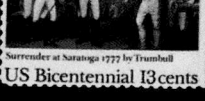

1724   **1723a**

1726   **1727**

1728

1729   **1730**

1732

1731

1733   **1732a**

1734

1735

1737

1738   1739   1740   1741   1742 1742a

1744

1745   1746

1747   1748   1748a

1750

1752

1749   1751   1752a

1753

1754

1755   1756

Issues of 1980			Un	U	PB/LP	#	FDC	Q(M)
Windmills Booklet Issue, Perf. 11								
1738	15¢ Virginia, 1720	02/07/80	.30	.15			1.00	
1739	15¢ Rhode Island, 1790	02/07/80	.30	.15			1.00	
1740	15¢ Massachusetts, 1793	02/07/80	.30	.15			1.00	
1741	15¢ Illinois, 1860	02/07/80	.30	.15			1.00	
1742	15¢ Texas, 1890	02/07/80	.30	.15			1.00	
a	Booklet pane of 10, #1738-42		3.50	3.00			3.50	

#1737-42 issued only in booklets. All stamps are imperf. top or bottom, or top or bottom and right side.

Issues of 1978 (continued), Coil Stamp, Perf. 10 Vertically								
1743	(15¢) "A" orange Eagle (1735)	05/22/78	.25	.15	.65	(2)	1.00	
a	Imperf. pair		100.00		—	(2)		
Black Heritage Issue, Perf. 10.5 x 11								
1744	13¢ Harriet Tubman and Cart Carrying Slaves	02/01/78	.25	.15	3.25	(12)	1.00	157
American Folk Art Issue, Quilts, Perf. 11								
1745	13¢ Basket design, red and orange	03/08/78	.25	.15			1.00	41
1746	13¢ Basket design, red	03/08/78	.25	.15			1.00	41
1747	13¢ Basket design, orange	03/08/78	.25	.15			1.00	41
1748	13¢ Basket design, brown	03/08/78	.25	.15			1.00	41
a	Block of 4, #1745-48		1.00	1.00	3.25	(12)	2.00	
American Dance Issue								
1749	13¢ Ballet	04/26/78	.25	.15			1.00	39
1750	13¢ Theater	04/26/78	.25	.15			1.00	39
1751	13¢ Folk	04/26/78	.25	.15			1.00	39
1752	13¢ Modern	04/26/78	.25	.15			1.00	39
a	Block of 4, #1749-52		1.00	1.00	3.25	(12)	1.75	
American Bicentennial Issue, French Alliance								
1753	13¢ King Louis XVI and Benjamin Franklin, by Charles Gabriel Sauvage	05/04/78	.25	.15	1.10	(4)	1.00	103
Perf. 10.5 x 11								
1754	13¢ Early Cancer Detection	05/18/78	.25	.15	1.10	(4)	1.00	152
Performing Arts Issue, Perf. 11								
1755	13¢ Jimmie Rodgers with Locomotive, Guitar and Brakeman's Cap	05/24/78	.25	.15	3.25	(12)	1.00	95
1756	15¢ George M. Cohan, "Yankee Doodle Dandy" and Stars	07/03/78	.25	.15	3.50	(12)	1.00	152

	ssues of 1978		Un	U	PE		FDC	Q(M)
	CAPEX '78 Souvenir Sheet, Perf. 11							
1757	13¢ Souvenir sheet of 8	06/10/78	2.00	2.00	2.25	(8)	2.75	15
a	13¢ Cardinal		.25	.15				15
b	13¢ Mallard		.25	.15				15
c	13¢ Canada Goose		.25	.15				15
d	13¢ Blue Jay		.25	.15				15
e	13¢ Moose		.25	.15				15
f	13¢ Chipmunk		.25	.15				15
g	13¢ Red Fox		.25	.15				15
h	13¢ Raccoon		.25	.15				15
i	Yellow, green, red, brown and black (litho.) omitted		6,500.00					
1758	15¢ Photography	06/26/78	.30	.15	4.00	(12)	1.50	163
1759	15¢ Viking Missions to Mars	07/20/78	.30	.15	1.35	(4)	2.00	159
	Wildlife Conservation Issue, American Owls							
1760	15¢ Great Gray Owl	08/26/78	.30	.15			1.00	47
1761	15¢ Saw-Whet Owl	08/26/78	.30	.15			1.00	47
1762	15¢ Barred Owl	08/26/78	.30	.15			1.00	47
1763	15¢ Great Horned Owl	08/26/78	.30	.15			1.00	47
a	Block of 4, #1760-63		1.25	1.25	1.40	(4)	2.00	
	American Trees Issue							
1764	15¢ Giant Sequoia	10/09/78	.30	.15			1.00	42
1765	15¢ White Pine	10/09/78	.30	.15			1.00	42
1766	15¢ White Oak	10/09/78	.30	.15			1.00	42
1767	15¢ Gray Birch	10/09/78	.30	.15			1.00	42
a	Block of 4, #1764-67		1.25	1.25	4.00	(12)	2.00	
b	As "a," imperf. horizontally		15,000.00					

On the fateful day in March 1887 when **Anne Sullivan** entered six-year-old **Helen Keller's** dark, silent world, a lifelong bond was forged that changed the way the world looked at the blind, deaf, and mute. The important role these two women played in crusading for the rights of the handicapped was commemorated in 1980 with a stamp by veteran stamp illustrator Paul Calle.

Anne first gave Helen the gift of language when she taught her the word for the cold, wet substance that came flowing from the pump by the house, "w-a-t-e-r." At that moment Helen's voracious appetite began, a hunger for learning that eventually lead to her graduating cum laude from Radcliffe College in 1904. Throughout Helen's education Anne was constantly by her side, acting as her eyes and ears at every level of schooling.

From Helen's graduation until shortly before Anne's death in 1936, the two women traveled around the United States and the world educating the general public and inspiring the disabled. Their early experiences were memorialized in Helen Keller's autobiography, *The Story of My Life*, a Pulitzer Prize-winning play, *The Miracle Worker*, and its acclaimed film adaptation.

a b c d

1757

e f g h

1758

1759

1760 **1761**

1762 **1763** **1763a**

1764 **1765**

1766 **1767** **1767a**

1768

1769

1770

1771

1772

1775   **1776**

1773   **1774**

1777   **1778**   **1778a**

1779   **1780**   **1783**   **1784**

1781   **1782**   **1782a**

1785   **1786**   **1786a**

Issues of 1978		Un	U	PB		FDC	Q(M)
Christmas Issues, Perf. 11							
1768 15¢ Madonna and Child with Cherubim, by Andrea della Robbia	10/18/78	.30	.15	4.00	(12)	1.00	963
a Imperf. pair		90.00					
1769 15¢ Child on Hobby Horse and Christmas Trees	10/18/78	.30	.15	4.00	(12)	1.00	917
a Imperf. pair		100.00					
b Vertical pair, imperf. horizontally		2,250.00					
Pair with full horizontal gutter between		—					
Issues of 1979, Perf. 11							
1770 15¢ Robert F. Kennedy	01/12/79	.30	.15	1.40	(4)	3.00	159
Black Heritage Issue, Martin Luther King, Jr.							
1771 15¢ Martin Luther King, Jr., and Civil Rights Marchers	01/13/79	.30	.15	4.00	(12)	2.50	166
a Imperf. pair		—					
1772 15¢ International Year of the Child	02/15/79	.30	.15	1.40	(4)	1.00	163
Literary Arts Issue, John Steinbeck, Perf. 10.5 x 11							
1773 15¢ John Steinbeck, by Philippe Halsman	02/27/79	.30	.15	1.40	(4)	1.25	155
1774 15¢ Albert Einstein	03/04/79	.30	.15	1.40	(4)	3.50	157
Pair with full horizontal gutter between		—					
American Folk Art Issue, Pennsylvania Toleware, Perf. 11							
1775 15¢ Straight-Spout Coffeepot	04/19/79	.30	.15			1.00	44
1776 15¢ Tea Caddy	04/19/79	.30	.15			1.00	44
1777 15¢ Sugar Bowl	04/19/79	.30	.15			1.00	44
1778 15¢ Curved-Spout Coffeepot	04/19/79	.30	.15			1.00	44
a Block of 4, #1775-78		1.25	1.25	3.25	(10)	2.00	
b As "a," imperf. horizontally		4,250.00					
American Architecture Issue							
1779 15¢ Virginia Rotunda, by Thomas Jefferson	06/04/79	.30	.15			1.00	41
1780 15¢ Baltimore Cathedral, by Benjamin Latrobe	06/04/79	.30	.15			1.00	41
1781 15¢ Boston State House, by Charles Bulfinch	06/04/79	.30	.15			1.00	41
1782 15¢ Philadelphia Exchange, by William Strickland	06/04/79	.30	.15			1.00	41
a Block of 4, #1779-82		1.25	1.25	1.40	(4)	2.00	
Endangered Flora Issue							
1783 15¢ Persistent Trillium	06/07/79	.30	.15			1.00	41
1784 15¢ Hawaiian Wild Broadbean	06/07/79	.30	.15			1.00	41
1785 15¢ Contra Costa Wallflower	06/07/79	.30	.15			1.00	41
1786 15¢ Antioch Dunes Evening Primrose	06/07/79	.30	.15			1.00	41
a Block of 4, #1783-86		1.25	1.25	4.00	(12)	2.00	
b As "a," imperf.		600.00					
As "a," full vertical gutter between		—					

	Issues of 1979		Un	UPE	PE		FDC	Q(M)
1787	15¢ Seeing Eye Dogs	06/15/79	.30	.15	6.50	(20)	1.00	162
a	Imperf. pair		425.00					
1788	15¢ Special Olympics	08/09/79	.30	.15	3.25	(10)	1.00	166
	American Bicentennial Issue, Perf. 11 x 12							
1789	15¢ John Paul Jones,							
	by Charles Willson Peale	09/23/79	.30	.15	3.25	(10)	1.25	160
a	Perf. 11		.30	.15	3.75	(10)		
b	Perf. 12		1,900.00	1,000.00				
c	Vertical pair, imperf. horizontally		200.00					
d	As "a," vertical pair,							
	imperf. horizontally		160.00					
	Numerous varieties of printer's waste of #1789 exist							
	Olympic Summer Games Issue, Perf. 11 (See also #C97)							
1790	10¢ Javelin Thrower	09/05/79	.20	.20	3.00	(12)	1.00	67
1791	15¢ Runner	09/28/79	.30	.15			1.00	47
1792	15¢ Swimmer	09/28/79	.30	.15			1.00	47
1793	15¢ Rowers	09/28/79	.30	.15			1.00	47
1794	15¢ Equestrian Contestant	09/28/79	.30	.15			1.00	47
a	Block of 4, #1791-94		1.25	1.25	4.00	(12)	2.00	
b	As "a," imperf.		1,750.00					
	Issues of 1980, Olympic Winter Games Issue, Perf. 11 x 10.5							
1795	15¢ Speed Skater	02/01/80	.35	.15			1.00	52
1796	15¢ Downhill Skier	02/01/80	.35	.15			1.00	52
1797	15¢ Ski Jumper	02/01/80	.35	.15			1.00	52
1798	15¢ Hockey Goaltender	02/01/80	.35	.15			1.00	52
a	Perf. 11		1.05	—				
b	Block of 4, #1795-98		1.50	1.40	4.50	(12)	2.00	
c	Block of 4, #1795a-98a		4.25	—	13.00	(12)		
	Issues of 1979 (continued), Christmas Issue, Perf. 11							
1799	15¢ Virgin and Child with							
	Cherubim, by Gerard David	10/18/79	.30	.15	4.00	(12)	1.00	874
a	Imperf. pair		100.00					
b	Vertical pair, imperf. horizontally		700.00					
c	pair, imperf. between		2,250.00					
1800	15¢ Santa Claus, Christmas							
	Tree Ornament	10/18/79	.30	.15	4.00	(12)	1.00	932
a	Green and yellow omitted		750.00					
b	Green, yellow and tan omitted		800.00					
	Performing Arts Issue							
1801	15¢ Will Rogers Portrait and							
	Rogers as a Cowboy							
	Humorist	11/04/79	.30	.15	4.00	(12)	1.50	161
a	Imperf. pair		225.00					
1802	15¢ Vietnam Veterans	11/11/79	.30	.15	3.25	(10)	4.00	173
	Issues of 1980 (continued), Performing Arts Issue							
1803	15¢ W.C. Fields Portrait							
	and Fields as a Juggler	01/29/80	.30	.15	4.00	(12)	1.75	169
	Black Heritage Issue							
1804	15¢ Benjamin Banneker Portrait							
	and Banneker as Surveyor	02/15/80	.30	.15	4.00	(12)	1.00	160
a	Horizontal pair, imperf. vertically		800.00					

1787

1788

1789

1791

1792

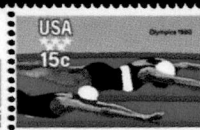

1790

1793

1794

1794a

1795

1796

1797

1798

1798b

1799

1800

1802

1801

1803

1804

1805 **1807** **1809**

1813 **1816**

1806 **1808** **1810**

1822

1818

1821 **1823**

1827 **1828**

1824 **1825** **1826**

1829 **1830** **1830a**

Issues of 1980		Un	U	PB/LP	#	FDC	Q(M)
Letter Writing Issue, Perf. 11							
1805	15¢ Letters Preserve Memories	02/25/80	.30	.15			1.00	39
1806	15¢ purple P.S. Write Soon	02/25/80	.30	.15			1.00	39
1807	15¢ Letters Lift Spirits	02/25/80	.30	.15			1.00	39
1808	15¢ green P.S. Write Soon	02/25/80	.30	.15			1.00	39
1809	15¢ Letters Shape Opinions	02/25/80	.30	.15			1.00	39
1810	15¢ red and blue P.S. Write Soon	02/25/80	.30	.15			1.00	39
a	Vertical Strip of 6, #1805-10		1.85	2.00	11.00	(36)	2.50	
Issues of 1980-81, Americana Issue, Coil Stamps, Perf. 10 Vertically							
(See also #1581-82, 1584-85, 1590-99, 1603-06, 1608, 1610-19, 1622-23, 1625)							
1811	1¢ dark blue, greenish Inkwelll							
	and Quill (1581)	03/06/80	.15	.15	.40	(2)	1.00	
a	Imperf. pair		*175.00*		*275.00*	(2)		
1812	Not assigned							
1813	3.5¢ Weaver Violins	06/23/80	.15	.15	1.00	(2)	1.00	
a	Untagged (Bureau precanceled)			.15				
b	Imperf. pair		*225.00*		*450.00*	(2)		
1814-15	Not assigned							
1816	12¢ red brown, *beige* Torch from							
	Statue of Liberty (1594)	04/08/81	.25	.15	1.50	(2)	1.00	
a	Untagged (Bureau precanceled)			.25				
b	Imperf. pair		*200.00*		*400.00*	(2)		
1817	Not assigned							
Issues of 1981, Perf. 11 x 10.5							
1818	(18¢) "B" Stamp	03/15/81	.35	.15	1.60	(4)	1.00	
Booklet Stamp, Perf. 10							
1819	(18¢) "B" Stamp (1818),							
	single from booklet	03/15/81	.40	.15			1.00	
a	Booklet pane of 8	03/15/81	3.50	1.75			3.00	
Coil Stamp, Perf. 10 Vertically							
1820	(18¢) "B" Stamp (1818)	03/15/81	.40	.15	1.60	(2)	1.00	
a	Imperf. pair		*120.00*		*275.00*	(2)		
Issues of 1980 (continued), Perf. 10.5 x 11							
1821	15¢ Frances Perkins	04/10/80	.30	.15	1.30	(4)	1.00	164
Perf. 11							
1822	15¢ Dolley Madison	05/20/80	.30	.15	1.40	(4)	1.00	257
1823	15¢ Emily Bissell	05/31/80	.30	.15	1.30	(4)	1.00	96
a	Vertical pair, imperf. horizontally		*400.00*					
1824	15¢ Helen Keller/Anne Sullivan	06/27/80	.30	.15	1.30	(4)	1.00	154
1825	15¢ Veterans Administration	07/21/80	.30	.15	1.30	(4)	1.50	160
a	Horizontal pair, imperf. vertically		*500.00*					
American Bicentennial Issue							
1826	15¢ General Bernardo de Galvez,							
	Battle of Mobile	07/23/80	.30	.15	1.30	(4)	1.00	104
a	Red, brown and blue omitted		*800.00*					
b	Bl., brn., red and yel. omitted		*1,400.00*					
Coral Reefs Issue							
1827	15¢ Brain Coral, Beaugregory							
	Fish	08/26/80	.30	.15			1.00	51
1828	15¢ Elkhorn Coral, Porkfish	08/26/80	.30	.15			1.00	51
1829	15¢ Chalice Coral, Moorish Idol	08/26/80	.30	.15			1.00	51
1830	15¢ Finger Coral, Sabertooth							
	Blenny	08/26/80	.30	.15			1.00	51
a	Block of 4, #1827-30		1.25	1.10	4.00	(12)	2.00	
b	As "a," imperf.		*1,000.00*					
c	As "a," imperf. between, vertically		—					
d	As "a," imperf. vertically		*3,000.00*					

ssues of 1980		Un	U	PB		FDC	Q(M)
1831 15¢ Organized Labor	09/01/80	.30	.15	3.50	(12)	1.00	167
a　Imperf. pair		375.00					
Literary Arts Issue, Edith Wharton, Perf. 10.5 x 11							
1832 15¢ Edith Wharton Reading							
Letter	09/05/80	.30	.15	1.30	(4)	1.00	163
Perf. 11							
1833 15¢ Education	09/12/80	.30	.15	1.90	(6)	1.00	160
a　Horizontal pair, imperf. vertically		250.00					
American Folk Art Issue, Pacific Northwest Indian Masks							
1834 15¢ Heiltsuk, Bella Bella Tribe	09/25/80	.30	.15			1.00	39
1835 15¢ Chilkat Tlingit Tribe	09/25/80	.30	.15			1.00	39
1836 15¢ Tlingit Tribe	09/25/80	.30	.15			1.00	39
1837 15¢ Bella Coola Tribe	09/25/80	.30	.15			1.00	39
a　Block of 4, #1834-37		1.25	1.25	3.50	(10)	2.00	
American Architecture Issue							
1838 15¢ Smithsonian Institution,							
by James Renwick	10/09/80	.30	.15			1.00	39
1839 15¢ Trinity Church, by Henry							
Hobson Richardson	10/09/80	.30	.15			1.00	39
1840 15¢ Pennsylvania Academy							
of Fine Arts, by Frank Furness	10/09/80	.30	.15			1.00	39
1841 15¢ Lyndhurst, by Alexander							
Jefferson Davis	10/09/80	.30	.15			1.00	39
a　Block of 4, #1838-41		1.25	1.25	1.50	(4)	2.00	
Christmas Issue							
1842 15¢ Madonna and Child							
from Epiphany Window,							
Washington Cathedral	10/31/80	.30	.15	4.00	(12)	1.00	693
a　Imperf. pair		85.00					
Pair with full vertical gutter between		—					
1843 15¢ Wreath and Toys	10/31/80	.30	.15	6.50	(20)	1.00	719
a　Imperf. pair		85.00					
b　Buff omitted		25.00					

In 1980 the U.S. Postal Service honored the **Smithsonian Institution** with a stamp, one of four celebrating American architecture. The stamp pays tribute to the Smithsonian Institution Building, popularly known as the Castle, and its architect, James Renwick. The Smithsonian has been

the subject of several stamps. A stamp issued in 1946 marked the Smithsonian's centennial; another issued in 1996 commemorated its sesquicentennial. All three stamps featured the Castle, the enduring symbol of the Smithsonian.

The Smithsonian Institution was established in 1846 with funds bequeathed to the United States by scientist James Smithson to found an institution for "the increase and diffusion of knowledge." James Renwick designed the Castle, the first Smithsonian building, in a medieval-revival style with towers, gables, battlements, arches, and stained-glass windows. Constructed of red sandstone, the Castle originally included a library, chemical laboratory, lecture halls, and museum galleries, and also served as the home of Joseph Henry, the Smithsonian's first Secretary. Today the Smithsonian encompasses 16 museums and galleries, several research facilities, and the National Zoo. The Castle, which now houses the Smithsonian Information Center, administrative offices, and James Smithson's crypt, remains one of Washington's best known landmarks.

1831

1832

1834   **1835**

1833

1836   **1837**   **1837a**

1838   **1839**

1840   **1841**   **1841a**

1842   **1843**

1844 **1845** **1846** **1847**

1848 **1849** **1850** **1851**

1852 **1853** **1854** **1855**

1856 **1857** **1858** **1859**

1860 **1861** **1862** **1863**

1864 **1865** **1866** **1867**

1868 **1869**

ssues of 1980-90		Un	U	PB		FDC

Great Americans Issue, Perf. 11 (See also #2168-73, 2176-80, 2182-86, 2188, 2190-92, 2194-97)

			Un	U	PB		FDC
1844	1¢ Dorothea Dix	09/23/83	.15	.15	.35	(6)	1.00
a	Imperf. pair		400.00				
b	Vertical pair, imperf. between		3,000.00				
	Perf. 11 x 10.5						
1845	2¢ Igor Stravinsky	11/18/82	.15	.15	.25	(4)	1.00
a	Vertical pair, full gutter between		—				
1846	3¢ Henry Clay	07/13/83	.15	.15	.45	(4)	1.00
1847	4¢ Carl Schurz	06/03/83	.15	.15	.50	(4)	1.00
1848	5¢ Pearl Buck	06/25/83	.15	.15	.50	(4)	1.00
	Perf. 11						
1849	6¢ Walter Lippman	09/19/85	.15	.15	.75	(6)	1.00
a	Vertical pair, imperf. between		2,250.00				
1850	7¢ Abraham Baldwin	01/25/85	.15	.15	.85	(6)	1.00
1851	8¢ Henry Knox	07/25/85	.15	.15	.85	(4)	1.00
1852	9¢ Sylvanus Thayer	06/07/85	.20	.15	1.30	(6)	1.00
1853	10¢ Richard Russell	05/31/84	.20	.15	1.50	(6)	1.00
a	Vertical pair, imperf. between		1,100.00				
b	Horizontal pair, imperf. between		2,250.00				
1854	11¢ Alden Partridge	02/12/85	.25	.15	1.25	(4)	1.00
	Perf. 11 x 10.5						
1855	13¢ Crazy Horse	01/15/82	.25	.15	1.50	(4)	1.50
	Perf. 11						
1856	14¢ Sinclair Lewis	03/21/85	.30	.15	2.25	(6)	1.00
b	Vertical pair, imperf. horizontally		150.00				
c	Horizontal pair, imperf. between		10.00				
d	Vertical pair, imperf. between		1,500.00				
	Perf. 11 x 10.5						
1857	17¢ Rachel Carson	05/28/81	.35	.15	1.75	(4)	1.00
1858	18¢ George Mason	05/07/81	.35	.15	2.25	(4)	1.00
1859	19¢ Sequoyah	12/27/80	.40	.15	2.25	(4)	1.50
1860	20¢ Ralph Bunche	01/12/82	.40	.15	3.25	(4)	1.00
1861	20¢ Thomas H. Gallaudet	06/10/83	.45	.15	3.25	(4)	1.25
	Perf. 11						
1862	20¢ Harry S. Truman	01/26/84	.40	.15	3.00	(6)	1.25
b	Overall tagging	1990	.40	—			
1863	22¢ John J. Audubon	04/23/85	.55	.15	3.50	(6)	1.00
d	Vertical pair, imperf. horizontally		2,500.00				
e	Vertical pair, imperf. between		—				
f	Horizontal pair, imperf. between		2,500.00				
1864	30¢ Frank C. Laubach	09/02/84	.55	.15	3.50	(6)	1.25
	Perf. 11 x 10.5						
1865	35¢ Charles R. Drew, MD	06/03/81	.70	.15	3.50	(4)	1.25
1866	37¢ Robert Millikan	01/26/82	.75	.15	3.50	(4)	1.25
	Perf. 11						
1867	39¢ Grenville Clark	03/20/85	.80	.15	5.50	(6)	1.25
a	Vertical pair, imperf. horizontally		600.00				
b	Vertical pair, imperf. between		2,000.00				
1868	40¢ Lillian M. Gilbreth	02/24/84	.80	.15	5.00	(6)	1.25
1869	50¢ Chester W. Nimitz	02/22/85	.95	.15	6.25	(4)	2.00
1870-73	Not assigned						

	Issues of 1981		Un	U	PB/PN		FDC	Q(M)
1874	15¢ Everett Dirksen	01/04/81	.30	.15	1.40	(4)	1.00	160
	Black Heritage Issue, Whitney Moore Young							
1875	15¢ Whitney Moore Young							
	at Desk	01/30/81	.30	.15	1.50	(4)	1.00	160
	Flower Issue							
1876	18¢ Rose	04/23/81	.35	.15			1.00	53
1877	18¢ Camellia	04/23/81	.35	.15			1.00	53
1878	18¢ Dahlia	04/23/81	.35	.15			1.00	53
1879	18¢ Lily	04/23/81	.35	.15			1.00	53
a	Block of 4, #1876-79		1.40	1.25	1.75	(4)	2.50	
	Wildlife Booklet Issue							
1880	18¢ Bighorn Sheep	05/14/81	.55	.15			1.00	
1881	18¢ Puma	05/14/81	.55	.15			1.00	
1882	18¢ Harbor Seal	05/14/81	.55	.15			1.00	
1883	18¢ Bison	05/14/81	.55	.15			1.00	
1884	18¢ Brown Bear	05/14/81	.55	.15			1.00	
1885	18¢ Polar Bear	05/14/81	.55	.15			1.00	
1886	18¢ Elk (Wapiti)	05/14/81	.55	.15			1.00	
1887	18¢ Moose	05/14/81	.55	.15			1.00	
1888	18¢ White-Tailed Deer	05/14/81	.55	.15			1.00	
1889	18¢ Pronghorn Antelope	05/14/81	.55	.15			1.00	
a	Booklet pane of 10, #1880-89		8.00	7.00			5.00	

#1880-89 issued only in booklets. All stamps are imperf. at one side or imperf. at one side and bottom.

	Flag and Anthem Issue							
1890	18¢ "...for amber waves							
	of grain"	04/24/81	.35	.15	2.25	(6)	1.00	
a	Imperf. pair		110.00					
b	Vertical pair, imperf. horizontally		1,000.00					
	Coil Stamp, Perf. 10 Vertically							
1891	18¢ "...from sea to shining sea"	04/24/81	.35	.15	4.50	(3)	1.00	
a	Imperf. pair		25.00					

Beginning with #1891, all coil stamps except 1947 feature a small plate number at the bottom of the design at varying intervals in a roll, depending on the press used. The basic "plate number coil" (PNC) collecting unit is a strip of three stamps, with the plate number appearing on the middle stamp. PNC values are for the most common plate number.

	Booklet Stamps, Perf. 11							
1892	6¢ USA Circle of Stars,							
	single from booklet (1893a)	04/24/81	.50	.15			1.00	
1893	18¢ "...for purple mountain majesties,"							
	single from booklet (1893a)	04/24/81	.30	.15			1.00	
a	Booklet pane of 8 (2 #1892 & 6 #1893)		3.00	2.25			2.50	
b	As "a," imperf. vertically between		75.00					

#1892-93 issued only in booklets. All stamps are imperf. at one side or imperf. at one side and bottom.

	Flag Over Supreme Court Issue							
1894	20¢ Flag Over Supreme Court	12/17/81	.40	.15	2.75	(6)	1.00	
a	Imperf. pair		35.00					
b	Vertical pair, imperf. horizontally		600.00					
c	Dark blue omitted		90.00					
d	Black omitted		325.00					
	Coil Stamp, Perf. 10 Vertically							
1895	20¢ Flag Over Supreme							
	Court (1894)	12/17/81	.35	.15	4.25	(3)	1.00	
b	Untagged (Bureau precanceled)		.50	.50	57.50	(3)		
d	Imperf. pair		9.00					
f	Black omitted		55.00					
g	Blue omitted		1,500.00					

1876   1877

USA 15c
Everett Dirksen

Whitney Moore Young

Black Heritage USA 15c

Rose USA 18c   Camellia USA 18c

Dahlia USA 18c   Lily USA 18c

1874   1875

1878   1879   1879a

1880

1881

1882

1883

1884

1885

1886

1887

1888

1889

1889a

1892

6¢
USA

6¢
USA

USA 18c   USA 18c

...for purple mountain majesties   ...for purple mountain majesties

USA 18c   USA 18c

...for purple mountain majesties   ...for purple mountain majesties

USA 18c   USA 18c

...for purple mountain majesties   ...for purple mountain majesties

1893   1893a

USA 18c

...for amber waves of grain

USA 18c

...from sea to shining sea

USA 20c

1890   1891   1894

1981-1984

1897

1897A

1898

Stagecoach 1890s
USA 4c
1898A

1899

1900

1901

1902

1903

1904

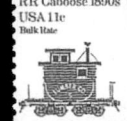
1905

1906

1907

1908

1909

1910

1911

Issues of 1981-82		Un	U	PB/PNC/LP	#	FDC	Q(M)
Booklet Stamp, Perf. 11 x 10.5							
1896	20¢ Flag over Supreme Court						
	(1894), single from booklet	12/17/81	.35	.15			1.00
a	Booklet pane of 6	12/17/81	2.50	2.00			6.00
b	Booklet pane of 10	06/01/82	4.25	3.25			*10.00*
Issues of 1981-84, Perf. 10 Vertically							
Coil Stamps, Transportation Issue (See also #2123-36, 2225-26, 2228, 2231, 2252-66,							
2452-53A, 2457, 2464, 2468)							
1897	1¢ Omnibus 1880s	08/19/83	.15	.15	.45	(3)	1.00
b	Imperf. pair		*675.00*		—	(2)	
1897A	2¢ Locomotive 1870s	05/20/82	.15	.15	.50	(3)	1.50
e	Imperf. pair		*60.00*		—	(2)	
1898	3¢ Handcar 1880s	03/25/83	.15	.15	.70	(3)	1.00
1898A	4¢ Stagecoach 1890s	08/19/82	.15	.15	1.40	(3)	1.00
b	Untagged (Bureau precanceled)		.15	.15	7.00	(3)	
c	As "b," imperf. pair		*750.00*				
d	Imperf. pair		*925.00*	—			
1899	5¢ Motorcycle 1913	10/10/83	.15	.15	1.10	(3)	2.00
a	Imperf. pair		*2,750.00*				
1900	5.2¢ Sleigh 1880s	03/21/83	.15	.15	7.50	(3)	1.00
a	Untagged (Bureau precanceled)		.15	.15	12.00	(3)	
1901	5.9¢ Bicycle 1870s	02/17/82	.20	.15	9.00	(3)	1.50
a	Untagged (Bureau precanceled)		.20	.20	27.50	(3)	
b	As "a," imperf. pair		*200.00*		—	(2)	
1902	7.4¢ Baby Buggy 1880s	04/07/84	.20	.15	8.50	(3)	1.00
a	Untagged (Bureau precanceled)		.20	.20	4.25	(3)	
1903	9.3¢ Mail Wagon 1880s	12/15/81	.30	.15	9.00	(3)	1.00
a	Untagged (Bureau precanceled)		.25	.25	3.00	(3)	
b	As "a," imperf. pair		*125.00*		*200.00*	(2)	
1904	10.9¢ Hansom Cab 1890s	03/26/82	.25	.15	18.00	(3)	1.00
a	Untagged (Bureau precanceled)		.25	.25	30.00	(3)	
b	As "a," imperf. pair		*150.00*			(2)	
1905	11¢ RR Caboose 1890s	02/03/84	.25	.15	4.00	(3)	1.50
a	Untagged (Bureau precanceled)		.25	.15	2.25	(3)	
1906	17¢ Electric Auto 1917	06/25/81	.35	.15	2.25	(3)	1.00
a	Untagged (Bureau precanceled)		.35	.35	4.00	(3)	
b	Imperf. pair		*165.00*		—	(2)	
c	As "a," imperf. pair		*650.00*		—	(2)	
1907	18¢ Surrey 1890s	05/18/81	.35	.15	3.25	(3)	1.00
a	Imperf. pair		*160.00*		—	(2)	
1908	20¢ Fire Pumper 1860s	12/10/81	.35	.15	3.00	(3)	3.00
a	Imperf. pair		*110.00*		*300.00*	(2)	
Values for plate # coil strips of 3 stamps for #1897-1908 are for the most common plate numbers.							
Other plate #s and strips of 5 stamps may have higher values.							
Issue of 1983, Express Mail Booklet Issue, Perf. 10 Vertically							
1909	$9.35 Eagle and Moon,						
	single from booklet	08/12/83	21.00	14.00			45.00
a	Booklet pane of 3		65.00	—			*125.00*
#1909 issued only in booklets. All stamps are imperf. at top and bottom or imperf. at top,							
bottom and right side.							
Issues of 1981, Perf. 10.5 x 11							
1910	18¢ American Red Cross	05/01/81	.35	.15	1.50	(4)	1.00	165
Perf. 11							
1911	18¢ Savings and Loans	05/08/81	.35	.15	1.50	(4)	1.00	107

1981

1928 **1929**

1930 **1931** **1931a**

1932 **1933**

1934 **1935** **1936**

1937 **1938** **1938a**

1939 **1940**

1941

Issues of 1981		Un	U	PB		FDC	Q(M)
American Architecture Issue, Perf. 11							
1928 18¢ NYU Library, by							
Sanford White	08/28/81	.40	.15			1.00	42
1929 18¢ Biltmore House, by							
Richard Morris Hunt	08/28/81	.40	.15			1.00	42
1930 18¢ Palace of the Arts,							
by Bernard Maybeck	08/28/81	.40	.15			1.00	42
1931 18¢ National Farmer's Bank,							
by Louis Sullivan	08/28/81	.40	.15			1.00	42
a Block of 4, #1928-31		1.65	1.50	2.10	(4)	2.50	
American Sports Issue, Babe Zaharias and Bobby Jones, Perf. 10.5 x 11							
1932 18¢ Babe Zaharias Holding							
Trophy	09/22/81	.35	.15	3.00	(4)	7.00	102
1933 18¢ Bobby Jones Teeing off	09/22/81	.35	.15	3.00	(4)	8.00	99
Perf. 11							
1934 18¢ Frederic Remington	10/09/81	.35	.15	1.60	(4)	1.00	101
a Vertical pair, imperf. between		275.00					
b Brown omitted		550.00					
1935 18¢ James Hoban	10/13/81	.35	.15	1.60	(4)	1.00	101
1936 20¢ James Hoban	10/13/81	.35	.15	1.65	(4)	1.00	167
American Bicentennial Issue, Yorktown-Virginia Capes							
1937 18¢ Battle of Yorktown 1781	10/16/81	.35	.15			1.00	81
1938 18¢ Battle of the Virginia							
Capes 1781	10/16/81	.35	.15			1.00	81
a Attached pair, #1937-38		.90	.75	2.00	(4)	1.50	
b As "a," black omitted		400.00					
Christmas Issue							
1939 20¢ Madonna and Child,							
by Botticelli	10/28/81	.40	.15	1.75	(4)	1.00	598
a Imperf. pair		125.00					
b Vertical pair, imperf. horizontally		1,650.00					
1940 20¢ Felt Bear on Sleigh	10/28/81	.40	.15	1.75	(4)	1.00	793
a Imperf. pair		350.00					
b Vertical pair, imperf. horizontally		2,500.00					
1941 20¢ John Hanson	11/05/81	.40	.15	1.75	(4)	1.00	167

The 1970 Christmas issue by the U.S. Post Office Department included four stamps depicting **antique toys**. Who can think of Christmas without remembering favorite toys? Running downstairs and discovering a dollhouse under the tree; reaching into a Christmas stocking and pulling out a toy soldier; unwrapping a package with shiny paper and finding a teddy bear: these are the memories of which Christmas are made.

The toys on these stamps are American classics, but the horse on wheels and the doll carriage also have a longer history. Wheeled toys existed in the ancient world. Dolls also were part of many ancient cultures. Some may have been used in religious ceremonies.

The stamps were illustrated by the late Stevan Dohanos. He worked on many other projects for the Postal Service, including John F. Kennedy (1967), Maine Statehood (1970), Santa Claus (1972), and Sleigh Full of Presents (1989).

	ssues of 1982		Ur	U	FDC	Q(M)
	State Birds & Flowers Issue (continued)					
1978	20¢ Montana: Western Meadowlark & Bitterroot	04/14/82	.50	.25	1.25	13
1979	20¢ Nebraska: Western Meadowlark & Goldenrod	04/14/82	.50	.25	1.25	13
1980	20¢ Nevada: Mountain Bluebird & Sagebrush	04/14/82	.50	.25	1.25	13
1981	20¢ New Hampshire: Purple Finch & Lilac	04/14/82	.50	.25	1.25	13
1982	20¢ New Jersey: American Goldfinch & Violet	04/14/82	.50	.25	1.25	13
1983	20¢ New Mexico: Roadrunner & Yucca Flower	04/14/82	.50	.25	1.25	13
1984	20¢ New York: Eastern Bluebird & Rose	04/14/82	.50	.25	1.25	13
1985	20¢ North Carolina: Cardinal & Flowering Dogwood	04/14/82	.50	.25	1.25	13
1986	20¢ North Dakota: Western Meadowlark & Wild Prairie Rose	04/14/82	.50	.25	1.25	13
1987	20¢ Ohio: Cardinal & Red Carnation	04/14/82	.50	.25	1.25	13
1988	20¢ Oklahoma: Scissor-tailed Flycatcher & Mistletoe	04/14/82	.50	.25	1.25	13
1989	20¢ Oregon: Western Meadowlark & Oregon Grape	04/14/82	.50	.25	1.25	13
1990	20¢ Pennsylvania: Ruffed Grouse & Mountain Laurel	04/14/82	.50	.25	1.25	13
1991	20¢ Rhode Island: Rhode Island Red & Violet	04/14/82	.50	.25	1.25	13
1992	20¢ South Carolina: Carolina Wren & Carolina Jessamine	04/14/82	.50	.25	1.25	13
1993	20¢ South Dakota: Ring-Necked Pheasant & Pasqueflower	04/14/82	.50	.25	1.25	13
1994	20¢ Tennessee: Mockingbird & Iris	04/14/82	.50	.25	1.25	13
1995	20¢ Texas: Mockingbird & Bluebonnet	04/14/82	.50	.25	1.25	13
1996	20¢ Utah: California Gull & Sego Lily	04/14/82	.50	.25	1.25	13
1997	20¢ Vermont: Hermit Thrush & Red Clover	04/14/82	.50	.25	1.25	13
1998	20¢ Virginia: Cardinal & Flowering Dogwood	04/14/82	.50	.25	1.25	13
1999	20¢ Washington: American Goldfinch & Rhododendron	04/14/82	.50	.25	1.25	13
2000	20¢ West Virginia: Cardinal & Rhododendron Maximum	04/14/82	.50	.25	1.25	13
2001	20¢ Wisconsin: Robin & Wood Violet	04/14/82	.50	.25	1.25	13
2002	20¢ Wyoming: Western Meadowlark & Indian Paintbrush	04/14/82	.50	.25	1.25	13
a	Any single, perf. 11		.55	.30		
b	Pane of 50 (with plate #)		25.00	—	30.00	
c	Pane of 50, perf. 11		27.50	—		
d	Pane of 50, imperf.		27,500.00			

Arizona
USA 20c
Cactus Wren &
Saguaro Cactus Blossom

Connecticut
USA 20c
Robin &
Mountain Laurel

Massachusetts
USA 20c
Black-Capped Chickadee &
Mayflower

New York
USA 20c
Eastern Bluebird &
Rose

In 1982 the U.S. Postal Service issued 50 stamps depicting **state birds and flowers** painted by Arthur and Alan Singer. Four of these stamps portray Arizona's cactus wren and saguaro cactus blossom, Connecticut's robin and mountain laurel, Massachusetts's black-capped chickadee and mayflower, and New York's eastern bluebird and rose.

The cactus wren has a white eye stripe and spotted breast. The giant saguaro cactus' white flowers remain open for less than a day.

The American robin can be identified by its familiar red breast. The mountain laurel is an evergreen shrub with white or pink blossoms.

The black-capped chickadee has a black cap, white cheeks, and black bib. Mayflower, also known as trailing arbutus or ground laurel, flowers in clusters of pink or white.

Bright blue above, chestnut and white below, the eastern bluebird is cherished for its brilliant plumage. Roses exist in many varieties, each with its distinctive color and shape.

Montana USA 20c — Western Meadowlark & Bitterroot — 1978

Nebraska USA 20c — Western Meadowlark & Goldenrod — 1979

Nevada USA 20c — Mountain Bluebird & Sagebrush — 1980

New Hampshire USA 20c — Purple Finch & Lilac — 1981

New Jersey USA 20c — American Goldfinch & Violet — 1982

New Mexico USA 20c — Roadrunner & Yucca Flower — 1983

New York USA 20c — Eastern Bluebird & Rose — 1984

North Carolina USA 20c — Cardinal & Flowering Dogwood — 1985

North Dakota USA 20c — Western Meadowlark & Wild Prairie Rose — 1986

Ohio USA 20c — Cardinal & Red Carnation — 1987

Oklahoma USA 20c — Scissor-tailed Flycatcher & Mistletoe — 1988

Oregon USA 20c — Western Meadowlark & Oregon Grape — 1989

Pennsylvania USA 20c — Ruffed Grouse & Mountain Laurel — 1990

Rhode Island USA 20c — Rhode Island Red & Violet — 1991

South Carolina USA 20c — Carolina Wren & Carolina Jessamine — 1992

South Dakota USA 20c — Ring-Necked Pheasant & Pasqueflower — 1993

Tennessee USA 20c — Mockingbird & Iris — 1994

Texas USA 20c — Mockingbird & Bluebonnet — 1995

Utah USA 20c — California Gull & Sego Lily — 1996

Vermont USA 20c — Hermit Thrush & Red Clover — 1997

Virginia USA 20c — Cardinal & Flowering Dogwood — 1998

Washington USA 20c — American Goldfinch & Rhododendron — 1999

West Virginia USA 20c — Cardinal & Rhododendron Maximum — 2000

Wisconsin USA 20c — Robin & Wood Violet — 2001

Wyoming USA 20c — Western Meadowlark & Indian Paintbrush — 2002

1982

2003

2004

2005

2006

2007

2008

2009

2009a

2010

2012

2011

2013

2014

2015

2016

2019

2020

2017

2018

2021

2022

2022a

Issues of 1982		Un	U	PB/PNC/LP	#	FDC Q(M)
Perf. 11						
2003 20¢ USA/The Netherlands	04/20/82	.40	.15	3.50	(6)	1.00 109
a Imperf. pair		325.00				
2004 20¢ Library of Congress	04/21/82	.40	.15	1.75	(4)	1.00 113
Coil Stamp, Perf. 10 Vertically						
2005 20¢ Consumer Education	04/27/82	.55	.15	30.00	(3)	1.00
a Imperf. pair		100.00		400.00	(2)	
Value for plate no. coil strip of 3 stamps is for most common plate nos. Other plate nos. and strips of 5 stamps may have higher values.						
Knoxville World's Fair Issue, Perf. 11						
2006 20¢ Solar Energy	04/29/82	.40	.15			1.00 31
2007 20¢ Synthetic Fuels	04/29/82	.40	.15			1.00 31
2008 20¢ Breeder Reactor	04/29/82	.40	.15			1.00 31
2009 20¢ Fossil Fuels	04/29/82	.40	.15			1.00 31
a Block of 4, #2006-09		1.65	1.50	2.00	(4)	2.50
2010 20¢ Horatio Alger	04/30/82	.40	.15	1.75	(4)	1.00 108
2011 20¢ Aging Together	05/21/82	.40	.15	1.75	(4)	1.00 173
Performing Arts Issue, The Barrymores						
2012 20¢ Portraits of John, Ethel and Lionel Barrymore	06/08/82	.40	.15	1.75	(4)	1.25 107
2013 20¢ Dr. Mary Walker	06/10/82	.40	.15	1.75	(4)	1.00 109
2014 20¢ International Peace Garden	06/30/82	.40	.15	1.75	(4)	1.00 183
a Black and green omitted		275.00				
2015 20¢ America's Libraries	07/13/82	.40	.15	1.75	(4)	1.00 169
a Vertical pair, imperf. horizontally		325.00				
Black Heritage Issue, Jackie Robinson, Perf. 10.5 x 11						
2016 20¢ Jackie Robinson Portrait and Robinson Stealing Home Plate	08/02/82	1.10	.15	5.50	(4)	6.00 164
Perf. 11						
2017 20¢ Touro Synagogue	08/22/82	.40	.15	11.00	(20)	1.00 110
a Imperf. pair		2,500.00				
2018 20¢ Wolf Trap Farm Park	09/01/82	.40	.15	1.75	(4)	1.00 111
American Architecture Issue						
2019 20¢ Fallingwater, by Frank Lloyd Wright	09/30/82	.40	.15			1.00 41
2020 20¢ Illinois Institute of Technology, by Ludwig Mies van der Rohe	09/30/82	.40	.15			1.00 41
2021 20¢ Gropius House, by Walter Gropius	09/30/82	.40	.15			1.00 41
2022 20¢ Dulles Airport by Eero Saarinen	09/30/82	.40	.15			1.00 41
a Block of 4, #2019-22		1.75	1.60	2.25	(4)	2.50

1983

2041

2042

2043

2044

2045

2046

2047

2048   **2049**

2050   **2051**   **2051a**

2052

2055   **2056**

2053

2057   **2058**   **2058a**

2054

ssues of 1983		Un	U	PB	#	FDC	Q(M)
2041	20¢ Brooklyn Bridge	05/17/83	.40	.15	1.75	(4)	1.00	182
2042	20¢ Tennessee Valley Authority	05/18/83	.40	.15	11.00	(20)	1.00	114
2043	20¢ Physical Fitness	05/14/83	.40	.15	3.00	(6)	1.00	112
	Black Heritage Issue, Scott Joplin							
2044	20¢ Scott Joplin Portrait							
	and Joplin Playing the Piano	06/09/83	.40	.15	1.75	(4)	1.00	115
a	Imperf. pair		475.00					
2045	20¢ Medal of Honor	06/07/83	.40	.15	1.75	(4)	3.75	109
a	Red omitted		300.00					
	American Sports Issue, Babe Ruth, Perf. 10.5 x 11							
2046	20¢ Babe Ruth Hitting							
	a Home Run	07/06/83	1.00	.15	6.00	(4)	5.00	185
	Literary Arts Issue, Nathaniel Hawthorne, Perf. 11							
2047	20¢ Nathaniel Hawthorne,							
	by Cephus Giovanni Thompson	07/08/83	.40	.15	1.70	(4)	1.00	111
	Olympic Summer Games Issue (See also #2082-85, C101-12)							
2048	13¢ Discus Thrower	07/28/83	.35	.15			1.00	99
2049	13¢ High Jumper	07/28/83	.35	.15			1.00	99
2050	13¢ Archer	07/28/83	.35	.15			1.00	99
2051	13¢ Boxers	07/28/83	.35	.15			1.00	99
a	Block of 4, #2048-51		1.50	1.25	1.75	(4)	2.50	
	American Bicentennial Issue, Treaty of Paris							
2052	20¢ Signing of Treaty of Paris							
	(John Adams, Benjamin Franklin							
	and John Jay observing David							
	Hartley), by Benjamin West	09/02/83	.40	.15	1.75	(4)	1.00	104
2053	20¢ Civil Service	09/09/83	.40	.15	3.00	(6)	1.00	115
2054	20¢ Metropolitan Opera	09/14/83	.40	.15	1.75	(4)	1.00	113
	American Inventors Issue							
2055	20¢ Charles Steinmetz							
	and Curve on Graph	09/21/83	.40	.15			1.00	48
2056	20¢ Edwin Armstrong and							
	Frequency Modulator	09/21/83	.40	.15			1.00	48
2057	20¢ Nikola Tesla and							
	Induction Motor	09/21/83	.40	.15			1.00	48
2058	20¢ Philo T. Farnsworth and							
	First Television Camera	09/21/83	.40	.15			1.00	48
a	Block of 4, #2055-58		1.60	1.25	2.00	(4)	2.50	
b	As "a," black omitted		400.00					

Joseph Louis Barrow, the quiet, unassuming son of an Alabama sharecropper, rose from humble origins to become the heavyweight boxing champion of the world from 1937 to 1949. Nicknamed the "Brown Bomber," Joe Louis's appeal transcended boxing. To white Americans he was seen as a symbol of racial harmony. To black Americans Louis represented triumph and hope in a segregated society. In his historic bouts with Germany's Max Schmeling, Louis symbolized democracy battling Nazism.

Joe Louis turned professional in 1934. He won 68 out of 71 professional bouts—54 by knockouts. He defended his title a record 25 times, scoring 21 knockouts, and held it for a record-breaking 12 years. Louis died in 1981 and was buried in Arlington National Cemetery by order of President Ronald Reagan. The Postal Service honored Louis in 1993 with a stamp illustrated by Thomas Blackshear.

Issues of 1983			Un	U	PB		FDC	Q(M)
Streetcars Issue, Perf. 11								
2059	20¢ First American Streetcar	10/08/83	.40	.15			1.00	52
2060	20¢ Early Electric Streetcar	10/08/83	.40	.15			1.00	52
2061	20¢ "Bobtail" Horsecar	10/08/83	.40	.15			1.00	52
2062	20¢ St. Charles Streetcar	10/08/83	.40	.15			1.00	52
a	Block of 4, #2059-62		1.70	1.40	2.00	(4)	2.50	
b	As "a," black omitted		425.00					
c	As "a," black omitted on #2059, 2061		—					
	Christmas Issue							
2063	20¢ Niccolini-Cowper Madonna, by Raphael	10/28/83	.40	.15	1.75	(4)	1.00	716
2064	20¢ Santa Claus	10/28/83	.40	.15	3.00	(6)	1.00	849
a	Imperf. pair		175.00					
2065	20¢ Martin Luther	11/11/83	.40	.15	1.75	(4)	3.00	165
	Issues of 1984							
2066	20¢ 25th Anniversary of Alaska Statehood	01/03/84	.40	.15	1.75	(4)	1.00	120
	Winter Olympic Games Issue, Perf. 10.5 x 11							
2067	20¢ Ice Dancing	01/06/84	.45	.15			1.00	80
2068	20¢ Alpine Skiing	01/06/84	.45	.15			1.00	80
2069	20¢ Nordic Skiing	01/06/84	.45	.15			1.00	80
2070	20¢ Hockey	01/06/84	.45	.15			1.00	80
a	Block of 4, #2067-70		1.85	1.50	2.50	(4)	2.50	
	Perf. 11							
2071	20¢ Federal Deposit Insurance Corporation	01/12/84	.40	.15	1.75	(4)	1.00	103

Cable cars, along with Alcatraz Island, Fisherman's Wharf, and the Golden Gate Bridge, serve as a distinctive reminder of San Francisco's unique and colorful past. In 1971 the U.S. Post Office Department celebrated this San Francisco landmark with a Historic Preservation stamp by Melbourne Brindle. The community

has rallied around the cable cars as a link to the city's rich history. Today commuters and tourists can ride over five miles of cable car tracks through the streets of San Francisco.

After witnessing a dramatic horse-drawn car crash on one of San Francisco's notoriously steep hills, inventor Andrew Smith Hallidie put his mind to creating a safer mass transit system. Hallidie's invention, the world's first cable car, was tested in the summer of 1873 and went into commercial service just a month later. The cable car network soon expanded and became a trademark of San Francisco.

2059　　　　　**2060**

2061　　　　　**2062**　　　　**2062a**

2063

2064

Martin Luther

1483-1983 USA 20c

2065

USA 20c

1959-1984
Alaska Statehood

2066

2067　　　　**2068**

2069　　　**2070**　**2070a**

FEDERAL DEPOSIT
INSURANCE
CORPORATION

USA 20c
50TH ANNIVERSARY

2071

2072

2073

2074

2075

2076

2077

2078

2079

2079a

2080

2081

2082

2083

2086

2087

2084

2085

2085a

Issues of 1984		Un	U	PB		FDC	Q(M)
Perf. 11 x 10.5							
2072	20¢ Love 01/31/84	.40	.15	11.50	(20)	2.00	555
a	Horizontal pair, imperf. vertically	175.00					
Black Heritage Issue, Carter G. Woodson, Perf. 11							
2073	20¢ Carter G. Woodson						
	Holding History Book 02/01/84	.40	.15	1.75	(4)	1.00	120
a	Horizontal pair, imperf. vertically	1,600.00					
2074	20¢ Soil and Water						
	Conservation 02/06/84	.40	.15	1.75	(4)	1.00	107
2075	20¢ 50th Anniversary						
	of Credit Union Act 02/10/84	.40	.15	1.75	(4)	1.00	107
	Orchids Issue						
2076	20¢ Wild Pink 03/05/84	45	.15			1.00	77
2077	20¢ Yellow Lady's-Slipper 03/05/84	.45	.15			1.00	77
2078	20¢ Spreading Pogonia 03/05/84	.45	.15			1.00	77
2079	20¢ Pacific Calypso 03/05/84	.45	.15			1.00	77
a	Block of 4, #2076-79	1.85	1.50	2.10	(4)	2.50	
2080	20¢ 25th Anniversary						
	of Hawaii Statehood 03/12/84	.40	.15	1.70	(4)	1.00	120
2081	20¢ National Archives 04/16/84	.40	.15	1.70	(4)	1.00	108
	Olympic Summer Games Issue (See also #2048-52, C101-12)						
2082	20¢ Diving 05/04/84	.50	.15			1.00	78
2083	20¢ Long Jump 05/04/84	.50	.15			1.00	78
2084	20¢ Wrestling 05/04/84	.50	.15			1.00	78
2085	20¢ Kayak 05/04/84	.50	.15			1.00	78
a	Block of 4, #2082-85	2.25	1.90	3.25	(4)	2.50	
2086	20¢ Louisiana World						
	Exposition 05/11/84	.40	.15	1.75	(4)	1.00	130
2087	20¢ Health Research 05/17/84	.40	.15	1.75	(4)	1.00	120

From an early age **John J. Audubon** (1785-1851) felt passionately about the natural world. He expressed that passion through sketching and painting what he saw in the vast American wilderness. Audubon's exquisite depictions of North American birds gained him his first taste of acclaim in 1826 when he unveiled his landmark folio, Birds of America. English engraver Robert Havell was able to enhance the lifelike qualities of Audubon's illustrations by picturing many of the birds in life-size.

By the time Birds of America was completed in 1838, Audubon was a celebrated artist. In the following decade Audubon traveled west to gather specimens and work on The Viviparous Quadrupeds of North America, two volumes of hand-colored lithographs of mammals. Audubon is venerated for his contributions to art and ornithology; his illustrations of birds and other wildlife are admired worldwide for their beauty and accuracy.

In 1985, the Postal Service honored one of America's finest naturalists and artists with a Great Americans stamp by Chris Calle. Audubon was also featured on stamps commemorating his importance as a scientist in 1940 and as an artist in 1963.

ssues of 1984		Un	U	PE		FDC	Q(M)
Performing Arts Issue, Perf. 11							
2088	20¢ Douglas Fairbanks Portrait						
	and Fairbanks in Pirate Role 05/23/84	.40	.15	12.00	(20)	1.00	117
American Sports Issue							
2089	20¢ Jim Thorpe						
	on Football Field 05/24/84	.40	.15	2.00	(4)	3.00	116
Performing Arts Issue							
2090	20¢ John McCormack Portrait						
	and McCormack in Tenor Role 06/06/84	.40	.15	1.75	(4)	1.00	117
2091	20¢ 25th Anniversary						
	of St. Lawrence Seaway 06/26/84	.40	.15	1.75	(4)	1.00	120
2092	20¢ Migratory Bird Hunting						
	and Preservation Act 07/02/84	.50	.15	2.50	(4)	1.25	124
a	Horizontal pair, imperf. vertically	400.00					
2093	20¢ Roanoke Voyages 07/13/84	.40	.15	1.75	(4)	1.00	120
	Pair with full horizontal gutter between	—					
Literary Arts Issue							
2094	20¢ Herman Melville 08/01/84	.40	.15	1.75	(4)	1.75	117
2095	20¢ Horace Moses 08/06/84	.45	.15	3.50	(6)	1.00	117
2096	20¢ Smokey the Bea 08/13/84	.40	.15	2.00	(4)	4.50	96
a	Horizontal pair, imperf. between	300.00					
b	Vertical pair, imperf. between	275.00					
c	Block of 4, imperf. between						
	vertically and horizontally	5,500.00					
d	Horizontal pair, imperf. vertically	1,750.00					
American Sports Issue							
2097	20¢ Roberto Clemente in Pirates Cap, Puerto						
	Rican Flag in Background 08/17/84	1.40	.15	7.00	(4)	9.00	119
a	Horizontal pair, imperf. vertically	1,900.00					
American Dogs Issue							
2098	20¢ Beagle and Boston Terrier 09/07/84	.40	.15			1.25	54
2099	20¢ Chesapeake Bay Retriever						
	and Cocker Spaniel 09/07/84	.40	.15			1.25	54
2100	20¢ Alaskan Malamute						
	and Collie 09/07/84	.40	.15			1.25	54
2101	20¢ Black and Tan Coonhound						
	and American Foxhound 09/07/84	.40	.15			1.25	54
a	Block of 4, #2098-2101	1.75	1.75	2.75	(4)	3.00	

Four stamps celebrating **American dogs** and illustrated by Roy Andersen were issued by the Postal Service in 1984. Featured together on one of the stamps are the **beagle and the Boston terrier**, breeds known for their affectionate natures.

Beagle, Boston Terrier

Beagles are small hounds that were initially bred to hunt, but are now popular as pets. Generally between 13 and 15 inches in height, they pack an enormous amount of energy into their small frames. As hunters, they have great stamina; as pets, they are eager playmates.

Like beagles, Boston terriers are popular pets, prized for their tenacity, playfulness, and loyalty. The breed, native to the United States, was developed from crossbreeding between bull terriers and bulldogs in Boston in the nineteenth century. Although they were originally bred to be fighting dogs, Boston terriers are now valued more for their intelligence and spirit than for their fighting prowess.

2088 **2089** **2090**

2091 **2092**

2093

2094 **2095** **2096** **2097**

2098 **2099**

2100 **2101** **2101a**

2102

2103

2104

2105

2106

2107

2108

2109

2110

2111

2114

2115b

2116

	ssues of 1984		Un	U	PB/PNC		FDC	Q(M)
2102	20¢ Crime Prevention	09/26/84	.40	.15	1.75	(4)	1.00	120
2103	20¢ Hispanic Americans	10/31/84	.40	.15	1.75	(4)	1.00	108
a	Vertical pair, imperf. horizontally		1,600.00					
2104	20¢ Family Unity	10/01/84	.40	.15	14.00	(20)	1.00	118
a	Horizontal pair, imperf. vertically		550.00					
2105	20¢ Eleanor Roosevelt	10/11/84	.40	.15	1.75	(4)	1.00	113
2106	20¢ A Nation of Readers	10/16/84	.40	.15	1.75	(4)	1.00	117
	Christmas Issue							
2107	20¢ Madonna and Child,							
	by Fra Filippo Lippi	10/30/84	.40	.15	1.70	(4)	1.00	751
2108	20¢ Santa Claus	10/30/84	.40	.15	1.70	(4)	1.00	786
a	Horizontal pair, imperf. vertically		950.00					
	Perf. 10.5							
2109	20¢ Vietnam Veterans'							
	Memorial	11/10/84	.40	.15	1.90	(4)	4.00	105
	Issues of 1985, Perf. 11							
	Performing Arts Issue, Jerome Kern							
2110	22¢ Jerome Kern Portrait and							
	Kern Studying Sheet Music	01/23/85	.40	.15	1.75	(4)	1.00	125
2111	(22¢)"D" Stamp	02/01/85	.55	.15	4.50	(6)	1.00	
a	Imperf. pair		45.00					
b	Vertical pair, imperf. horizontally		1,350.00					
	Coil Stamp, Perf. 10 Vertically							
2112	(22¢)"D" green Eagle (2111)	02/01/85	.60	.15	6.00	(3)	1.00	
a	Imperf. pair		50.00					
b	As "a," tagging omitted		140.00					
	Booklet Stamp, Perf. 11							
2113	(22¢)"D" green Eagle (2111),							
	single from booklet	02/01/85	.80	.15			1.00	
a	Booklet pane of 10	02/01/85	8.50	3.00			7.50	
b	As "a," imperf. between horizontally		—					
	Issues of 1985-87, Flag Over Capitol Issue							
2114	22¢ Flag Over Capitol	03/29/85	.40	.15	1.90	(4)	1.00	
	Pair with full horizontal gutter between							
	Coil Stamp, Perf. 10 Vertically							
2115	22¢ Flag Over Capitol (2114)	03/29/85	.40	.15	3.75	(3)	1.00	
a	Imperf. pair		15.00				1.00	
b	Inscribed "T" at bottom	05/23/87	.50	.15	4.00	(3)		
c	Black field of stars		—	—				
	#2115b issued for test on prephosphored paper. Paper is whiter and colors are brighter than on 2115.							
	Booklet Stamp, Perf. 10 Horizontally							
2116	22¢ Flag over Capitol,							
	single from booklet		.50	.15			1.00	
a	Booklet pane of 50	03/29/85	2.50	1.25			3.50	
	#2116 issued only in booklets. All stamps are imperf. at both sides or imperf. at both sides and bottom.							

	Issues of 1985		Un	U	PN		FDC
	Seashells Booklet Issue, Perf. 10						
2117	22¢ Frilled Dogwinkle	04/04/85	.40	.15			1.00
2118	22¢ Reticulated Helmet	04/04/85	.40	.15			1.00
2119	22¢ New England Neptune	04/04/85	.40	.15			1.00
2120	22¢ Calico Scallop	04/04/85	.40	.15			1.00
2121	22¢ Lightning Whelk	04/04/85	.40	.15			1.00
a	Booklet pane of 10		4.00	2.50			7.50
b	As "a," violet omitted		850.00				
c	As "a," imperf. between vertically		600.00				
e	Strip of 5, #2117-21		2.00	—			
	Express Mail Booklet Issue, Perf. 10 Vertically						
2122	$10.75 Eagle and Moon,						
	booklet single	04/29/85	17.00	7.00			40.00
a	Booklet pane of 3		52.50	—			95.00
	#2122 issued only in booklets. All stamps are imperf. at top and bottom or at top, bottom and one side.						
	Issues of 1985-89, Coil Stamps, Transportation Issue (See also #1897-1908, 2225-31, 2252-66, 2451-68)						
2123	3.4¢ School Bus 1920s	06/08/85	.15	.15	1.25	(3)	1.00
a	Untagged (Bureau precanceled)		.15	.15	6.75	(3)	
2124	4.9¢ Buckboard 1880s	06/21/85	.15	.15	1.10	(3)	1.00
a	Untagged (Bureau precanceled)		.20	.20	2.00	(3)	
2125	5.5¢ Star Route Truck 1910s	11/01/86	.15	.15	2.25	(3)	1.00
a	Untagged (Bureau precanceled)		.15	.15	1.90	(3)	
2126	6¢ Tricycle 1880s	05/06/85	.15	.15	1.65	(3)	1.50
a	Untagged (Bureau precanceled)		.15	.15	2.00	(3)	
b	As "a," imperf. pair		200.00				
2127	7.1¢ Tractor 1920s	02/06/87	.15	.15	2.75	(3)	1.00
a	Untagged (Bureau precanceled "Nonprofit org.")		.15	.15	3.50	(3)	
b	Untagged (Bureau precanceled "Nonprofit 5-Digit ZIP + 4")	05/26/89	.15	.15	2.25	(3)	5.00
2128	8.3¢ Ambulance 1860s	06/21/85	.20	.15	1.90	(3)	1.00
a	Untagged (Bureau precanceled)		.20	.20	2.25	(3)	
2129	8.5¢ Tow Truck 1920s	01/24/87	.20	.15	3.25	(3)	1.00
a	Untagged (Bureau precanceled)		.20	.20	3.50	(3)	
2130	10.1¢ Oil Wagon 1890s	04/18/85	.25	.15	3.00	(3)	1.00
a	Untagged (Bureau precanceled, black)		.25	.25	3.25	(3)	1.00
a	Untagged (Bureau precanceled, red)		.25	.25	2.75	(3)	1.00
b	As "a," black precancel, imperf. pair		100.00				
b	As "a," red precancel, imperf. pair		15.00				
2131	11¢ Stutz Bearcat 1933	06/11/85	.25	.15	2.00	(3)	1.25
2132	12¢ Stanley Steamer 1909	04/02/85	.25	.15	2.50	(3)	1.00
a	Untagged (Bureau precanceled)		.25	.25	2.75	(3)	
b	As "a," type II		.25	.25	21.00	(3)	
	Type II has "Stanley Steamer 1909" .5 mm shorter (17.5 mm) than #2132 (18mm).						
2133	12.5¢ Pushcart 1880s	04/18/85	.25	.15	3.25	(3)	1.25
a	Untagged (Bureau precanceled)		.25	.25	3.50	(3)	
b	As "a," imperf. pair		55.00				
2134	14¢ Iceboat 1880s	03/23/85	.30	.15	3.00	(3)	1.25
a	Imperf. pair		100.00				
2135	17¢ Dog Sled 1920s	08/20/86	.30	.15	3.50	(3)	1.25
a	Imperf. pair		550.00				
2136	25¢ Bread Wagon 1880s	11/22/86	.45	.15	4.00	(3)	1.25
a	Imperf. pair		10.00				

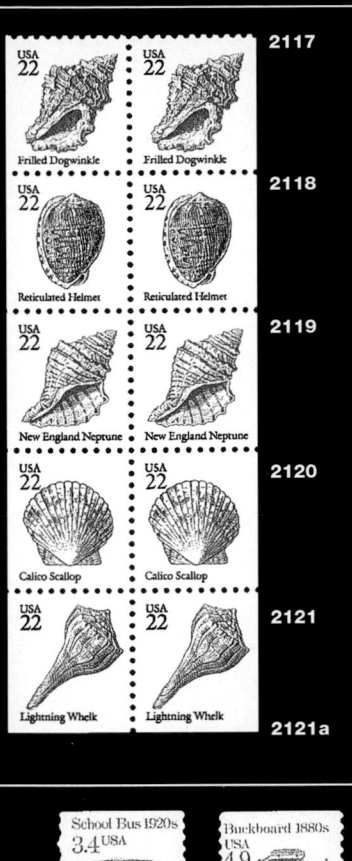

2117
Frilled Dogwinkle   Frilled Dogwinkle

2118
Reticulated Helmet   Reticulated Helmet

2119
New England Neptune   New England Neptune

2120
Calico Scallop   Calico Scallop

2121
Lightning Whelk   Lightning Whelk

2121a

2122

2123

2124

2125

2126

2127

2128

2129

2130

2131

2132

2133

2134

2135

2136

1985

2137

2138   **2139**

Broadbill Decoy — Folk Art USA 22

Mallard Decoy — Folk Art USA 22

Canvasback Decoy — Folk Art USA 22

Redhead Decoy — Folk Art USA 22

2140   **2141**   **2141a**

Winter Special Olympics

2142

LOVE USA 22

2143

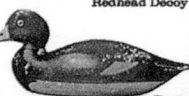

22 USA Rural Electrification Administration 1935 1985

2144

AMERIPEX 86
International Stamp Show, Chicago
May 22 to June 1, 1986.
USA 22

2145

Abigail Adams

2146

F.A. Bartholdi, Statue of Liberty Sculptor USA 22

2147

18 USA

2149

USA 21.1

2150

Veterans Korea USA 22

2152

Social Security Act 1935-1985 USA 22

2153

ssues of 1985			Un	U	PB/PN		FDC	Q(M)
Black Heritage Issue, Perf. 11								
2137	22¢ Mary McLeod Bethune Portrait	03/05/85	.40	.15	2.25	(4)	1.00	120
American Folk Art Issue, Duck Decoys								
2138	22¢ Broadbill Decoy	03/22/85	.60	.15			1.00	75
2139	22¢ Mallard Decoy	03/22/85	.60	.15			1.00	75
2140	22¢ Canvasback Decoy	03/22/85	.60	.15			1.00	75
2141	22¢ Redhead Decoy	03/22/85	.60	.15			1.00	75
a	Block of 4, #2138-41		3.75	2.25	6.00	(4)	2.75	
2142	22¢ Winter Special Olympics	03/25/85	.40	.15	1.75	(4)	1.00	121
a	Vertical pair, imperf. horizontally		650.00					
2143	22¢ Love	04/17/85	.40	.15	1.70	(4)	2.00	730
a	Imperf. pair		1,500.00					
2144	22¢ Rural Electrification							
	Administration	05/11/85	.45	.15	25.00	(20)	1.00	125
2145	22¢ AMERIPEX '86	05/25/85	.40	.15	1.75	(4)	1.00	203
a	Red, black and blue omitted		200.00					
b	Red and black omitted		1,250.00					
2146	22¢ Abigail Adams	06/14/85	.40	.15	1.90	(4)	1.00	126
a	Imperf. pair		275.00					
2147	22¢ Frederic A. Bartholdi	07/18/85	.40	.15	1.90	(4)	1.00	130
2148	Not assigned							
	Coil Stamps, Perf. 10 Vertically							
2149	18¢ George Washington,							
	Washington Monument	11/06/85	.35	.15	4.00	(3)	1.25	
a	Untagged (Bureau precanceled)		.35	.35	4.00	(3)		
b	Imperf. pair		950.00					
c	As "a," imperf. pair		800.00		5.50	(3)		
2150	21.1¢ Sealed Envelopes	10/22/85	.40	.15	4.00	(3)	1.25	
a	Untagged (Bureau precanceled)		.40	.40	4.25	(3)		
2151	Not assigned							
	Perf. 11							
2152	22¢ Korean War Veterans	07/26/85	.40	.15	1.90	(4)	3.00	120
2153	22¢ Social Security Act,							
	50th Anniversary	08/14/85	.40	.15	1.90	(4)	1.00	120

The bright, hopeful colors of the fourth **Love** stamp, issued in 1985, reflect the heart and mind of its creator, artist Corita Kent (1918–1986).

Corita Kent was born in Fort Dodge, Iowa. She became a nun when she was a young woman, and taught art at Immaculate Heart College in Los Angeles, where she eventually headed the art department. After leaving the sisterhood in 1968 she moved to Boston, where she became known for a brilliant rainbow-colored decoration of a natural gas tank along a highway. Her bold designs, which were also featured on posters and prints, conveyed messages of optimism and peace.

A highly principled woman, Corita Kent featured strong social and religious opinions in her work. Her message of love enjoyed enormous popularity: more than 700 million of the 1985 Love stamps were sold.

2167

2168

2169

2170

2171

2172

2173

2175

2176

2177

2178

2179

2180

2181

2182

2183

2184

2185

2186

2187

2188

2189

2190

2191

2192

2193

2194A

2195

2196

	ssues of 1986		Un	U	PB	#	FDC	Q(M)
2167	22¢ Arkansas Statehood	01/03/86	.40	.15	2.00	(4)	1.00	130
a	Vertical pair, imperf. horizontally		—					
	Issues of 1986-91, Great Americans Issue (See also #1844-69)							
2168	1¢ Margaret Mitchell	06/30/86	.15	.15	.25	(4)	1.50	
2169	2¢ Mary Lyon	02/28/87	.15	.15	.30	(4)	1.00	
2170	3¢ Paul Dudley White, MD	09/15/86	.15	.15	.40	(4)	1.00	
2171	4¢ Father Flanagan	07/14/86	.15	.15	.50	(4)	1.00	
2172	5¢ Hugo L. Black	02/27/86	.15	.15	.50	(4)	1.00	
2173	5¢ Luis Munoz Marin	02/18/90	.15	.15	.60	(4)	1.25	
2174	Not assigned							
2175	10¢ Red Cloud	08/15/87	.20	.15	.85	(4)	1.50	
a	Overall tagging	1990	.30	.15	10.00	(4)		
2176	14¢ Julia Ward Howe	02/12/87	.25	.15	1.25	(4)	1.00	
2177	15¢ Buffalo Bill Cody	06/06/88	.30	.15	1.40	(4)	2.00	
a	Overall tagging	1990	.30	—	3.25	(4)		
2178	17¢ Belva Ann Lockwood	06/18/86	.35	.15	1.75	(4)	1.00	
	Perf. 11 x 11.8							
2179	20¢ Virginia Apgar	10/24/94	.40	.15	2.00	(4)	1.25	
	Perf. 11							
2180	21¢ Chester Carlson	10/21/88	.40	.15	1.90	(4)	1.25	
2181	23¢ Mary Cassatt	11/04/88	.45	.15	2.00	(4)	1.25	
2182	25¢ Jack London	01/11/86	.45	.15	2.25	(4)	1.25	
a	Booklet pane of 10	05/03/88	4.50	3.75			6.00	
b	Tagging omitted	1990	—					
2183	28¢ Sitting Bull	09/28/89	.50	.15	2.50	(4)	1.50	
2184	29¢ Earl Warren	03/09/92	.55	.15	2.50	(4)	1.25	
2185	29¢ Thomas Jefferson	04/13/93	.50	.15	2.50	(4)	1.25	
2186	35¢ Dennis Chavez	04/03/91	.65	.15	3.25	(4)	1.25	
2187	40¢ Claire Lee Chennault	09/06/90	.70	.15	3.25	(4)	2.00	
2188	45¢ Harvey Cushing, MD	06/17/88	.85	.15	3.75	(4)	1.25	
a	Overall tagging	1990	1.65	.15				
2189	52¢ Hubert H. Humphrey	06/03/91	1.10	.15	5.00	(4)	1.35	
2190	56¢ John Harvard	09/03/86	1.10	.15	5.00	(4)	2.50	
2191	65¢ H.H. 'Hap' Arnold	11/05/88	1.20	.20	5.00	(4)	1.50	
2192	75¢ Wendell Willkie	02/16/92	1.30	.20	5.50	(4)	1.50	
2193	$1 Bernard Revel	09/23/86	2.25	.50	10.00	(4)	3.00	
2194	$1 Johns Hopkins	06/07/89	1.75	.50	7.00	(4)	3.00	
b	Overall tagging	1990	1.75	—	7.00	(4)		
2195	$2 William Jennings Bryan	03/19/86	3.50	.50	15.00	(4)	5.00	
2196	$5 Bret Harte	08/25/87	8.00	1.00	32.50	(4)	20.00	
	Booklet Stamp, Perf. 10							
2197	25¢ Jack London (2182),single from booklet		.45	.15			1.25	
a	Booklet pane of 6	05/03/88	3.00	2.25			4.00	

	ssues of 1986		Un	U	PE		FDC	Q(M)
	United States — Sweden Stamp Collecting Booklet Issue, Perf. 10 Vertically							
2198	22¢ Handstamped Cover	01/23/86	.45	.15			1.00	17
2199	22¢ Boy Examining							
	Stamp Collection	01/23/86	.45	.15			1.00	17
2200	22¢ #836 Under Magnifying							
	Glass	01/23/86	.45	.15			1.00	17
2201	22¢ 1986 Presidents							
	Miniature Sheet	01/23/86	.45	.15			1.00	17
a	Booklet pane of 4, #2198-2201		2.00	1.75			4.00	17
b	As "a," black omitted							
	on #2198, 2201		55.00					
c	As "a," blue omitted							
	on #2198-2200		2,500.00					
d	As "a," buff omitted		—					

#2198-2201 issued only in booklets. All stamps are imperf. at top and bottom or imperf. at top, bottom and right side.

	Perf. 11							
2202	22¢ Love	01/30/86	.40	.15	1.75	(4)	1.75	949
	Black Heritage Issue, Sojourner Truth							
2203	22¢ Sojourner Truth Portrait							
	and Truth Lecturing	02/04/86	.40	.15	1.75	(4)	1.00	130
2204	22¢ Republic of Texas,							
	150th Anniversary	03/02/86	.40	.15	1.75	(4)	1.25	137
a	Horizontal pair, imperf. vertically		1,100.00					
b	Dark red omitted		2,750.00					
c	Dark blue omitted		8,500.00					
	Fish Booklet Issue, Perf. 10 Horizontally							
2205	22¢ Muskellunge	03/21/86	.50	.15			1.00	44
2206	22¢ Atlantic Cod	03/21/86	.50	.15			1.00	44
2207	22¢ Largemouth Bass	03/21/86	.50	.15			1.00	44
2208	22¢ Bluefin Tuna	03/21/86	.50	.15			1.00	44
2209	22¢ Catfish	03/21/86	.50	.15			1.00	44
a	Booklet pane of 5, #2205-09		4.50	2.75			2.50	44

#2205-09 issued only in booklets. All stamps are imperf. at sides or imperf. at sides and bottom.

	Perf. 11							
2210	22¢ Public Hospitals	04/11/86	.40	.15	1.75	(4)	1.00	130
a	Vertical pair, imperf. horizontally		325.00					
b	Horizontal pair, imperf. vertically		1,350.00					
	Performing Arts Issue, Duke Ellington							
2211	22¢ Duke Ellington Portrait							
	and Piano Keys	04/29/86	.40	.15	1.90	(4)	1.75	130
a	Vertical pair, imperf. horizontally		1,000.00					
2212-15	Not assigned							

2198	2199	2200	2201	2201a

2202	2203	2204

2205

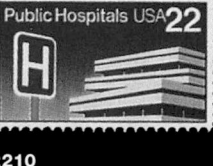

2210

2206

2207

2208

2209

2209a

2211

USA22
George Washington 1789-1797

2216a

USA22
John Adams 1797-1801

2216b

USA22
Thomas Jefferson 1801-1809

2216c

USA22
James Madison 1809-1817

2216d

USA22
James Monroe 1817-1825

2216e

USA22
John Quincy Adams 1825-1829

2216f

USA22
Andrew Jackson 1829-1837

2216g

USA22
Martin Van Buren 1837-1841

2216h

USA22
William Henry Harrison 1841-1841

2216i

USA22
John Tyler 1841-1845

2217a

USA22
James K. Polk 1845-1849

2217b

USA22
Zachary Taylor 1849-1850

2217c

USA22
Millard Fillmore 1850-1853

2217d

USA22
Franklin Pierce 1853-1857

2217e

USA22
James Buchanan 1857-1861

2217f

USA22
Abraham Lincoln 1861-1865

2217g

USA22
Andrew Johnson 1865-1869

2217h

USA22
Ulysses S. Grant 1869-1877

2217i

Issues of 1986		Un	U	FDC	Q(M)
AMERIPEX '86 Issue, Presidents Miniature Sheets, Perf. 11					
2216	Sheet of 9	05/22/86	3.75	—	4.00	6
a	22¢ George Washington		.40	.25	1.50	
b	22¢ John Adams		.40	.25	1.50	
c	22¢ Thomas Jefferson		.40	.25	1.50	
d	22¢ James Madison		.40	.25	1.50	
e	22¢ James Monroe		.40	.25	1.50	
f	22¢ John Quincy Adams		.40	.25	1.50	
g	22¢ Andrew Jackson		.40	.25	1.50	
h	22¢ Martin Van Buren		.40	.25	1.50	
i	22¢ William H. Harrison		.40	.25	1.50	
j	Blue omitted		3,500.00			
k	Black inscription omitted		2,000.00			
l	Imperf.		10,500.00			
2217	Sheet of 9	05/22/86	3.75	—	4.00	6
a	22¢ John Tyler		.40	.25	1.50	
b	22¢ James Polk		.40	.25	1.50	
c	22¢ Zachary Taylor		.40	.25	1.50	
d	22¢ Millard Fillmore		.40	.25	1.50	
e	22¢ Franklin Pierce		.40	.25	1.50	
f	22¢ James Buchanan		.40	.25	1.50	
g	22¢ Abraham Lincoln		.40	.25	1.50	
h	22¢ Andrew Johnson		.40	.25	1.50	
i	22¢ Ulysses S. Grant		.40	.25	1.50	

Presidents of
the United States: I

AMERIPEX 86
International
Stamp Show
Chicago, Illinois
May 22–June 1, 1986

#2216

Presidents of
the United States: II

AMERIPEX 86
International
Stamp Show
Chicago, Illinois
May 22–June 1, 1986

#2217

ssues of 1986		Un	U	FDC	Q(M)
AMERIPEX '86 Issue (continued), Presidents Miniature Sheets					
2218 Sheet of 9	05/22/86	3.75	—	4.00	6
a	22¢ Rutherford B. Hayes	.40	.25	1.50	
b	22¢ James A. Garfield	.40	.25	1.50	
c	22¢ Chester A. Arthur	.40	.25	1.50	
d	22¢ Grover Cleveland	.40	.25	1.50	
e	22¢ Benjamin Harrison	.40	.25	1.50	
f	22¢ William McKinley	.40	.25	1.50	
g	22¢ Theodore Roosevelt	.40	.25	1.50	
h	22¢ William H. Taft	.40	.25	1.50	
i	22¢ Woodrow Wilson	.40	.25	1.50	
j	Brown omitted	—			
k	Black inscription omitted	3,000.00			
2219 Sheet of 9	05/22/86	3.75	—	4.00	6
a	22¢ Warren G. Harding	.40	.25	1.50	
b	22¢ Calvin Coolidge	.40	.25	1.50	
c	22¢ Herbert Hoover	.40	.25	1.50	
d	22¢ Franklin D. Roosevelt	.40	.25	1.50	
e	22¢ White House	.40	.25	1.50	
f	22¢ Harry S. Truman	.40	.25	1.50	
g	22¢ Dwight D. Eisenhower	.40	.25	1.50	
h	22¢ John F. Kennedy	.40	.25	1.50	
i	22¢ Lyndon B. Johnson	.40	.25	1.50	

#2218

#2219

2218a

2218b

2218c

2218d

2218e

2218f

2218g

2218h

2218i

2219a

2219b

2219c

2219d

2219e

2219f

2219g

2219h

2219i

2220   2221

Liberty
1886-1986

USA 22

2224

Omnibus 1880s
1 USA

2225

2222   2223   2223a

Locomotive 1870s
2 USA

2226

2235   2236

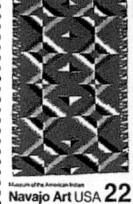

Navajo Art USA 22

Navajo Art USA 22

Navajo Art USA 22

Navajo Art USA 22

T.S. Eliot

22 USA

2239

2240   2241

Folk Art USA 22   Folk Art USA 22

Folk Art USA 22   Folk Art USA 22

2237   2238   2238a

2242   2243   2243a

CHRISTMAS 22 USA

Perugino, National Gallery

2244

GREETINGS

2245

USA 22

1837-1987
Michigan Statehood

2246

22 USA

Pan American Games Indianapolis 1987

2247

LOVE

USA 22

2248

Jean Baptiste
Pointe Du Sable 22

Black Heritage USA

2249

Enrico
Caruso
22 USA

2250

GIRL SCOUTS USA 22

2251

	Issues of 1986,		Un	U	PB/PNC	#	FDC	Q(M)
Arctic Explorers Issue, Perf. 11								
2220	22¢ Elisha Kent Kane	05/28/86	.65	.15			1.00	33
2221	22¢ Adolphus W. Greely	05/28/86	.65	.15			1.00	33
2222	22¢ Vilhjalmur Stefansson	05/28/86	.65	.15			1.00	33
2223	22¢ Robt. Peary, Matt. Henson	05/28/86	.65	.15			1.00	33
a	Block of 4, #2220-23		2.75	2.25	4.50	(4)	2.50	
b	As "a," black omitted		9,500.00					
2224	22¢ Statue of Liberty	07/04/86	.40	.15	2.25	(4)	3.00	221
Issues of 1986-87, Reengraved Transportation Issue, Coil Stamps, Perf. 10 Vertically								
(See also #1897-1908, 2123-36, 2252-66, 2452-53A, 2457, 2464, 2468)								
2225	1¢ Omnibus	11/26/86	.15	.15	.90	(5)	1.00	
2226	2¢ Locomotive	03/06/87	.15	.15	.75	(5)	1.50	
2227, 2229-30, 2232-34 Not assigned								
2228	4¢ Stagecoach (1898A)	08/86	.15	.15	1.50	(5)		
2231	8.3¢ Ambulance (2128)							
	(Bureau precanceled)	08/29/86	.20	.20	4.50	(5)		
On #2228, "Stagecoach 1890s" is 17mm long; on #1898A, it is 19.5mm long. On #2231,								
"Ambulance 1860s" is 18mm long; on #2128, it is 18.5mm long.								
American Folk Art Issue, Navajo Blankets, Perf. 11								
2235	22¢ Navajo Art, four "+" marks							
	horizontally through middle	09/04/86	.45	.15			1.00	60
2236	22¢ Navajo Art, vertical							
	diamond pattern	09/04/86	.45	.15			1.00	60
2237	22¢ Navajo Art, horizontal							
	diamond pattern	09/04/86	.45	.15			1.00	60
2238	22¢ Navajo Art, jagged line							
	horizontally through middle	09/04/86	.45	.15			1.00	60
a	Block of 4, #2235-38		2.25	2.00	3.00	(4)	2.50	
b	As "a," black omitted		450.00					
Literary Arts Issue, T.S. Eliot								
2239	22¢ T.S. Eliot Portrait	09/26/86	.40	.15	1.90	(4)	1.00	132
American Folk Art Issue, Wood-Carved Figurines								
2240	22¢ Highlander Figure	10/01/86	.40	.15			1.00	60
2241	22¢ Ship Figurehead	10/01/86	.40	.15			1.00	60
2242	22¢ Nautical Figure	10/01/86	.40	.15			1.00	60
2243	22¢ Cigar Store Figure	10/01/86	.40	.15			1.00	60
a	Block of 4, #2240-43		1.75	1.75	3.00	(4)	2.50	
b	As "a," imperf. vertically		1,500.00					
Christmas Issue								
2244	22¢ Madonna and Child	10/24/86	.40	.15	2.00	(4)	1.00	690
2245	22¢ Village Scene	10/24/86	.40	.15	1.90	(4)	1.00	882
Issues of 1987								
2246	22¢ Michigan Statehood	01/26/87	.40	.15	1.90	(4)	1.00	167
Pair with full vertical gutter between								
2247	22¢ Pan American Games	01/29/87	.40	.15	1.90	(4)	1.00	167
a	Silver omitted		1,500.00					
Perf. 11.5 x 11								
2248	22¢ Love	01/30/87	.40	.15	1.90	(4)	1.75	842
Black Heritage Issue, Jean Baptiste Point Du Sable, Perf. 11								
2249	22¢ Portrait of Du Sable							
	and Chicago Settlement	02/20/87	.40	.15	1.90	(4)	1.00	143
Performing Arts Issue, Enrico Caruso								
2250	22¢ Caruso as the Duke							
	of Mantua in Rigoletti	02/27/87	.40	.15	1.90	(4)	1.00	130
2251	22¢ Girl Scouts	03/12/87	.40	.15	1.90	(4)	2.50	150

	Issues of 1987-88		Un	U	PN		FDC	Q(M)

Coil Stamps, Transportation Issue, Perf. 10 Vertically (See also #1897-1908, 2123-36, 2225-31, 2451-68)

2252	3¢ Conestoga Wagon 1800s	02/29/88	.15	.15	1.00	(5)	1.00	
2253	5¢ Milk Wagon 1900s	09/25/87	.15	.15	1.10	(5)	1.00	
2254	5.3¢ Elevator 1900s,							
	Bureau precanceled	09/16/88	.15	.15	1.50	(5)	1.25	
2255	7.6¢ Carreta 1770s,							
	Bureau precanceled	08/30/88	.15	.15	2.50	(5)	1.25	
2256	8.4¢ Wheel Chair 1920s,							
	Bureau precanceled	08/12/88	.15	.15	2.25	(5)	1.25	
a	Imperf. pair		750.00					
2257	10¢ Canal Boat 1880s	04/11/87	.20	.15	1.75	(5)	1.00	
2258	13¢ Patrol Wagon 1880s,							
	Bureau precanceled	10/29/88	.25	.25	3.00	(5)	1.50	
2259	13.2¢ Coal Car 1870s,							
	Bureau precanceled	07/19/88	.25	.25	3.00	(5)	1.50	
a	Imperf. pair		100.00					
2260	15¢ Tugboat 1900s	07/12/88	.25	.15	2.75	(5)	1.25	
2261	16.7¢ Popcorn Wagon 1902,							
	Bureau precanceled	07/07/88	.30	.30	3.75	(5)	1.25	
a	Imperf. pair		225.00					
2262	17.5¢ Racing Car 1911	09/25/87	.30	.15	4.00	(5	1.00	
a	Untagged (Bureau precanceled)		.30	.30	4.25	(5)		
b	Imperf. pair		2,250.00					
2263	20¢ Cable Car 1880s	10/28/88	.35	.15	4.00	(5)	1.25	
a	Imperf. pair		75.00					
2264	20.5¢ Fire Engine 1920s,							
	Bureau precanceled	09/28/88	.40	.40	4.00	(5)	2.00	
2265	21¢ Railroad Mail Car 1920s,							
	Bureau precanceled	08/16/88	.40	.40	4.00	(5)	1.50	
a	Imperf. pair		65.00					
2266	24.1¢ Tandem Bicycle 1890s,							
	Bureau precanceled	10/26/88	.45	.45	4.00	(5)	1.75	

Issues of 1987 (continued), Special Occasions Booklet Issue, Perf. 10

2267	22¢ Congratulations!	04/20/87	.55	.15		1.00	1,222
2268	22¢ Get Well!	04/20/87	.55	.15		1.00	611
2269	22¢ Thank you!	04/20/87	.55	.15		1.00	611
2270	22¢ Love You, Dad!	04/20/87	.55	.15		1.00	611
2271	22¢ Best Wishes!	04/20/87	.55	.15		1.00	611
2272	22¢ Happy Birthday!	04/20/87	.55	.15		1.00	1,222
2273	22¢ Love You, Mother!	04/20/87	.55	.15		1.00	611
2274	22¢ Keep In Touch!	04/20/87	.55	.15		1.00	611
a	Booklet pane of 10, #2268-71, 2273-74						
	and 2 each of #2267, 2272		8.00	5.00		5.00	611

#2267-74 issued only in booklets. All stamps are imperf. at one or two sides or imperf. at sides and bottom.

Conestoga Wagon 1800s 3 USA

Milk Wagon 1900s 5 USA

Elevator 1900s 5.3 USA Nonprofit Carrier Route Sort

Carreta 1770s 7.6 USA Nonprofit

Wheel Chair 1920s 8.4 USA Nonprofit

2252 **2253** **2254** **2255** **2256**

Canal Boat 1880s 10 USA

Patrol Wagon 1880s USA 13 Presorted First-Class

2257 **2258**

2267

Congratulations! USA 22

Coal Car 1870s 13.2 Bulk Rate USA

Tugboat 1900s USA 15

2259 **2260**

2268

Get Well! USA 22

Thank You! USA 22

2269

Popcorn Wagon 16.7 USA 1902 Bulk Rate

Racing Car 1911 USA 17.5

2261 **2262**

2270

Love You, Dad! USA 22

Best Wishes! USA 22

Happy Birthday! USA 22

2271 **2272**

USA 20 Cable Car 1880s

Fire Engine 1900s 20.5 USA ZIP+4 Presort

2263 **2264**

2273

Love You, Mother! USA 22

Keep In Touch! USA 22

Happy Birthday! USA 22

2274

Railroad Mail Car 1920s Presorted First-Class 21 USA

Tandem Bicycle 1890s 24.1 USA ZIP+4

2265 **2266**

Congratulations! USA 22

2274a

2275

2276

2277

2278

2279

2280

2281

2283

2283c

2282a

2285b

2284   **2285**

ssues of 1987		Un	U	PB/PNC	#	FDC	Q(M)
2275	22¢ United Way	04/28/87	.40	.15	1.90	(4)	1.00	157
2276	22¢ Flag with Fireworks	05/09/87	.40	.15	1.90	(4)	1.00	
a	Booklet pane of 20	11/30/87	8.50	—			8.00	
Issues of 1988-89 (All issued in 1988 except #2280 on prephosphored paper)								
2277	(25¢) "E" Stamp	03/22/88	.45	.15	2.00	(4)	1.25	
2278	25¢ Flag with Clouds	05/06/88	.45	.15	1.90	(4)	1.25	
	Pair with full vertical gutter between		—					
Coil Stamps, Perf. 10 Vertically								
2279	(25¢) "E" Earth	03/22/88	.45	.15	3.00	(5)	1.25	
a	Imperf. pair		90.00					
2280	25¢ Flag over Yosemite	05/20/88	.45	.15	4.00	(5)	1.25	
a	Prephosphored paper	02/14/89	.45	.15	4.00	(5)	1.25	
b	Imperf. pair, large block tagging		35.00					
e	Black trees		100.00	—				
2281	25¢ Honeybee	09/02/88	.45	.15	3.25	(3)	1.25	
a	Imperf. pair		45.00					
b	Black omitted		65.00					
d	Pair, imperf. between		1,000.00					
Booklet Stamp, Perf. 10								
2282	(25¢) "E" Earth (#2277), single from booklet		.50	.15			1.25	
a	Booklet pane of 10	03/22/88	6.50	3.50			6.00	
Pheasant Booklet Issue, Perf. 11								
2283	25¢ Pheasant, single from booklet		.50	.15			1.25	
a	Booklet pane of 10	04/29/88	6.50	3.50			6.00	
b	Single, red removed from sky		6.00	.15				
c	As "b," booklet pane of 10		65.00	—				
d	As "a," imperf. horizontally between	2,250.00						
#2283 issued only in booklets. All stamps have one or two imperf. edges. Imperf. and part perf. pairs and panes exist from printer's waste.								
Owl and Grosbeak Booklet Issue, Perf. 10								
2284	25¢ Grosbeak, single from booklet		.45	.15			1.25	
2285	25¢ Owl, single from booklet		.45	.15			1.25	
b	Booklet pane of 10, 5 each of #2284, 2285	05/28/88	4.50	3.50			6.00	
#2284 and 2285 issued only in booklets. All stamps are imperf. at one side or imperf. at one side and bottom.								
2285A	25¢ Flag with Clouds (#2278), single from booklet		.45	.15			1.25	
c	Booklet pane of 6	07/05/88	2.75	2.00			4.00	

A controversial thinker, professor, and author, **W.E.B. Du Bois,** is considered one of the leading African American intellectuals and social reformers of the 20th century. A brilliant scholar and essayist, he was dedicated to gaining equal treatment for black people in a white-dominated world. A founding member of the National Association for the Advancement of Colored People (NAACP), he also edited its magazine, The Crisis, for 24 years. In his career as a writer and orator he criticized imperialism, supported socialism and civil rights, and called for greater independence for black nations.

In 1961 he joined the Communist party and moved to Ghana at the invitation of President Kwame Nkruma. In 1992, the Postal Service honored Du Bois by featuring him on a stamp in the Black Heritage series. Barbara Higgins-Bond illustrated the stamp.

	Issues of 1987		Un	U	FDC	Q(M)
	American Wildlife Issue, Perf. 11					
2286	22¢ Barn Swallow	06/13/87	.85	.15	1.50	13
2287	22¢ Monarch Butterfly	06/13/87	.85	.15	1.50	13
2288	22¢ Bighorn Sheep	06/13/87	.85	.15	1.50	13
2289	22¢ Broad-tailed Hummingbird	06/13/87	.85	.15	1.50	13
2290	22¢ Cottontail	06/13/87	.85	.15	1.50	13
2291	22¢ Osprey	06/13/87	.85	.15	1.50	13
2292	22¢ Mountain Lion	06/13/87	.85	.15	1.50	13
2293	22¢ Luna Moth	06/13/87	.85	.15	1.50	12
2294	22¢ Mule Deer	06/13/87	.85	.15	1.50	13
2295	22¢ Gray Squirrel	06/13/87	.85	.15	1.50	13
2296	22¢ Armadillo	06/13/87	.85	.15	1.50	13
2297	22¢ Eastern Chipmunk	06/13/87	.85	.15	1.50	13
2298	22¢ Moose	06/13/87	.85	.15	1.50	13
2299	22¢ Black Bear	06/13/87	.85	.15	1.50	13
2300	22¢ Tiger Swallowtail	06/13/87	.85	.15	1.50	13
2301	22¢ Bobwhite	06/13/87	.85	.15	1.50	13
2302	22¢ Ringtail	06/13/87	.85	.15	1.50	13
2303	22¢ Red-winged Blackbird	06/13/87	.85	.15	1.50	13
2304	22¢ American Lobster	06/13/87	.85	.15	1.50	13
2305	22¢ Black-tailed Jack Rabbit	06/13/87	.85	.15	1.50	13
2306	22¢ Scarlet Tanager	06/13/87	.85	.15	1.50	13
2307	22¢ Woodchuck	06/13/87	.85	.15	1.50	13
2308	22¢ Roseate Spoonbill	06/13/87	.85	.15	1.50	13
2309	22¢ Bald Eagle	06/13/87	.85	.15	1.50	13
2310	22¢ Alaskan Brown Bear	06/13/87	.85	.15	1.50	13

Visionary **Walt Disney** (1901-1966) rode the wave of early animation to new heights. The legendary animator and producer helped define the medium of animated cartoons. With lovable characters like Mickey Mouse, Donald Duck, and Goofy, he built a vast entertainment empire that expanded into films, television programs, books, and an endless array of merchandise for children. In 1937 he produced *Snow White and the Seven Dwarfs*, Disney's first full-length animated film. He followed the success of this film with others such as, *Pinocchio, Fantasia*, and *Cinderella*. Disney's characters came to life in two famous amusement parks, Disneyland in California and Walt Disney World in Florida. The legacy of Walt Disney continues today.

In 1968 the U.S. Post Office Department honored Walt Disney with a commemorative stamp. The stamp was designed by Robert C. Moore and Paul E. Wenzel.

2286   2287   2288   2289   2290

2291   2292   2293   2294   2295

2296   2297   2298   2299   2300

2301   2302   2303   2304   2305

2306   2307   2308   2309   2310

22 USA *Iiwi* — 2311
22 USA *Badger* — 2312
22 USA *Pronghorn* — 2313
22 USA *River Otter* — 2314
22 USA *Ladybug* — 2315

22 USA *Beaver* — 2316
22 USA *White-tailed Deer* — 2317
22 USA *Blue Jay* — 2318
22 USA *Pika* — 2319
22 USA *Bison* — 2320

22 USA *Snowy Egret* — 2321
22 USA *Gray Wolf* — 2322
22 USA *Mountain Goat* — 2323
22 USA *Deer Mouse* — 2324
22 USA *Black-tailed Prairie Dog* — 2325

22 USA *Box Turtle* — 2326
22 USA *Wolverine* — 2327
22 USA *American Elk* — 2328
22 USA *California Sea Lion* — 2329
22 USA *Mockingbird* — 2330

22 USA *Raccoon* — 2331
22 USA *Bobcat* — 2332
22 USA *Black-footed Ferret* — 2333
22 USA *Canada Goose* — 2334
22 USA *Red Fox* — 2335

	Issues of 1987		Un	U	FDC	Q(M)
	American Wildlife Issue (continued), Perf. 11					
2311	22¢ Iiwi	06/13/87	.85	.15	1.50	13
2312	22¢ Badger	06/13/87	.85	.15	1.50	13
2313	22¢ Pronghorn	06/13/87	.85	.15	1.50	13
2314	22¢ River Otter	06/13/87	.85	.15	1.50	13
2315	22¢ Ladybug	06/13/87	.85	.15	1.50	13
2316	22¢ Beaver	06/13/87	.85	.15	1.50	13
2317	22¢ White-tailed Deer	06/13/87	.85	.15	1.50	13
2318	22¢ Blue Jay	06/13/87	.85	.15	1.50	13
2319	22¢ Pika	06/13/87	.85	.15	1.50	13
2320	22¢ Bison	06/13/87	.85	.15	1.50	13
2321	22¢ Snowy Egret	06/13/87	.85	.15	1.50	13
2322	22¢ Gray Wolf	06/13/87	.85	.15	1.50	13
2323	22¢ Mountain Goat	06/13/87	.85	.15	1.50	13
2324	22¢ Deer Mouse	06/13/87	.85	.15	1.50	13
2325	22¢ Black-tailed Prairie Dog	06/13/87	.85	.15	1.50	13
2326	22¢ Box Turtle	06/13/87	.85	.15	1.50	13
2327	22¢ Wolverine	06/13/87	.85	.15	1.50	13
2328	22¢ American Elk	06/13/87	.85	.15	1.50	13
2329	22¢ California Sea Lion	06/13/87	.85	.15	1.50	13
2330	22¢ Mockingbird	06/13/87	.85	.15	1.50	13
2331	22¢ Raccoon	06/13/87	.85	.15	1.50	13
2332	22¢ Bobcat	06/13/87	.85	.15	1.50	13
2333	22¢ Black-footed Ferret	06/13/87	.85	.15	1.50	13
2334	22¢ Canada Goose	06/13/87	.85	.15	1.50	13
2335	22¢ Red Fox	06/13/87	.85	.15	1.50	13
a	Pane of 50, #2286-2335		47.50		50.00	
b	Any single, red omitted		—			

Example of 2335a

ssues of 1987-90		Un	U	PB		FDC	Q(M)
Constitution Bicentennial Issue, Ratification of the Constitution, Perf. 11							
2336	22¢ Delaware	07/04/87	.40	.15	2.00	(4)	1.00	168
2337	22¢ Pennsylvania	08/26/87	.40	.15	2.25	(4)	1.00	187
2338	22¢ New Jersey	09/11/87	.40	.15	2.00	(4)	1.00	184
a	Black omitted		6,000.00					
2339	22¢ Georgia	01/06/88	.40	.15	2.00	(4)	1.00	169
2340	22¢ Connecticut	01/09/88	.40	.15	2.00	(4)	1.25	155
2341	22¢ Massachusetts	02/06/88	.40	.15	2.00	(4)	1.00	102
2342	22¢ Maryland	02/15/88	.40	.15	2.25	(4)	1.00	103
2343	25¢ South Carolina	05/23/88	.45	.15	2.00	(4)	1.25	162
2344	25¢ New Hampshire	06/21/88	.45	.15	2.00	(4)	1.25	153
2345	25¢ Virginia	06/25/88	.45	.15	2.25	(4)	1.25	160
2346	25¢ New York	07/26/88	.45	.15	2.00	(4)	1.25	183
2347	25¢ North Carolina	08/22/89	.45	.15	2.00	(4)	1.25	
2348	25¢ Rhode Island	05/29/90	.45	.15	2.00	(4)	1.25	164
2349	22¢ Friendship with Morocco	07/18/87	.40	.15	1.75	(4)	1.00	157
a	Black omitted		350.00					
Issues of 1987, Literary Arts Issue								
2350	22¢ William Faulkner	08/03/87	.40	.15	1.75	(4)	1.00	156
American Folk Art Issue, Lacemaking								
2351	22¢ Squash Blossoms	08/14/87	.45	.15			1.00	41
2352	22¢ Floral Piece	08/14/87	.45	.15			1.00	41
2353	22¢ Floral Piece	08/14/87	.45	.15			1.00	41
2354	22¢ Dogwood Blossoms	08/14/87	.45	.15			1.00	41
a	Block of 4, #2351-54		1.90	1.90	3.25	(4)	2.75	
b	As "a," white omitted		1,000.00					

Fallingwater is one of the most admired works of architect Frank Lloyd Wright. It was built for department-store owner Edgar J. Kaufmann and his family as a weekend retreat in western Pennsylvania. Fallingwater is depicted on one of four stamps by Walter Dubois Richards that were issued by the Postal Service in 1982 to celebrate American architecture. One of the most famous houses in the world, Fallingwater exemplifies Wright's philosophy of organic architecture.

Wright's architectural style uses contemporary designs and materials, harmonizes with its surroundings, and serves the people who use it. Fallingwater meets these criteria admirably. It has a bold contemporary design and reinforced concrete terraces. Wright designed the house to be constructed over a waterfall in Bear Run, where the Kaufmanns enjoyed swimming and sunbathing. He made a boulder the hearthstone of the fireplace and installed stairs from the living room down to the water. The design brings the inhabitants close to the surrounding water and woods and expresses harmony with nature. Fallingwater was later donated to the state and is now open to visitors who marvel at its innovative design.

Dec 7, 1787 USA
Delaware 22
2336

22 USA
Dec 12, 1787
Pennsylvania
2337

Dec 28, 1787 USA
New Jersey 22
2338

22 USA
January 2, 1788
Georgia
2339

22 USA
January 9, 1788
Connecticut
2340

22 USA
Feb 6, 1788
Massachusetts
2341

April 28, 1788 USA
Maryland 22
2342

25 USA
May 23, 1788
South Carolina
2343

25 USA
June 21, 1788
New Hampshire
2344

June 25, 1788 USA
Virginia 25
2345

July 26, 1788 USA
New York 25
2346

25 USA
November 21, 1789
North Carolina
2347

25 USA
May 29, 1790
Rhode Island
2348

Friendship
with Morocco
1787-1987
USA 22
2349

William Faulkner
USA 22
2350

2351   **2352**

Lacemaking USA 22   Lacemaking USA 22

Lacemaking USA 22   Lacemaking USA 22

2353   **2354**   **2354a**

The Bicentennial
of the Constitution of
the United States
of America
1787-1987 USA 22   **2355**

We the people
of the United States,
in order to form
a more perfect Union...
Preamble, U.S. Constitution   USA 22   **2356**

Establish justice,
insure domestic tranquility,
provide for the common defense,
promote the general welfare...
Preamble, U.S. Constitution   USA 22   **2357**

And secure
the blessings of liberty
to ourselves
and our posterity...
Preamble, U.S. Constitution   USA 22   **2358**

Do ordain
and establish this
Constitution for the
United States of America.
Preamble, U.S. Constitution   USA 22   **2359**

2359a

2360   **2361**

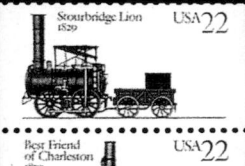

Stourbridge Lion
1829   USA 22   **2362**

Best Friend
of Charleston
1830   USA 22   **2363**

John Bull
1831   USA 22   **2364**

Brother Jonathan
1832   USA 22   **2365**

Gowan & Marx
1839   USA 22   **2366**

2366a

CHRISTMAS 2.2 USA
Moroni, National Gallery

2367

USA 22 GREETINGS

2368

ssues of 1987			Un	U	PB		FDC	Q(M)
Constitution Bicentennial Issue, Drafting of the Constitution Booklet Issue, Perf. 10 Horizontally								
2355	22¢ "The Bicentennial..."	08/28/87	.50	.15			1.00	122
2356	22¢ "We the people..."	08/28/87	.50	.15			1.00	122
2357	22¢ "Establish justice..."	08/28/87	.50	.15			1.00	122
2358	22¢ "And secure..."	08/28/87	.50	.15			1.00	122
2359	22¢ "Do ordain..."	08/28/87	.50	.15			1.00	122
a	Booklet pane of 5, #2355-59		2.50	*2.25*			3.00	122
	#2355-59 issued only in booklets. All stamps are imperf. at sides or imperf. at sides and bottom.							
	Signing of the Constitution, Perf. 11							
2360	22¢ Constitution and Signer's Hand-Holding Quill Pen	09/17/87	.40	.15	2.00	(4)	1.00	169
2361	22¢ Certified Public Accountants	09/21/87	*1.90*	.15	*9.00*	(4)	3.50	163
a	Black omitted		*900.00*					
	Locomotives Booklet Issue, Perf. 10 Horizontally							
2362	22¢ Stourbridge Lion, 1829	10/01/87	.55	.15			1.50	143
2363	22¢ Best Friend of Charleston, 1830	10/01/87	.55	.15			1.50	143
2364	22¢ John Bull, 1831	10/01/87	.55	.15			1.50	143
2365	22¢ Brother Jonathan, 1832	10/01/87	.55	.15			1.50	143
2366	22¢ Gowan & Marx, 1839	10/01/87	.55	.15			1.50	143
a	Booklet pane of 5, #2362-66		2.75	*2.50*			4.50	143
b	As "a," black omitted on #2366		—					
	#2362-66 issued only in booklets. All stamps are imperf. at sides or imperf. at sides and bottom.							
	Christmas Issue, Perf. 11							
2367	22¢ Madonna and Child, by Moroni	10/23/87	.40	.15	2.00	(4)	1.00	529
2368	22¢ Christmas Ornaments	10/23/87	.40	.15	1.75	(4)	1.00	978
	Pair with full vertical gutter between		—					

During the summer of 1787 the 55 delegates to the Constitutional Convention pulled together 12 of the 13 loosely allied states (Rhode Island did not participate) into a republic. **The Constitution,** signed on September 17th, was made effective by the formation of a new government in the spring of 1789. The document set forth a framework for the American system of government. Power would be divided between the states and the federal government, each of which would consist of legislative, judicial, and executive branches. Each branch would check and balance the others' power.

The Framers also made it a flexible document, allowing for amendments. Ratified in 1791 and comprised of the first ten amendments, the Bill of Rights safeguards individual freedoms.

The U.S. Postal Service's stamp commemorates the bicentennial of this truly momentous and unprecedented accomplishment; the formation of a nation by its citizenry. Illustrated by Howard Koslow, the stamp was issued in 1987.

	ssues of 1988		Un	U	PE		FDC	Q(M)
	Winter Olympic Games Issue, Perf. 11							
2369	22¢ Skier and Olympic Rings	01/10/88	.40	.15	1.75	(4)	1.00	159
2370	22¢ Australia Bicentennial	01/10/88	.40	.15	1.75	(4)	1.00	146
	Black Heritage Issue							
2371	22¢ Portrait of James Weldon Johnson and Music from "Lift Ev'ry Voice and Sing"	02/02/88	.40	.15	1.75	(4)	1.00	97
	American Cats Issue							
2372	22¢ Siamese and Exotic Shorthair	02/05/88	.45	.15			2.00	40
2373	22¢ Abyssinian and Himalayan	02/05/88	.45	.15			2.00	40
2374	22¢ Maine Coon and Burmese	02/05/88	.45	.15			2.00	40
2375	22¢ American Shorthair and Persian	02/05/88	.45	.15			2.00	40
a	Block of 4, #2372-75		1.90	1.90	3.75	(4)	4.50	
	American Sports Issue							
2376	22¢ Knute Rockne Holding Football on Field	03/09/88	.40	.15	2.25	(4)	3.50	97
	Francis Ouimet							
2377	25¢ Portrait of Ouimet and Ouimet Hitting Fairway Shot	06/13/88	.45	.15	2.50	(4)	3.50	153
2378	25¢ Love	07/04/88	.45	.15	1.90	(4)	1.75	841
2379	45¢ Love	08/08/88	.65	.20	3.25	(4)	1.75	180
	Summer Olympic Games Issue							
2380	25¢ Gymnast on Rings	08/19/88	.45	.15	1.90	(4)	1.25	157

Four stamps celebrating **American cats** were issued by the Postal Service in 1988. Featured on one stamp were the **Siamese and the exotic shorthair**. The Siamese is one of the best-known breeds of cat in the world.

Siamese originated in Asia and were treasured by the royal family of Siam (now Thailand). They first came to England from Siam in the late 19th century and by the early 20th century were appearing in American cat shows.

Cherished for their beauty, Siamese are long and slim with a short, fine coat and blue, almond-shaped eyes. They are outgoing and affectionate pets, intelligent and playful.

The artist for the American Cats stamps was John D. Dawson, who has worked on other Postal Service projects: Idaho Statehood (1990), Flowering Trees (1998), and Sonoran Desert and Pacific Coast Rain Forest, both from The Nature of America series (1999 and 2000).

2370

2369

2371

2372　　　　**2373**

2374　　　　**2375**　　**2375a**

2378

2376　　　　**2377**　　　　**2379**

2380

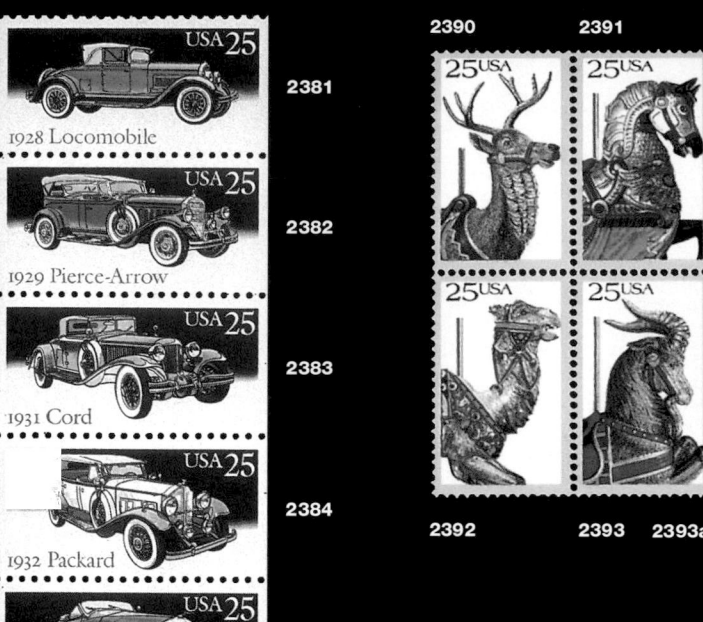

2381 — 1928 Locomobile
2382 — 1929 Pierce-Arrow
2383 — 1931 Cord
2384 — 1932 Packard
2385 — 1935 Duesenberg

2385a

2390 2391
2392 2393 2393a

2386 2387
Nathaniel Palmer — Lt. Charles Wilkes
Richard E. Byrd — Lincoln Ellsworth
2388 2389 2389a

ssues of 1988			Un	U	PB	#	FDC	Q(M)
Classic Cars Booklet Issue, Perf. 10 Horizontally								
2381	25¢ 1928 Locomobile	08/25/88	.50	.15			1.25	127
2382	25¢ 1929 Pierce-Arrow	08/25/88	.50	.15			1.25	127
2383	25¢ 1931 Cord	08/25/88	.50	.15			1.25	127
2384	25¢ 1932 Packard	08/25/88	.50	.15			1.25	127
2385	25¢ 1935 Duesenberg	08/25/88	.50	.15			1.25	127
a	Booklet pane of 5, #2381-85		5.25	2.25			3.00	127
#2381-85 issued only in booklets. All stamps are imperf. at sides or imperf. at sides and bottom.								
Antarctic Explorers Issue, Perf. 11								
2386	25¢ Nathaniel Palmer	09/14/88	.65	.15			1.25	41
2387	25¢ Lt. Charles Wilkes	09/14/88	.65	.15			1.25	41
2388	25¢ Richard E. Byrd	09/14/88	.65	.15			1.25	41
2389	25¢ Lincoln Ellsworth	09/14/88	.65	.15			1.25	41
a	Block of 4, #2386-89		2.75	2.00	4.50	(4)	3.00	
b	As "a," black omitted		1,500.00					
c	As "a," imperf. horizontally		3,000.00					
American Folk Art Issue, Carousel Animals								
2390	25¢ Deer	10/01/88	.65	.15			2.50	76
2391	25¢ Horse	10/01/88	.65	.15			2.50	76
2392	25¢ Camel	10/01/88	.65	.15			2.50	76
2393	25¢ Goat	10/01/88	.65	.15			2.50	76
a	Block of 4, #2390-93		3.00	2.00	4.00	(4)	5.00	

In the 1920s and '30s the Pierce-Arrow Motor Car Company designed and manufactured some of the most elegant automobiles in the world. By 1929 the company had established a reputation for its luxury cars. Known for their signature fender-mounted headlamps and well-crafted chassis, Pierce-Arrows were a symbol of status and wealth. A **1929 Pierce-Arrow** was one of five automobiles featured on the 1988 Classic Cars stamps.

Pierce-Arrow's 1929 line was strikingly popular, selling almost 10,000 in that year. The company then created a stir in 1933 when it introduced its stylishly designed Silver Arrow. Although only five were produced, the elegant Silver Arrow became a lasting part of the company's legacy. By the late 1930s, the Great Depression and increased competition from larger engines and more innovative styles pushed Pierce-Arrow into bankruptcy.

Ken Dallison, the Classic Cars' artist, is a respected and experienced illustrator. His work has appeared in such publications as Redbook, National Geographic, Esquire, and Sports Illustrated. His automotive projects include commissioned works for Mercedes Benz, Rolls Royce, and the Indianapolis 500. Car and Driver and Road and Track magazines also have published his work.

ssues of 1988		Un	U	PE		FDC	Q(M)
2394 $8.75 Express Mail	10/04/88	13.50	8.00	54.00	(4)	25.00	
Special Occasions Booklet Issue							
2395 25¢ Happy Birthday	10/22/88	.50	.15			1.25	120
2396 25¢ Best Wishes	10/22/88	.50	.15			1.25	120
a Booklet pane of 6, 3 #2395 and							
3 #2396 with gutter between		3.50	3.25			4.00	
2397 25¢ Thinking of You	10/22/88	.50	.15			2.00	120
2398 25¢ Love You	10/22/88	.50	.15			2.00	120
a Booklet pane of 6, 3 #2397 and							
3 #2398 with gutter between		3.50	3.25			5.00	
b As "a," imperf. horizontally		—					
#2395-98a issued only in booklets. All stamps are imperf. on one side or on one side and top or bottom.							
Christmas Issue							
2399 25¢ Madonna and Child,							
by Botticelli	10/20/88	.45	.15	1.90	(4)	1.25	844
a Gold omitted		30.00					
2400 25¢ One-Horse Open							
Sleigh and Village Scene	10/20/88	.45	.15	1.90	(4)	1.25	1,038
Pair with full vertical gutter between		—					

In January 2000 the U.S. Postal Service issued a pane of 15 stamps commemorating the **1980s** as a part of the **Celebrate The Century®** program. Featuring several illustrations by Robert Rodriguez, the 1980s stamps capture the spirit of the decade—from entertainment and sports to science and technology.

The 1980s were a time of profound change. The first space shuttle was launched in 1981, Sandra Day O'Connor became the first female justice on the U.S. Supreme Court, and Sally Ride became the first American woman in space. It was also a time to reflect on the past and ponder the future: The **Vietnam Veterans Memorial** in Washington, D.C., was dedicated in 1982, Martin Luther King Day was first celebrated in January 1986, and the fall of the **Berlin Wall** in 1989 presaged the end of the Cold War.

It was also a decade marked by new cultural trends and notable moments in entertainment. Audiences were touched by the film *E.T. The Extra-Terrestrial* and charmed by the Broadway musical *Cats*. Video games mesmerized people both in arcades and at home, and Cabbage Patch Kids® set off a shopping frenzy during the 1983-84 holiday season. The Cosby Show was one of the decade's most popular TV programs, and hip-hop culture spread across the country.

2394

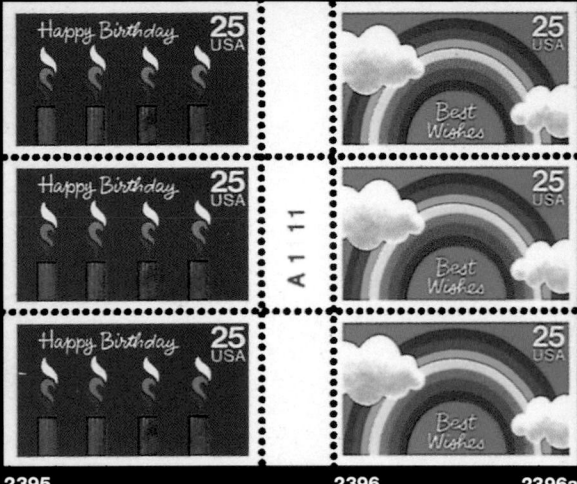

2395   2396   2396a

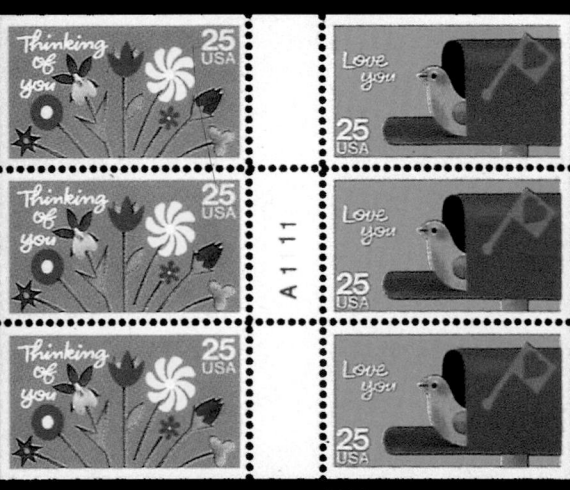

2397   2398   2398a

2399

2400

2401

2402

2403

2404

2405

2406

2407

2408

2409

2409a

2410

2411

2412

2413

2414

2415

2416

2417

2418

Issues of 1989		Un	U	PB		FD	Q(M)
2401 25¢ Montana Statehood	01/15/89	.45	.15	2.00	(4)	1.25	165
Black Heritage Issue							
2402 25¢ Portrait of A. Philip Randolph, Pullman							
Porters and Railroad Cars	02/03/89	.45	.15	2.00	(4)	1.25	152
2403 25¢ North Dakota Statehood	02/21/89	.45	.15	1.90	(4)	1.25	163
2404 25¢ Washington Statehood	02/22/89	.45	.15	2.00	(4)	1.25	265
Steamboats Booklet Issue, Perf. 10 Horizontally							
2405 25¢ Experiment 1788-90	03/03/89	.45	.15			1.25	159
2406 25¢ Phoenix 1809	03/03/89	.45	.15			1.25	159
2407 25¢ New Orleans 1812	03/03/89	.45	.15			1.25	159
2408 25¢ Washington 1816	03/03/89	.45	.15			1.25	159
2409 25¢ Walk in the Water 1818	03/03/89	.45	.15			1.25	159
a Booklet pane of 5, #2405-09		2.25	1.75			4.00	159
#2405-09 issued only in booklets. All stamps are imperf. at sides or imperf. at sides and bottom.							
Perf. 11							
2410 25¢ World Stamp Expo '89	03/16/89	.45	.15	1.90	(4)	1.25	164
Performing Arts Issue							
2411 25¢ Portrait of Arturo Toscanini							
Conducting with Baton	03/25/89	.45	.15	2.00	(4)	1.25	152
Issues of 1989-90, Constitution Bicentennial Issue							
2412 25¢ U.S. House of							
Representatives	04/04/89	.45	.15	1.90	(4)	1.25	139
2413 25¢ U.S. Senate	04/06/89	.45	.15	2.00	(4)	1.25	138
2414 25¢ Executive Branch, George							
Washington	04/16/89	.45	.15	2.00	(4)	1.25	139
2415 25¢ Supreme Court, Chief Justice							
John Marshall	02/02/90	.45	.15	1.90	(4)	1.25	151
Issues of 1989 (continued)							
2416 25¢ South Dakota							
Statehood	05/03/89	.45	.15	1.90	(4)	1.25	165
American Sports Issue							
2417 25¢ Portrait of Lou Gehrig,							
Gehrig Swinging Bat	06/10/89	.50	.15	3.00	(4)	4.00	263
Literary Arts Issue							
2418 25¢ Portrait of Ernest Hemingway, African							
Landscape in Background	07/17/89	.45	.15	2.00	(4)	1.25	192

Ernest Hemingway (1899-1961), a distinctive prose stylist and winner of the Nobel Prize for Literature, was honored by the Postal Service with a stamp issued in 1989. Part of the Literary Arts series, this stamp, illustrated by Greg Rudd, portrays Hemingway in an African landscape. The setting recalls Hemingway's safaris to Africa, a subject he explored in *Green Hills of Africa*.

Hemingway began his writing career as a reporter in Kansas City. During World War I, he was an ambulance driver for the Red Cross. After the war, he moved to Paris, where his first book, *Three Stories and Ten Poems,* was published in 1923. He subsequently wrote such novels as *The Sun Also Rises*, *A Farewell to Arms, For Whom the Bell Tolls*, and *The Old Man and the Sea,* for which he won a Pulitzer Prize. Hemingway was also acknowledged as a master of the short story.

Hemingway's stoic protagonists and understated prose are hallmarks of his writing. His heroes show courage in the face of adversity, a quality that Hemingway described as "grace under pressure." Hemingway's prose is concrete and spare, unemotional yet evocative. His style has been a major influence on twentieth-century writers.

	ssues of 1989		Un	U	PE		FDC	Q(M)
	Priority Mail Issue, Perf. 11 x 11.5							
2419	$2.40 Moon Landing	07/20/89	4.00	2.00	16.00	(4)	9.00	
a	Black omitted		2,500.00					
b	Imperf. pair		750.00					
	Perf. 11							
2420	25¢ Letter Carriers	08/30/89	.45	.15	1.90	(4)	1.25	188
	Constitution Bicentennial Issue, Drafting of the Bill of Rights							
2421	25¢ Stylized U.S. Flag, Eagle							
	With Quill Pen in Mouth	09/25/89	.45	.15	3.00	(4)	1.25	192
a	Black omitted		375.00					
	Prehistoric Animals Issue							
2422	25¢ Tyrannosaurus	10/01/89	.65	.15			1.50	102
2423	25¢ Pteranodon	10/01/89	.65	.15			1.50	102
2424	25¢ Stegosaurus	10/01/89	.65	.15			1.50	102
2425	25¢ Brontosaurus	10/01/89	.65	.15			1.50	102
a	Block of 4, #2422-25		3.00	2.00	3.50	(4)	3.00	
b	As "a," black omitted		1,150.00					
	America/PUAS Issue (See also #C121)							
2426	25¢ Southwest Carved Figure							
	(A.D. 1150-1350), Emblem of the							
	Postal Union of the Americas	10/12/89	.45	.15	2.00	(4)	1.25	137
	Christmas Issue, Perf. 11.5							
2427	25¢ Madonna and							
	Child, by Caracci	10/19/89	.45	.15	2.00	(4)	1.25	913
a	Booklet pane of 10		4.75	3.50			6.00	
	Perf. 11							
2428	25¢ Sleigh Full of Presents	10/19/89	.45	.15	1.90	(4)	1.25	900
a	Vertical pair, imperf.							
	horizontally		2,000.00					
	Booklet Stamp Issue, Perf. 11.5							
2429	25¢ Single from booklet							
	pane (#2428)	10/19/89	.45	.15			1.25	399
a	Booklet pane of 10		4.75	3.50			6.00	40
b	As "a," imperf. horiz. between		—					
d	As "a," red omitted		—					
	In #2429, runners on sleigh are twice as thick as in 2428; bow on package at rear of sleigh							
	is same color as package; board running underneath sleigh is pink.							
2430	Not assigned							
	Self-Adhesive, Die-Cut							
2431	25¢ Eagle and Shield	11/10/89	.50	.20			1.25	75
a	Booklet pane of 18		11.00					
b	Vertical pair, no							
	die-cutting between		850.00					
2432	Not assigned							

2419

2420

2421

2422   2423

2424   2425   2425a

2426

2427

2428

2431

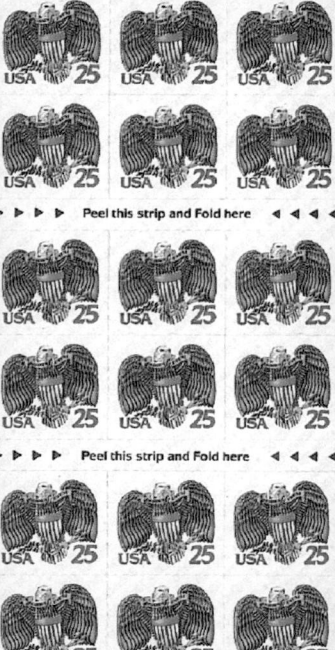

2431a

2431 (coil)

WORLD STAMP EXPO'89 SM

The classic 1869 U.S. Abraham Lincoln stamp is reborn in these four larger versions commemorating World Stamp Expo'89, held in Washington, D.C. during the 20th Universal Postal Congress of the UPU. These stamps show the issued colors and three of the trial proof color combinations.

USPS 1988

2433

2434   **2435**

2436   **2437**   **2437a**

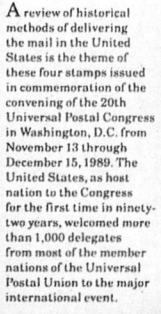

20th Universal Postal Congress

A review of historical methods of delivering the mail in the United States is the theme of these four stamps issued in commemoration of the convening of the 20th Universal Postal Congress in Washington, D.C. from November 13 through December 15, 1989. The United States, as host nation to the Congress for the first time in ninety-two years, welcomed more than 1,000 delegates from most of the member nations of the Universal Postal Union to the major international event.

2438

IDAHO

USA 25 1890

2439

L O V E
USA 25

2440

Ida B. Wells

Black Heritage USA 25

2442

USA 15

2443

Issues of 1989		Un	U	PB	#	FDC	Q(M)
World Stamp Expo '89 Issue Souvenir Sheet, Imperf.							
2433	Reproduction of #122, 90¢ Lincoln,						
	and three essays of #122	11/17/89	14.00	9.00			7.00	2
a-d	Single stamp from sheet		2.00	1.75				
	20th UPU Congress Issues, Classic Mail Transportation, Perf. 11							
	(See also #C122-25)							
2434	25¢ Stagecoach	11/19/89	.45	.15			1.25	41
2435	25¢ Paddlewheel Steamer	11/19/89	.45	.15			1.25	41
2436	25¢ Biplane	11/19/89	.45	.15			1.25	41
2437	25¢ Depot-Hack Type							
	Automobile	11/19/89	.45	.15			1.25	41
a	Block of 4, #2434-37		2.00	1.00	3.75	(4)	3.00	
b	As "a," dark blue omitted		1,000.00					
	Souvenir Sheet, Imperf. (See also #C126)							
2438	Designs of #2434-37	11/28/89	4.00	1.75			2.00	2
a-d	Single stamp from sheet		.65	.25				
	Issues of 1990, Perf. 11							
2439	25¢ Idaho Statehood	01/06/90	.45	.15	2.00	(4)	1.25	173
	Perf. 12.5 x 13							
2440	25¢ Love	01/18/90	.45	.15	2.00	(4)	1.25	886
a	Imperf. pair		850.00					
	Booklet Stamp, Perf. 11.5							
2441	25¢ Love, single from booklet	01/18/90	.45	.15			1.25	995
a	Booklet pane of 10	01/18/90	4.75	3.50			6.00	
b	As "a," bright pink omitted		2,250.00					
	Black Heritage Issue, Perf. 11							
2442	25¢ Portrait of Ida B. Wells,							
	Marchers in Background	02/01/90	.45	.15	2.00	(4)	1.25	153
	Beach Umbrella Booklet Issue, Perf. 11.5 x 11							
2443	15¢ Beach Umbrella,							
	single from booklet	02/03/90	.30	.15			1.25	
a	Booklet pane of 10	02/03/90	3.00	2.00			4.25	
b	As "a," blue omitted		2,000.00					

#2443 issued only in booklets. All stamps are imperf. at one side or imperf. at one side and bottom.

Transportation has played an essential role in the delivery of mail in the United States from the Revolutionary era to the present. Roads, waterways, rails, and the air have opened up new postal routes. The U.S. Postal Service (once the U.S. Post Office Department) has used the latest systems of transportation and contributed to their development. In 1989 the Postal Service issued four stamps depicting historical methods of mail transportation: stagecoach, paddlewheel steamer, biplane, and depot-hack type automobile.

These stamps, illustrated by Mark Hess, commemorated the convening in 1989 of the **20th Universal Postal Congress** in Washington, D.C. The Universal Postal Congress is the legislative body of the Universal Postal Union, a specialized institution of the United Nations that regulates postal service throughout the world. The United States, as host to the Congress in 1989, welcomed delegates from member nations to this major international event.

	Issues of 1990		Un	U	PB		FDC	Q(M)
	Perf 11							
2444	25¢ Wyoming Statehood	02/23/90	.45	.15	2.00	(4)	1.25	169
	Classic Films Issue							
2445	25¢ The Wizard of Oz	03/23/90	1.00	.15			2.50	44
2446	25¢ Gone With the Wind	03/23/90	1.00	.15			2.50	44
2447	25¢ Beau Geste	03/23/90	1.00	.15			2.50	44
2448	25¢ Stagecoach	03/23/90	1.00	.15			2.50	44
a	Block of 4, #2445-48		4.50	3.50	6.00	(4)	5.00	
	Literary Arts Issue							
2449	25¢ Portrait of Marianne Moore	04/18/90	.45	.15	2.00	(4)	1.25	150
2450	Not assigned							
	Issues of 1990-95, Transportation Issue, Coil Stamps, Perf. 9.8 Vertically							
2451	4¢ Steam Carriage 1866	01/25/91	.15	.15	1.25	(5)	1.25	
a	Imperf. pair		700.00					
2452	5¢ Circus Wagon 1900s, intaglio printing	08/31/91	.15	.15	1.40	(5)	1.40	
2452B	5¢ Circus Wagon (2452), gravure printing	12/08/92	.15	.15	1.60	(5)	1.50	
2452D	5¢ Circus Wagon (2452), gravure printing	03/20/95	.15	.15	1.60	(5)	1.50	
2453	5¢ Canoe 1800s, precanceled, intaglio printing	05/25/91	.15	.15	1.75	(5)	1.25	
2454	5¢ Canoe 1800s, precanceled, gravure printing	10/22/91	.15	.15	1.60	(5)	1.25	
2455-56	Not assigned							
2457	10¢ Tractor Trailer, Bureau precanceled, intaglio printing	05/25/91	.20	.20	2.10	(5)	1.25	
2458	10¢ Tractor Trailer, Bureau precanceled, gravure printing	05/25/94	.20	.20	2.25	(5)	1.25	
2459-62	Not assigned							
2463	20¢ Cog Railway Car 1870s	06/09/95	.40	.15	4.00	(5)	1.25	
a	Imperf. pair		150.00					
2464	23¢ Lunch Wagon 1890s	04/12/91	.45	.15	4.00	(5)	1.25	
b	Imperf. pair		175.00					
2465	Not assigned							
2466	32¢ Ferryboat 1900s		.60	.15	6.50	(5)	1.25	
2467	Not assigned							
2468	$1 Seaplane 1914	04/20/90	1.75	.50	10.00	(5)	2.50	
2469	Not assigned							
	Issues of 1990, Lighthouses Booklet Issue, Perf. 10 Vertically							
2470	25¢ Admiralty Head, WA	04/26/90	.45	.15			1.75	147
2471	25¢ Cape Hatteras, NC	04/26/90	.45	.15			1.75	147
2472	25¢ West Quoddy Head, ME	04/26/90	.45	.15			1.75	147
2473	25¢ American Shoals, FL	04/26/90	.45	.15			1.75	147
2474	25¢ Sandy Hook, NJ	04/26/90	.45	.15			1.75	147
a	Booklet pane of 5, #2470-74		2.50	2.00			4.50	147
b	As "a," white (USA 25) omitted		75.00					

2444

2445   **2446**

2449

2447   **2448**   **2448a**

2451

2452

2452D

2453

2454

2457

2463

2464

2466

2468

2474a

2470   **2471**   **2472**   **2473**   **2474**

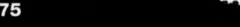

2475

2476   **2477**

2478

2479

2480   **2481**   **2482**

2483

2484

2485

2486

2487

2488

2489

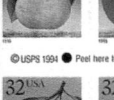

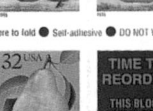

2487-88a

2490

2491

2492

2496

2497

2498

2499

2500   **2500a**

2501

2502

2503

2504

2505   **2505a**

ssues of 1990-1995		Un	U	PB		FDC	Q(M)
Self-Adhesive Issue, Die-Cut							
2475	25¢ Flag, single from pane	05/18/90	.50	.25			1.25	36
a	Pane of 12	05/18/90	6.00				
Flora and Fauna Issues, Perf. 11							
2476	1¢ American Kestrel	06/22/91	.15	.15	.15	(4)	1.25
2477	1¢ American Kestrel	05/10/95	.15	.15	.15	(4)	1.25
2478	3¢ Eastern Bluebird	06/22/91	.15	.15	.30	(4)	1.25
Perf. 11.5 x 11							
2479	19¢ Fawn	03/11/91	.35	.15	1.75	(4)	1.25
2480	30¢ Cardinal	06/22/91	.50	.15	2.25	(4)	1.25
Perf. 11							
2481	45¢ Pumpkinseed Sunfish	12/02/92	.80	.15	3.90	(4)	1.75
a	Black omitted		600.00	—			
2482	$2 Bobcat	06/01/90	3.00	1.25	12.00	(4)	5.00
Perf. 10.9 x 9.8							
2483	20¢ Blue Jay	06/15/95	.40	.15			1.25
a	Booklet pane of 10		4.00	2.25			
Wood Duck Booklet Issue, Perf. 10							
2484	29¢ Black and multicolored	04/12/91	.50	.15			1.25
a	Booklet pane of 10		5.50	3.75			5.00
Perf. 11							
2485	29¢ Red and multicolored	04/12/91	.50	.15			1.25
a	Booklet pane of 10		5.50	4.00			5.00
#2484-85a issued only in bklts. All stamps are imperf. top or bottom, or top or bottom and right edge.							
Perf. 10 x 11							
2486	29¢ African Violet	10/08/93	.50	.15			1.25
a	Booklet pane of 10		5.50	4.00			5.00
2487	32¢ Peach	07/08/95	.60	.15			1.25
2488	32¢ Pear	07/08/95	.60	.15			1.25
a	Booklet pane, 5 each #2487-88		6.00	4.25			7.50
b	Pair, #2487-88		1.25	.30			
Issues of 1993 (Self-Adhesive), Die-Cut							
2489	29¢ Red Squirrel	06/25/93	.50	.15			1.25
2490	29¢ Red Rose	08/19/93	.50	.15			1.25
2491	29¢ Pine Cone	11/05/93	.50	.15			1.25
Serpentine Die-Cut							
2492	32¢ Pink Rose	06/02/95	.60	.15			1.25
a	Booklet pane of 20 plus label		12.00				
Issues of 1995 (Self Adhesive), Serpentine Die-Cut							
2493	32¢ Peach	07/08/95	.60	.15			
2494	32¢ Pear	07/08/95	.60	.15			
Coil Stamps, Serpentine Die Cut Vert.							
2495	32¢ Peach	07/08/95	.60	.15			
2495A	32¢ Pear	07/08/95	.60	.15	5.25	(5)	
Issues of 1990, Olympians Issue, Perf. 11							
2496	25¢ Jesse Owens	07/06/90	.60	.15			1.25	36
2497	25¢ Ray Ewry	07/06/90	.60	.15			1.25	36
2498	25¢ Hazel Wightman	07/06/90	.60	.15			1.25	36
2499	25¢ Eddie Eagan	07/06/90	.60	.15			1.25	36
2500	25¢ Helene Madison	07/06/90	.60	.15			1.25	36
a	Strip of 5, #2496-2500		3.25	2.50	8.00	(10)	3.00	7
Indian Headdresses Booklet Issue							
2501	25¢ Assiniboine Headdress	08/17/90	.55	.15			1.25	124
2502	25¢ Cheyenne Headdress	08/17/90	.55	.15			1.25	124
2503	25¢ Comanche Headdress	08/17/90	.55	.15			1.25	124
2504	25¢ Flathead Headdress	08/17/90	.55	.15			1.25	124
2505	25¢ Shoshone Headdress	08/17/90	.55	.15			1.25	124
a	Booklet pane of 10, 2 each of #2501-05		5.50	3.50			6.00	62
b	As "a," black omitted		2,500.00				
#2501-05 issued only in booklets. All stamps imperf. top or bottom, or top or bottom and right edge.							

	Issues of 1990		Un	U	PB		FDC	Q(M)
	Micronesia/Marshall Islands Issue, Perf. 11							
2506	25¢ Canoe and Flag of the							
	Federated States of Micronesia	09/28/90	.45	.15			1.25	76
2507	25¢ Stick Chart, Canoe and							
	Flag of the Marshall Islands	09/28/90	.45	.15			1.25	76
a	Pair, #2506-07		.90	.60	2.25	(4)	2.00	61
b	As "a" black omitted		4,000.00					
	Creatures of the Sea Issue							
2508	25¢ Killer Whales	10/03/90	.45	.15			1.25	70
2509	25¢ Northern Sea Lions	10/03/90	.45	.15			1.25	70
2510	25¢ Sea Otter	10/03/90	.45	.15			1.25	70
2511	25¢ Common Dolphin	10/03/90	.45	.15			1.25	70
a	Block of 4, #2508-11		1.90	1.75	2.50	(4)	3.00	70
b	As "a," black omitted		900.00					
	America/PUAS Issue, (See also #C127) 1990-1991							
2512	25¢ Grand Canyon	10/12/90	.45	.15	2.00	(4)	1.25	151
2513	25¢ Dwight D. Eisenhower	10/13/90	.45	.15	2.75	(4)	1.25	143
a	Imperf. pair		2,250.00					
	Christmas Issue, Perf. 11.5							
2514	25¢ Madonna and							
	Child, by Antonello	10/18/90	.45	.15	2.00	(4)	1.25	500
a	Booklet pane of 10		5.00	3.25			5.00	23
	Perf. 11							
2515	25¢ Christmas Tree	10/18/90	.45	.15	2.00	(4)	1.25	599
	Booklet Stamp, Perf. 11.5 x 11 on two or three sides							
2516	Single (2515) from booklet pane	10/18/90	.45	.15	1.25			
a	Booklet pane of 10	10/18/90	5.00	3.25			6.00	32
	Issues of 1991, Perf. 13							
2517	(29¢) "F" Stamp	01/22/91	.50	.15	2.50	(4)	1.25	
	Coil Stamp, Perf. 10 Vertically							
2518	(29¢) "F" Tulip (2517)	01/22/91	.50	.15	4.25	(5)	1.25	
	Booklet Stamps, Perf. 11 on two or three sides							
2519	(29¢) "F", single from booklet		.50	.15			1.25	
a	Booklet pane of 10	01/22/91	6.50	4.50			7.25	
2520	(29¢) "F", single from booklet		.50	.15			1.25	
a	Booklet pane of 10	01/22/91	18.00	4.50			7.25	
	#2519 has bull's-eye perforations that measure approximately 11.2. #2520 has less-pronounced							
	black lines in the leaf, which is a much brighter green than on #2519.							
	Perf. 11							
2521	(4¢) Makeup Rate	01/22/91	.15	.15	.40	(4)	1.25	
	Self-Adhesive, Die-Cut, Imperf.							
2522	(29¢) F Flag, single from pane		.55	.25			1.25	
a	Pane of 12	01/22/91	7.00					
	Coil Stamps, Perf. 10 Vertically							
2523	29¢ Flag Over Mt. Rushmore,							
	intaglio printing	03/29/91	.50	.15	4.75	(5)	1.25	
b	Imperf. pair		22.50					
2523A	29¢ Flag Over Mt. Rushmore,							
	gravure printing	07/04/91	.50	.15	5.25	(5)	1.25	

2506   2507   2507a

2508   2509   2511a

2510   2511

2512

2513

2514   2515

   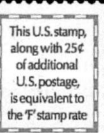

2517   2519   2520   2521

2522

2523   2523A

ssues of 1995		Un	U	PB		FDC	Q(M)
Perf. 11.2							
2544 $3 Space Shuttle *Challenger*	06/22/95	5.25	2.25	21.00	(4)	7.00	
Express Mail Rate, Perf. 11							
2544A $10.75 Space Shuttle *Endeavour*	08/04/95	17.50	7.50			15.00	
Issues of 1991, Fishing Flies Booklet Issue, Perf. 11 Horizontally							
2545 29¢ Royal Wulff	05/31/91	.55	.15			1.25	149
2546 29¢ Jock Scott	05/31/91	.55	.15			1.25	149
2547 29¢ Apte Tarpon Fly	05/31/91	.55	.15			1.25	149
2548 29¢ Lefty's Deceiver	05/31/91	.55	.15			1.25	149
2549 29¢ Muddler Minnow	05/31/91	.55	.15			1.25	149
a Booklet pane of 5, #2545-49		3.00	*2.50*			3.00	149
#2545-49 were issued only in booklets. All stamps are imperf. at sides or imperf. at sides and bottom.							
Performing Arts Issue, Perf. 11							
2550 29¢ Portrait of Cole Porter at Piano, Sheet Music	06/08/91	.50	.15	2.50	(4)	1.25	150
a Vertical pair, imperf. horizontally		*650.00*					
2551 29¢ Operations Desert Shield/ Desert Storm	07/02/91	.50	.15	2.50	(4)	2.50	200
Booklet Stamp, Perf. 11 on one or two sides							
2552 29¢ Operations Desert Shield/Desert Storm (2551), single from booklet	07/02/91	.50	.15			2.50	200
a Booklet pane of 5	07/02/91	2.75	*2.25*			4.50	40
Summer Olympic Games Issue, Perf. 11							
2553 29¢ Pole Vaulter	07/12/91	.50	.15			1.25	34
2554 29¢ Discus Thrower	07/12/91	.50	.15			1.25	34
2555 29¢ Women Sprinters	07/12/91	.50	.15			1.25	34
2556 29¢ Javelin Thrower	07/12/91	.50	.15			1.25	34
2557 29¢ Women Hurdlers	07/12/91	.50	.15			1.25	34
a Strip of 5, #2553-57		2.75	2.25	7.50	(10)	3.00	34
2558 29¢ Numismatics	08/13/91	.50	.15	2.50	(4)	1.25	150
World War II Issue, 1941: A World at War, Miniature Sheet, Perf. 11							
2559 Sheet of 10 and central label	09/03/91	5.25	4.50			7.00	15
a 29¢ Burma Road		.50	.30			1.50	15
b 29¢ America's First Peacetime Draft		.50	.30			1.50	15
c 29¢ Lend-Lease Act		.50	.30			1.50	15
d 29¢ Atlantic Charter		.50	.30			1.50	15
e 29¢ Arsenal of Democracy		.50	.30			1.50	15
f 29¢ Destroyer *Reuben James*		.50	.30			1.50	15
g 29¢ Civil Defense		.50	.30			1.50	15
h 29¢ Liberty Ship		.50	.30			1.50	15
i 29¢ Pearl Harbor		.50	.30			1.50	15
j 29¢ U.S. Declaration of War		.50	.30			1.50	15

Born Ethel Agnes Zimmermann, **Ethel Merman** was a secretary who began her showbiz career in small stage roles. Her big break came in 1930 when George Gershwin hired her for the musical *Girl Crazy*. Her brassy performance of "I Got Rhythm" brought down the house, prompting Gershwin to implore her never to ruin her distinctive style with voice lessons.

Merman was a Broadway superstar, singing the songs of theater luminaries such as Cole Porter, Irving Berlin, and George and Ira Gershwin. She appeared in classics such as *Anything Goes* and *Gypsy*. Ethel Merman appeared along with Nat "King" Cole, Ethel Waters, Bing Crosby, and Al Jolson on the 1994 Popular Singers stamps in the Legends of American Music series. The stamps were illustrated by Chris Payne.

2544

2544A

Cole Porter
USA 29

2550

2545 Royal Wulff

2546 Jock Scott

2547 Apte Tarpon Fly

2548 Lefty's Deceiver

2549 Muddler Minnow

2549a

Honoring
Those Who Served
Desert Shield ★ Desert Storm

2551

NUMISMATICS

2558

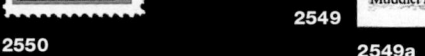

2553   2554   2555   2556   2557   2557a

a   b   c   d   e

1941: A World at War

f   g   h   i   j   **2559**

313

2561

2560

2567

2562　　　　**2563**　　　　**2564**　　　　**2565**　　　**2566**　**2566a**

2568　　　**2569**　　　　**2570**　　　　**2571**　　　　**2572**

    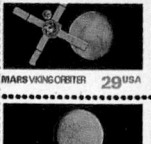

2573　　　　**2574**　　　　**2575**　　　　**2576**　　　　**2577**　**2577a**

2578

2579　　　　**2580**　　　　**2581**　　　**2581a**

2582　　　　**2583**　　　　**2584**　　　　**2585**

	ssues of 1991		Un	U	PB	#	FDC	Q(M)
2560	29¢ Basketball	08/28/91	.50	.15	2.50	(4)	2.00	150
2561	29¢ District of Columbia	09/07/91	.50	.15	2.50	(4)	1.25	149
	Comedians Booklet Issue, Perf. 11 on two or three sides							
2562	29¢ Stan Laurel and Oliver Hardy	08/29/91	.50	.15			1.25	140
2563	29¢ Edgar Bergen and							
	Dummy Charlie McCarthy	08/29/91	.50	.15			1.25	140
2564	29¢ Jack Benny	08/29/91	.50	.15			1.25	140
2565	29¢ Fanny Brice	08/29/91	.50	.15			1.25	140
2566	29¢ Bud Abbott and Lou Costello	08/29/91	.50	.15			1.25	140
a	Booklet pane of 10, 2 each of #2562-66		5.50	*3.50*			6.00	70
b	As "a," scarlet and bright violet omitted		*900.00*					
	#2562-66 issued only in booklets. All stamps are imperf. at top or bottom, or at top or bottom and right side.							
	Black Heritage Issue, Perf. 11							
2567	29¢ Portrait of Jan Matzeliger and							
	Shoe-Lasting Machine Diagram	09/15/91	.50	.15	2.50	(4)	1.25	149
	Space Exploration Booklet Issue							
2568	29¢ Mercury, Mariner 10	10/01/91	.50	.15			1.25	33
2569	29¢ Venus, Mariner 2	10/01/91	.50	.15			1.25	33
2570	29¢ Earth, Landsat	10/01/91	.50	.15			1.25	33
2571	29¢ Moon, Lunar Orbiter	10/01/91	.50	.15			1.25	33
2572	29¢ Mars, Viking Orbiter	10/01/91	.50	.15			1.25	33
2573	29¢ Jupiter, Pioneer 11	10/01/91	.50	.15			1.25	33
2574	29¢ Saturn, Voyager 2	10/01/91	.50	.15			1.25	33
2575	29¢ Uranus, Voyager 2	10/01/91	.50	.15			1.25	33
2576	29¢ Neptune, Voyager 2	10/01/91	.50	.15			1.25	33
2577	29¢ Pluto	10/01/91	.50	.15			1.25	33
a	Booklet pane of 10, #2568-77		5.50	*3.50*			5.00	33
	#2568-77 issued only in booklets. All stamps are imperf. at top or bottom, or at top or bottom and right side.							
	Christmas Issue, Perf. 11							
2578	29¢ Madonna and Child,							
	by Romano	10/17/91	.50	.15	2.50	(4)	1.25	401
a	Booklet pane of 10		5.50	*3.25*				30
2579	29¢ Santa Claus Sliding							
	Down Chimney	10/17/91	.50	.15	2.50	(4)	1.25	900
	Booklet Stamps							
2580	29¢ Santa Claus (2579),							
	Type I, single from booklet	10/17/91	1.75	.15			1.25	
2581	29¢ Santa Claus (2579),							
	Type II, single from booklet	10/17/91	1.75	.15			1.25	
a	Pair, #2580, 2581	10/17/91	3.50	.25				28
	The extreme left brick in top row of chimney is missing from Type II, #2581.							
2582	29¢ Santa Claus Checking							
	List, single from booklet	10/17/91	.50	.15			1.25	
a	Booklet pane of 4	10/17/91	2.00	*1.25*			2.50	28
2583	29¢ Santa Claus Leaving Present							
	Under Tree, single from booklet	10/17/91	.50	.15			1.25	
a	Booklet pane of 4	10/17/91	2.00	*1.25*			2.50	28
2584	29¢ Santa Claus Going Up							
	Chimney, single from booklet	10/17/91	.50	.15			1.25	
a	Booklet pane of 4	10/17/91	2.00	*1.25*			2.50	28
2585	29¢ Santa Claus Flying Away							
	in Sleigh, single from booklet	10/17/91	.50	.15			1.25	
a	Booklet pane of 4	10/17/91	2.00	*1.25*			2.50	28
	#2582-85 issued only in booklets. All stamps are imperf. at top or bottom, or at top or bottom and right side.							

	Issue of 1995		Un	U	PB		FDC	Q(M)
	Perf. 11.2							
2587	32¢ James K. Polk	11/02/95	.60	.15	3.00	(4)	1.25	
	Issues of 1994, Perf. 11.5							
2590	$1 Victory at Saratoga	05/05/94	1.90	.50	7.60	(4)	2.00	
2592	$5 Washington and Jackson	08/19/94	8.00	2.50	40.00	(4)	9.00	
	Issue of 1992, Perf. 10							
2593	29¢ Pledge of Allegiance	09/08/92	.50	.15			1.25	
a	Booklet of 10		5.25	4.25			5.00	
	Issue of 1993, Perf. 11 x 10							
2594	29¢ Pledge of Allegiance	04/08/93	.50	.15				
a	Booklet of 10		5.25	4.25				
	Issues of 1992, Self-Adhesive Booklet and Coil Stamps							
2595	29¢ Eagle and Shield							
	(brown lettering)	09/25/92	.50	.25			1.25	
a	Pane of 17 + label		13.00					
2596	29¢ Eagle and Shield							
	(green lettering)	09/25/92	.50	.25			1.25	
a	Pane of 17 + label		12.00					
2597	29¢ Eagle and Shield							
	(red lettering)	09/25/92	.50	.25			1.25	
a	Pane of 17 + label		10.00					
	Issues of 1994, Perf. 10							
2598	29¢ Eagle, Self-Adhesive	02/04/94	.50	.15			1.25	
2599	29¢ Statue of Liberty	06/24/94	.50	.15			1.25	
	Issues of 1991-93, Perf. 10 Vertically							
2602	10¢ Eagle and Shield							
	(inscribed "Bulk Rate USA")	12/13/91	.20	.20	3.50	(5)	1.25	
2603	10¢ Eagle and Shield							
	(inscribed "USA Bulk Rate")	05/29/93	.20	.20	4.00	(5)	1.25	
2604	10¢ Eagle and Shield (metallic,							
	inscribed "USA Bulk Rate")	05/29/93	.20	.20	3.50	(5)	1.25	
2605	23¢ Flag, Presorted First-Class	09/27/91	.40	.40	4.25	(5)	1.25	
	Issues of 1992, Perf. 11							
2606	23¢ USA	07/21/92	.40	.40	4.75	(5)	1.25	
2607	23¢ USA (Bureau)							
	(In #2607, "23" is 7mm long)	10/09/92	.40	.40	4.75	(5)	1.25	
2608	23¢ USA (violet)	05/14/93	.40	.40	4.75	(5)	1.25	
2609	29¢ Flag Over White House	04/23/92	.50	.15	4.75	(5)	1.25	
	Winter Olympic Games Issue							
2611	29¢ Hockey	01/11/92	.50	.15			1.25	32
2612	29¢ Figure Skating	01/11/92	.50	.15			1.25	32
2613	29¢ Speed Skating	01/11/92	.50	.15			1.25	32
2614	29¢ Skiing	01/11/92	.50	.15			1.25	32
2615	29¢ Bobsledding	01/11/92	.50	.15			1.25	32
a	Strip of 5, #2611-15		2.75	2.25	6.50	(10)	3.00	
2616	29¢ World Columbian							
	Stamp Expo	01/24/92	.50	.15	2.50	(4)	1.25	149
	Black Heritage Issue							
2617	29¢ W.E.B. DuBois	01/31/92	.50	.15	2.50	(4)	1.25	150
2618	29¢ Love	02/06/92	.50	.15	2.50	(4)	1.25	835
2619	29¢ Olympic Baseball	04/03/92	.50	.15	2.75	(4)	1.25	160

2587

2590

2592

2593

2594

2595

2596

2597

2598

2599

2602

2603

2604

2605

2606

2607

2608

2609

2611

2612

2613

2614

2615

2615a

2616

2617

2618

2619

2620   2621

2622   2623   2623a

2624   2625

2626   2627

2628   2629

ssues of 1984		Un	U	PB		FDC	Q(M)
First Voyage of Christopher Columbus Issue, Perf. 11 x 10.5							
2620 29¢ Seeking Queen Isabella's							
Support	04/24/92	.50	.15			1.25	40
2621 29¢ Crossing The Atlantic	04/24/92	.50	.15			1.25	40
2622 29¢ Approaching Land	04/24/92	.50	.15			1.25	40
2623 29¢ Coming Ashore	04/24/92	.50	.15			1.25	40
a Block of 4, #2620-23		2.00	1.90	2.50	(4)	2.75	
The Voyages of Columbus Souvenir Sheets, Perf. 10.5							
2624 First Sighting of Land,							
sheet of 3	05/22/92	1.75	—			2.10	2
a 1¢ deep blue		.15	.15			1.25	
b 4¢ ultramarine		.15	.15			1.25	
c $1 salmon		1.65	1.00			2.00	
2625 Claiming a New World,							
sheet of 3	05/22/92	6.75	—			8.10	2
a 2¢ brown violet		.15	.15			1.25	
b 3¢ green		.15	.15			1.25	
c $4 crimson lake		6.50	4.00			8.00	
2626 Seeking Royal Support,							
sheet of 3	05/22/92	1.40	—			1.70	2
a 5¢ chocolate		.15	.15			1.25	
b 30¢ orange brown		.50	.30			1.25	
c 50¢ slate blue		.80	.50			1.50	
2627 Royal Favor Restored,							
sheet of 3	05/22/92	5.25	—			6.25	2
a 6¢ purple		.15	.15			1.25	
b 8¢ magenta		.15	.15			1.25	
c $3 yellow green		4.75	3.00			6.00	
2628 Reporting Discoveries,							
sheet of 3	05/22/92	3.75	—			4.50	2
a 10¢ black brown		.15	.15			1.25	
b 15¢ dark green		.25	.15			1.25	
c $2 brown red		3.25	2.00			4.00	
2629 $5 Christopher Columbus,							
sheet of 1	05/22/92	8.50	—			10.00	2

As part of the celebrations surrounding the 500th anniversary of **Christopher Columbus's first voyage** to the New World, the Postal Service issued four stamps commemorating this historic journey in 1992. Part of a joint issue with Italy and illustrated by Richard Schlecht, these stamps trace the development of Columbus's journey.

Columbus's original intention was to reach eastern Asia, then called the Indies, by sailing west. After seeking a patron to finance his voyages, Columbus received financial support from the Spanish throne. He set sail on August 3, 1492, with three ships: the *Niña, Pinta*, and *Santa Maria*. After reaching the Canary Islands, the three vessels were not to see land again until October 12, when a small Caribbean island was sighted.

Over the course of four voyages, Columbus explored several Caribbean islands and sailed along the coast of South America. Nonetheless, he never accepted that the Indies were not Asia.

ssues of 1992		Un	U	PB		FDC	Q(M)
Perf. 11							
2630 29¢ New York Stock Exchange							
Bicentennial	05/17/92	.50	.15	2.50	(4)	1.75	148
Space Adventures Issue							
2631 29¢ Cosmonaut, US Space							
Shuttle	05/29/92	.50	.15			1.50	37
2632 29¢ Astronaut, Russian							
Space Station	05/29/92	.50	.15			1.50	37
2633 29¢ Sputnik, Vostok, Apollo							
Command and Lunar Modules	05/29/92	.50	.15			1.50	37
2634 29¢ Soyuz, Mercury and							
Gemini Spacecraft	05/29/92	.50	.15			1.50	37
a Block of 4, #2631-34		2.00	1.75	2.50	(4)	2.75	
2635 29¢ Alaska Highway, 50th							
Anniversary	05/30/92	.50	.15	2.50	(4)	1.25	147
a Black (engr.) omitted		500.00					
2636 29¢ Kentucky Statehood							
Bicentennial	06/01/92	.50	.15	2.50	(4)	1.25	160
Summer Olympic Games Issue							
2637 29¢ Soccer	06/11/92	.50	.15			1.25	32
2638 29¢ Gymnastics	06/11/92	.50	.15			1.25	32
2639 29¢ Volleyball	06/11/92	.50	.15			1.25	32
2640 29¢ Boxing	06/11/92	.50	.15			1.25	32
2641 29¢ Swimming	06/11/92	.50	.15			1.25	32
a Strip of 5, #2637-41		2.50	2.25	5.50	(10)	3.00	
Hummingbirds Issue							
2642 29¢ Ruby-Throated	06/15/92	.50	.15			1.25	88
2643 29¢ Broad-Billed	06/15/92	.50	.15			1.25	88
2644 29¢ Costa's	06/15/92	.50	.15			1.25	88
2645 29¢ Rufous	06/15/92	.50	.15			1.25	88
2646 29¢ Calliope	06/15/92	.50	.15			1.25	88
a Booklet pane of 5, #2642-46		2.75	2.25			3.00	

When the lunar module *Eagle* landed on the surface of the moon on July 20, 1969, it fulfilled the commitment President John F. Kennedy made in 1961 to put a man on the moon. In 1989 the Postal Service issued a **Moon Landing** stamp illustrated by Chris Calle to celebrate the twentieth anniversary of this historic American achievement. Calle's son, Paul, is also a stamp designer; the two shared credit for designing 1994's First Moon Landing stamp.

Manned by Neil Armstrong, Michael Collins, and Edwin "Buzz" Aldrin, Jr., the *Apollo 11* spacecraft's landing on the Moon was televised worldwide. People all around the world were thrilled by Armstrong's dramatic message to Mission Control, "The *Eagle* has landed."

Not only was the mission itself a remarkable technological accomplishment, but the astronauts set up instruments and took moon rock samples that would help scientists gain insight into the lunar landscape. As he stepped onto the surface of the moon, Armstrong, the first man to make this momentous step, famously said, "One small step for a man, one giant leap for mankind." It was a fitting statement for such a proud moment in human history.

2636

2635

2637   2638   2639   2640   2641   2641a

2642   2643   2644   2645   2646   2646a

Indian Paintbrush
USA 29

Fragrant Water Lily
USA 29

Meadow Beauty
USA 29

Jack-in-the-Pulpit
USA 29

California Poppy
USA 29

2647   **2648**   **2649**   **2650**   **2651**

Large-flowered Trillium
USA 29

Tickseed
USA 29

Shooting Star
USA 29

Stream Violet
USA 29

Bluets
USA 29

2652   **2653**   **2654**   **2655**   **2656**

Herb Robert
USA 29

Marsh Marigold
USA 29

Sweet White Violet
USA 29

Claret Cup Cactus
USA 29

White Mountain Avens
USA 29

2657   **2658**   **2659**   **2660**   **2661**

Sessile Bellwort
USA 29

Blue Flag
USA 29

Harlequin Lupine
USA 29

Twinflower
USA 29

Common Sunflower
USA 29

2662   **2663**   **2664**   **2665**   **2666**

Sego Lily
USA 29

Virginia Bluebells
USA 29

Ohi'a Lehua
USA 29

Rosebud Orchid
USA 29

Showy Evening Primrose
USA 29

2667   **2668**   **2669**   **2670**   **2671**

ssues of 1992			Un	U	FDC	Q(M)
Wildflowers Issue, Perf. 11						
2647	29¢ Indian Paintbrush	07/24/92	.50	.15	1.25	11
2648	29¢ Fragrant Water Lily	07/24/92	.50	.15	1.25	11
2649	29¢ Meadow Beauty	07/24/92	.50	.15	1.25	11
2650	29¢ Jack-in-the-Pulpit	07/24/92	.50	.15	1.25	11
2651	29¢ California Poppy	07/24/92	.50	.15	1.25	11
2652	29¢ Large-Flowered Trillium	07/24/92	.50	.15	1.25	11
2653	29¢ Tickseed	07/24/92	.50	.15	1.25	11
2654	29¢ Shooting Star	07/24/92	.50	.15	1.25	11
2655	29¢ Stream Violet	07/24/92	.50	.15	1.25	11
2656	29¢ Bluets	07/24/92	.50	.15	1.25	11
2657	29¢ Herb Robert	07/24/92	.50	.15	1.25	11
2658	29¢ Marsh Marigold	07/24/92	.50	.15	1.25	11
2659	29¢ Sweet White Violet	07/24/92	.50	.15	1.25	11
2660	29¢ Claret Cup Cactus	07/24/92	.50	.15	1.25	11
2661	29¢ White Mountain Avens	07/24/92	.50	.15	1.25	11
2662	29¢ Sessile Bellwort	07/24/92	.50	.15	1.25	11
2663	29¢ Blue Flag	07/24/92	.50	.15	1.25	11
2664	29¢ Harlequin Lupine	07/24/92	.50	.15	1.25	11
2665	29¢ Twinflower	07/24/92	.50	.15	1.25	11
2666	29¢ Common Sunflower	07/24/92	.50	.15	1.25	11
2667	29¢ Sego Lily	07/24/92	.50	.15	1.25	11
2668	29¢ Virginia Bluebells	07/24/92	.50	.15	1.25	11
2669	29¢ Ohi'a Lehua	07/24/92	.50	.15	1.25	11
2670	29¢ Rosebud Orchid	07/24/92	.50	.15	1.25	11
2671	29¢ Showy Evening Primrose	07/24/92	.50	.15	1.25	11

They called her "Lady Day." Her voice combined the emotional depth of the blues with the spontaneity and phrasing of a jazz instrumental soloist. Inspired by Bessie Smith and Louis Armstrong, **Billie Holiday** was one of the first jazz vocalists, and perhaps was the greatest singer the genre has ever produced.

Billie Holiday was born in Baltimore, Maryland, in 1915 to teenage parents. Her traumatic childhood foreshadowed the lifelong struggle that she would have with drugs and alcohol. As a teenager she moved to New York City with her mother and began singing in clubs in Harlem. In 1933 she was discovered by a producer, John Hammond, who recorded her with Benny Goodman's band. She made later recordings with various all-star groups led by Teddy Wilson. These sides, recorded between 1935 and 1942, are considered the quintessential Holiday recordings.

In 1994 the U.S. Postal Service honored Billie Holiday and seven other jazz and blues singers with stamps in the **Legends of American Music** series. Howard Koslow illustrated the Holiday, Bessie Smith, Mildred Bailey, and Jimmy Rushing stamps, while Julian Allen was responsible for Muddy Waters, Robert Johnson, Ma Rainey, and Howlin' Wolf.

	ssues of 1992		Un	U	FDC	Q(M)
	Wildflowers Issue (continued)					
2672	29¢ Fringed Gentian	07/24/92	.50	.15	1.25	11
2673	29¢ Yellow Lady's Slipper	07/24/92	.50	.15	1.25	11
2674	29¢ Passionflower	07/24/92	.50	.15	1.25	11
2675	29¢ Bunchberry	07/24/92	.50	.15	1.25	11
2676	29¢ Pasqueflower	07/24/92	.50	.15	1.25	11
2677	29¢ Round-Lobed Hepatica	07/24/92	.50	.15	1.25	11
2678	29¢ Wild Columbine	07/24/92	.50	.15	1.25	11
2679	29¢ Fireweed	07/24/92	.50	.15	1.25	11
2680	29¢ Indian Pond Lily	07/24/92	.50	.15	1.25	11
2681	29¢ Turk's Cap Lily	07/24/92	.50	.15	1.25	11
2682	29¢ Dutchman's Breeches	07/24/92	.50	.15	1.25	11
2683	29¢ Trumpet Honeysuckle	07/24/92	.50	.15	1.25	11
2684	29¢ Jacob's Ladder	07/24/92	.50	.15	1.25	11
2685	29¢ Plains Prickly Pear	07/24/92	.50	.15	1.25	11
2686	29¢ Moss Campion	07/24/92	.50	.15	1.25	11
2687	29¢ Bearberry	07/24/92	.50	.15	1.25	11
2688	29¢ Mexican Hat	07/24/92	.50	.15	1.25	11
2689	29¢ Harebell	07/24/92	.50	.15	1.25	11
2690	29¢ Desert Five Spot	07/24/92	.50	.15	1.25	11
2691	29¢ Smooth Solomon's Seal	07/24/92	.50	.15	1.25	11
2692	29¢ Red Maids	07/24/92	.50	.15	1.25	11
2693	29¢ Yellow Skunk Cabbage	07/24/92	.50	.15	1.25	11
2694	29¢ Rue Anemone	07/24/92	.50	.15	1.25	11
2695	29¢ Standing Cypress	07/24/92	.50	.15	1.25	11
2696	29¢ Wild Flax	07/24/92	.50	.15	1.25	11
a	Pane of 50, #2647-96		25.00		30.00	11

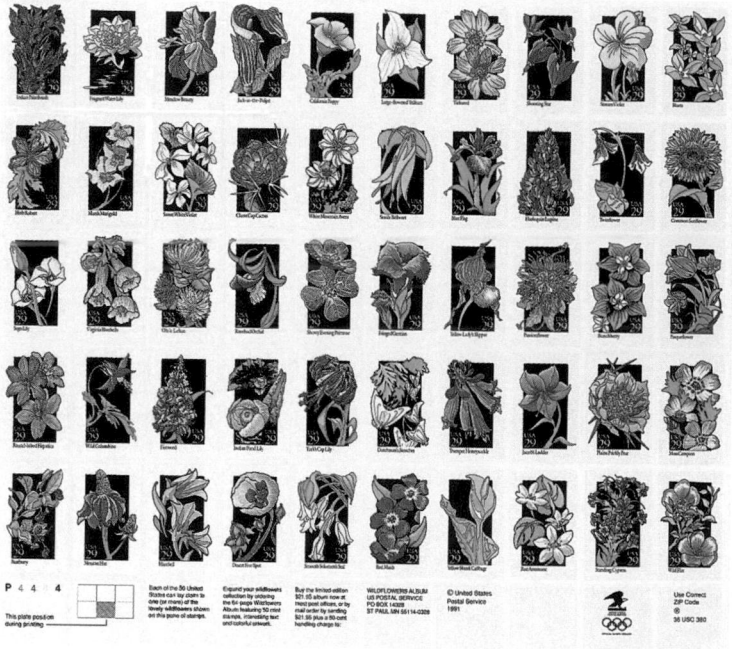

Example of #2696a

Fringed Gentian
USA 29

Yellow Lady's Slipper
USA 29

Passionflower
USA 29

Bunchberry
USA 29

Pasqueflower
USA 29

2672	2673	2674	2675	2676

Round-lobed Hepatica
USA 29

Wild Columbine
USA 29

Fireweed
USA 29

Indian Pond Lily
USA 29

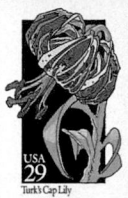
Turk's Cap Lily
USA 29

2677	2678	2679	2680	2681

Dutchman's Breeches
USA 29

Trumpet Honeysuckle
USA 29

Jacob's Ladder
USA 29

Plains Prickly Pear
USA 29

Moss Campion
USA 29

2682	2683	2684	2685	2686

Bearberry
USA 29

Mexican Hat
USA 29

Harebell
USA 29

Desert Five Spot
USA 29

Smooth Solomon's Seal
USA 29

2687	2688	2689	2690	2691

Red Maids
USA 29

Yellow Skunk Cabbage
USA 29

Rue Anemone
USA 29

Standing Cypress
USA 29

Wild Flax
USA 29

2692	2693	2694	2695	2696

a

29 USA
B-25s take off to raid Tokyo April 18, 1942

b

29 USA
Food and other commodities rationed, 1942

c

29 USA
U.S. wins Battle of the Coral Sea May 1942

d

29 USA
Corregidor falls to Japanese May 6, 1942

e

29 USA
Japan invades Aleutian Islands June 1942

ASIA

Supplies flown to China over the "Hump"

CHINA

HONG KONG

GUAM

WAKE I.

SINGAPORE

PHILIPPINES

Singapore falls February 15.

AUSTRALIA

Doolittle carries out daring raid on Tokyo with B-25s launched from U.S.S. Hornet April 18.

PACIFIC

TOKYO

Battle of Midway decisive defeat for Japan June 3–6.

HONOLULU

Philippines fall to Japanese: Bataan, April 9; Corregidor, May 6.

Battle of the Coral Sea halts Japanese advance southward May 4–8.

U.S. Marines land on Guadalcanal August 7.

Note: Red areas controlled by enemy.

CANADA

OTTAWA

UNITED STATES

WASHINGTON

EQUATOR

SOUTH AMERICA

ATLANTIC

OCEAN

AFRICA

Desperate struggle waged against German U-boats as Allies convoy supplies across North Atlantic.

U.S. and Allies land more than 100,000 troops in North Africa November 8.

British defeat German forces at Battle of El Alamein October 23–November 4.

Extent of German expansion, Summer 1942.

Massive RAF raids strike German cities.

LENINGRAD

MOSCOW

BERLIN

U.S.S.R.

Russian defenders battle German forces at Stalingrad, Summer 1942.

INDIA

INDIAN OCEAN

1942: Into the Battle

29 USA
Allies decipher secret enemy codes, 1942

29 USA
Yorktown lost, U.S. wins at Midway, 1942

29 USA
Millions of women join war effort, 1942

29 USA
Marines land on Guadalcanal Aug. 7, 1942

29 USA
Allies land in North Africa November 1942

f   g   h   i   j   2697

29 USA
Dorothy Parker
American Writer 1893-1967

2698

Theodore von Kármán
Aerospace Scientist

USA 29

2699

2700   **2701**

Minerals USA 29
Azurite

Minerals USA 29
Copper

Minerals USA 29
Variscite

Minerals USA 29
Wulfenite

2702   **2703**   **2703a**

Explorer of California 1542
29 USA
Juan Rodríguez
CABRILLO

2704

	Issues of 1992		Un	U	PB	#	FDC	Q(M)
World War II Issue, 1942: Into the Battle, Miniature Sheet, Perf. 11								
2697	Sheet of 10 and central label	08/17/92	5.25	4.50			7.00	12
a	29¢ B-25s Take Off to Raid Tokyo		.50	.30			1.50	12
b	29¢ Food and Other Commodities Rationed		.50	.30			1.50	12
c	29¢ U.S. Wins Battle of the Coral Sea .		50	.30			1.50	12
d	29¢ Corregidor Falls to Japanese		.50	.30			1.50	12
e	29¢ Japan Invades Aleutian Islands		.50	.30			1.50	12
f	29¢ Allies Decipher Secret Enemy Codes		.50	.30			1.50	12
g	29¢ *Yorktown* Lost		.50	.30			1.50	12
h	29¢ Millions of Women Join War Effort		.50	.30			1.50	12
i	29¢ Marines Land on Guadalcanal		.50	.30			1.50	12
j	29¢ Allies Land in North Africa		.50	.30			1.50	12
	Literary Arts Issue							
2698	29¢ Dorothy Parker	08/22/92	.50	.15	2.50	(4)	1.25	105
2699	29¢ Dr. Theodore von Karman	08/31/92	.50	.15	2.50	(4)	1.25	143
	Minerals Issue							
2700	29¢ Azurite	09/17/92	.50	.15			1.25	37
2701	29¢ Copper	09/17/92	.50	.15			1.25	37
2702	29¢ Variscite	09/17/92	.50	.15			1.25	37
2703	29¢ Wulfenite	09/17/92	.50	.15			1.25	37
a	Block of 4, #2700-03		2.00	1.75	2.50	(4)	2.75	
2704	29¢ Juan Rodriguez Cabrillo	09/28/92	.50	.15	2.50	(4)	1.25	85

In 1991, the U.S. Postal Service issued a stamp jointly with Russia. Illustrated by Ren Wicks and part of the Literary Arts series, the stamp honored **William Saroyan** (1908-1981). In his short stories, plays, novels, and memoirs, Saroyan expressed his affection for common people and his belief in their basic goodness. His mastery of colloquial speech brought his characters to life.

Saroyan was born in California to Armenian immigrant parents. He left school determined to become a writer. His first book of short stories, *The Daring Young Man on the Flying Trapeze*, brought him fame in 1934 and was followed by several other collections of stories.

Saroyan achieved equal renown in the theater. In 1939 *My Heart's in the Highlands* and *The Time of Your Life* were produced to great acclaim. *The Time of Your Life* won a Pulitzer Prize, which he refused.

He also wrote novels and memoirs. His best-known novel was *The Human Comedy* (1943). Its evocation of small-town America appealed to its wartime readers. One of his later books, *Obituaries* (1979), was nominated for an American Book Award shortly before Saroyan's death.

ssues of 1992		Un	U	PB		FDC	Q(M)
Wild Animals Issue, Perf. 11 Horizontally							
2705	29¢ Giraffe	10/01/92	.50	.15			1.25	80
2706	29¢ Giant Panda	10/01/92	.50	.15			1.25	80
2707	29¢ Flamingo	10/01/92	.50	.15			1.25	80
2708	29¢ King Penguins	10/01/92	.50	.15			1.25	80
2709	29¢ White Bengal Tiger	10/01/92	.50	.15			1.25	80
a	Booklet pane of 5, #2705-09		2.50	2.00			4.00	
Christmas Issue, Perf. 11.5 x 11							
2710	29¢ Madonna and Child by Giovanni Bellini	10/22/92	.50	.15	2.50	(4)	1.25	300
a	Booklet pane of 10		5.25	3.50			7.25	349
2711	29¢ Horse and Rider	10/22/92	.50	.15			1.25	125
2712	29¢ Toy Train	10/22/92	.50	.15			1.25	125
2713	29¢ Toy Steamer	10/22/92	.50	.15			1.25	125
2714	29¢ Toy Ship	10/22/92	.50	.15			1.25	125
a	Block of 4, #2711-14		2.00	1.10	2.50	(4)	2.75	
Perf. 11							
2715	29¢ Horse and Rider	10/22/92	.50	.15			1.25	102
2716	29¢ Toy Train	10/22/92	.50	.15			1.25	102
2717	29¢ Toy Steamer	10/22/92	.50	.15			1.25	102
2718	29¢ Toy Ship	10/22/92	.50	.15			1.25	102
a	Booklet pane of 4, #2715-18		2.25	1.25			2.75	
2719	29¢ Toy Train (self-adhesive)	10/22/92	.60	.15			1.25	22
a	Booklet pane of 18		11.00					
Lunar New Year Issue							
2720	29¢ Year of the Rooster	12/30/92	.50	.15	2.00	(4)	1.50	

In 1992, the Postal Service issued five stamps by Robert Giusti that celebrate wild animals. Featured on two of the stamps are a flamingo and **pair of king penguins**, birds known for their striking appearance. A flamingo has a long neck and legs; large, curved bill; and pink and crimson feathers. A king penguin does not have the brilliant plumage of the flamingo, but is still more colorful than most penguins. Its yellow and orange collar contrasts with its dark back and white front.

Flamingos are wading birds that live mainly near saltwater lakes and lagoons, where they use their webbed feet to stir up debris and their bills as a sieve to filter food. Flamingos nest in large colonies. Parents feed their young with a secretion from their crop called flamingo's milk.

King penguins also nest in large colonies, but they are found on subantarctic islands and are swimmers. They spend most of their life in and around the sea, coming ashore to molt, breed, incubate their eggs, and raise their chicks. The female lays one egg, which the parents take turns holding on top of their feet and warming with a layer of skin and feathers.

2705

2706

2707

2708

2709

Giraffe

Giant Panda

Flamingo

King Penguins

White Bengal Tiger

2710

2709a

2711 2712

2713 2714 2714a

2715 2716

2717 2718 2718a

2719

2720

2721

2722

2723

2724   2725   2726   2727   2728

2729   2730

 2731

 2732

 2733

 2734

 2735

2736

2737

2731

2737a   2737b

ssues of 1993		Un	U	PB	#	FDC	Q(M)
Legends of American Music Series, Perf. 11							
2721 29¢ Elvis Presley	01/08/93	.50	.15	2.50	(4)	1.75	517
Perf. 10							
2722 29¢ *Oklahoma!*	03/30/93	.50	.15	2.50	(4)	1.25	150
2723 29¢ Hank Williams	06/09/93	.50	.15	2.50	(4)	1.25	152
Legends of American Music Series, Rock & Roll/Rhythm & Blues Issue							
2724 29¢ Elvis Presley	06/16/93	.50	.15			1.25	14
2725 29¢ Bill Haley	06/16/93	.50	.15			1.25	14
2726 29¢ Clyde McPhatter	06/16/93	.50	.15			1.25	14
2727 29¢ Ritchie Valens	06/16/93	.50	.15			1.25	14
2728 29¢ Otis Redding	06/16/93	.50	.15			1.25	14
2729 29¢ Buddy Holly	06/16/93	.50	.15			1.25	14
2730 29¢ Dinah Washington	06/16/93	.50	.15			1.25	14
a Vertical strip of 7, #2724-30		3.50	—	5.00	(10)	5.00	
Perf. 11 Horizontal							
2731 29¢ Elvis Presley	06/16/93	.50	.15			1.25	99
2732 29¢ Bill Haley (2725)	06/16/93	.50	.15			1.25	33
2733 29¢ Clyde McPhatter (2726)	06/16/93	.50	.15			1.25	33
2734 29¢ Ritchie Valens (2727)	06/16/93	.50	.15			1.25	33
2735 29¢ Otis Redding	06/16/93	.50	.15			1.25	66
2736 29¢ Buddy Holly	06/16/93	.50	.15			1.25	66
2737 29¢ Dinah Washington	06/16/93	.50	.15			1.25	66
a Booklet pane, 2 #2731, 1 each #2732-37		4.25	2.25			5.25	
b Booklet pane of 4, #2731, 2735-37		2.25	*1.50*			2.75	
2738-40 Not assigned							

With ***Oklahoma!***, Richard Rodgers and Oscar Hammerstein II ushered in a new era for the Broadway musical with their innovative integration of music and plot. The show, which had originally been titled *Away We Go!*, opened on Broadway on March 31, 1943, and ran for more than 2,200 performances. With its simple story about the relationship between a farm woman and a cowboy complicated by a jealous farmhand, the show charmed

audiences for years. Many of its songs, including the title song and "Oh, What a Beautiful Mornin'," remain emblazoned on the American consciousness. For the 1955 film version of *Oklahoma!*, the show's choreographer, Agnes de Mille, recreated the dance sequences made famous by the stage production.

Composer Rodgers and lyricist Hammerstein collaborated numerous times and enjoyed several other successes, including *Carousel* (1945), the Pulitzer Prize-winning *South Pacific* (1949), *The King and I* (1951), and *The Sound of Music* (1959). As a part of the Legends of American Music series, *Oklahoma!* was honored by the U.S. Postal Service on one of four 1993 stamps, illustrated by Wilson McLean, celebrating Broadway Musicals. Rodgers and Hammerstein were honored on the Broadway Songwriters stamps in 1999.

	ssues of 1993		Un	U	PE		FDC	Q(M)
	Space Fantasy Issue, Perf. 11 Vertical on 1 or 2 sides							
2741	29¢ multicolored	01/25/93	.50	.15			1.25	140
2742	29¢ multicolored	01/25/93	.50	.15			1.25	140
2743	29¢ multicolored	01/25/93	.50	.15			1.25	140
2744	29¢ multicolored	01/25/93	.50	.15			1.25	140
2745	29¢ multicolored	01/25/93	.50	.15			1.25	140
a	Booklet pane of 5, #2741-45		2.50	2.00			3.25	
2746	29¢ Percy Lavon Julian	01/29/93	.50	.15	2.50	(4)	1.25	105
2747	29¢ Oregon Trail	02/12/93	.50	.15	2.50	(4)	1.25	110
2748	29¢ World University Games	02/25/93	.50	.15	2.50	(4)	1.25	110
2749	29¢ Grace Kelly	03/25/93	.50	.15	2.50	(4)	1.50	173
	Circus Issue, Perf. 11							
2750	29¢ Clown	04/06/93	.50	.15			1.50	66
2751	29¢ Ringmaster	04/06/93	.50	.15			1.50	66
2752	29¢ Trapeze Artist	04/06/93	.50	.15			1.50	66
2753	29¢ Elephant	04/06/93	.50	.15			1.50	66
a	Block of 4, #2750-53		2.00	1.75	3.50	(6)	3.00	
2754	29¢ Cherokee Strip	04/17/93	.50	.15	2.00	(4)	1.25	110
2755	29¢ Dean Acheson	04/21/93	.50	.15	2.50	(4)	1.25	116
b	As "a," black omitted		—					
	Sporting Horses Issue, Perf. 11 x 11.5							
2756	29¢ Steeplechase	05/01/93	.50	.15			1.75	40
2757	29¢ Thoroughbred Racing	05/01/93	.50	.15			1.75	40
2758	29¢ Harness Racing	05/01/93	.50	.15			1.75	40
2759	29¢ Polo	05/01/93	.50	.15			1.75	40
a	Block of 4, #2756-59		2.00	1.75	2.50	(4)	3.50	

A form of horse racing originating in the United States, **harness racing** developed in the early 19th century. In 1993, as part of the Sports Horse issue, the U.S. Postal Service commemorated this competition of precision, speed, and strategy with a stamp illustrated by C. Michael Dudash.

The breed raised for harness racing, the standardbred, is usually smaller, stronger, and less high-strung than the thoroughbred saddle horse. Horses are trained in one of two gaits that mark the two forms of the competition: Pacers move both legs on one side together and trotters move their left front leg and right rear leg together. Pulling a rider in a two-wheeled cart called a sulky, they must maintain speed for a long distance without breaking into a gallop, which can disqualify them.

2741   2742   2743   2744   2745   2745a

2747

2748

2746   2749

2750   2751

2754

2755

2752   2753   2753a

2756   2757

2758   2759   2759a

29 USA Hyacinth 29 USA Daffodil 29 USA Tulip 29 USA Iris 29 USA Lilac

2764a

2760   2761   2762   2763   2764

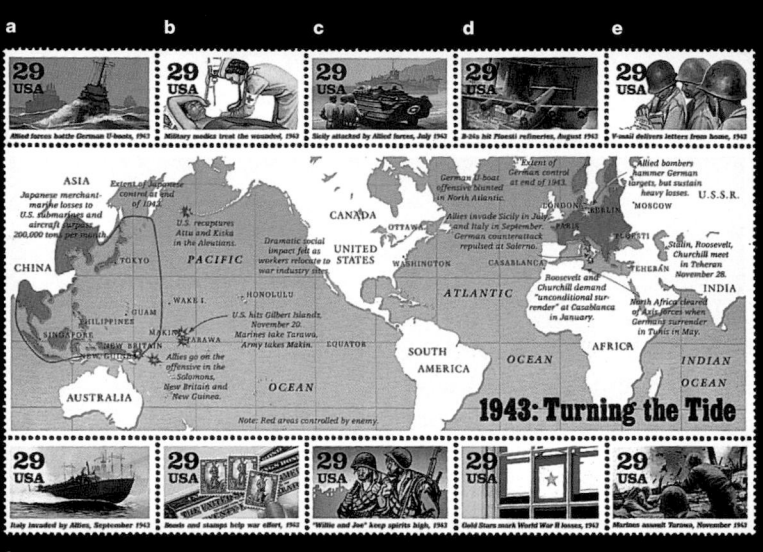

a   b   c   d   e

Allied forces battle German U-boats, 1943   Military medics treat the wounded, 1943   Sicily attacked by Allied forces, July 1943   B-24s hit Ploesti refineries, August 1943   V-mail delivers letters from home, 1943

1943: Turning the Tide

Italy invaded by Allies, September 1943   Bonds and stamps help war effort, 1943   "Willie and Joe" keep spirits high, 1943   Gold Stars mark World War II losses, 1943   Marines assault Tarawa, November 1943

f   g   h   i   j   2765

JOE LOUIS

USA 29

2766

2767

2768

2769

2770

2770a

	ssues of 1993		Un	U	PB		FDC	Q(M)
	Garden Flowers Issue, Perf. 11 Vertical							
2760	29¢ Hyacinth	05/15/93	3.50	.15			1.25	200
2761	29¢ Daffodil	05/15/93	.50	.15			1.25	200
2762	29¢ Tulip	05/15/93	.50	.15			1.25	200
2763	29¢ Iris	05/15/93	.50	.15			1.25	200
2764	29¢ Lilac	05/15/93	.50	.15			1.25	200
a	Booklet pane of 5, #2760-64		2.50	*2.00*			3.25	
b	As "a," black omitted		*375.00*					
c	As "a," imperf.		*2,500.00*					
	World War II Issue, 1943: Turning The Tide, Miniature Sheet, Perf. 11							
2765	Sheet of 10 and central label	05/31/93	5.25	4.50			7.00	
a	29¢ Allied Forces Battle German U-boats			.50	.30		1.50	12
b	29¢ Military Medics Treat the Wounded.		50	.30			1.50	12
c	29¢ Sicily Attacked by Allied Forces		.50	.30			1.50	12
d	29¢ B-24s Hit Ploesti Refineries		.50	.30			1.50	12
e	29¢ V-Mail Delivers Letters from Home.		50	.30			1.50	12
f	29¢ Italy Invaded by Allies		.50	.30			1.50	12
g	29¢ Bonds and Stamps Help War Effort		.50	.30			1.50	12
h	29¢ "Willie and Joe" Keep Spirits High .		50	.30			1.50	12
i	29¢ Gold Stars Mark World War II Losses		.50	.30			1.50	12
j	29¢ Marines Assault Tarawa		.50	.30			1.50	12
2766	29¢ Joe Louis	06/22/93	.50	.15	2.50	(4)	1.50	160
	Legends of American Music Series, Broadway Musicals Issue, Perf. 11 Horizontal							
2767	29¢ *Show Boat*	07/14/93	.50	.15			1.25	129
2768	29¢ *Porgy & Bess*	07/14/93	.50	.15			1.25	129
2769	29¢ *Oklahoma!*	07/14/93	.50	.15			1.25	129
2770	29¢ *My Fair Lady*	07/14/93	.50	.15			1.25	129
a	Booklet pane of 4, #2767-70		2.50	*2.00*			3.25	

In 1993 the U.S. Postal Service issued ten stamps commemorating the third year of America's participation in World War II. The ninth stamp depicted a **gold star** displayed to honor a family member who died in service to our country. One gold star family, the Sullivans of Waterloo, Iowa, is remembered for its extraor-  dinary sacrifice. After a friend was killed at Pearl Harbor, the five Sullivan brothers—Joseph, Francis, Albert, Madison, and George—joined the Navy and insisted on being assigned to the same ship. They were serving together on the USS Juneau in November 1942 when it was hit off Guadalcanal. All five brothers perished.

ssues of 1993		Un	U	PE		FDC	Q(M)
Legends of American Music Series, Country & Western Issue, Perf. 10							
2771	29¢ Hank Williams (2775)	09/25/93	.50	.15			1.25	25
2772	29¢ Patsy Cline (2777)	09/25/93	.50	.15		1.25	25
2773	29¢ The Carter Family (2776)	09/25/93	.50	.15		1.25	25
2774	29¢ Bob Willis (2778)	09/25/93	.50	.15		1.25	25
a	Block or horiz. strip of 4, #2771-74		2.00	1.75	2.00	(4)	2.75	
Booklet Stamps, Perf. 11 Horizontal							
2775	29¢ Hank Williams	09/25/93	.50	.15		1.25	170
2776	29¢ The Carter Family	09/25/93	.50	.15		1.25	170
2777	29¢ Patsy Cline	09/25/93	.50	.15		1.25	170
2778	29¢ Bob Willis	09/25/93	.50	.15		1.25	170
a	Booklet pane of 4, #2775-78		2.50	2.00			2.75	
National Postal Museum Issue, Perf. 11							
2779	Independence Hall, Benjamin Franklin, Printing Press, Colonial Post Rider	07/30/93	.50	.15		1.25	38
2780	Pony Express Rider, Civil War Soldier, Concord Stagecoach	07/30/93	.50	.15		1.25	38
2781	Biplane, Charles Lindbergh, Railway Mail Car, 1931 Model A Ford Mail Truck	07/30/93	.50	.15		1.25	38
2782	California Gold Rush Miner's Letter, Barcode and Circular Date Stamp	07/30/93	.50	.15		1.25	38
a	Block or strip of 4, #2779-82		2.00	1.75	2.00	(4)	2.75	
American Sign Language Issue, Perf. 11.5							
2783	29¢ Recognizing Deafness	09/20/93	.50	.15		1.25	42
2784	29¢ American Sign Language	09/20/93	.50	.15		1.25	42
a	Pair, #2783-84		1.00	.65	2.00	(4)	2.00	
Classic Books Issues, Perf. 11							
2785	29¢ Rebecca of Sunnybrook Farm	10/23/93	.50	.15		1.25	38
2786	29¢ Little House on the Prairie	10/23/93	.50	.15		1.25	38
2787	29¢ The Adventures of Huckleberry Finn	10/23/93	.50	.15		1.25	38
2788	29¢ Little Women	10/23/93	.50	.15		1.25	38
a	Block or horiz. strip of 4, #2785-88		2.00	1.75	3.75	(4)	2.75	

Little House on the Prairie, the second book in a series by Laura Ingalls Wilder, chronicled the adventures, joys, and hardships of pioneer life. Written from the perspective of a child growing up in the American Midwest during the 1870s and 1880s, each of Wilder's semi-autobiographical books were instant successes.

Born in Wisconsin in 1867, Laura Ingalls Wilder did not begin writing the books that made her famous until she was in her 60s. Following the publication of the first book, *Little House in Big Woods*, in 1932, she wrote seven more in eleven years, including a book about the childhood of her husband, Almanzo. Serving as a wonderful time capsule, her books still resonate with children today.

Little House on the Prairie was featured in 1993 on the Youth Classics stamps, which commemorate beloved books that describe life in America from the middle of the 19th century to the beginning of the 20th century. Artist Jim Lamb faithfully represented three other works on these stamps: *Rebecca of Sunnybrook Farm* by Kate Douglas Smith Wiggin, *The Adventures of Huckleberry Finn* by Mark Twain, and *Little Women* by Louisa May Alcott.

2771 2772

2775

2776

2777

2773 2774 2774a

2778

2778a

2779 2780

2781 2782 2782a

2783 2784 2784a

2785 2786

2787 2788 2788a

2789

2791   2792

2795   2796

2790

2793   2794

2797   2798

2799   2800

2801   2802

2802a

2803

2804

2805

2806

2806a

	ssues of 1993		Un	U	PB	#	FDC	Q(M)
	Christmas Issue, Perf. 11							
2789	29¢ Madonna and Child	10/21/93	.50	.15	2.50	(4)	1.25	500
	Booklet Stamps, Perf. 11.5 x 11 on 2 or 3 sides							
2790	29¢ Madonna and Child (2789)	10/21/93	.50	.15			1.25	500
a	Booklet pane of 4		2.25	*1.75*			2.00	
	Perf. 11.5							
2791	29¢ Jack-in-the-Box	10/21/93	.50	.15			1.25	250
2792	29¢ Red-Nosed Reindeer	10/21/93	.50	.15			.1.25	250
2793	29¢ Snowman	10/21/93	.50	.15			1.25	250
2794	29¢ Toy Soldier	10/21/93	.50	.15			1.25	250
a	Block or strip of 4, #2791-94		2.00	1.75	2.75	(4)	2.75	
	Booklet Stamps, Perf. 11 x 10 on 2 or 3 sides							
2795	29¢ Toy Soldier (2794)	10/21/93	.50	.15			1.25	200
2796	29¢ Snowman (2793)	10/21/93	.50	.15			1.25	200
2797	29¢ Red-Nosed Reindeer (2792)	10/21/93	.50	.15			1.25	200
2798	29¢ Jack-in-the-Box (2791)	10/21/93	.50	.15			1.25	200
a	Booklet pane, 3 each #2795-96,							
	2 each #2797-98		5.00	*4.00*			6.50	
b	Booklet pane, 3 each #2797-98,							
	2 each #2795-96		5.00	*4.00*			6.50	
	Self-Adhesive							
2799	29¢ Snowman	10/28/93	.50	.15			1.25	120
2800	29¢ Toy Soldier	10/28/93	.50	.15			1.25	120
2801	29¢ Jack-in-the-Box	10/28/93	.50	.15			1.25	120
2802	29¢ Red-Nosed Reindeer	10/28/93	.50	.15			1.25	120
a	Booklet pane, 3 each #2799-2802		7.00					
2803	29¢ Snowman	10/28/93	.50	.15			1.25	18
a	Booklet pane of 18	10.00						
	Perf. 11							
2804	29¢ Northern Mariana Islands	11/04/93	.50	.15	2.00	(4)	1.25	88
2805	29¢ Columbus Landing in							
	Puerto Rico	11/19/93	.50	.15	2.50	(4)	1.25	105
2806	29¢ AIDS Awareness	12/01/93	.50	.15	2.50	(4)	1.25	100
a	Booklet version		.50	.15			1.25	250
b	Booklet pane of 5		2.50	*2.00*			3.25	

	ssues of 1994		Un	U	PB		FDC	Q(M)
	Winter Olympic Games Issue, Perf. 11.2							
2807	29¢ Slalom	01/06/94	.50	.15			1.25	36
2808	29¢ Luge	01/06/94	.50	.15			1.25	36
2809	29¢ Ice Dancing	01/06/94	.50	.15			1.25	36
2810	29¢ Cross-Country Skiing	01/06/94		.15			1.25	36
2811	29¢ Ice Hockey	01/06/94		.15			1.25	36
a	Strip of 5, #2807-11		2.50	2.25	5.00	(10)	3.00	36
2812	29¢ Edward R. Murrow	01/21/94	.50	.15	2.50	(4)	1.25	151
2813	29¢ Love Sunrise	01/27/94	.50	.15	6.00	(5)	1.25	358
a	Booklet of 18 (self-adhesive)		11.00					
	Perf. 10.9 x 11.1							
2814	29¢ Love Stamp	02/14/94	.50	.15			1.25	830
a	Booklet pane of 10		5.50	3.50			6.50	
	Perf. 11.1							
2814C	29¢ Love Stamp	06/11/94	.50	.15	2.50	(4)	1.25	300
	Perf. 11.2							
2815	52¢ Love Birds	02/14/94	1.00	.20	5.00	(4)	1.35	175
2816	29¢ Dr. Allison Davis	02/01/94	.50	.15	2.00	(4)	1.25	156
	Lunar New Year Issue							
2817	29¢ Year of the Dog	02/05/94	.50	.15	2.00	(4)	1.75	105
	Perf. 11.5 x 11.2							
2818	29¢ Buffalo Soldiers	04/22/94	.50	.15	2.00	(4)	1.50	186
	Stars of the Silent Screen Issue, Perf. 11.2							
2819	29¢ Rudolph Valentino	04/27/94	.50	.15			1.50	19
2820	29¢ Clara Bow	04/27/94	.50	.15			1.50	19
2821	29¢ Charlie Chaplin	04/27/94	.50	.15			1.50	19
2822	29¢ Lon Chaney	04/27/94	.50	.15			1.50	19
2823	29¢ John Gilbert	04/27/94	.50	.15			1.50	19
2824	29¢ Zasu Pitts	04/27/94	.50	.15			1.50	19
2825	29¢ Harold Lloyd	04/27/94	.50	.15			1.50	19
2826	29¢ Keystone Cops	04/27/94	.50	.15			1.50	19
2827	29¢ Theda Bara	04/27/94	.50	.15			1.50	19
2828	29¢ Buster Keaton	04/27/94	.50	.15			1.50	19
a	Block of 10 #2819-2828		5.00	4.00	5.00	(10)	6.50	19
b	As "a" black (litho.) omitted		—					
c	As "a" black (litho.) and red & brt. vio (engr.) omitted		—					

Born in Parsons, Kansas, in 1898, **ZaSu Pitts** was a star of the silent screen known for her comedic talents. Her film career began in 1917, and for decades, ZaSu Pitts stole scenes and delighted audiences.

Though best remembered for being a visually expressive comedienne, Pitts also appeared in dramas. Her popularity and versatility as an actress survived the transition into sound motion pictures later in her career, and she even appeared on television in the 1950s. ZaSu Pitts died in Hollywood in 1963.

In 1994, famed caricaturist Al Hirschfeld of New York City captured the essence of ZaSu Pitts and several of her fellow performers on the **Stars of the Silent Screen** stamps. Alongside Pitts were Rudolph Valentino, Clara Bow, Charlie Chaplin, Lon Chaney, John Gilbert, Harold Lloyd, the Keystone Cops, Theda Bara, and Buster Keaton.

2807   2808   2809   2810   2811   2811a

           2813   2814   2814C

2812

2815

         2817

2816   2818

2819   2820   2821   2822   2823

2824   2825   2826   2827   2828

                                            2828a

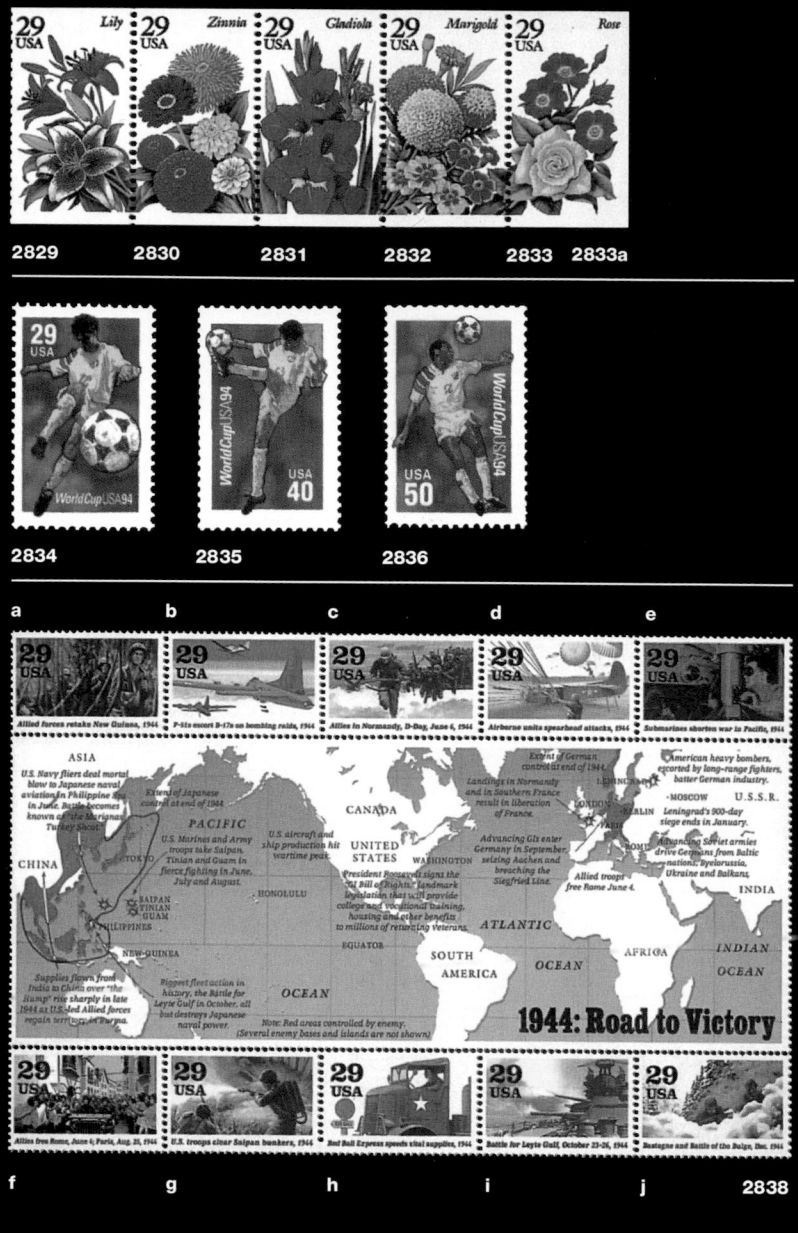

2829   2830   2831   2832   2833   2833a

2834   2835   2836

a   b   c   d   e

1944: Road to Victory

f   g   h   i   j   2838

ssues of 1994		Un	U	PE		#	FDC	Q(M)
Garden Flowers Booklet Issue, Perf. 10.9 Vertical								
2829	29¢ Lily	04/28/94	.50	.15			1.25	166
2830	29¢ Zinnia	04/28/94	.50	.15			1.25	166
2831	29¢ Gladiola	04/28/94	.50	.15			1.25	166
2832	29¢ Marigold	04/28/94	.50	.15			1.25	166
2833	29¢ Rose	04/28/94	.50	.15			1.25	166
a	Booklet pane of 5, #2829-2833		2.50	2.00				
1994 World Cup Soccer Championships Issue, Perf. 11.1								
2834	29¢ Soccer Player	05/26/94	.50	.15	2.00	(4)	1.25	201
2835	40¢ Soccer Player	05/26/94	.80	.20	3.20	(4)	1.25	300
2836	50¢ Soccer Player	05/26/94	1.00	.20	4.00	(4)	1.35	269
2837	Souvenir Sheet of 3,							
	#2834-2836	05/26/94	2.50	2.00			2.50	60
a	29¢ Soccer Player							
b	40¢ Soccer Player							
c	50¢ Soccer Player							
World War II Issue, 1944: Road to Victory Miniature, Sheet, Perf. 10.9								
2838	Sheet of 10 and central label	06/06/94	5.25	4.50			7.00	12
a	29¢ Allies Retake New Guinea		.50	.30			1.50	12
b	29¢ Bombing Raids		.50	.30			1.50	12
c	29¢ Allies in Normandy, D-Day		.50	.30			1.50	12
d	29¢ Airborne Units		.50	.30			1.50	12
e	29¢ Submarines Shorten War		.50	.30			1.50	12
f	29¢ Allies Free Rome, Paris		.50	.30			1.50	12
g	29¢ Troops Clear Siapan Bunkers		.50	.30			1.50	12
h	29¢ Red Ball Express		.50	.30			1.50	12
i	29¢ Battle for Leyte Gulf		.50	.30			1.50	12
j	29¢ Battle of the Bulge		.50	.30			1.50	12

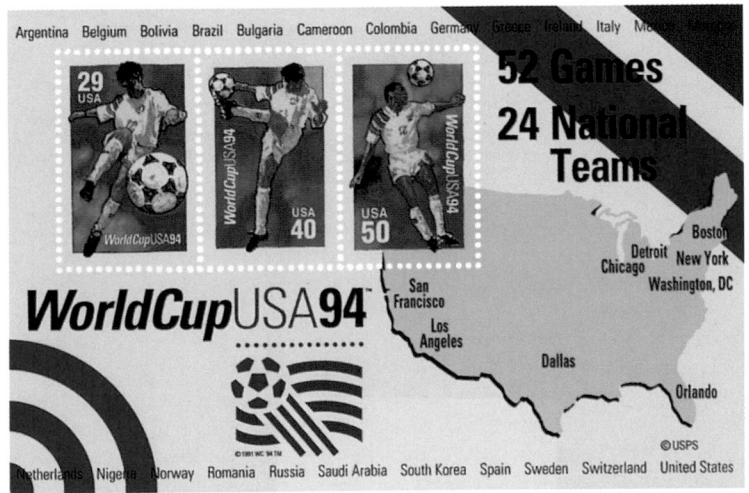

Example of #2837

ssues of 1994		Un	U	PE		FDC	Q(M)
Norman Rockwell Issue, Perf. 10.9 x 11.1							
2839 29¢ Rockwell Self-Portrait	07/01/94	.50	.15	2.50	(4)	1.25	209
2840 Four Freedoms souvenir sheet	07/01/94	4.00	2.75			3.50	20
a 50¢ Freedom from Want		1.00	.65			1.50	20
b 50¢ Freedom from Fear		1.00	.65			1.50	20
c 50¢ Freedom of Speech		1.00	.65			1.50	20
d 50¢ Freedom of Worship		1.00	.65			1.50	20
First Moon Landing Issue, Perf. 11.2 x 11.1							
2841 29¢ sheet of 12	07/20/94	7.50	—			6.50	13
a Single stamp		.60	.60			1.50	155
Perf. 10.7 x 11.1							
2842 $9.95 Moon Landing	07/20/94	17.50	7.50	70.00	(4)	15.00	101
Locomotives Issue, Perf. 11 Horizontal							
2843 29¢ Hudson's General	07/28/94	.50	.15			1.25	159
2844 29¢ McQueen's Jupiter	07/28/94	.50	.15			1.25	159
2845 29¢ Eddy's No. 242	07/28/94	.50	.15			1.25	159
2846 29¢ Ely's No. 10	07/28/94	.50	.15			1.25	159
2847 29¢ Buchanan's No. 999	07/28/94	.50	.15			1.25	159
a Booklet pane of 5, #2843-2847		2.50	2.00			3.25	159
Perf. 11.1 x 11							
2848 29¢ George Meany	08/16/94	.50	.15	2.50	(4)	1.25	151
Legends of American Music Series, Popular Singers Issue, Perf. 10.1 x 10.2							
2849 29¢ Al Jolson	09/01/94	.50	.15			1.25	35
2850 29¢ Bing Crosby	09/01/94	.50	.15			1.25	35
2851 29¢ Ethel Waters	09/01/94	.50	.15			1.25	35
2852 29¢ Nat "King" Cole	09/01/94	.50	.15			1.25	35
2853 29¢ Ethel Merman	09/01/94	.50	.15			1.25	35
a Vert. strip of 5, #2849-2853		2.50	2.00			3.25	

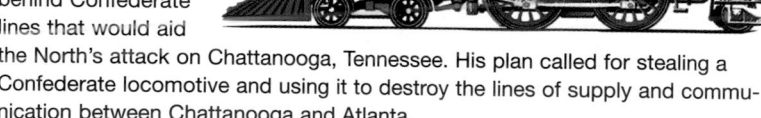

Designed by William S. Hudson, **Hudson's General** became the centerpiece of one of the Civil War's most famous episodes. James Andrews, a Union spy, planned a daring raid behind Confederate lines that would aid the North's attack on Chattanooga, Tennessee. His plan called for stealing a Confederate locomotive and using it to destroy the lines of supply and communication between Chattanooga and Atlanta.

The early stages of the raid went according to plan, with Andrews and his band commandeering the General at a rail depot in Georgia. But after a costly delay things started to go wrong for Andrews and his band. The general alarm was raised and the raiders were forced to make a dash for the Union lines. What followed can only be called a high-speed train chase. Andrews and his men desperately tried to outrun or derail the locomotive on their tail. Eventually, the raiders were captured, but not before leading their Confederate pursuers on one of the most harrowing chases of the war.

At least two film versions of the chase have been made, including Buster Keaton's 1927 silent masterpiece *The General*. Illustrated by Richard Leech, Hudson's General is one of five Locomotives stamps issued in 1994.

2839

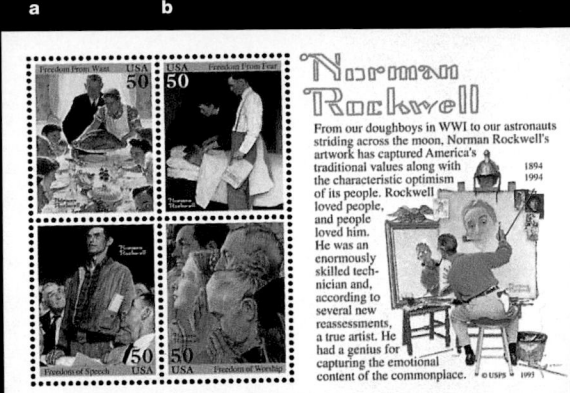

a　　　　b

c　　　　d　　　　2840

First Moon Landing, 1969

2841a

25th Anniversary First Moon Landing,1969

2842

HUDSON'S GENERAL　1855, 1870　2843

McQUEEN'S JUPITER　1969　2844

EDDY'S Nº 242　1874　2845

ELY'S Nº 10　1881　2846

BUCHANAN'S Nº 999　1893　2847

2847a

George Meany

Labor Leader USA 29

2848

AL JOLSON　2849

BING CROSBY　2850

ETHEL WATERS　2851

NAT 'KING' COLE　2852

ETHEL MERMAN　2853

2853a

2854 2855 2856 2857 2858

2859 2860 2861

2862

2863 2864

2865 2866 2866a

2867 2868

2870g

a b c d e 2869
f g h i j
k l m n o
p q r s t

ssues of 1994			Un	U	PB	#	FDC	Q(M)
Legends of American Music Series, Jazz and Blues Singers Issue, Perf. 11 x 10.8								
2854	29¢ Bessie Smith	09/17/94	.50	.15			1.25	25
2855	29¢ Muddy Waters	09/17/94	.50	.15			1.25	25
2856	29¢ Billie Holiday	09/17/94	.50	.15			1.25	25
2857	29¢ Robert Johnson	09/17/94	.50	.15			1.25	20
2858	29¢ Jimmy Rushing	09/17/94	.50	.15			1.25	20
2859	29¢ "Ma" Rainey	09/17/94	.50	.15			1.25	20
2860	29¢ Mildred Bailey	09/17/94	.50	.15			1.25	20
2861	29¢ Howlin' Wolf	09/17/94	.50	.15			1.25	20
a	Block of 9, #2854-2861							
	+ 1 additional stamp		4.50	3.50	6.50	(10)	6.00	
Literary Arts Issue, Perf. 11								
2862	29¢ James Thurber	09/10/94	.50	.15	2.50	(4)	1.25	151
Wonders of the Sea Issue, Perf. 11 x 10.9								
2863	29¢ Diver, Motorboat	10/03/94	.50	.15			1.25	56
2864	29¢ Diver, Ship	10/03/94	.50	.15			1.25	56
2865	29¢ Diver, Ship's Wheel	10/03/94	.50	.15			1.25	56
2866	29¢ Diver, Coral	10/03/94	.50	.15			1.25	56
a	Block of 4, #2963-2966		2.00	1.50	2.00	(4)	2.75	56
b	As "a" imperf.		2,250.00					
Cranes Issue, Perf. 10.8 x 11								
2867	29¢ Black-Necked Crane	10/09/94	.50	.15			1.25	78
2868	29¢ Whooping Crane	10/09/94	.50	.15			1.25	78
a	Pair, #2867-2868		1.00	.65	2.00	(4)	2.00	78
b	Black and magenta (engr.) omitted		—					
Legends of the West Issue, Perf. 10.1 x 10								
2869	Sheet of 20	10/18/94	12.00	—			14.00	20
a	29¢ Home on the Range		.60	.15			1.75	20
b	29¢ Buffalo Bill Cody		.60	.15			1.75	20
c	29¢ Jim Bridger		.60	.15			1.75	20
d	29¢ Annie Oakley		.60	.15			1.75	20
e	29¢ Native American Culture		.60	.15			1.75	20
f	29¢ Chief Joseph		.60	.15			1.75	20
g	29¢ Bill Pickett		.60	.15			1.75	20
h	29¢ Bat Masterson		.60	.15			1.75	20
i	29¢ John C. Fremont		.60	.15			1.75	20
j	29¢ Wyatt Earp		.60	.15			1.75	20
k	29¢ Nellie Cashman		.60	.15			1.75	20
l	29¢ Charles Goodnight		.60	.15			1.75	20
m	29¢ Geronimo		.60	.15			1.75	20
n	29¢ Kit Carson		.60	.15			1.75	20
o	29¢ Wild Bill Hickok		.60	.15			1.75	20
p	29¢ Western Wildlife		.60	.15			1.75	20
q	29¢ Jim Beckwourth		.60	.15			1.75	20
r	29¢ Bill Tilghman		.60	.15			1.75	20
s	29¢ Sacagawea		.60	.15			1.75	20
t	29¢ Overland Mail		.60	.15			1.75	20
2870	29¢ Sheet of 20 (recalled)	10/18/94	190.00	—				0.1

	Issues of 1994		Un	U	PB		FDC	Q(M)
	Christmas Issue, Perf. 11.1							
2871	29¢ Madonna and Child	10/20/94	.50	.15	2.50	(4)	1.25	
a	Perf. 9.8 x 10.8		.50	.15			1.25	
b	As "a," booklet pane of 10		5.25	3.50				50
c	As "a," Imperf.		—					
2872	29¢ Stocking	10/20/94	.50	.15	2.50	(4)	1.25	603
a	Booklet pane of 20		10.50	3.00				30
	Self-Adhesive							
2873	29¢ Santa Claus	10/20/94	.50	.15	6.00	(5)	1.25	240
a	Booklet pane of 12		6.25					20
2874	29¢ Cardinal in Snow	10/20/94	.50	.15			1.25	36
a	Booklet pane of 18		9.50					2
	Bureau of Engraving and Printing Issue, Perf.11							
2875	$2.00 Sheet of 4	11/03/94	15.00	—			12.00	5
a	Single stamp		3.00	1.25				20
	Lunar New Year Issue, Perf. 11.2 x 11.1							
2876	29¢ Year of the Boar	12/30/94	.50	.15	2.00	(4)	1.50	80
	Untagged, Perf. 11 x 10.8							
2877	(3¢) Dove Make-Up Rate	12/13/94	.15	.15	.30	(4)	1.25	
	Perf. 10.8 x 10.9							
2878	(3¢) Dove Make-Up Rate	12/13/94	.15	.15	.30	(4)	1.25	
	Tagged, Perf. 11.2 x 11.1							
2879	(20¢) Old Glory Postcard Rate	12/13/94	.40	.15	5.00	(4)	1.25	
	Perf. 11 x 10.9							
2880	(20¢) Old Glory Postcard Rate	12/13/94	.45	.15	7.50	(4)	1.25	
	Perf. 11.2 x 11.1							
2881	(32¢) "G" Old Glory	12/13/94	.70	.15	30.00	(4)	1.25	
a	Booklet pane of 10		6.00	3.75			7.50	
	Perf. 11 x 10.9							
2882	(32¢) "G" Old Glory	12/13/94	.60	.15	3.00	(4)	1.25	
	Booklet Stamps, Perf. 10 x 9.9 on 2 or 3 sides							
2883	(32¢) "G" Old Glory	12/13/94	.60	.15			1.25	
a	Booklet pane of 10		6.25	3.75			7.50	
	Perf. 10.9							
2884	(32¢) "G" Old Glory	12/13/94	.60	.15			1.25	
a	Booklet pane of 10		6.00	3.75			7.50	
	Perf. 11 x 10.9							
2885	(32¢) "G" Old Glory	12/13/94	.60	.15			1.25	
a	Booklet pane of 10		6.00	3.75			7.50	
	Self-Adhesive, Die-Cut							
2886	(32¢) "G" Old Glory	12/13/94	.60	.15	5.75	(5)	1.25	
a	Booklet pane of 18		11.50					
2887	(32¢) "G" Old Glory	12/13/94	.60	.15			1.25	
a	Booklet pane of 18		11.50					
	Coil Stamps, Perf. 9.8 Vertical							
2888	(25¢) Old Glory First-Class Presort	12/13/94	.50	.15	5.00	(5)	1.25	
2889	(32¢) Black "G"	12/13/94	.60	.15	5.50	(5)	1.25	
2890	(32¢) Blue "G"	12/13/94	.60	.15	5.75	(5)	1.25	
2891	(32¢) Red "G"	12/13/94	.60	.15	5.75	(5)	1.25	
	Rouletted							
2892	(32¢) Red "G"	12/13/94	.60	.15	5.75	(5)	1.25	
	Issue of 1995, Perf. 9.8 Vertical							
2893	(5¢) Green	01/12/95	.15	.15				

2871

2873

2875

2872

2874

2876

2877

2878

2879

2880

2881

2882

2883

2884

2885

2886

2887

2888

2889

2890

2891

2892

2893

For details and illustrations of the new 1998 issues, see pages 20-43.

2897

2902

2903

2904

2905

2906

2907

2908

2909

2910

2911

2912

2913

2914

2915

2916

2919

2920

2921

2933

2934

2935

2936

2938

2940

2941

	Issues of 1995-97		Un	U	PB	#	FDC	Q(M)
	Perf. 10.4							
2897	32¢ Flag Over Porch	05/19/95	.60	.15	3.00	(4)	1.25	
	Coil Stamps, Perf. 9.8 Vertically							
2902	(5¢) Butte	03/10/95	.15	.15	1.60	(5)	1.25	
a	Imperf. pair		750.00					
	Serpentine Die-Cut 11.5							
2902B	(5¢) Butte	06/15/96	.15	.15	1.60	(5)	1.25	550
2903	(5¢) Mountain, purple and multi	03/16/96	.20	.20	1.60	(5)	1.25	150
2904	(5¢) Mountain, blue and multi	03/16/96	.20	.20	1.60	(5)	1.25	150
	Self-Adhesive Serpentine Die-Cut 11.2							
2904A	(5¢) Mountain, purple and multi	06/15/96	.20	.15	1.60	(5)	1.25	
	Self-Adhesive Serpentine Die-Cut 9.8 Vertically							
2904B	(5¢) Mountain, purple and multi	01/24/97	.20	.15	1.60	(5)	1.25	148
2905	(10¢) Automobile	03/10/95	.20	.20	2.75	(5)	1.25	
2906	(10¢) Automobile	06/15/96	.20	.20	2.75	(5)	1.25	450
2907	(10¢) Eagle and Shield	05/21/96	.20	.20	2.75	(5)	1.25	450
2908	(15¢) Auto Tail Fin, bureau printing	03/17/95	.30	.30	3.25	(5)	1.25	
2909	(15¢) Auto Tail Fin, private printing	03/17/95	.30	.30	3.25	(5)	1.25	
2910	(15¢) Auto Tail Fin	06/15/96	.30	.30	3.25	(5)	1.25	450
2911	(25¢) Juke Box, bureau printing	03/17/95	.50	.50	4.50	(5)	1.25	
2912	(25¢) Juke Box, private printing	03/17/95	.50	.50	4.50	(5)	1.25	
	Serpentine Die-Cut 11.5							
2912A	(25¢) Juke Box	06/15/96	.50	.50	4.50	(5)	1.25	550
	Self-Adhesive Serpentine Die-Cut 9.8 Vertically							
2912B	(25¢) Juke Box	01/24/97	.50	.50	4.00	(5)	1.25	200
	Perf. 9.9 Vertically							
2913	32¢ Flag Over Porch	05/19/95	.60	.15	5.75	(5)	1.25	
a	Imperf. pair		70.00					
2914	32¢ Flag Over Porch	05/19/95	.60	.15	5.25	(3)	1.25	
	Self-Adhesive, Serpentine Die-Cut Vertically							
2915	32¢ Flag Over Porch	04/18/95	.60	.30	5.25	(5)	1.25	
	Self-Adhesive Serpentine Die-Cut 9.8 Vertically							
2915D	32¢ Flag Over Porch	01/24/97	.60	.15	5.25	(5)	1.25	300
	Booklet Stamps, Perf. 10.8 x 9.8							
2916	32¢ Flag Over Porch	05/19/95	.60	.15			1.25	
a	Booklet pane of 10		6.00				7.50	
b	As "a," imperf.		—					
	Self-Adhesive, Die-Cut							
2919	32¢ Flag Over Field	03/17/95	.60	.15			1.25	
a	Booklet pane of 18		11.00					
	Self-Adhesive, Serpentine Die-Cut 8.8							
2920	32¢ Flag Over Porch	04/18/95	.60	.15			1.25	
a	Booklet pane of 20 + label		12.00					
b	Small date		1.75	.15				
c	As "b," booklet pane of 20 + label		42.50					
d	Serpentine die-cut 11.3	01/20/96	.60	.15				789
	Coil Stamps, Serpentine Die-Cut Perf. 9.8 on 2 or 3 sides							
2921	32¢ Flag Over Porch	05/21/96	.60	.15			1.25	7,344
a	Booklet pane of 10		6.00					
	Great Americans Issue, Perf. 11.1							
2933	32¢ Milton S. Hershey	09/13/95	.60	.15	3.00	(4)	1.25	
2934	32¢ Cal Farley	04/26/96	.60	.15	3.00	(4)	1.25	150
2935	32¢ Henry R. Luce	04/03/98	.60	.15	2.40	(4)	1.25	
2936	32¢ Lila and DeWitt Wallace	07/16/98	.60	.15	2.40	(4)	1.25	
2938	46¢ Ruth Benedict	10/20/95	.90	.15	4.50	(4)	1.35	
2940	55¢ Alice Hamilton, MD	07/11/95	1.10	.20	5.50	(4)	1.35	
	Self-Adhesive Serpentine Die-Cut 11.5							
2941	55¢ Justin S. Morrill	07/17/99	1.10	.15	4.40	(4)		

	ssues of 1995		Un	U	PE		FDC
	Perf. 11.8 x 11.6						
2942	77¢ Mary Breckenridge	11/09/98	1.50	.20			1.75
	Perf. 11.1						
2943	78¢ Alice Paul	08/18/95	1.60	.20	7.50	(4)	1.50
	Love Issue, Perf. 11.2						
2948	32¢ Love, Cherub from						
	Sistine Madonna, by Raphael	02/01/95	.60	.15	3.00	(4)	1.25
	Self-Adhesive, Die-Cut						
2949	32¢ Love, Cherub from						
	Sistine Madonna, by Raphael	02/01/95	.60	.15			1.25
a	Booklet pane of 20 + label		12.00				
b	As "a," red (engr.) omitted		—				
	Perf. 11.1						
2950	32¢ Florida Statehood,						
	150th Anniversary	03/03/95	.60	.15	2.40	(4)	1.25
	Kids Care Earth Day Issue						
2951	32¢ Earth Clean-Up	04/20/95	.60	.15			1.25
2952	32¢ Solar Energy	04/20/95	.60	.15			1.25
2953	32¢ Tree Planting	04/20/95	.60	.15			1.25
2954	32¢ Beach Clean-Up	04/20/95	.60	.15			1.25
a	Block of 4, #2951-54		2.40	1.75	2.40	(4)	2.75
	Perf. 11.2						
2955	32¢ Richard Nixon	04/26/95	.60	.15	3.00	(4)	1.25
	Black Heritage Issue						
2956	32¢ Bessie Coleman	04/27/95	.60	.15	3.00	(4)	1.25
	Love Issue						
2957	32¢ Love, Cherub from						
	Sistine Madonna, by Raphael	05/12/95	.60	.15	3.00	(4)	1.25
2958	55¢ Love, Cherub from						
	Sistine Madonna, by Raphael	05/12/95	1.10	.15	5.50	(4)	1.35
	Booklet Stamps, Perf. 9.8 x 10.8						
2959	32¢ Love, Cherub from						
	Sistine Madonna, by Raphael	05/12/95	.60	.15			1.25
a	Booklet pane of 10		6.00	3.25			7.50
	Self-Adhesive, Die-Cut						
2960	55¢ Love, Cherub from						
	Sistine Madonna, by Raphael	05/12/95	1.10	.15			1.35
a	Booklet pane of 20 + label		22.50				
	Recreational Sports Issue, Perf. 11.2						
2961	32¢ Volleyball	05/20/95	.60	.15			1.50
2962	32¢ Softball	05/20/95	.60	.15			1.50
2963	32¢ Bowling	05/20/95	.60	.15			1.50
2964	32¢ Tennis	05/20/95	.60	.15			1.50
2965	32¢ Golf	05/20/95	.60	.15			1.50
a	Vertical strip of 5, #2961-65		3.00	2.00	6.00	(10)	3.25
2966	32¢ Prisoners of War						
	and Missing in Action	05/29/95	.60	.15	2.40	(4)	2.00
	Pane of 20		12.00	—			

2942

2943

2948

2950

2951 2952

2953 2954 2954a

2955

2965a

2956

2958

2961

2962

2963

2965

2964

2966

2967a

2967

2968

2969   **2970**   **2971**   **2972**   **2973**   **2973a**

Issues of 1995		Un	U	PB	#	FDC
Legends of Hollywood Issue, Perf. 11.1						
2967 32¢ Marilyn Monroe	06/01/95	.60	.15	4.00	(4)	2.00
a Imperf., pair		600.00				
Perf. 11.2						
2968 32¢ Texas Statehood	06/16/95	.60	.15	2.40	(4)	1.25
Great Lakes Lighthouses Issue, Perf. 11.2 Vertically						
2969 32¢ Split Rock, Lake Superior	06/17/95	.60	.15			1.75
2970 32¢ St. Joseph, Lake Michigan	6/17/95	.60	.15			1.75
2971 32¢ Spectacle Reef, Lake Huron	06/17/95	.60	.15			1.75
2972 32¢ Marblehead, Lake Erie	06/17/95	.60	.15			1.75
2973 32¢ Thirty Mile Point,1.25 Lake Ontario	06/17/95	.60	.15			1.75
a Booklet pane of 5, #2969-73		3.00	2.25			5.00

Born in 1926, Norma Jeane Mortenson dropped out of high school to assemble airplanes in California during World War II. It was there that an Army photographer selected her to pose for an article on women workers for YANK magazine. A talent scout noticed her and arranged for her first silent screen test with Ben Lyon of Twentieth Century Fox, who suggested she change her name to "Marilyn." She added her mother's maiden name and on August 26, 1946, Norma Jeane Mortenson became **Marilyn Monroe**.

Rising through small parts in two 1950 films, *The Asphalt Jungle* and *All About Eve*, Monroe became increasingly popular after her performance in the 1953 film *Gentlemen Prefer Blondes*. Soon after, she ventured on a tour of U.S. Army posts in South Korea, where her image as a sex symbol became international. Some of her most popular films included *Bus Stop*, *Some Like It Hot*, and *The Misfits*. Though she died from an overdose of sleeping pills at age 36, she remains one of the most recognizable icons of the silver screen.

In 1995, the U.S. Postal Service honored Marilyn Monroe with the first stamp in the **Legends of Hollywood** series, featuring an illustration by Michael Deas.

ssues of 1995		Un	U	PE		FDC
2974	32¢ United Nations,					
	50th Anniversary	06/26/95	.60	.15	2.40	(4)	1.25
	Civil War Issue, Perf. 10.1					
2975	Sheet of 20	06/29/95	12.00	—		13.00
a	32¢ *Monitor and Virginia*		.60	.15		1.50
b	32¢ Robert E. Lee		.60	.15		1.50
c	32¢ Clara Barton		.60	.15		1.50
d	32¢ Ulysses S. Grant		.60	.15		1.50
e	32¢ Battle of Shiloh		.60	.15		1.50
f	32¢ Jefferson Davis		.60	.15		1.50
g	32¢ David Farragut		.60	.15		1.50
h	32¢ Frederick Douglass		.60	.15		1.50
i	32¢ Raphael Semmes		.60	.15		1.50
j	32¢ Abraham Lincoln		.60	.15		1.50
k	32¢ Harriet Tubman		.60	.15		1.50
l	32¢ Stand Watie		.60	.15		1.50
m	32¢ Joseph E. Johnston		.60	.15		1.50
n	32¢ Winfield Hancock		.60	.15		1.50
o	32¢ Mary Chesnut		.60	.15		1.50
p	32¢ Battle of Chancellorsville		.60	.15		1.50
q	32¢ William T. Sherman		.60	.15		1.50
r	32¢ Phoebe Pember		.60	.15		1.50
s	32¢ "Stonewall" Jackson		.60	.15		1.50
t	32¢ Battle of Gettysburg		.60	.15		1.50

The most traumatic event in the history of the United States was the **Civil War**, which raged from 1861 to 1865. At least 623,000 soldiers perished-more than have died in any other war in American history. In 1995 the U.S. Postal Service issued 20 stamps, illustrated by Mark Hess, that portrayed heroes and battles of this historic conflict.

Union **General Ulysses S. Grant** (1822-1885) gained fame with his victory at Fort Donelson, where he demanded "unconditional surrender." On April 9, 1865, he accepted the surrender of Confederate General Robert E. Lee's army at Appomattox Court House. After the war, Grant served two terms as U.S. President.

Abraham Lincoln (1809-1865), 16th President of the United States, pursued the war vigorously to restore the Union "of the people, by the people, for the people," as he proclaimed in his famous Gettysburg Address. He was assassinated five days after Lee's surrender.

Former slave and abolitionist **Frederick Douglass** (circa 1818-1895) campaigned tirelessly with his oratory and journalism for the rights of African Americans and women. He strongly supported the Union cause, recruiting African Americans troops.

Confederate **General Robert E. Lee** (1807-1870) was Commander of the Army of Northern Virginia. His key victories included the Seven Days' Campaign and the battles of Second Manassas and Chancellorsville. After Lee's surrender to Grant, he became president of Washington College (later Washington and Lee University) in Virginia.

2974

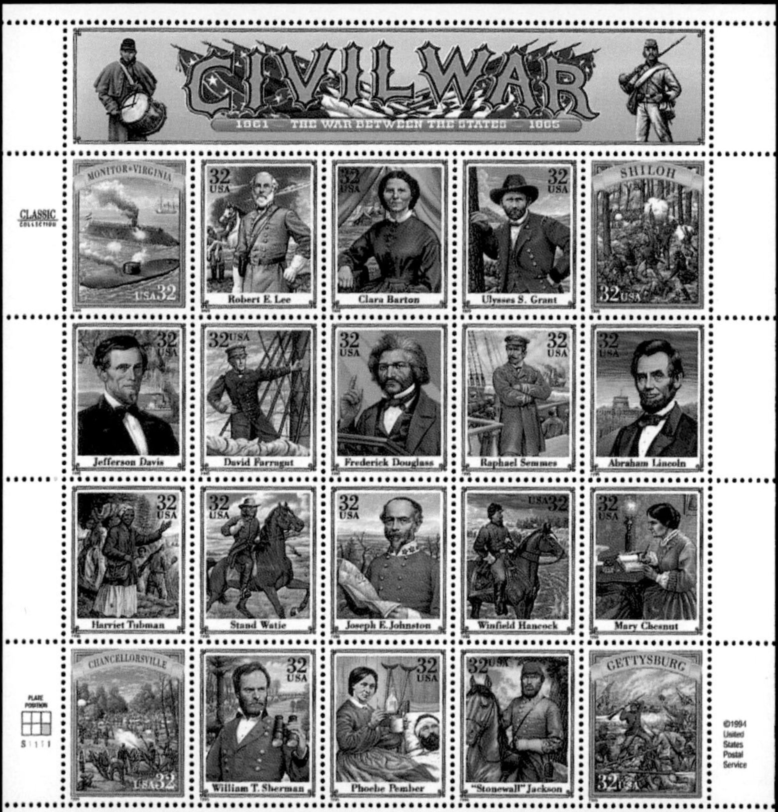

CIVIL WAR

1861 THE WAR BETWEEN THE STATES 1865

CLASSIC COLLECTION

MONITOR • VIRGINIA
USA 32

Robert E. Lee
32 USA

Clara Barton
32 USA

Ulysses S. Grant
32 USA

SHILOH
32 USA

Jefferson Davis
32 USA

David Farragut
32 USA

Frederick Douglass
32 USA

Raphael Semmes
32 USA

Abraham Lincoln
32 USA

Harriet Tubman
32 USA

Stand Watie
32 USA

Joseph E. Johnston
32 USA

Winfield Hancock
USA 32

Mary Chesnut
32 USA

PLATE POSITION
S1111

CHANCELLORSVILLE
32 USA

William T. Sherman
32 USA

Phoebe Pember
32 USA

"Stonewall" Jackson
32 USA

GETTYSBURG
32 USA

©1994
United
States
Postal
Service

a   b   c   d   e   2975
f   g   h   i   j
k   l   m   n   o
p   q   r   s   t

2976   **2977**

2978   **2979**

2979a

2980

a   b   c   d   e

f   g   h   i   j

2981

ssues of 1995		Un	U	PB		FDC
Carousel Horse Issue, Perf. 11						
2976	32¢ Golden Horse with Roses 07/21/95	.60	.15			1.25
2977	32¢ Black Horse with Gold Bridle 07/21/95	.60	.15			1.25
2978	32¢ Horse with Armor 07/21/95	.60	.15			1.25
2979	32¢ Brown Horse with					
	Green Bridle 07/21/95	.60	.15			1.25
a	Block of 4, #2976-79	2.40	1.75	2.40	(4)	3.25
Perf. 11.1 x 11						
2980	32¢ Women's Suffrage 08/26/95	.60	.15	3.00	(4)	1.25
a	Black (engr.) omitted	425.00				
World War II Issue, 1945: Victory at Last, Miniature Sheet, Perf. 11.1						
2981	Block of 10 and central label 09/02/95	6.00	4.50			7.00
a	32¢ Marines Raise					
	Flag on Iwo Jima	.60	.30			1.50
b	32¢ Fierce Fighting Frees Manila					
	by March 3, 1945	.60	.30			1.50
c	32¢ Soldiers Advancing: Okinawa,					
	the Last Big Battle	.60	.30			1.50
d	32¢ Destroyed Bridge: U.S. and					
	Soviets Link Up at Elbe River	.60	.30			1.50
e	32¢ Allies Liberate Holocaust					
	Survivors	.60	.30			1.50
f	32¢ Germany Surrenders at Reims	.60	.30			1.50
g	32¢ Refugees: By 1945, World 1.25					
	War II Has Uprooted Millions	.60	.30			1.50
h	32¢ Truman Announces Japan's					
	Surrender	.60	.30			1.50
i	32¢ Sailor Kissing Nurse: News of					
	Victory Hits Home	.60	.30			1.50
j	32¢ Hometowns Honor Their					
	Returning Veterans	.60	.30			1.50

Wooden carousels flourished in the United States from the late 19th century through the 1920s. **Carousel animals** were carved and painted by master craftsmen. Although most of the figures were horses, carousels also featured an assortment of domestic and wild animals. During the Great Depression, new technology and economic pressures caused carousel manufacturers to switch to cast-metal animals, which are cheaper to produce and maintain than the traditional wooden figures. Wooden carousels were replaced or deteriorated from lack of maintenance.

In the 1960s carousel animals were newly seen as important cultural artifacts. Since then museums, collectors, and carousel enthusiasts have preserved this legacy by restoring the surviving wooden carousels and exhibiting carousel animals as art. The U.S. Postal Service honored carousel art in its **American Folk Art** issue of 1988 with four stamps illustrated by Paul Calle.

ssues of 1995		Un	U	PB		FDC	Q(M)
Legends of American Music Series, Perf. 11.1 x 11							
2982	32¢ Louis Armstrong,						
	white denomination	09/01/95	.60	.15	2.40	(4)	1.25	
2983	32¢ Coleman Hawkins	09/16/95	.60	.15			1.25
2984	32¢ Louis Armstrong,						
	black denomination	09/16/95	.60	.15			1.25
2985	32¢ James W. Johnson	09/16/95	.60	.15			1.25
2986	32¢ Jelly Roll Morton	09/16/95	.60	.15			1.25
2987	32¢ Charlie Parker	09/16/95	.60	.15			1.25
2988	32¢ Eubie Blake	09/16/95	.60	.15			1.25
2989	32¢ Charles Mingus	09/16/95	.60	.15			1.25
2990	32¢ Thelonious Monk	09/16/95	.60	.15			1.25
2991	32¢ John Coltrane	09/16/95	.60	.15			1.25
2992	32¢ Erroll Garner	09/16/95	.60	.15			1.25
a	Vertical block of 10, #2983-92		6.00	—	6.00	(10)	6.50
	Pane of 20		12.00	—			
Garden Flowers Issue, Perf. 10.9 Vertically							
2993	32¢ Aster	09/19/95	.60	.15			1.25	800
2994	32¢ Chrysanthemum	09/19/95	.60	.15			1.25	800
2995	32¢ Dahlia	09/19/95	.60	.15			1.25	800
2996	32¢ Hydrangea	09/19/95	.60	.15			1.25	800
2997	32¢ Rudbeckia	09/19/95	.60	.15			1.25	800
a	Booklet pane of 5, #2993-97		3.00	2.25			4.00
	Perf. 11.1						
2998	60¢ Eddie Rickenbacker,						
	Aviator	09/25/95	1.25	.25	6.25	(4)	1.50
2999	32¢ Republic of Palau	09/29/95	.60	.15	3.00	(4)	1.25

They called him "Satchmo," "Dippermouth," and "Pops." Perhaps more than any other figure in jazz, Louis Armstrong left a legacy that intertwined a man with his music. It was his beautiful tone, commanding presence, and bright smile that lit up stages around the world with a whole new sound.

Born **Louis Armstrong** in the "Back o' Town" section of New Orleans on August 4, 1901, he went on to become one of the most famous jazzmen of the 20th century. He broke onto the emerging jazz scene when he traveled north to Chicago and joined Joe "King" Oliver's band in 1922. He later formed his own groups, the Hot Five and Hot Seven.

His unique brand of improvising and "scat" singing gave Armstrong multifaceted appeal that landed him roles in films, on radio, and later in television. The brilliance of his trumpet and vocal solos, combined with his endearing personality, earned him the distinction of being one of America's finest musicians. Louis Armstrong died on July 6, 1971.

In 1995 the U.S. Postal Service honored Louis Armstrong and nine other jazz greats with stamps in the Legends of American Music series. The stamps were designed by Thomas Blackshear and Dean Mitchell.

2982

2983
2984
2985
2986
2987
2988
2989
2990
2991
2992

2992a

2993 **2994** **2995** **2996** **2997** **2997a**

2998

2999

COMIC STRIP CLASSICS

 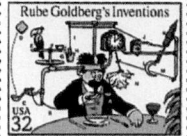  

a   b   c   d   3000
 e   f   g   h
  i   j   k   l
  m   n   o   p
   q   r   s   t

3001

3002

ssues of 1995		Un	U	PB		FDC
Comic Strip Classics Issue, Perf. 10						
3000 Pane of 20	10/01/95	12.00	—			13.00
a	32¢ The Yellow Kid	.60	.15			1.75
b	32¢ Katzenjammer Kids	.60	.15			1.75
c	32¢ Little Nemo in Slumberland	.60	.15			1.75
d	32¢ Bringing Up Father	.60	.15			1.75
e	32¢ Krazy Kat	.60	.15			1.75
f	32¢ Rube Goldberg's Inventions	.60	.15			1.75
g	32¢ Toonerville Folks	.60	.15			1.75
h	32¢ Gasoline Alley	.60	.15			1.75
i	32¢ Barney Google	.60	.15			1.75
j	32¢ Little Orphan Annie	.60	.15			1.75
k	32¢ Popeye	.60	.15			1.75
l	32¢ Blondie	.60	.15			1.75
m	32¢ Dick Tracy	.60	.15			1.75
n	32¢ Alley Oop	.60	.15			1.75
o	32¢ Nancy	.60	.15			1.75
p	32¢ Flash Gordon	.60	.15			1.75
q	32¢ Li'l Abner	.60	.15			1.75
r	32¢ Terry and the Pirates	.60	.15			1.75
s	32¢ Prince Valiant	.60	.15			1.75
t	32¢ Brenda Starr, Reporter	.60	.15			1.75
Perf 10.9						
3001 32¢ U.S. Naval Academy, 150th Anniversary	10/10/95	.60	.15	2.40	(4)	1.25
Literary Arts Issue, Perf 11.1						
3002 32¢ Tennessee Williams	10/13/95	.60	.15	2.40	(4)	1.25

On July 5, 1954, 19-year-old **Elvis Presley** walked into Sun Records in Memphis, Tennessee. The music that he recorded combined elements of blues and country with a raw energy and driving beat. It helped ignite a new sound, rock & roll, that would change the face of popular culture.

Born in 1935 in Tupelo, Mississippi, Elvis Presley rose to stardom by age 21. His early singles for Sun Records and his appearances on Shreveport's Louisiana Hayride radio show, made him a regional success. In 1955 his recording contract was sold to RCA for $35,000, an unprecedented amount.

Elvis's move to RCA was his springboard to fame. Over the next few years he recorded many, hits including "Heartbreak Hotel," "Love Me Tender," "Jailhouse Rock," "Don't Be Cruel," and "Hound Dog." Elvis bought Graceland, a church converted to a 23-room mansion in Memphis, in March 1957. He was drafted into the Army a year later. He served in West Germany for 18 months, and while there met his future wife, Priscilla.

After his return from the Army, Elvis spent much of the 1960s making movies. His loyal public made sure these films were profitable. Following a successful television special in 1968, Elvis returned to the stage, performing in Las Vegas and on the road.

1995

One of the earliest American automobiles, the **1893 Duryea** was constructed by Charles E. and J. Frank Duryea. The two brothers are credited with founding the American automobile industry. Their groundbreaking automobile was commemorated by the U.S. Postal Service in 1995 on an **Antique Automobiles** stamp illustrated by Ken Dallison.

On September 21, 1893, the Duryea prototype was taken for a brief test drive in Springfield, Massachusetts. Some claim that this quarter-mile drive represents the first time a gas-powered car was driven in the United States. Regardless of whether or not this is true, the Duryea brothers can still be credited as America's first automobile manufacturers. The Duryea Motor Wagon Company produced and sold 13 later versions of the Duryea design in 1896.

Today, production models of early Duryeas are preserved in the collections of the Smithsonian Institution and the Henry Ford Museum.

3003

3004   **3005**

3007a

3006   **3007**

3011a   **3008**   **3009**   **3010**   **3011**

3012   **3013**

3019

3020

3021

3022

3023

3023a

3024

| 3025 | 3026 | 3027 | 3028 | 3029 | 3029a |

| 3030 | 3032 | 3033 | 3036 | 3044 |

| 3048 | 3049 | 3050 | 3052 |

Issues of 1995-1996		Un	U	PB	#	FDC	Q(M)
Antique Automobiles Issue							
3019	32¢ 1893 Duryea	11/03/95	.60	.15			1.25	
3020	32¢ 1894 Haynes	11/03/95	.60	.15			1.25	
3021	32¢ 1898 Columbia	11/03/95	.60	.15			1.25	
3022	32¢ 1899 Winton	11/03/95	.60	.15			1.25	
3023	32¢ 1901 White	11/03/95	.60	.15			1.25	
a	Vertical or horizontal strip of 5, #3019-23		3.00	2.00			3.25	
3024	32¢ Utah Statehood	01/04/96	.60	.15	3.00	(4)	1.25	
Issues of 1996, Garden Flowers Issue, Perf 10.9 Vertically							
3025	32¢ Crocus	01/19/96	.60	.15			1.25	
3026	32¢ Winter Asconite	01/19/96	.60	.15			1.25	
3027	32¢ Pansy	01/19/96	.60	.15			1.25	
3028	32¢ Snowdrop	01/19/96	.60	.15			1.25	
3029	32¢ Anemone	01/19/96	.60	.15			1.25	
a	Booklet pane of 5, #3025-3029		3.00	2.25			4.00	
Love Issue, Serpentine Die-Cut Perf. 11.3							
3030	32¢ Love Cherub from Sistine							
	Madonna, by Raphael	01/20/96	.60	.15			1.25	
Flora and Fauna Issue, Perf. 11.1							
Self-Adhesive Serpentine Die-Cut							
3031	1¢ American Kestral	11/19/99	.20	.20				120
3032	2¢ Red-Headed Woodpecker	02/02/96	.15	.15	.25	(4)	1.25	311
3033	3¢ Eastern Bluebird	04/03/96	.15	.15	.25	(4)	1.25	317
Self-Adhesive Serpentine Die-Cut 11.5 x 11.3							
3036	$1 Red Fox	08/14/98	2.00	.50				
Coil Stamps, Perf. 9.75 Vert.							
3044	1¢ American Kestral	01/20/96	.15	.15	.65	(5)	1.25	
Serpentine Die-Cut 10.4 x 10.8 on 3 Sides							
3045	2¢ Red-Headed Woodpecker	6/22/99	.20	.20	.75	(5)	1.25	100
3048	20¢ Blue Jay	08/02/96	.40	.15			1.25	491
a	Booklet pane of 10		4.00					
Serpentine Die-Cut 11.3 x 11.7							
3049	32¢ Yellow Rose	10/24/96	.60	.15			1.25	2,900
a	Booklet pane of 20 and label		12.00					
Serpentine Die-Cut 11.2 on 3 Sides							
3050	20¢ Ring-neck Pheasant	07/31/98	.40	.20				
a	Booklet pane of 10		4.00					
Perf. 11.6 Vertically							
Booklet Stamps, Self-Adhesive Serpentine Die Cut 10.5 x 11 on 3 sides							
3051	20¢ Ring-neck Pheasant	07/99	.40	.20				634
Booklet Stamps, Self-Adhesive Serpentine Die Cut 11. x 1.5 on 2, 3 or 4 Sides							
3052	33¢ Coral Pink Rose	8/13/99	.65	.15				1,000
a	Booklet pane of 4			2.60				
3053	20¢ Blue Jay	08/02/96	.40	.15	3.25	(5)	1.25	330

Issued in 1996, the **Winter Garden Flowers** stamps feature five different flowers known for blooming despite cold temperatures and less hospitable conditions. Gardens featuring these plants yield a different, often more subtle, sense of pleasure than summer gardens. To many gardeners winter is the least promising season, but it has its own colorful rewards, including the crocus, winter aconite, pansy, snowdrop, and anemone.

The Winter Garden Flowers stamps are the fourth, and final, component of a stamp series that depicts garden flowers across the seasons. Garden flowers stamps were first issued in 1993 and continued each year until 1996. All four sets were painted by Ned Seidler of Hampton Bay, New York. If placed end to end, the stamps illustrate the changes a garden undergoes over the course of a year without losing any of its color or beauty.

ssues of 1996		Un	U	PE		FDC	Q(M)
Black Heritage Issue, Perf. 11.1							
3058 32¢ Ernest E. Just	02/01/96	.60	.15	2.40	(4)	1.25	92
3059 32¢ Smithsonian Institution	02/07/96	.60	.15	2.40	(4)	1.25	115
Lunar New Year Issue							
3060 32¢ Year of the Rat	02/08/96	.60	.15	2.40	(4)	1.50	93
Pioneers of Communication Issue, Perf. 11.1 x 11							
3061 32¢ Eadweard Muybridge	02/22/96	.60	.15			1.25	96
3062 32¢ Ottmar Mergenthaler	02/22/96	.60	.15			1.25	96
3063 32¢ Frederic E. Ives	02/22/96	.60	.15			1.25	96
3064 32¢ William Dickson	02/22/96	.60	.15			1.25	96
a Block or strip of 4, #3061-3064		2.40	1.75	2.40	(4)	3.25	
Perf. 11.1							
3065 32¢ Fulbright Scholarships	02/28/96	.60	.15	3.00	(4)	1.25	130
Pioneers of Aviation Issue							
3066 50¢ Jacqueline Cochran	03/09/96	1.00	.20	5.00	(4)	1.35	314
3067 32¢ Marathon	04/11/96	.60	.15	2.40	(4)	1.25	209

EADWEARD MUYBRIDGE (1830-1904) Photography

In the late 19th century, several brilliant inventors turned their attention toward communications. These trailblazers, and their contributions to these world-changing technologies, were commemorated on four **Pioneers of Communication** stamps. Illustrated by Fred Otnes, the stamps were issued in 1996.

Eadweard Muybridge was famous for his photographs of Yosemite Valley, California, and for introducing some important innovations into stop-motion photography. He made photographic studies of animals and humans and later used the pictures to create the illusion of moving images. His device for creating this illusion, the zoopraxiscope, was the first machine to project sequential, still photographs into moving pictures on a screen.

In one of his more famous projects, Muybridge, at railroad magnate Leland Stanford's request, proved that there are moments in a running horse's stride when all its hooves are in the air. Later, Muybridge went on to produce photographs depicting human movement that both artists and scientists found useful.

3059

3060

3058

3063   3064

3064a

3061   3062

3066

3065   3067

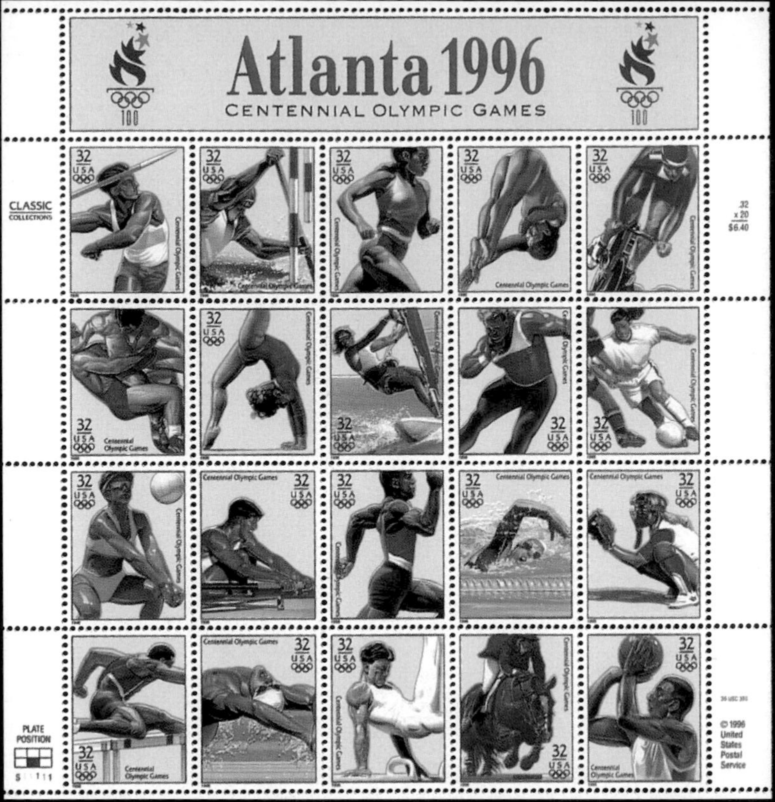

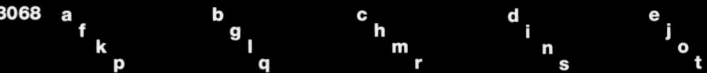

3068 a f b c d e
k g l h m i n j o
p q r s t

3069

3070

3072

3073

3074

3075

3076 3076a

	ssues of 1996		Un	U	PB	#	FDC	Q(M)
	Summer Olympic Games Issue, Perf. 11.1							
3068	Pane of 20	05/02/96	12.00	—			13.00	324
a	32¢ Decathlon		.60	.15			1.25	
b	32¢ Canoeing		.60	.15			1.25	
c	32¢ Women's running		.60	.15			1.25	
d	32¢ Women's diving		.60	.15			1.25	
e	32¢ Cycling		.60	.15			1.25	
f	32¢ Freestyle wrestling		.60	.15			1.25	
g	32¢ Women's gymnastic		.60	.15			1.25	
h	32¢ Women's sailboarding		.60	.15			1.25	
i	32¢ Shot put		.60	.15			1.25	
j	32¢ Women's soccer		.60	.15			1.25	
k	32¢ Beach volleyball		.60	.15			1.25	
l	32¢ Rowing		.60	.15			1.25	
m	32¢ Sprinting		.60	.15			1.25	
n	32¢ Women's swimming		.60	.15			1.25	
o	32¢ Women's softball		.60	.15			1.25	
p	32¢ Hurdles		.60	.15			1.25	
q	32¢ Swimming		.60	.15			1.25	
r	32¢ Gymnastics		.60	.15			1.25	
s	32¢ Equestrian		.60	.15			1.25	
t	32¢ Basketball		.60	.15			1.25	
	Perf. 11.6 x 11.4							
3069	32¢ Georgia O'Keeffe	05/23/96	.60	.15	2.40	(4)	1.25	156
	Perf. 11.1							
3070	32¢ Tennessee Statehood	05/31/96	.60	.15	3.00	(4)	1.25	100
	Serpentine Die-Cut 9.9 x 10.8, Self-Adhesive							
3071	32¢ Tennessee Statehood	05/31/96	.60	.30			1.25	60
a	Booklet pane of 20		12.00					
	American Indian Dances Issue, Perf. 11.1							
3072	32¢ Fancy Dance	06/07/96	.60	.15			1.25	139
3073	32¢ Butterfly Dance	06/07/96	.60	.15			1.25	139
3074	32¢ Traditional Dance	06/07/96	.60	.15			1.25	139
3075	32¢ Raven Dance	06/07/96	.60	.15			1.25	139
3076	32¢ Hoop Dance	06/07/96	.60	.15			1.25	139
a	Strip of 5, #3072-3076		3.00	1.75	6.00	(10)	3.50	139

In ancient Greece, a race was run in honor of Zeus every four years at Olympia. The winner was crowned with an olive wreath cut with a golden knife. Other games were eventually added to this quadrennial event, which became known as the Olympic Games. The first modern Olympic Games were held in 1896, in Athens, as a symbolic nod to their Greek origin. In the summer of 1996, Atlanta, Georgia hosted the **Centennial Olympic Games**.

Atlanta won the honor of hosting the 1996 Centennial Games partly through the use of a virtual reality program that allowed Olympic Committee members to visit Atlanta without leaving home.

In 1996 the U.S. Postal Service honored the Centennial Olympic Games with 20 stamps designed by Richard Waldrep portraying men's and women's Olympic sports. Two stamps depicted women's gymnastics, an audience favorite, and **men's hurdles**, traditionally a strong event for American athletes.

ssues of 1996			Un	U	PB		FDC	Q(M)
Prehistoric Animals Issue, Perf. 11.1 x 11								
3077	32¢ Eohippus	06/08/96	.60	.15			1.25	150
3078	32¢ Woolly Mammoth	06/08/96	.60	.15			1.25	150
3079	32¢ Mastodon	06/08/96	.60	.15			1.25	150
3080	32¢ Saber-tooth cat	06/08/96	.60	.15			1.25	150
a	Block or strip of 4, #3077-3080		2.40	1.50	2.40	(4)	3.25	150
	Pane of 20		12.00	—				
Perf. 11.1								
3081	32¢ Breast Cancer Awareness	06/15/96	.60	.15	2.40	(4)	1.25	96
Legends of Hollywood Issue, Perf. 11.1								
3082	32¢ James Dean	06/24/96	.60	.15	2.40	(4)	1.75	300
	Pane of 20		12.00	—				
Folks Heroes Issue, Perf. 11.1 x 11								
3083	32¢ Mighty Casey	07/11/96	.60	.15			1.25	113
3084	32¢ Paul Bunyan	07/11/96	.60	.15			1.25	113
3085	32¢ John Henry	07/11/96	.60	.15			1.25	113
3086	32¢ Pecos Bill	07/11/96	.60	.15			1.25	113
a	Block or strip of 4, #3083-3086		2.40	1.50	2.40	(4)	3.25	
Centennial Olympic Games Issue, Perf. 11.1								
3087	32¢ Centennial Olympic Games	07/11/96	.60	.15	2.75	(4)	2.40	134
	Pane of 20		13.00	—				
3088	32¢ Iowa Statehood	08/01/96	.60	.15	3.00	(4)	1.25	103
Booklet Stamp, Self-Adhesive Serpentine Die-Cut 11.6 x 11.4								
3089	32¢ Iowa Statehood	08/01/96	.60	.30			1.25	60
a	Booklet pane of 20		12.00	—				
Perf. 11.2 x 11				.15				
3090	32¢ Rural Free Delivery	08/07/96	.60	.15	2.40	(4)	1.25	134

American folk heroes were America's earliest supermen. They were larger than life, brave and strong, clever and proud, with the endurance and skill necessary to conquer their wild country. Even though they are imaginary or exaggerated, they are important to any understanding of the American character. These indomitable figures were commemorated by the Postal Service in 1996 with four stamps illustrated by Dave La Fleur.

Before the days of big machines, the railroads connecting cities and towns were built by strong backs and muscle. A man who did such work was a kind of hero. When machines took the hardest work away, such men became legendary. **John Henry**, who lost his life in an epic battle with a steam drill is a symbol of all who died while working hard to build America, and of the African-American contribution to the industrialization of this country.

3077   3078

3079   3080   3080a

3081

3082

3083

3086a

3086

3085

JOHN HENRY   PAUL BUNYAN   3084

3087

3088

3090

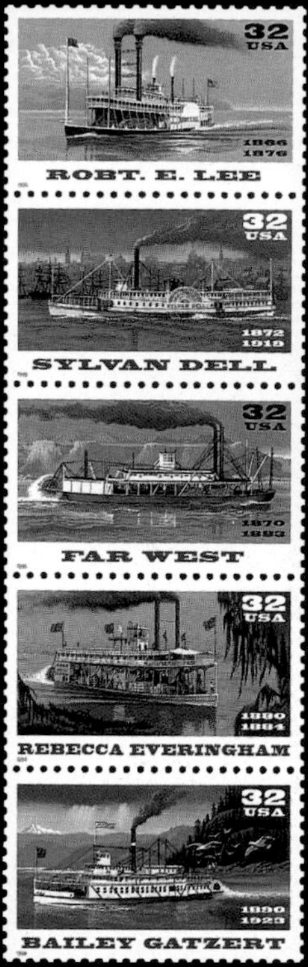

3091

ROBT. E. LEE

3092

SYLVAN DELL

3093

FAR WEST

3094

REBECCA EVERINGHAM

3095

BAILEY GATZERT

3095a

3096   3097

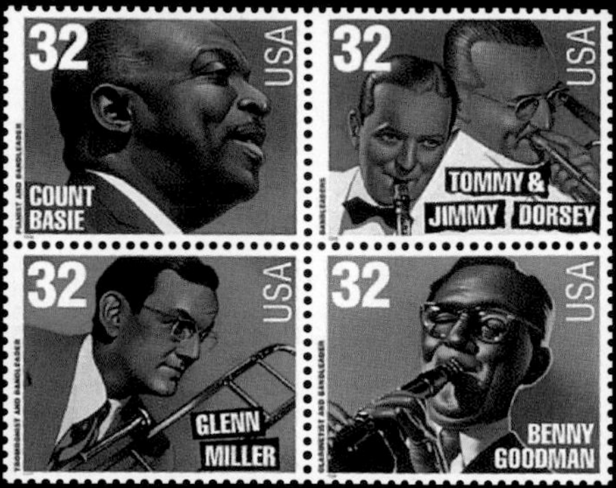

COUNT BASIE   TOMMY & JIMMY DORSEY

3098   3099   3099a

GLENN MILLER   BENNY GOODMAN

3100   3101

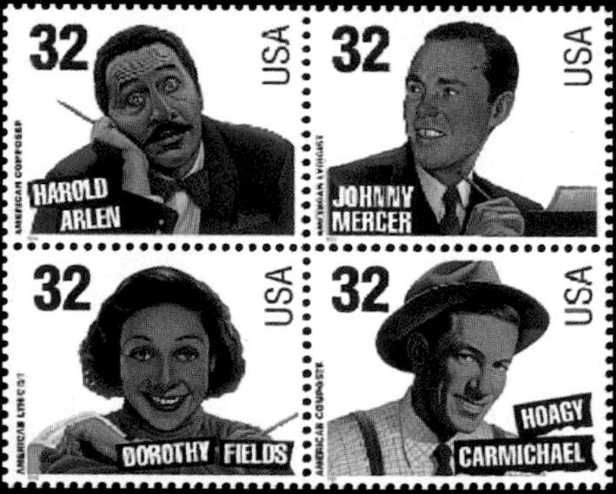

HAROLD ARLEN   JOHNNY MERCER

3102   3103   3103a

DOROTHY FIELDS   HOAGY CARMICHAEL

F SCOTT FITZGERALD
23
USA

3104

ssues of 1996		Un	U	PB	#	FDC	Q(M)
Riverboats Issue, Serpentine Die-Cut 11 x 11.1							
3091	32¢ Robert E. Lee	08/22/96	.60	.15			1.25	160
3092	32¢ Sylvan Dell	08/22/96	.60	.15			1.25	160
3093	32¢ Far West	08/22/96	.60	.15			1.25	160
3094	32¢ Rebecca Everingham	08/22/96	.60	.15			1.25	160
3095	32¢ Bailey Gatzert	08/22/96	.60	.15			1.25	160
a	Vertical strip of 5, #3091-3095		3.00		6.00	(10)	3.50	
American Music Series Issue, Perf. 11.1 x 11							
Big Band Leaders							
3096	32¢ Count Basie	09/11/96	.60	.15			1.25	92
3097	32¢ Tommy and Jimmy Dorsey	09/11/96	.60	.15			1.25	92
3098	32¢ Glenn Miller	09/11/96	.60	.15			1.25	92
3099	32¢ Benny Goodman	09/11/96	.60	.15			1.25	92
a	Block or strip of 4, #3096-3099		2.40	1.50	2.40	(4)	3.25	
Songwriters							
3100	32¢ Harold Arlen	09/11/96	.60	.15			1.25	92
3101	32¢ Johnny Mercer	09/11/96	.60	.15			1.25	92
3102	32¢ Dorothy Fields	09/11/96	.60	.15			1.25	92
3103	32¢ Hoagy Carmichael	09/11/96	.60	.15			1.25	92
a	Block or strip of 4, #3100-3103		2.40	1.50	2.40	(4)	3.25	
Literary Arts Issue, Perf. 11.1							
3104	23¢ F. Scott Fitzgerald	09/11/96	.45	.15	2.25	(4)	1.25	300

ROBT. E. LEE

SYLVAN DELL

Riverboats were an essential means of transporting passengers and cargo during the 19th century. Sometimes towering above and extending out over the waterline, riverboats quickly became a familiar silhouette in American waters. In 1996 the Postal Service issued five stamps illustrated by Dean Ellis commemorating the role these vessels played in America's history. Pictured on the stamps are the *Robt. E. Lee, Sylvan Dell, Far West, Rebecca Everingham*, and *Bailey Gatzert*.

One of the fastest riverboats on the Mississippi River, the **Robt. E. Lee** was famous for beating the *Natchez* in a race from New Orleans to St. Louis in 1870. Both the *Lee* and *Natchez* were side-wheelers and burned coal or wood for power. Their race captured national attention and enhanced the glamour of Mississippi River riverboats.

The **Sylvan Dell**, built in 1872, carried passengers along the Delaware River and New York's East River. Until elevated trains were introduced in New York City, commuters used the *Sylvan Dell* to travel between Harlem and lower Manhattan.

With the spread of railroads, automobiles, and trucks, riverboats became less important to the business of carrying passengers and freight. Now riverboats occupy a nostalgic place in American history, symbols of enterprise and ambition from our past.

	Issues of 1996		Un	U	PB		FDC	
	Endangered Species Issue, Perf. 11.1 x 11							
3105	Pane of 15	10/02/96	9.00	—			7.50	224
a	32¢ Black-footed ferret		.60	.15			1.25	
b	32¢ Thick-billed parrot		.60	.15			1.25	
c	32¢ Hawaiian monk seal		.60	.15			1.25	
d	32¢ American crocodile		.60	.15			1.25	
e	32¢ Ocelot		.60	.15			1.25	
f	32¢ Schaus swallowtail butterfly		.60	.15			1.25	
g	32¢ Wyoming toad		.60	.15			1.25	
h	32¢ Brown pelican		.60	.15			1.25	
i	32¢ California condor		.60	.15			1.25	
j	32¢ Gilatrout		.60	.15			1.25	
k	32¢ San Francisco garter snake		.60	.15			1.25	
l	32¢ Woodland caribou		.60	.15			1.25	
m	32¢ Florida panther		.60	.15			1.25	
n	32¢ Piping plover		.60	.15			1.25	
o	32¢ Florida manatee		.60	.15			1.25	
	Perf. 10.9 x 11.1							
3106	32¢ Computer Technology	10/08/96	.60	.15	3.00	(4)		94
	Christmas Issue, Perf. 11.1 x 11.2							
3107	32¢ Madonna and Child by Paolo de Matteis	10/08/96	.60	.15	3.00	(4)	1.25	848
	Perf. 11.3							
3108	32¢ Family at Fireplace	10/08/96	.60	.15			1.25	226
3109	32¢ Decorating Tree	10/08/96	.60	.15			1.25	226
3110	32¢ Dreaming of Santa Claus	10/08/96	.60	.15			1.25	226
3111	32¢ Holiday Shopping	10/08/96	.60	.15			1.25	226
a	Block or strip of 4, #3108-3111		2.40	1.50	3.00	(4)	3.25	
	Self-Adhesive Booklet Stamps, Serpentine Die-Cut 10 on 2, 3 or 4 sides							
3112	32¢ Madonna and Child by Paolo de Matteis	10/08/96	.60	.15			1.25	244
3113	32¢ Family at Fireplace	10/08/96	.60	.15			1.25	1,805
3114	32¢ Decorating Tree	10/08/96	.60	.15			1.25	1,805
3115	32¢ Dreaming of Santa Claus	10/08/96	.60	.15			1.25	1,805
3116	32¢ Holiday Shopping	10/08/96	.60	.15			1.25	1,805
a	Booklet pane, 5 ea #3113-3116		12.00				3.25	
	Die-Cut							
3117	32¢ Skaters	10/08/96	.60	.15			1.25	495
a	Booklet pane of 18		11.00					
	Serpentine Die-Cut 11.1							
3118	32¢ Hanukkah	10/22/96	.60	.15	2.40	(4)	1.25	104
	Cycling Issue, Perf. 11 x 11.1							
3119	32¢ Souvenier sheet of 2	11/01/96	2.00	2.00			2.50	
a	50¢ orange		1.00	1.00			1.50	
b	50¢ blue and green		1.00	1.00			1.50	

Endangered Species

3105

National Stamp Collecting Month 1996 highlights these 15 species to promote awareness of endangered wildlife. Each generation must work to protect the delicate balance of nature, so that future generations may share a sound and healthy planet.

a   b   c

d   e   f

g   h   i

j   k   l

m   n   o

3106

3107

3108   3111

3111a

3109   3110

3117

3118

3119a

3119b

3120

3121

3122

3123

3124

3125

3126

3127

3130

3131

3132

3133

3134

3135

ssues of 1997			Un	UPB			DC	Q(M)
Lunar New Year Issue, Perf. 11.2								
3120	32¢ Year of the Ox	01/05/97	.60	.15	2.40	(4)	1.50	106
Black Heritage Issue, Serpentine Die-Cut 11.4								
3121	32¢ Brig. Gen. Benjamin							
	O. Davis Sr.	01/28/97	.60	.15	2.40	(4)	1.25	112
Self Adhesive Booklet Stamps, Serpentine Die-Cut 11 on 2, 3 or 4 sides								
3122	32¢ Statue of Liberty,							
	Type of 1994	02/01/97	.60	.15			1.25	2,855
a	Booklet panel of 20 + label		12.00					
b	Booklet pane of 4		2.50					
c	Booklet pane of 5 + label		3.00					
d	Booklet pane of 6		3.60					
Self Adhesive, Serpentine Die-Cut 11.8 x 11.6 on 2, 3 or 4 sides								
3123	32¢ Love Swans	02/04/97	.60	.15			1.25	1,660
a	Booklet pane of 20 + label		12.00					
Serpentine Die-Cut, Perf. 11.6 x 11.8 on 2, 3 or 4 sides								
3124	55¢ Love Swans	02/04/97	1.00	.15			1.50	814
a	Booklet pane of 20 + label		21.00					
Self Adhesive, Serpentine Die-Cut, Perf. 11.6 x 11.7								
3125	32¢ Helping Children Learn	02/18/97	.60	.15	2.40	(4)	1.25	122
Merian Botanical Print Issues, Self Adhesive,								
Serpentine Die-Cut 10.9 x 10.2 on 2, 3 or 4 sides								
3126	32¢ Citron, Roth, Larvae,							
	Pupa, Beetle	03/03/97	.60	.15			1.25	2,048
3127	32¢ Flowering Pineapple,							
	Cockroaches	03/03/97	.60	.15			1.25	2,048
Serpentine Die-Cut 11.2 x 10.8 on 2 or 3 sides								
3128	32¢ Citron, Roth, Larvae,							
	Pupa, Beetle	03/03/97	.60	.15			1.25	30
3129	32¢ Flowering Pineapple,							
	Cockroaches	03/03/97	.60	.15			1.25	30
b	Booklet pane of 5,							
	2 each #3128-29, 1 #3129a		3.00					
Pacific 97 Issues, Perf. 11.2								
3130	32¢ Sailing Ship	03/13/97	.60	.15			1.25	130
3131	32¢ Stagecoach	03/13/97	.60	.15			1.25	130
a	Pair #3130-31		1.25	.30	2.50	(4)	1.75	
Self Adhesive Coil Stamps, Imperf.								
3132	25¢ Juke Box	03/14/97	.50	.50	4.50	(5)	1.25	24
Coil Stamps, Tagged, Serpentine Die-Cut 9.9 Vertically								
3133	32¢ Flag Over Porch	03/14/97	.60	.15	4.75	(5)	1.25	1
Literary Arts Issue, Perf. 11.1								
3134	32¢ Thornton Wilder	04/17/97	.60	.15	2.40	(4)	1.25	98
3135	32¢ Raoul Wallenberg	04/24/97	.60	.15	2.40	(4)	1.25	96

1997

Issues of 1997			Un	U	FDC	Q(M)
The World of Dinosaurs Issue, Perf. 11 x 11.1						
3136	Sheet of 15	05/01/97	9.00	—	7.50	219
a	32¢ Ceratosaurus		.60	.15	1.25	
b	32¢ Camptosaurus		.60	.15	1.25	
c	32¢ Camarasaurus		.60	.15	1.25	
d	32¢ Brachiosaurus		.60	.15	1.25	
e	32¢ Goniopholis		.60	.15	1.25	
f	32¢ Stegosaurus		.60	.15	1.25	
g	32¢ Allosaurus		.60	.15	1.25	
h	32¢ Opisthias		.60	.15	1.25	
i	32¢ Edmontonia		.60	.15	1.25	
j	32¢ Einiosaurus		.60	.15	1.25	
k	32¢ Daspletosaurus		.60	.15	1.25	
l	32¢ Palaeosaniwa		.60	.15	1.25	
m	32¢ Corythosaurus		.60	.15	1.25	
n	32¢ Ornithominus		.60	.15	1.25	
o	32¢ Parasaurolophus		.60	.15	1.25	
Looney Tunes Issue, Serpentine Die-Cut 11						
3137	Bugs Bunny Pane of 10	05/22/97	6.00			265
a	32¢ single		60	.15	1.75	
b	Booklet pane of 9		5.40			
c	Booklet pane of 1		.60			
	Die-cutting on #3137b does not extend through the backing paper.					
3138	Pane of 10	05/22/97	125.00			
a	32¢ single		2.00			
b	Booklet pane of 9					
c	Booklet pane of 1, imperf.					
	Die-cutting on #3138b extends through the backing paper.					

Issued in 1997 and illustrated by James Gurney the **World of Dinosaurs** stamps show two scenes, one from about 150 million years ago during the Jurassic Period in Colorado and the other from about 75 million years ago during the Cretaceous Period in Montana. These scenes portray prehistoric ecosystems by depicting dinosaurs with plants, insects, frogs, turtles, crocodiles, birds, pterosaurs, and mammals.

The Jurassic Period was remarkable for its large sauropods, herbivores with long necks and tails. The giant *Brachiosaurus* and the smaller *Camarasaurus* are the two sauropods pictured on the stamps. *Brachiosaurus* was one of the largest land animals. Its front legs were longer than its hind legs, helping this giraffe-like sauropod to browse in the forest canopy. *Camarasaurus* was closely related to *Brachiosaurus*, but had a shorter neck and tail. Its thick, spoon-shaped teeth were adapted for eating fibrous plants. Also depicted on the stamps are the horned *Ceratosaurus* , the powerfully built *Camptosaurus*, the sharp-clawed *Allosaurus*, the crocodilian *Goniopholis*, the lizard relative *Opisthias*, and *Stegosaurus*, with its plated back and spiked tail.

The Cretaceous Period was inhabited by such dinosaurs as the armored herbivore *Edmontonia* and the ostrich-like *Ornithomimus*, both of which are depicted on the stamps. *Edmontonia* was protected by strong, flexible armor on its back and threatening spikes on its shoulders. *Ornithomimus's* long hind legs made it a fast runner. It had toothless, beak-like jaws, like a modern bird. Also pictured on the stamps are the horned *Einiosaurus*, the powerful, sharp-toothed *Daspletosaurus*, the crested duckbills *Parasaurolophus* and *Corythosaurus*, and *Palaeosaniwa*, which is related to the modern monitor lizard.

3136   a   b   c   d   f   g
                                          e   h

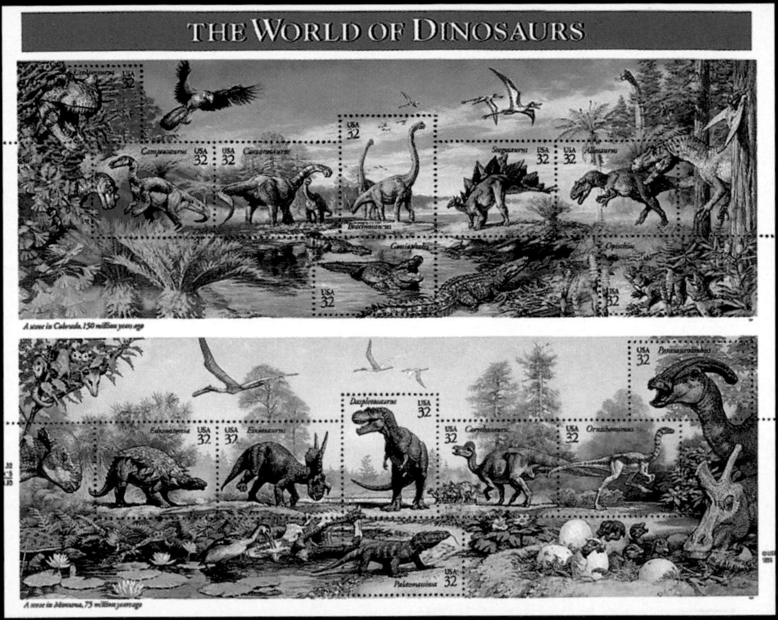

THE WORLD OF DINOSAURS

A scene in Colorado, 150 million years ago

A scene in Montana, 75 million years ago

        i   j   k   m   n   o
                   l

3137

3139

3140

3141

Issues of 1997		Un	U	PB		FDC	Q(M)
Pacific 97 Issue, Perf. 10.5 x 10.4							
Benjamin Franklin							
3139 Sheet of 12	05/29/97	12.00	—			12.00	56
a 50¢ single		1.00	.50			2.00	
George Washington							
3140 Sheet of 12	05/30/97	14.50	—			14.50	56
a 60¢ single		1.20	.60			2.50	
The Marshall Plan, 50th Anniversary Issue, Perf. 11.1							
3141 32¢ The Marshall Plan	06/04/97	.60	.15	2.40	(4)	1.25	45

The 15th **Love stamp**, issued in 1997, features a heart formed by the necks of two swans as they gaze into each other's eyes. Marvin Mattelson illustrated this beautiful and compelling image that reminds us of the role of nature in love—and the role of love in nature.

Swans are a fitting choice to appear on a stamp about love. Through their courtship and enduring relationships, these large, regal birds have become the very embodiment of eternal love. The male swan, called a "cob," and the female, a "pen," undertake a unique courtship. They glide across still waters with a natural elegance, performing a ritual that involves the intricate posturing

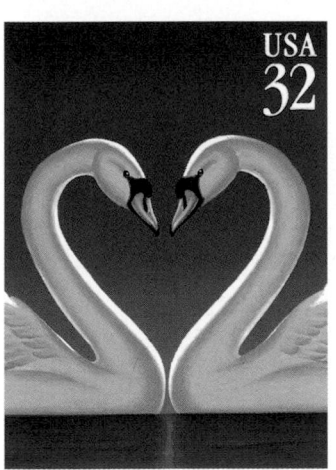

of their heads. Once they find their ideal partner, they remain together. Most swans mate for life; if one swan in a pair dies, the other mourns for a period of time, sometimes never seeking another mate.

ssues of 1997		Un	U	PE		FDC	Q(M)
Classic American Aircraft Issue, Perf. 10.1							
3142	Pane of 20	07/19/97	12.00	—			9.50	161
a	32¢ Mustang		.60	.15			1.25	
b	32¢ Model B		.60	.15			1.25	
c	32¢ Cub		.60	.15			1.25	
d	32¢ Vega		.60	.15			1.25	
e	32¢ Alpha		.60	.15			1.25	
f	32¢ B-10		.60	.15			1.25	
g	32¢ Corsair		.60	.15			1.25	
h	32¢ Stratojet		.60	.15			1.25	
i	32¢ Gee Bee		.60	.15			1.25	
j	32¢ Staggerwing		.60	.15			1.25	
k	32¢ Flying Fortress		.60	.15			1.25	
l	32¢ Stearman		.60	.15			1.25	
m	32¢ Constellation		.60	.15			1.25	
n	32¢ Lightning		.60	.15			1.25	
o	32¢ Peashooter		.60	.15			1.25	
p	32¢ Tri-Motor		.60	.15			1.25	
q	32¢ DC-3		.60	.15			1.25	
r	32¢ 314 Clipper		.60	.15			1.25	
s	32¢ Jenny		.60	.15			1.25	
t	32¢ Wildcat		.60	.15			1.25	
Legendary Football Coaches Issue, Perf. 11.2							
3143	32¢ Bear Bryant	07/25/97	.60	.15			1.25	90
3144	32¢ Pop Warner	07/25/97	.60	.15			1.25	90
3145	32¢ Vince Lombardi	07/25/97	.60	.15			1.25	90
3146	32¢ George Halas	07/25/97	.60	.15			1.25	90
a	Block or strip of 4, #3143-3146		2.40	—	2.40	(4)	3.25	

From the crude engineering of the Wright brothers' Model B to the graceful lines of the 314 Clipper, aircraft enjoy an important and romantic place in our history. Both the sleek designs of fighter aircraft and the muscular contours of bombers immediately call to mind the daring of our nation's military fliers. The planes shown here are important for their engineering and for the changes they introduced to one of America's most important hobbies, traveling.

The **Curtiss JN-4** "Jenny," originally a trainer for World War I pilots, became an official air mail plane. The Jenny was also popular with barnstomers, and it became a familiar sight wherever the public gathered to watch aerobatics. The **Ford Tri-Motor** was one of the great successes of the late 1920s aviation boom. Nicknamed the "Tin Goose,"

the Tri-Motor was an all-metal response to Fokker's similar wood-winged plane.

The Jenny and Tri-Motor were issued in 1997 as a part of the **Classic American Aircraft** pane. Respected aviation artist William Phillips illustrated the stamps. The Jenny appeared previously on a 1968 issue commemorating 50 years of air mail and on a 1918 issue that produced a famous stamp error: a Jenny inverted within the stamp frame.

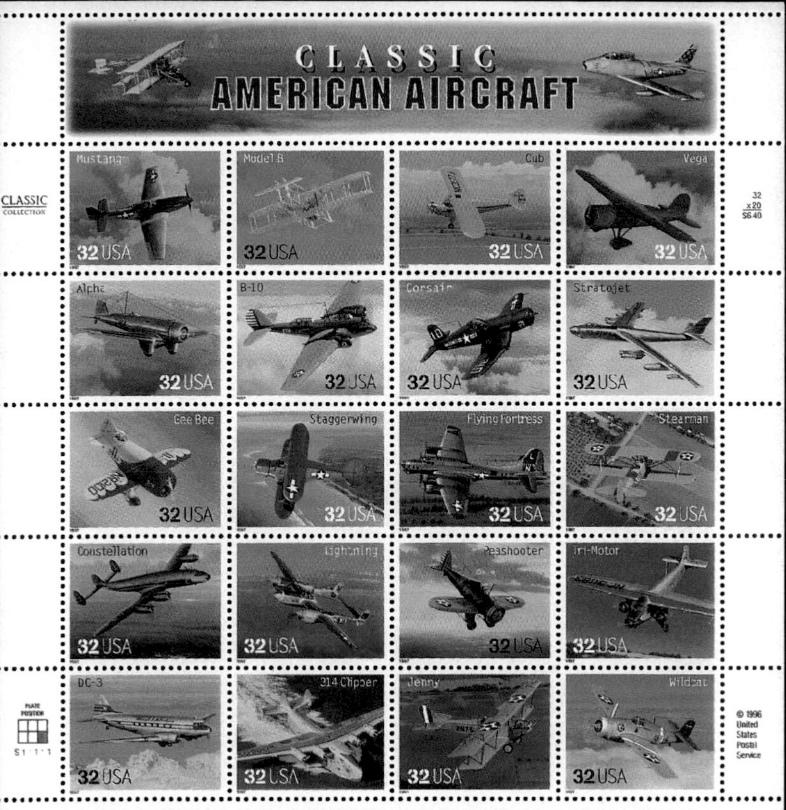

3147

3148

3149

3150

3151 a   b   c   d   e
      f   g   h   i   j
      k   l   m   n   o

ssues of 1997		Un	U	PB		FDC	Q(M)
Legendary Football Coaches Issue with Red Bar above Coach's Name, Perf. 11							
3147 32¢ Vince Lombardi	08/05/97	.60	.30	2.40	(4)	1.50	20
3148 32¢ Bear Bryant	08/07/97	.60	.30	2.40	(4)	1.50	20
3149 32¢ Pop Warner	08/08/97	.60	.30	2.40	(4)	1.50	10
3150 32¢ George Halas	08/16/97	.60	.30	2.40	(4)	1.50	10
Classic American Dolls Issue, Perf. 10.9 x 11.1							
3151 Pane of 15	07/28/97	9.00	—			8.00	105
a 32¢ "Alabama Baby," and doll							
by Martha Chase		.60	.15			1.50	
b 32¢ "Columbian Doll"		.60	.15			1.50	
c 32¢ Johnny Gruelle's "Raggedy Ann"		60	.15			1.50	
d 32¢ Doll by Martha Chase		.60	.15			1.50	
e 32¢ "American Child"		.60	.15			1.50	
f 32¢ "Baby Coos"		.60	.15			1.50	
g 32¢ Plains Indian		.60	.15			1.50	
h 32¢ Doll by Izannah Walker		.60	.15			1.50	
i 32¢ "Babyland Rag"		.60	.15			1.50	
j 32¢ "Scootles"		.60	.15			1.50	
k 32¢ Doll by Ludwig Greiner		.60	.15			1.50	
l 32¢ "Betsy McCall"		.60	.15			1.50	
m 32¢ Percy Crosby's "Skippy"		.60	.15			1.50	
n 32¢ "Maggie Mix-up"		.60	.15			1.50	
o 32¢ Dolls by Albert Schoenhut		.60	.15			1.50	

In 1997 the U.S. Postal Service honored **Vince Lombardi** with a Legendary Football Coaches stamp illustrated by Daniel Moore. Lombardi, an exceptional motivator, was famous for getting the most out of his players. During the 1960s his Green Bay Packers dominated professional football. Many people consider Vince Lombardi to be pro football's greatest coach.

Born in Brooklyn, New York in 1913, Lombardi attended Fordham University where he played football and was a member of the famous line, "the Seven Blocks of Granite." In 1959 Vince Lombardi took over the head coaching job in Green Bay. In an amazing nine-year stretch, Lombardi coached the Packers to five NFL titles and victories in the first two Super Bowls. Today, Super Bowl winners receive the coveted Lombardi Trophy, created in his memory.

ssues of 1997		Un	U	PE		FDC	Q(M)
Legends of Hollywood Issue, Perf. 11.1							
3152	32¢ Humphrey Bogart	07/31/97	.60	.15	2.40	(4)	1.25	195
3153	32¢ "The Stars and Stripes							
	Forever"	08/21/97	.60	.15	3.00	(4)	1.25	323
American Music Series Issue, Opera Singers, Perf. 11							
3154	32¢ Lily Pons	09/10/97	.60	.15			1.25	86
3155	32¢ Richard Tucker	09/10/97	.60	.15			1.25	86
3156	32¢ Lawrence Tibbett	09/10/97	.60	.15			1.25	86
3157	32¢ Rosa Ponselle	09/10/97	.60	.15			1.25	86
a	Block or strip of 4, #3154-3157		2.40	—	2.40	(4)	3.25	

A mesmerizing performer who embodied the lonely, misunderstood outsider, **James Dean** became an American film icon. In 1951, 20-year-old Dean moved from California to New York to look for work in the theater. A year later he was selected to study at the prestigious Actors Studio. Dean appeared in numerous television shows and in two Broadway plays before landing the role of Cal Trask in *East of Eden*. Released in 1955, the film would earn him critical and public acclaim and catapult him to stardom.

Dean starred in only two other films, *Rebel Without a Cause* and *Giant*, both released after his untimely death in an automobile accident in 1955 at age 24. Both films earned him Academy Award nominations for his performances. In his three films, produced in the span of only two years, Dean personified the edgy, restless youth of his generation.

In 1996, James Dean followed Marilyn Monroe as the second stamp in the U.S. Postal Service's **Legends of Hollywood** series. Artist Michael Deas successfully captured both the intensity of James Dean as an actor and the moody, tempestuous nature of the characters he portrayed.

3152

3153

3154   3155

3156   3157

3157a

3158   3159   3160   3161

3162   3163   3164   3165   3165a

3167

3166

3169   3170   3171   3172   3168

ssues of 1997		Un	U	PB		DC	Q(M)
American Music Series Issue, Classical Composers & Conductors, Perf. 11							
3158 32¢ Leopold Stokowski	09/12/97	.60	.15			1.25	86
3159 32¢ Arthur Fiedler	09/12/97	.60	.15			1.25	86
3160 32¢ George Szell	09/12/97	.60	.15			1.25	86
3161 32¢ Eugene Ormandy	09/12/97	.60	.15			1.25	86
3162 32¢ Samuel Barber	09/12/97	.60	.15			1.25	86
3163 32¢ Ferde Grofç	09/12/97	.60	.15			1.25	86
3164 32¢ Charles Ives	09/12/97	.60	.15			1.25	86
3165 32¢ Louis Moreau Gottschalk	09/12/97	.60	.15			1.25	86
a Block of 8, #3158-3165		4.80	—	4.80	(8)	5.25	
Perf. 11.2							
3166 32¢ Padre Félix Varela	09/15/97	.60	.15	2.40	(4)	1.25	2,855
Department of the Air Force, 50th Anniversary Issue, Perf. 11.2 x 11.1							
3167 32¢ Thunderbirds Aerial Demonstration Squadron	09/18/97	.60	.15	2.40	(4)	1.25	45
Classic Movie Monsters Issue, Perf. 10.2							
3168 32¢ Lon Chaney as the Phantom of the Opera	09/30/97	.60	.15			1.25	145
3169 32¢ Bela Lugosi as Dracula	09/30/97	.60	.15			1.25	145
3170 32¢ Boris Karloff as Frankenstein's Monster	09/30/97	.60	.15			1.25	145
3171 32¢ Boris Karloff as the Mummy	09/30/97	.60	.15			1.25	145
3172 32¢ Lon Chaney Jr. as the Wolf Man	09/30/97	.60	.15			1.25	145
a Strip of 5, #3168-3172		3.00	—	6.00	(10)	3.75	

Beginning with No. 3167, a hidden 3-D design can be seen on some stamps when they are viewed with a special viewer sold by the post office.

Dracula and **Frankenstein** were two of the five stamps that Thomas Blackshear illustrated for the **Classic Movie Monsters** issue of 1997. The two characters have much in common: each is strongly associated with a single actor, originated in 19th-century British novels, and has been remade in numerous later versions.

Bela Lugosi thrilled and chilled stage and screen audiences in the title role of Dracula. Directed by Tod Browning in the 1931 film, Lugosi's elegant portrayal of the menacing vampire became his signature role. Bram Stoker created the infamous count in his 1897 novel.

Boris Karloff starred as the monster in the first sound version of Mary Shelley's 1818 novel, *Frankenstein*. The movie was a hit in 1931. The monster's trademark makeup and lurching gait have become film icons. Frankenstein was just one of the movie monsters that Karloff would play in his career.

Issues of 1997-98		Un	U	PE		FDC	Q(M)
	Serpentine Die-Cut 11.4						
3173	32¢ First Supersonic Flight, 50th Anniversary	10/14/97	.60	.15	2.40	(4)	1.25	173
	Perf. 11.1						
3174	32¢ Women in Military Service	10/18/97	.60	.15	2.40	(4)	1.25	
	Self Adhesive, Serpentine Die-Cut 11						
3175	32¢ Kwanzaa	10/22/97	.60	.15	3.00	(4)	1.25	133
	Holiday Traditional, Self Adhesive, Serpentine Die-Cut 9.9 on 2, 3 or 4 sides						
3176	32¢ Madonna and Child by Sano di Pietro	10/09/97	.60	.15			1.25	883
a	Booklet pane of 20 + label		12.00					
	Holiday Contemporary, Serpentine Die-Cut 11.2 x 11.8 on 2, 3 or 4 sides						
3177	32¢ American Holly	10/30/97	.60	.15			1.25	180
a	Booklet pane of 20 + label		12.00					
b	Booklet pane of 4		2.50					
c	Booklet pane of 5 + label		3.00					
d	Booklet pane of 6		3.75					
	Mars Pathfinder, Perf 11 x 11.1						
3178	$3 Mars Rover Sojourner	12/10/97	6.00	—			6.00	15
	Lunar New Year Issue, Perf. 11.2						
3179	32¢ Year of the Tiger	01/05/98	.60	.15	2.40	(4)	1.25	

One of the most intimidating obstacles facing aeronautical engineers and pilots in the years following World War II was the sound barrier. Scientists knew that objects like bullets and rockets could be propelled faster than the speed of sound, but they were unsure that they could design an airplane capable of withstanding the enormous pressures that velocity would produce.

Working in secrecy with the military, the Bell Aircraft Corporation built the X-1 aircraft. A revolutionary design, the X-1 resembled a rocket and was fueled with liquid oxygen and alcohol propellants. In order to conserve fuel, a B-29 bomber carried the X-1 aloft and then released the smaller plane.

In October 1947 pilot Chuck Yeager, flying an X-1 named *Glamorous Glennis*, became the first pilot to **break the sound barrier**. Because of the secrecy surrounding the project, the news of Yeager's historic flight was not released until June 1948.

In 1997 the Postal Service commemorated the 50th anniversary of this important aeronautical achievement with a commemorative stamp illustrated by Paul Salmon. Salmon, an experienced illustrator, has also worked with the National Air and Space Museum and NASA.

3173

3174

3175

3176

3177

3178

3179

3180

3181

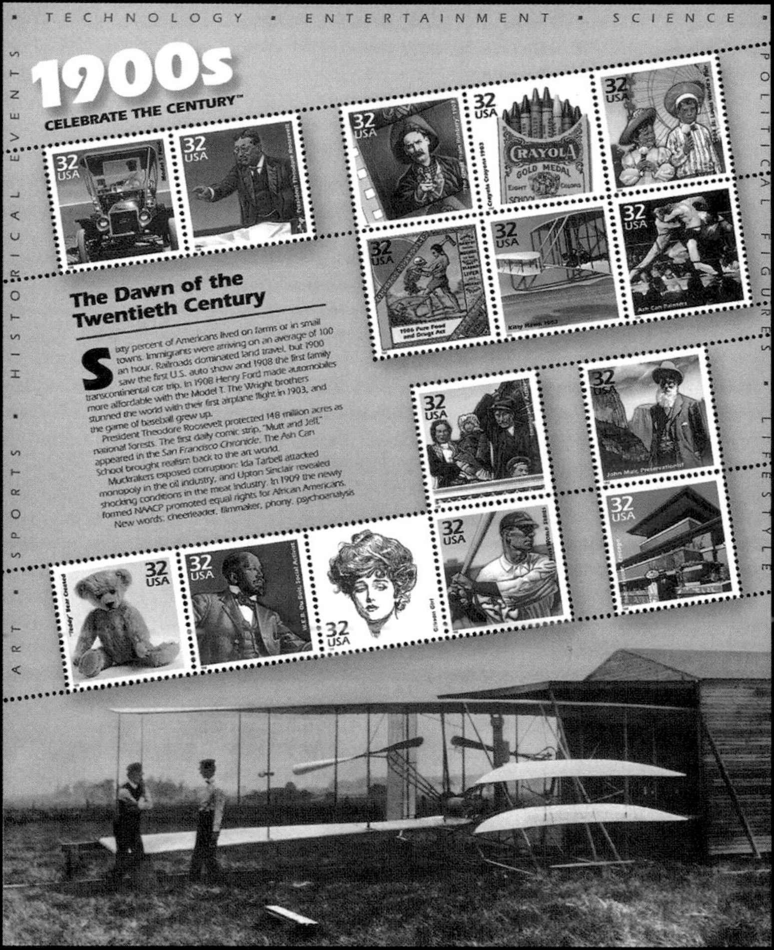

- TECHNOLOGY · ENTERTAINMENT · SCIENCE ·

1900s
CELEBRATE THE CENTURY™

POLITICAL FIGURES · LIFESTYLE

HISTORICAL EVENTS · SPORTS · ART

The Dawn of the Twentieth Century

Sixty percent of Americans lived on farms or in small towns. Immigrants were arriving on an average of 100 an hour. Railroads dominated land travel, but 1900 saw the first U.S. auto show and 1908 the first family transcontinental car trip. In 1908 Henry Ford made automobiles more affordable with the Model T. The Wright brothers stunned the world with their first airplane flight in 1903, and the game of baseball grew up.

President Theodore Roosevelt protected 148 million acres as national forests. The first daily comic strip, "Mutt and Jeff," appeared in the San Francisco Chronicle. The Ash Can School brought realism back to the art world.

Muckrakers exposed corruption: Ida Tarbell attacked monopoly in the oil industry, and Upton Sinclair revealed shocking conditions in the meat industry. In 1909 the newly formed NAACP promoted equal rights for African Americans. New words: cheerleader, filmmaker, phony, psychoanalysis.

3182   a   b   c   d   e

f   g   h

i   j

k   l   m   n   o

ssues of 1998		Un	U	PB	#	FDC	Q(M)
3180 32¢ Winter Sports-Skiing	1/2/98	.60	.15	2.40	(4)	1.25	80
Black Heritage Issue, Serpentine Die-Cut 11.6 x 11.3							
3181 32¢ Madam C. J. Walker	1/28/98	.60	.15	2.40	(4)	1.25	45
CelebrateThe Century® Issue, Perf. 11.6							
3182 Pane of 15, 1900-1909	2/3/98	9.00	—			7.50	188
a 32¢ Model T Ford		.60	.30			1.25	
b 32¢ Theodore Roosevelt		.60	.30			1.25	
c 32¢ Motion picture, "The Great Train Robbery"		.60	.30			1.25	
d 32¢ Crayola Crayons introduced, 1903		.60	.30			1.25	
e 32¢ St. Louis World's Fair, 1904		.60	.30			1.25	
f 32¢ Design used on Hunt's Remedy stamp (#RS56), Pure Food & Drug Act, 1906		.60	.30			1.25	
g 32¢ Wright Brothers first flight, Kitty Hawk, 1903		.60	.30			1.25	
h 32¢ Boxing match shown in painting "Stag at Sharkey's," by George Bellows of the Ash Can School		.60	.30			1.25	
i 32¢ Immigrants arrive		.60	.30			1.25	
j 32¢ John Muir, preservationist		.60	.30			1.25	
k 32¢ "Teddy" Bear created		.60	.30			1.25	
l 32¢ W.E.B. Du Bois, social activist		.60	.30			1.25	
m 32¢ Gibson Girl		.60	.30			1.25	
n 32¢ First baseball World Series, 1903		.60	.30			1.25	
o 32¢ Robie House, Chicago, designed by Frank Lloyd Wright		.60	.30			1.25	

The first decade of the 20th century saw new developments in technology, society, and arts and entertainment. In 1903, the Wright brothers stunned the world with the first powered airplane flight. The Model T Ford, which debuted in 1908, made automobiles more affordable for the average American.

Important social movements were underway. Congress passed the Pure Food and Drug Act of 1906. President Roosevelt also protected 148 million acres of land as national forests. W.E.B. Du Bois promoted equal rights for African Americans and helped found the National Association for the Advancement of Colored People (NAACP) in 1909. Immigrants poured into the United States, arriving on an average of 100 an hour.

Changes also took place in the arts and entertainment. Painters of the Ash Can School brought realism back to the art world. Frank Lloyd Wright designed the Robie House in Chicago. *The Great Train Robbery* was one of the first commercially successful story films. The championship baseball games of 1903 became known as the **First World Series**. The St. Louis World's Fair of 1904 popularized the ice cream cone, and illustrator Charles Dana Gibson set the fashion for American women with his Gibson Girl. Children delighted in the newly invented Crayola crayons. The Teddy bear was named for President Roosevelt.

A pane of 15 stamps commemorating the **1900s** was released in 1998 as part of the **Celebrate The Century®** program. It featured illustrations by Richard Waldrep, whose other projects for the U.S. Postal Service include Summer Olympic Games (1992), Country & Western Music (1993), and Centennial Olympic Games (1996).

			Un	U	FDC	Q(M)
	Celebrate The Century® Issue, Perf. 11.6					
3183	Pane of 15, 1910-1919	2/3/98	9.00	—	7.50	188
a	32¢ Charlie Chaplin as the Little Tramp		.60	.30	1.25	
b	32¢ Federal Reserve System created, 1913		.60	.30	1.25	
c	32¢ George Washington Carver		.60	.30	1.25	
d	32¢ Avant-garde art introduced at Armory Show, 1913		.60	.30	1.25	
e	32¢ First transcontinental telephone line, 1914		.60	.30	1.25	
f	32¢ Panama Canal opens, 1914		.60	.30	1.25	
g	32¢ Jim Thorpe wins decathlon at Stockholm Olympics, 1912		.60	.30	1.25	
h	32¢ Grand Canyon National Park, 1919		.60	.30	1.25	
i	32¢ U.S. enters World War I		.60	.30	1.25	
j	32¢ Boy Scouts started in 1910, Girl Scouts formed in 1912		.60	.30	1.25	
k	32¢ Woodrow Wilson		.60	.30	1.25	
l	32¢ First crossword puzzle published, 1913		.60	.30	1.25	
m	32¢ Jack Dempsey wins heavyweight title, 1919		.60	.30	1.25	
n	32¢ Construction toys		.60	.30	1.25	
o	32¢ Child labor reform		.60	.30	1.25	

The **1910s** saw rapid changes in American society. Workers began moving from farms to factories. The national landscape changed forever as the first transcontinental telephone line was completed in 1914. The Federal Reserve System was established. Lewis W. Hine's photographs of children working prompted efforts to regulate child labor. The Grand Canyon was designated a national park in 1919. Botanist George Washington Carver improved the economy of the South by demonstrating the commercial possibilities of peanuts and sweet potatoes.

America also looked beyond its borders. The Panama Canal was constructed, connecting the Atlantic and Pacific Oceans. The sinking of *Lusitania* led to U.S. involvement in World War I. **President Woodrow Wilson** was awarded the Nobel Peace Prize for his promotion of the League of Nations, the precursor to the United Nations.

New forms of art and recreation attracted a following. The 1913 Armory Show introduced avant-garde art to this country. Charlie Chaplin created his famous film character, the Little Tramp. The Boy Scouts and Girl Scouts introduced American youth to a variety of outdoor activities and promoted self-reliance and resourcefulness.

The decade produced famous athletes. Jack Dempsey won the world heavyweight boxing championship. Jim Thorpe was hailed as the greatest athlete in the world after he won the pentathlon and decathlon in 1912 at Stockholm.

In 1998, the U.S. Postal Service issued a pane of 15 stamps to commemorate the 1910s as part of the **Celebrate The Century®** program. The stamp pane featured illustrations by Dennis Lyall, whose many projects for the Postal Service include American Inventors (1983), Arctic Explorers (1986), Antarctic Explorers (1988), and Women in Military Service (1997).

TECHNOLOGY • ENTERTAINMENT • SCIENCE

1910s
CELEBRATE THE CENTURY™

America Looks
Beyond its Borders

Halley's comet lit up the sky to begin the decade. American workers began moving from farms to factories. The Ford Motor Co. refined the automobile assembly line. Traffic lights and white line dividers became part of the American landscape. Scientific and technological achievements changed society. In 1911, in New York, fingerprint evidence alone was used for the first time in the United States to arrest a burglar. Jim Thorpe was an international sports star, but Tarzan was an even more popular hero.

The accidental sinking of the luxury liner Titanic shocked the nation, but it was the sinking of another ship, the Lusitania, that upset society, leading to U.S. involvement in World War I. Two million American soldiers fought in Europe and more than 116,500 lost their lives. Americans saw the light as the decade ended: Daylight saving time was instituted in 1918.

New words: camouflage, electronics, troublemaker

3183
a   b   c

d   e   f

g   h   i   j   k

l   m   n   o

3184 a   b   c   d   e

      f   g   h   i   j

      k   l   m

      n   o

Issues of 1998		Un	U	FDC	Q(M)
Celebrate The Century® Issue, Perf. 11.6					
3184 Pane of 15, 1920-1929	5/28/98	9.00	—	7.50	188
a	32¢ Babe Ruth	.60	.30	1.25	
b	32¢ The Gatsby style	.60	.30	1.25	
c	32¢ Prohibition enforced	.60	.30	1.25	
d	32¢ Electric toy trains	.60	.30	1.25	
e	32¢ Nineteenth Amendment (woman voting)	.60	.30	1.25	
f	32¢ Emily Post's Etiquette	.60	.30	1.25	
g	32¢ Margaret Mead, anthropologist	.60	.30	1.25	
h	32¢ Flappers do the Charleston	.60	.30	1.25	
i	32¢ Radio entertains America	.60	.30	1.25	
j	32¢ Art Deco style (Chrysler Building)	.60	.30	1.25	
k	32¢ Jazz flourishes	.60	.30	1.25	
l	32¢ Four Horsemen of Notre Dame	.60	.30	1.25	
m	32¢ Lindbergh flies the Atlantic	.60	.30	1.25	
n	32¢ American realism (The Automat, by Edward Hopper)	.60	.30	1.25	
o	32¢ Stock Market crash, 1929	.60	.30	1.25	

The U.S. Postal Service issued a pane of 15 stamps in 1998 to commemorate the **1920s** as a part of the **Celebrate The Century®** program. Davis Meltzer and Keith Birdsong illustrated this decade filled with thrill-seekers, heroes, and important cultural milestones.

They didn't call it the Roaring Twenties for nothing. In 1927 Charles Lindbergh flew alone and nonstop across the Atlantic and Babe Ruth hit 60 home runs, just one year after Gertrude Ederle swam across the English Channel faster than any man. Audiences enjoyed the first feature-length film with talking parts with the release of *The Jazz Singer*, and the first Academy Awards were presented. *The Great Gatsby* by F. Scott Fitzgerald was published in 1925, exposing the lavish and insensitive lifestyle of the rich and glamorous, while Emily Post wrote about proper manners and conduct.

The **Chrysler Building** in New York City illustrates the Art Deco style that was embraced in architecture and in decorative arts during this period, and jazz became the sound of the 1920s. The public crowded around radios to listen to comedy shows, newscasts, and presidential speeches.

The manufacture and sale of alcoholic beverages became illegal with the 18th Amendment, and the 19th Amendment gave women the right to vote. The stock market crashed on October 29, 1929, ending prosperous times and leading the country into the Great Depression of the 1930s.

Davis Meltzer has illustrated several stamps for the U.S. Postal Service, including Balloons (1983), Eddie Rickenbacker (1995), and Prehistoric Animals (1996). Keith Birdsong's other projects for the Postal Service include American Indian Dances (1996), General Joseph Stilwell (1998), and Celebrate The Century: The 1960s (1999).

ssues of 1998		Un	U	DC	Q(M)
Celebrate The Century Issue®, Perf. 11.6					
3185	Pane of 15, 1930-1939 9/10/98	9.00	—	7.50	188
a	32¢ Franklin D. Roosevelt	.60	.30	1.25	
b	32¢ The Empire State Building	.60	.30	1.25	
c	32¢ First Issue of Life Magazine, 1936	.60	.30	1.25	
d	32¢ Eleanor Roosevelt	.60	.30	1.25	
e	32¢ FDR's New Deal	.60	.30	1.25	
f	32¢ Superman arrives, 1938	.60	.30	1.25	
g	32¢ Household conveniences	.60	.30	1.25	
h	32¢ "Snow White and the Seven Dwarfs," 1937	.60	.30	1.25	
i	32¢ "Gone with the Wind," 1936	.60	.30	1.25	
j	32¢ Jesse Owens	.60	.30	1.25	
k	32¢ Streamline design	.60	.30	1.25	
l	32¢ Golden Gate Bridge	.60	.30	1.25	
m	32¢ America survives the Depression	.60	.30	1.25	
n	32¢ Bobby Jones wins Grand Slam, 1938	.60	.30	1.25	
o	32¢ The Monopoly Game	.60	.30	1.25	

The **1930s** brought hardship to many Americans. By 1933 the average wage was 60 percent less than in 1929, and unemployment had skyrocketed to 25 percent. Dust storms forced many farmers to give up their land. President Franklin Roosevelt fought the Great Depression with his New Deal programs. First Lady Eleanor Roosevelt championed the rights of women, youths, minorities, and the disadvantaged. The decade ended with many Americans anxious about the growing war in Europe.

The decade saw impressive technological achievements. The Empire State Building rose above the Manhattan skyline and the **Golden Gate Bridge** spanned the San Francisco Bay. Stressing efficiency and speed, streamlined designs were used for cars, planes, trains, buildings, and even household appliances

Americans escaped the harsh realities of the depression years by playing Monopoly and attending movies such as *Gone With the Wind* and *Snow White and the Seven Dwarfs*, this country's first feature-length animated film. Bobby Jones became the first-and-only person to win the Grand Slam of golf. On the afternoon of May 25, 1935, Ohio State University's track star Jesse Owens was credited with setting five world records and tying another. Children thrilled to the exploits of comic book hero Superman; their parents enjoyed LIFE magazine, which opened a new era of photojournalism.

In 1998 the U.S. Postal Service issued a pane of 15 stamps to commemorate the 1930s as a part of the **Celebrate The Century®** program. The stamp pane featured illustrations by Paul Calle, whose other projects for the Postal Service include Robert Frost (1974), International Year of the Child (1979), Vietnam Veterans Memorial (1984), Carousel Horses (1995), and Lila and DeWitt Wallace (1998).

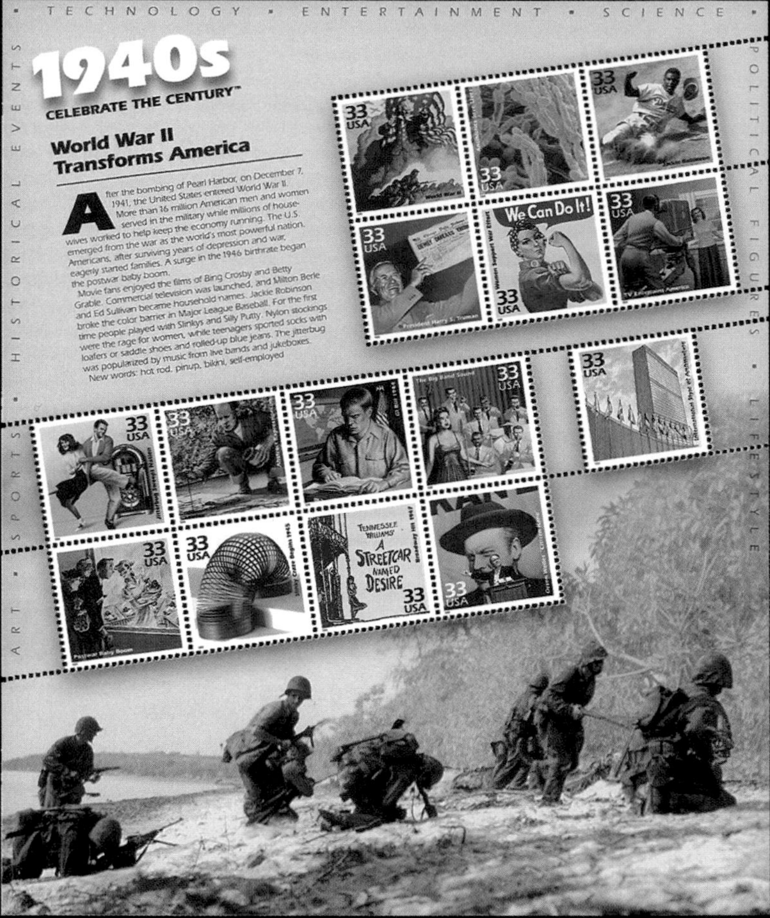

1940s
CELEBRATE THE CENTURY™

World War II Transforms America

After the bombing of Pearl Harbor, on December 7, 1941, the United States entered World War II. More than 16 million American men and women served in the military while millions of housewives worked to help keep the economy running. The U.S. emerged from the war as the world's most powerful nation. Americans, after surviving years of depression and war, eagerly started families. A surge in the 1946 birthrate began the postwar baby boom.

Movie fans enjoyed the films of Bing Crosby and Betty Grable. Commercial television was launched, and Milton Berle and Ed Sullivan became household names. Jackie Robinson broke the color barrier in Major League Baseball. For the first time people played with Slinkys and Silly Putty. Nylon stockings were the rage for women, while teenagers sported socks with loafers or saddle shoes and rolled-up blue jeans. The jitterbug was popularized by music from live bands and jukeboxes.

New words: hot rod, pinup, bikini, self-employed

3186

ssues of 1999			Un	U	FDC	Q(M)
Celebrate The Century®, Perf. 11.6						
3186 Pane of 15, 1940-1949		2/18/99	9.75			12.5
a.	33¢ World War II		.65	.30		
b.	33¢ Antibiotics save lives		.65	.30		
c.	33¢ Jackie Robinson		.65	.30		
d.	33¢ Harry S. Truman		.65	.30		
e.	33¢ Women support war effort		.65	.30		
f.	33¢ TV entertains America		.65	.30		
g.	33¢ Jitterbug sweeps nation		.65	.30		
h.	33¢ Jackson Pollock, Abstract Expressionist		.65	.30		
i.	33¢ GI Bill, 1944		.65	.30		
j.	33¢ The Big Band Sound		.65	.30		
k.	33¢ International style of architecture		.65	.30		
l.	33¢ Postwar baby boom		.65	.30		
m.	33¢ Slinky craze begins 1945		.65	.30		
n.	33¢ Broadway Hit 1947		.65	.30		
o.	33¢ Orson Welles' "Citizen Kane"		.65	.30		

After the bombing of Pearl Harbor on December 7, 1941, the United States entered **World War II**. More than 16 million American men and women served in the military. On the home front, millions of women—more than one-third of the civilian work force—worked to keep the economy running. President **Harry S. Truman** guided the nation through the end of World War II and the beginning of the Cold War. Returning GIs married and started families, and a surge in the 1946 birthrate began the postwar baby boom.

It was a decade of social accomplishment as well. The GI Bill of 1944 helped approximately 2.25 million war veterans attend college, while millions of others received job training; home, business, and farm loans; and unemployment benefits. In 1947 Jackie Robinson broke the color barrier in Major League Baseball; he earned the National League's Most Valuable Player award in 1949. Doctors used the antibiotics penicillin and streptomycin to treat bacterial infections.

The 1940s saw new developments in arts and entertainment. Abstract Expressionism was marked by a range of individual styles of modern painting and sculpture. Jackson Pollock created his most famous abstract paintings by pouring paint onto canvas laid on his studio floor. Architects of the International Style were concerned with function and simple shapes and utilized materials such as glass, steel, and concrete. Released in 1941, Orson Welles' film *Citizen Kane* was hailed for its artistic and technical innovations. Tennessee Williams' powerful play, *A Streetcar Named Desire*, won the 1948 Pulitzer Prize for drama.

Big band music was popular and the jitterbug was a fast-paced dance that bridged the eras of swing and rock 'n' roll. Commercial television formally began July 1, 1941, and by the end of 1949 more than three million American homes had sets. A new toy, the Slinky, caused a sensation when it was first marketed in 1945.

In 1999 the U.S. Postal Service issued a pane of 15 stamps commemorating the **1940s** as part of the **Celebrate The Century®** program. The stamps featured illustrations by Howard Koslow, whose other projects for the Postal Service include Wolf Trap Farm (1972), Rural Electrification Administration (1985), Jazz and Blues Singers (1994), and Great Lakes Lighthouses (1995).

ssues of 1999		Un	U	FDC	Q(M)
Celebrate The Century®, Perf. 11.6					
3187 Pane of 15, 1950-1959	5/26/99	9.75			12.5
a.	33¢ Polio vaccine developed	.65	.30		
b.	33¢ Teen fashions	.65	.30		
c.	33¢ The "Shot Heard 'Round the World"	.65	.30		
d.	33¢ U.S. launches satellites	.65	.30		
e.	33¢ Korean War	.65	.30		
f.	33¢ Desegregating public schools	.65	.30		
g.	33¢ Tail fins, chrome	.65	.30		
h.	33¢ Dr. Seuss' "The Cat in the Hat"	.65	.30		
i.	33¢ Drive-in movies	.65	.30		
j.	33¢ World Series rivals	.65	.30		
k.	33¢ Rocky Marciano, undefeated	.65	.30		
l.	33¢ "I Love Lucy"	.65	.30		
m.	33¢ Rock 'n Roll	.65	.30		
n.	33¢ Stock car racing	.65	.30		
o.	33¢ Movies go 3-D	.65	.30		

During the **1950s**, America struggled for freedom on several fronts. The Supreme Court declared segregation in public schools unconstitutional, Dr. Jonas Salk developed a vaccine against polio, and the first successful U.S. satellite was launched into space. Americans fought with other United Nations forces to oppose the invasion of South Korea by Communist troops.

Meanwhile, Americans enjoyed their postwar prosperity with sporting events and other forms of entertainment. The New York Giants beat the Brooklyn Dodgers in the 1951 National League pennant race when, in the ninth inning of the deciding game, Bobby Thomson hit a three-run homer. Between 1949 and 1956, the Dodgers and their crosstown rivals, the New York Yankees, met five times in the World Series. The Dodgers won once, in 1955. Boxer Rocky Marciano held the world heavyweight title from September 1952 to April 1956, defending his crown six times. The 1950s witnessed a boom in stock car racing; the first Daytona 500 was held in 1959.

The movies remained a popular form of entertainment. Audiences were thrilled by the new 3-D movies with images that seemed to jump off the screen. **Drive-in movies** attracted families and teenage couples; the cars they drove to get there were large and ornate with tail fins and chrome trim. The small screen moved into American homes as *I Love Lucy* became one of the most popular shows in television history. A new form of music, rock 'n' roll, captivated teenagers and upset their parents. Children were delighted by *The Cat in the Hat*, an imaginative masterpiece by Dr. Seuss (Theodor Seuss Geisel).

The **1950s** were commemorated by a pane of 15 stamps released in 1998 as a part of the **Celebrate The Century®** program. It featured illustrations by Dean Ellis, whose other projects for the U.S. Postal Service include Arkansas River Navigation (1968), Jefferson Memorial (1973), and Riverboats (1996).

1999

TECHNOLOGY • ENTERTAINMENT • SCIENCE

1950s
CELEBRATE THE CENTURY

Family Fun, Suburbia, and Nuclear Threats

The 1950s were, for the most part, years of peace and prosperity. Millions of families moved to the suburbs. Americans liked President Dwight D. Eisenhower, their kindly war-hero President.

Television became popular; *I Love Lucy* and *Gunsmoke* were hits. Teenagers chose their own fashions and music. Elvis Presley thrilled young people and shocked their elders.

The decade also had a serious side. The Korean War took more than 50,000 American lives. The first hydrogen bomb was detonated. In 1954 the U.S. Supreme Court declared racial segregation in public schools unconstitutional, and in 1955, in Montgomery, Alabama, Rosa Parks refused to give up her bus seat to a white man. But in 1957 President Eisenhower had to use the Arkansas National Guard and paratroopers to enforce integration at a Little Rock high school.

In January 1959 Alaska was admitted as the 49th state, and in August Hawaii became the 50th state.

New words: brainwashing, ballpoint, high-rise, centerfold

3187

a   b   c   d   e

f   g   h

3188

a   b   c   d   e

f   g   h   i   j

ssues of 1999			Un	U	FDC	Q(M)
Celebrate The Century®, Perf. 11.6						
3188	Pane of 15, 1960-1969	9/17/99	9.75			8
a.	33¢ "I have a dream"		.65	.30		
b.	33¢ Woodstock		.65	.30		
c.	33¢ Man walks on the moon		.65	.30		
d.	33¢ Green Bay Packers		.65	.30		
e.	33¢ Star Trek		.65	.30		
f.	33¢ The Peace Corps		.65	.30		
g.	33¢ The Vietnam War		.65	.30		
h.	33¢ Ford Mustang		.65	.30		
i.	33¢ Barbie Doll		.65	.30		
j.	33¢ The integrated circuit		.65	.30		
k.	33¢ Lasers		.65	.30		
l.	33¢ Super Bowl I		.65	.30		
m.	33¢ Peace Symbol		.65	.30		
n.	33¢ Roger Maris, 61 in '61		.65	.30		
o.	33¢ The Beatles		.65	.30		

The **1960s** were marked by poignant moments and national conflict. In 1965, U.S. ground troops were deployed to active combat in Vietnam, beginning the longest military conflict in U.S. history and sparking protests stateside. The hostilities in Vietnam, Cambodia, and Laos claimed more than 58,000 American lives, and another 304,000 were wounded. The decade also saw the assassination of great leaders: President John F. Kennedy in 1963 and civil rights leader Martin Luther King in 1968.

But the 1960s also saw triumphs for America. President Kennedy's commitment to put a man on the moon by the end of the decade was fulfilled. The Peace Corps was established in 1961 and the Civil Rights Act was passed in 1964.

In 1999 the U.S. Postal Service issued a pane of 15 stamps to commemorate the 1960s as a part of the **Celebrate The Century®** program. The stamp pane featured illustrations by Keith Birdsong.

1999

ssues of 1999		Un	U	FDC	Q(M)
Celebrate The Century®, Perf. 11.6					
3189 Pane of 15, 1970-1979	11/18/99	9.75			6
a.	33¢ Earth Day celebrated	.65	.30		
b.	33¢ TV series "All in the Family"	.65	.30		
c.	33¢ "Sesame Street"	.65	.30		
d.	33¢ Disco music	.65	.30		
e.	33¢ Steelers win four Super Bowls	.65	.30		
f.	33¢ U.S. celebrates 200th birthday	.65	.30		
g.	33¢ Secretariat wins the Triple Crown	.65	.30		
h.	33¢ VCRs transform entertainment	.65	.30		
i.	33¢ Pioneer 10	.65	.30		
j.	33¢ Women's Rights Movement	.65	.30		
k.	33¢ 1970s fashions	.65	.30		
l.	33¢ "Monday Night Football"	.65	.30		
m.	33¢ America smiles	.65	.30		
n.	33¢ Jumbo jet	.65	.30		
o.	33¢ Medical imaging	.65	.30		

In 1999 the U.S. Postal Service issued a pane of 15 stamps commemorating the **1970s** as a part of the **Celebrate The Century®** program. Illustrator Kazuhiko Sano captured the style and substance of the decade, from disco music and 1970s fashion to technological leaps such as jumbo jets and the Pioneer 10 space probe.

Some of the changes and developments of the 1970s included the 26th Amendment, which lowered the voting age for all elections to 18; a new commitment to protecting the environment, as exemplified by the first Earth Day; and the women's rights movement. The introduction of the jumbo jet allowed for more convenient travel, and the videocassette recorder allowed people to tape their favorite TV shows. *All in the Family* was an innovative look at controversial topics, and *Sesame Street* displayed a revolutionary combination of education and entertainment.

People were also watching accomplishments in sports during the 1970s. ABC's *Monday Night Football* made its television debut, and the Pittsburgh Steelers won four Super Bowls, dominating pro football in the second half of the decade. Secretariat was named Horse of the Year in 1972, and won the Triple Crown in 1973.

On July 4, 1976, the United States of America celebrated its 200th birthday. To remember the Bicentennial, people all over the country gathered to celebrate. In New York City, a magnificent procession of ships sailed into the harbor; Chicago held a naturalization ceremony; and fireworks lit up the skies from coast to coast.

Kazuhiko Sano has illustrated a wide range of media, including book covers, posters, and advertisements. He has received numerous awards and teaches illustration at the Academy of Art in San Francisco, California.

3192

3193   **3194**   **3195**   **3196**   **3197**   **3197a**

3198   **3199**   **3200**   **3201**   **3202**   **3202a**

3203

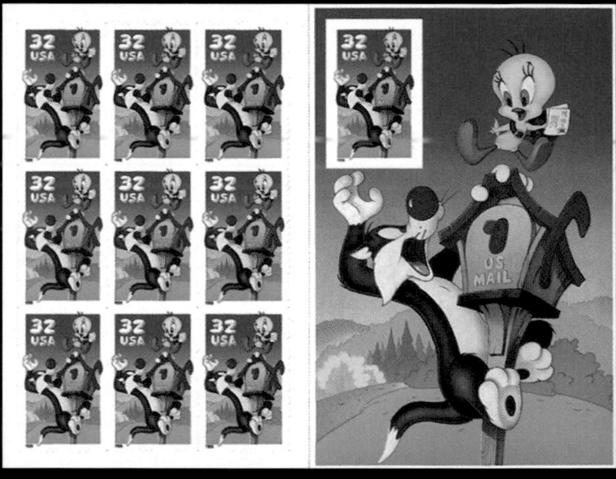

3204b

ssues of 1998		Un	U	PB		DC	Q(M)
Perf. 11.2 x 11							
3192 "Remember the Maine"							
Spanish-American War	2/15/98	.60	.15	2.40	(4)	1.25	30
Flowering Trees Issue, Die-Cut, Perf. 11.3							
3193 32¢ Southern Magnolia	3/19/98	.60	.15			1.25	
3194 32¢ Blue Paloverde	3/19/98	.60	.15			1.25	
3195 32¢ Yellow Poplar	3/19/98	.60	.15			1.25	
3196 32¢ Prairie Crab Apple	3/19/98	.60	.15			1.25	
3197 32¢ Pacific Dogwood	3/19/98	.60	.15			1.25	
a Strip of 5, #3193-3197	3/19/98	3.00		6.00	(10)	3.75	250
Alexander Calder Issue, Perf. 10.2							
3198 32¢ Black Cascade	3/25/98	.60	.15			1.25	
3199 32¢ Untitled	3/25/98	.60	.15			1.25	
3200 32¢ Rearing Stallion	3/25/98	.60	.15			1.25	
3201 32¢ Portrait of a Young Man	3/25/98	.60	.15			1.25	
3202 32¢ Un Effet du Japonais	3/25/98	.60	.15			1.25	
a Strip of 5, #3198-3202	3/25/98	3.00		6.00	(10)	3.75	80
Perf. 11.7 x 10.9							
3203 32¢ Cinco de Mayo	4/16/98	.60	.15	2.40	(4)	1.25	85
Looney Tunes Issue, Serpentine Die-Cut 11.1							
3204 Sylvester & Tweety Pane of 10	4/27/98	6.00					300
a 32¢ single		.60	.15			1.25	
b Booklet pane of 9, #3204a		5.40					
c Booklet pane of 1, #3204a		.60					

In 1979 the U.S. Postal Service issued four stamps commemorating **Endangered Flora**. The stamps depicted four flowering plants: **Persistent Trillium**, **Hawaiian Wild Broadbean**, **Contra Costa Wallflower**, and **Antioch Dunes Evening Primrose**. Two of these plants, the Contra Costa Wallflower and the Antioch Dunes Evening Primrose, are native to California and found only in that state. They are both perennial herbs that grow in dune habitats.

Since the passage of the Endangered Species Act in 1973, Americans have become increasingly aware of the importance of protecting fish, wildlife, and plants that are in danger of extinction. A critical element in this protection is conservation of the habitat on which endangered species depend; for example, the Antioch Dunes National Wildlife Refuge in Newark, California, provides an isolated dunes ecosystem that protects the Contra Costa Wallflower and the Antioch Dunes Evening Primrose.

Issues of 1998			Un	U	PB		FDC	Q(M)
	Serpentine Die-Cut 10.8 x 10.9							
3206	32¢ Wisconsin Statehood	5/29/98	.60	.30	2.40	(4)	1.25	16
	American Scenes Issue, Perf. 10 Vertically							
3207	5¢ Wetlands (Nonprofit)	6/5/98	.15	.15	1.65	(5)	1.25	
	American Scenes Issue, Perf. 9.7 Vertically							
3207A	5¢ Wetlands (Nonprofit)	12/4/98	.15	.15				650
	American Culture Issue, Perf. 10 Vertically							
3208	25¢ Diner	6/5/98	.50	.50	4.00	(5)	1.25	400
	American Culture Issue, Serpentine Die-Cut 9.7 Vertically							
3208A	25¢ Diner	9/30/98	.50	.50	4.00	(5)		
	1898 Trans-Mississippi Reissue, Perf. 12 x 12.4							
3209	Sheet of 9	6/18/98	7.75	5.00			6.50	19.8
a	1¢ Marquette on the Mississippi		.15	.15			1.25	
b	2¢ Mississippi River Bridge		.15	.15			1.25	
c	4¢ Indian Hunting Buffalo		.15	.15			1.25	
d	5¢ Fremont on the Rocky Mountains		.15	.15			1.25	
e	8¢ Troops Guarding Train		.15	.15			1.25	
f	10¢ Hardships of Emigration		.20	.15			1.25	
g	50¢ Western Mining Prospector		1.00	.60			1.50	
h	$1 Western Cattle in Storm		2.00	1.25			2.00	
i	$2 Farm in the West		4.00	2.50			4.00	
3210	Sheet of 9 #3209h	6/18/98	18.00	—			15.00	
	Perf. 11.2							
3211	32¢ Berlin Airlift	6/26/98	.60	.15	2.40	(4)	1.25	30

Merchant, fur trader, and settler, **Jean Baptiste Pointe Du Sable** fashioned a successful trading enterprise on the banks of the Chicago River. His vigor and vision created a community that grew to be the cornerstone of America's heartland—Chicago. This resourceful and enterprising individual was honored in the **Black Heritage** series with a stamp in 1997 illustrated by Thomas Blackshear.

Born around 1750 in what is now Haiti to an African-born slave mother and a French mariner father, he may have been educated in France. Sometime in the 1770s Du Sable made his way to the Great Lakes region and settled there. He married Catherine, a member of the Potawatomi tribe, and established a settlement and thriving business supplying Indians, traders, and trappers.

At the turn of the century, he sold his property and business and moved to Missouri, where he lived until his death in 1818.

3206

3207A

3208A

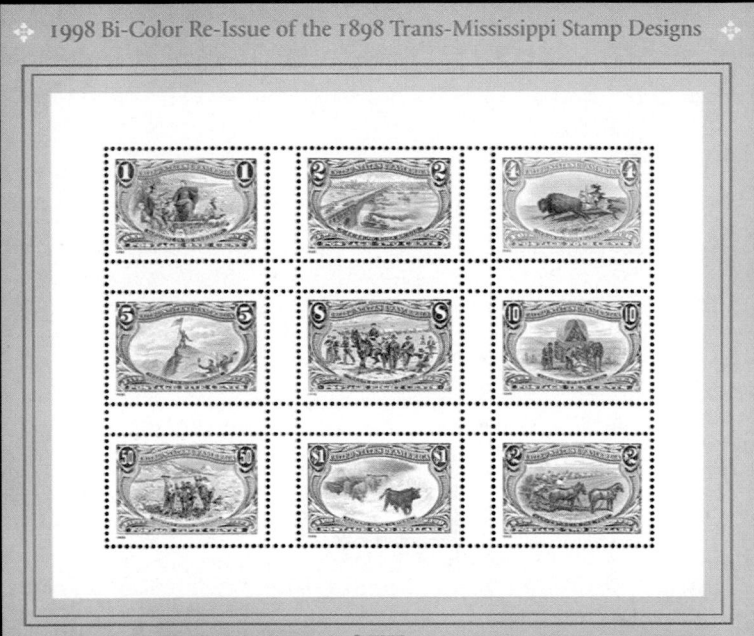

1998 Bi-Color Re-Issue of the 1898 Trans-Mississippi Stamp Designs

3209

a	b	c
d	e	f
g	h	i

3210

3211

3212   3213

3214   3215   3215a

3219   3218

3216   3217   3219a

3220   3221

3222   3223

3224   3225   3225a

Issues of 1998		Un	U	PB	#	FDC	Q(M)
American Music Series, Folk Musicians, Perf. 10.1 x 10.2							
3212	32¢ Huddie "Leadbelly"						
	Ledbetter	6/26/98	.60	.15			1.25	
3213	32¢ Woody Guthrie	6/26/98	.60	.15			1.25	
3214	32¢ Sonny Terry	6/26/98	.60	.15			1.25	
3215	32¢ Josh White	6/26/98	.60	.15			1.25	
a	Block or strip of 4, #3212-3215 6/26/98		2.40	—	2.40	(4)	3.25	45
American Music Series, Gospel Singers, Perf. 10.1 x 10.3							
3216	32¢ Mahalia Jackson	7/15/98	.60	.15			1.25	
3217	32¢ Roberta Martin	7/15/98	.60	.15			1.25	
3218	32¢ Clara Ward	7/15/98	.60	.15			1.25	
3219	32¢ Sister Rosetta Tharpe	7/15/98	.60	.15			1.25	
a	Block or strip of 4, #3216-3219 7/15/98		2.40	—	2.40	(4)	3.25	45
	Perf. 11.2							
3220	32¢ Spanish Settlement of						
	the Southwest	7/11/98	.60	.15	2.40	(4)	1.25	46
	Literary Arts Series, Perf. 11.2							
3221	32¢ Stephen Vincent Benét	7/22/98	.60	.15	2.40	(4)	1.25	
	Tropical Birds Issue, Perf. 11.2							
3222	32¢ Antillean Euphonia	7/29/98	.60	.15			1.25	
3223	32¢ Green-throated Carib	7/29/98	.60	.15			1.25	
3224	32¢ Crested Honeycreeper	7/29/98	.60	.15			1.25	
3225	32¢ Cardinal Honeyeater	7/29/98	.60	.15			1.25	
a	Block of 4, #3222-3225		2.40	—	2.40	(4)	3.25	70

Born in Okemah, Oklahoma, in 1912, **Woody Guthrie** was the consummate folk singer, voicing the sentiments of the dispossessed and telling the stories and struggles of the common people. Many of his songs, including "Tom Joad" and "So Long (It's Been Good To Know Yuh)," have become folk classics.

Although its hopeful, unifying message is atypical of its author, Guthrie's song "This Land Is Your Land" has become an unofficial national anthem. Of the roughly 1,000 songs written by Guthrie, this one surfaced as a beacon of promise during the lean years of the Great Depression. In the song's lyrics, Guthrie invoked his travels across the United States, particularly through the far West. The song has taken on a life of its own, transcending political and social divisions and becoming emblematic of the ideal America.

Guthrie died in Queens, New York, in 1967. His son Arlo Guthrie continued his father's musical legacy and was himself considerably successful as a folk musician.

In 1998, the U.S. Postal Service honored Woody Guthrie alongside Sonny Terry, Josh White, and Huddie Ledbetter (more commonly known as "Leadbelly") on the Folk Musicians stamps in the **Legends of American Music** series. The stamps were illustrated by Bernie Fuchs.

Issues of 1998		Un	U	FDC	Q(M)
Legends of Hollywood Issue, Perf. 11.1					
3226	32¢ Alfred Hitchcock	8/3/98	.60	.15	1.25	65
Self-Adhesive, Serpentine Die-Cut 11.7					
3227	32¢ Organ & Tissue Donation	8/5/98	.60	.15	1.25	25
Self-Adhesive, Serpentine Die-Cut 9.8 Vertically					
3228	(10¢) Green Bicycle	8/14/98	.20	.15	1.25	
Perf. 9.9 vert.					
3229	(10¢) Green Bicycle	8/14/98	.20	.15	1.25	
Bright Eyes Issue, Self-Adhesive, Serpentine Die-Cut 9.9					
3230	32¢ Dog	8/20/98	.60	.15	1.25	
3231	32¢ Goldfish	8/20/98	.60	.15	1.25	
3232	32¢ Cat	8/20/98	.60	.15	1.25	
3233	32¢ Parakeet	8/20/98	.60	.15	1.25	
3234	32¢ Hamster	8/20/98	.60	.15	1.25	
a	Strip of 5, #3230-3234	8/20/98	3.00		3.25	180
Perf. 11.1					
3235	32¢ Klondike Gold Rush	8/21/98	.60	.15	1.25	28

The final decade of the 20th century saw surprising developments in America and around the world. The Soviet Union collapsed, effectively ending the Cold War, and American astronauts joined Russian cosmonauts on the Mir space station. The United States deployed troops in the **Persian Gulf**, Somalia, and the Balkans.

American culture underwent significant changes. The World Wide Web and e-mail revolutionized communications. Moviegoers flocked to see films such as *Titanic* and *Jurassic Park* and enjoyed *Seinfeld* on television. The decade ended amid an economic boom, and fears of possible Y2K computer glitches faded as the year 2000 began with no major technical problems.

In 2000 the U.S. Postal Service issued a pane of 15 stamps to commemorate the **1990s** as a part of the **Celebrate The Century®** program. The stamp pane featured illustrations by Drew Struzan, who is best known for his popular movie posters.

3226

3227

3228

3234a

3230

3231

3232

3233

3234

3235

FOUR CENTURIES OF
American Art

(Sheet of 20 stamps, 32¢ each, depicting American artworks with artist names and dates)

3236

a	b	c	d	e
f	g	h	i	j
k	l	m	n	o
p	q	r	s	t

3237

Issues of 1998		Un	U	FDC	Q(M)
Four Centuries of American Art Issue, Perf. 10.2					
3236 Pane of 20	8/27/98	12.00	—	9.50	80
a 32¢ "Portrait of Richard Mather," by John Foster		.60	.15	1.25	
b 32¢ "Mrs. Elizabeth Freake and Baby Mary," by The Freake Limner		.60	.15	1.25	
c 32¢ "Girl in Red Dress with Cat and Dog," by Ammi Phillips		.60	.15	1.25	
d 32¢ "Rubens Peale with a Geranium," by Rembrandt Peale		.60	.15	1.25	
e 32¢ "Long-billed Curlew, Numenius Longrostris," by John James Audubon		.60	.15	1.25	
f 32¢ "Boatmen on the Missouri," by George Caleb Bingham		.60	.15	1.25	
g 32¢ "Kindred Spirits," by Asher B. Durand		.60	.15	1.25	
h 32¢ "The Westwood Children," by Joshua Johnson		.60	.15	1.25	
i 32¢ "Music and Literature," by William Harnett		.60	.15	1.25	
j 32¢ "The Fog Warning," by Winslow Homer		.60	.15	1.25	
k 32¢ "The White Cloud, Head Chief of the Iowas," by George Catlin		.60	.15	1.25	
l 32¢ "Cliffs of Green River," by Thomas Moran		.60	.15	1.25	
m 32¢ "The Last of the Buffalo," by Alfred Bierstadt		.60	.15	1.25	
n 32¢ "Niagara," by Frederic Edwin Church		.60	.15	1.25	
o 32¢ "Breakfast in Bed," by Mary Cassatt		.60	.15	1.25	
p 32¢ "Nighthawks," by Edward Hopper		.60	.15	1.25	
q 32¢ "American Gothic," by Grant Wood		.60	.15	1.25	
r 32¢ "Two Against the White," by Charles Sheeler		.60	.15	1.25	
s 32¢ "Mahoning," by Franz Kline		.60	.15	1.25	
t 32¢ "No. 12" by Mark Rothko		.60	.15	1.25	
Perf. 10.9 x 11.1					
3237 32¢ Ballet	9/16/98	.60	.15	1.25	130

	ssues of 1998		Un	U	PE		FDC	Q(M)
	Space Discovery Issue, Perf. 11.1							
3238	32¢ Multicolored	10/1/98	.60	.15			1.25	
3239	32¢ Multicolored	10/1/98	.60	.15			1.25	
3240	32¢ Multicolored	10/1/98	.60	.15			1.25	
3241	32¢ Multicolored	10/1/98	.60	.15			1.25	
3242	32¢ Multicolored	10/1/98	.60	.15			1.25	
a	Strip of 5, #3238-3242		3.00				3.75	
	Self-adhesive, Serpentine Die-Cut 11.1							
3243	32¢ Philanthropy,							
	Giving and Sharing	10/7/98	.60	.15			1.25	50
	Holiday Traditional, Serpentine Die-Cut 10.1 x 9.9 on 2, 3 or 4 sides							
3244	32¢ The Madonna and Child							
	by Hans Memling	10/15/98	.60	.15			1.25	925.2
a	Booklet pane of 20 + label		12.00					
	Holiday Contemporary, Serpentine Die-Cut 11.3 x 11.6 on 2 or 3 sides							
3245	32¢ Evergreen Wreath	10/15/98	.60	.15			1.25	
3246	32¢ Victorian Wreath	10/15/98	.60	.15			1.25	
3247	32¢ Chili Pepper Wreath	10/15/98	.60	.15			1.25	
3248	32¢ Tropical Wreath	10/15/98	.60	.15			1.25	
a	Booklet pane of 4, #3245-3248		2.50				3.25	
b	Booklet pane of 5, #3245, #3246,							
	3248, 2 #3247 and label		3.00					
c	Booklet pane of 6, #3247-3248,							
	2 each #3245-3246		3.60					
	Serpentine Die-Cut 11.4 x 11.6 on 2, 3 or 4 sides							
3249	32¢ Evergreen Wreath	10/15/98	.60	.15			1.25	
3250	32¢ Victorian Wreath	10/15/98	.60	.15			1.25	
3251	32¢ Chili Pepper Wreath	10/15/98	.60	.15			1.25	
3252	32¢ Tropical Wreath	10/15/98	.60	.15			1.25	
a	Block of 4, #3249-3252		2.40				3.25	
b	Booklet pane, 5 each #3249-3252		12.00					
	Perf. 11.2							
3257	(1¢) Make-Up Rate Weathervane	11/9/98	.15	.15			1.25	
3258	(1¢) Make-Up Rate Weathervane	11/9/98	.15	.15			1.25	
	#3257 is 18mm high, has thin letters, white USA, and black 1998.							
	#3258 is 17mm high, has thick letters, pale blue USA, and blue 1998.							
	Coil Stamps, Self-Adhesive Serpentine Die-Cut 10.8							
3259	22¢ Uncle Sam	11/9/98	.45	.15			1.25	
	Perf. 11.2							
3260	(33¢) H-Series		.65	.15			1.25	

3242a

3238 3239 3240 3241 3242

3243

3245 3246

3244

3248a

3247 3248

3258

3259

3260

3261

3262

B1

ssues of 1998		Un	U	PB	#	FDC	Q(M)
Priority Mail, Self-Adhesive Serpentine Die-Cut 11.5							
3261 ($3.20) Space Shuttle Landing	11/9/98	6.00	3.00			6.00	245
Self-Adhesive Serpentine Die-Cut 11.5							
3262 ($11.75) Express Mail	11/19/98	22.50	11.50			12.00	21
Self-Adhesive Serpentine Die-Cut 9.9 Vertically							
3263 22¢ Uncle Sam	11/9/98	.45	.15			1.25	
Perf. 9.8 Vertically							
3264 33¢ Unce Sam's Hat	11/9/98	.65	.15			1.25	
Self-Adhesive Serpentine Die-Cut 9.9 Vertically							
3265 (33¢) H-Series	11/9/98	.65	.15			1.25	
Serpentine Die Cut 9.9 Vertically							
3266 33¢ Uncle Sam's Hat	11/9/98	.65	.15			1.25	
Booklet Stamps, Self-Adhesive Serpentine Die-Cut 9.9 on 2 or 3 Sides							
3267 (33¢) H-Series	11/9/98	.65	.15			1.25	
a Booklet pane of 10		6.50					
Serpentine Die Cut 11.2 on 2, 3 or 4 Sides							
3268 33¢ Uncle Sam's Hat	11/9/98	.65	.15			1.25	
Die Cut 8 on 2, 3 or 4 Sides							
3269 33¢ Uncle Sam's Hat	11/9/98	.65	.15			1.25	
Coil Stamps, Perf. 9.9 Vertically							
3270 (10¢) Eagle with Shield	12/14/98	.20	.20			1.25	
Self-Adhesive Serpentine Die-Cut 9.9 Vertically							
3271 (10¢) Eagle with Shield	12/14/98	.20	.20			1.25	
Self-Adhesive Serpentine Die-Cut 11							
B1 (32¢ + 8¢) Breast Cancer							
Awareness	7/29/98	.80	.60	3.25	(4)		200

Submarines played a crucial role in establishing American naval superiority in the Pacific during World War II. The massive damage inflicted on American surface ships during the Japanese attack on Pearl Harbor pushed the Submarine Force into prominence. Despite representing only 1.6 percent of our Navy, American

subs sank a third of Japan's Navy and nearly two-thirds of her merchant marine. By the end of the war, seven American submariners had earned the Medal of Honor, the United States' highest award for bravery.

The Submarine Force had many wartime responsibilities besides hunting enemy ships. By ferrying raiders and commandos into hostile territory and rescuing downed pilots (one of whom was future President George Bush), submarines expanded their role in the eventual Allied victory.

Armed with deck guns and ten torpedo tubes, the 307-foot long *Gato* class subs played a pivotal role in American naval superiority. One of five different stamps included in the U.S. Postal Service's first-ever prestige booklet, the *Gato* class stamp honors the contributions of America's World War II submariners. Other stamps in the booklet include the USS *Holland*, an S class sub, and modern **Los Angeles** and *Ohio* class boats.

Issues of 1999		Un	U	PB		FDC	Q(M)
Lunar New Year Issue, Perf. 11.2							
3272	33¢ Year of the Rabbit	1/5/99	.65	.20	2.60	(4)	1.25	51
Black Heritage Issue, Serpentine Die Cut 11.4							
3273	33¢ Malcolm X	1/20/99	.65	.20	2.60	(4)	1.25	100
Self-Adhesive Die Cut							
3274	33¢ Love	1/28/99	.65	.20			1.25	1,500
3275	55¢ Love	1/20/99	1.10	.20	4.40	(4)	2.00	300
Serpentine Die Cut 11.4							
3276	33¢ Hospice Care	2/9/99	.65	.20	2.60	(4)	1.25	100
Perf. 11.2							
3277	33¢ City Flag	2/25/99	.65	.20	2.60	(4)	1.25	200
Self-Adhesive Serpentine Die Cut 11.1 on 2, 3 or 4 Sides							
3278	33¢ City Flag	2/25/99	.65	.20	2.60	(4)	1.25	
Booklet Stamps, Self-Adhesive Serpentine Die Cut 9.8 on 2 or 3 Sides							
3279	33¢ City Flag	2/25/99	.65	.20			1.25	
a.	Booklet pane of 10		6.50					
Coil Stamps, Perf. 9.9 Vert.							
3280	33¢ City Flag	2/25/99	.65	.20	4.75	(5)	1.25	
Serpentine Die Cut 9.8 Vert.							
3281	33¢ City Flag	2/25/99	.65	.20	4.75	(5)	1.25	
3282	33¢ City Flag	2/25/99	.65	.20	4.75	(5)	1.25	
	Rounded corners.							
Booklet Stamp, Serpentine Die Cut 7.9 on 2, 3 or 4 Sides							
3283	33¢ Flag and Chalkboard	3/13/99	.65	.20			1.25	306
Perf. 11.2							
3286	33¢ Irish Immigration	2/26/99	.65	.20	2.60	(4)	1.25	40.4
3287	33¢ Lunt & Fontanne	3/2/99	.65	.20	2.60	(4)	1.25	42.5

The eighth in a twelve-stamp series commemorating the Lunar New Year, the **Year of the Dragon** stamp was issued in 2000. Clarence Lee created the stamp art by combining grass-style calligraphy with an intricate paper-cut design of a dragon. One of the twelve animals associated with the Chinese calendar, the dragon is an auspicious symbol of power and nobility. According to tradition, those born in the Year of the Dragon (for example, 1940, 1952, 1964, 1976, or 1988) are expected to be natural leaders with strong wills, self-confidence, and good fortune. February 5, 2000, was the first day in the Year of the Dragon.

The **Lunar New Year** is celebrated not just by those of Chinese descent, but also by Koreans, Vietnamese, Tibetans, and Mongolians. New Year's festivities are complex celebrations with many traditions. On New Year's Eve, families gather together to enjoy specially prepared foods and venerate their forebears. The next day, public celebrations often include the performance of the traditional dragon dance. Accompanied by choruses of firecrackers, pounding drums, and crashing cymbals, the dragons are sometimes more than 100 feet long and are cast in many colors.

3272

3273

3274

3275

3276

3277

3278

3279

3280

3286

3287

| 3288 | 3289 | 3290 | 3291 | 3292 |

ssues of 1999		Un	U	PB	#	FDC	Q(M)
Arctic Animals Issue, Perf. 11							
3288 33¢ Arctic Hare	3/12/99	.65	.20			1.25	15.3
3289 33¢ Arctic Fox	3/12/99	.65	.20			1.25	15.3
3290 33¢ Snowy Owl	3/12/99	.65	.20			1.25	15.3
3291 33¢ Polar Bear	3/12/99	.65	.20			1.25	15.3
3292 33¢ Gray Wolf	3/12/99	.65	.20			1.25	15.3
a. Strip of 5, #3288-3292		3.25				3.75	

The Arctic consists of treeless tundra regions and is,in general, located north of the Arctic Circle in Alaska, Canada, Greenland, and Eurasia. This area includes the high arctic islands, the ice-covered Arctic Ocean, and adjacent land areas and bodies of water. Here, in one of nature's most forbidding climates, live some of the most unique animals on Earth the arctic hare, arctic fox, snowy owl, polar bear, and gray wolf. These **arctic animals** have adapted to survive the region's brutal winters, with strong winds and temperatures that plunge to below -50 degrees Fahrenheit. Their thick fur or feathers and short appendages help reduce heat loss. Many arctic animals turn white during the winter and blend with the snowy landscapes. They must breed and grow during the short summer season.

The arctic hare is the largest hare in North America. It has strong claws that allow it to dig through snow for food, primarily willow twigs, grasses, sedges, and other plants. The arctic fox is a solitary animal that lives in burrows in summer. It often ventures onto the sea ice in winter to eat the remains of seals killed by polar bears. One of the largest owls, the snowy owl nests on the open ground during the summer. It attacks from the air, killing prey with its sharp talons and beak. The polar bear weighs up to 1,400 pounds and stands about four feet at the shoulder. It is considered a marine mammal, because it lives most of the time on sea ice and depends on the sea for its food, feasting primarily on seals. The gray wolf is an intelligent and social animal. It travels in packs of a few to ten or more animals that cover territories of 100 to 1,000 square miles.

The stamp sheet was designed by Derry Noyes of Washington, DC.

	ssues of 1999		Un	U	PB		FDC	Q(M
	Sonoran Desert Issue, Self-Adhesive Serpentine Die Cut Perf. 11.2							
3293	Pane of 10	4/6/99	6.50				6.75	10.3
a.	33¢ Cactus Wren, brittlebush,							
	teddy bear cholla		.65	.20			1.25	
b.	33¢ Desert tortoise		.65	.20			1.25	
c.	33¢ White-winged dove		.65	.20			1.25	
d.	33¢ Gambel quail		.65	.20			1.25	
e.	33¢ Saguaro cactus		.65	.20			1.25	
f.	33¢ Desert mule deer		.65	.20			1.25	
g.	33¢ Desert cottontail, hedgehog cactus		.65	.20			1.25	
h.	33¢ Gila monster		.65	.20			1.25	
i.	33¢ Western diamondback rattlesnake,							
	cactus mouse		.65	.20			1.25	
j.	33¢ Gila woodpecker		.65	.20			1.25	
	Fruit Berries Issue, Self-Adhesive Serpentine Die Cut 11.2 x 11.7 on 2, 3 or 4 Sides							
3294	33¢ Blueberries	4/10/99	.65	.20			1.25	
3295	33¢ Raspberries	4/10/99	.65	.20			1.25	
3296	33¢ Strawberries	4/10/99	.65	.20			1.25	
3297	33¢ Blackberries	4/10/99	.65	.20			1.25	
a.	Booklet pane, 5 each #3294-3297 + label		13.00	—			3.25	
	Serpentine Die Cut 9/5 on 2 or 3 Sides							
3298	33¢ Blueberries	4/10/99	.65	.20			1.25	
3299	33¢ Raspberries	4/10/99	.65	.20			1.25	
3300	33¢ Strawberries	4/10/99	.65	.20			1.25	
3301	33¢ Blackberries	4/10/99	.65	.20			1.25	
a.	Booklet pane of 15, 4 each							
	#3298-3300, 3 #3301		10.00	—			3.25	
	Coil Stamps, Serpentine Die Cut 8.5 Vert.							
3302	33¢ Blueberries	4/10/99	.65	.20			1.25	
3303	33¢ Raspberries	4/10/99	.65	.20			1.25	
3304	33¢ Strawberries	4/10/99	.65	.20			1.25	
3305	33¢ Blackberries	4/10/99	.65	.20			1.25	
a.	Strip of 4		2.60				3.25	

SONORAN DESERT

FIRST IN A SERIES

N A T U R E   O F   A M E R I C A

```
              e
        c           f                    j
   a        b       d       g        h
                                i
```

3294   **3296**

3297a

3295   **3297**

3305a

3306a

3308

3309

3310   **3311**

3314

3312   **3313**   **3313a**

3315

3316

3320a

ssues of 1999		Un	U	PB	#	FDC	Q(M)
	Self-Adhesive Serpentine Die Cut 11.1						
3306	Pane of 10	4/16/99	6.50				
a.	33¢ Daffy Duck		.65	.20		1.25	427
	Perf. 11.2						
3308	33¢ Ayn Rand	4/22/99	.65	.20	2.60	(4)	1.25	42.5
	Serpentine Die Cut 11.6 x 11.3						
3309	33¢ Cinco De Mayo	4/27/99	.65	.20	2.60	(4)	1.25	113
	Tropical Flowers Issue, Self-Adhesive Serpentine Die Cut 10.9 on 2 or 3 Sides						
3310	33¢ Bird of Paradise	5/1/99	.65	.20		1.25	
3311	33¢ Royal Poinciana	5/1/99	.65	.20		1.25	
3312	33¢ Gloriosa Lily	5/1/99	.65	.20		1.25	
3313	33¢ Chinese Hibiscus	5/1/99	.65	.20		1.25	
a.	Block of 4 #3310-3313		2.60			3.25	
b.	Booklet pane of 5 #3313a		13.00				
	Self-Adhesive, Perf. 11.5						
3314	33¢ John & William Bartram	5/18/99	.65	.20	2.60	(4)	1.25	145
	Self-Adhesive, Perf. 11						
3315	33¢ Prostate Cancer Awareness	5/28/99	.65	.20	2.60	(4)	1.25	78
	Perf. 11.25						
3316	33¢ California Gold Rush 1849	6/18/99	.65	.20	2.60	(4)	1.25	89
	Aquarium Fish Issue, Self-Adhesive Serpentine Die Cut 11.5						
3317	33¢ Yellow fish, red fish, cleaner shrimp	6/24/99	.65	.20		1.25	39
3318	33¢ Fish, thermometer	6/24/99	.65	.20		1.25	39
3319	33¢ Red fish, blue & yellow fish	6/24/99	.65	.20		1.25	39
3320	33¢ Fish, heater/aerator	6/24/99	.65	.20		1.25	39
a.	Strip of 4, #3317-3320		2.60		5.20	(8)	3.50	

"My philosophy, in essence," wrote Ayn Rand, "is the concept of man as a heroic being, with his own happiness as the moral purpose of his life, with productive achievement as his noblest activity, and reason as his only absolute."

Born in Russia in 1905, **Ayn Rand** graduated from St. Petersburg University. After attending a cinema academy for a year, she received permission in 1925 to visit America.

After struggling at various jobs, Rand sold her first screenplay in 1932, and her first play was produced on Broadway in 1935. She began to publish novels in 1936, but it was *The Fountainhead* (1943) that brought her lasting recognition as a champion of individualism.

Although she considered herself primarily a fiction writer, Rand realized that in order to create heroic characters, she had to identify the philosophic principles that make such people possible. Thus she developed "Objectivism," a philosophy advocating reason, individualism, self-interest, and capitalism. *Atlas Shrugged* (1957), considered her greatest literary achievement, dramatized her unique philosophy in an intellectual mystery story in which Rand attempted to integrate ethics, metaphysics, epistemology, politics, economics, and sex.

In 1999, the U.S. Postal Service honored Ayn Rand with a stamp in the Literary Arts series, illustrated by Nicholas Gaetano.

1999

	Issues of 1999		Un	U	PE		FDC	Q(M)
	Extreme Sports Issue, Self-Adhesive Serpentine Die Cut 11							
3321	33¢ Skateboarding	6/25/99	.65	.20			1.25	38
3322	33¢ BMX Biking	6/25/99	.65	.20			1.25	38
3323	33¢ Snowboarding	6/25/99	.65	.20			1.25	38
3324	33¢ Inline Skating	6/15/99	.65	.20			1.25	38
a.	Block of 4, #3321-3324		2.60		2.60	(4)	3.50	
	American Glass Issue, Perf. 11							
3325	33¢ Free-Blown Glass	6/29/99	.65	.20			1.25	29
3326	33¢ Mold-Blown Glass	6/29/99	.65	.20			1.25	29
3327	33¢ Pressed Glass	6/29/99	.65	.20			1.25	29
3328	33¢ Art Glass	6/29/99	.65	.20			1.25	29
a.	Strip or block of 4, #3325-3328		2.60				3.50	
	Legends of Hollywood Issue, Perf. 11							
3329	33¢ James Cagney	7/22/99	.65	.20	2.60	(4)	1.25	75.5
	Pioneers of Aviation Issue, Serpentine Die Cut 9.75 x 10							
3330	55¢ Gen. William "Billy" L. Mitchell	7/30/99	1.10	.20	4.40	(4)	1.25	101
	Self-Adhesive Serpentine Die Cut 11							
3331	33¢ Honoring Those Who Served	8/16/99	.65	.20	2.60	(4)	1.25	102
	Perf. 11							
3332	45¢ Universal Postal Union	8/25/99	.90	.20				43
	All Aboard!: Twentieth Century Trains Issue, Perf. 11							
3333	33¢ Daylight	8/26/99	.65	.20				24
3334	33¢ Congressional	8/26/99	.65	.20				24
3335	33¢ 20th Century Limited	8/26/99	.65	.20				24
3336	33¢ Hiawatha	8/26/99	.65	.20				24
3337	33¢ Super Chief	8/26/99	.65	.20				24
a.	Strip of 5, #3333-3337		3.25					

Designed to compete with automobiles and airplanes, the Art Deco-inspired passenger trains of the 1930s and ´40s were notable for both their speed and beauty. Railroads spared almost no expense in outfitting these supertrains with the most luxurious appointments. Streamliners, as they were known, looked sleek enough to fly. The Postal Service celebrated the **Twentieth Century Limited** and **Super Chief** in two of the five **All Aboard!** stamps illustrated by Ted Rose and issued in 1999.

Known as a "National Institution" and the "Most Famous Train in the World," the Twentieth Century Limited was renowned for its speed, luxury, and dependability. Serving the New York-Chicago route, it was the New York Central's crown jewel.

Running between Chicago and Los Angeles, the Super Chief's glamorous clientele earned it the nickname "Train of the Stars." Reliable diesel engines and famously comfortable accommodations made the Super Chief one of the most appealing trains of its time.

3321 3322

3325 3326

3323 3324 3324a

3327 3328 3328a

3329  3330

3331

3332

3333

3334

3335

3336

3337

3337a

3338

3344a

3339

3340

3341

3342

3343

3344

3350a

3345

3346

3347

3348

3349

3350

ssues of 1999			Un	U	PB	#	FDC	Q(M)
Perf. 11								
3338	33¢ Frederck Law Olmstead	9/13/99	.65	.20				42.5
Hollywood Composers Issue, Perf. 11								
3339	33¢ Max Steiner	9/16/99	.65	.20				
3340	33¢ Dimitri Tiomkin	9/16/99	.65	.20				
3341	33¢ Bernard Herrmann	9/16/99	.65	.20				
3342	33¢ Franz Waxman	9/16/99	.65	.20				
3343	33¢ Alfred Newman	9/16/99	.65	.20				
3344	33¢ Erich Wolfgang Korngold	9/16/99	.65	.20				
a.	Block of 6, #3339-3344		3.90					
Broadway Songwriters Issue, Perf. 11								
3345	33¢ Ira & George Gershwin	9/21/99	.65	.65				
3346	33¢ Lerner & Lowe	9/21/99	.65	.65				
3347	33¢ Lorenz Hart	9/21/99	.65	.65				
3348	33¢ Rodgers & Hammerstein	9/21/99	.65	.65				
3349	33¢ Meredith Willson	9/21/99	.65	.65				
3350	33¢ Frank Loesser	9/21/99	.65	.65				
a.	Block of 6, #3345-3350		3.90					

A challenging and rewarding hobby, aquariums require close attention in order to achieve the delicate balance in which fish, coral, live rock, and plants can survive. In 1999, the Postal Service issued four stamps commemorating this popular American pastime.

These four stamps depict a reef tank holding delicate corals, life-encrusted live rock, fish, and other specimens that populate reefs in different parts of the world. This type of marine tank has become popular among casual hobbyists because of recent improvements in filtration systems, lighting, and nutrition. The featherduster worm, flame angelfish, longhorn cowfish, and red hermit crab are just a few of the species depicted in these stamps.

Illustrated by Teresa Fasolino, these **Aquarium fish** stamps form one continuous scene from a well-stocked reef tank. To guarantee the accuracy of the stamps, Fasolino worked with experts from the National Aquarium in Baltimore, Maryland.

ssues of 1999		Un	L	PE		FDC	Q(M
Insects & Spiders Issue, Perf. 11							
3351 Pane of 20	10/1/99	13.00					4.23
a.	Black widow	.65	.20				
b.	Elderberry longhorn	.65	.20				
c.	Lady beetle	.65	.20				
d.	Yellow garden spider	.65	.20				
e.	Dogbane beetle	.65	.20				
f.	Flower Fly	.65	.20				
g.	Assassin bug	.65	.20				
h.	Ebony jewelwing	.65	.20				
i.	Velvet ant	.65	.20				
j.	Monarch caterpillar	.65	.20				
k.	Monarch butterfly	.65	.20				
l.	Eastern Hercules beetle	.65	.20				
m.	Bombardier beetle	.65	.20				
n.	Dung beetle	.65	.20				
o.	Spotted water beetle	.65	.20				
p.	True katydid	.65	.20				
q.	Spinybacked spider	.65	.20				
r.	Periodical cicada	.65	.20				
s.	Scorpionfly	.65	.20				
t.	Jumping spider	.65	.20				

Second in the **Nature of America** series, the **Pacific Coast Rain Forest** stamp pane issued in 2000 depicts one of the largest remaining temperate rain forests in the world. The rain forest occupies a narrow strip between the ocean and the mountains and stretches from northern California to the Gulf of Alaska. One of the characteristic features of this ecosystem is the Sitka spruce, a conifer that is among North America's largest trees.

The rain forest's climate is mild and wet—the temperature rarely goes above 80° or below freezing and the average annual precipitation ranges from 80 to 160 inches. Summer fogs are common, and intense winter storms bring large amounts of rain and strong winds. Immense old-growth conifers form a dense canopy over a luxuriant understory of ferns, mosses, herbs, and shrubs. This ecosystem supports the greatest accumulation of organic material per square mile in the world. Numerous streams and rivers abound with fish and amphibians, including such notable species as cutthroat trout and chinook salmon.

Artist John D. Dawson worked with thousands of reference photographs, lists of species prepared by scientists, and his own imagination to create this temperate rain forest scene.

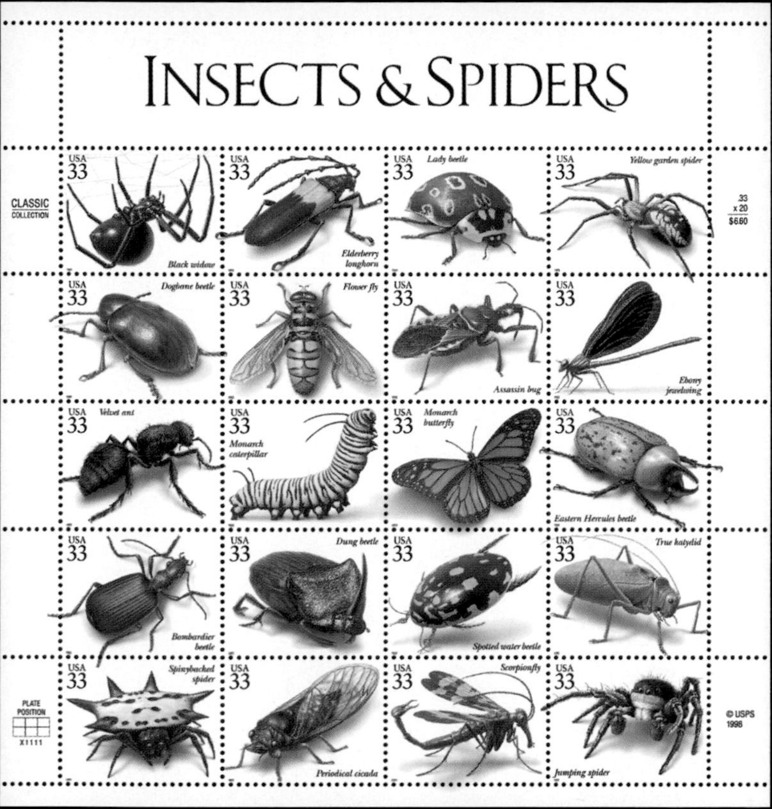

INSECTS & SPIDERS

CLASSIC
COLLECTION

.33
x 20
$6.60

USA 33 — Black widow
USA 33 — Elderberry longhorn
USA 33 — Lady beetle
USA 33 — Yellow garden spider

USA 33 — Dogbane beetle
USA 33 — Flower fly
USA 33 — Assassin bug
USA 33 — Ebony jewelwing

USA 33 — Velvet ant
USA 33 — Monarch caterpillar
USA 33 — Monarch butterfly
USA 33 — Eastern Hercules beetle

USA 33 — Bombardier beetle
USA 33 — Dung beetle
USA 33 — Spotted water beetle
USA 33 — True katydid

USA 33 — Spinybacked spider
USA 33 — Periodical cicada
USA 33 — Scorpionfly
USA 33 — Jumping spider

PLATE POSITION X1111

© USPS 1998

3351a

a   b   c   d

e   f   g   h

i   j   k   l

3352

3353

3354

3355

3359a

3368

ssues of 1999		Un	U	PB		DC	Q(M)
Self-Adhesive Serpentine Die Cut 11							
3352 33¢ Hanukkah	10/8/99	.65	.20				65
Coil Stamp, Perf. 9.75							
3353 22¢ Uncle Sam	10/8/99	.45	.20				150
Perf. 11.25							
3354 33¢ NATO 50th Anniversary	10/13/99	.65	.20				44.6
Holiday Traditional, Self-Adhesive Serpentine Die Cut 11.25 on 2 or 3 sides							
3355 33¢ Madonna and child by							
Bartolomeo Vivarini	10/20/99	.65	.20				1,556
a. Booklet pane of 20		13.00					
Holiday Contemporary, Self-Adhesive Serpentine Die Cut 11.25							
3356 33¢ Red Deer	10/20/99	.65	.20				
3357 33¢ Blue Deer	10/20/99	.65	.20				
3358 33¢ Purple Deer	10/20/99	.65	.20				
3359 33¢ Green Deer	10/20/99	.65	.20				
a. Block or strip, #3356-3359		2.60					
Booklet Stamps, Serpentine Die Cut 11.25 on 2, 3 or 4 sides							
3360 33¢ Red Deer	10/20/99	.65	.20				
3361 33¢ Blue Deer	10/20/99	.65	.20				
3362 33¢ Purple Deer	10/20/99	.65	.20				
3363 33¢ Green Deer	10/20/99	.65	.20				
a. Booklet pane of 20		13.00					
Serpentine Die Cut 11.5 x 11.25 on 2 or 3 sides							
3364 33¢ Red Deer	10/20/99	.65	.20				
3365 33¢ Blue Deer	10/20/99	.65	.20				
3366 33¢ Purple Deer	10/20/99	.65	.20				
3367 33¢ Green Deer	10/20/99	.65	.20				
a. Booklet pane of 15		9.75					
Serpentine Die Cut 11							
3368 33¢Kwaanza	10/29/99	.65	.20				95

Lou Gehrig was one of the greatest first basemen of all time. Known as the "Iron Horse," he played in an astounding 2,130 consecutive games for the New York Yankees. The record would stand for over 50 years until it was broken in 1996 by Cal Ripken, Jr. of the Baltimore Orioles.

Gehrig was born in New York City in 1903. After an outstanding college career he signed with the Yankees. He began his famous streak on May 31, 1925. Gehrig and teammate Babe Ruth formed one of the most powerful offensive duos in Major League Baseball history. Gehrig drove in at least 100 runs for 13 seasons in a row, and set an American League record with 184 RBI in 1931. He hit 493 career home runs, including a Major League record 23 grand slams. He once hit four home runs in one game.

On May 2, 1939, Gehrig took himself out of the lineup. He was suffering from a terminal disease that would later be named for him. He died in 1941. In 1989 the U.S. Postal Service honored Lou Gehrig with a stamp illustrated by Bart Forbes.

Celebrate
The Century®

Celebrate 1900-1999 with the Celebrate The Century® stamps.

The American public voted for many of the 150 subjects featured on ten panes of fifteen stamps— the most memorable people, places, things, and events of the last century!

Airmail and Special Delivery Stamps

1918-1938

C1 **C2** **C3** **C3a**

C4 **C5** **C6** **C7**

C10 **C12**

C11

C13 **C14**

C15 **C18**

C20 **C21** **C23**

ssues of 1918		Un	U	PE		FDC	Q(M)
Perf. 11							
For prepayment of postage on all mailable matter sent by airmail. All unwatermarked.							
C1	6¢ Curtiss Jenny	12/10/18	75.00	30.00	800.00	(6)	*32,500.00*	3
	Double transfer		95.00	45.00				
C2	16¢ Curtiss Jenny	07/11/18	105.00	35.00	1,250.00	(6)	*32,500.00*	4
C3	24¢ Curtiss Jenny	05/13/18	105.00	35.00	500.00	(4)	*27,500.00*	2
a	Center Inverted		*150,000.00*		*1,100,000.00*	(4)		0.0001
Issues of 1923							
C4	8¢ Airplane Radiator and							
	Wooden Propeller	08/15/23	27.50	14.00	275.00	(6)	500.00	6
C5	16¢ Air Service Emblem	08/17/23	105.00	30.00	2,000.00	(6)	725.00	5
C6	24¢ De Havilland Biplane	08/21/23	120.00	30.00	2,600.00	(6)	900.00	5
Issues of 1926-27							
C7	10¢ Map of U.S. and							
	Two Mail Planes	02/13/26	3.00	.35	35.00	(6)	55.00	42
	Double transfer		5.75	1.10				
C8	15¢ olive brown (C7)	09/18/26	3.50	2.50	37.50	(6)	75.00	16
C9	20¢ yellow green (C7)	01/25/27	9.00	2.00	85.00	(6)	100.00	18
Issue of 1927-28							
C10	10¢ Lindbergh's							
	"Spirit of St. Louis"	06/18/27	8.50	2.50	105.00	(6)	20.00	20
a	Booklet pane of 3	05/26/28	85.00	65.00	825.00			
Issue of 1928							
C11	5¢ Beacon on Rocky							
	Mountains	07/25/28	5.25	.75	175.00	(8)	55.00	107
	Recut frame line at left		6.75	1.25				
Issues of 1930							
C12	5¢ Winged Globe	02/10/30	11.00	.50	145.00	(6)	12.50	98
a	Horizontal pair, imperf. between		*4,500.00*					
Graf Zeppelin Issue							
C13	65¢ Zeppelin over							
	Atlantic Ocean	04/19/30	250.00	160.00	2,300.00	(6)	1,900.00	0.09
C14	$1.30 Zeppelin							
	Between Continents	04/19/30	500.00	375.00	5,750.00	(6)	1,350.00	0.07
C15	$2.60 Zeppelin							
	Passing Globe	04/19/30	800.00	575.00	8,250.00	(6)	1,600.00	0.06
Issues of 1931-32, Perf. 10.5 x 11							
C16	5¢ violet (C12)	08/19/31	5.50	.60	80.00	(4)	175.00	57
C17	8¢ olive bister (C12)	09/26/32	2.50	.40	27.50	(4)	15.00	77
Issue of 1933, Century of Progress Issue, Perf. 11							
C18	50¢ Zeppelin, Federal Building							
	at Chicago Exposition and							
	Hangar at Friedrichshafen	10/02/33	75.00	70.00	575.00	(6)	225.00	0.3
	Beginning with #C19, unused values are for never-hinged stamps.							
Issue of 1934, Perf. 10.5 x 11							
C19	6¢ dull orange (C12)	06/30/34	3.50	.25	22.50	(4)	*200.00*	302
Issues of 1935-37, Trans-Pacific Issue, Perf. 11							
C20	25¢ "China Clipper"							
	over the Pacific	11/22/35	1.40	1.00	22.50	(6)	20.00	10
C21	20¢ "China Clipper"							
	over the Pacific	02/15/37	11.00	1.75	105.00	(6)	20.00	13
C22	50¢ carmine (C21)	02/15/37	10.00	5.00	105.00	(6)	20.00	9
Issue of 1938							
C23	6¢ Eagle Holding Shield,							
	Olive Branch and Arrows	05/14/38	.50	.15	8.00	(4)	15.00	350
a	Vertical pair, imperf. horizontally		350.00					
b	Horizontal pair, imperf. vertically		*12,500.00*		*37,500.00*	(4)		
	6¢ ultramarine and carmine		150.00					

	Issue of 1939		Un	U	PB/LP		FDC	Q(M)
	Transatlantic Issue							
C24	30¢ Winged Globe	05/16/39	10.50	1.50	140.00	(6)	45.00	20
	Issues of 1941-44, Perf. 11 x 10.5							
C25	6¢ Twin-Motor Transport	06/25/41	.15	.15	.65	(4)	2.25	4,477
a	Booklet pane of 3	03/18/43	5.00	1.50			25.00	
	Singles of #C25a are imperf. at sides or imperf. at sides and bottom.							
b	Horizontal pair, imperf. between		2,250.00					
C26	8¢ olive green (C25)	03/21/44	.20	.15	1.10	(4)	3.75	1,745
C27	10¢ violet (C25)	08/15/41	1.25	.20	7.00	(4)	8.00	67
C28	15¢ brn. carmine (C25)	08/19/41	2.75	.35	13.50	(4)	10.00	78
C29	20¢ bright green (C25)	08/27/41	2.25	.30	11.00	(4)	12.50	42
C30	30¢ blue (C25)	09/25/41	2.50	.35	12.00	(4)	20.00	60
C31	50¢ orange (C25)	10/29/41	11.00	3.00	65.00	(4)	40.00	11
	Issue of 1946							
C32	5¢ DC-4 Skymaster	09/25/46	.15	.15	.45	(4)	2.00	865
	Issues of 1947, Perf. 10.5 x 11							
C33	5¢ DC-4 Skymaster	03/26/47	.15	.15	.50	(4)	2.00	972
	Perf. 11 x 10.5							
C34	10¢ Pan American Union Bldg., Washington, D.C. and Martin 2-0-2	08/30/47	.25	.15	1.10	(4)	2.00	208
C35	15¢ Statue of Liberty, N.Y. Skyline and Lockheed Constellation	08/20/47	.35	.15	1.25	(4)	2.00	756
a	Horizontal pair, imperf. between		2,000.00					
b	Dry printing		.55	.15	2.50	(4)		
C36	25¢ San Francisco-Oakland Bay Bridge and Boeing Stratocruiser	07/30/47	.85	.15	3.50	(4)	2.75	133
	Issues of 1948, Coil Stamp, Perf. 10 Horizontally							
C37	5¢ carmine (C33)	01/15/48	1.00	.80	10.00	(2)	2.00	33
	Perf. 11 x 10.5							
C38	5¢ New York City	07/31/48	.15	.15	3.75	(4)	1.75	38
	Issues of 1949, Perf. 10.5 x 11							
C39	6¢ carmine (C33)	01/18/49	.15	.15	.50	(4)	1.50	5,070
a	Booklet pane of 6	11/18/49	10.00	5.00	9.00			
b	Dry printing		.50	.15	2.25	(4)		
c	As "a," dry printing		15.00	—				
	Perf. 11 x 10.5							
C40	6¢ Alexandria, Virginia	05/11/49	.15	.15	.50	(4)	1.25	75
	Coil Stamp, Perf. 10 Horizontally							
C41	6¢ carmine (C33)	08/25/49	3.25	.15	15.00	(2)	1.25	260
	Universal Postal Union Issue, Perf. 11 x 10.5							
C42	10¢ Post Office Dept. Bldg.	11/18/49	.20	.20	1.40	(4)	2.00	21
C43	15¢ Globe and Doves Carrying Messages	10/07/49	.30	.25	1.25	(4)	3.00	37
C44	25¢ Boeing Stratocruiser and Globe	11/30/49	.50	.40	5.75	(4)	4.00	16
C45	6¢ Wright Brothers	12/17/49	.15	.15	.65	(4)	3.50	80
	Issue of 1952							
C46	80¢ Diamond Head, Honolulu, Hawaii	03/26/52	5.00	1.25	25.00	(4)	20.00	19
	Issue of 1953							
C47	6¢ Powered Flight	05/29/53	.15	.15	.55	(4)	1.50	78
	Issue of 1954							
C48	4¢ Eagle in Flight	09/03/54	.15	.15	1.40	(4)	1.00	50

C24

C25

C32

C33

C34

C35

C36

C38

C40

C42

C43

C44

C45

C46

C47

C48

1957-1964

C49

C51

C53

C54

C55

C56

C57

C58

C59

C61

C62

C63

C64

C66

C67

C68

C69

446

	ssue of 1957		Un	U	PB/LP		FDC	Q(M)
C49	6¢ Air Force	08/01/57	.15	.15	.75	(4)	2.00	63
	Issues of 1958							
C50	5¢ rose red (C48)	07/31/58	.15	.15	1.40	(4)	1.00	72
	Perf. 10.5 x 11							
C51	7¢ Jet Airliner	07/31/58	.15	.15	.60	(4)	1.00	1,327
a	Booklet pane of 6		14.00	7.00			9.50	221
	Coil Stamp, Perf. 10 Horizontally							
C52	7¢ blue (C51)	07/31/58	2.25	.15	15.00	(2)	1.00	157
	Issues of 1959, Perf. 11 x 10.5							
C53	7¢ Alaska Statehood	01/03/59	.15	.15	.60	(4)	1.00	90
	Perf. 11							
C54	7¢ Balloon Jupiter	08/17/59	.15	.15	.60	(4)	1.10	79
	Perf. 11 x 10.5							
C55	7¢ Hawaii Statehood	08/21/59	.15	.15	.60	(4)	1.00	85
	Perf. 11							
C56	10¢ Pan American Games	08/27/59	.25	.25	1.25	(4)	1.00	39
	Issues of 1959-66							
C57	10¢ Liberty Bell	06/10/60	1.25	.70	5.50	(4)	1.25	40
C58	15¢ Statue of Liberty	11/20/59	.35	.20	1.50	(4)	1.25	98
C59	25¢ Abraham Lincoln	04/22/60	.50	.15	2.00	(4)	1.75	
a	Tagged	12/29/66	.60	.30	2.50	(4)	15.00	
	Issues of 1960, Perf. 10.5 x 11							
C60	7¢ carmine (C61)	08/12/60	.15	.15	.60	(4)	1.00	1,289
	Pair with full horizontal gutter between							
a	Booklet pane of 6	08/19/60	17.50	8.00			9.50	
	Coil Stamp, Perf. 10 Horizontally							
C61	7¢ Jet Airliner	10//22/60	4.25	.25	35.00	(2)	1.00	87
	Issues of 1961-67, Perf. 11							
C62	13¢ Liberty Bell	06/28/61	.40	.15	1.65	(4)	1.00	
a	Tagged	02/15/67	.75	.50	5.00	(4)	10.00	
C63	15¢ Statue of Liberty	01/13/61	.30	.15	1.25	(4)	1.00	
a	Tagged	01/11/67	.35	.20	1.50	(4)	15.00	
b	As "a," horiz. pair, imperf. vertically	15,000.00						
	#C63 has a gutter between the two parts of the design; C58 does not.							
	Issues of 1962-65, Perf. 10.5 x 11							
C64	8¢ Jetliner over Capitol	12/05/62	.15	.15	.65	(4)	1.00	
a	Tagged	08/01/63	.15	.15	.65	(4)	4.50	
b	Bklt. pane of 5 + label		7.00	3.00			3.50	
c	As "b," tagged	1964	2.00	.75				
	Coil Stamp, Perf. 10 Horizontally							
C65	8¢ carmine (C64)	12/05/62	.40	.15	3.75	(2)	1.00	
a	Tagged	01/14/65	.35	.15	1.50	(2)		
	Issue of 1963, Perf. 11							
C66	15¢ Montgomery Blair	05/03/63	.60	.55	2.75	(4)	1.10	42
	Issues of 1963-67, Perf. 11 x 10.5							
C67	6¢ Bald Eagle	07/12/63	.15	.15	1.80	(4)	1.00	
a	Tagged	02/15/67	4.00	3.00	55.00	(4)	15.00	
	1963 continued, Perf. 11							
C68	8¢ Amelia Earhart	07/24/63	.20	.15	1.00	(4)	2.25	64
	Issue of 1964							
C69	8¢ Robert H. Goddard	10/05/64	.40	.15	1.75	(4)	2.25	62

1967-1976

	Issues of 1967		Un		PB/LP		FDC	Q(M)
C70	8¢ Alaska Purchase	03/30/67	.25	.15	1.40	(4)	1.00	56
C71	20¢ "Columbia Jays,"							
	by Audubon, (See also #1241)	04/26/67	.80	.15	3.50	(4)	2.00	165
	Issues of 1968, Unwmk., Perf. 11 x 10.5							
C72	10¢ 50-Star Runway	01/05/68	.20	.15	.90	(4)	1.00	
b	Booklet pane of 8		2.00	.75			3.50	
c	Booklet pane of 5 + label	01/06/68	3.75	.75			125.00	
	Coil Stamp, Perf. 10 Vertically							
C73	10¢ carmine (C72)	01/05/68	.30	.15	1.70	(2)	1.00	
a	Imperf. pair		600.00		900.00	(2)		
	Perf. 11							
C74	10¢ U.S. Air Mail Service	05/15/68	.25	.15	2.00	(4)	1.50	
a	Red (tail stripe) omitted		—					
C75	20¢ USA and Jet	11/22/68	.35	.15	1.75	(4)	1.10	
	Issue of 1969							
C76	10¢ Moon Landing	09/09/69	.25	.15	1.10	(4)	5.00	152
a	Rose red omitted		500.00	—				
	Issues of 1971-73, Perf. 10.5 x 11							
C77	9¢ Delta Wing Plane	05/15/71	.20	.15	.90	(4)	1.00	
	Perf. 11 x 10.5							
C78	11¢ Silhouette of Jet	05/07/71	.20	.15	.90	(4)	1.00	
a	Booklet pane of 4 + 2 labels		1.25	.75			1.75	
C79	13¢ Winged Airmail Envelope	11/16/73	.25	.15	1.10	(4)	1.00	
a	Booklet pane of 5 + label	12/27/73	1.50	.75			1.75	
b	Untagged (Bureau precanceled)			.30				
	Perf. 11							
C80	17¢ Statue of Liberty	07/13/71	.30	.15	1.40	(4)	1.00	
C81	21¢ USA and Jet	05/21/71	.35	.15	1.65	(4)	1.00	
	Coil Stamps, Perf. 10 Vertically							
C82	11¢ carmine (C78)	05/07/71	.25	.15	.80	(2)	1.00	
a	Imperf. pair		250.00		375.00	(2)		
C83	13¢ carmine (C79)	12/27/73	.30	.15	1.20	(2)	1.00	
a	Imperf. pair		80.00		150.00	(2)		
	Issues of 1972, National Parks Centennial Issue, Perf. 11 (See also #1448-54)							
C84	11¢ Kii Statue and Temple at City							
	of Refuge Historical National Park,							
	Honaunau, Hawaii	05/03/72	.20	.15	.90	(4)	1.00	78
a	Blue and green omitted		1,000.00					
	Olympic Games Issue, Perf. 11 x 10.5 (See also #1460-62)							
C85	11¢ Skiers and Olympic Rings	08/17/72	.20	.15	2.25	(10)	1.00	96
	Issues of 1973, Progress in Electronics Issue, Perf. 11 (See also #1500-02)							
C86	11¢ DeForest Audions	07/10/73	.20	.15	.95	(4)	1.00	59
a	Vermilion and green omitted		1,400.00					
	Issues of 1974							
C87	18¢ Statue of Liberty	01/11/74	.35	.25	1.50	(4)	1.00	
C88	26¢ Mount Rushmore							
	National Memorial	01/02/74	.50	.15	2.25	(4)	1.25	
	Issues of 1976							
C89	25¢ Plane and Globes	01/02/76	.45	.15	2.10	(4)	1.25	
C90	31¢ Plane, Globes and Flag	01/02/76	.50	.15	2.25	(4)	1.25	

C70

C71

C72

C74

C75

FIRST MAN ON THE MOON

C76

C77

C78

C79

C80

C81

C84

C85

C86

C87

C88

C89

C90

449

C91 **C93** **C95**

C97

Philip Mazzei
Patriot Remembered

USA airmail 40c

C98

C92 C92a C94 C94a C96 C96a

28c
USAirmail
Blanche Stuart Scott
Pioneer Pilot

C99

Glenn Curtiss
Aviation
Pioneer

USAirmail 35c

C100

C101 C102

C105 C106

Olympics 84
USA
40c
Airmail

Olympics 84
USA
40c
Airmail

Olympics 84
USA
40c
Airmail

Olympics 84
USA
40c
Airmail

C107 **C108 C108a**

Olympics 84
USA
28c
Airmail

Olympics 84
USA
28c
Airmail

Olympics 84
USA
28c
Airmail

Olympics 84
USA
28c
Airmail

C103 C104 C104a

C109 C110

Olympics 84
USA
35c
Airmail

Olympics 84
USA
35c
Airmail

Olympics 84
USA
35c
Airmail

Olympics 84
USA
35c
Airmail

C111 C112 C112a

	ssues of 1978		Un	U	PB	#	FDC	Q(M)
	Aviation Pioneers Issue, Perf. 11 (See also #C93-96)							
C91	31¢ Wright Brothers, Flyer A	09/23/78	.60	.30			3.00	157
C92	31¢ Wright Brothers, Flyer A							
	and Shed	09/23/78	.60	.30			3.00	157
a	Vert. pair, #C91-92		1.20	1.10	2.75	(4)	4.00	
b	As "a," ultramarine and black omitted	800.00						
c	As "a," black omitted	—						
d	As "a," black, yellow, magenta,							
	blue and brown omitted	2,250.00						
	Issues of 1979, Aviation Pioneers Issue							
C93	21¢ Octave Chanute and Biplane							
	Hang-Glider	03/29/79	.70	.30			3.00	29
C94	21¢ Biplane Hang-Glider							
	and Chanute	03/29/79	.70	.30	3.25	(4)	3.00	29
a	Attached pair, #C93-94		1.40	1.10			4.00	
b	As "a," ultramarine and black omitted	4,500.00						
	Aviation Pioneers Issue (See also #C99-100)							
C95	25¢ Wiley Post and							
	"Winnie Mae"	11/20/79	1.10	.35			3.00	32
C96	25¢ NR-105-W, Post in							
	Pressurized Suit and Portrait	11/20/79	1.10	.35	8.00	(4)	3.00	32
a	Attached pair, #C95-96		2.25	1.25			4.00	
	Olympic Summer Games Issue (See also #1790-94)							
C97	31¢ High Jumper	11/01/79	.65	.30	9.50	(12)	1.25	47
	Issues of 1980-82							
C98	40¢ Philip Mazzei	10/13/80	.75	.15	9.50	(12)	1.35	81
a	Perf. 10.5 x 11	1982	5.00	—	90.00	(12)		
b	Imperf. pair	3,250.00						
	Issues of 1980, Aviation Pioneers Issues							
C99	28¢ Blanche Stuart Scott							
	and Biplane	12/30/80	.55	.15	8.50	(12)	1.25	20
	Glenn Curtiss (See also #C113-14)							
C100	35¢ Portrait of Curtiss							
	and "Pusher" Biplane	12/30/80	.60	.15	8.00	(12)	1.25	23
	Issues of 1983, Olympic Summer Games Issue (See also #2048-51 and 2082-85)							
C101	28¢ Gymnast	06/17/83	1.00	.30			1.25	43
C102	28¢ Hurdler	06/17/83	1.00	.30			1.25	43
C103	28¢ Basketball Player	06/17/83	1.00	.30			1.25	43
C104	28¢ Soccer Player	06/17/83	1.00	.30			1.25	43
a	Block of 4, #C101-04		4.50	2.00	6.75	(4)	3.75	
	Olympic Summer Games Issue (See also #2048-51 and 2082-85)							
C105	40¢ Shotputter	04/08/83	.90	.40			1.35	67
C106	40¢ Gymnast	04/08/83	.90	.40			1.35	67
C107	40¢ Swimmer	04/08/83	.90	.40			1.35	67
C108	40¢ Weightlifter	04/08/83	.90	.40			1.35	67
a	Block of 4, #C105-08		4.25	2.50	4.75	(4)	5.00	
b	As "a," imperf.	1,250.00						
	Olympic Summer Games Issue (See also #2048-51 and 2082-85)							
C109	35¢ Fencer	11/04/83	.90	.50			1.25	43
C110	35¢ Bicyclist	11/04/83	.90	.50			1.25	43
C111	35¢ Volleyball Players	11/04/83	.90	.50			1.25	43
C112	35¢ Pole Vaulter	11/04/83	.90	.50			1.25	43
a	Block of 4, #C109-12		4.00	3.00	6.75	(4)	4.50	

ssues of 1985		Un	U	PB		FDC	Q(M)
Aviation Pioneers Issues, Perf. 11							
C113 33¢ Portrait of Alfred Verville							
and Airplane Diagram	02/13/85	.65	.20	3.25	(4)	1.25	168
a	Imperf. pair		900.00				
C114 39¢ Lawrence and							
Elmer Sperry	02/13/85	.75	.25	3.50	(4)	1.35	168
a	Imperf. pair		1,400.00				
C115 44¢ Transpacific Airmail	02/15/85	.85	.25	4.00	(4)	1.50	209
a	Imperf. pair		900.00				
C116 44¢ Junipero Serra	08/22/85	1.00	.30	8.50	(4)	1.50	164
a	Imperf. pair		1,500.00				
Issues of 1988							
C117 44¢ New Sweden	03/29/88	1.00	.25	7.00	(4)	1.35	137
Aviation Pioneers Issues (See also #C128-29)							
C118 45¢ Samuel P. Langley	05/14/88	.90	.20	4.25	(4)	1.40	406
C119 36¢ Igor Sikorsky	06/23/88	.70	.20	3.25	(4)	2.50	179
Issues of 1989, Perf. 11.5 x 11							
C120 45¢ French Revolution	07/14/89	.95	.20	4.75	(4)	1.40	38
America/PUAS Issue, Perf. 11 (See also #2426)							
C121 45¢ Southeast Carved Wood Figure,							
Key Marco Cat (A.D. 700-1450),							
Emblem of the Postal Union of the							
Americas and Spain	10/12/89	.90	.20	5.50	(4)	1.40	39
20th UPU Congress Issue, Future Mail Transportation (See also #2434-38)							
C122 45¢ Hypersonic Airliner	11/27/89	1.00	.40			1.40	27
C123 45¢ Air-Cushion Vehicle	11/27/89	1.00	.40			1.40	27
C124 45¢ Surface Rover	11/27/89	1.00	.40			1.40	27
C125 45¢ Shuttle	11/27/89	1.00	.40			1.40	27
a	Block of 4, #C122-25		4.00	3.00	5.00	(4)	5.00
b	As "a," light blue omitted		1,000.00				

In 1907 American inventor Lee De Forest (1873–1961) patented the first triode vacuum tube, which he named the **Audion.** De Forest's invention made possible the effective transmission of the human voice. In 1973 the U.S. Postal Service honored the Audion with a stamp in

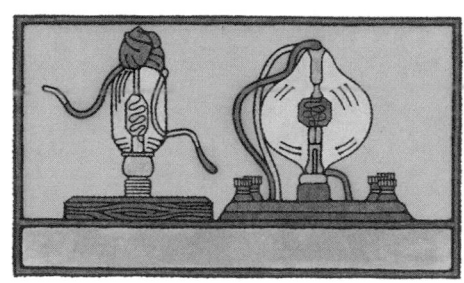

its **Progress in Electronics** issue.

When attached to a radio receiver, the Audion amplified weak electronic signals, making easier the detection of radio waves. The sensitive Audion enabled the transmission of high quality voice vibrations, music, and other sounds. It revolutionized radio and telephone equipment and was the basis of television, radar, and the first computers.

De Forest, who held many patents for inventions in fields including wireless telegraphy, radio telephony, talking pictures, and radar, formed the De Forest Wireless Telegraph Company in 1902. He broadcast a performance by Enrico Caruso from New York's Metropolitan Opera House and the first news by radio.

C113

C114

C115

C116

C117

C118

C119

C120

C121

C122

C123

C124

C125

C125a

20th Universal Postal Congress

A glimpse at several potential mail delivery methods of the future is the theme of these four stamps issued by the U.S. in commemoration of the convening of the 20th Universal Postal Congress in Washington, D.C. from November 13 through December 14, 1989. The United States, as host nation to the Congress for the first time in ninety-two years, welcomed more than 1,000 delegates from most of the member nations of the Universal Postal Union to the major international event.
©USPS 1989

C126

C127

C128

C129

C130

C131

C133

C134

CE1

CE2

	Issues of 1989		Un	U	PB		FDC	Q(M)
	20th UPU Congress Issue Souvenir Sheet, Imperf.							
C126	Designs of #C122-25	11/24/89	4.25	3.25			3.00	2
a-d	Single stamp from sheet		1.00	.50				
	Issue of 1990, America/PUAS Issue, Perf. 11 (See also #2512)							
C127	45¢ Tropical Coast	10/12/90	.90	.20	6.75	(4)	1.40	39
	Issues of 1991, Aviation Pioneers Issues							
C128	50¢ Harriet Quimby							
	and Early Plane	04/27/91	1.00	.25	5.00	(4)	1.35	
b	50¢ Harriet Quimby (C128)	04/27/91	1.00	.25	5.00	(4)		
C129	40¢ William T. Piper							
	and Piper Cub Airplane	05/17/91	.80	.20	4.00	(4)	1.25	
C130	50¢ Antarctic Treaty	06/21/91	1.00	.25	5.00	(4)	1.35	113
	Issues of 1991-93, America/PUAS Issue							
C131	50¢ Eskimo and Bering							
	Land Bridge	10/12/91	1.00	.25	5.25	(4)	1.35	15
C132	40¢ Portrait of Piper	1993	1.00	.90	7.00	(4)		
	Issues of 1999, Self-Adhesive, Perf. 11							
C133	48¢ Niagra Falls	5/12/99	.95	.20	4.00	(4)		
	Serpentine Die Cut 11							
C134	40¢ RioGrande	7/30/99	.80	.60	3.20	(4)		
	Airmail Special Delivery Stamps							
	Issues of 1934							
CE1	16¢ Great Seal of the							
	United States	08/30/34	.60	.65	15.00	(6)	25.00	
	For imperforate variety see #77							
	Issue of 1936							
CE2	16¢ red and blue	02/10/36	.40	.25	6.50	(4)	17.50	
a	Horizontal pair, imperf. vertically	*4,000.00*						
	Special Delivery Stamps							
	Issue of 1885, Perf. 12, Unwmkd.							
E1	10¢ Messenger Running	10/01/85	300.00	45.00	*14,000.00*	(8)	8,500.00	
	Issue of 1888							
E2	10¢ blue Messenger Running (E3)	09/06/88	275.00	17.50	*11,500.00*	(8)		
	Issue of 1893							
E3	10¢ Messenger Running	01/24/93	180.00	22.50	*7,250.00*	(8)		
	Issue of 1894, Line under "Ten Cents"							
E4	10¢ Messenger Running	10/10/94	650.00	30.00	*14,000.00*	(6)		

Although we take them for granted today, street boxes for mail collection did not begin to appear in large cities until 1858. In 1863, free city delivery was instituted in 49 of the nation's largest cities; by the turn of the century many more post offices were delivering mail to city residents. The **City Mail Delivery** stamp, issued in 1963, celebrates 100 years of this indispensable service with artwork by beloved American illustrator Norman Rockwell (1894–1978).

Rockwell's work has appeared on several stamps, including one honoring the Boy Scouts of America in 1960 and another honoring Mark Twain's *Tom Sawyer* in 1972. A stamp featured his self-portrait in 1994, the same year his famous Four Freedoms were issued as a souvenir sheet. One of his paintings also appeared on a stamp honoring the Peace Corps as a part of the Celebrate The Century®: The 1960s stamp pane in 1999.

	Issue of 1895		Un	U	PB		FDC
	Perf. 12, Wmkd. (191)						
E5	10¢ bl. Messenger Running (E4)	08/16/95	160.00	3.50	*4,000.00*	(6)	
	Double transfer		—	16.00			
	Line of color through "POSTAL DELIVERY"		210.00	12.50			
	Dots in curved frame above messenger		200.00	9.00			
	Issue of 1902						
E6	10¢ Messenger on Bicycle	12/09/02	105.00	3.25	*2,400.00*	(6)	
	Damaged transfer under "N" of "CENTS"		140.00	3.75			
	Issue of 1908						
E7	10¢ Mercury Helmet and						
	Olive Branch	12/12/08	60.00	40.00	*925.00*	(6)	
	Issue of 1911, Wmkd. (190)						
E8	10¢ ultramarine Messenger						
	on Bicycle (E6)	01/11	100.00	5.25	*2,000.00*	(6)	
	Top frame line missing		140.00	12.50			
	Issue of 1914, Perf. 10						
E9	10¢ ultramarine Messenger						
	on Bicycle (E6)	09/14	175.00	6.50	*3,250.00*	(6)	
	Issue of 1916, Unwmkd.						
E10	10¢ ultramarine Messenger						
	on Bicycle (E6)	10/19/16	275.00	27.50	*5,000.00*	(6)	
	Issue of 1917, Perf. 11						
E11	10¢ ultramarine Messenger						
	on Bicycle (E6)	05/02/17	19.00	.50	225.00	(6)	
c	Blue		50.00	2.50	550.00	(6)	
d	Perf. 10 at left		—				
	Issue of 1922						
E12	10¢ Postman and Motorcycle	07/12/22	32.50	.50	400.00	(6)	425.00
a	10¢ deep ultramarine		37.50	.60	425.00	(6)	
	Double transfer		—	—			
	Issues of 1925						
E13	15¢ Postman and Motorcycle	04/11/25	27.50	1.00	325.00	(6)	240.00
E14	20¢ Post Office Truck	04/25/25	2.00	.85	32.50	(6)	95.00
	Issue of 1927, Perf. 11 x 10.5						
E15	10¢ gray violet Postman						
	and Motorcycle (E12)	11/29/27	.60	.15	4.00	(4)	110.00
c	Horizontal pair, imperf. between		300.00				
	Cracked plate		35.00				
	Issue of 1931						
E16	15¢ or. Postman and						
	Motorcycle (E13)	08/13/31	.70	.15	3.75	(4)	125.00
	Beginning with #E17, unused values are for never-hinged stamps.						
	Issues of 1944						
E17	13¢ Postman and Motorcycle	10/30/44	.60	.15	3.00	(4)	12.00
E18	17¢ Postman and Motorcycle	10/30/44	2.75	1.75	22.50	(4)	12.00
	Issue of 1951						
E19	20¢ blk. Post Office Truck (E14)	11/30/51	1.25	.15	5.50	(4)	5.00
	Issues of 1954-57						
E20	20¢ Delivery of Letter	10/13/54	.40	.15	2.00	(4)	3.00
E21	30¢ Delivery of Letter	09/03/57	.50	.15	2.40	(4)	2.25
	Issues of 1969-71, Perf. 11						
E22	45¢ Arrows	11/21/69	1.25	.25	5.50	(4)	3.50
E23	60¢ Arrows	05/10/71	1.25	.20	5.50	(4)	3.50

E6   E7

E12   E13

E14   E18

E20   E21

E22   E23

Registration, Certified Mail and Postage Due Stamps

1879-1959

F1

FA1

J2

J19

J25

J33

J69

J78

J88

J98

J101

	Issue of 1911		Un	U	PB		DC	Q(M)

Perf. 12, Wmkd. (190)

Registration Stamp

Issued for the prepayment of registry; not usable for postage. Sale discontinued May 28, 1913.

			Un	U	PB		DC	Q(M)
F1	10¢ Bald Eagle	12/01/11	75.00	7.50	*1,600.00*	(6)	*8,000.00*	

Certified Mail Stamp

For use on First-Class mail for which no indemnity value was claimed, but for which proof of mailing and proof of delivery were available at less cost than registered mail.

Issue of 1955, Perf. 10.5 x 11

			Un	U	PB		DC	Q(M)
FA1	15¢ Letter Carrier	06/06/55	.45	.30	4.50	(4)	3.25	54

Postage Due Stamps

For affixing by a postal clerk to any mail to denote amount to be collected from addressee because of insufficient prepayment of postage.

Issues of 1879, Printed by American Bank Note Co., Design of #J2, Perf. 12, Unwmkd.

			Un	U	PB	
J1	1¢ brown		50.00	8.50	*1,000.00*	(10)
J2	2¢ Figure of Value		325.00	7.50		
J3	3¢ brown		45.00	4.50	*950.00*	(10)
J4	5¢ brown		525.00	45.00		
J5	10¢ brown	09/19/79	550.00	25.00		
a	Imperf. pair		*1,750.00*			
J6	30¢ brown	09/19/79	275.00	50.00	*3,700.00*	(10)
J7	50¢ brown	09/19/79	425.00	60.00	*9,750.00*	(10)

Special Printing, Soft, Porous Paper

		Un
J8	1¢ deep brown	*7,000.00*
J9	2¢ deep brown	*5,000.00*
J10	3¢ deep brown	*7,500.00*
J11	5¢ deep brown	*5,000.00*
J12	10¢ deep brown	*2,750.00*
J13	30¢ deep brown	*2,750.00*
J14	50¢ deep brown	*2,750.00*

Issues of 1884, Design of #J19

		Un	U	PB	
J15	1¢ red brown	50.00	4.50	*1,100.00*	(10)
J16	2¢ red brown	60.00	4.50	*1,250.00*	(10)
J17	3¢ red brown	850.00	175.00		
J18	5¢ red brown	425.00	25.00		
J19	10¢ Figure of Value	400.00	17.50	*11,000.00*	(10)
J20	30¢ red brown	150.00	50.00	*2,500.00*	(10)
J21	50¢ red brown	1,500.00	175.00		

Issues of 1891, Design of #J25

		Un	U	PB	
J22	1¢ bright claret	22.50	1.00	*500.00*	(10)
J23	2¢ bright claret	27.50	1.00	*600.00*	(10)
J24	3¢ bright claret	55.00	8.00	*850.00*	(10)
J25	5¢ Figure of Value	67.50	8.00	*1,000.00*	(10)
J26	10¢ bright claret	110.00	17.50	*1,750.00*	(10)
J27	30¢ bright claret	425.00	150.00	*6,750.00*	(10)
J28	50¢ bright claret	450.00	150.00	*8,000.00*	(10)

Issues of 1894, Printed by the Bureau of Engraving and Printing, Design of #J33, Perf. 12

		Un	U	PB	
J29	1¢ vermilion	1,400.00	400.00	*6,000.00*	(6)
J30	2¢ vermilion	600.00	125.00	5,250.00	(6)

Issues of 1894-95, Design of #J33, Unwmkd., Perf. 12

			Un	U	PB	
J31	1¢ deep claret	08/14/94	45.00	6.00	400.00	(6)
J32	2¢ deep claret	07/20/94	37.50	4.00	350.00	(6)
J33	3¢ Figure of Value	04/27/95	150.00	30.00	1,500.00	(6)

	Issues of 1894-95		Un	U	PE	#
	Design of #J33, Unwmkd., Perf. 12					
J34	5¢ deep claret	04/27/95	225.00	35.00	1,750.00	(6)
J35	10¢ deep claret	09/24/94	225.00	25.00	1,750.00	(6)
J36	30¢ deep claret	04/27/95	375.00	90.00		
b	30¢ pale rose		310.00	85.00	2,500.00	(6)
J37	50¢ deep claret	04/27/95	1,100.00	250.00		
a	50¢ pale rose		1,050.00	250.00	8,500.00	(6)
	Issues of 1895-97, Design of #J33, Wmkd. (191)					
J38	1¢ deep claret	08/29/95	8.00	.75	225.00	(6)
J39	2¢ deep claret	09/14/95	8.00	.70	225.00	(6)
J40	3¢ deep claret	10/30/95	55.00	1.75	550.00	(6)
J41	5¢ deep claret	10/15/95	60.00	1.75	575.00	(6)
J42	10¢ deep claret	09/14/95	62.50	3.50	600.00	(6)
J43	30¢ deep claret	08/21/97	500.00	50.00	4,750.00	(6)
J44	50¢ deep claret	03/17/96	325.00	37.50	3,250.00	(6)
	Issues of 1910-12, Design of #J33, Wmkd. (190)					
J45	1¢ deep claret	08/30/10	30.00	3.00		
a	1¢ rose carmine		27.50	3.00	450.00	(6)
J46	2¢ deep claret	11/25/10	30.00	1.00		
a	2¢ rose carmine		27.50	1.00	425.00	(6)
J47	3¢ deep claret	08/31/10	550.00	30.00	5,000.00	(6)
J48	5¢ deep claret	08/31/10	85.00	6.50		
a	5¢ rose carmine		80.00	6.50	875.00	(6)
J49	10¢ deep claret	08/31/10	110.00	12.50	1,300.00	(6)
J50	50¢ deep claret	09/23/12	850.00	120.00	8,250.00	(6
	Issues of 1914, Design of #J33, Perf. 10					
J52	1¢ carmine lake		55.00	11.00	500.00	(6)
J53	2¢ carmine lake		45.00	.40	425.00	(6)
J54	3¢ carmine lake		825.00	37.50	7,000.00	(6)
J55	5¢ carmine lake		36.00	2.50	325.00	(6)
	5¢ deep claret		—	—		
J56	10¢ carmine lake		55.00	2.00	625.00	(6)
J57	30¢ carmine lake		225.00	17.50	2,500.00	(6)
J58	50¢ carmine lake		9,500.00	800.00	66,000.00	(6)
	Issues of 1916, Design of #J33, Unwmkd.					
J59	1¢ rose		2,400.00	325.00	16,500.00	(6)
	Experimental Bureau precancel,					
	New Orleans			210.00		
J60	2¢ rose		150.00	20.00	1,400.00	(6)
	Issues of 1917-25, Design of #J33, Perf. 11					
J61	1¢ carmine rose		2.75	.25	45.00	(6)
J62	2¢ carmine rose		2.50	.25	40.00	(6)
J63	3¢ carmine rose		11.00	.25	100.00	(6)
J64	5¢ carmine		11.00	.25	100.00	(6)
J65	10¢ carmine rose		17.00	.30	160.00	(6)
	Double transfer		—	—		
J66	30¢ carmine rose		87.50	.75	725.00	(6)
J67	50¢ carmine rose		110.00	.30	900.00	(6)
J68	½¢ dull red	04/13/25	1.00	.25	12.50	(6)

ssue of 1930-31		Un	U	PB	#
	Design of #J69, Perf. 11				
J69	½¢ Figure of Value	4.50	1.40	42.50	(6)
J70	1¢ carmine	3.00	.25	30.00	(6)
J71	2¢ carmine	4.00	.25	45.00	(6)
J72	3¢ carmine	21.00	1.75	275.00	(6)
J73	5¢ carmine	19.00	2.50	250.00	(6)
J74	10¢ carmine	40.00	1.00	450.00	(6)
J75	30¢ carmine	110.00	2.00	1,000.00	(6)
J76	50¢ carmine	140.00	.75	1,400.00	(6)
	Design of #J78				
J77	$1 carmine	30.00	.25	225.00	(6)
a	$1 scarlet	25.00	.25	275.00	(6)
J78	$5 "FIVE" on $	37.50	.25	300.00	(6)
a	$5 scarlet	32.50	.25	250.00	(6)
b	As "a," wet printing	35.00	.25	275.00	(6)
	Issues of 1931-56, Design of #J69, Perf. 11 x 10.5				
J79	½¢ dull carmine	.90	.15	22.50	(4)
J80	1¢ dull carmine	.20	.15	1.75	(4)
J81	2¢ dull carmine	.20	.15	1.75	(4)
J82	3¢ dull carmine	.25	.15		
a	3¢ scarlet	.25	.15	2.50	(4)
b	3¢ scarlet, wet printing	.30	.15		
J83	5¢ dull carmine	.40	.15	3.25	(4)
J84	10¢ dull carmine	1.10	.15	6.75	(4)
b	scarlet, wet printing	1.25	.15		
J85	30¢ dull carmine	7.50	.25	35.00	(4)
J86	50¢ dull carmine	10.00	.25		
a	50¢ scarlet	10.00	.25	52.50	(4)
	Design of J78, Perf. 10.5 x 11				
J87	$1 scarlet	32.50	.25	200.00	(4)
	Beginning with #J88, unused values are for never-hinged stamps.				
	Issues of 1959, Designs of #J88, J98 and J101, Perf. 11 x 10.5				
J88	½¢ Figure of Value	06/19/59	1.50	1.10	180.00	(4)
J89	1¢ carmine rose	06/19/59	.15	.15	.35	(4)
a	"1 CENT" omitted		350.00			
b	Pair, one without "1 CENT"		600.00			
J90	2¢ carmine rose	06/19/59	.15	.15	.45	(4)
J91	3¢ carmine rose	06/19/59	.15	.15	.50	(4)
J92	4¢ carmine rose	06/19/59	.15	.15	.60	(4)
J93	5¢ carmine rose	06/19/59	.15	.15	.65	(4)
J94	6¢ carmine rose	06/19/59	.15	.15	.70	(4)
a	Pair, one without "6 CENTS"		850.00			
J95	7¢ carmine rose	06/19/59	.20	.15	.80	(4)
J96	8¢ carmine rose	06/19/59	.20	.15	.90	(4)
J97	10¢ carmine rose	06/19/59	.20	.15	1.00	(4)
J98	30¢ Figure of Value	06/19/59	.75	.15	2.75	(4)
J99	50¢ carmine rose	06/19/59	1.10	.15	5.00	(4)
	Design of #J101					
J100	$1 carmine rose	06/19/59	2.00	.15	8.75	(4)
J101	$5 Outline Figure of Value	06/19/59	9.00	.20	45.00	(4)
	Issues of 1978-85, Designs of #J98					
J102	11¢ carmine rose	01/02/78	.25	.20	2.00	(4)
J103	13¢ carmine rose	01/02/78	.25	.20	2.00	(4)
J104	17¢ carmine rose	06/10/85	.40	.35	25.00	(4)

Official and Penalty Mail Stamps

1873-1995

O3

O7

O11

O14

O16

O18

O25

O34

O37

O44

O47

O52

O57

O74

O76

O87

O91

O121

O124

O125

O126

O127

O129A

O139

O140

O143

O146A

O151

O152

O153

O154

O155

O156

O157

Issues of 1873	Un	U

Thin, Hard Paper, Perf. 12, Unwmkd.

Official Stamps

The franking privilege having been abolished as of July 1, 1873, these stamps were provided for each of the departments of government for the prepayment on official matter. These stamps were supplanted on May 1, 1879, by penalty envelopes and on July 5, 1884, were declared obsolete.

Department of Agriculture Issue: Yellow

		Un	U
O1	1¢ Franklin	160.00	125.00
	Ribbed paper	170.00	135.00
O2	2¢ Jackson	130.00	50.00
O3	3¢ Washington	115.00	9.50
	Double transfer	—	—
O4	6¢ Lincoln	125.00	40.00
O5	10¢ Jefferson	26000	160.00
	10¢ golden yellow	275.00	170.00
	10¢ olive yellow	290.00	180.00
O6	12¢ Clay	350.00	200.00
	12¢ golden yellow	375.00	210.00
O7	15¢ Webster	290.00	170.00
	15¢ olive yellow	325.00	190.00
O8	24¢ Scott	290.00	160.00
	24¢ golden yellow	325.00	170.00
O9	30¢ Hamilton	375.00	225.00
	30¢ olive yellow	425.00	240.00

Executive Dept. Issue: Carmine

		Un	U
O10	1¢ Franklin	575.00	350.00
O11	2¢ Jackson	375.00	160.00
	Double transfer	—	—
O12	3¢ Washington	450.00	160.00
O13	6¢ Lincoln	675.00	425.00
O14	10¢ Jefferson	625.00	500.00

Dept. of the Interior Issue: Vermilion

		Un	U
O15	1¢ Franklin	35.00	8.00
	Ribbed paper	40.00	9.50
O16	2¢ Jackson	30.00	9.00
O17	3¢ Washington	47.50	5.00
O18	6¢ Lincoln	35.00	5.00
O19	10¢ Jefferson	35.00	15.00
O20	12¢ Clay	50.00	7.75
O21	15¢ Webster	85.00	17.00
	Double transfer of left side	140.00	25.00
O22	24¢ Scott	62.50	14.00
O23	30¢ Hamilton	85.00	14.00
O24	90¢ Perry	190.00	37.50

Dept. of Justice Issue: Purple

		Un	U
O25	1¢ Franklin	105.00	77.50
O26	2¢ Jackson	175.00	82.50
O27	3¢ Washington	175.00	17.00
O28	6¢ Lincoln	160.00	25.00

Issues of 1873	Un	U

Dept. of Justice Issue: Purple (continued)

		Un	U
O29	10¢ Jefferson	180.00	55.00
	Double transfer	—	—
O30	12¢ Clay	140.00	37.50
O31	15¢ Webster	275.00	125.00
O32	24¢ Scott	700.00	275.00
O33	30¢ Hamilton	600.00	160.00
	Double transfer at top	625.00	175.00
O34	90¢ Perry	900.00	425.00

Navy Dept. Issue: Ultramarine

		Un	U
O35	1¢ Franklin	75.00	37.50
a	1¢ dull blue	85.00	40.00
O36	2¢ Jackson	60.00	17.00
a	2¢ dull blue	70.00	15.00
	2¢ gray blue	65.00	15.00
O37	3¢ Washington	60.00	8.00
a	3¢ dull blue	70.00	11.00
O38	6¢ Lincoln	60.00	14.00
a	6¢ dull blue	70.00	14.50
	Vertical line through "N" of "NAVY"	100.00	20.00
O39	7¢ Stanton	375.00	140.00
a	7¢ dull blue	425.00	150.00
O40	10¢ Jefferson	80.00	27.50
a	10¢ dull blue	85.00	27.50
	Plate scratch	*170.00*	—
O41	12¢ Clay	95.00	25.00
	Double transfer of left side	160.00	45.00
O42	15¢ Webster	175.00	50.00
O43	24¢ Scott	175.00	55.00
a	24¢ dull blue	200.00	—
O44	30¢ Hamilton	140.00	27.50
O45	90¢ Perry	700.00	175.00
a	Double impression		*3,750.00*

Post Office Dept. Issue: Black

		Un	U
O47	1¢ Figure of Value	12.50	7.50
O48	2¢ Figure of Value	16.00	7.00
a	Double impression	325.00	300.00
O49	3¢ Figure of Value	5.25	1.00
	Cracked plate	—	—
O50	6¢ Figure of Value	16.00	6.00
	Vertical ribbed paper	—	11.00
O51	10¢ Figure of Value	70.00	40.00
O52	12¢ Figure of Value	35.00	8.25
O53	15¢ Figure of Value	47.50	14.00
	Double transfer	—	—
O54	24¢ Figure of Value	60.00	17.00
O55	30¢ Figure of Value	60.00	17.00
O56	90¢ Figure of Value	90.00	14.00

Issues of 1873	Un	U
Dept. of State Issue: Green, Perf. 12		
O57 1¢ Franklin	110.00	40.00
O58 2¢ Jackson	210.00	60.00
O59 3¢ Washington	85.00	17.00
Double paper	—	—
O60 6¢ Lincoln	80.00	19.00
O61 7¢ Stanton	160.00	40.00
Ribbed paper	180.00	45.00
O62 10¢ Jefferson	125.00	27.50
Short transfer	160.00	40.00
O63 12¢ Clay	200.00	82.50
O64 15¢ Webster	210.00	55.00
O65 24¢ Scott	425.00	140.00
O66 30¢ Hamilton	400.00	110.00
O67 90¢ Perry	750.00	250.00
O68 $2 Seward	850.00	650.00
O69 $5 Seward	6,000.00	3,250.00
O70 $10 Seward	4,000.00	2,250.00
O71 $20 Seward	3,250.00	1,700.00
Treasury Dept. Issue: Brown		
O72 1¢ Franklin	37.50	4.50
Double transfer	45.00	6.25
O73 2¢ Jackson	47.50	4.50
Double transfer	—	7.75
Cracked plate	65.00	—
O74 3¢ Washington	32.50	1.25
Shaded circle outside		
right frame line	—	—
O75 6¢ Lincoln	42.50	2.25
Worn plate	37.50	4.00
O76 7¢ Stanton	90.00	22.50
O77 10¢ Jefferson	90.00	7.75
O78 12¢ Clay	90.00	6.00
O79 15¢ Webster	85.00	7.75
O80 24¢ Scott	425.00	65.00
O81 30¢ Hamilton	145.00	9.00
Short transfer top right	—	—
O82 90¢ Perry	150.00	10.00
War Dept. Issue: Rose		
O83 1¢ Franklin	140.00	7.25
O84 2¢ Jackson	125.00	9.50
Ribbed paper	135.00	11.50
O85 3¢ Washington	130.00	2.75
O86 6¢ Lincoln	425.00	6.00
O87 7¢ Stanton	125.00	72.50
O88 10¢ Jefferson	42.50	15.00

Issues of 1873	Un	U
War Dept. Issue (continued): Rose		
O89 12¢ Clay	145.00	9.00
Ribbed paper	160.00	10.50
O90 15¢ Webster	37.50	11.00
Ribbed paper	42.50	14.00
O91 24¢ Scott	37.50	6.75
O92 30¢ Hamilton	40.00	6.75
O93 90¢ Perry	90.00	40.00
Issues of 1879, Soft, Porous Paper		
Dept. of Agriculture: Yellow		
O94 1¢ Franklin, issued		
without gum	3,000.00	
O95 3¢ Washington	290.00	55.00
Dept. of the Interior Issue: Vermilion		
O96 1¢ Franklin	210.00	190.00
O97 2¢ Jackson	4.00	1.25
O98 3¢ Washington	3.50	1.00
O99 6¢ Lincoln	5.25	5.50
O100 10¢ Jefferson	65.00	60.00
O101 12¢ Clay	125.00	90.00
O102 15¢ Webster	300.00	225.00
Double transfer	350.00	—
O103 24¢ Scott	*3,000.00*	
O104-05 Not assigned		
Dept. of Justice Issue: Bluish Purple		
O106 3¢ Washington	85.00	55.00
O107 6¢ Lincoln	190.00	160.00
Post Office Dept. Issue: Black		
O108 3¢ Figure of Value	15.00	5.00
Treasury Dept. Issue: Brown		
O109 3¢ Washington	45.00	6.75
O110 6¢ Lincoln	85.00	35.00
O111 10¢ Jefferson	125.00	40.00
O112 30¢ Hamilton	1,250.00	275.00
O113 90¢ Perry	2,000.00	275.00
War Dept. Issue: Rose Red		
O114 1¢ Franklin	3.50	2.75
O115 2¢ Jackson	5.00	3.25
O116 3¢ Washington	5.00	1.20
b Double impression	*750.00*	
Double transfer	8.00	4.75
O117 6¢ Lincoln	4.50	1.00
O118 10¢ Jefferson	37.50	37.50
O119 12¢ Clay	30.00	10.00
O120 30¢ Hamilton	80.00	67.50

Issues of 1910-85	Un	U
Perf. 12		
Official Postal Savings Mail		

These stamps were used to prepay postage on official correspondence of the Postal Savings Division of the Post Office Department. Discontinued Sept. 23, 1914.

		Un	U
O121	2¢ Postal Savings	14.00	1.50
	Double transfer	19.00	2.50
O122	50¢ dark green	140.00	40.00
O123	$1 ultramarine	130.00	11.00
	Wmkd. (190)		
O124	1¢ dark violet	7.50	1.50
O125	2¢ Postal Savings (O121)	45.00	5.50
O126	10¢ carmine	17.00	1.60
	Penalty Mail Stamps		

Stamps for use by government departments were reinstituted in 1983. Now known as Penalty Mail stamps, they help provide a better accounting of actual mail costs for official departments and agencies, etc.

Beginning with #O127, unused values are for never-hinged stamps.

Issues of 1983-85, Unwmkd., Perf. 11 x 10.5, O129A is Perf. 11			
O127	1¢, Jan. 12, 1983	.15	.15
O128	4¢, Jan. 12, 1983	.15	.25
O129	13¢, Jan. 12, 1983	.45	.75
O129A	14¢, May 15, 1985	.45	.50
O130	17¢, Jan. 12, 1983	.55	.40

Issues of 1983-95	Un	U
Perf. 11 x 10.5		
O131, O134, O137, O142 Not assigned		
O132 $1, Jan. 12, 1983	2.00	1.00
O133 $5, Jan. 12, 1983	9.00	5.00
Coil Stamps, Perf. 10 Vertically		
O135 20¢, Jan. 12, 1983	1.75	*2.00*
a Imperf. pair	*2,000.00*	
O136 22¢, May 15, 1985	.70	*2.00*
Perf. 11		
O138 "D" postcard rate		
(14¢) Feb. 4, 1985	5.25	5.00
Coil Stamps, Perf. 10 Vertically		
O138A 15¢, June 11, 1988	.45	.50
O138B 20¢, May 19, 1988	.45	.30
O139 "D" (22¢), Feb. 4, 1985	5.25	*3.00*
O140 "E" (25¢), Mar. 22, 1988	.75	*2.00*
O141 25¢, June 11, 1988	.65	.50
Perf. 11		
O143 1¢, July 5, 1989	.15	.15
Perf. 10		
O144 "F" (29¢), Jan. 22, 1991	.75	.50
O145 29¢, May 24, 1991	.65	.30
Perf. 11		
O146 4¢, Apr. 6, 1991	.15	.30
O146A 10¢, Oct. 19, 1993	.25	.30
O147 19¢, May 24, 1991	.40	.50
O148 23¢, May 24, 1991	.45	.30
O151 $1, Sept., 1993	2.00	.75
O152 (32¢), Dec. 13, 1994	.65	—
O153 32¢, May 9, 1995	.65	.30
O154 1¢, May 9, 1995	.15	.15
O155 20¢, May 9, 1995	.45	.30
O156 23¢, May 9, 1995	.50	.30
O157 33¢, Oct. 8, 1999	.65	—

Variable Rate Coil Stamps

These are coil postage stamps printed without denominations. The denomination is imprinted by the dispensing equipment called a Postage and Mailing Center (PMC). Denominations can be set between 1¢ and $99.99. In 1993, the minimum denomination was adjusted to 19¢ (the postcard rate at the time).

Date of Issue:
August 20, 1992
Printing: Intaglio

Date of Issue:
February 19, 1994
Printing: Gravure

Date of Issue:
January 26, 1996
Printing: Gravure

Parcel Post and
Special Handling Stamps

1913-1955

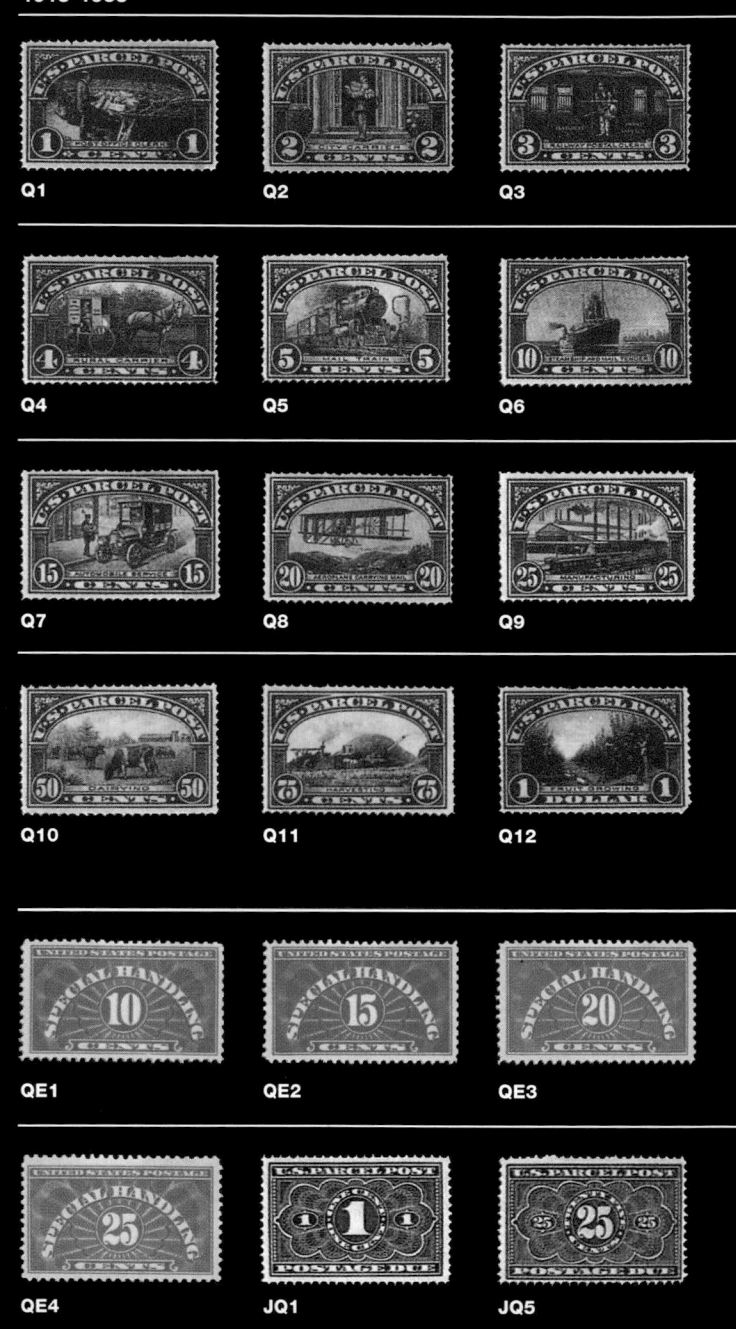

Q1

Q2

Q3

Q4

Q5

Q6

Q7

Q8

Q9

Q10

Q11

Q12

QE1

QE2

QE3

QE4

JQ1

JQ5

ssues of 1913			Un	U	PB	#	FDC
Wmkd. (190), Perf. 12							

Parcel Post Stamps

Issued for the prepayment of postage on parcel post packages only. Beginning
July 1, 1913 these stamps were valid for all postal purposes.

			Un	U	PB	#	FDC
Q1	1¢ Post Office Clerk	07/01/13	5.00	1.50	40.00	(4)	1,500.00
	Double transfer		8.50	4.00			
Q2	2¢ City Carrier	07/01/13	6.50	1.25	45.00	(4)	1,500.00
	2¢ lake		—				
	Double transfer		—	—			
Q3	3¢ Railway Postal Clerk	04/05/13	12.50	5.75	95.00	(4)	3,250.00
	Retouched at lower right corner		25.00	14.50			
	Double transfer		25.00	14.50			
Q4	4¢ Rural Carrier	07/01/13	35.00	3.00	350.00	(4)	3,250.00
	Double transfer		—	—			
Q5	5¢ Mail Train	07/01/13	30.00	2.25	325.00	(4)	3,250.00
	Double transfer		42.50	6.25			
Q6	10¢ Steamship and Mail Tender		50.00	3.00	425.00	(4)	
	Double transfer		—	—			
Q7	15¢ Automobile Service	07/01/13	65.00	12.00	675.00	(4)	
Q8	20¢ Aeroplane Carrying Mail		135.00	25.00	1,400.00	(4)	
Q9	25¢ Manufacturing		65.00	6.75	2,600.00	(6)	
Q10	50¢ Dairying	03/15/13	275.00	40.00	1,900.00	(4)	
Q11	75¢ Harvesting		90.00	35.00	3,900.00	(6)	
Q12	$1 Fruit Growing	01/03/13	350.00	30.00	20,000.00	(6)	

Special Handling Stamps

Issued for use on parcel post packages to secure the same expeditious handling
accorded first class mail matter.

Issues of 1925, 1928-29, 1955, Unwmkd., Perf. 11,							
QE1	10¢ Special Handling	1955	1.50	1.00	20.00	(6)	
a	Wet printing	06/25/28	3.25	1.00			45.00
QE2	15¢ Special Handling	1955	1.75	.90	30.00	(6)	
a	Wet printing	06/25/28	3.25	.90			45.00
QE3	20¢ Special Handling	1955	2.75	1.50	32.50	(6)	
a	Wet printing	06/25/28	4.00	1.50			45.00
QE4	25¢ Special Handling	1929	20.00	7.50	260.00	(6)	
a	25¢ deep grn.	04/11/25	30.00	5.50	330.00	(6)	225.00
	"A" and "T" of "STATES" joined at top		47.50	22.50			
	"T" and "A" of "POSTAGE" joined at top		47.50	45.00			

Parcel Post Postage Due Stamps

Issued for affixing by a postal clerk to any parcel post package to denote the amount to be
collected from the addressee because of insufficient prepayment of postage. Beginning
July 1, 1913 these stamps were valid for use as regular postage due stamps.

Issues of 1913, Wmkd. (190), Perf. 12							
JQ1	1¢ Figure of Value	11/27/13	10.00	4.50	550.00	(6)	
JQ2	2¢ dark green	12/09/13	80.00	17.50	3,750.00	(6)	
JQ3	5¢ dark green	11/27/13	14.50	5.50	600.00	(6)	
JQ4	10¢ dark green	12/12/13	165.00	45.00	9,500.00	(6)	
JQ5	25¢ Figure of Value	12/16/13	95.00	5.00	4,750.00	(6)	

1934-1949

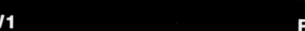

RW1

RW3

RW10

RW13

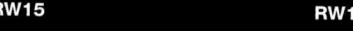

RW15

RW16

Issues of 1934-1955		Un	U	PB	#	Q(M)
Department of Agriculture Duck Stamps						
RW1 $1 Mallards Alighting	1934	700.00	125.00	11,000.00	(6)	0.6
a	Imperf. pair	—				
b	Vert. pair, imperf. horiz.	—				
RW2 $1 Canvasbacks	1935	650.00	130.00	8,500.00	(6)	0.4
RW3 $1 Canada Geese	1936	325.00	72.50	2,750.00	(6)	0.6
RW4 $1 Scaup Ducks	1937	275.00	57.50	2,100.00	(6)	0.8
RW5 $1 Pintail Drake and Hen Alighting	1938	350.00	57.50	2,500.00	(6)	1
Department of the Interior Duck Stamps						
RW6 $1 Green-winged Teal	1939	200.00	45.00	1,700.00	(6)	1
RW7 $1 Black Mallards	1940	200.00	45.00	1,600.00	(6)	1
RW8 $1 Ruddy Ducks	1941	200.00	45.00	1,600.00	(6)	1
RW9 $1 Baldpates	1942	200.00	45.00	1,600.00	(6)	1
RW10 $1 Wood Ducks	1943	75.00	40.00	575.00	(6)	1
RW11 $1 White-fronted Geese	1944	87.50	27.50	625.00	(6)	1
RW12 $1 Shoveller Ducks	1945	60.00	25.00	400.00	(6)	2
RW13 $1 Redhead Ducks	1946	45.00	14.00	290.00	(6)	2
RW14 $1 Snow Geese	1947	45.00	14.00	290.00	(6)	2
RW15 $1 Buffleheads in Flight	1948	50.00	14.00	325.00	(6)	2
RW16 $2 Goldeneye Ducks	1949	60.00	14.00	350.00	(6)	2
RW17 $2 Trumpeter Swans	1950	72.50	11.00	450.00	(6)	2
RW18 $2 Gadwall Ducks	1951	72.50	11.00	475.00	(6)	2
RW19 $2 Harlequin Ducks	1952	72.50	11.00	475.00	(6)	2
RW20 $2 Blue-winged Teal	1953	75.00	10.00	475.00	(6)	2
RW21 $2 Ring-necked Ducks	1954	75.00	9.50	475.00	(6)	2
RW22 $2 Blue Geese	1955	75.00	9.50	475.00	(6)	2

Migratory Bird hunting and Conservation Stamps (popularity known as "Duck Stamps") are sold as hunting permits. While they are sold through many post offices, they are not usable for postage.

Issues of 1956-1982		Un	U	PB	#	Q(M)
Department of the Interior Duck Stamps (continued)						
RW23 $2 American Merganser	1956	75.00	9.50	475.00	(6)	2
RW24 $2 American Eider	1957	75.00	9.50	475.00	(6)	2
RW25 $2 Canada Geese	1958	72.50	9.00	475.00	(6)	2
RW26 $3 Labrador Retriever						
Carrying Mallard Drake	1959	92.50	9.50	450.00	(4)	2
RW27 $3 Redhead Ducks	1960	80.00	9.50	375.00	(4)	2
RW28 $3 Mallard Hen and Ducklings	1961	82.50	9.50	400.00	(4)	1
RW29 $3 Pintail Drakes	1962	95.00	10.50	450.00	(4)	1
RW30 $3 Pair of Brant Landing	1963	95.00	10.50	450.00	(4)	1
RW31 $3 Hawaiian Nene Geese	1964	95.00	10.50	2,100.00	(6)	2
RW32 $3 Three Canvasback Drakes	1965	92.50	10.00	450.00	(4)	2
RW33 $3 Whistling Swans	1966	92.50	10.50	450.00	(4)	2
RW34 $3 Old Squaw Ducks	1967	100.00	10.00	450.00	(4)	2
RW35 $3 Hooded Mergansers	1968	57.50	9.00	275.00	(4)	2
RW36 $3 White-winged Scoters	1969	57.50	7.00	250.00	(4)	2
RW37 $3 Ross's Geese	1970	57.50	7.00	260.00	(4)	2
RW38 $3 Three Cinnamon Teal	1971	40.00	7.00	190.00	(4)	2
RW39 $5 Emperor Geese	1972	25.00	7.00	140.00	(4)	2
RW40 $5 Steller's Eiders	1973	21.00	7.00	100.00	(4)	2
RW41 $5 Wood Ducks	1974	20.00	6.00	82.50	(4)	2
RW42 $5 Canvasbacks Decoy,						
3 Flying Canvasbacks	1975	15.00	6.00	65.00	(4)	2
RW43 $5 Canada Geese	1976	14.00	6.00	57.50	(4)	2
RW44 $5 Pair of Ross's Geese	1977	15.00	6.00	60.00	(4)	2
RW45 $5 Hooded Merganser Drake	1978	12.50	6.00	55.00	(4)	2
RW46 $7.50 Green-winged Teal	1979	14.00	6.00	57.50	(4)	2
RW47 $7.50 Mallards	1980	14.00	6.00	57.50	(4)	2
RW48 $7.50 Ruddy Ducks	1981	14.00	6.00	57.50	(4)	2
RW49 $7.50 Canvasbacks	1982	15.00	6.00	60.00	(4)	2

DUCK STAMP DOLLARS
BUY WETLANDS
FOR WATERFOWL.

IT IS UNLAWFUL TO HUNT
WATERFOWL UNLESS YOU
SIGN YOUR NAME IN INK
ON THE FACE OF THIS STAMP.

RW26-34

BUY DUCK STAMPS
SAVE WETLANDS
•
SEND IN ALL BIRD BANDS
•
SIGN YOUR DUCK STAMP

IT IS UNLAWFUL TO HUNT WATERFOWL UNLESS YOU
SIGN YOUR NAME IN INK ON THE FACE OF THIS STAMP

RW37-53

TAKE PRIDE IN AMERICA
BUY DUCK STAMPS
SAVE WETLANDS
•
SEND IN ALL BIRD BANDS
•
SIGN YOUR DUCK STAMPS

IT IS UNLAWFUL TO HUNT WATERFOWL OR USE THIS STAMP
AS A NATIONAL WILDLIFE ENTRANCE PASS UNLESS YOU
SIGN YOUR NAME IN INK ON THE FACE OF THIS STAMP

RW57

TAKE PRIDE IN AMERICA
BUY DUCK STAMPS
SAVE WETLANDS
•
SEND IN ALL BIRD BANDS
•

IT IS UNLAWFUL TO HUNT WATERFOWL OR USE THIS STAMP
AS A NATIONAL WILDLIFE REFUGE ENTRANCE PASS UNLESS
YOU SIGN YOUR NAME IN INK ON THE FACE OF THIS STAMP.

RW58-present

RW23

RW26

RW33

RW36

RW38

RW54

RW57

RW58

RW59

RW60

RW61

RW62

RW63

RW65

RW66

ssues of 1983-1998			Un	U	PB	#	Q(M)
Department of the Interior Duck Stamps (continued)							
RW50	$7.50 Pintails	1983	15.00	6.00	60.00	(4)	2
RW51	$7.50 Widgeons	1984	15.00	6.00	62.50	(4)	2
RW52	$7.50 Cinnamon Teal	1985	14.00	6.00	57.50	(4)	2
RW53	$7.50 Fulvous Whistling Duck	1986	15.00	6.00	60.00	(4)	2
a	Black omitted		3,750.00				
RW54	$10 Redheads	1987	15.00	9.00	62.50	(4)	2
RW55	$10 Snow Goose	1988	16.00	9.00	65.00	(4)	1
RW56	$12.50 Lesser Scaup	1989	19.00	10.00	77.50	(4)	1
RW57	$12.50 Black Bellied						
	Whistling Duck	1990	19.00	10.00	77.50	(4)	1
RW58	$15 King Eiders	1991	22.50	11.00	92.50	(4)	1
RW59	$15 Spectacled Eider	1992	22.50	11.00	92.50	(4)	1
RW60	$15 Canvasbacks	1993	22.50	11.00	92.50	(4)	1
RW61	$15 Red-breasted Merganser	1994	22.50	11.00	92.50	(4)	1
RW62	$15 Mallards	1995	22.50	11.00	92.50	(4)	
RW63	$15 Surf Scoters	1996	22.50	11.00	92.50	(4)	
RW64	$15 Canada Goose	1997	22.50	11.00	92.50	(4)	
RW65	$15 Barrow's Goldeneye	1998	22.50	11.00	92.50	(4)	
RW66	$15 Greater Scaup	1999	22.50	11.00	100.00	(4)	

At the age of 21, Adam Grimm of Elyria, Ohio, became the youngest person ever to win the Federal Duck Stamp Competition, while at the same time becoming the first Junior Duck Stamp participant to cross over and win the Federal! His winning entry will appear on the **2000-2001 Millennium Federal Duck Stamp**. Adam's entry features a drake mottled duck flapping his wings on the water, a common behavior to relieve excess water trapped on feathers after bathing.

In 1934, with the passage of the Migratory Bird Hunting Stamp Act (Act), an increasingly concerned nation took firm action to stop the destruction of migratory waterfowl and the wetlands so vital to their survival. Under the Act, all waterfowl hunters 16 years of age and over must annually purchase and carry a Federal Duck Stamp.

Approximately 98 cents of every Duck Stamp dollar goes directly into the Migatory Bird Conservation Fund to purchase wetlands and wildlife habitat for inclusion into the National Wildlife Refuge System—a fact that ensures this land will be protected and available for all generations to come. Since 1934, better than $500 million has gone into that Fund to purchase more than 4.5 million acres of habitat.

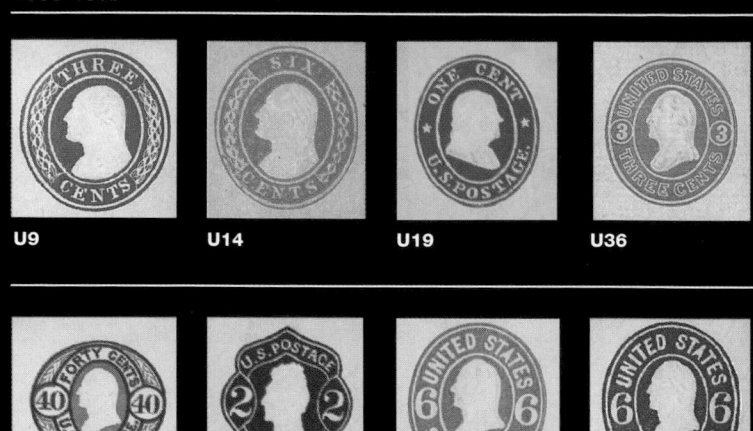

U9   U14   U19   U36

U45   U46   U62   U64

 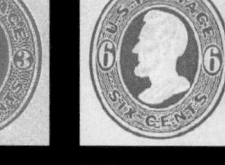 

U84   U85   U97

U103   U113   U142

Issues of 1853-65		Un	U

Represented below is only a partial listing of stamped envelopes. At least one example is listed for most die types; most die types exist on several colors of envelope paper. Values are for cut squares; prices for entire envelopes are higher. Color in italic is the color of the envelope paper; when no color is specified, envelope paper is white. "W" with catalog number indicates wrapper instead of envelope.

		Un	U
U1	3¢ red Washington (top label 13mm wide), *buff*	250.00	20.00
U4	3¢ red Washington (top label 15mm wide) *buff*	275.00	20.00
U5	3¢ red (label has octagonal ends)	4,500.00	375.00
U7	3¢ red (label 20mm wide)	750.00	85.00
U9	3¢ red (label 14½mm)	35.00	3.00
U12	6¢ red Washington, *buff*	130.00	55.00
U14	6¢ green Washington, *buff*	200.00	80.00
U15	10¢ green Washington (label 15½mm wide)	225.00	70.00
U17	10¢ green (label 20mm)	275.00	100.00
a	10¢ pale green	225.00	100.00
U19	1¢ blue Franklin (period after "POSTAGE"), *buff*	32.50	15.00
U23	1¢ blue (bust touches inner frame line), *orange*	450.00	350.00
U24	1¢ blue (no period after "POSTAGE"), *buff*	225.00	90.00
U27	3¢ red, no label, *buff*	22.50	12.50
U28	3¢ + 1¢ (U12 and U9)	350.00	240.00
U30	6¢ red Wash., no label	2,400.00	1,250.00
U33	10¢ green, no label, *buff*	1,100.00	250.00
U34	3¢ pink Washington (outline lettering)	22.50	5.50
U36	3¢ pink, blue (letter sheet)	80.00	50.00
U39	6¢ pink Washington, *buff*	70.00	60.00
U40	10¢ yellow green Wash.	35.00	30.00
U42	12¢ red, brn. Wash., *buff*	190.00	160.00
U44	24¢ Washington, *buff*	200.00	175.00
U45	40¢ blk., red Wash., *buff*	300.00	300.00
U46	2¢ black Jackson ("U.S. POSTAGE" downstroke, tail of "2" unite near point)	35.00	17.50
U49	2¢ black ("POSTAGE" downstroke and tail of "2" touch but do not merge), *orange*	1,200.00	
U50	2¢ blk. Jack. ("U.S. POST." stamp 24-25mm wide), *buff*	14.00	9.00
W51	2¢ blk. Jack. ("U.S. POST." stamp 24-25mm wide), *buff*	175.00	150.00
U54	2¢ blk. Jack. ("U.S. POST." stp. 25½-26½mm), *buff*	14.00	9.00
W55	2¢ blk. Jack. ("U.S. POST." stp. 25½-26½mm), *buff*	75.00	55.00
U58	3¢ pink Washington (solid lettering)	8.00	1.50
U60	3¢ brown Washington	45.00	27.50
U62	6¢ pink Washington	70.00	27.50

Issues of 1863-86		Un	U
U64	6¢ purple Washington	50.00	27.50
U66	9¢ lemon Washington, *buff*	425.00	250.00
U67	9¢ orange Washington, *buff*	100.00	80.00
U68	12¢ brn. Wash., *buff*	350.00	250.00
U69	12¢ red brown Wash., *buff*	90.00	55.00
U70	18¢ red Washington, *buff*	90.00	90.00
U71	24¢ bl. Washington, *buff*	95.00	80.00
U72	30¢ green Washington, *buff*	75.00	75.00
U73	40¢ rose Washington, *buff*	92.50	300.00
U75	1¢ blue Franklin (bust points to end of "N" of "ONE"), *amber*	32.50	27.50
U78	2¢ brown Jackson (bust narrow at back; small, thick numerals)	37.50	15.00
U84	3¢ grn. Washington ("ponytail" projects below bust), *cream*	9.50	4.00
U85	6¢ dark red Lincoln (neck very long at back)	22.50	16.00
a	6¢ vermilion	17.50	16.00
U88	7¢ verm. Stanton (figures 7 normal), *amber*	47.50	*180.00*
U89	10¢ olive blk. Jefferson	550.00	425.00
U92	10¢ brown Jefferson, *amber*	72.50	50.00
U93	12¢ plum Clay (chin prominent)	110.00	82.50
U97	15¢ red orange Webster (has side whiskers), *amber*	140.00	180.00
U99	24¢ purple Scott (locks of hair project, top of head)	130.00	120.00
U103	30¢ black Hamilton (back of bust very narrow), *amber*	200.00	250.00
U105	90¢ carmine Perry (front of bust very narrow, pointed)	140.00	225.00
U113	1¢ lt. blue Frank. (lower part of bust points to end of "E" in "ONE")	1.60	.75
a	1¢ dark blue	7.50	7.50
U114	1¢ lt. blue (lower part of bust points to end of "E" in "Postage"), *amber*	4.25	4.00
U122	2¢ brown Jackson (bust narrow at back; numerals thin)	90.00	37.50
U128	2¢ brown Jackson (numerals in long ovals)	45.00	32.50
U132	2¢ brown, die 3 (left numeral touches oval)	60.00	27.50
U134	2¢ brown Jackson (similar to U128-31 but "O" of "TWO" has center netted instead of plain)	575.00	135.00
U139	2¢ brown (bust broad; numerals short, thick)	40.00	32.50
U142	2¢ verm. Jackson (U139)	6.00	2.75

1874-1886

W155

U159

U172

U190

U204

U218

U250

U294

U314

U348

U351

U358

U368

U374

U377

U379

U386

U390

U393

U398

U400

U406

U416

U429

U447

U468

W485

U522

U523

U524

Issues of 1899-1906	Un	U
U379 1¢ green Franklin, horizontal oval	.70	.20
U386 2¢ carm. Wash. (1 short, 2 long vertical lines at right of "CENTS"), *amber*	1.90	.20
U390 4¢ chocolate Grant	22.50	11.00
U393 5¢ blue Lincoln	20.00	12.50
U398 2¢ carm. Washington, recut die (lines at end of "TWO CENTS" all short), *blue*	3.50	.90
U400 1¢ grn. Frank., oval, die 1 (wide "D" in "UNITED")	.30	.15
U401a 1¢ grn. Frank., die 2 (narrow "D"), *amber*	.90	.70
U402b 1¢, grn. die 3 (wide "S" in "STATES"), *oriental buff*	6.50	1.50
U403c 1¢, die 4 (sharp angle at back of bust, "N," "E" of "ONE" are parallel), *blue*	4.25	1.25
U406 2¢ brn. red Wash., die 1 (oval "O" in "TWO" and "C" in "CENTS")	.80	.15
U407a 2¢, die 2 (like die 1, but hair recut in 2 distinct locks, top of head), *amb.*	100.00	45.00
U408b 2¢, die 3 (round "O" in "TWO" and "C" in "CENTS," coarse letters), *or. buff*	6.50	2.50
U411c 2¢ carmine, die 4 (like die 3 but lettering, hair lines fine, clear)	.40	.20
U412d 2¢ carmine Wash., die 5 (all S's wide), *amber*	.60	.35
U413e 2¢ carm., die 6 (like die 1 but front of bust narrow), *oriental buff*	.55	.35
U414f 2¢ carm., die 7 (like die 6 but upper corner of front of bust cut away), *blue*	12.50	7.50
g 2¢ carm., die 8 (like die 7 but lower stroke of "S" in "CENTS" straight line; hair as in die 2), *blue*	12.50	7.50
U416 4¢ blk. Wash., die 2 ("F" is 1¾mm from left "4")	4.00	2.25
a 4¢, die 1 ("F" is 1mm from left "4")	4.50	3.00
U420 1¢ grn. Frank., round, die 1 ("UNITED" nearer inner circle than outer circle)	.15	.15
U421a 1¢, die 2 (large "U"; "NT" closely spaced), *amber*	300.00	175.00
U423a 1¢ grn. die 3 (knob of hair at back of neck; large "NT" widely spaced), *blue*	.75	.45
b 1¢, die 4 ("UNITED" nearer outer circle than inner)	1.25	.65
c 1¢, die 5 (narrow, oval "C")	.80	.35

Issues of 1907-32	Un	U
U429 2¢ carmine Washington, die 1 (letters broad, numerals vertical, "E" closer than "N" to inner circle)	.15	.15
a 2¢, die 2 (like die 1 but "U" far from left circle), *amber*	9.00	6.00
b 2¢, die 3 (like die 2 but inner circles very thin)	30.00	25.00
U430b 2¢, die 4 (like die 1 but "C" very close to left circle), *amber*	20.00	10.00
c 2¢, die 5 (small head, 8¾mm from tip of nose to back of neck; "TS" of "CENTS" close at bottom)	1.10	.35
U431d 2¢, die 6 (like die 6 but "TS" of "CENTS" far apart at bottom; left numeral slopes right), *oriental buff*	3.00	2.00
e 2¢, die 7 (large head, both numerals slope right, T's have short top strokes)	2.75	1.75
U432h 2¢, die 8 (like die 7 but all T's have long top strokes), *blue*	.60	.25
i 2¢, die 9 (narrow, oval "C")	.90	.30
U436 3¢ dk. violet Washington, die 1 (as 2¢)	.55	.20
U440 4¢ black Washington	1.50	.60
U447 2¢ on 3¢ dark violet, rose surcharge	7.75	6.50
U458 Same as U447, black surcharge, bars 2mm apart	.50	.35
U468 Same as U458, bars 1½mm apart	.70	.45
U481 1½¢ brown Washington, die 1 (as U429)	.15	.15
W485 1½¢ brown, *manila*	.80	.15
U490 1½¢ on 1¢ grn. Franklin, black surcharge	4.00	3.50
U499 1½¢ on 1¢, *manila*	12.50	6.00
U510 1½¢ on 1¢ grn., outline numeral in surcharge	2.40	1.25
U522 2¢ carmine Liberty Bell	1.10	.50
a 2¢, center bar of "E" of "Postage" same length as top bar	7.00	3.75
U523 1¢ ol. grn. Mount Vernon	1.00	.80
U524 1½¢ choc. Mount Vernon	2.00	1.50

Issues of 1916-62		Un	U
U525	2¢ carmine Mount Vernon	.40	.20
a	2¢, die 2 "S" of		
	"POSTAGE" raised	70.00	16.00
U526	3¢ violet Mount Vernon	2.00	.35
U527	4¢ black Mount Vernon	18.00	16.00
U528	5¢ dark blue Mount Vernon	4.00	3.50
U529	6¢ orange Washington	5.50	4.00
U530	6¢ orange Wash., *amber*	11.00	8.00
U531	6¢ or. Washington, *blue*	11.00	10.00
U532	1¢ green Franklin	5.00	1.75
U533	2¢ carmine Wash. (oval)	.75	.25
U534	3¢ dk. violet Washington, die 4		
	(short N in UNITED,thin		
	crossbar in A of STATES)	.40	.20
U535	1½¢ brown Washington	5.00	3.50
U536	4¢ red violet Franklin	.80	.20
U537	2¢ + 2¢ Wash. (U429)	3.25	1.50
U538	2¢ + 2¢ Washington (U533)	.75	.20
U539	3¢ + 1¢ purple, die 1		
	(4½mm tall, thick "3")	15.00	11.00
U540	3¢ + 1¢ purple, die 3		
	(4mm tall, thin "3")	.50	.15
a	Die 2 (4½mm tall,		
	thin "3" in medium		
	circle), entire	*1,000.00*	—
U541	1¼¢ turquoise Franklin	.75	.50
a	Die 2 ("4" 3½mm		
	high), precanceled		1.50
U542	2½¢ dull blue Washington	.85	.50
U543	4¢ brn. Pony Express Rider	.60	.30
U544	5¢ dark blue Lincoln	.85	.20
c	With albino impression		
	of 4¢ U536)	50.00	—
U545	4¢ + 1¢, type 1 (U536)	1.40	.50
U546	5¢ New York World's Fair	.60	.40
U547	1¼¢ brown Liberty Bell		.15
U548	1⁴⁄₁₀¢ brown Liberty Bell		.15
U548A	1⁶⁄₁₀¢ orange Liberty Bell		.15
U549	4¢ blue Old Ironsides	.75	.15
U550	5¢ purple Eagle	.75	.15
a	Tagged	1.25	.15
U551	6¢ green Statue of Liberty	.70	.15
U552	4¢ + 2¢ brt. bl. (U549)	3.75	2.00
U553	5¢ + 1¢ brt. pur. (U550)	3.50	2.50
U554	6¢ lt. blue Herman Melville	.50	.15
U555	6¢ Youth Conference	.75	.15
U556	1⁷⁄₁₀¢ lilac Liberty Bell		.15
U557	8¢ ultramarine Eagle	.40	.15
U561	6¢ + (2¢) lt. grn.	1.00	.30
U562	6¢ + (2¢) lt. blue	2.00	1.60
U563	8¢ rose red Bowling	.50	.15
U564	8¢ Aging Conference	.50	.15
U565	8¢ Transpo '72	.50	.15
U566	8¢ + 2¢ brt. ultra.	.40	.15
U567	10¢ emerald Liberty Bell	.40	.15
U568	1⁸⁄₁₀¢ Volunteer Yourself		.15

Issues of 1962-78		Un	U
U569	10¢ Tennis Centenary	.30	.20
U571	10¢ Compass Rose	.30	.15
a	Brown "10¢/USA"		
	omitted, entire	*125.00*	
U572	13¢ Quilt Pattern	.35	.15
U573	13¢ Sheaf of Wheat	.35	.15
U574	13¢ Mortar and Pestle	.35	.15
U575	13¢ Tools	.35	.15
U576	13¢ Liberty Tree	.30	.15
U577	2¢ red Nonprofit		.15
U578	2.1¢ yel. green Nonprofit		.15
U579	2.7¢ green Nonprofit		.15
U580	15¢ orange Eagle, A	.40	.15
U581	15¢ red Uncle Sam	.40	.15
U582	13¢ emerald Centennial	.35	.15
U583	13¢ Golf	.45	.20
U584	13¢ Energy Conservation	.40	.15
d	Blk, red omitted, ent.	*425.00*	
U585	13¢ Energy Development	.40	.15
U586	15¢ on 16¢ blue USA	.35	.15
U587	15¢ Auto Racing	.35	.15
a	Black omitted, entire	*120.00*	
U588	15¢ on 13¢ (U576)	.35	.15
U589	3.1¢ ultramarine nonprofit		.15
U590	3.5¢ purple Violins		.15
U591	5.9¢ Auth Nonprofit Org		.15
U592	18¢ violet Eagle, B	.45	.20
U593	18¢ dark blue Star	.45	.20
U594	20¢ brown Eagle, C	.45	.15
U595	15¢ Veterinary Medicine	.35	.15
U596	15¢ Summer Oly. Games	.60	.15
a	Red, grn. omitted, ent.	*225.00*	
U597	15¢ Highwheeler Bicycle	.40	.15
a	Blue "15¢ USA"		
	omitted, entire	*100.00*	
U598	15¢ America's Cup	.40	.15
U599	Brown 15¢ Honeybee	.35	.15
a	Brown "15¢ USA"		
	omitted, entire	*125.00*	
U600	18¢ Blind Veterans	.45	.20
U601	20¢ Capitol Dome	.45	.15
U602	20¢ Great Seal of U.S.	.45	.15
U603	20¢ Purple Heart	.45	.15
U604	5.2¢ Auth Nonprofit Org		.15
U605	20¢ Paralyzed Veterans	.45	.15
U606	20¢ Small Business	.50	.15
U607	22¢ Eagle, D	.55	.15
U608	22¢ Bison	.55	.15
U609	6¢ USS Constitution		.15
U610	8.5¢ Mayflower		.15
U611	25¢ Stars	.60	.15
U612	8.4¢ USF Constellation		.15
U613	25¢ Snowflake	.60	.25
U614	25¢ USA, Stars (Philatelic Mail)	.50	.25

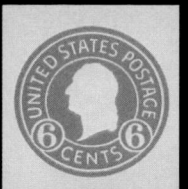

U530

U531

U541

U542

U543

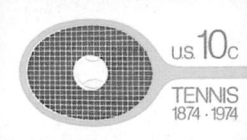

U569

U576

U581

U587

U601

U609

U610

U611

U614

U616

U617

U631

U632

U634

U635

U636

Issues of 1989-92	Un	U
U615 25¢ Stars (lined paper)	.50	.25
U616 25¢ Love	.50	.25
U617 25¢ Space hologram	.60	.30
U618 25¢ Football hologram	.50	.25
U619 29¢ Star	.60	.30
U620 11.1¢ Birds		.20
U621 29¢ Love	.60	.30
U622 29¢ Magazine Industry	.60	.30
U623 29¢ Star and Bars	.60	.30
U624 29¢ Country Geese	.60	.60
U625 29¢ Space Shuttle	.60	.25
U626 29¢ Western Americana	.60	.30
U627 29¢ Protect the Environment	.60	.30
U628 19.8¢ Bulk Rate precanceled		.40

Issues of 1992-95	Un	U
U629 29¢ Disabled Americans	.60	.30
U630 29¢ Kitten	.60	.30
U631 29¢ Football	.60	.30
U632 32¢ Liberty Bell	.65	.30
U634 32¢ Old Glory	.65	.30
U635 5¢ Nonprofit		.15
U636 10¢ Graphic Eagle		.15
U637 32¢ Spiral Heart	.65	.30

Issues of 1995-99	Un	U
U639 32¢ Space Shuttle	.65	.35
U640 32¢ Save Our Environment	.60	.30
U641 32¢ 1996 Paralympic Games	.60	.30
U642 33¢ Flag (yellow, red, blue)	.65	.30

Issues of 1999	Un	U
U643 33¢ Flag (blue & red)	.65	.30
U644 33¢ Victorian Love	.65	.30
U645 33¢ Lincoln	.65	.30

With her strong and emotive voice, **Patsy Cline** took country music to new places. As the first female country singer to successfully cross over to the pop mainstream, Patsy Cline helped blaze a trail for women in country music to follow.

Patsy Cline, whose real name was Virginia Patterson Hensley, was born in 1932, in Winchester, Virginia. She began performing in public as a youngster and made her first records in 1954. Her first big break came in 1957 when she sang "Walking After Midnight" on the television program, *Arthur Godfrey's Talent Scout Show*. The song made both the country and pop charts and established Cline's crossover appeal. She put together a string of hits including, "I Fall to Pieces," "Sweet Dreams," and "Crazy." These songs were examples of the new "Nashville sound," which fused country and pop musical elements.

Patsy Cline died in a plane crash in 1963. She expanded the boundaries of country music and her music continues to influence women singers today. The U.S. Postal Service honored Patsy Cline with a commemorative stamp by Richard Waldrep in 1993. The Patsy Cline stamp is one of four Country & Western stamps, a part of the **Legends of American Music** series.

U639

U640

U641

U642

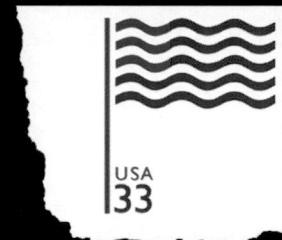

U643

U644

U645

Legends

Get Your Legends
of Baseball Classic
Collection Here!

*Twenty members
of the Baseball
Hall of Fame.*

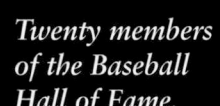

*Join the United States
Postal Service and
Major League Baseball®
in celebrating our
national pastime.*

All twenty players are
nominees to Major League
Baseball's All-Century Team™.

Don't Strike Out!
Get your stamps and
collectibles honoring 20
of baseball's greatest stars.

Collect the stamps and
stamped cards with descrip-
tions on the back of the most
significant achievements in
the careers of each player.
And, for your convenience
and collecting pleasure, we've
created matted panes, press
sheets, and first day covers.

*Major League Baseball trademarks and copyrights are used with permission of
Major League Baseball Properties, Inc.*

Baseball

To order or for more
information visit us at
www.stampsonline.com or
Call 1-800-STAMP-24

*Collection includes
pane of stamps,
matted pane,
stamped card set,
and first day covers
(set of 20).

Item		Price	No.
Full Pane		$6.60	560340
First Day Covers	(Set of 20)	$10.80	560363
Stamped Cards	(Set of 20)	$8.95	560366
Matted Pane		$16.95	560382
Press Sheet		$39.60	560384
Collection*		$38.95	560389

Airmail Envelopes and Aerogrammes

1929-1973

UC1

UC3

UC7

UC8

UC14

UC21

UC25

UC26

UC30

UC39

UC46

Issues of 1946-58	Un	U
UC1 5¢ blue Airplane, die 1		
(vertical rudder is not		
semicircular)	3.50	2.00
1933 wmk., entire	*700.00*	700.00
1937 wmk., entire	—	2,000.00
Bicolored border		
omitted, entire	600.00	
UC2 5¢ blue, die 2 (vertical		
rudder is semicircular)	11.00	5.00
1929 wmk., entire	—	*1,500.00*
1933 wmk., entire	*600.00*	—
UC3 6¢ orange Airplane, die 2a		
("6" is 6½mm wide)	1.45	.40
a With #U436a added		
impression	*3,000.00*	
UC4 6¢ orange, die 2b		
("6" is 6mm wide)	2.75	2.00
UC5 6¢ orange, die 2c		
("6" is 5mm wide)	.75	.30
UC6 6¢ orange, die 3 (vertical		
rudder leans forward)	1.00	.35
a 6¢ orange, *blue*,		
entire	*3,500.00*	2,400.00
UC7 8¢ olive green Airplane	13.00	3.50
UC8 6¢ on 2¢ carm.		
Washington (U429)	1.25	.65
a 6¢ on 1¢ green		
(U420)	*1,750.00*	
c 6¢ on 3¢ purple		
(U437a)	*3,000.00*	
UC9 6¢ on 2¢ Wash. (U525)	75.00	40.00
UC10 5¢ on 6¢ orange (UC3)	2.75	1.50
a Double surcharge	60.00	
Issues of 1946-58		
UC11 5¢ on 6¢ orange (UC4)	9.00	5.50
UC13 5¢ on 6¢ orange (UC6)	.80	.60
a Double surcharge	60.00	
UC14 5¢ carm. DC-4, die 1		
(end of wing on right		
is smooth curve)	.75	.20
UC16 10¢ red, DC-4		
2-line back inscription,		
entire, *pale blue*	7.50	6.00
a "Air Letter" on face,		
4-line back inscription	16.00	14.00
Die-cutting reversed	275.00	
b 10¢ chocolate	400.00	
c "Air Letter" and		
"Aerogramme" on face	45.00	12.50
d 3-line back inscription	8.00	8.00

Issues of 1946-58	Un	U
UC17 5¢ Postage Centenary	.40	.25
UC18 6¢ carm. Airplane (UC14),		
type I (6's lean right)	.35	.15
a Type II (6's upright)	.75	.25
UC20 6¢ on 5¢ (UC15)	.80	.50
a 6¢ on 6¢ carmine,		
entire	*1,500.00*	—
b Double surcharge	*250.00*	
UC21 6¢ on 5¢ (UC14)	27.50	17.50
UC22 6¢ on 5¢ (UC14)	3.50	2.50
a Double surcharge	75.00	
UC23 6¢ on 5¢ (UC17)	*1,850.00*	
UC25 6¢ red Eagle	.75	.50
UC26 7¢ blue (UC14)	.65	.50
Issues of 1958-73		
UC27 6¢ + 1¢ orange (UC3)	250.00	225.00
UC28 6¢ + 1¢ orange (UC4)	65.00	75.00
UC29 6¢ + 1¢ orange (UC5)	37.50	50.00
UC30 6¢ + 1¢ (UC5)	1.00	.50
UC32 10¢ Jet Airliner, back		
inscription in 2 lines	6.00	5.00
a Type 1, entire	10.00	5.00
UC33 7¢ blue Jet Silhouette	.60	.25
UC34 7¢ carmine (UC33)	.60	.25
UC35 11¢ Jet, Globe, entire	2.75	2.25
a Red omitted	*875.00*	
Die-cutting reversed	35.00	
UC36 8¢ red Jet Airliner	.55	.15
UC37 8¢ red Jet in Triangle	.35	.15
a Tagged	1.25	.30
UC39 13¢ John Kennedy, entire	3.00	2.75
a Red omitted	*500.00*	
UC40 10¢ Jet in Triangle	.50	.15
UC41 8¢ + 2¢ (UC37)	.65	.15
UC42 13¢ Human Rights, entire	8.00	4.00
Die-cutting reversed	75.00	
UC43 11¢ Jet in Circle	.50	.15
UC44 15¢ gray, red, white		
and blue Birds in Flight	1.50	1.10
UC45 10¢ + (1¢) (UC40)	1.50	.20
UC46 15¢ red, white, bl.	.75	.40

1973-1999

Issues of 1973-83		Un	U
UC47	13¢ red Bird in Flight	.30	.15
UC48	18¢ USA, entire	.90	.30
UC50	22¢ red and bl. USA, entire	.90	.40
UC51	22¢ blue USA, entire	.70	.25
	Die-cutting reversed	25.00	
UC52	22¢ Summer Olympic		
	Games	1.50	.25
UC53	30¢ blue, red, brn. Tour		
	the United States, entire	.65	.30
a	Red "30" omitted	75.00	
UC54	30¢ *yellow, magenta, blue*		
	and *black* (UC53), entire	.65	.30
	Die-cutting reversed	20.00	
UC55	30¢ Made in USA, entire	.65	.30
UC56	30¢ World Communications		
	Year, entire	.65	.30
	Die-cutting reversed	25.00	

Issues of 1983-99		Un	U
UC57	30¢ Olympic Games, entire	.65	.30
UC58	36¢ Landsat, entire	.70	.35
UC59	36¢ Tourism Week, entire	.70	.35
UC60	36¢ Mark Twain/		
	Halley's Comet, entire	.70	.35
UC61	39¢ Envelope	.80	.40
UC62	39¢ Montgomery Blair	.80	.40
UC63	45¢ Eagle, entire, *blue*	.90	.45
a	White paper	.90	.45
UC64	50¢ Thaddeus Lowe,		
	Balloonist	1.00	.50
UC65	60¢ Voyageurs Nat'l Park,		
	Minnesota	1.25	.65

Born in Hungary in 1899, **Eugene Ormandy** was a professor of violin at Budapest Royal Academy by the age of 17. In 1921, Ormandy went to New York City, where he played violin with, and later conducted, the Capitol Theater Orchestra. After working with Arturo Toscanini in Philadelphia, he conducted an orchestra in Minnesota from 1931 to 1936.

In 1936, he returned to the Philadelphia Orchestra and remained for decades, becoming conductor laureate in 1980. Ormandy guest-conducted and traveled the world over, but always concentrated on taking the Philadelphia Orchestra to new heights. He had a reputation for learning scores quickly, and sometimes conducted from memory. Ormandy was also known for his conservative choices of music, favoring Romanticism over the avant-garde. When he died in 1985, the New York Times called him "the last of the old-fashioned conductors."

In 1997, the U.S. Postal Service issued the **Classical Composers and Conductors** stamps, honoring Eugene Ormandy and seven other musical legends. All eight of the stamps were created by Burton Silverman, an artist whose work for the Postal Service includes the Raoul Wallenberg and Igor Stravinsky stamps.

UC48

UC52

UC53

UC56

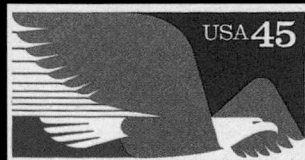

UC57

UC59

UC63

UC65

UC64

UO1

UO16

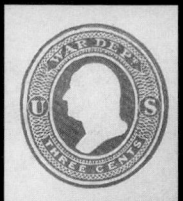

UO20

UO73

UO84

UO88

UO89

Issues of 1873-1875	Un	U
Official Envelopes		
Post Office Department		
Numeral 9½mm high		
UO1 2¢ black, *lemon*	15.00	8.00
Numeral 10½mm high		
UO5 2¢ black, *lemon*	6.00	4.00
UO9 3¢ black, *amber*	45.00	35.00
Postal Service		
UO16 blue, *amber*	50.00	30.00
War Department		
UO20 3¢ dk. red Washington	60.00	40.00
UO26 12¢ dark red Clay	110.00	50.00
UO39 10¢ vermilion Jefferson	200.00	
UO48 2¢ red Jackson, *amber*	25.00	14.00
UO55 3¢ red Washington, *fawn*	4.50	2.75

Issues of 1983-99	Un	U
Penalty Mail Envelopes		
UO73 20¢ blue Great Seal	1.25	30.00
UO74 22¢ (seal embossed)	.90	5.00
UO75 22¢ (seal typographed)	1.00	20.00
UO76 "E" (25¢) Great Seal	1.20	20.00
UO77 25¢ black, blue Great Seal (seal embossed)	.80	5.00
UO78 25¢ (seal typographed)	1.00	25.00
UO79 45¢ (stars illegible)	1.25	—
UO80 65¢ (stars illegible)	1.75	—
UO81 45¢ (stars clear)	1.25	—
UO82 65¢ (stars clear)	1.60	—
UO83 "F" (29¢) Great Seal	1.10	20.00
UO84 29¢ black, blue, entire	.75	10.00
UO88 32¢ Official Mail	.75	10.00
UO89 33¢ Official Mail	.75	—

UX5

UX6

UX11

UX14

UX16

UX18

UX25   **UX27**

UX28

UX37

UX43

UX44

UX45   **UX46**

UX48

UX49

UX50

UX56

Issues of 1873-1917	Un	U

Represented below is only a partial listing of postal cards. Values are for entire cards. Color in italic is color of card. Cards preprinted with written address or message usually sell for much less.

		Un	U
UX1	1¢ brown Liberty, wmkd. (90 x 60mm)	325.00	17.50
UX3	1¢ brown Liberty, wmkd. (53 x 36mm)	70.00	2.25
UX4	1¢ blk. Liberty, wmkd., USPOD in monogram	2,000.00	300.00
UX5	1¢ blk. Liberty, unwmkd.	60.00	.40
UX6	2¢ blue Liberty, *buff*	25.00	17.50
a	2¢ dark blue, *buff*	30.00	19.00
UX7	1¢ (UX5), inscribed "Nothing But The Address"	60.00	.35
a	23 teeth below "One Cent"	500.00	30.00
b	Printed on both sides	*575.00*	*400.00*
UX8	1¢ brown Jefferson, large "one-cent" wreath	45.00	1.25
c	1¢ chocolate	85.00	6.00
UX9	1¢ blk. Jefferson, *buff*	17.50	.55
a	1¢ blk., *dark buff*	20.00	1.25
UX10	1¢ black Grant	32.50	1.40
UX11	1¢ blue Grant	12.50	2.50
UX12	1¢ black Jefferson, wreath smaller than UX14	35.00	.45
UX13	2¢ blue Liberty, *cream*	135.00	75.00
UX14	1¢ Jefferson	25.00	.40
UX15	1¢ black John Adams	40.00	15.00
UX16	2¢ black Liberty	10.00	9.00
UX17	1¢ black McKinley	*4,500.00*	*2,500.00*
UX18	1¢ black McKinley, facing left	12.00	.30
UX19	1¢ black McKinley, triangles in top corners	37.50	.50
UX20	1¢ (UX19), correspondence space at left	50.00	4.00
UX21	1¢ blue McKinley, shaded background	90.00	6.50
a	1¢ bronze blue, *bluish*	165.00	12.50
UX22	1¢ blue McKinley, white background	13.00	.30
UX23	1¢ red Lincoln, solid background	8.00	5.50
UX24	1¢ red McKinley	9.00	.30
UX25	2¢ red Grant	1.25	8.50
UX26	1¢ green Lincoln, solid background	10.00	6.00
UX27	1¢ Jefferson, *buff*	.25	.25
a	1¢ green, *cream*	3.50	.60
UX27C	1¢ green Jefferson, *gray*, die I	2,000.00	150.00
UX28	1¢ green Lincoln, *cream*	.60	.30
a	1¢ green, *buff*	1.50	.60
UX29	2¢ red Jefferson, *buff*	40.00	2.00
a	2¢ lake, *cream*	47.50	2.50
c	2¢ vermilion, *buff*	275.00	60.00

Issues of 1918-68	Un	U

		Un	U
UX30	2¢ red Jefferson, *cream*	27.50	1.50
	Surcharged in one line by canceling machine.		
UX31	1¢ on 2¢ red Jefferson	3,500.00	3,500.00
	Surcharged in two lines by canceling machine.		
UX32	1¢ on 2¢ red Jeff., *buff*	50.00	12.50
a	1¢ on 2¢ vermilion	*95.00*	60.00
b	Double surcharge		82.50
UX33	1¢ on 2¢ red Jefferson, *cream*	12.00	1.90
a	Inverted surcharge	55.00	
b	Double surcharge	55.00	35.00
d	Triple surcharge	350.00	
	Surcharged in two lines by press printing.		
UX34	1¢ on 2¢ red (UX29)	500.00	47.50
UX35	1¢ on 2¢ red Jefferson, *cream*	200.00	32.50
UX36	1¢ on 2¢ red (UX25)		28,500.00
UX37	3¢ red McKinley, *buff*	4.00	*10.00*
UX38	2¢ carmine rose Franklin	.35	.25
a	Double impression	200.00	
	Surcharged by canceling machine in light green.		
UX39	2¢ on 1¢ green Jefferson, *buff*	.50	.35
b	Double surcharge	17.50	20.00
UX40	2¢ on 1¢ green (UX28)	.65	.45
	Surcharged typographically in dark green.		
UX41	2¢ on 1¢ green Jefferson, *buff*	4.50	1.75
a	Inverted surcharge lower left	75.00	125.00
UX42	2¢ on 1¢ green (UX29)	5.00	2.50
b	Surcharged on back	80.00	
UX43	2¢ carmine Lincoln	.30	*1.00*
UX44	2¢ FIPEX	.25	*1.00*
b	Dk. vio. blue omitted	450.00	225.00
UX45	4¢ Statue of Liberty	1.50	*40.00*
UX46	3¢ purple Statue of Liberty	.50	.20
a	"N GOD WE TRUST"	15.00	25.00
UX47	2¢ + 1¢ carmine rose Franklin	185.00	250.00
UX48	4¢ red violet Lincoln	.25	.20
UX49	7¢ World Vacationland	3.75	*35.00*
UX50	4¢ U.S. Customs	.50	*1.00*
a	Blue omitted	450.00	
UX51	4¢ Social Security	.40	*1.00*
b	Blue omitted	*700.00*	
UX52	4¢ blue & red Coast Guard	.30	*1.00*
UX53	4¢ Bureau of the Census	.30	*1.00*
UX54	8¢ blue & red (UX49)	3.75	*35.00*
UX55	5¢ emerald Lincoln	.30	.50
UX56	5¢ Women Marines	.35	*1.00*

Issues of 1970-83		Un	U
UX57	5¢ Weather Services	.30	*1.00*
a	Yellow, black omitted	700.00	
b	Blue omitted	650.00	
c	Black omitted	600.00	
UX58	6¢ brown Paul Revere	.30	1.00
a	Double impression	300.00	
UX59	10¢ blue & red (UX49)	4.00	35.00
UX60	6¢ America's Hospitals	.30	*1.00*
a	Blue, yellow omitted	700.00	
UX61	6¢ USF *Constellation*	.85	*3.00*
a	Address side blank	300.00	
UX62	6¢ black Monument Valley	.40	*3.00*
UX63	6¢ Gloucester, MA	.40	*3.00*
UX64	6¢ blue John Hanson	.25	*1.00*
UX65	6¢ magenta Liberty	.25	*1.00*
UX66	8¢ orange Samuel Adams	.25	*1.00*
UX67	12¢ Visit USA/		
	Ship's Figurehead	.35	30.00
UX68	7¢ Charles Thomson	.30	5.00
UX69	9¢ John Witherspoon	.25	*1.00*
UX70	9¢ blue Caesar Rodney	.25	*1.00*
UX71	9¢ Federal Court House	.25	*1.00*
UX72	9¢ green Nathan Hale	.25	*1.00*
UX73	10¢ Cincinnati Music Hall	.30	*1.00*
UX74	10¢ John Hancock	.30	*1.00*
UX75	10¢ John Hancock	.30	.15
UX76	14¢ Coast Guard Eagle	.40	15.00
UX77	10¢ Molly Pitcher	.30	*1.00*
UX78	10¢ George Rogers Clark	.30	*1.00*
UX79	10¢ Casimir Pulaski	.30	*1.00*
UX80	10¢ Olympic Sprinter	.60	*1.00*
UX81	10¢ Iolani Palace	.30	*1.00*
UX82	14¢ Olympic Games	.60	10.00
UX83	10¢ Salt Lake Temple	.25	*1.00*
UX84	10¢ Landing of Rochambeau	.25	*1.00*
UX85	10¢ Battle of Kings Mtn.	.25	*1.00*
UX86	19¢ Drake's Golden Hinde	.65	10.00
UX87	10¢ Battle of Cowpens	.25	2.50
UX88	12¢ violet Eagle,		
	nondenominated	.30	.50
UX89	12¢ lt. bl. Isaiah Thomas	.30	.50
UX90	12¢ Nathanael Greene	.30	*1.00*
UX91	12¢ Lewis and Clark	.30	*3.00*
UX92	13¢ buff Robert Morris	.30	.50
UX93	13¢ buff Robert Morris	.30	.50
UX94	13¢ "Swamp Fox"		
	Francis Marion	.30	.75
UX95	13¢ LaSalle Claims		
	Louisiana	.30	.75
UX96	13¢ Academy of Music	.30	.75
UX97	13¢ Old Post Office,		
	St. Louis, Missouri	.30	.75
UX100	13¢ Olympic Yachting	.30	.75

Issues of 1984-90		Un	U
UX101	13¢ *Ark* and *Dove*, Maryland	.30	.75
UX102	13¢ Olympic Torch	.30	.75
UX103	13¢ Frederic Baraga	.30	.75
UX104	13¢ Dominguez Adobe	.30	.75
UX105	14¢ Charles Carroll	.30	.50
UX106	14¢ green Charles Carroll	.45	.25
UX107	25¢ Clipper *Flying Cloud*	.70	5.00
UX108	14¢ brt. grn. George Wythe	.30	.50
UX109	14¢ Settlement of		
	Connecticut	.30	.75
UX110	14¢ Stamp Collecting	.30	.75
UX111	14¢ Francis Vigo	.30	.75
UX112	14¢ Settling of Rhode Island	.30	.75
UX113	14¢ Wisconsin Territory	.30	.75
UX114	14¢ National Guard	.30	.75
UX115	14¢ Self-Scouring Plow	.30	.50
UX116	14¢ Constitutional		
	Convention	.30	.50
UX117	14¢ Stars and Stripes	.30	.50
UX118	14¢ Take Pride in		
	America	.30	.50
UX119	14¢ Timberline Lodge	.30	.50
UX120	15¢ Bison and Prairie	.30	.50
UX121	15¢ Blair House	.30	.50
UX122	28¢ *Yorkshire*	.60	3.00
UX123	15¢ Iowa Territory	.30	.50
UX124	15¢ Ohio, Northwest Terr.	.30	.50
UX125	15¢ Hearst Castle	.30	.50
UX126	15¢ The Federalist Papers	.30	.50
UX127	15¢ Hawk and Desert	.30	.50
UX128	15¢ Healy Hall	.30	.50
UX129	15¢ Blue Heron and Marsh	.30	.50
UX130	15¢ Settling of Oklahoma	.30	.50
UX131	21¢ Geese and Mountains	.40	3.00
UX132	15¢ Seagull and Seashore	.30	.50
UX133	15¢ Deer and Waterfall	.30	.50
UX134	15¢ Hull House, Chicago	.30	.50
UX135	15¢ Ind. Hall, Philadelphia	.30	.50
UX136	15¢ Inner Harbor, Baltimore	.30	.50
UX137	15¢ Bridge, New York	.30	.50
UX138	15¢ Capitol, Washington	.30	.50
	#UX139-42 issued in sheets of 4 plus 2		
	inscribed labels, rouletted 9½ on 2 or		
	3 sides.		
UX139	15¢ (UX135)	3.25	.90
UX140	15¢ The White House	3.25	.90
UX141	15¢ (UX137)	3.25	.90
UX142	15¢ (UX138)	3.25	.90
a	Sheet of 4,		
	#UX139-42	13.00	
UX143	15¢ The White House	1.00	1.00
UX144	15¢ Jefferson Memorial	1.00	1.00
UX145	15¢ Papermaking	.30	.30
UX146	15¢ World Literacy Year	.30	.50

UX70

UX79

UX81

UX83

UX94

UX109

UX112

UX113

UX115

UX116

UX118

UX119

America the Beautiful USA**21**

UX131

UX143

UX144

UX143 (picture side)

UX144 (picture side)

1926-1998

UX174

UX175

UX176

UX177

UX198

UX199

UX219A

UX220

UX241

UX263

UX280

UX262

UX282

UX283

UX290

UX292

UX298

Issues of 1990-93	Un	U
UX147 15¢ George Caleb Bingham	1.00	1.00
UX148 15¢ Isaac Royall House	.30	.50
UX150 15¢ Stanford University	.30	.50
UX151 15¢ Constitution Hall	1.00	1.00
UX152 15¢ Chicago Orchestra Hall	.30	.50
UX153 19¢ Flag	.40	.50
UX154 19¢ Carnegie Hall	.40	.50
UX155 19¢ Old Red, UT-Galveston	.40	.50
UX156 19¢ Bill of Rights	.40	.50
UX157 19¢ Notre Dame	.40	.50
UX158 30¢ Niagara Falls	.75	1.40
UX159 19¢ The Old Mill	.40	.50
UX160 19¢ Wadsworth Atheneum	.40	.50
UX161 19¢ Cobb Hall	.40	.50
UX162 19¢ Waller Hall	.40	.50
UX163 19¢ America's Cup	1.00	1.75
UX164 19¢ Columbia River Gorge	.40	.50
UX165 19¢ Ellis Island	.40	.50
UX166 19¢ National Cathedral	.40	.50
UX167 19¢ Wren Building	.40	.50
UX168 19¢ Holocaust Memorial	1.00	1.75
UX169 19¢ Fort Recovery	.40	.50
UX170 19¢ Playmakers Theatre	.40	.50
UX171 19¢ O'Kane Hall	.40	.50

Issues of 1993-98	Un	U
UX172 19¢ Beecher Hall	.40	.50
UX173 19¢ Massachusetts Hall	.40	.50
UX174 19¢ Lincoln's Home	.40	.50
UX175 19¢ Wittenberg University	.40	.50
UX176 19¢ Canyon de Chelly	.40	.50
UX177 19¢ St. Louis Union Station	.40	.50
UX198 20¢ Red Barn	.40	.40
UX199 20¢ Old Glory	.60	.40
UX219A 50¢ Soaring Eagle	1.00	1.50
UX220 20¢ American Clipper Ships	.40	.40
UX241 20¢ Winter Scene	.40	.40
UX262 20¢ St. John's College	.40	.40
UX263 20¢ Princeton University	.40	.40
UX280 20¢ City College of New York	.40	.40
UX281 20¢ Bugs Bunny	.40	.40
UX282 20¢ Pacific 97 Golden Gate Bridge in Daylight	.40	.40
UX283 50¢ Pacific 97 Golden Gate Bridge at Sunset	1.00	1.00
UX284 20¢ Fort McHenry	.40	.40
UX290 20¢ University of Mississippi	.40	.40
UX291 20¢ Sylvester & Tweety	1.20	1.75
UX292 20¢ Girard College	.40	.40
UX298 20¢ Northeastern University	.40	.40

To many, the music of bandleader **Glenn Miller** (1904-1944) is synonymous with the sentimental, romantic yearnings of the World War II era.

Best remembered for performing songs like "In the Mood" and "Moonlight Serenade," Miller's band featured a lead clarinet that became its musical trademark. The band was extremely popular, and even appeared on the silver screen, first in the 1941 film Sun Valley Serenade, which featured the hit "Chattanooga Choo Choo," and in Orchestra Wives in 1942.

During World War II, Miller put together an all-soldier orchestra. Even after his death, his band continued entertaining troops.

In 1996, the U.S. Postal Service honored Glenn Miller when he appeared alongside Count Basie, Benny Goodman, and Tommy and Jimmy Dorsey on the Big Band Leaders stamps. Illustrated by Bill Nelson, these stamps were part of the American Music series.

Issues of 1998-99	Un	U
UX299 20¢ Brandeis University	.40	.40
UX301 20¢ University of		
Wisconsin-Madison	.40	.40
UX302 20¢ Washington and		
Lee University	.40	.40
UX303 20¢ Redwood Library		
& Anthenæum	.40	.40
UX305 20¢ Mount Vernon	.40	.40
UX306 20¢ Block Island Lighthouse	.40	.40

Issues of 1949-66	Un	U
Airmail Postal Cards		
UXC1 4¢ orange Eagle	.50	.75
UXC2 5¢ red Eagle (C48)	1.75	.75
UXC3 5¢ UXC2 redrawn "Air		
Mail-Postal Card" omitted	6.00	2.00
UXC4 6¢ red Eagle	.60	.75
UXC5 11¢ Visit The USA	.60	12.50

 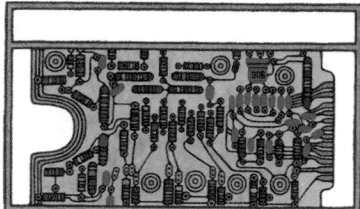

The 1973 **Progress in Electronics** issue celebrates technological advances that changed society. The Marconi spark coil and spark gap, featured on one stamp, were key features of Guglielmo Marconi's wireless telegraphy, which transmitted the electric telegraph signal without wires and led to others' invention of voice radio.

Another stamp depicted transistors and the printed circuit board items that replaced the vacuum tubes and wires used in early radios and computers.

The small size and power requirements of transistors and printed circuits revolutionized electronics. The items shown on the third stamp—microphone, radio speaker, radio tube, and TV camera tube—recall early tools of radio and television broadcasting.

The stamps were illustrated by Naiad and Walter Einsel. Naiad Einsel also illustrated the 1981 Christmas issue, Felt Teddy Bear on Sleigh, while Walter Einsel's Postal Service projects included 50th Anniversary Year of Talking Pictures (1977) and Centennial of Sound Recording (1977).

UX299

UX301

UX302

UX303

UX305

UX306

UXC1

UXC2

UXC4

UXC5

UXC6

UXC7

UXC8

UXC9

UXC10

UXC11

UXC12

UXC13

UXC19

UXC20

UXC23

UXC25

UXC27

UY12

UY41

UZ6

Issues of 1967-1999		Un	U
UXC6	6¢ Virgin Islands	.40	6.00
a	Red, yellow omitted	1,700.00	
UXC7	6¢ Boy Scout		
	World Jamboree	.40	6.00
UXC8	13¢ blue & red (UXC5)	1.25	8.00
UXC9	8¢ Stylized Eagle	.60	2.00
UXC10	9¢ red & blue (UXC5)	.50	1.00
UXC11	15¢ Travel Service	1.75	12.50
UXC12	9¢ black Grand Canyon	.50	8.00
UXC13	15¢ black Niagara Falls	.65	15.00
UXC14	11¢ Stylized Eagle	.70	2.00
UXC15	18¢ Eagle Weather Vane	.85	7.00
UXC16	21¢ Angel Weather Vane	.80	7.50
UXC17	21¢ Curtiss Jenny	.75	6.00
UXC18	21¢ Olympic Gymnast	1.00	10.00
UXC19	28¢ First Transpacific Flight	.90	4.00
UXC20	28¢ Gliders	.90	3.00
UXC21	28¢ Olympic Speed Skater	.90	2.00
UXC22	33¢ China Clipper	.90	2.00
UXC23	33¢ AMERIPEX '86	.65	2.00
UXC24	36¢ DC-3	.70	2.00
UXC25	40¢ Yankee Clipper	.80	1.00
UXC27	Mt. Rainier	1.10	1.00

Issues of 1892-1995		Un	U
Paid Reply Postal Cards			
	Prices are: Un=unsevered,		
	U=severed card.		
UY1	1¢ + 1¢ black Grant	35.00	9.00
UY6	1¢ + 1¢ green G. and M.		
	Washington, double		
	frame line around		
	instructions	150.00	25.00
UY7	1¢ + 1¢ green G. and M.		
	Washington, single		
	frame line	1.25	.50
UY12	3¢ + 3¢ red McKinley	9.00	25.00
UY18	4¢ + 4¢ Lincoln	3.00	2.50
UY23	6¢ + 6¢ John Adams	.90	2.00
UY31	"A" (12¢ + 12¢) Eagle	.75	2.00
UY39	15¢ + 15¢ Bison and Prairie	.75	1.00
UY40	19¢ + 19¢ Flag	.75	1.00
UY41	20¢ Red Barn	.80	1.25
Issues of 1913-95			
Official Mail Postal Cards			
UZ1	1¢ black Numeral	325.00	175.00
UZ2	13¢ blue Great Seal	.60	
UZ3	14¢ blue Great Seal	.60	
UZ4	15¢ blue Great Seal	.60	35.00
UZ5	19¢ blue Great Seal	.55	30.00
UZ6	20¢ Official Mail	.40	30.00

SOUVENIR PAGES SUBSCRIPTION PROGRAM
Collect Every First Day Issue

- Features every stamp issued each year
- Complete with First Day cancellation and informative text
- A convenient, affordable way to collect

The U.S. Postal Service's Souvenir Pages Subscription Program is your ticket to all the year's stamp issues. It's a great way to collect and learn about the stamps and stamp subjects honored during the year.

FUN AND ATTRACTIVE

A Souvenir Page is issued for every stamp—all definitives and commemoratives, peel and stick stamps, coil stamps and booklet panes. Each Souvenir Page includes the featured stamp(s), postmarked with a First Day of Issue cancellation, mounted on an 8" x 10½" page. Information on relevant philatelic specifications and a lively narrative about the history of the stamp's subject are included.

AFFORDABLE COLLECTIBLES

Souvenir Pages are printed in a limited quantity each year. The cost of a Souvenir Page currently is approximately $1.50 per page. (In the rare event that the face value of the stamp[s] affixed exceeds $1.50 the price will be the face value.)

MONEY-BACK GUARANTEE

If you are ever dissatisfied, return your Souvenir Pages within 30 days for a full refund. For more information and an order form, fill out the request card in this book, or call toll-free:

1-800-STAMP24

or visit us at www.stampsonline.com

Souvenir Pages

The Postal Service offers Souvenir Pages for new stamps. The series began with a page for the Yellowstone Park Centennial stamp issued March 1, 1972. The Pages feature one or more stamps tied by the first day cancel, along with technical data and information on the subject of the issue. More than just collectors' items, Souvenir Pages make wonderful show and conversation pieces. Souvenir Pages are issued in limited editions. Number in parentheses ( ) indicates the number of stamps on page if there are more than one.

The identifying numbers used below are based on the Postal Service's numbering system for Souvenir Pages; therefore, they do not follow the Scott numbering system.

	1972	
72-00	Family Planning	450.00
72-01	Yellowstone Park	85.00
72-01a	Yellowstone Park with DC cancel	—
72-02	2¢ Cape Hatteras	70.00
72-03	14¢ Fiorello LaGuardia	75.00
72-04	11¢ City of Refuge Park	75.00
72-05	6¢ Wolf Trap Farm Park	27.50
72-06	Colonial Craftsmen (4)	14.00
72-07	15¢ Mount McKinley	20.00
72-08	6¢-15¢ Olympic Games (4)	10.50
72-08E	Olympic Games with broken red circle on 6¢ stamp	—
72-09	PTA	5.50
72-10	Wildlife Conservation (4)	6.75
72-11	Mail Order	5.50
72-12	Osteopathic Medicine	5.50
72-13	Tom Sawyer	5.50
72-14	7¢ Benjamin Franklin	6.25
72-15	Christmas (2)	6.75
72-16	Pharmacy	5.25
72-17	Stamp Collecting	5.50
	1973	
73-01	$1 Eugene O'Neill	12.50
73-01E	$1 Eugene O'Neill picture perf. error	—
73-02	Love	6.50
73-03	Pamphleteer	4.25
73-04	George Gershwin	5.00
73-05	Broadside	5.75
73-06	Copernicus	4.75
73-07	Postal Employees	5.50
73-08	Harry S. Truman	4.25
73-09	Post Rider	5.50
73-10	21¢ Amadeo Gianninni	4.50
73-11	Boston Tea Party (4)	5.50
73-12	6¢-15¢ Electronics (4)	6.25
73-13	Robinson Jeffers	4.00
73-14	Lyndon B. Johnson	3.50
73-15	Henry O. Tanner	5.00
73-16	Willa Cather	3.25
73-17	Colonial Drummer	4.00
73-18	Angus Cattle	3.50
73-19	Christmas (2)	5.75
73-20	13¢ Winged Envelope airmail	2.75
73-21	10¢ Crossed Flags	2.75
73-22	10¢ Jefferson Memorial	2.50
73-23	13¢ Winged Envelope airmail coil (2)	2.75
	1974	
74-01	26¢ Mount Rushmore airmail	4.75
74-02	ZIP Code	3.25
74-02E	ZIP Code with date error 4/4/74	—
74-03	18¢ Statue of Liberty airmail	5.50
74-04	18¢ Elizabeth Blackwell	2.00
74-05	VFW	2.50
74-06	Robert Frost	2.50
74-07	Expo '74	2.50
74-08	Horse Racing	3.75
74-09	Skylab	5.25
74-10	UPU (8)	4.75
74-11	Mineral Heritage (4)	5.00
74-12	Fort Harrod	2.50
74-13	Continental Congress (4)	4.00
74-14	Chautauqua	1.90
74-15	Kansas Wheat	1.90
74-16	Energy Conservation	1.90
74-17	6.3¢ Liberty Bell coil (2)	2.75
74-18	Sleepy Hollow	2.75
74-19	Retarded Children	2.00
74-20	Christmas (3)	5.00
	1975	
75-01	Benjamin West	2.25
75-02	Pioneer/Jupiter	5.00
75-03	Collective Bargaining	2.50
75-04	8¢ Sybil Ludington	2.50
75-05	Salem Poor	2.50
75-06	Haym Salomon	2.75
75-07	18¢ Peter Francisco	3.25
75-08	Mariner 10	4.25
75-09	Lexington & Concord	2.50
75-10	Paul Dunbar	3.25
75-11	D.W. Griffith	2.50
75-12	Bunker Hill	2.50
75-13	Military Uniforms (4)	5.00
75-14	Apollo Soyuz (2)	5.00
75-15	International Women's Year	2.00
75-16	Postal Service Bicentennial (4)	3.25
75-17	World Peace Through Law	2.00
75-18	Banking & Commerce (2)	2.00
75-19	Christmas (2)	3.00
75-20	3¢ Francis Parkman	2.50
75-21	11¢ Freedom of the Press	2.00
75-22	24¢ Old North Church	1.90
75-23	Flag over Independence Hall (2)	2.00
75-24	9¢ Freedom to Assemble (2)	2.00
75-25	Liberty Bell coil (2)	2.00
75-26	Eagle & Shield	2.50
	1976	
76-01	Spirit of '76 (3)	3.25
76-01E	Spirit of '76 with cancellation error Jan. 2, 1976 (3)	—
76-02	25¢ and 31¢ Plane and Globes airmails (2)	2.75
76-03	Interphil '76	2.50
76-04	State Flags, DE to VA (10)	7.00
76-05	State Flags, NY to MS (10)	7.00
76-06	State Flags, IL to WI (10)	7.00
76-07	State Flags, CA to SD (10)	7.00
76-08	State Flags, MT to HI (10)	7.00
76-09	9¢ Freedom to Assemble coil (2)	1.75

76-10	Telephone Centennial	1.75
76-11	Commercial Aviation	2.00
76-12	Chemistry	1.75
76-13	7.9¢ Drum coil (2)	1.90
76-14	Benjamin Franklin	1.75
76-15	Bicentennial souvenir sheet	8.00
76-15E	13¢ Bicentennial souvenir sheet with perforation and numerical errors	—
76-16	18¢ Bicentennial souvenir sheet	8.00
76-17	24¢ Bicentennial souvenir sheet	8.00
76-18	31¢ Bicentennial souvenir sheet	8.00
76-19	Declaration of Independence (4)	4.00
76-20	Olympics (4)	4.25
76-21	Clara Maass	1.75
76-22	Adolph S. Ochs	1.75
76-23	Christmas (3)	2.25
76-24	7.7¢ Saxhorns coil (2)	1.75
1977		
77-01	Washington at Princeton	1.90
77-02	Flag over Capitol booklet pane (9¢ and 13¢) Perf. 10 (8)	16.00
77-03	Sound Recording	1.75
77-04	Pueblo Pottery (4)	2.25
77-05	Lindbergh Flight	2.75
77-06	Colorado Centennial	1.90
77-07	Butterflies (4)	2.00
77-08	Lafayette	1.75
77-09	Skilled Hands (4)	2.25
77-10	Peace Bridge	1.65
77-11	Battle of Oriskany	1.65
77-12	Alta, CA, First Civil Settlement	1.65
77-13	Articles of Confederation	1.75
77-14	Talking Pictures	2.50
77-15	Surrender at Saratoga	2.50
77-16	Energy (2)	1.65
77-17	Christmas, Mailbox and Christmas, Valley Forge, Omaha cancel (2)	2.00
77-18	Same, Valley Forge cancel	—
77-19	10¢ Petition for Redress coil (2)	2.75
77-20	10¢ Petition for Redress sheet (2)	2.25
77-21	1¢-4¢ Americana (5)	2.00
1978		
78-01	Carl Sandburg	2.00
78-02	Indian Head Penny	2.00
78-03	Captain Cook, Anchorage cancel (2)	2.00
78-04	Captain Cook, Honolulu cancel (2)	2.00
78-05	Harriet Tubman	3.00
78-06	American Quilts (4)	2.50
78-07	16¢ Statue of Liberty sheet and coil (2)	1.90
78-08	29¢ Sandy Hook Lighthouse	1.90
78-09	American Dance (4)	2.50
78-10	French Alliance	1.90
78-11	Early Cancer Detection	2.50
78-12	"A" (15¢) sheet and coil (2)	4.50
78-13	Jimmie Rodgers	3.00
78-14	CAPEX '78 (8)	6.25
78-15	Oliver Wendell Holmes coil	1.90
78-16	Photography	1.90
78-17	Fort McHenry Flag sheet and coil (2)	2.00
78-18	George M. Cohan	1.65
78-19	Rose booklet single	2.50
78-20	8.4¢ Piano coil (2)	2.00
78-21	Viking Missions	3.75
78-22	28¢ Remote Outpost	2.00
78-23	American Owls (4)	2.50
78-24	31¢ Wright Brothers airmails (2)	2.75
78-25	American Trees (4)	2.75
78-26	Christmas, Madonna	2.00
78-27	Christmas, Hobby Horse	2.00
78-28	$2 Kerosene Lamp	5.25
1979		
79-01	Robert F. Kennedy	2.00
79-02	Martin Luther King, Jr.	3.50
79-03	International Year of the Child	1.90
79-04	John Steinbeck	1.90
79-05	Albert Einstein	2.25
79-06	21¢ Octave Chanute airmails (2)	2.75
79-07	Pennsylvania Toleware (4)	2.25
79-08	American Architecture (4)	2.25
79-09	Endangered Flora (4)	2.50
79-10	Seeing Eye Dogs	1.90
79-11	Candle & Holder	4.25
79-12	Special Olympics	1.90
79-13	$5 Lantern	10.50
79-14	30¢ Schoolhouse	3.00
79-15	10¢ Summer Olympics (2)	2.75
79-16	50¢ Whale Oil Lamp	3.25
79-17	John Paul Jones	2.00
79-18	Summer Olympics (4)	3.75
79-19	Christmas, Madonna	2.50
79-20	Christmas, Santa Claus	2.50
79-21	3.1¢ Guitar coil (2)	3.50
79-22	31¢ Summer Olympics airmail	4.00
79-23	Will Rogers	1.90
79-24	Vietnam Veterans	1.90
79-25	25¢ Wiley Post airmails (2)	3.25
1980		
80-01	W.C. Fields	2.00
80-02	Winter Olympics (4)	5.00
80-03	Windmills booklet pane (10)	4.00
80-04	Benjamin Banneker	3.50
80-05	Letter Writing (6)	2.25
80-06	1¢ Ability to Write (2)	1.65
80-07	Frances Perkins	1.50
80-08	Dolley Madison	3.00
80-09	Emily Bissell	1.90
80-10	3.5¢ Violins coil (2)	2.50
80-11	Helen Keller/ Anne Sullivan	1.90
80-12	Veterans Administration	1.50
80-13	General Bernardo de Galvez	1.50
80-14	Coral Reefs (4)	1.90
80-15	Organized Labor	3.25
80-16	Edith Wharton	3.00
80-17	Education	3.00
80-18	Indian Masks (4)	2.50
80-19	American Architecture (4)	1.90
80-20	40¢ Philip Mazzei airmail	2.75
80-21	Christmas, Madonna	2.50
80-22	Christmas, Antique Toys	2.50
80-23	Sequoyah	1.50
80-24	28¢ Blanche Scott airmail	1.65
80-25	35¢ Glenn Curtiss airmail	1.65
1981		
81-01	Everett Dirksen	1.50
81-02	Whitney M. Young	3.25
81-03	"B" (18¢) sheet and coil (3)	2.00
81-04	"B" (18¢) booklet pane (8)	2.25
81-05	12¢ Freedom of Conscience sheet and coil (3)	1.90
81-06	Flowers block (4)	2.00
81-07	Flag and Anthem sheet and coil (3)	2.50
81-08	Flag and Anthem booklet pane (8 - 6¢ and 18¢)	2.50
81-09	American Red Cross	1.50
81-10	George Mason	1.50
81-11	Savings & Loans	1.50
81-12	Wildlife booklet pane (10)	—
81-13	Surrey coil (2)	2.75
81-14	Space Achievement (8)	6.75
81-15	17¢ Rachel Carson (2)	1.40
81-16	35¢ Charles Drew, MD	2.50
81-17	Professional Management	1.40
81-18	17¢ Electric Auto coil (2)	3.25
81-19	Wildlife Habitat (4)	2.00
81-20	International Year of the Disabled	1.50
81-21	Edna St. Vincent Millay	2.50
81-22	Alcoholism	2.50
81-23	American Architecture (4)	2.50
81-24	Babe Zaharias	4.25
81-25	Bobby Jones	4.25
81-26	Frederic Remington	1.50
81-27	"C" (20¢) sheet and coil (3)	3.25
81-28	"C" (18¢) booklet pane (10)	3.25
81-29	18¢ and 20¢ Hoban (2)	1.65
81-30	Yorktown/ Virginia Capes (2)	2.00
81-31	Christmas, Madonna	2.75
81-32	Christmas, Bear on Sleigh	3.00
81-33	John Hanson	1.40
81-34	Fire Pumper coil (2)	5.00
81-35	Desert Plants (4)	2.50

81-36	9.3¢ Mail Wagon coil (3)	3.75
81-37	Flag over Supreme Court sheet and coil (3)	3.75
81-38	Flag over Supreme Court booklet pane (6)	3.25

1982

82-01	Sheep booklet pane (10)	3.00
82-02	Ralph Bunche	4.00
82-03	13¢ Crazy Horse (2)	1.65
82-04	37¢ Robert Millikan	1.40
82-05	Franklin D. Roosevelt	1.50
82-06	Love	1.50
82-07	5.9¢ Bicycle coil (4)	5.75
82-08	George Washington	3.25
82-09	10.9¢ Hansom Cab coil (2)	4.25
82-10	Birds & Flowers, AL-GE (10)	10.00
82-11	Birds & Flowers, HI-MD (10)	10.00
82-12	Birds & Flowers, MA-NJ (10)	10.00
82-13	Birds & Flowers, NM-SC (10)	10.00
82-14	Birds & Flowers, SD-WY (10)	10.00
82-15	USA/Netherlands	1.50
82-16	Library of Congress	1.40
82-17	Consumer Education coil (2)	3.25
82-18	Knoxville World's Fair (4)	1.75
82-19	Horatio Alger	1.50
82-20	2¢ Locomotive coil (2)	3.50
82-21	Aging Together	1.50
82-22	The Barrymores	2.50
82-23	Mary Walker	1.65
82-24	Peace Garden	1.65
82-25	America's Libraries	1.40
82-26	Jackie Robinson	14.00
82-27	4¢ Stagecoach coil (3)	4.00

82-28	Touro Synagogue	1.50
82-29	Wolf Trap Farm Park	1.40
82-30	American Architecture (4)	2.00
82-31	Francis of Assisi	1.40
82-32	Ponce de Leon	1.40
82-33	13¢ Kitten & Puppy (2)	2.75
82-34	Christmas, Madonna	2.50
82-35	Christmas, Seasons Greetings (4)	2.75
82-36	2¢ Igor Stravinsky (2)	2.00

1983

83-01	1¢, 4¢, 13¢ Penalty Mail (5)	2.50
83-02	17¢ Penalty Mail (4)	2.25
83-03	Penalty Mail coil (2)	3.25
83-04	$1 Penalty Mail	4.00
83-05	$5 Penalty Mail	9.50
83-06	Science & Industry	1.65
83-07	5.2¢ Antique Sleigh coil (4)	4.75
83-08	Sweden/USA Treaty	2.00
83-09	3¢ Handcar coil (3)	3.25
83-10	Balloons (4)	1.90
83-11	Civilian Conservation Corps	1.25
83-12	40¢ Olympics airmails (4)	2.75
83-13	Joseph Priestley	1.65
83-14	Volunteerism	1.50
83-15	Concord/German Immigration	1.50
83-16	Physical Fitness	1.65
83-17	Brooklyn Bridge	2.00
83-18	TVA	1.50
83-19	4¢ Carl Schurz (5)	1.50
83-20	Medal of Honor	2.50
83-21	Scott Joplin	3.25
83-22	Thomas H. Gallaudet	1.50
83-23	28¢ Olympics (4)	3.00
83-24	5¢ Pearl S. Buck (4)	1.65

83-25	Babe Ruth	10.00
83-26	Nathaniel Hawthorne	1.65
83-27	3¢ Henry Clay (7)	1.40
83-28	13¢ Olympics (4)	3.25
83-29	$9.35 Eagle booklet single	110.00
83-30	$9.35 Eagle booklet pane (3)	140.00
83-31	1¢ Omnibus coil (3)	3.50
83-32	Treaty of Paris	1.90
83-33	Civil Service	1.50
83-34	Metropolitan Opera	1.90
83-35	Inventors (4)	2.00
83-36	1¢ Dorothea Dix (3)	1.90
83-37	Streetcars (4)	2.25
83-38	5¢ Motorcycle coil (4)	4.75
83-39	Christmas, Madonna	2.00
83-40	Christmas, Santa Claus	1.90
83-41	35¢ Olympics airmails (4)	2.50
83-42	Martin Luther	2.50
83-43	Flag over Supreme Court booklet pane (10)	3.00

1984

84-01	Alaska Statehood	2.00
84-02	Winter Olympics (4)	2.25
84-03	FDIC	1.65
84-04	Harry S. Truman	1.50
84-05	Love	1.65
84-06	Carter G. Woodson	3.25
84-07	11¢ RR Caboose coil (2)	3.50
84-08	Soil & Water Conservation	1.65
84-09	Credit Union Act	1.65
84-10	40¢ Lillian M. Gilbreth	1.40
84-11	Orchids (4)	2.25
84-12	Hawaii Statehood	1.65
84-13	7.4¢ Baby Buggy coil (3)	3.50
84-14	National Archives	1.50

84-15	20¢ Summer Olympics (4)	3.50	85-29	14¢ and 22¢ Penalty Mail sheet and coil (4)	3.25	
84-16	New Orleans World's Fair	1.50	85-30	AMERIPEX '86	1.65	
84-17	Health Research	1.50	85-31	9¢ Sylvanus Thayer (3)	2.00	
84-18	Douglas Fairbanks	1.90	85-32	3.4¢ School Bus coil (7)	4.25	
84-19	Jim Thorpe	7.75	85-33	11¢ Stutz Bearcat coil (2)	3.50	
84-20	10¢ Richard Russell (2)	1.25	85-34	Abigail Adams	1.50	
84-21	John McCormack	2.00	85-35	4.9¢ Buckboard coil (5)	4.25	
84-22	St. Lawrence Seaway	1.65	85-36	8.3¢ Ambulance coil (3)	4.00	
84-23	Migratory Bird Hunting and Conservation Stamp Act	4.00	85-37	Frederic Bartholdi	3.25	
84-24	Roanoke Voyages	1.65	85-38	8¢ Henry Knox (3)	1.50	
84-25	Herman Melville	1.75	85-39	Korean War Veterans	2.50	
84-26	Horace Moses	1.65	85-40	Social Security Act	2.00	
84-27	Smokey Bear	4.75	85-41	44¢ Father Junipero Serra airmail	2.00	
84-28	Roberto Clemente	11.00	85-42	World War I Veterans	2.00	
84-29	30¢ Frank C. Laubach	1.40	85-43	6¢ Walter Lippmann (4)	1.75	
84-30	Dogs (4)	3.25	85-44	Horses (4)	3.50	
84-31	Crime Prevention	2.00	85-45	Public Education	2.00	
84-32	Family Unity	2.50	85-46	International Youth Year (4)	2.50	
84-33	Eleanor Roosevelt	2.50	85-47	Help End Hunger	2.00	
84-34	Nation of Readers	2.25	85-48	21.1¢ Letters coil (2)	2.50	
84-35	Christmas, Madonna	2.25	85-49	Christmas, Madonna	2.00	
84-36	Christmas, Santa Claus	2.25	85-50	Christmas, Poinsettias	2.50	
84-37	Hispanic Americans	1.50	85-51	18¢ Washington/ Washington Monument coil (2)	2.25	
84-38	Vietnam Veterans Memorial	2.75	**1986**			

1985			86-01	Arkansas Statehood	1.50	
85-01	Jerome Kern	2.50	86-02	25¢ Jack London	1.75	
85-02	7¢ Abraham Baldwin (3)	2.50	86-03	Stamp Collecting booklet pane (4)	4.00	
85-03	"D" (22¢) sheet and coil (3)	2.25	86-04	Love	2.25	
85-04	"D" (22¢) booklet pane (10)	3.75	86-05	Sojourner Truth	2.75	
85-05	"D" (22¢) Penalty Mail sheet and coil (3)	1.65	86-06	5¢ Hugo L. Black (5)	2.50	
85-06	11¢ Alden Partridge (2)	1.50	86-07	Republic of Texas (2)	1.50	
85-07	33¢ Alfred Verville airmail	1.65	86-08	$2 William Jennings Bryan	3.75	
85-08	39¢ Lawrence & Elmer Sperry airmail	2.00	86-09	Fish booklet pane (5)	3.50	
85-09	44¢ Transpacific airmail	2.00	86-10	Public Hospitals	1.25	
85-10	50¢ Chester Nimitz	1.75	86-11	Duke Ellington	3.25	
85-11	Mary McLeod Bethune	2.50	86-12	Presidents, Washington- Harrison (9)	4.25	
85-12	39¢ Grenville Clark	1.25	86-13	**Presidents, Tyler-Grant (9)**	4.25	
85-13	14¢ Sinclair Lewis (2)	1.50	86-14	Presidents, Hayes-Wilson (9)	4.25	
85-14	Duck Decoys (4)	2.25	86-15	Presidents, Harding-Johnson (9)	4.25	
85-15	14¢ Iceboat coil (2)	3.50	86-16	Polar Explorers (4)	3.25	
85-16	Winter Special Olympics	2.00	86-17	17¢ Belva Ann Lockwood (2)	2.25	
85-17	Flag over Capitol sheet and coil (3)	2.25	86-18	1¢ Margaret Mitchell (3)	1.90	
85-18	Flag over Capitol booklet pane (5)	2.50	86-19	Statue of Liberty	3.00	
85-19	12¢ Stanley Steamer coil (2)	3.75	86-20	4¢ Father Flanagan (3)	1.65	
85-20	Seashells booklet pane (10)	3.75	86-21	17¢ Dog Sled coil (2)	3.00	
85-21	Love	3.25	86-22	56¢ John Harvard	1.75	
85-22	10.1¢ Oil Wagon coil (3)	2.75	86-23	Navajo Blankets (4)	2.75	
85-23	12.5¢ Pushcart coil (2)	3.25	86-24	3¢ Paul Dudley White, MD (8)	2.00	
85-24	John J. Audubon	1.90	86-25	**$1 Bernard Revel**	**2.00**	
85-25	$10.75 Eagle booklet single	37.50	86-26	T.S. Eliot	1.50	
85-26	$10.75 Eagle booklet pane (3)	72.50	86-27	Wood-Carved Figurines (4)	2.00	
85-27	6¢ Tricycle coil (4)	3.25				
85-28	Rural Electrification Administration	1.65				

86-28	Christmas, Madonna	2.25				
86-29	Christmas, Village Scene	2.25				
86-30	5.5¢ Star Route Truck coil (4)	3.25				
86-31	25¢ Bread Wagon coil	3.25				
1987						
87-01	8.5¢ Tow Truck coil (5)	2.50				
87-02	Michigan Statehood	2.50				
87-03	Pan American Games	2.50				
87-04	Love	3.00				
87-05	7.1¢ Tractor coil (5)	2.50				
87-06	14¢ Julia Ward Howe (2)	1.50				
87-07	Jean Baptiste Pointe Du Sable	4.50				
87-08	Enrico Caruso	2.00				
87-09	2¢ Mary Lyon (3)	2.00				
87-10	Reengraved 2¢ Locomotive coil (6)	2.75				
87-11	Girl Scouts	3.25				
87-12	10¢ Canal Boat coil (5)	3.00				
87-13	Special Occasions booklet pane (10)	4.50				
87-14	United Way	1.75				
87-15	Flag with Fireworks	1.75				
87-16	Flag over Capitol coil, prephosphored paper (2)	—				
87-17	Wildlife, Swallow-Squirrel (10)	5.00				
87-18	Wildlife, Armadillo-Rabbit (10)	5.00				
87-19	Wildlife, Tanager-Ladybug (10)	5.00				
87-20	Wildlife, Beaver-Prairie Dog (10)	5.00				
87-21	Wildlife, Turtle-Fox (10)	5.00				
87-22	Delaware Statehood	1.90				
87-23	U.S./Morocco Friendship	1.75				
87-24	William Faulkner	1.75				
87-25	Lacemaking (4)	3.25				
87-26	10¢ Red Cloud (3)	1.50				
87-27	$5 Bret Harte	9.50				
87-28	Pennsylvania Statehood	2.00				
87-29	Drafting of the Constitution booklet pane (5)	3.25				
87-30	New Jersey Statehood	2.50				
87-31	Signing of Constitution	2.00				
87-32	Certified Public Accountants	3.75				
87-33	5¢ Milk Wagon and 17.5¢ Racing Car coils (4)	3.00				
87-34	Locomotives booklet pane (5)	6.75				
87-35	Christmas, Madonna	2.00				
87-36	Christmas, Ornaments	1.75				
87-37	Flag with Fireworks booklet-pair	2.75				
1988						
88-01	Georgia Statehood	2.00				
88-02	Connecticut Statehood	2.00				
88-03	Winter Olympics	1.75				
88-04	Australia Bicentennial	1.90				
88-05	James Weldon Johnson	3.00				
88-06	Cats (4)	3.50				
88-07	Massachusetts Statehood	2.25				

88-08	Maryland Statehood	2.25
88-09	3¢ Conestoga Wagon coil (8)	2.50
88-10	Knute Rockne	5.00
88-11	"E" (25¢) Earth sheet and coil (3)	2.00
88-12	"E" (25¢) Earth booklet pane (10)	4.75
88-13	"E" (25¢) Penalty Mail coil (2)	2.00
88-14	44¢ New Sweden airmail	2.00
88-15	Pheasant booklet pane (10)	4.25
88-16	Jack London booklet pane (6)	3.25
88-17	Jack London booklet pane (10)	4.25
88-18	Flag with Clouds	1.65
88-19	45¢ Samuel Langley airmail	2.00
88-19A	20¢ Penalty Mail coil (2)	2.25
88-20	Flag over Yosemite coil (2)	2.00
88-21	South Carolina Statehood	2.00
88-22	Owl & Grosbeak booklet pane (10)	4.00
88-23	15¢ Buffalo Bill Cody (2)	1.90
88-24	15¢ and 25¢ Penalty Mail coils (4)	2.75
88-25	Francis Ouimet	6.00
88-26	45¢ Harvey Cushing, MD	1.65
88-27	New Hampshire Statehood	2.00
88-28	36¢ Igor Sikorsky airmail	2.75
88-29	Virginia Statehood	2.00
88-30	10.1¢ Oil Wagon coil, precancel (3)	—
88-31	Love	2.00
88-32	Flag with Clouds booklet pane (6)	4.00
88-33	16.7¢ Popcorn Wagon coil (2)	2.50
88-34	15¢ Tugboat coil (2)	2.00
88-35	13.2¢ Coal Car coil (2)	3.00
88-36	New York Statehood	2.50
88-37	45¢ Love	2.00
88-38	8.4¢ Wheelchair coil (3)	2.50
88-39	21¢ Railroad Mail Car coil (2)	3.00
88-40	Summer Olympics	2.00
88-41	Classic Cars booklet pane (5)	4.75
88-42	7.6¢ Carreta coil (4)	3.00
88-43	Honeybee coil (2)	4.25
88-44	Antarctic Explorers (4)	2.75
88-45	5.3¢ Elevator coil (5)	3.00
88-46	20.5¢ Fire Engine coil (2)	3.50
88-47	Carousel Animals (4)	3.25
88-48	$8.75 Eagle	20.00
88-49	Christmas, Madonna	2.00
88-50	Christmas, Snow Scene	2.00
88-51	21¢ Chester Carlson	1.50
88-52	Special Occasions booklet pane (6), Love You, Thinking of You	9.25
88-53	Special Occasions booklet pane (6), Happy Birthday, Best Wishes	14.00
88-54	24.1¢ Tandem Bicycle coil (2)	3.00
88-55	20¢ Cable Car coil (2)	3.00
88-56	13¢ Patrol Wagon coil (2)	3.00
88-57	23¢ Mary Cassatt	1.90
88-58	65¢ H.H. "Hap" Arnold	2.25
1989		
89-01	Montana Statehood	1.75
89-02	A. Philip Randolph	3.25
89-03	Flag over Yosemite coil, prephosphored paper (2)	2.50
89-04	North Dakota Statehood	1.90
89-05	Washington Statehood	1.90
89-06	Steamboats booklet pane (5)	3.50
89-07	World Stamp Expo '89	2.00
89-08	Arturo Toscanini	1.75
89-09	U.S. House of Representatives	2.25
89-10	U.S. Senate	2.25
89-11	Executive Branch	2.25
89-12	South Dakota Statehood	2.00
89-13	7.1¢ Tractor coil, precancel (4)	2.50
89-14	$1 Johns Hopkins	2.50
89-15	Lou Gehrig	9.25
89-16	1¢ Penalty Mail	2.75
89-17	45¢ French Revolution airmail	3.00
89-18	Ernest Hemingway	1.65
89-19	$2.40 Moon Landing	12.50
89-20	North Carolina Statehood	2.00
89-21	Letter Carriers	1.65
89-22	28¢ Sitting Bull	1.75
89-23	Drafting of the Bill of Rights	2.00
89-24	Prehistoric Animals (4)	7.50
89-25	25¢ and 45¢ PUAS-America (2)	2.50
89-26	Christmas, Madonna	7.00
89-27	Christmas, Antique Sleigh	6.75
89-28	Eagle and Shield, self-adhesive	2.25
89-29	World Stamp Expo '89 souvenir sheet	7.00
89-30	Classic Mail Transportation (4)	2.75
89-31	Future Mail Transportation souvenir sheet	5.25
89-32	45¢ Future Mail Transportation airmails (4)	5.25
89-33	Classic Mail Transportation souvenir sheet	5.75
1990		
90-01	Idaho Statehood	2.00
90-02	Love sheet and booklet pane (10)	4.75
90-03	Ida B. Wells	3.75
90-04	U.S. Supreme Court	2.00
90-05	15¢ Beach Umbrella booklet pane (10)	3.50
90-06	5¢ Luis Munoz Marin (5)	2.00
90-07	Wyoming Statehood	2.00
90-08	Classic Films (4)	5.00
90-09	Marianne Moore	2.00
90-10	$1 Seaplane coil (2)	5.75
90-11	Lighthouses booklet pane (5)	5.00
90-12	Plastic Flag stamp	3.25
90-13	Rhode Island Statehood	2.75
90-14	$2 Bobcat	5.00
90-15	Olympians (5)	5.75
90-16	Indian Headdresses booklet pane (10)	6.50
90-17	5¢ Circus Wagon coil (5)	3.25
90-18	40¢ Claire Lee Chennault	3.25
90-19	Federated States of Micronesia/ Marshall Islands (2)	2.75
90-20	Creatures of the Sea (4)	4.75
90-21	25¢ and 45¢ PUAS/America (2)	3.00
90-22	Dwight D. Eisenhower	2.25
90-23	Christmas, Madonna, sheet and booklet pane (11)	5.75
90-24	Christmas, Yule Tree, sheet and booklet pane (11)	5.75
1991		
91-01	"F" (29¢) Flower sheet and coil (3)	3.25
91-02	"F" (29¢) Flower booklet panes (20)	11.00
91-03	4¢ Makeup	2.25
91-04	"F" (29¢) ATM booklet single	2.75
91-05	"F" (29¢) Penalty Mail coil (2)	3.25
91-06	4¢ Steam Carriage coil (7)	3.25
91-07	50¢ Switzerland	2.75
91-08	Vermont Statehood	2.75
91-09	19¢ Fawn (2)	2.75
91-10	Flag over Mount Rushmore coil (2)	2.75
91-11	35¢ Dennis Chavez	2.50
91-12	Flower sheet and booklet pane (10)	6.25
91-13	4¢ Penalty Mail (8)	2.50
91-14	Wood Duck booklet panes (10)	11.00
91-15	23¢ Lunch Wagon coil (2)	2.75
91-16	Flag with Olympic Rings booklet pane (10)	6.25
91-17	50¢ Harriet Quimby	2.75
91-18	Savings Bond	2.25
91-19	Love sheet and booklet pane, 52¢ Love (12)	9.25
91-20	19¢ Balloon booklet pane (10)	4.50
91-21	40¢ William Piper airmail	2.75
91-22	William Saroyan	2.75
91-23	Penalty Mail coil and 19¢ and 23¢ sheet (4)	3.50
91-24	5¢ Canoe and 10¢ Tractor Trailer coils (4)	3.25
91-25	Flags on Parade	2.75
91-26	Fishing Flies booklet pane (5)	5.25

91-27	52¢ Hubert H. Humphrey	2.75
91-28	Cole Porter	2.75
91-29	50¢ Antarctic Treaty airmail	3.25
91-30	1¢ Kestrel, 3¢ Bluebird and 30¢ Cardinal (3)	2.75
91-31	Torch ATM booklet single	2.75
91-32	Desert Shield/ Desert Storm sheet and booklet pane (11)	5.75
91-33	Flag over Mount Rushmore coil, gravure printing (darker, 3)	2.75
91-34	Summer Olympics (5)	5.75
91-35	Flower coil, slit perforations (3)	2.75
91-36	Numismatics	2.50
91-37	Basketball	5.75
91-38 through 91-47 are unassigned		
91-48	19¢ Fishing Boat coil (3)	3.00
91-49	Comedians booklet pane (10)	6.75
91-50	World War II miniature sheet (10)	7.25
91-51	District of Columbia	2.50
91-52	Jan Matzeliger	4.50
91-53	$1 USPS/ Olympic Logo	4.00
91-54	Space Exploration booklet pane (10)	6.75
91-55	50¢ PUASP/America airmail	2.75
91-56	Christmas, Madonna sheet and booklet pane (10)	8.50
91-57	Christmas, Santa Claus sheet and booklet pane (11)	12.50
91-58	5¢ Canoe coil, gravure printing (red, 6)	3.25
91-59	29¢ Eagle and Shield, self-adhesive (3)	6.00
91-60	23¢ Flag presort	3.25
91-61	$9.95 Express Mail	22.50
91-62	$2.90 Priority Mail	7.50
91-63	$14.00 Express Mail International	30.00
1992		
92-01	Winter Olympic Games (5)	4.75
92-02	World Columbian Stamp Expo '92	2.75
92-03	W.E.B. DuBois	5.75
92-04	Love	2.75
92-05	75¢ Wendell Willkie	3.25
92-06	29¢ Flower coil, round perforations (2)	2.75
92-07	Earl Warren	3.75
92-08	Olympic Baseball	12.50
92-09	Flag over White House, coil (2)	2.75
92-10	First Voyage of Christopher Columbus (4)	4.00
92-11	New York Stock Exchange	2.50
92-12	Columbian-Columbus	12.00
92-13	Columbian-Seeking Royal Support (3)	12.00
92-14	Columbian-First Sighting of Land (3)	12.00
92-15	Columbian-Claiming New World (3)	12.00

92-16	Columbian-Reporting Discoveries (3)	12.00
92-17	Columbian-Royal Favor Restored (3)	12.00
92-18	Space Adventures (4)	4.75
92-19	Alaska Highway	2.50
92-20	Kentucky Statehood	2.50
92-21	Summer Olympic Games (5)	4.75
92-22	Hummingbirds booklet pane (5)	5.50
92-22A	23¢ Presort (3)	3.25
92-23	Wildflowers (10)	6.50
92-24	Wildflowers (10)	6.50
92-25	Wildflowers (10)	6.50
92-26	Wildflowers (10)	6.50
92-27	Wildflowers (10)	6.50
92-28	World War II miniature sheet (10)	8.00
92-29	29¢ Variable Rate	2.75
92-30	Dorothy Parker	2.75
92-31	Theodore von Karman	4.25
92-32	Pledge of Allegiance (10)	10.00
92-33	Minerals (4)	4.75
92-34	Eagle and Shield (3)	3.50
92-35	Juan Rodriguez Cabrillo	2.50
92-36	Wild Animals booklet pane (5)	5.50
92-37	23¢ Presort (3)	4.00
92-38	Christmas Contemporary, sheet and booklet pane (8)	7.50
92-39	Christmas Traditional, sheet and booklet pane (11)	8.75
92-40	Pumpkinseed Sunfish	2.75
92-41	Circus Wagon	3.50
92-42	Year of the Rooster	6.00
1993		
93-01	Elvis	11.00
93-02	Space Fantasy (5)	7.00
93-03	Percy Lavon Julian	4.75
93-04	Oregon Trail	3.50
93-05	World University Games	3.75
93-06	Grace Kelly	5.50
93-07	Oklahoma!	3.75
93-08	Circus	5.50
93-09	Thomas Jefferson	3.50
93-10	Cherokee Strip	3.50
93-11	Dean Acheson	3.50
93-12	Sporting Horses	5.50
93-13	USA Coil	3.50
93-14	Garden Flowers, booklet pane (5)	5.50
93-15	Eagle and Shield, coil	3.25
93-16	World War II miniature sheet (10)	6.75
93-17	Futuristic Space Shuttle	10.00
93-18	Hank Williams, sheet	6.00
93-19	Rock & Roll/Rhythm & Blues, sheet single, booklet pane (8)	10.00
93-20	Joe Louis	7.50
93-21	Red Squirrel	4.00
93-22	Broadway Musicals, booklet pane (4)	6.75
93-23	National Postal Museum, strip (4)	4.75
93-24	Rose	4.00
93-25	American Sign Language, pair	3.50
93-26	Country & Western Music, sheet and booklet pane (4)	9.25
93-27	African Violets, booklet pane (10)	6.00

93-28	10¢ Official Mail	3.25
93-29	Contemporary Christmas, booklet pane (10), sheet and self-adhesive stamps	8.50
93-30	Traditional Christmas, sheet, booklet pane (4)	6.25
93-31	Classic Books, strip (4)	5.50
93-32	Mariana Islands	4.25
93-33	Pine Cone	4.00
93-34	Columbus' Landing in Puerto Rico	4.75
93-35	AIDS Awareness	7.50
1994		
94-01	Winter Olympics	5.50
94-02	Edward R. Murrow	3.50
94-03	Love, self-adhesive	3.50
94-04	Dr. Allison Davis	6.00
94-05	29¢ Eagle, self-adhesive	5.25
94-06	Year of the Dog	5.25
94-07	Love, booklet pane (10), single sheet stamp	8.00
94-08	Postage and Mailing Center	5.00
94-09	Buffalo Soldiers	8.00
94-10	Silent Screen Stars	7.25
94-11	Garden Flowers, booklet pane (5)	8.50
94-12	Victory at Saratoga	7.00
94-13	10¢ Tractor Trailer gravure printing	5.00
94-14	World Cup Soccer	8.75
94-15	World Cup Soccer souvenir sheet	9.25
94-16	World War II miniature sheet (10)	5.50
94-17	Love, sheet stamp	5.25
94-18	Statue of Liberty	5.25
94-19	Fishing Boat, reissue	5.25
94-20	Norman Rockwell	8.00
94-21	$9.95 and 29¢ Moon Landing	15.00
94-22	Locomotives (5)	7.00
94-23	George Meany	5.25
94-24	$5.00 Washington/ Jackson	11.00
94-25	Popular Singers (5)	10.00
94-26	James Thurber	5.25
94-27	Jazz Singers/Blues Singers (10)	14.00
94-28	Wonders of the Sea (4)	8.75
94-29	Chinese/Joint Issue (2)	—
94-30	Holiday Traditional (10)	14.00
94-31	Holiday Contemporary (4)	12.00
94-32	Holiday, self-adhesive	9.25
94-33	20¢ Virginia Apgar	—
94-34	BEP Centennial	17.50
94-35	Year of the Boar	9.00
94-G1	G1 (4) Rate Change	12.00
94-G2	G2 (6) Rate Change	12.00
94-G3	G3 (5) Rate Change	12.00
94-G4	G4 (2) Rate Change	12.00
94-36	Legends of West	12.00
1995		
95-01	Love (2)	12.00
95-02	Florida State	12.00
95-03	Butte (7)	12.00
95-04	Automobile (4)	12.00
95-05	Flag Over Field, self-adhesive	12.00
95-06	Juke Box (2+2)	12.00
95-07	Tail Fin (2+2)	12.00
95-08	Circus Wagon (7)	6.00

No.	Description	Value
95-09	Kids Care (4)	12.00
95-10	Richard Nixon	12.00
95-11	Bessie Coleman	12.00
95-12	Official Mail	12.00
95-13	Kestrel with cent sign	8.00
95-14	Love 1 oz. and 2 oz.	12.00
95-15	Flag Over Porch	12.00
95-16	Recreational Sports (5)	12.00
95-17	POW & MIA	12.00
95-18	Marilyn Monroe	12.00
95-19	Pink Rose	8.00
95-20	Ferry Boat (3)	8.00
95-21	Cog Railway Car (3)	8.00
95-22	Blue Jay (10)	8.00
95-23	Texas Statehood	12.00
95-24	Great Lake Lighthouses (5)	12.00
95-25	Challenger Shuttle	12.00
95-26	United Nations	12.00
95-27	Civil War (front and back)	16.00
95-28	Two Fruits	8.00
95-29	Alice Hamilton	12.00
95-30	Carousel Horses	12.00
95-31	Endeavor Shuttle	24.00
95-32	Alice Paul	12.00
95-33	Women's Suffrage	12.00
95-34	Louis Armstrong	12.00
95-35	World War II	12.00
95-36	Milton Hershey	12.00
95-37	Jazz Musicians	14.00
95-38	Fall Garden Flowers (5)	12.00
95-39	Eddie Rickenbacker (airmail)	12.00
95-40	Republic of Palau	12.00
95-41	Holiday Contemporary/Santa (4)	14.00
95-42	American Comic Strips	20.00
95-43	Naval Academy	12.00
95-44	Tennessee Williams	12.00
95-45	Holiday Children Sledding	12.00
95-46	Holiday Traditional sheet and booklet pane (10)	14.00
95-47	Holiday Midnight Angel	12.00
95-48	Ruth Bendict	12.00
95-49	James K. Polk	12.00
95-50	Antique Automobiles, strip (5)	14.00

1996

No.	Description	Value
96-01	Utah Statehood	12.00
96-02	Garden Flowers	14.00
96-03	Love/Kestrel	16.00
96-04	Postage and Mailing Center (3)	5.00
96-05	Ernest E. Just	12.00
96-06	Woodpecker	14.00
96-07	Smithsonian Institution	12.00
96-08	Year of the Rat	12.00
96-09	Pioneers of Communication	14.00
96-10	Fulbright Scholarships	12.00
96-11	Jacqueline Cochran	12.00
96-12	Mountain	—
96-13	Bluebird	6.00
96-14	Marathon	6.00
96-15	Flag over Porch/Eagle & Shield	—
96-16	Cal Farley	6.00
96-17	Classic Olympic Collection	8.00
96-18	Georgia O'Keefe Art	6.00
96-19	Tennessee	6.00
96-20	American Indian Dances	9.00
96-21	Prehistoric Animals	9.00
96-22	Breast Cancer Awareness	6.00
96-23	Flag over Porch/Juke Box/Butte/Tail Fin Automobile/Mountain	9.00
96-24	James Dean	6.00
96-25	Folk Heroes	9.00
96-26	Olympic/Discus	6.00
96-27	Iowa	6.00
96-28	Blue Jay	6.00
96-29	Rural Free Delivery	6.00
96-30	Riverboats	9.00
96-31	Big Band Leaders	9.00
96-32	Songwriters	9.00
96-33	F. Scott Fitzgerald	6.00
96-34	Endangered Species	10.00
96-35	Computer Technology	6.00
96-36	Family Scenes	7.50
96-37	Skaters	6.00
96-38	Hanukkah	6.00
96-39	Madonna and Child	7.50
96-40	Yellow Rose	6.00
96-41	Cycling	10.00

1997

No.	Description	Value
97-01	Year of the Ox	6.00
97-02	Flag Over Porch/Juke Box/Mountain	—
97-03	Benjamin O. Davis Sr.	6.00
97-04	Statue of Liberty	6.00
97-05	Love Swans	6.00
97-06	Helping Children Learn	6.00
97-07	Merian Botanical Plants	7.50
97-08	Pacific 97 - Stagecoach and Ship	7.50
97-09	Linerless Flag Over Porch/Juke Box	9.00
97-10	Thornton Wilder	6.00
97-11	Raoul Wallenberg	6.00
97-12	Dinosaurs	10.00
97-13	Pacific '97 - Franklin	15.00
97-14	Pacific '97 - Washington	15.00
97-15	Bugs Bunny	6.00
97-16	The Marshall Plan	6.00
97-17	Humphrey Bogart	6.00
97-18	Classic Aircraft	15.00
97-19	Classic American Dolls	15.00
97-20	Football Coaches	7.50
97-20A	George Halas	6.00
97-20B	Vince Lombardi	6.00
97-20C	Pop Warner	6.00
97-20D	Bear Bryant	6.00
97-21	Yellow Rose	6.00
97-22	"Stars and Stripes Forever"	6.00
97-23	Padre Félix Varela	6.00
97-24	Composers and Conductors	7.50
97-25	Opera Singers	7.50
97-26	Air Force	6.00
97-27	Movie Monsters	7.50
97-28	Supersonic Flight	6.00
97-29	Women in Military	6.00
97-30	Kwanzaa	6.00
97-31	Holiday Traditional, Madonna and Child	6.00
97-32	Holly	6.00
97-33	Mars Pathfinder	12.00

1998

No.	Description	Value
98-01	Year of the Tiger	6.00
98-02	Winter Sports	6.00
98-03	Madam C. J. Walker	6.00
98-03A	Celebrate The Century 1900s	10.00
98-03B	Celebrate The Century 1910s	10.00
98-04	Spanish American War	6.00
98-05	Flowering Trees	6.00
98-06	Alexander Calder	6.00
98-07	Henry R. Luce	6.00
98-08	Cinco De Mayo	6.00
98-09	Sylvester & Tweety	6.00
98-09A	Celebrate The Century 1920s	10.00
98-10	Wisconsin	6.00
98-11	Trans-Mississippi Reissue of 1898	10.00
98-12	Trans-Mississippi (single stamp)	6.00
98-13	Folk Singers	6.00
98-14	Berlin Airlift	6.00
98-15	Diner/Wetlands coil	6.00
98-16	Spanish Settlement of the Southwest	6.00
98-17	Gospel Singers	6.00
98-18	The Wallaces	6.00
98-19	Stephen Vincent Benet	6.00
98-20	Tropical Birds	6.00
98-21	Breast Cancer Research (semi-postal)	6.00
98-22	Ring-Neck Pheasant	6.00
98-23	Alfred Hitchcock	6.00
98-24	Organ Donations	6.00
98-24A	Red Fox	6.00
98-24B	Green Bicycle coil	6.00
98-25	Bright Eyes	7.50
98-26	Klondike Gold Rush	6.00
98-26A	Celebrate The Century 1930s	10.00
98-27	American Art	6.00
98-28	Ballet	6.00
98-28A	Diner coil	6.00
98-29	Space Fantasy	7.50
98-30	Philanthropy	6.00
98-31	Holiday Traditional	6.00
98-32	Holiday Contemporary	7.50
98-33	Hat Rate Change "H" Series/Makeup Rate	10.00
98-34	Uncle Sam — Rate Change	6.00
98-35	Hat Rate Change "H" Series	10.00
98-36	Hat Rate Change "H" Series	10.00
98-37	Mary Breckinridge	6.00
98-38	Space Shuttle Landing	10.00
98-39	Shuttle Piggyback	20.00
98-40	Wetlands non-denominated nonprofit coil and Eagle & Shield non-denominated presort coil	10.00

1999

No.	Description	Value
99-01	Year of the Hare	6.00
99-02	Malcolm X	6.00
99-03	33¢ Victorian — Love	6.00
99-04	55¢ Victorian — Love	6.00
99-05	Hospice Care	6.00
99-06	Celebrate The Century 1940s	10.00
99-07	City Flag	6.00
99-08	Irish Immigration	6.00
99-09	Alfred Lunt and Lynn Fontanne	6.00
99-10	Arctic Animals	6.00
99-10A	Classroom Flag	6.00
99-11	Nature of America Sonoran Desert	10.00
99-11A	Fruit Berries	—
99-12	Daffy Duck	—
99-13	Ayn Rand	—
99-14	Cinco de Mayo	—

Note: Numbers and prices may be changed without notice due to additional USPS stamp issues and/or different information that may become available on older issues.

American Commemorative Panels

The Postal Service offers American Commemorative Panels for each new commemorative stamp and special Holiday and Love stamp issued. The series began in 1972 with the Wildlife Commemorative Panel. The panels feature mint stamps complemented by fine reproductions of steel line engravings and the stories behind the commemorated subjects.

The identifying numbers used below are based on the Postal Service's numbering system for American Commemorative Panels; therefore, they do not follow the Scott numbering system.

1972

1	Wildlife	6.00
2	Mail Order	5.75
3	Osteopathic Medicine	5.75
4	Tom Sawyer	5.25
5	Pharmacy	6.00
6	Christmas, Angels	9.00
7	Christmas, Santa Claus	9.00
7E	Same with error date (1882)	—
8	Stamp Collecting	5.50

1973

9	Love	6.75
10	Pamphleteers	5.50
11	George Gershwin	6.00
12	Posting a Broadside	5.50
13	Copernicus	5.50
14	Postal People	5.25
15	Harry S. Truman	7.50
16	Post Rider	5.00
17	Boston Tea Party	15.00
18	Electronics	5.50
19	Robinson Jeffers	5.50
20	Lyndon B. Johnson	5.00
21	Henry O. Tanner	5.50
22	Willa Cather	5.50
23	Drummer	8.25
24	Angus Cattle	5.50
25	Christmas, Madonna	8.75
26	Christmas Tree, Needlepoint	8.75

1974

27	VFW	5.75
28	Robert Frost	5.75
29	Expo '74	6.50
30	Horse Racing	7.00
31	Skylab	8.50
32	Universal Postal Union	7.00
33	Mineral Heritage	5.00
34	First Kentucky Settlement	5.75

35	Continental Congress	7.00
35A	Same with corrected logo	—
36	Chautauqua	5.75
37	Kansas Wheat	5.75
38	Energy Conservation	5.75
39	Sleepy Hollow	5.75
40	Retarded Children	5.75
41	Christmas, Currier & Ives	8.50
42	Christmas, Angel Altarpiece	8.50

1975

43	Benjamin West	5.50
44	Pioneer	8.50
45	Collective Bargaining	5.75
46	Contributors to the Cause	5.50
47	Mariner 10	6.50
48	Lexington & Concord	6.25
49	Paul Laurence Dunbar	7.00
50	D.W. Griffith	5.75
51	Bunker Hill	6.25
52	Military Uniforms	5.00
53	Apollo Soyuz	8.25
54	World Peace Through Law	5.50
54A	Same with August 15, 1975 date	—
55	Women's Year	5.75
56	Postal Service Bicentennial	7.00
57	Banking and Commerce	7.00
58	Early Christmas, Card	7.75
59	Christmas, Madonna	7.75

1976

60	Spirit of '76	8.50
61	Interphil 76	7.50
62	State Flags	9.50

63	Telephone	6.75
64	Commercial Aviation	9.25
65	Chemistry	8.00
66	Benjamin Franklin	7.75
67	Declaration of Independence	7.50
68	12th Winter Olympics	7.50
69	Clara Maass	7.00
70	Adolph S. Ochs	8.25
70A	Same with charter logo	—
71	Christmas, Winter Pastime	8.75
71A	Same with charter logo	—
72	Christmas, Nativity	8.75
72A	Same with charter logo	—

1977

73	Washington at Princeton	13.00
73A	Same with charter logo	—
74	Sound Recording	17.50
74A	Same with charter logo	—
75	Pueblo Art	55.00
75A	Same with charter logo	—
76	Solo Transatlantic Lindbergh Flight	60.00
77	Colorado Statehood	14.00
78	Butterflies	14.00
79	Lafayette	14.00
80	Skilled Hands	14.00
81	Peace Bridge	14.00
82	Battle of Oriskany	14.00
83	Alta, CA, Civil Settlement	14.00
84	Articles of Confederation	15.00
85	Talking Pictures	20.00
86	Surrender at Saratoga	15.00
87	Energy	14.00

88 Christmas, Valley Forge	14.00	
89 Christmas, Mailbox	25.00	

1978

90 Carl Sandburg	8.00
91 Captain Cook	14.00
92 Harriet Tubman	8.50
93 Quilts	15.00
94 Dance	10.00
95 French Alliance	10.00
96 Early Cancer Detection	8.25
97 Jimmie Rodgers	11.00
98 Photography	8.00
99 George M. Cohan	14.00
100 Viking Missions	26.00
101 Owls	26.00
102 Trees	26.00
103 Christmas, Madonna	12.00
104 Christmas, Hobby Horse	12.00

1979

105 Robert F. Kennedy	7.25
106 Martin Luther King, Jr.	7.50
107 International Year of the Child	6.75
108 John Steinbeck	6.75
109 Albert Einstein	7.25
110 Pennsylvania Toleware	6.75
111 Architecture	6.50
112 Endangered Flora	8.00
113 Seeing Eye Dogs	8.00
114 Special Olympics	8.00
115 John Paul Jones	8.25
116 15¢ Olympics	9.50
117 Christmas, Madonna	9.50
118 Christmas, Santa Claus	9.50
119 Will Rogers	8.00
120 Vietnam Veterans	9.50
121 10¢, 31¢ Olympics	10.00

1980

122 W.C. Fields	7.50
123 Winter Olympics	7.50
124 Benjamin Banneker	10.00
125 Frances Perkins	6.75
126 Emily Bissell	6.75
127 Helen Keller/ Anne Sullivan	6.75
128 Veterans Administration	6.75
129 General Bernardo de Galvez	6.75
130 Coral Reefs	8.00
131 Organized Labor	6.25
132 Edith Wharton	5.75
133 Education	6.00
134 Indian Masks	5.00
135 Architecture	6.75
136 Christmas, Epiphany Window	10.00
137 Christmas, Toys	6.50

1981

138 Everett Dirksen	7.25
139 Whitney Moore Young	7.25
140 Flowers	8.25
141 Red Cross	7.50
142 Savings & Loans	6.75
143 Space Achievement	10.00
144 Professional Management	6.75
145 Wildlife Habitats	10.50
146 Int'l. Year of Disabled Persons	6.25
147 Edna St. Vincent Millay	6.25
148 Architecture	6.50
149 Babe Zaharias/ Bobby Jones	12.50
150 James Hoban	6.75
151 Frederic Remington	6.75
152 Battle of Yorktown/ Virginia Capes	6.75
153 Christmas, Madonna	9.25
154 Christmas, Bear and Sleigh	6.50
155 John Hanson	7.00
156 U.S. Desert Plants	8.00

1982

157 Roosevelt	8.25
158 Love	10.00
159 George Washington	9.50
160 State Birds & Flowers	17.00
161 U.S./ Netherlands	10.00
162 Library of Congress	10.50
163 Knoxville World's Fair	10.00
164 Horatio Alger	8.75
165 Aging Together	11.00
166 The Barrymores	12.00
167 Dr. Mary Walker	10.00
168 Peace Garden	11.00
169 America's Libraries	11.00
170 Jackie Robinson	24.00
171 Touro Synagogue	10.50
172 Architecture	12.00
173 Wolf Trap Farm Park	12.00
174 Francis of Assisi	12.00
175 Ponce de Leon	12.00
176 Christmas, Madonna	14.00
177 Christmas, Season's Greetings	14.00
178 Kitten & Puppy	14.00

1983

179 Science and Industry	5.25
180 Sweden/ USA Treaty	5.75
181 Balloons	6.00

182 Civilian Conservation Corps	5.25
183 40¢ Olympics	6.50
184 Joseph Priestley	5.25
185 Voluntarism	4.50
186 Concord/German Immigration	5.25
187 Physical Fitness	4.25
188 Brooklyn Bridge	6.00
189 TVA	5.25
190 Medal of Honor	6.50
191 Scott Joplin	9.00
192 28¢ Olympics	6.50
193 Babe Ruth	10.00
194 Nathaniel Hawthorne	5.75
195 13¢ Olympics	8.00
196 Treaty of Paris	6.50
197 Civil Service	6.50
198 Metropolitan Opera	6.50
199 Inventors	6.75
200 Streetcars	8.00
201 Christmas, Madonna	8.75
202 Christmas, Santa Claus	8.75
203 35¢ Olympics	8.00
204 Martin Luther	8.00

1984

205 Alaska Statehood	4.50
206 Winter Olympics	5.00
207 FDIC	4.75
208 Love	4.00
209 Carter G. Woodson	6.75
210 Soil and Water Conservation	4.75
211 Credit Union Act	4.75
212 Orchids	6.75
213 Hawaii Statehood	6.25
214 National Archives	4.50
215 20¢ Olympics	6.75
216 Louisiana World Exposition	6.00
217 Health Research	4.75
218 Douglas Fairbanks	5.25
219 Jim Thorpe	8.25
220 John McCormack	4.75
221 St. Lawrence Seaway	6.25
222 Preserving Wetlands	7.50
223 Roanoke Voyages	4.75
224 Herman Melville	4.75
225 Horace Moses	5.25
226 Smokey Bear	5.00
227 Roberto Clemente	13.00
228 Dogs	6.25
229 Crime Prevention	5.25
230 Family Unity	6.25
231 Christmas, Madonna	6.75
232 Christmas, Santa Claus	6.75
233 Eleanor Roosevelt	5.50
234 Nation of Readers	5.50
235 Hispanic Americans	5.25
236 Vietnam Veterans Memorial	8.25

1985

237 Jerome Kern 5.75
238 Mary McLeod
    Bethune 7.00
239 Duck Decoys 7.25
240 Winter
    Special Olympics 6.00
241 Love 5.00
242 Rural Electrification
    Administration 5.00
243 AMERIPEX '86 6.75
244 Abigail Adams 4.75
245 Frederic Auguste
    Bartholdi 6.50
246 Korean War
    Veterans 6.25
247 Social Security
    Act 5.00
248 World War I
    Veterans 5.75
249 Horses 9.00
250 Public
    Education 4.50
251 Youth 6.75
252 Help End Hunger 5.00
253 Christmas,
    Madonna 8.00
254 Christmas,
    Poinsettias 5.00

1986

255 Arkansas
    Statehood 5.25
256 Stamp Collecting
    Booklet 6.75
257 Love 5.00
258 Sojourner Truth 7.50
259 Republic of Texas 6.25
260 Fish Booklet 6.75
261 Public Hospitals 4.75
262 Duke Ellington 7.50
263 U.S. Presidents'
    Sheet #1 6.25
264 U.S. Presidents'
    Sheet #2 6.25
265 U.S. Presidents'
    Sheet #3 6.25
266 U.S. Presidents'
    Sheet #4 6.25
267 Polar Explorers 6.75
268 Statue of Liberty 7.50
269 Navajo Blankets 6.75
270 T.S. Eliot 6.25
271 Wood-Carved
    Figurines 6.00
272 Christmas,
    Madonna 5.75
273 Christmas,
    Village Scene 5.75

1987

274 Michigan
    Statehood 5.75
275 Pan American
    Games 3.50
276 Love 7.00
277 Jean Baptiste
    Pointe Du Sable 5.00
278 Enrico Caruso 3.50
279 Girl Scouts 4.00
280 Special Occasions
    Booklet 6.00

281 United Way 4.75
282 #1 American
    Wildlife 6.50
283 #2 American
    Wildlife 6.50
284 #3 American
    Wildlife 6.50
285 #4 American
    Wildlife 6.50
286 #5 American
    Wildlife 6.50
287 Delaware
    Statehood 5.75
288 Morocco/U.S.
    Diplomatic
    Relations 4.75
289 William Faulkner 4.75
290 Lacemaking 4.75
291 Pennsylvania
    Statehood 5.25
292 Constitution
    Booklet 4.75
293 New Jersey
    Statehood 5.75
294 Signing of
    the Constitution 4.75
295 Certified Public
    Accountants 5.75
296 Locomotives
    Booklet 5.75
297 Christmas,
    Madonna 6.25
298 Christmas,
    Ornaments 5.75

1988

299 Georgia Statehood 6.25
300 Connecticut
    Statehood 6.25
301 Winter Olympics 6.25
302 Australia 5.75
303 James Weldon
    Johnson 5.00
304 Cats 6.50
305 Massachusetts
    Statehood 6.25
306 Maryland
    Statehood 6.25
307 Knute Rockne 9.50
308 New Sweden 5.75
309 South Carolina
    Statehood 6.25
310 Francis Ouimet 12.00
311 New Hampshire
    Statehood 6.25
312 Virginia
    Statehood 6.25
313 Love 7.00
314 New York
    Statehood 6.25
315 Summer
    Olympics 6.25
316 Classic Cars
    Booklet 6.75
317 Antarctic Explorers 6.25
318 Carousel Animals 6.75
319 Christmas,
    Madonna, Sleigh 7.00
320 Special Occasions
    Booklet 6.75

1989

321 Montana
    Statehood 6.25
322 A. Philip Randolph 8.75
323 North Dakota
    Statehood 6.25
324 Washington
    Statehood 6.25
325 Steamboats
    Booklet 8.00
326 World Stamp
    Expo '89 6.25
327 Arturo Toscanini 6.25
328 U.S. House of
    Representatives 7.25
329 U.S. Senate 7.25
330 Executive
    Branch 7.25
331 South Dakota
    Statehood 6.25
332 Lou Gehrig 15.00
333 French Revolution 7.50
334 Ernest Hemingway 7.25
335 North Carolina
    Statehood 6.25
336 Letter Carriers 7.25
337 Drafting of the
    Bill of Rights 7.25
338 Prehistoric
    Animals 9.50
339 25¢ and 45¢
    America/PUAS 7.25
340 Christmas,
    Traditional and
    Contemporary 8.50
341 Classic Mail
    Transportation 7.25
342 Future Mail
    Transportation 8.00

1990

343 Idaho Statehood 7.25
344 Love 7.25
345 Ida B. Wells 11.00
346 U.S. Supreme
    Court 7.25
347 Wyoming
    Statehood 6.25
348 Classic Films 9.25
349 Marianne Moore 6.25
350 Lighthouses
    Booklet 10.00
351 Rhode Island
    Statehood 6.75
352 Olympians 10.00
353 Indian
    Headdresses
    Booklet 8.75
354 Micronesia/
    Marshall Islands 8.75
355 25¢ and 45¢
    America/PUAS 7.50
356 Eisenhower 8.25
357 Creatures
    of the Sea 13.00
358 Christmas,
    Traditional and
    Contemporary 9.50

1991

No.	Description	Price
359	Switzerland	8.75
360	Vermont Statehood	7.25
361	Savings Bonds	6.25
362	29¢ and 52¢ Love	8.00
363	Saroyan	7.50
364	Fishing Flies Booklet	7.50
365	Cole Porter	8.00
366	Antarctic Treaty	8.00
367	Desert Shield/ Desert Storm	20.00
368	Summer Olympics	8.75
369	Numismatics	7.50
370	Basketball	10.50
371	World War II Miniature Sheet	12.00
372	Comedians Booklet	9.50
373	District of Columbia	8.00
374	Jan Matzeliger	7.50
375	Space Exploration Booklet	11.00
376	America/PUAS	8.00
377	Christmas, Traditional and Contemporary	9.50

1992

No.	Description	Price
378	Winter Olympics	10.00
379	World Columbian Stamp Expo '92	8.75
380	W.E.B. Du Bois·	8.75
381	Love	8.75
382	Olympic Baseball	15.00
383	Columbus' First Voyage	15.00
384	Space Adventures	12.00
385	New York Stock Exchange	11.00
386	Alaska Highway	8.75
387	Kentucky Statehood	8.75
388	Summer Olympics	10.50
389	Hummingbirds Booklet	11.00
390	World War II Miniature Sheet	10.00
391	Dorothy Parker	8.75
392	Theodore von Karman	10.00
393	Minerals	9.50
394	Juan Rodriguez Cabrillo	10.00
395	Wild Animals Booklet	12.50
396	Christmas, Traditional and Contemporary	9.25
397	Columbus Souvenir Sheets	21.00
398	Columbus Souvenir Sheets	21.00
399	Columbus Souvenir Sheets	21.00
400	Wildflowers #1	10.50
401	Wildflowers #2	10.50
402	Wildflowers #3	10.50
403	Wildflowers #4	10.50
404	Wildflowers #5	10.50
405	Happy New Year	10.00

1993

No.	Description	Price
406	Elvis	22.50
407	Space Fantasy	12.50
408	Percy Julian	12.50
409	Oregon Trail	10.50
410	World Univ.Games	11.00
411	Grace Kelly	13.00
412	Oklahoma!	12.00
413	Circus	12.00
414	Cherokee Strip	9.25
415	Dean Acheson	10.50
416	Sport Horses	13.00
417	Garden Flowers	13.00
418	World War II	13.00
419	Hank Williams	13.00
420	Rock & Roll/R&B	17.00
421	Joe Louis	14.00
422	Broadway Musicals	14.00
423	National Postal Museum	12.00
424	Deaf Communication	12.00
425	Country Western	14.00
426	Christmas, Traditional	13.00
427	Youth Classics	13.00
428	Mariana Islands	12.00
429	Columbus Landing In Puerto Rico	10.50
430	AIDS Awareness	12.00

1994

No.	Description	Price
431	Winter Olympics	12.00
432	Edward R. Murrow	9.50
433	Dr. Allison Davis	10.00
434	Year of the Dog	14.00
435	Love	9.50
436	Buffalo Soldiers	16.00
437	Silent ScreenStars	14.00
438	Garden Flowers	12.00
439	World Cup Soccer	12.50
440	World War II	15.00
441	Norman Rockwell	13.00
442	Moon Landing	16.00
443	Locomotives	13.00
444	George Meany	13.00
445	Popular Singers	14.00
446	James Thurber	13.00
447	Jazz/Blues	16.00
448	Wonders of the Sea	13.00
449	Birds (Cranes)	13.00
450	Christmas, Madonna	13.00
451	Christmas, Stocking	13.00
452	Year of the Boar	13.00

1995

No.	Description	Price
453	Florida Statehood	17.50
454	Bessie Coleman	17.50
455	Kids Care!	17.50
456	Richard Nixon	17.50
457	Love	17.50
458	Recreational Sports	17.50
459	POW & MIA	17.50
460	Marilyn Monroe	20.00
461	Texas Statehood	17.50
462	Great Lakes Lighthouses	20.00
463	United Nations	17.50
464	Carousel Horses	20.00
465	Jazz Musicians	20.00
466	Women's Suffrage	17.50
467	Louis Armstrong	17.50
468	World War II	17.50
469	Fall Garden Flowers	17.50
470	Republic of Palau	17.50
471	Christmas, Contemporary	20.00
472	Naval Academy	17.50
473	Tennessee Williams	17.50
474	Christmas, Traditional	17.50
475	James K. Polk	17.50
476	Antique Automobiles	20.00

1996

No.	Description	Price
477	Utah Statehood	17.50
478	Winter Garden Flowers	20.00
479	Ernest E. Just	17.50
480	Smithsonian Institution	17.50
481	Year of the Rat	17.50
482	Pioneers of Communication	17.50
483	Fulbright Scholarships	17.50
484	Olympics	17.50
485	Marathon	17.50
486	Georgia O'Keefe	17.50
487	Tennessee Statehood	17.50
488	James Dean	17.50
489	Prehistoric Animals	17.50
490	Breast Cancer Awareness	17.50
491	American Indian Dances	17.50
492	Folk Heroes	17.50
493	Centennial Games (Discus)	17.50
494	Iowa Statehood	17.50
495	Rural Free Delivery	17.50
496	Riverboats	17.50
497	Big Band Leaders	17.50
498	Songwriters	17.50
499	Endangered Species	20.00
500	Family Scenes (4 designs)	17.50
501	Hanukkah	17.50
502	Madonna and Child	17.50
503	Cycling	15.00
503A	F. Scott Fitzgerald	15.00
503B	Computer Technology	15.00

1997

504	Year of the Ox	15.00
505	Benjamin O. Davis	15.00
506	Love	17.50
507	Helping Children Learn	15.00
508	Pacific 97 Triangle Stamps	17.50
509	Thornton Wilder	15.00
510	Raoul Wallenberg	15.00
511	Dinosaurs	-
512	Bugs Bunny	15.00
513	Pacific 97 Franklin	-
514	Pacific 97 Washington	-
515	The Marshall Plan	15.00
516	Classic Aircraft	17.50
517	Football Coaches	15.00
518	Dolls	17.50
519	Humphrey Bogart	15.00
520	Stars and Stripes	15.00
521	Opera Singers	15.00
522	Composers and Conductors	15.00
523	Padre Varela	15.00
524	Air Force	15.00
525	Movie Monsters	15.00
526	Supersonic Flight	15.00
527	Women in the Military	15.00
528	Holiday Kwanzaa	15.00
529	Holiday, Traditional	15.00
530	Holiday Holly	15.00

1998

531	Year of the Tiger	15.00
532	Winter Sports	15.00
533	Madam C.J. Walker	15.00
533A	Celebrate The Century 1900s	25.00
533B	Celebrate The Century 1910s	25.00
534	Spanish American War	15.00
535	Flowering Trees	15.00
536	Alexander Calder	15.00
537	Cinco de Mayo	15.00
538	Sylvester & Tweety	15.00
538A	Celebrate The Century 1920s	25.00
539	Wisconsin Statehood	16.00
540	Trans-Mississippi	26.00
541	Folk Singers	16.00
542	Berlin Airlift	16.00
543	Spanish Settlement of the Southwest	16.00
544	Gospel Singers	16.00
545	Stephen Vincent Benet	16.00
546	Tropical Birds	16.00
546A	Breast Cancer Research	16.00
547	Alfred Hitchcock	16.00
548	Organ Donations	16.00
549	Bright Eyes	16.00

550	Klondike Gold Rush	16.00
551	American Art	20.00
551A	Celebrate The Century 1930s	25.00
552	Ballet	16.00
553	Space Discovery	16.00
554	Philanthropy	16.00
555	Holiday, Traditional	20.00
556	Holiday, Contemporary	16.00

1999

557	Year of the Hare	16.00
558	Malcolm X	16.00
559	33¢ Victorian - Love	20.00
560	55¢ Victorian - Love	16.00
561	Hospice Care	16.00
562	Celebrate The Century 1940s	25.00
563	Irish Immigration	16.00
564	Alfred Lunt and Lynn Fontanne	16.00
565	Arctic Animals	16.00
566	Nature of America Sonoran Desert	25.00
567	Daffy Duck	25.00
568	Ayn Rand	16.00
569	Cinco de Mayo	16.00
570	John and William Bartram	16.00
571	Celebrate The Century 1950s	-
572	Prostate Cancer	-
573	California Gold Rush	-
574	Aquarium Fish	-
575	Xtreme Sports	-
576	American Glass	-
577	James Cagney	-
578	Honoring Those Who Served	-
579	All Aboard!	-
580	Frederick Law Olmsted	-
581	Hollywood Composers	-
582	Celebrate The Century 1960s	-
583	Broadway Songwriters	-
584	Insects and Spiders	-
585	Hanukkah	-
586	Nato	-
587	Holiday Traditional, Bartolomeo Vivarini	-
588	Holiday Contemporary, Deer	-
589	Kwanzaa	-
590	Celebrate The Century 1970s	-

Glossary

Accessories
The tools used by stamp collectors, such as tongs, hinges, etc.

Aerophilately
Stamp collecting that focuses on stamps or postage relating to airmail.

Airmail
Mail which has been transported by air, as distinct from "surface" mail. Most long-distance mail is now transported by air; in the U.S., the distinction (and premium) for domestic airmail ceased in the late 1970s, and for foreign mail in the mid-1990s (now generically called "international rate").

Album
A book designed to hold stamps and covers.

Approvals
Stamps sent by a dealer to a collector for examination. Approvals must either be bought or returned to the dealer within a specified time.

Auction
A sale at which philatelic material is sold to the highest bidder.

Block
An unseparated group of stamps, at least two stamps high and two stamps wide.

Bogus
A completely fictitious, worthless "stamp," created only for sale to collectors. Bogus stamps include labels for nonexistent values added to regularly issued sets, issues for nations without postal systems, etc.

Booklet Pane
A small sheet of stamps specially cut to be sold in booklets.

Bourse
A marketplace, such as a stamp exhibition, where stamps are bought, sold or exchanged.

Cachet (ka-shay')
A design on an envelope describing an event. Cachets appear on first day of issue, first flight and stamp exhibition covers, etc.

Cancellation
A mark placed on a stamp by a postal authority to show that it has been used.

Centering
The position of the design on a postage stamp. On perfectly centered stamps the design is exactly in the middle.

Cinderella
Any stamp-like label without an official postal value.

Classic
An early stamp issue. Most people consider these to be rare stamps, but classic stamps aren't necessarily rare.

Coils
Stamps issued in rolls (one stamp wide) for use in dispensers or vending machines.

Commemoratives
Stamps that honor anniversaries, important people, special events or aspects of national culture.

Compound Perforations
Different gauge perforations on different (normally adjacent) sides of a single stamp.

Condition
Condition is the most important characteristic in determining the value of a stamp. It refers to the state of a stamp regarding such details as centering, color and gum.

Cover
An envelope that has been sent through the mail.

Cracked Plate
A term used to describe stamps which show evidence that the plate from which they were printed was cracked.

Definitives
Regular issues of postage stamps, usually sold over long periods of time.

Denomination
The postage value appearing on a stamp, such as 5 cents.

Die Cut
Scoring of self-adhesive stamps that allows stamp separation from liner.

Directory Markings
Postal markings that indicate a failed delivery attempt, stating reasons such as "No Such Number" or "Address Unknown."

Double Transfer
The condition on a printing plate that shows evidence of a duplication of all or part of the design.

Duplicates
Extra copies of stamps that can be sold or traded. Duplicates should be examined carefully for color and perforation variations.

Entire
An intact piece of postal stationery, in contrast to a cut-out of the printed design.

Error
A stamp with some-thing incorrect in its design or manufacture.

Exploded (booklet)
A stamp booklet that has been separated into its various components for display.

Face Value
The monetary value or denomination of a stamp.

Fake
A genuine stamp that has been altered in some way to make it more attractive to collectors. It may be repaired, reperfed or regummed to resemble a more valuable variety.

First Day Cover (FDC)
An envelope with a new stamp and cancellation showing the date the stamp was issued.

Foreign Entry
When original transfers are erased incompletely from a plate, they can appear with new transfers of a different design which are subsequently entered on the plate.

Franks
Marking on the face of a cover, indicating it is to be carried free of postage. Franks may be written, hand-stamped, imprinted or represented by special adhesives. Such free franking is usually limited to official correspondence, such as the President's mail.

Freak
An abnormal variety of stamps occurring because of paper fold, over-inking, perforation shift, etc., as opposed to a continually appearing variety or a major error.

Grill
A pattern of small, square pyramids in parallel rows impressed or embossed on the stamp to break paper fibers, allowing cancellation ink to soak in and preventing washing and reuse.

Gum
The coating of glue on the back of an unused stamp.

Hinges
Small strips of gummed material used by collectors to affix stamps to album pages.

Imperforate
Indicates stamps without perforations or separating holes. They usually are separated by scissors and collected in pairs.

Label
Any stamp-like adhesive that is not a postage stamp.

Laid Paper
When held to the light, the paper shows alternate light and dark crossed lines.

Line Pairs (LP)
Most coil stamp rolls prior to 1981 freature a line of ink (known as a "joint line") printed between two stamps at various intervals, caused by the joining of two or more curved plates around the printing cylinder.

Liner
The backing paper for self-adhesive stamps.

Linerless Coil
Self-adhesive roll of coil stamps without a liner.

Miniature Sheet
A single stamp or block of stamps with a margin on all sides bearing some special wording or design.

On Paper
Stamps "on paper" are those that still have portions of the original envelope or wrapper stuck to them.

Overprint
Additional printing on a stamp that was not part of the original design.

Packet

A presorted unit of all different stamps. One of the most common and economical ways to begin a collection.

Pane

A full "sheet" of stamps as sold by a Post Office. Four panes typically make up the original sheet of stamps as printed.

Par Avion

French for mail transported "by air."

Perforations

Lines of small holes or cuts between rows of stamps that make them easy to separate.

Philately

The collection and study of postage stamps and other postal materials.

Pictorials

Stamps with a picture of some sort, other than portraits or static designs such as coats of arms.

Plate Block (PB) (or Plate Number Block)

A block of stamps with the margin attached that bears the plate number used in printing that sheet.

Plate Number Coils (PNC)

For most coil stamp rolls beginning with #1891, a small plate number appears at varying intervals in the roll in the design of the stamp.

Postage Due

A stamp issued to collect unpaid postage.

Postal Stationery

Envelopes, postal cards and aerogrammes with stamp designs printed or embossed on them.

Postal Cards

See "stamped cards."

Postcards

Commercially-produced mailable cards, but without imprinted postage (postage must be affixed).

Postmark

A mark put on envelopes or other mailing pieces showing the date and location of the post office where it was mailed.

Precancels

Cancellations applied to stamps before the stamps were affixed to mail.

Presort Stamp

A discounted stamp used by qualified mailers who presort mail.

Registered Mail

First class mail with a numbered receipt, including a valuation of the registered item. This guarantees customers will get their money back if an item is lost in the mail.

Reissue

An official reprinting of a stamp that was no longer being printed.

Replicas

Reproductions of stamps sold during the early days of collecting. Usually printed in one color on a sheet containing a number of different designs. Replicas were never intended to deceive either the post office or the collector.

Reprint

A stamp printed from the original plate after the issue is no longer valid for postage. Official reprints are sometimes made for presentation purposes, official collections, etc., and are often distinguished in some way from the "real" ones.

Revenue Stamps

Stamps not valid for postal use but issued for collecting taxes.

Ribbed Paper

Paper which shows fine parallel ridges on one or both sides of a stamp.

Se-tenant

An attached pair, strip or block of stamps that differ in design, value or surcharge.

Secret Marks

Many stamps have included tiny reference points in their designs to foil attempts at counterfeiting and to differentiate issues.

Self-Adhesive Stamp

A stamp with a pressure sensitive adhesive.

Selvage

The unprinted paper around panes of stamps, sometimes called the margin.

Series

A number of individual stamps or sets of stamps having a common purpose or theme, issued over an extended period of time (generally a year or more), including all variations of design and/or denomination.

Set

A group of stamps with a common design or theme issued at one time for a common purpose or over a limited perid of time (generally less than a year).

Souvenir Sheet

A small sheet of stamps with a commemorative inscription of some sort.

Special Issues

Stamps which supplement definitives, while meeting specific needs and having a more commemorative appearance. These include Christmas, Love, Holiday Celebration, airmail, international rate, Express Mail and Priority Mail stamps.

Speculative

A stamp or issue released primarily for sale to collectors, rather than to meet any legitimate postal need.

Stamped Cards

The current term for postal cards, which are mailable cards with postage imprinted directly on them.

Stamped Envelopes

Mailable envelopes with postage embossed and/or imprinted on them.

Strip

Three or more unseparated stamps in a row.

Surcharge

An overprint that changes the denomination of a stamp from its original face value.

Sweatbox

A closed box with a grill over which stuck-together unused stamps are placed. A wet, sponge-like material under the grill creates humidity so the stamps can be separated without removing the gum.

Thematic

A stamp collection that relates to a specific theme and is arranged to present a logical story and progression.

Tied On

Indicates a stamp whose postmark touches the envelope.

Tongs

A tool, used to handle stamps, that resembles a tweezers with rounded or flattened tips.

Topicals

Indicates a group of stamps with the same theme—space travel, for example.

Unhinged

A stamp without hinge marks, but not necessarily with original gum.

Unused

The condition of a stamp that has no cancellation or other sign of use.

Used

The condition of a stamp that has been canceled.

Variety

A stamp which varies in some way from its standard or original form. Varieties can include missing colors or perforations, constant plate flaws, changes in ink or paper, differences in printing method or in format, such as booklet and coil "varieties" of the same stamp.

Want List

A list of philatelic material needed by a collector.

Watermark

A design pressed into stamp paper during its manufacture.
Water Activated Gum
Water soluable adhesives such as sugar based starches on back of unused stamps.

Water Activated Gum

Water soluable adhesives such as sugar based starches on back of unused stamps.

Wove Paper

A uniform paper which, when held to the light, shows no light or dark figures.

Organizations, Publications and Resources

For your information . . .
Here's a list of philatelic resources that can increase your
knowledge of stamps as well as your collecting enjoyment.

Organizations

*Please enclose a stamped,
self-addressed envelope
when writing to these organizations.*

American Air Mail Society
Rudy Roy
P.O. Box 5367
Virginia Beach, VA
23471-0367
(p) 757/499-5234
AAMSInformation@aol.com
http://ourworld.compuserve.
com/homepages/aams/

*Specializes in all phases of
aerophilately. Membership
services include Advance
Bulletin Service, Auction
Service, free want ads, Sales
Department, monthly jour-
nal, discounts on Society
publications, translation
service.*

**American First Day Cover
Society**
Douglas Kelsey
Executive Director
P.O. box 65960
Tucson, AZ 85728-5960
(p) 520/321-0880
(f) 520/321-0879
AFDCS@aol.com
www.afdcs.org

*A full-service, not-for-profit,
noncommercial society
devoted exclusively to First
Day Covers and First Day
Cover collecting. Publishes
90-page magazine, First
Day, eight times a year.
Offers information on 300
current cachet producers,
expertizing, foreign covers,
translation service, color
slide programs and archives
covering First Day Covers.*

**American Ceremony Program
Society**
Monte Eiserman
14359 Chadbourne
Houston, TX 77079-6611
Montelou@wt.net

*Interested in learning about
First Day Ceremonies and
Ceremony Programs?
The American Ceremony
Program Society (ACPS) is
just such a learning place.*

American Philatelic Society
Robert E. Lamb
Executive Director
P.O. Box 8000
State College, PA
16803-8000
(p) 814/237-3803
(f) 814/237-6128
relamb@stamps.org
www.stamps.org

*A full complement of serv-
ices and resources for stamp
collectors. Annual membership offers: library services,
educational seminars and
correspondence courses,
expertizing service, estate
advisory service, translation
service, a stamp theft
committee that functions as
a clearinghouse for philatelic
crime information,
intramember sales service
and a monthly journal, The
American Philatelist, sent to
all members. Membership
57,000 worldwide.*

**American Society for
Philatelic Pages and Panels**
Gerald Blankenship
P.O. Box 475
Crosby, TX 77532-0475
(p) 281/324-2709
gblank1941@aol.com

*Focuses on souvenir pages
and commemorative panels.
Free ads, member auction,
publishes a quarterly journal
sent to all members with
reports on new issues,
varieties, errors, oddities
and discoveries.*

**American Stamp Dealers
Association**
Joseph B. Savarese
3 School St., Suite 205
Glen Cove, NY
11542-2548
(p) 516/759-7000
(f) 516/759-7014
asdashows@erols.com
www.asdaonline.com

*Association of dealers
engaged in every facet of
philately, with 11 regional
chapters nationwide.
Sponsors national and local
shows. Will send you a
complete listing of dealers in
your area or collecting specialty. A #10 SASE must
accompany your request.*

American Topical Association
Paul E. Tyler
Executive Director
P.O. Box 50820
Albuquerque, NM
87181-0820
(p) 505/323-8595
(f) 505/323-8795
ATAStamps@juno.com
http://home.prcn.org/~pauld/
ata

*A service organization con-
centrating on the specialty
of topical stamp collecting.
Offers handbooks and
checklists on specific topics;
exhibition awards; Topical
Time, a bimonthly publication dealing with topical
interest areas; a slide loan
service, and information,
translation and sales
services.*

**Ebony Society of Philatelic
Events and Reflections**
Sanford L. Byrd
P.O. Box 8888
Corpus Christi, TX
78468-8888
(p) 361/980-3962
esper@attglobal.net
http://slsabyrd.com

Junior Philatelists of America
Jennifer Arnold
Executive Secretary
P.O. Box 2625
Albany, OR 97321-0643
Exec.sec@jpastamps.org
www.jpastamps.org/

*Publishes a bimonthly
newsletter,* The Philatelic
Observer, *and offers auction, exchange, pen pal
and other services to young
stamp collectors. Adult
supporting membership
and gift memberships are
available. The Society also
publishes various brochures
on stamp collecting.*

Mailer's Postmark Permit Club
Joseph LoPreiato
165 Old Farm Drive
Newington, CT
06111-1819
(p) 860/666-5244
(f) 860/666-7041
EnotriaLP@aol.com

*Publishes bimonthly
newsletter,* Permit Patter, *which covers all aspects of
mailer's precancel post-
marks, as well as a catalog
and two checklists.*

Postal History Society
Kalman V. Illyefalvi
8207 Daren Court
Pikesville, MD 21208-2211
(p) 410/653-0665
kalphyl@freewwweb.com

*Devoted to the study of
various aspects of the development of the mails and
local, national and international postal systems; UPU
treaties; and means of transporting mail.*

**The Souvenir Card Collectors
Society, Inc.**
Dana M. Marr
P.O. Box 4155
Tulsa, OK 74159-0155
(p) 918/664-6724
DMARR5569@aol.com

*Provides member auctions,
a quarterly journal and
access to limited-edition
souvenir cards.*

Stamp Services
United States Postal Service
475 L'Enfant Plaza SW
Washington, D.C.
20260-2437

**United Postal Stationery
Society**
Joann Thomas
P.O. Box 48
Redlands, CA 92373-0601

**Universal Ship Cancellation
Society**
David Kent
P.O. Box 127
New Britian, CT
06050 0127
(p) 860/667-1400
kentdave@aol.com
www.uscs.org

*Specializes in naval ship
postmarks.*

United States Stamp Society
Formerly "Business Issues
Association"
Executive Secretary
P.O. Box 722
Westfield, NJ 07091-0722
www.usstamps.org

*Devoted to the study of all
U.S. stamps, principally
those produced by the
Bureau of Engraving and
Printing.*

Expertisers

**American Philatelic
Expertizing Service (APEX)**
P.O. Box 8000
State College, PA
16803-8000
(p) 814/237-3803
(f) 814/237-6128
www.stamps.org

Mercer Bristow
Director of Expertizing
Ambristo@stamps.org

Krystal Harter
Expertizing Coordinator
Krharter@stamps.org

*A joint project of the
American Philatelic Society
and the American Stamp
Dealers' Association, APEX
utilizes the high-tech equipment and outstanding reference collection at APS head-
quarters in conjunction with
the nation's best philatelic
scholars to pass judgement
on the identification,
authenticity and condition
of stamps from all countries.
APEX certificates are
accepted by all legitimate
auction firms, dealers and
collectors and are the least
expensive of all leading
expertization services.*

Philatelic Foundation
Attention: Chairman
501 Fifth Ave. Rm. 1901
New York, NY
10017-6102
(p) 212/867-3699

*A nonprofit organization
known for its excellent
expertization service.
The Foundation's broad
resources, including extensive reference collections,
5,000-volume library and
Expert Committee, provide
collectors with comprehen-
sive consumer protection.
Slide and cassette programs
are available on such subjects as the Pony Express,
classic U.S. stamps,
Confederate Postal History
and collecting basics for
beginners. Book series
include expertizing case
histories in Opinions,
Foundation seminar subjects
in "textbooks" and
specialized U.S. subjects
in monographs.*

**Professional Stamp Experts,
Inc.**
P.O. Box 6170
Newport Beach, CA 92658
(p) 877/782-6788
www.collectors.com/pse

*A for-profit organization
comprised of more than 70
of the leading philatelic
experts in the U.S. in the
identification and authentication of all U.S. and British
Commonwealth postage
stamps, covers, revenues,
etc. The PSE's expansive
resources include a 2,500-
volume reference library
plus postagestamp reference
collection for direct compar-
ison, examination and
authentication. PSE issues
a Certificate of Authenticity
on each submission it
receives. These expert opinions are accepted by all
legitimate auction firms,
dealers and collectors. All
submissions are fully insured
once reviewed by PSE until
items are returned to the
original submitter.*

Periodicals

The following publications will send you a free copy of their magazine or newspaper upon request.

Global Stamp News
P.O. Box 97
Sidney, OH 45365-0097
(p) 937/492-3183
global@bright.net

America's largest-circulation monthly stamp magazine featuring U.S. as well as foreign issues.

Linn's Stamp News
P.O. Box 29
Sidney, OH 45365-0097
(p) 937/498-0801
(f) 800/340-9501 (US only)
(f) 937/498-0814 (outside US)
linns@linns.com
www.linns.com

The largest weekly stamp newspaper.

Mekeel's & Stamps Magazine
John Dunn
P.O. Box 5050-fa
White Plains, NY
10602-5050
Stampnews@aol.com
www.stampnews.com

World's oldest stamp weekly, for intermediate and advanced collectors.

Stamp Collector
Wayne Youngblood
Publisher, Stamps Dept.
700 E. State St.
Iola, WI 54990-0001
(p) 715/445-2214
youngblood@krause.com

For beginning and advanced collectors of all ages.

Stamp Wholesaler
Wayne Youngblood
Publisher, Stamps Dept.
700 E. State St.
Iola, WI 54990-0001
(p) 715/445-2214
youngblood@krause.com

For dealers of all levels and those interested in the stamp business.

USA Philatelic
Information Fulfillment
Dept. 6270
U.S. Postal Service
P.O. box 219014
Kansas City, MO
64121-9014
(p) 1 800 STAMP-24

U.S. Stamp News
John Dunn
P.O. Box 5050-fb
White Plains, NY
10602-5050
Stampnews@aol.com
www.stampnews.com

Monthly magazine for all collectors of U.S. stamps, covers and postal history.

Museums, Libraries and Displays

Please contact the institutions before visiting to confirm hours and any entry fees.

American Philatelic Research Library
Robert E. Lamb
P.O. Box 8000
State College, PA
16803-8000
(p) 814/237-3803
(f) 814/237-6128
Relamb@stamps.org
www.stamps.org

Founded in 1968; now the largest philatelic library in the U.S. Currently receives more than 400 worldwide periodical titles and houses extensive collections of bound journals, books, auction catalogs and dealer pricelists. Directly serves members of the APS and APRL (library members also receive the quarterly Philatelic Literature Review). The public may purchase photocopies directly or borrow materials through the national interlibrary loan system.

Cardinal Spellman Philatelic Museum
Viki Sand
Executive Director
235 Wellesley Street
Weston, MA 02193-1538
(p) 781/768-8367
(f) 781/768-7332
laura.rundall@spellman.org
www.spellman.org

Hours: Th-S 12 noon-5 p.m. (closed holidays)

Adults: $5; students/seniors: $3; members/16 and under: free.

Located on the campus of Regis College. America's first fully accredited museum devoted to the display, collection and preservation of stamps and postal history. The three galleries' exhibitions feature international rarities, United States, and worldwide collections. Philatelic research library and family activity center open with admission. Museum Store and Post Office has collectibles, collecting supplies, and U.S. postage stamps.

The Collectors Club
Irene Bromberg
Executive Secretary
22 E. 35th Street
New York, NY
10016-3806
(p) 212/683-0559
(f) 212/481-1269
collectorsclub@nac.net
www.collectorsclub.org

Bimonthly journal, publication of various reference works, one of the most extensive reference libraries in the world, reading and study rooms. Regular meetings on the first and third Wednesdays of each month at 6:30 p.m., except July and August.

Friends of the Western Philatelic Library
P.O. Box 2219
Sunnyvale, CA 94087-2219
(p) 408/733-0336
www.fwpl.org/

National Postal Museum
Smithsonian Institution
2 Massachusetts Ave. NE
Washington, D.C.
20560-0570
(p) 202/633-9360
www.si.edu/postal/

Hours: 7 days 10:00 a.m.-
5:30 p.m., except 12/25

Houses more than 16
million items for exhibition
and study purposes.
Research may be conducted
by appointment only on
materials in the collection
and library. This new
museum, which is housed in
the old Washington, D.C.
Post Office next to Union
Station, opened to the public
in mid-1993.

The Postal History Foundation
Betsy Towle
P.O. Box 40725
Tucson, AZ 85717-0725
(p) 520/623-6652
(f) 520/623-6652
phf@azstarnet.com

Hours: M-F 8:00 a.m.-
3:00 p.m.

Regular services include a
library, USPS contract post
office, philatelic sales,
archives, artifacts and
collections and a Youth
Department. Membership
includes subscription to a
quarterly journal, The
Heliograph.

San Diego County Philatelic Library
Ralph H. Armington
7403C Princess View Drive
San Diego, CA 92120-1345
(p) 619/229-8813

Hours: M-Th 6:00 p.m.-
9:00 p.m. and Sat noon to
3 p.m.

Western Philatelic Library
P.O. Box 2219
Sunnyvale, CA 94087-2219
(p) 408/733-0336
stulev@ix.netcom.com
www.pbbooks.com/wpl.htm

Wineburgh Philatelic Research Library
Carol Thomas
University of Texas at Dallas
P.O. Box 830643
Mailstation: MC33
Richardson, TX
75083-0643
(p) 972/883-2570
sall@utdallas.edu
www.utdallas.edu/library/
special/wprl.html

Hours: M-T 9:00 a.m. 6:00
p.m.; F 9:00 a.m.-5:00 p.m.

Exchange Service

Stamp Master
Charles Bergeron
P.O. Box 17
Putnam Hall, FL
32185-0017
Cbergero@bellsouth.net

An "electronic connection"
for philatelists via modem
and computer to
display/review members'
stamp inventories for trad-
ing purposes, etc.

Literature

ArtCraft First Day Cover Price List
Washington Press
2 Vreeland Road
Florham Park, NJ
07932-1501
(p) 973/966-0001
info@washpress.com
www.washingtonpress.com

Includes Presidential
Inaugural covers.

Basic Philately
Wayne Youngblood
Publisher, Stamps Dept.
700 E. State St.
Iola, WI 54990-0001
(p) 715/445-2214
youngblood@krause.com

Brookman's 1st Edition Black Heritage First Day Cachet Cover Catalog
Arlene Dunn
Brookman/Barrett & Worthen
10 Chestnut Drive
Bedford, NH 03110-5566
(p) 603/472-5575
(f) 603/472-8795

Illustrated 170-page perfect
bound book.

Brookman's 2nd Edition Price Guide for Disney Stamps
Arlene Dunn
Brookman/Barrett & Worthen
10 Chestnut Drive
Bedford, NH 03110-5566
(p) 603/472-5575
(f) 603/472-8795

Illustrated 248-page perfect
bound book.

2001 Brookman Price Guide of U.S., U.N. and Canada Stamps and Postal Collectibles
Arlene Dunn
Brookman/Barrett & Worthen
10 Chestnut Drive
Bedford, NH 03110-5566
(p) 603/472 5575
(f) 603/472-8795

Illustrated 280-page catalog.

Commemorative Cancellation Catalog
Paul Brenner
General Image, Inc.
P.O. Box 335
Maplewood, NJ
07040-0335
Postmark1@earthlink.net
http://home.earthlink.net/~
postmark1 (How-to-do-it is
excellent for beginners)

Catalog covering all picto-
rial cancellations used in the
U.S. during 1988-1989 is
available. Please send self-
addressed, stamped envelope
for prices and description.
Weekly newsletter is avail-
able which also provides
descriptive information on
U.S. pictorial postmarks.

Compilation of U.S. Souvenir Cards
P.O. Box 4155
Tulsa, OK 74159-4155

Durland Plate Number Catalog
c/o US Stamp Society
Executive Director
P.O. Box 722
Westfield, NJ 07091-0722
www.stamps.org

Fleetwood's Standard First Day Cover Catalog
Fleetwood
Unicover Corporation
1 Unicover Center
Cheyenne, WY 82008-0001
(p) 307/771-3000
www.unicover.com

The Hammarskjold Invert
Washington Press
2 Vreeland Road
Florham Park, NJ
07932-1501
(p) 973/966-0001
info@washpress.com
www.washingtonpress.com

Tells the story of the Dag Hammarskjold error/invert. FREE for #10 SASE.

Linn's U.S. Stamp Yearbook
P.O. Box 29
Sidney, OH 45365-0097
(p) 937/498-0801
(f) 800/340-9501 (US only)
(f) 937/498-0814 (outside US)
linns@linns.com
www.linns.com

A series of books providing facts and annual figures on every collectible variety of U.S. stamps, postal stationery and souvenir cards issued since 1983.

Linn's World Stamp Almanac
P.O. Box 29
Sidney, OH 45365-0097
(p) 937/498-0801
(f) 800/340-9501 (US only)
(f) 937/498-0814 (outside US)
linns@linns.com
www.linns.com

The most useful single reference source for stamp collectors. Contains detailed information on U.S. stamps.

19th Century Envelopes Catalog
Joann Thomas
P.O. Box 48
Redlands, CA 92373-0601

Postage Stamp Identifier and Dictionary of Philatelic Terms
Washington Press
2 Vreeland Road
Florham Park, NJ
07932-1501
(p) 973/966-0001
info@washpress.com
www.washingtonpress.com

1992 edition, with new country listings.

Precancel Stamp Society Catalogs
Dick Laetsch
108 Ashwamp Road
Scarborough, ME 04070
(p) 207/883-2505
precancel@aol.com
http://members.aol.com/precancel

Scott Specialized Catalogue of U.S. Stamps
P.O. Box 828
Sidney, OH 45365-0828
(p) 937/498-0802
(p) 800/572-6885
(f) 800/488-5349
ssm@scottonline.com
www.scottonline.com

Scott Stamp Monthly
P.O. Box 828
Sidney, OH 45365-0828
(p) 937/498-0802
(p) 800/572-6885
(f) 800/488-5349
ssm@scottonline.com
www.scottonline.com

Scott Standard Postage Stamp Catalogue
P.O. Box 828
Sidney, OH 45365-0828
(p) 937/498-0802
(p) 800/572-6885
(f) 800/488-5349
ssm@scottonline.com
www.scottonline.com

Stamp Collecting Made Easy
P.O. Box 29
Sidney, OH 45365-0029

An illustrated, easy-to-read, 96-page booklet for beginning collectors.

The 24¢ 1918 Air Mail Invert
Washington Press
2 Vreeland Road
Florham Park, NJ
07932-1501
(p) 973/966-0001
info@washpress.com
www.washingtonpress.com

Tells all there is to know about this famous stamp. FREE for #10 SASE.

20th Century Envelops Catalog
Joann Thomas
P.O. Box 48
Redlands, CA 92373-0601

U.S. Postal Card Catalog
Joann Thomas
P.O. Box 48
Redlands, CA 92373-0601

The U.S. Transportation Coils
Washington Press
2 Vreeland Road
Florham Park, NJ
07932-1501
(p) 973/966-0001
info@washpress.com
www.washingtonpress.com

FREE for #10 SASE.

White Ace Souvenir Card Album
Washington Press
2 Vreeland Road
Florham Park, NJ
07932-1501
(p) 973/966-0001
info@washpress.com
www.washingtonpress.com

Philatelic Centers

In addition to the more than 20,000 postal facilities authorized to sell philatelic products, the Postal Service also maintains Philatelic Centers located in major population centers. These Philatelic Centers have been established to serve stamp collectors and make it convenient for them to acquire an extensive range of current postage stamps, postal stationery and philatelic products issued by the Postal Service.

Centers are located at Main Post Offices with a ZIP + 4 of 9998 unless otherwise indicated. For questions about a Philatelic Center near you, call 800-275-8777.

Please note that Philatelic Centers in this listing include offices that may have only one philatelic window or limited hours dedicated to philatelic services.

Alabama
351 24th St. N
Birmingham, AL
35203-9816

379 N. Oates St.
Dothan, AL
36302-

Downtown Station
615 Clinton Ave. W
Huntsville, AL
35801-

250 St. Joseph St.
Mobile, AL
36601-

6701 Winton Blount
Blvd.
Montgomery, AL
36124-

Alaska
315 Barnette St.
Fairbanks, AK
99701-4532

Downtown Station
344 W. 3rd Ave.
Anchorage, AK
99510-2337

Arizona
2400 N. Postal Blvd.
Flagstaff, AZ
86004-4300

Osborne Station
3905 N. 7th Ave.
Phoenix, AZ
85013-3349

General Mail Facility
4949 E. Van Buren St.
Phoenix, AZ
85026-9800

1501 S. Cherrybell St.
Tucson, AZ
85726-9713

Arkansas
600 E. Capitol Ave.
Little Rock, AR
72202-

California
1180 W. Ball Rd.
Anaheim, CA
92812-2730

W. Tregallas Rd.
Antioch, CA
94509-4912

3400 Pegasus Dr.
Bakersfield, CA
93380-

2000 Allston Way
Berkeley, CA
94704-1418

2140 N. Hollywood Way
Burbank, CA
91505-

18122 Carmenita Rd.
Cerritos, CA
90703-6330

Fountain Square Dr.
Citrus Heights, CA
95621-5500

2121 Meridian Park
Blvd.
Concord, CA
94520-5708

2020 Fifth St.
Davis, CA
95616-

8111 Firestone Blvd.
Downey, CA
90241-

401 W. Lexington Ave.
El Cajon, CA
92020-4415

Cutten Station
3901 Walnut Dr.
Eureka, CA
95501-9991

600 Kentucky St.
Fairfield, CA
94533-5531

1900 E. St.
Fresno, CA
93706-2028

313 E. Broadway
Glendale, CA
91205-1010

Hillcrest Station
300 E. Hillcrest Blvd.
Inglewood, CA
50301-

300 N. Long Beach Blvd.
Long Beach, CA
90802-2427

900 N. Alameda St.
Los Angeles, CA
90012-2904

Village Station
11100 W. Wilshire Blvd.
Los Angeles, CA
90024-

Worldway Philatelic
Center
5800 Century Blvd.
Ste. 12
Los Angeles, CA
90009-

407 C St.
Marysville, CA
95901-

2334 M St.
Merced, CA
95340-

715 Kearney Ave.
Modesto, CA
95350-

Napa Station
1625 Trancas St.
Napa, CA
94558-

Civic Center Annex
201 13th St.
Oakland, CA
94612-3921

211 Brooks St.
Oceanside, CA
92054-3404

281 E. Colorado Blvd.
Pasadena, CA
91101-1903

4300 Black Ave.
Pleasanton, CA
94566-6103

2323 Churn Creek Rd.
Redding, CA
96049-

1201 N. Catalina
Redondo Beach, CA
90277-

2000 Royal Oaks Dr.
Sacramento, CA
95813-0100

1164 N. E. St.
San Bernardino, CA
92410-3508

2535 Midway Dr.
San Diego, CA
92111-3223

180 Steuart St.
San Francisco, CA
94105-1239

1750 Maridian Ave.
San Jose, CA
95125-

40 Bellum Blvd.
San Rafael, CA
94901-

12935 Alcosta Blvd.
San Ramon, CA
94583-

Spurgeon Station
615 Bush St.
Santa Ana, CA
92701-4103

836 Anacapa St.
Santa Barbara, CA
93102-

201 E. Battles Rd.
Santa Maria, CA
93454-7203

730 Second St.
Santa Rosa, CA
95402-

200 Prairie Ct.
Vacaville, CA
95687-

15701 Sherman Way
Van Nuys, CA
91409-

396 S. California Ave.
West Covina, CA
91793-9000

Colorado

16890 E. Alameda Pkwy.
Aurora, CO
80017-

1905 15th St.
Boulder, CO
80302-

201 E. Pikes Peak Ave.
Rm. 205
Colorado Springs, CO
80903-1933

1823 Stout St.
Denver, CO
80202-2500

7500 E. 53rd Place
Denver, CO
80217-

222 W. Eighth St.
Durango, CO
81301-

301 E. Broadwalk Dr.
Fort Collins, CO
80528-

241 N. Fourth St.
Grand Junction, CO
81501-

5753 S. Prince St.
Littleton, CO
80120-1927

1905 15th St.
Longmont, CO
80501-

Connecticut

70 Water St.
Danielson, CT
06239-

141 Weston St.
Hartford, CT
06101-9000

11 Silver St.
Middletown, CT
06457-

50 Brewery St.
New Haven, CT
06511-

469 Main St.
Ridgefield, CT
06877-4513

Springfield Station
1004 Hope St.
Stamford, CT
06901-9991

411 Barnum Ave. Cut-Off
Stratford, CT
06614-9991

Elmwood Station
121 Shield St.
W. Hartford, CT
06110-

135 Grand St.
Waterbury, CT
06701-9991

Delaware

55 The Plaza
Dover, DE
19901-

Wilmington P&DC
147 Quigley Blvd.
New Castle, DE
19720-9696

Rodney Square Station
1101 N. King St.
Wilmington, DE
19801-

District of Columbia

Pavillion Postique
1100 Penn. Ave. NW
Washington, DC
20004-2501

Postal Square
2 Mass. Ave. NE
Washington, DC
20002-9997

Florida

321 Montgomery Rd.
Altamonte Springs, FL
32714-

Bradenton MOWU
824 Manatee Ave.
W. Bradenton, FL
34205-

Brooksville MOWU
19101 Cortez Blvd.
Brooksville, FL
34601-

Clearwater MOWU
100 South Belcher Rd.
Clearwater, FL
33765-

Deland Postal Store
336 E. New York Ave.
Deland, FL
32724-

1900 W. Oakland Pk.
Blvd.
Fort Lauderdale, FL
33310-0116

Renaissance Contract
Postal Unit
8695 College Pkwy
Ste. 131
Fort Myers, FL
33919-4892

5000 W. Midway Rd.
Fort Pierce, FL 34981-

1801 Polk St.
Hollywood, FL
33022-0079

Downtown Station
210 N. Missouri Ave.
Lakeland, FL
33815-

Leesburg Station
1201 S. 14th St.
Leesburg, FL
34748-9996

Longwood Wekiva
Station
920 Wekiva Springs Rd.
Longwood, FL
32779-9996

2200 NW 72nd Ave.
Miami, FL
33152-9000

1200 Goodlette Rd. N
Naples, FL
34102-5254

New Port Richey
MOWU
6550 Nebraska Ave.
New Port Richey, FL
34653-

1335 Kingsley Ave.
Orange Park, FL
32073-4507

Downtown Station
46 E. Robinson St.
Orlando, FL
32801-

Sebring Post Office
518 N. Ridgewood Dr.
Sebring, FL
33870-

St. Petersburg MOWU
3135 First Ave. N
St. Petersburg, FL
33730-

Tampa Airport MOWU
Postal Store
5201 W. Spruce St.
Tampa, FL
33630-

Titusville Postal Store
1538 Harrison Ave.
Titusville, FL
32780-

3200 Summit Blvd.
W. Palm Beach, FL
33406-

Georgia

1072 W. Peachtree St.
NW
Atlanta, GA
30309-

Perimeter Branch
4707 Ashford
Dunwoody Rd.
Atlanta, GA
31146-

3470 McClure Bridge Rd.
Duluth, GA
30136-

364 Green St. NE
Gainesville, GA
30501-

451 College St.
Macon, GA
31213-9812

257 Lawrence St. NE
Marietta, GA
30060-

2 N. Farm St., Rm 14
Savannah, GA
31402-

Hawaii

335 Merchant St.
Honolulu, HI
96813-

Idaho

770 S. 13th St.
Boise, ID
83708-

220 E. Fifth St.
Moscow, ID
83843-

730 E. Clark St.
Pocatello, ID
83201-

Illinois

909 W. Euclid Ave.
Arlington Heights, IL
60004-

525 N. Broadway
Aurora, IL
60507-

Moraine Valley Station
7401 W. 100th Place
Bridgeview, IL
60455-

1301 E. Main St.
Carbondale, IL
62901-

Loop Station
11 S. Clark St.
Chicago, IL
60604-

433 W. Harrison St.
2nd Fl.
Chicago, IL
60607-9208

1000 E. Oakton St.
Des Plaines, IL
60018-

1101 Davis St.
Evanston, IL
60201-

2359 Madison Ave.
Granite City, IL
62040-

2000 McDonough St.
Joliet, IL
60436-

1750 W. Ogden Ave.
Naperville, IL
60540-

123 Indianwood Blvd.
Park Forest, IL
60466-

N. University Station
6310 N. University St.
Peoria, IL
61614-3454

401 William
River Forest, IL
60305-1900

5225 Harrison Ave.
Rockford, IL
61125-

1956 2nd Ave.
Rock Island, IL
61201-9700

450 W. Schaumburg Rd.
Schaumburg, IL
60194-

2105 E. Cook St.
Springfield, IL
62703-

326 N. Genesee St.
Waukegan, IL
60085-

Indiana

North Park Branch
4490 First Ave.
Evansville, IN
47710-

Fort Wayne Facility
1501 S. Clinton St.
Fort Wayne, IN
46802-

5530 Sohl St.
Hammond, IN
46320-

3450 State Rd. 26 E
Lafayette, IN
47901-

424 S. Michigan St.
South Bend, IN
46624-

Iowa

615 6th Ave. SE
Cedar Rapids, IA
52401-9830

1165 Second Ave.
Des Moines, IA
50318-9755

214 Jackson St.
Sioux City, IA
51101-

Kansas

6029 Broadmoor St.
Shawnee Mission, KS
66202-

424 S. Kansas Ave.
Topeka, KS
66603-

Downtown Station
330 W. 2nd St. N
Wichita, KS
67202-

Kentucky

1088 Nandino Blvd.
Lexington, KY
40511-

St. Mathews Station
4600 Shelbyville Rd.
Louisville, KY
40207-

Louisiana

3401 Government St.
Alexandria, LA
71302-9996

8101 Bluebonnet St.
Baton Rouge, LA
70826-2830

1105 Moss St.
Lafayette, LA
70501-

921 Moss St.
Lake Charles, LA
70601-

3301 17th St.
Metairie, LA
70009-

501 Sterlington Rd.
Monroe, LA
71201-

Carrollton Station
3400 S. Carrollton Ave.
New Orleans, LA
70118-4581

701 Loyola Ave.
New Orleans, LA
70113-

Vieux Carre Station
1022 Iberville St.
New Orleans, LA
70112-3145

2400 Texas Ave.
Shreveport, LA
71102-9711

Maine

40 Western Ave.
Augusta, ME
04330-

125 Forest Ave.
Portland, ME
04101-

Maryland

1 Church Cir.
Annapolis, MD
21401-

900 E. Fayette St.
Baltimore, MD
21233-9713

215 Park St.
Cumberland, MD
21502-

Riverdale Station
6411 Baltimore Ave.
Riverdale, MD
20737-

100 E. Carroll St.
Salisbury, MD
21801-

Massachusetts

McCormack Office
90 Devonshire St.
Boston, MA
02109-

120 Commercial St.
Brockton, MA
02402-9997

5 Bedford St.
Burlington, MA
01803-9996

2 Government Center
Fall River, MA
02722-

881 Main St.
Fitchburg, MA
01420-

P.O. Box 465
Lawrence, MA
01842-9996

P.O. Box 9998
Lowell, MA
01853-

695 Pleasant St.
New Bedford, MA
02740-

212 Fenn St.
Pittsfield, MA
01201-

2 Margin St.
Salem, MA
01270-

Main St. Station
1883 Main St.
Springfield, MA
01101-

178 Ave. A
Turner Falls, MA
01376-

4 E. Central St.
Worcester, MA
01613-

Michigan

2075 W. Stadium Blvd.
Ann Arbor, MI
48106-

90 S. McCamly St.
Battle Creek, MI
49016-

26200 Ford Rd.
Dearborn Hgts., MI
48127-

1401 W. Fort St.
Detroit, MI
48233-

250 E. Boulevard Dr.
Flint, MI
48502-

225 Michigan NW
Grand Rapids, MI
49599-

113 W. Michigan Ave.
Jackson, MI
49201-

1121 Miller Rd.
Kalamazoo, MI
49001-

General Mail Facility
4800 Collins Rd.
Lansing, MI
48924-

2900 Rodd St.
Midland, MI
48640-

735 W. Huron St.
Pontiac, MI
48343-9997

1300 Military St.
Port Huron, MI
48060-

30550 Gratiot St.
Roseville, MI
48066-

200 W. 2nd St.
Royal Oak, MI
48068-6800

1233 S. Washington St.
Saginaw, MI
48605-2510

6300 Wayne Rd.
Westland, MI
48185-3169

Minnesota

2800 W. Michigan
Duluth, MN
55806-1742

100 S. First St.
Minneapolis, MN
55401-2037

Mississippi

401 E. South St.
Jackson, MS
39205-5200

Missouri

401 S. Washington St.
Chillicothe, MO
64601-

2300 Bernadette Dr.
Columbia, MO
65203-4607

315 W. Pershing Rd.
Kansas City, MO
64108-

Northwest Plaza Station
500 Northwest Plaza
St. Ann, MO
63074-2209

201 S. Eighth St.
St. Joseph, MO
64501-

Clayton Branch
7750 Maryland Ave.
St. Louis, MO
63105-

500 W. Chestnut
Expwy.
Springfield, MO
65801-

Montana

841 S. 26th
Billings, MT
59101-9614

215 First Ave. N
Stop 1
Great Falls, MT
59401-9911

Nebraska

W. South Front St.
Grand Island, NE
68801-

700 R St.
Lincoln, NE
68501-9804

300 E. Third St.
North Platte, NE
69101-4000

1124 Pacific St.
Omaha, NE
68108-9630

Nevada

1001 E. Sunset Rd.
Rm 1053
Las Vegas, NV
89199-

2000 Vassar St.
Reno, NV
89510-

New Hampshire

955 Goffs Falls Rd.
Manchester, NH
03103-9713

New Jersey
1701 Atlantic Ave.
Atlantic City, NJ
08401-

421 Beningo Blvd.
Bellmawr, NJ
08031-2520

25 Veterans Plaza
Bergenfield, NJ
07621-

3 Miln St.
Cranford, NJ
07016-

21 Kilmore Rd.
Edison, NJ
08899-9706

229 Main St.
Fort Lee, NJ
07024-

65 Hazlet Ave.
Hazlet, NJ
07730-

5 Wannamaker
Municipal Complex
Island Heights, NJ
08732-0001

69 Montgomery St.
Jersey City, NJ
07303-

160 Maplewood Ave.
Maplewood, NJ
07040-2532

Morristown/Convent
Station
1 Convent Rd.
Morristown, NJ
07961-9999

Nutley Branch
372 Franklin Ave.
Nutley, NJ
07110-1663

171 Broad St.
Red Bank, NJ
07701-

680 US Highway Rt. 130
Trenton, NJ
08650-9611

150 Pompton Plains
Cross Rd.
Wayne, NJ
07470-9994

155 Clinton Rd.
W. Caldwell, NJ
07006-

Woodbury Station
35 N. Broad St.
Woodbury, NJ
08096-

411 Greenwood Ave.
Wyckoff, NJ
07481-

New Mexico

1135 Broadway SE
Albuquerque, NM
87101-

200 E. Las Cruces Ave.
Las Cruces, NM
88001-9994

415 N. Pennsylvania Ave.
Roswell, NM
88201-4752

New York

50001 Colonie Ctr. Mall
Albany, NY
12205-

Empire State Plaza
Albany, NY
12220-

1620 Grand Ave. N
Baldwin, NY
11510-1807

345 Hicksville Rd.
Bethpage, NY
11714-3401

115 Henry St.
Binghamton, NY
13902-

Bronx General PO
558 Grand Concourse
Bronx, NY
10451-

1200 William St.
Buffalo, NY
14240-8500

124 Grove Ave.
Cedarhurst, NY
11516-2315

297 Larkfield Rd.
East Northport, NY
11731-2417

Downtown Station
55 Clemens Center Pkwy.
Elmira, NY
14902-3091

41-65 Main St.
Flushing, NY
11351-0001

Roosevelt Field Mall
630 Old Country Rd.
Unit 507
Garden City, NY
11530-3500

16 Hudson Ave.
Glen Falls, NY
12801-4356

P.O. Box 9998
Glenham, NY
12527-

185 W. John St.
Hicksville, NY
11801-9671

445 Furrows Rd.
Holbrook, NY
11741-2720

55 Gerard St.
Huntington, NY
11743-6978

888 E. Hericho Turnpike
Huntingon Station, NY
11746-7505

8840 164th St.
Jamaica, NY
11431-4049

300 E. 3rd St.
Jamestown, NY
14701-5552

65 E. Hoffman Ave.
Lindenhurst, NY
11747-5005

324 Broadway
Monticello, NY
12701-1183

Church St. Station
90 Church St.
New York, NY
10007-

441 8th Ave.
New York, NY
10001-9291

Rockefeller Center
610 Fifth Ave.
New York, NY
10020-9991

909 Third Ave.

New York, NY
10022-

352 Main St.
Oneonta, NY
13820-

33 S. Main St.
Pearl River, NY
10965-2456

10 Miller St.
Plattsburgh, NY
12901-1820

55 Mansion St.
Poughkeepsie, NY
12601-

1335 Jefferson Rd.
Rochester, NY
14692-9205

29 Jay St.
Schenectady, NY
12305-1912

25 Route 111
Smithtown, NY
11787-3712

550 Manor Rd.
Staten Island, NY
10314-9648

40 Queens St.
Syosset, NY
11791-3006

5640 E. Taft Rd.
Syracuse, NY
13220-9800

108 Main St.
Warwick, NY
10990-1370

100 Fisher Ave.
White Plains, NY
10602-1907

79-81 Main St.
Yonkers, NY
10701-2740

North Carolina
West Asheville Station
1302 Patton Ave.
Asheville, NC
28806-2604

Starmount Finance Unit
6241 S. Blvd.
Charlotte, NC
28224-9798

Four Seasons Station
301 Four Seasons Town Ctr.
Greensboro, NC
27427-

311 New Bern Ave.
Raleigh, NC
27601-1442

North Dakota
220 E. Rosser Ave.
Bismarck, ND
58502-

675 2nd Ave. N
Fargo, ND
58102-4701

Ohio
675 Wolf Ledges Pky.
Akron, OH
44309-9902

4420 Dressier Rd. NW
Canton, OH
44718-

525 Vine St. (Skywalk)
Cincinnati, OH
45202-3905

2400 Orange Ave.
Cleveland, OH
44101-9997

6316 Nicholas Dr.
Columbus, OH
43235-

1111 E. Fifth St.
Rm. 212A
Dayton, OH
45401-9712

345 E. Bridge St.
Elyria, OH
44035-5222

200 N. Diamond St.
Mansfield, OH
44901-9996

150 N. Third St.
Steubenville, OH
43952-

435 S. St. Clair St.
Toledo, OH
43601-0101

201 High St. NE
Warren OH
44481-

99 S. Walnut St.
Youngstown, OH
44501-9713

Oklahoma

115 W. Broadway
Enid, OK
73701-

525 E. Okmulgee St.
Muskogee, OK
74401-

129 W. Gray
Norman, OK
73069-

Postique
320 SW Fifth Ave.
Oklahoma City, OK
73125-9100

333 W. 4th St.
Tulsa, OK
74103-9612

Oregon

520 Willamette St.
Eugene, OR
97401-2627

751 NW Hoyt St.
Portland, OR
97208-

Pennsylvania

442 W. Hamilton St.
Allentown, PA
18101-1611

535 Wood St.
Bethlehem, PA
18616-

115 Boylston St.
Bradford, PA
16701-

229 Beaver Dr.
Du Bois, PA
15801-2517

1314 Griswold Plaza
Erie, PA
16501-1730

1025 Valley Forge Rd.
Fairview Village, PA
19409-

238 S. Pennsylvania
Greensburg, PA
15601-

1425 Crooked Hill Rd.
Harrisburg, PA
17107-9714

111 Franklin St.
Johnstown, PA
15901-

Downtown Station
4 W. Chestnut St.
Lancaster, PA
17603-3581

980 Wheeler Way
Langhorne, PA
19047-

Lehigh Valley Post
Office Philatelic Center
17 S. Commerce Way
Lehigh Valley, PA
18002-9999

435 S. Cascade St.
New Castle, PA
16108-

501 11th St.
New Kensington, PA
15068-

Grant Street Station
700 Grant St., Ste. B
Pittsburgh, PA
15219-1906

William Penn Annex
Station
900 Market St.
Philadelphia, PA
19107-

Gus Yatron Facility
2100 N. 13th St.
Reading PA
19612-

Southeastern Window
Unit
1000 W. Valley Rd.
Southeastern, PA
19399-

237 S. Fraser St.
State College, PA
16801-4827

701 Ann St.
Stroudsburg, PA
18360-2016

300 S. Main St.
Wilkes Barre, PA
18701-

Center City Finance
Station
621 Hepburn St.
Williamsport, PA
17703-

200 S. George St.
York, PA
17405-5554

Puerto Rico

585 Ave. Fed.
Roosevelt, Ste. 180
San Juan, PR
00936-9711

Rhode Island

320 Thames St.
Newport, RI
02840-

40 Montgomery St.
Pawtucket, RI
02860-

24 Corliss St.
Providence, RI
02904-9713

South Carolina

7075 Cross County Rd.
Charleston, SC
29423-

1601 Assembly St.
Columbia, SC
29201-9713

600 W. Washington St.
Greenville, SC
29602-9918

South Dakota

320 S. 2nd Ave.
Sioux Falls, SD
57104-

Tennessee

General Mail Facility
6050 Shallowford Rd.
Chattanooga, TN
37421-5500

200 Martin Luther
King Dr.
Jackson, TN
38301-6921

530 E. Main St.
Johnson City, TN
37601-

General Mail Facility
1237 E. Weisgarber Rd.
Knoxville, TN
37950-8502

Colonial Station
4695 Southern Ave.
Memphis, TN
38124-4809

Crosstown Station
1520 Union Ave.
Memphis, TN
38124-3700

Broadway Station
901 Broadway
Nashville, TN
37203-3806

Texas

3401 Pine St.
Abilene, TX
79604-9996

2301 S. Ross
Amarillo, TX
79120-9604

300 E. South St.
Arlington, TX
76004-

510 Guadolupe St.
Austin, TX
78701-

1535 Los Ebanos Blvd.
Brownsville, TX
78520-8634

2121 E. Wm. J. Bryan Pky.
Bryan, TX
77801-

809 Nueces Bay Blvd.
Corpus Christi, TX
78469-

400 N. Ervay St.
Dallas, TX
75201-

Olla Podrida Post Office
12215 Coit Rd.
Dallas, TX
75251-

Golden Triangle
Finance Unit
Denton, TX
76206-

8401 Boeing Dr.
El Paso, TX
79910-

251 W. Lancaster Ave.
Fort Worth, TX
76102-

401 Franklin Ave.
Houston, TX
77201-9901

300 N. 10th
Killeen, TX
76541-5217

601 E. Pecan
McAllen, TX
78501-9995

100 E. Wall St.
Midland, TX
79701-

433 Belle Grove Dr.
Richardson, TX
75080-

1 S. Bryant Blvd.
San Angelo, TX
76902-

Downtown Station
615 E. Houston
San Antonio, TX
78205-

10410 Perrin Beitel Rd.
San Antonio, TX
78284-

430 W. State Hwy. 6
Waco, TX
76702-

202 E. Erwin St.
Tyler, TX
75702-

1000 Lamar St.
Wichita Falls, TX
76301-

Utah

3680 Pacific Ave.
Ogden, UT
84401-

1760 W. 2100 S.
Salt Lake City, UT
84199-

Vermont

204 Main St.
Brattleboro, VT
05301-2837

11 Elmwood Ave.
Burlington, VT
05401-5700

10 Sykes Mountain Ave.
White River Junction, VT
05001-

Virginia

111 Sixth St.
Bristol, VA
24201-9996

1155 Seminole Tr.
Charlottesville, VA
22906-9996

1425 Battlefield Blvd.
N. Chesapeake, VA
23327-

700 Main St.
Danville, VA
24542-

809 Aberdeen Rd.
Hampton, VA
23670-

300 Odd Fellows Rd.
Lynchburg, VA
24506-9996

Denigh Station
14104 Warwick Blvd.
Newport News, VA
23608-

600 Church St.
Norfolk, VA
23501-

29 Franklin St.
Petersburg, VA
23804-

933 Broad St.
Portsmouth, VA
23707-

901 First St.
Radford, VA
24141-

1801 Brook Rd.
Richmond, VA
23232-

419 Rutherford Ave. NE.
Roanoke, VA
24022-9993

501 Viking Dr.
Virginia Beach, VA
23451-

1430 N. Augusta
Staunton, VA
24401-2401

425 N Boundary St.
Williamsburg, VA
23187-

Washington

11 3rd St. NW
Auburn, WA
98002-4033

15800 NE 8th St.
Bellevue, WA
98008-3906

315 Prospect St.
Bellingham, WA
98225-4001

3102 Hoyt Ave.
Everett, WA
98225-

3500 W. Court
Pasco, WA
99301-

424 E. 1st St.
Port Angeles, WA
98362-

301 Union St.
Seattle, WA 9
98101-2205

904 N. Riverdale Ave.
Spokane, WA
99201-

1102 A St.
Tacoma, WA
98402-

205 W. Washington Ave.
Yakima, WA
98903-

West Virginia

3010 E. Cumberland Rd.
Bluefield, WV
24701-9995

1057 Charleston Town
Ctr.
Charleston, WV
25357-

500 W Pike St.
Clarksburg, WV
26301-9995

1000 Virginia Ave. W.
Huntington, WV
25704-1726

1355 Old Courthouse
Sq.
Martinsburg, WV
25401-9995

Wisconsin

126 N. Barstow St.
Eau Claire, WI
54703-3572

425 State St.
La Crosse, WI
54601-3346

3902 Milwaukee St.
Madison, WI
53714-

345 W. St. Paul Ave.
Milwaukee, WI
53203-3096

1025 W. 20th Ave.
Oshkosh, WI
54901-6617

235 Forrest St.
Wausau, WI
54403-

Wyoming

2120 Capitol Ave.
Cheyenne, WY
82001-9996

Subject Index

The Numbers listed next to the stamp description are the Scott numbers, and the numbers in the parentheses are the numbers of the pages on which the stamps are listed.

A

A Stamp, 1735 (220), 1736 (220)
Abbott & Costello, 2566 (315)
Abstract Expressionist, Jackson Pollock, 3186h (403)
Abyssinian Cat, 2373 (292)
Acadia National Park, 746 (112), 762 (115)
Acheson, Dean, 2755 (332)
Acoma Pot, 1709 (217)
Adams
  Abigail, 2146 (267)
  John, 806 (120), 841 (123), 850 (123), 1687a (210), 2201 (272), 2216b (275)
  John Quincy, 811 (120), 846 (123), 2201 (272), 2216f (275)
Addams, Jane, 878 (124)
Admiralty Head Lighthouse (WA), 2470 (304), 2474 (304)
Adventures of Huckleberry Finn, The, 348 (2787)
Adoption, 3398 (35)
African
  Americans, 873 (124), 902 (127), 953 (134), 1085 (149), 1233 (161), 1290 (166), 1361 (174), 1372 (174), 1486 (189), 1490-1491 (189), 1493 (189), 1495 (189), 1554 (194), 1560 (197), 1772 (227), 1790-1791 (228), 1860 (235), 1865 (235), 2027 (252), 2043 (255), 2051 (255), 2083-2084 (259), 2097 (260), 2164 (268), 2211 (272), 2223 (279), 2275 (283), 2420 (300), 2496 (307), 2746 (332), 2766 (335), 3121 (379), 3175 (392), 3181 (395), 3186c (403), 3188a (407), 3273 (424), 3371 (24), C97 (451), C102-C103 (451), C105 (451)

Elephant Herd, 1388 (177)
  Violet, 2486 (307)
Agave Cactus, 1943 (244)
Aging Together, 2011 (251)
AIDS Awareness, 2806 (339)
Air
  Cushion Vehicle, C123 (452), C126 (455)
  Force, 1013 (141), 3167 (391), C49 (447)
  Mail Service, US, C74 (448)
  Save Our, 1413 (178)
  Service Emblem, C5 (443)
Aircraft Gun 90mm, Anti, 900 (127)
Aircrafts, Classic American, 3142a-t (384)
Airliner, Hypersonic, C122 (452), C126 (455)
Airmail Envelopes
  and Aerogrammes, UC1-UC46 (489), UC47-UC65 (490)
  Official, UO1 (493), UO5 (493), UO9 (493), UO16 (493), UO20 (493), UO26 (493), UO39 (493), UO48 (493), UO55 (493), UO73-UO84 (493), UO88-UO89 (493)
Airmail
  Stamps, C1-C23 (443), C24-C48 (444), C49-C69 (447), C70-C90 (448), C91-C112 (451), C113-C125 (452), C126-C134 (455)
  Special Delivery, CE1-CE2 (455)
Alabama, 1654 (206), 1953 (247)
"Alabama Baby," 3151a (387)
Alamo, The, 776 (116), 778 (116), 1043 (142)
Alaska
  American Bicentennial, 1681 (209), 1954 (247)
  Cook, Captain James, 1732-1733 (220)

Highway, 2635 (320)
  Purchase, C70 (448)
  Statehood, 2066 (256), C53 (447)
  Territory, 800 (119)
  -Yukon-Pacific Exposition, 370 (82), 371 (82)
Alaskan Malamute, 2100 (260)
Albania, 918 (128)
Alcoholism, You Can Beat It, 1927 (240)
Alcott, Louisa May, 862 (124)
Alexandria, C40 (444)
Alger, Horatio, 2010 (251)
All Aboard!: Twentieth Century Trains, 3333-3337 (432)
  Congressional, 3334 (432)
  Daylight, 3333 (432)
  Hiawatha, 3336 (432)
  Super Chief, 3337 (432)
  20th Century Limited, 3335 (432)
Allegiance, Pledge of, 2594 (316)
Allen, Ethan, 1071 (146)
Alliance
  for Progress, 1234 (161)
  French, 1753 (223)
Allied
  Nations, 537 (95), 907 (127)
  Victory, 537 (95)
Alligator, 1428 (181)
"All in the Family" TV Series, 3189b (408)
Allosaurus, 1390 (177), 3136g (380)
Alpha, 3142e (384)
Alta, California, 1st Civil Settlement, 1725 (220)
Amateur Radio, 1260 (165)
Ambulance, 2128 (264), 2231 (279)
Amendment, Nineteenth, 2980 (359)
America
  Beautification of, 1318 (170), 1365 (174), 1366 (174)
  Nature of, 3293a-j (428), 3378 (28), 3378a-j (28)

Bright Eyes, 3230-3234 (416)
Brittlebush, 3293a (428)
Broad-billed Hummingbird, 2643 (320)
Broadbill Decoy, 2138 (267)
Broadway Hit 1947, 3186n (403)
Broadway Songwriters, 3345-3350 (435)
  Frank Loesser, 3350 (435)
  Ira & George Gershwin, 3345 (435)
  Lerner & Lowe, 3346 (435)
  Lorenz Hart, 3347 (435)
  Meredith Willson, 3349 (435)
  Rodgers & Hammerstein, 3348 (435)
Brontosaurus, 1390 (177), 2425 (300)
Brooklyn
  Bridge, 1012 (141), 2041 (255)
  Battle of, 1003 (138)
Brother Jonathan, 2365 (291)
Brown
  Bear, 1884 (236)
  Horse with Green Bridle, 2979 (359)
  Pelican, 1466 (186)
Brussels Universal and International Exhibition, 1104 (150)
Bryan, William Jennings, 2195 (271)
Bryant, Bear, 3143 (384), 3148 (387)
Buchanan
  James, 820 (120), 2217f (275)
  James (Wheatland), 1081 (149)
Buchanan's No. 999, 2847 (344)
Buck, Pearl, 1848 (235)
Buckboard, 2124 (264)
Buffalo, 287 (72), 700 (108), 1392 (177), 1883 (236)
  Bill Cody, 2178 (271), 2869 (347)
  Soldiers, 2818 (340)
Bug, Assassin, 3351g (436)
Buggy, 1360 (174), 1370 (174), 1505 (190), 1902 (239)
  Baby, 1418 (181), 1902 (239)
Bugs Bunny, 3137-3138 (380)
Bulfinch, Charles, 1781 (227)
Bull, John, 2364 (291)
Bunche, Ralph, 1860 (235)
Bunker Hill, 1034 (142), 1056 (145)
  Flag, 1351 (173)
Bunyan, Paul, 3084 (372)
Burbank, Luther, 876 (124)
Burgoyne Campaign, 644 (104), 1728 (220)
Burma Road, 2559a (312)
Burmese, 2374 (292)
Butte, 2902 (351)
Butterflies, 1712-1715 (217)
Butterfly, Monarch, 3351k (436)
Butterfly Dance, 3073 (371)

Byrd
  Antarctic Expedition II, 733 (111), 735 (112), 753 (115), 768 (115)
  Richard E., 2388 (295)

<hr/>

C

<hr/>

C (20¢) Stamp, 1946-1948 (244)
Cab, Hansom, 1904 (239)
Cable Car, San Francisco, 1442 (182), 2263 (280)
Caboose, RR, 1905 (239)
Cabrillo, Juan Rodriguez, 2704 (327)
Cactus
  Hedgehog, 3293g (428)
  Mouse, 3293i (428)
  Saguaro, 3293e (428)
  Wren, 3293a (428)
Cadillac, Landing of, 1000 (138)
Cagney, James, 3329 (432)
Calder, Alexander, 3198-3202 (411)
Calico Scallop, 2120 (264)
California, 1663 (206), 1957 (247)
  Condor, 1430 (181)
  Gold, 954 (134)
  Gold Rush, 3316 (431)
  Pacific International Exposition, 773 (116), 778 (116)
  Settlement, 1373 (174)
  Statehood, (44), 997 (138)
  Yosemite National Park, 740 (112), 751 (112), 756 (115), 769 (115)
Calliope Hummingbird, 2446 (320), 2643 (320)
Camarasaurus, 3136c (380)
Camel, 2392 (295)
Camellia, 1877 (236), 1935 (247)
Cameras, Motion Picture, 1555 (194)
Camp Fire Girls, 1167 (157), 2163 (268)
Camptosaurus, 3136b (380)
Canada, 1324 (170)
  Goose, 1757 (224), 1757c (224)
  US Friendship, 961 (134)
Canal, 298 (77), 398 (85), 681 (107), 856 (123)
  Boat, 2257 (280)
  Erie, 1325 (170)
Cancer
  Breast, Awareness, 3081 (372)
  Breast, Research, B1 (423)
  Early Detection, 1754 (223)
  Crusade Against, 1263 (165)
  Prostate, Awareness, 3315 (431)
Candle, 1205 (161), 2395 (296)

Holder, Rush Lamp and, 1610 (201)
Cannon, 629-630 (103), 1178 (158), 1181 (158)
Canoe, 1356 (174), 2163 (268), 2353A (304), 2453 (304)
Canoeing, 3068b (371)
Canvasback Decoy, 2140 (267)
Cape Hatteras, 1448-1451 (185), 2471 (304)
CAPEX '78, 1757-1757h (224)
Capitol, 572 (99), 989 (138), 992 (138), 1202 (161), 1365 (174), 1503 (190), 1590-1591 (198), 1616 (202), 1623 (202), 2114-2116 (263), 2561 (315), C64-C65 (447)
  National Sesquicentennial, 989-992 (138)
  Statue of Freedom on Dome, 989 (138)
Cardinal, 1465 (186), 1757 (224), 1757a (224), 1965-1966 (247), 1969 (247), 1985 (248), 1987-1998 (248), 2000 (248), 2480 (307)
  in Snow, 2874 (348)
Cards, Postal, (503), UX1-UX56 (495), UX57-UX146 (496), UX147-UX263 (499), UX280-UX284 (499), UX290-UX292 (499), UY1 (503), UY6-UY7 (503), UY12 (503), UY18 (503), UY23 (503), UY31 (503), UY39-UY41 (503), UXC1-UXC5 (500), UXC6-UXC27 (503), UZ1-UZ6 (503)
CARE, 1439 (182)
Carlson, Chester, 2180 (271)
Carlyle House, John, C40 (444)
Carmel, Man and Children of, 1485 (189)
Carmichael, Hoagy, 3103 (375)
Carnegie, Andrew, 1171 (157)
Carolina
  Charter, 1230 (161)
  -Charleston, 683 (107)
Carousel
  Animals, 2390-2393 (295)
  Horses, 2976-2979a (359)
Carpenters' Hall, 1543 (194)
Carreta, 2255 (280)
Carriage, Steam, 2451 (304)
Carrier, Letter, 1238 (162), 1490 (189), 1497 (189), 2420 (300)
Cars, Classic, 2381-2385 (295)
Carson
  Kit, 2869 (347)
  Rachel, 1857 (235)
  Rachel, Valley, NV, 999 (138)
Carter Family, The, 2773 (336), 2776 (336)
Carteret, Philip, Landing of, 1247 (162)

Polo, 2759 (332)
Pony Express, 894 (127), 1154 (157)
Rider, 2780 (336)
Pons, Lily, 3154 (388)
Ponselle, Rosa, 3157 (388)
Poor, Salem, 1560 (197)
Popcorn Wagon, 2261 (280)
Porgy & Bess, 1484 (189), 2768 (335)
Porkfish, 1828 (231)
Porter
  Cole, 2550 (312)
  David D., 792 (119)
Portrait of Richard Mather, 3236a (419)
Post Office
  Dept. Bldg., C42 (444)
  First Automated, 1164 (157)
Post
  Rider, 113 (58), 1478 (186)
  Wiley, C95-C96 (451)
Postage
  Due Stamps, J1-J33 (459), J34-J68 (460), J69-J104 (461)
  Stamp Centenary, 947-948 (134)
Postal Cards, (503) UX1-UX56 (495), UX57-UX146 (496), UX147-UX263 (499), UX280-UX284 (499), UX290-UX292 (499), UX298 (499), UX299 (500), UX301-UX303 (500), UX305-UX306 (500)
  Airmail, UXC1-UXC5 (500), UXC6-UXC27 (503)
  Paid Reply, UY1 (503), UY6-UY7 (503), UY12 (503), UY18 (503), UY23 (503), UY31 (503), UY39-UY41 (503)
  Official Mail, UZ1-UZ6 (503)
  Conference, International, C66 (447)
  Service, 1164 (157), 1238 (162), 1396 (178), 1489-1498 (189), 1572-1575 (198), 2420 (300), 2539 (311)
Postal Union, Universal, 3332 (432)
Posting a Broadside, 1477 (186)
Post's, Emily, Etiquette, 3184f (399)
Postwar Baby Boom, 3186l (403)
Potomac River, 1366 (174)
Poultry Industry, 968 (137)
POW-MIAs, 1422 (181), 2966 (352)
Powatan, USS, 792 (119)
Powered Flight, C47 (444)
Preamble to the Constitution, 2355-2359 (291)
Prehistoric Animals, 2422-2425 (300), 3077-3080 (372)

Preservation of Wildlife Habitats, 1921-1924 (240)
Preservationist, John Muir, 3182j (395)
Preserve the Environment (Expo '74), 1527 (193)
Presidential Issue '38, 803-804 (120), 806-824 (120), 826-834 (123), 839-851 (123)
Presidents Miniature Sheets '86, 2216-2217 (275), 2218-2219 (276)
  (Stamp Collecting), 2201 (272)
Presley, Elvis, 2721 (331), 2724 (331), 2731 (331)
Pressed Glass, 3327 (432)
Prevent Drug Abuse, 1438 (182)
Priestley, Joseph, 2038 (252)
Princeton
  University (Nassau Hall), 1083 (149)
  George Washington at, 1704 (214)
Printed Circuit Board, 1501 (190)
Printing, 857 (123)
Press, 857 (123), 1014 (141), 1119 (153), 1476 (186), 1593 (198), 2779 (336)
Priority Mail, 2419 (300), 2540 (311)
Prisoners of War, 2966 (352)
Proclamation
  of Peace, American Revolution, 727 (111), 752 (115)
  Emancipation, 1233 (161)
Professional
  Baseball, 1381 (177)
  Management, 1920 (240)
Progress
  in Electronics, 1500-1502 (190), C86 (448)
  of Women, 959 (134)
  Alliance for, 1232 (161), 1234 (161)
Prohibition Enforced, 3184c (399)
Project Mercury, 1193 (158)
Prominent Americans, 1278-1294 (166), 1299 (169), 1303-1305C (169), 1393-1395 (178), 1397-1402 (178)
Pronghorn Antelope, 1078 (149), 1889 (236)
Propeller, Wooden, and Airplane Radiator, C4 (443)
Prostate Cancer Awareness, 3315 (431)
Providence, RI, 1164 (157)
Pteranodon, 2423 (300)
PUAS, America, 2426 (300), 2512 (308), C121 (452), C127 (455), C131 (455)
Public
  Education, 2159 (268)

Hospitals, 2210 (272)
Schools, Desegregating, 3187f (404)
Pueblo Pottery, 1706-1709 (217)
Puerto Rico
  Clemente, Roberto, 2097 (260)
  Columbus Landing in, 2805 (339)
  De Leon, Ponce, 2024 (252)
  Election, 983 (137)
  Marin, Luis Munoz, 2173 (271)
  San Jaun, 1437 (182)
  Territory, 801 (119)
Pulaski, General, 690 (108)
Pulitzer, Joseph, 946 (131)
Puma, 1881 (236)
Pumper, Fire, 1908 (239)
Pumpkinseed Sunfish, 2481 (307)
Puppy and Kitten, 2025 (252)
Pure Food and Drugs, Act, 1906, 3182f (395)
  Laws, 1080 (149)
Purple Deer, 3358 (439), 3362 (439), 3366 (439)
Pushcart, 2133 (264)
Putnam, Rufus, 795 (119)
Pyle, Ernie, 1398 (178)

Q

Quail, Gambel, 3293d (428)
Quarter
  Horse, 2155 (268)
  Seated, 1578 (198)
Quill
  Pen, 1099 (150), 1119 (153), 1230 (161), 1250 (162), 2360 (291), 2421 (300)
  Inkwell and, 1535 (193), 1581 (198), 1811 (231)
Quilts, American, 1745-1748 (223)
  Basket Design, 1745-1748 (223)
Quimby, Harriet, C128 (455)

R

Raccoon, 1757h (224)
Racing
  Car, 2262 (280)
  Horse, 1528 (193), 3189g (408)
  Stock Car, 3187n (404)
Radiator, Airplane, and Wooden Propeller, C4 (443)
Radio
  Amateur, 1260 (165)
  Entertains America, 3184i (399)

S

Wulfenite, 2703 (327)
Wyoming, 1676 (209), 2002
    (248)
  Statehood, 2444 (304)
  Yellowstone National Park,
      744 (112), 760 (115), 1453
      (185)

of the Ox, 3120 (379)
of the Rabbit, 3272 (424)
of the Rat, 3060 (368)
of the Rooster, 2720 (328)
of the Tiger, 3179 (395)
International Women's, 1571
    (198)
Yellow
  Fish, 3317 (431)
  Garden Spider, 3351d (436)
  Lady's-Slipper, 2077 (259)
  Rose, 3049 (367)
Yellowstone National Park, 744
    (112), 760 (115), 1453 (185)
YMCA Youth Camping, 2160
    (268)
Yorktown, Battle of, 703 (108),
    1937 (243)
  Surrender of Cornwallis at,
      703 (108), 1686 (210)
  -Virginia Capes, Battle of, 703
      (108), 1937-1938 (243)
Yosemite
  Flag over, 2280 (283)
  National Park, 740 (112), 751
      (112), 756 (115), 769 (115)
Young, Whitney Moore, 1875
    (236)
Youth

Camping, YMCA, 2160
    (268)
Year, International, 2160-2163
    (268)
Salute to, 963 (134)
Support our, 1342 (173)
Team Sports, 3399-3402 (36),
    3402a (36)
Yugoslavia, Oct. 26, 917 (128)
Yukon-Pacific, Exposition,
    Alaska-, 370-371 (82)

Postmasters General of the United States

Appointed by the Continental Congress

1775 Benjamin Franklin, PA
1776 Richard Bache, PA
1782 Ebenezer Hazard, NY

Appointed by the President with the advice and consent of the Senate

1789 Samuel Osgood, MA
1791 Timothy Pickering, PA
1795 Joseph Habersham, GA
1801 Gideon Granger, CT
1814 Return J. Meigs, Jr., OH
1823 John McLean, OH
1829 William T. Barry, KY
1835 Amos Kendall, KY
1840 John M. Niles, CT
1841 Francis Granger, NY
1841 Charles A. Wickliffe, KY
1845 Cave Johnson, TN
1849 Jacob Collamer, VT
1850 Nathan K. Hall, NY
1852 Samuel D. Hubbard, CT
1853 James Campbell, PA
1857 Aaron V. Brown, TN
1859 Joseph Holt, KY
1861 Horatio King, ME
1861 Montgomery Blair, DC
1864 William Dennison, OH
1866 Alexander W. Randall, WI
1869 John A.J. Creswell, MD
1874 James W. Marshall, NJ
1874 Marshall Jewell, CT
1876 James N. Tyner, IN
1877 David McK. Key, TN
1880 Horace Maynard, TN
1881 Thomas L. James, NY
1882 Timothy O. Howe, WI
1883 Walter Q. Gresham, IN
1884 Frank Hatton, IA
1885 William F. Vilas, WI
1888 Don M. Dickinson, MI
1889 John Wanamaker, PA
1893 Wilson S. Bissell, NY
1895 William L. Wilson, WV
1897 James A. Gary, MD
1898 Charles Emory Smith, PA
1902 Henry C. Payne, WI
1904 Robert J. Wynne, PA
1905 George B. Cortelyou, NY
1907 George von L. Meyer, MA
1909 Frank H. Hitchcock, MA
1913 Albert S. Burleson, TX
1921 Will H. Hays, IN
1922 Hubert Work, CO
1923 Harry S. New, IN
1929 Walter F. Brown, OH
1933 James A. Farley, NY
1940 Frank C. Walker, PA
1945 Robert E. Hannegan, MO
1947 Jesse M. Donaldson, IL
1953 Arthur E. Summerfield, MI
1961 J. Edward Day, CA
1963 John A. Gronouski, WI
1965 Lawrence F. OíBrien, MA
1968 W. Marvin Watson, TX
1969 Winton M. Blount, AL

Selected by the Presidentially appointed U.S. Postal Service Board of Governors

1971 Elmer T. Klassen, MA
1975 Benjamin Franklin Bailar, MD
1978 William F. Bolger, CT
1985 Paul N. Carlin, WY
1986 Albert V. Casey, MA
1986 Preston R. Tisch, NY
1988 Anthony M. Frank, CA
1992 Marvin Runyon, TN
1998 William J. Henderson, NC

Acknowledgments

This stamp collecting catalog was produced by Public Affairs and Communications, Stamp Services, United States Postal Service.

United States Postal Service

William J. Henderson
Postmaster General and Chief Executive Officer

Deborah K. Willhite
Senior Vice President, Government Relations and Public Policy

Azeezaly S. Jaffer
Vice President, Public Affairs and Communications

James C. Tolbert, Jr.
Executive Director, Stamp Services

Terrence McCaffrey
Manager, Stamp Development

Kelly Spinks
Project Manager and Editor

HarperCollins Publishers

Megan Newman
Editorial Director, HarperResource

Greg Chaput
Associate Editor, HarperResource

Lucy Albanese
Design Director, General Books Group

Roberto de Vicq de Cumptich
Art Director, HarperResource

Design and Production Services

Roberta Wojtkowski Design & Associates
10992 Thrush Ridge Road
Reston, VA 20191-4718

Research and Writing Services

PhotoAssist, Inc.
4400 Jenifer Street NW
Washington, DC 20015-2133

Color Separation and Digital Prepress Services

Dodge Color
4827 Rugby Avenue
Bethesda, MD 20814

Printing and Binding

R. R. Donnelly & Sons Company
Crawfordsville, IN 47933

Notes